D1596772

Also by William D. Green
Published by the University of Minnesota Press

*A Peculiar Imbalance:*
*The Fall and Rise of Racial Equality*
*in Minnesota, 1837–1869*

*Degrees of Freedom:*
*The Origins of Civil Rights*
*in Minnesota, 1865–1912*

# THE
# CHILDREN
## OF LINCOLN

WHITE PATERNALISM AND THE
LIMITS OF BLACK OPPORTUNITY
IN MINNESOTA, 1860–1876

WILLIAM D. GREEN

University of Minnesota Press
Minneapolis
London

The University of Minnesota Press gratefully acknowledges
financial assistance provided for the publication of this book
from the Office of the Provost, Augsburg University.

Frontispiece: The Emancipation statue, Washington, D.C.
Photograph by Karen Bleier/AFP/Getty Images.

Copyright 2018 by William D. Green

All rights reserved. No part of this publication may be reproduced,
stored in a retrieval system, or transmitted, in any form or by any means,
electronic, mechanical, photocopying, recording, or otherwise,
without the prior written permission of the publisher.

Published by the University of Minnesota Press
111 Third Avenue South, Suite 290
Minneapolis, MN 55401-2520
http://www.upress.umn.edu

Printed in the United States of America on acid-free paper

The University of Minnesota is an equal-opportunity educator and employer.

24 23 22 21 20 19 18    10 9 8 7 6 5 4 3 2 1

Library of Congress Cataloging-in-Publication Data
Names: Green, William D. (William Davis), author.
Title: The children of Lincoln : white paternalism and the limits of black opportunity
in Minnesota, 1860–1876 / William D. Green.
Description: Minneapolis, MN : University of Minnesota Press, [2018] | Includes
bibliographical references and index.
Identifiers: LCCN 2018001571 (print) | ISBN 978-1-5179-0528-6 (hc/j)
Subjects: LCSH: African Americans—Civil rights—Minnesota—History—19th century.
| Racism—Minnesota—History—19th century. | Wilkinson, Morton S. (Morton Smith),
1819–1894. | Montgomery, Thomas, 1841–1907. | Merrill, Daniel D. (Daniel David),
1834–1896. | Stearns, Sarah B.
Classification: LCC E185.93.M55 G74 2018 (print) | DDC 323.196/07307760904—dc23
LC record available at https://lccn.loc.gov/2018001571

With love, to Judi,
who held my hand
every step of the way

(T.F.M.M., A.)

*We fully comprehend the relation of Abraham Lincoln both to ourselves and to the white people of the United States . . . The race to which we belong were not the special objects of his consideration . . . You are the children of Abraham Lincoln. We are only at best his step-children; children by adoption, children of circumstances and necessity.*

FREDERICK DOUGLASS
"ORATION IN MEMORY OF ABRAHAM LINCOLN"
DELIVERED AT THE UNVEILING OF THE
FREEDMAN'S MONUMENT IN MEMORY OF ABRAHAM LINCOLN
LINCOLN PARK, WASHINGTON, D.C., APRIL 14, 1876

# CONTENTS

PART III

# The Man on the Seal
### Morton S. Wilkinson, 1865–1869

PART IV

# The Man in the Shadows
### Daniel D. Merrill, 1864–1871

PART V

# The Buried Citizen
### Sarah Burger Stearns, 1866–1875

PART VI

# *The Changed Man*

### Morton S. Wilkinson, 1869–1876

EPILOGUE

# ACKNOWLEDGMENTS

I thank Professor Annette Atkins for urging me to find confidence in writing this history and the courage to present it in my own "voice," and Professor William Jones for his insights into the nuance of race relations in the postwar North. As always, I wish to express appreciation to all of the researchers and archivists at the Minnesota Historical Society who were always ready to provide me with assistance to my work. I am especially indebted to Erik Anderson for believing in this book. His calm reassurance, wise advice, and simple kindness made the project quite doable.

# "WE HAVE DONE OUR PART"

*You have chosen the anniversary of the great Proclamation*
*of Emancipation, and if in this city the majority was*
*against you, the grand agricultural people were for you.*

MORTON S. WILKINSON, 1869

St. Paul, Minnesota.

January 1, 1869, six years to the day that President Abraham Lincoln issued the Emancipation Proclamation.

Ingersoll Hall was alive with the jubilation of the black men and women of Minnesota who had crowded into the large auditorium in which they would normally not have been allowed. This evening they were there to hear and cheer the political leadership of the state welcoming them at last into the community of Minnesota citizens. The enthusiasm of the audience did not dim even after the sixth speech. But now, late into the program, with the introduction of the next speaker, the crowd's enthusiasm reached an even higher pitch, not because he was the most entertaining orator of the day—that honor went to the last speaker of the evening, Ignatius Donnelly—but because he was the one political leader who did more to persuade the white men of the state to extend the right to vote to black men. To a sustained ovation, Morton Smith Wilkinson, former U.S. senator, recently elected member to the House of Representatives, and a genuine hero to black equality, took center stage and prepared to speak, as he always did, not from notes but from the fire deep within his combative heart.

All eyes were cast upon him—including, it seemed, those from the four banners hanging overhead that displayed the weathered faces of generals Ulysses S. Grant and Philip Sheridan, Frederick Douglass, the conscience of America, and their beloved Abraham Lincoln; but Wilkinson seemed unaffected by it all. He was accustomed to speaking before large crowds and being a witness and, on occasion, a participant to historic events; and he was not one to be impressed by great men. Whether on the battlefield or in the president's office, Wilkinson had ventured into both quarters to scold the men in charge for not being more aggressive against the rebels and the Dakota in 1862 and 1863. Wilkinson now viewed the banners—even the beatific likeness of the martyred president, perhaps even the blacks seated before him, as symbols— stained fibers of the bloody shirt, indeed icons—so fundamental to a political party that had lost its way.[1] He and the Republicans were indeed at odds.

His slender frame, prominent forehead and chin, and broad, thin-lipped mouth that on most recent occasions appeared severe and humorless, reflected the intensity through which he delivered words that could fill the packed hall with the fervor of an Old Testament prophet. His visage was in stark contrast to the triumphant celebration now occurring within the very city that had for fifteen years mocked the abolition of slavery and rejected black suffrage. But at forty-nine years of age, he was their champion, the general of their occupying army. Yet, while he embraced their freedom and their right to vote as the highest principles of the American experiment, he knew little about the people for whom the great struggle had been fought. Not since his youth in central New York, where his father harbored and then led fugitive slaves to freedom, had he had an African American in his home, and even then, he was but a child looking on as they hid, huddled and muted in the shadows within his father's barn. From that time onward grew his abiding faith in the nobility of the American farmer. It would be with that noble figure in mind that Wilkinson, responding to the moment tonight, would proclaim two simple messages. The first, to the survivors of slavery: nothing less than a commitment to hard work could erase the yoke of prejudice and bring them closer to full equality; the second: all that could be done for black Minnesotans had been done, and now it was left to them to do the rest. "So far as Minnesota is concerned, we have done our part in the enfranchisement of the colored race. The solution of that question [of how your race can gain respect] remains with you."[2]

It was a message and moment to get through. But even as he spoke, even as he drew tearful and cheering black men and women to their feet, his mind was already elsewhere. Only those in the hall who knew him best could sense within him the welling up of that pugnacious restlessness that always came with the advent of a new crusade. For him, the page of black equality had already been turned.[3] From that day forward, the only blacks he might speak to were the porters who carried his bags or the barbers who trimmed his hair. As the iconic likeness of Lincoln draped high above the stage, perfunctorily hung like a talismanic fixture of the civic religion that the Republican Party was becoming, Wilkinson had already become an apostate.

◆ ◆ ◆ ◆ ◆

Writers talk of that moment during the process of reworking a manuscript when a new interpretation of an otherwise all-too-familiar passage in the text suddenly hits them like a rock through a windshield. This happened to me when I was working on another book. I was transcribing a quote—"We have done our part"—made by former U.S. senator Morton S. Wilkinson in a speech delivered before the Convention of Colored Citizens in 1869, when it dawned on me that he meant something altogether different than I once assumed. Instead of "We have done our part [but we will continue to stand ready to help whenever you need us]," he meant, "We have done our part [and now we leave you to prosper or perish on your own]." Indeed, the staging of the moment was filled with paradox. They convened in a city that had largely voted against black suffrage. They were there to celebrate a franchise that had largely been delivered by voters in Minnesota's farmland who nevertheless had discouraged and would continue to discourage black homesteaders from settling among them, usually by subtlety and misdirection. And these farmland voters had just returned Wilkinson to Congress, where he had opposed both Lincoln's colonization plan and a senate resolution to relocate freedmen to northern states. The small number of black Minnesotans during the second half of the nineteenth century had found a safe harbor in the North Star State, but they did not live as equals amid an accepting white population. There were a lot of pieces to the puzzle that I had not yet fitted together.

In hindsight, it seems strange, even embarrassing, that my previous assumption was so naive and wrong. The fact is, I was superimposing the traits of a twenty-first-century liberal on the liberal of the nineteenth century, assuming that those in the past shared the present sense of Minnesota exceptionalism, and I was wrong to do that. Minnesota Nice had not yet become the restrained manner in which whites talked to blacks when sentiment was shrouded within circumspect agreeability: Wilkinson, sometimes hyperbolic but always blunt, meant what he said.

His "part" meant giving black people freedom from slavery and black men the ballot and the legal right to acquire a farm; in terms of helping to defeat

Lincoln's policy on colonization, Wilkinson adamantly believed that America was the rightful home of African Americans. These provisions were all that were needed and it was indeed a significant list. What one did with these opportunities, the degree to which one was industrious and sober, made all the difference between one's success and failure. In Wilkinson's mind, racism was adversity to be overcome, no different from a crop failure or a business forced to close. One's duty as a "hard-handed" Republican, a true American, was to persevere. Life was hard, and it was supposed to be, for it was only through adversity that one showed one's character. The clearest indicator of a man's success could be measured in how far he had risen from his previous state of wretchedness. If, despite all the opportunities he had been provided, a man remained poor, then he deserved his impecunious state and the opprobrium of society. Nothing more could—indeed, should—be done for him. And unto such a man—indeed, his entire race if with all of their opportunities the majority remained wretched—one could affix, without equivocation, the well-deserved label "inferior."

Wilkinson's rigid view of self-help, very much in keeping with Republican ideals that valued landownership, economic individualism, and hard work, was nevertheless a perspective that, at least, permitted discrimination to become accepted convention and, at worst, enabled violent white supremacy to act with impunity. If opportunity eluded the grasp of African Americans, it was their fault and no one else's. If stewardship of their fate was neglected, the consequence of them being few in numbers made their welfare negligible.

It was a harsh assessment and one Wilkinson did not level against the farmer who, despite the opportunities granted by the Homestead Act and the whiteness of his skin, experienced debilitating hardship and failure caused by both nature and monopolies. In the face of their adversity and in their name, he saw injustice and could demand fair play. In their name, he distinguished between the economic laws of Social Darwinism and corrupt practices of privilege. Their failure to prosper was not their fault. To him the culprit was the Republican Party—a willing handmaiden to corporate greed, a far greater issue for him than its complaisance toward the emergence in the South of white supremacy. To him, as with other men who had called themselves Radicals, Reconstruction had become a ploy by the party to secure votes in order to continue enriching its friends. Less than a year after celebrating black suffrage in Minnesota, Wilkinson voted in Congress to defeat a bill that would allocate funds for martial law in Louisiana that had protected black and white Republicans from mob violence.

*We have done our part.*

In the wake of the Civil War it had seemed that African Americans had at long last overcome; that after surviving centuries of enslavement, now through emancipation and enfranchisement, black men were not just free but equal to white men. The Confederacy, and therefore the government of the enslavers, had been defeated. The Union had prevailed. The political and civil rights of black men had been ratified. And even with a Democratic president, the Republicans, the nation's most powerful political party, embarked on creating a new nation that befitted the vision of their beloved martyred president. Within the land of their birth, the land where since its founding social custom and law imprinted their skin into an immutable badge of inferiority, African Americans had, without leaving the country, finally, essentially, reached the Promised Land.

Then, almost as soon as it began, it all changed. White supremacy sprouted and spread throughout the South with a hitherto unseen bestial vengeance. Within this climate, the newfound rights were curtailed and eventually lost when Southern states amended their respective constitutions and by a federal judiciary that distorted the intent of the Fourteenth and Fifteenth Amendments. The Freedmen's Bureau, which was intended to redistribute land and educate the freedman to manage his affairs, buckled under an unreasonable multitude of duties, working with a meager annual budget and relying on overworked agents harassed and brutalized by white mobs. Within ten years after Appomattox, African Americans throughout the South were being forced back into a position of subjugation, except this time Jim Crow had replaced Simon Legree.

The quality of life for African Americans throughout the North was also different. Their political rights remained unfettered, and during the 1870s they were largely free from mob violence. However, small populations in the cities and towns had no political influence, organizational clout, or training to compete against white native- and foreign-born workers for a share of economic opportunities, and in most Northern cities black children were required to attend segregated and ill-equipped schools that limited the quality of their education. Those who worked on farms tended to do so as laborers, not owners. As Southern blacks made their way to Northern cities, these people from the countryside were transformed into an urban underclass. Simply put, for most, the right to vote did not result in farm ownership, jobs, adequate housing, and harassment-free education for their children.

It was becoming clear that African Americans were entering into a new era of unanticipated darkness. Notwithstanding that it all happened on the watch of the Party of Lincoln, the decline occurred in plain view of the white patrons of emancipation and black enfranchisement, many of whom had acquired positions of status, comfort, and privilege. In 1877, the year when Reconstruction ended and well into the decade when Southern white supremacy terrorized black citizens and rolled back their rights, Henry Ward Beecher wrote to fellow abolitionist Wendell Phillips, "Ah, Phillips, we are getting old . . . for I feel that there is nothing left now to fight against—nothing that excites my antagonism as did those questions of our younger days. They are settled, and you and I are no account any longer."[4] And Minnesota's fiery liberal congressman Ignatius Donnelly, and occasional ally of the taciturn Morton Wilkinson, echoed the sentiment, adding that a new great struggle now needed to be engaged. "The struggle between the North and South having ended the struggle between the East and West commences. It will not be a conflict of arms but of ideas a contest of interests—a struggle of intelligence—one side defending itself from the greed of the other."[5]

*We have done our part.*

In fact, Republican-led Minnesota fit into the broader regional and national story of black citizenship when it extended voting rights to black male residents and ended school segregation.[6] Nonetheless blacks were denied opportunities to acquire skills and purchase farms, though not by legal decree. Rather, racial prejudice on the part of the seller or land agents proved to be as prohibitive as any Jim Crow law. Even "friends of the black man" (as illustrated by Thomas Montgomery, one of the subjects of this book) exploited their positions in acquiring land that trusting blacks thought was available to them; and Wilkinson simply bowed to political expediency. Like so many Lincoln Republicans, he believed that blacks had a right to homestead on America's public lands; yet as a senator he spearheaded the removal of the Dakota and Winnebago, who had possessed the rich farmland of the state's southwestern counties, opened it for homesteading, but deferred to the racial animus of whites who wanted to reserve it for white settlement. Indeed, as this book points out, after the Civil War, many whites, just as many Indians at the outset of the Dakota War, felt that blacks received resources that should have gone to them.

The "bridge of gold"—a phrase Donnelly coined to describe the path of opportunity for immigrant farmers to settle in agrarian Minnesota—for most newly arriving blacks led to urban areas and poverty. By 1870 the city had indeed become the new promised land for African Americans with, in fact, a new kind of challenge. "Locked into a rigid socioeconomic class structure," historian David Taylor wrote, "black people were generally unable to procure employment above low wage levels."[7] In Lowertown, the section of St. Paul where they lived with other impoverished immigrants, blacks in the coming years would be left behind as their ethnic neighbors moved out into the city's residential, political, and, for many, economical mainstream.[8] Within this emerging American city a new housing and socioeconomic arrangement that later scholars would call the ghetto became their promised land.[9]

By 1870 the white patrons—satisfied that their black brethren were free, if not equal—went their own way to pursue their own financial and political interests, never to return to the cause, allowing the momentum they had created on behalf of equality to slow to a crawl, leaving that work unfinished, even blaming the unfinished work on the failed effort of what many came to view as an "unfortunate and unindustrious" race. Some, like Thomas Montgomery and Daniel D. Merrill, lost interest and moved on to other work. Others, like Wilkinson and Sarah Burger Stearns, grew hostile to black equality for they felt it (in the guise of the "bloody shirt") was used by cynical Republican bosses to maintain their hold on power at the expense of the interests of other constituencies. Still others simply did not have a vision for what should come after enfranchisement. In 1873 clerks in two St. Paul hotels denied rooms to Frederick Douglass on account of his race. The proprietors of both hotels were Republicans, one even a friend of Douglass. Humiliated by the incident, the Republican-dominated legislature considered whether to sponsor a resolution to ban discrimination in public accommodations. The intent to resolve to debate the issue was tabled.[10]

A year after Congress had dropped a provision that would federally prohibit school segregation, Douglass's oration in memory of Abraham Lincoln on April 14, 1876, was a tour de force of both soaring praise, gratitude, and restraint: "I refer to the past not in malice, for this is no day for malice, but simply to place more distinctly in front the gratifying and glorious change which had come both to our white fellow-citizens and ourselves, and to congratulate all upon the contrast between now and then."[11] Within the year, as a bargain to keep a Republican in the White House, president-elect Rutherford B. Hayes, from whom Douglass would benefit through patronage and access, withdrew federal troops from the South, leaving the fate of millions of African Americans within that region in the hands of white supremacists.

Everyone, it seemed, who had served on the right side of history and now celebrated themselves in the visage of martyrs cast in bronze, nonetheless lived in parallel worlds. For white patrons: in this monument to Lincoln they could see their noble legacy of emancipation and, without full self-awareness, seemingly intransient paternalism toward the emancipated. For blacks: as if a reminder of a life of caution they had lived for the past decade and would continue to live even in the North, the shackles of the huddled freedman, though broken, remained fixed on his wrists even in freedom, for time immemorial. He was never to forget what Lincoln and, by extension, his Children had done for him. Yet, even in the uplifting course of ennobling deeds, it was their persistent though often tastefully discreet belief in the inferiority of the African American that actually slowed black advancement, the freed chattel forever huddled at the knee of his emancipator, free but forever not equal.

Douglass declared, "Truth compels me to admit, even here in the presence of the monument we have erected to his memory, Abraham Lincoln was not, in the fullest sense of the word, either our man or our model. In his interests, in his associations, in his habits of thought, and in his prejudices, he was a white man . . . preeminently the white man's President, entirely devoted to the welfare of white men."[12] Even as such, in the days immediately preceding his assassination, the multidimensional Lincoln that few of his day fully understood—his "children" or "stepchildren"—was already moved, as Eric Foner notes, "to ask the entire nation to confront unblinkingly the legacy of the long history of slavery."[13] He had led a nation to abolish an institution that had been a fixture in the minds of his compatriots, but he did not live long enough to leave a road map or even a singular vision of how to secure the need for full opportunity for black Americans. That legacy would have to be left to his otherwise preoccupied "children."

It would therefore be easy to condemn the Lincoln Republicans as a whole for the failure of shortsighted principle in racial justice: ratifying progressive laws ("all men are created equal . . .") without modeling progressive behavior (. . . *as long as the freedmen tactfully knew their place*) was akin to dousing a flame but leaving embers unattended. In fairness, by thinking that they had done their part, they turned their attention to other pressing matters, often taking opposing sides on such issues as economic inequity, women's suffrage, immigration, political corruption, sectional reconciliation, conquest of Indian lands, and entrepreneurial pursuits. In Minnesota the list of issues with which they contended would include the five-year ordeal of grasshopper infestation and railroad regulation. As significant as each of these was, I believe many of these issues to a greater or lesser degree were conjoined with a gnawing sense of "negro fatigue," a profound desire to get on with life, and willful blindness to the resilient and corrosive nature of unattended racism. Government, they strongly felt, could not nor should not control the hearts of citizens. During the postwar era, Lincoln Republicans, far from being monolithic, would prove to be quite divergent and even willing to engage in political fratricide. Yet, by 1862, when Lincoln finally issued the Preliminary Emancipation Proclamation, thereby elevating the purpose of the war to a struggle to create a nation in which all men were free, they came together, for the time being, as one.

◆ ◆ ◆ ◆ ◆

I was interested in looking at Minnesota's Children of Lincoln, a group from a state that historians tended to overlook in American history and during the postwar era, in particular. It is understandable that they did so. Minnesota, with a short history, was, as defined by size of population, small compared to other midwestern states. Because of its remote location in the far north-western corner of the contiguous states, but for now far from the wave of western migration, it seemed insignificant to nineteenth-century national political leaders. Lincoln never set foot in Minnesota. Likewise, latter-day scholars seemed to find no relevance to the Minnesota experience. Three seminal works on the Reconstruction era—*Battle Cry of Freedom* by James McPherson (a graduate of my alma mater, Gustavus Adolphus College in southwestern Minnesota), Kenneth Stampp's *The Era of Reconstruction, 1865–1877*, and Eric Foner's monumental *Reconstruction: America's Unfinished Revolution, 1863–1877*—mention the state only in passing. Nevertheless, Minnesota's "obscurity," and its leaders' "insignificance," never weakened the investment in the national debate that the "Children" themselves had, most having relocated from New York and New England, where reform was deeply rooted. Under their leadership, Minnesota was the first state in the Union to respond to the call to arms after Fort Sumter fell, and four years later, the first to extend the franchise to the black men of their state by popular vote, doing so even though the black population was minuscule and growing in proportion even smaller as native- and foreign-born settlers flooded into the region. I felt it was time for history to recognize their work.

To do this, I wanted to make this an intimate history of individuals rather than a conventional panoramic display of leaders and events so characteristic of the canon of Minnesota history. The works of William Watts Folwell and Theodore Blegen continue to hold a significant place in our understanding of state history. I felt it was time, however, to delve more deeply into that history. Thus, I chose to focus on four Minnesotans, warts and all, using four criteria: they played noteworthy roles in black freedom and equality; their work illuminated hitherto unexamined corners of Minnesota history; they left records detailing how they saw their duty to black Minnesotans; and yet their names were not prominent in the annals of Minnesota history.

Accordingly, because civil rights were as a whole a political and legal matter, I selected Morton S. Wilkinson, the first practicing attorney in preterritorial Minnesota, the first Republican to represent Minnesota in the U.S. Senate, and, as highlighted at the beginning of the introduction, a champion of black suffrage. His association with black rights ended almost at the moment of its highest point as another crusade—farmer equity—consumed his focus and energy. Wilkinson viewed all federal intervention into state matters as actions of moral corruption.

Because of the fast-growing immigrant population who settled in rural Minnesota, I chose Thomas Montgomery, an Irish Protestant immigrant whose family settled in Le Sueur County and who served as an enlisted soldier in the Dakota War and an officer in a colored regiment during the Civil War. For him service in the colored regiment was a stepping-stone into the middle class. Once securely there, his interest in the welfare of the African American vanished.

In that race relations had a moral basis, I selected Daniel D. Merrill, a church and business leader in St. Paul who also served on the city board of education. What began as a mission to help black people launch their church ended when he was drawn to start other churches. Though the church edifice was constructed, the leadership of the congregation would not be the black man who led them to Minnesota, the choice of the members, but Merrill's father-in-law, who had not been hired by any other church.

Last but not least, political equality was defined only in terms of black male suffrage nudging women's suffrage to the sidelines. "This is the Negro Hour," insisted abolitionist leader Wendell Phillips, rankling Susan B. Anthony and Elizabeth Cady Stanton, and straining up-to-then strong alliances.[14] The trajectory of the work of Sarah Burger Stearns to establish women's suffrage in Minnesota paralleled the tensions between advocates for black male suffrage and women's suffrage that never fully healed, Stearns occasionally using racially charged stories to denigrate black men.

Through their lives, this book details the history of Minnesota between 1860 and 1876, roughly encompassing the Civil and Dakota wars and the era of Reconstruction. I have used extended quotes, perhaps more so than in traditional histories; but I feel in this telling of the history, they in fact help bring across the figures, their personalities, characters, and voices in a way that paraphrasing simply cannot do. Moreover, through the extended quotes (which nevertheless I believe I use with a light hand), my intent is to help these figures come to life for the modern reader. To this end I sought to achieve a balance between the vernacular of their time and ours today. The history will not be conventionally told in a strictly chronological manner. I present each profile separately; yet like scraps of cloth, when stitched together by the narrative of history, they form a large quilt. In this they are at once unique, yet a significant part of the whole.

All identified themselves as Lincoln Republicans, though Stearns and Wilkinson until 1863 were often frustrated with the president's apparent ambivalence to ending slavery. Merrill, a New Englander by descent, lived in the same region of Michigan where native New Yorkers Wilkinson and later Stearns lived, a region noted in the 1850s for protecting fugitive slaves from their Southern masters. Stearns's husband, Ozora, like Montgomery, served as an officer in a U.S. Colored Troops and, like Wilkinson, served as a U.S. senator. All but Merrill lived in southern Minnesota, and none was a farmer. Though Montgomery (similar to Wilkinson) grew up on his family's farm prior to his enlistment, he never returned, rejecting that way of life for himself (as Wilkinson had done), choosing instead to relocate to neighboring St. Peter, where he sold land to farmers. Stearns was a journalist and Merrill was a prominent businessman. All four were Protestants. Only Montgomery was an immigrant, and the only one of the four to bear arms during both the Civil and Dakota Wars. None, it could be said, had a friend who was a black man or woman, not even Montgomery or Merrill, whose associations with the African American were unequal, with both men filling superior roles in their respective relationships. Thus, what they knew about black people was superficial. Though the paths of the four white patrons at times crossed, there is no indication that they had more than a passing awareness of each other. Still, their lives conveyed a deceptively complex history befitting a state that underwent its own postwar reconstruction.

In this sense, the book looks into corners of Minnesota history not otherwise known—Wilkinson's often turbulent but ultimately loyal relationship with Lincoln that did not transfer to the keepers of the president's legacy; Montgomery's sense of opportunism in being an officer over colored troops while holding a casual admiration for the Southern way; Merrill's apparent ease in blurring lines between the pragmatism of doing business and politics within Democrat-controlled St. Paul and principles of his ethical beliefs; Stearns's struggle to advance women's suffrage against a churlish Republican leadership who bestowed political favor on her husband while chastising her for wanting what black men had received.

As each character takes center stage, standing in the wings are black men and women for whom history has recorded very few if any lines. The black leaders who serenaded Wilkinson as he received them from the balcony of his

St. Paul hotel that denied black patronage, a policy I examined in my previous book, *Degrees of Freedom*. The contraband Lizzie Estell who Montgomery felt was ungrateful when she wanted to return south after working on his Minnesota farm, because her children had been discovered and her husband, Will, Montgomery's corporal, was dying of cholera. Robert Hickman, who as a slave could preach to his flock in slaveholding Missouri but was prohibited to do so on the free soil of Minnesota: Merrill would help him build his church but installed his father-in-law as its pastor, relegating Hickman to a peripheral role. Martha Hall, the long-term maid of Senator Alexander Ramsey, who due to her race, status, and duty to her employer, consigns women's suffrage to a privilege to be enjoyed only by white women of means. The relationships between the African Americans and the central figures of this book characterize the full scope of white activism, its eventual limits and failures.

All of this looks like a study of duplicity. But, much to my surprise, I reached a different conclusion: the charge of "duplicity" can at times be an unjust reading of the complicated human impulses of not always agreeable people. In the end, it was my intent to resist the conceit of painting over their motives with a broad brush, but rather to try understanding the whole person engaged in their life and time. In their individual and collective stories, we have, I hope, a portrait of Minnesota as a microcosm of America, and perhaps even a glimpse into ourselves.

PART I

# *The Unforgiving Radical*
## Morton S. Wilkinson
### 1860–1863

# 1

# THE CANDIDATE

*I regard Lincoln as very widely misunderstood in*
*one of the most important attributes of his character.*

ALEXANDER McCLURE
REPUBLICAN LEADER FROM PENNSYLVANIA

On Saturday, May 18, 1860, George Ashmun, a congressman from Massachusetts, colleague and friend of Lincoln since the 1840s, and president of the National Republican Convention, arrived in Springfield with the committee of exhausted delegates who were there to perform their official function. As they worked their way through the Springfield crowd that had assembled in front of the modest two-story house, the moment weighed on the men in a manner that was in stark contrast to the raucous day before, which had culminated, once the ballot that put Lincoln over the top had been tallied, with cheers and the stomping of feet, boisterous demonstrations and blasting cannons. The committee members now showed no sign of the celebration they had left behind in Chicago, for the gravity of what they were about to witness cast a reverential pall over all of them. Lincoln's sober demeanor set the tone. Not even Lincoln's playful sons, Tad and Willie, brought much levity to the moment.[1]

After the delegates crowded into the "large north parlor," which was plainly though tastefully furnished, there was a moment of awkward confusion and embarrassment as they looked at Lincoln and he at them. Standing at the rear of the back parlor bowing in jerks, pale, with compressed lips, he seemed an ordinary man. The delegates shifted uneasily and nervously looked around for Ashmun, who was urged forward to make the official notification. Lincoln heard him with folded hands and inclined head, his eyes so deep they might have been closed. Then he stepped forward, accepted the nomination, shook each by hand, and hearkened to each name, all with an attentive ease and grace that surprised some of them, his face conveying to those who then for the first time met him, "an impression," as contemporary David Brainerd Williamson sentimentally wrote, "of that sincere, loving nature which those who had known him long and well had learned in some measure to comprehend and revere."[2]

Morton Wilkinson, a member of the delegation whose presence was intended to symbolize party unity—he, like all of the other Minnesota Republicans, was initially a Seward man—likely did not share these impressions. But his reservations were not founded on malice. Quite the contrary. He had known Lincoln for years through his brothers, who knew him from political circles in Illinois. Through their prompting, Lincoln had endorsed Wilkinson's St. Paul law practice in 1850. And even though the presidential candidate had not yet declared his support for the abolition of slavery—virtually the entire political career of William Seward, a fellow New Yorker, included his advocacy for emancipation—the reservation of the radical Wilkinson toward the moderate Lincoln was more tactically cautious: he had instructed his men to "keep cool under all conditions" and not offend the Minnesotans who he knew belonged to Seward.[3] As recently as the day before, the candidate had sent a note to his men at the convention commenting on the position of his chief rival on the issue of slavery: "I agree with Seward in his 'Irrepressible Conflict,' but I do not endorse his 'Higher Law' doctrine. Make no contracts that will bind me."[4] Nonetheless, Wilkinson understood that it was in the nature of coalition politics to have to settle, if one was lucky, for the second choice. But not even this got to the source of Wilkinson's reservation. As long as he had known the candidate, the Illinoisan, despite his folksy manner, somehow remained inaccessible. Now, in these uncertain times, it was unnerving to be led by a man one did not really know, whose moderation could easily be viewed as weakness to the detriment of the nation.[5]

Most Republican leaders in Minnesota never took to Lincoln wholeheartedly as one of their own, for he was not really like them at all: he was a westerner, and by virtue of their residency, they were as well. But they were Eastern-born men who had moved to Minnesota to claim and secure the land for freedom and opportunity. They arrived with skills or professions that could be plied to transform the savage wilderness into an enlightened civilization as well as launch them into a lifestyle that afforded them relative comfort, social standing, and the sensibility to pursue high-minded goals. For the most part they were not men who had struggled with the hand-to-mouth drudgery of the desperately poor and illiterate. They embraced reform, education, temperance, and the abiding belief that all men deserved just treatment from their fellows. Above all they believed in a society in which a man willing to work hard enough and show industry and sober comportment could move beyond his desperate origins. In this, Lincoln, with his rough-hewn, rugged-individual persona who would lead the nation as its president, embodied their greatest ideals. And yet, it was perhaps this early life experience—self-made, self-taught, self-counseled—that imbued Lincoln's deportment, a character trait that somehow rendered him inaccessible, enigmatic.

"A well-controlled and intensely private man," observes historian Eric Foner, "he seldom disclosed his innermost thoughts, even to close friends." David Davis, who knew Lincoln well, described him as "the most reticent, secretive man I ever saw or expect to see."[6] Hardly the heroic and dashing figure one imagined to lead a crusade against the tyranny of Southern slavocracy. Yet, Lincoln was now their standard bearer, this distant, cunning, genial but awkward man against whom they voted in Chicago on the first, second, and third ballots. It would take a leap of faith for loyal party members to accept that the national leaders best understood the calculus for political victory, the reward being keeping free soil free, and, purely on a provincial level, the prospect of acquiring wealth and power through patronage. Beyond this few could anticipate the full extent to which the America that he would lead, then leave because of the assassin's bullet, would be transformed.

Reflecting on how deeply the Minnesotans had been committed to Seward, and how the New Yorker's speech on that rainy day in St. Paul later on September 18—intended to be part of a canvass for Abraham Lincoln—instead amplified their disappointment that Seward would not lead them in the fall elections, one could not help thinking of the challenge Lincoln faced in marshaling his party with different loyalties, divergent interests, and a general but fundamental skepticism of him, his vision, and his ability to lead, in the best of times.[7] The challenge, of course, would seem insurmountable in a period of national crisis, especially if the cause for war was slavery, as Wilkinson felt it should be. Though Republicans were determined to prohibit the spread of that institution onto free soil and into the territories, they—including Minnesota Republicans as a whole—were mixed on the issues of absolute emancipation, black political equality, black military service, black resettlement to Northern states, and colonization. Lincoln understood this about his amorphous Northern constituency. Indeed, many of their prejudices were his.

Nonetheless, his political calculations were often checked by an acute pragmatism that monitored just how far it was prudent for him to go. Though it would always anger the radicals, Lincoln's political North Star would always be holding the nation together by maintaining solid footing with most of his party. In those uncertain times, the politics of the candidate, Wilkinson understood, would be one of compromise.[8]

Concluding the formalities of the evening, Lincoln said, "Mrs. Lincoln will be pleased to see you in the other room, gentlemen. You must be thirsty after your journey." They passed into the library and met Mrs. Lincoln, who, offering light refreshments, as one delegate mentioned, was "a distinguished ornament of the White House." Earlier friends had delivered hampers of wine and liquors so that Lincoln could extend "the usually expected hospitality." But the teetotaler Lincoln had returned the gifts, and instead made ready for the reception according to his own ideas of hospitality. No one said a word when the only drink offered was water. Wilkinson, a temperance man, was at least pleased with this gesture. By midnight, after many speeches and a brilliant fireworks display in the sky over Springfield, the committee members boarded the cars for Chicago.[9]

# 2

# IN DEFENSE
# OF THE UNION

*I see no way to still the hands of traitors.*

MORTON S. WILKINSON TO ALEXANDER RAMSEY,

JANUARY 17, 1861

It was unavoidable. For all the pandering to the Southerners, the facts clearly showed that they were intent on leaving the Union. In his short time in Washington, Wilkinson had worked among rebel sympathizers in the Senate. He had heard their epithets against the Union and had seen the resolve in the red veins of their eyes. Only a fool would take those men lightly, and Wilkinson was no fool. As early as December 1860, he described all the ominous signs to Mankato law partner Cameron Burt, and predicted that war now was inevitable: "The Republican members here in Congress are firm. They will not concede anything nor will they back down from the position heretofore assured by our party."[1]

A month later, he observed to Ramsey the curious impact of the treacherous rumblings of the people in the capital, even on the Democratic president of the United States: "[Buchanan] became terribly frightened, so much so, indeed, that I am credibly informed that he was afraid of personal violence." He saw the same fear within the other senator from Minnesota. "[Democrat Henry] Rice I think is frightened. He told me so also that he feared [there] would be an attack made on the Capitol. There are all kinds of stories afloat of this nature, but still I do not fear any such [event]. I believe the old ship will yet right up and get on her course again."[2] It was about to be the most meaningful time of his life.

Over the past month news reports from across the South were quite troubling, "an array of facts which startled the country and the ears of the senators as they occurred."[3] It was no longer a war of words. The assault against the government was not just widespread but also orchestrated; and there was a deepening gnawing sense that the capital was next to be seized, as Rice had predicted. "The clouds are thick enough," a somber Wilkinson wrote to Ramsey on January 17. "It looks to me as though the Government would be dismembered on the line dividing the free and slave states. . . . I see no way to stay the hand of traitors."[4]

It seemed that the rebels could appear anywhere. They seemed to strike at will.[5] So far all the targets that rebels seized were in the South, but the worrisome phrase was "so far."[6] Wilkinson worried for the safety of the home front in Minnesota. "I think soon there should be . . . in our State . . . the organization of a militia. We should have war in all probability." More immediate was the fact that the nation's capital was surrounded by slaveholding states. Though he would later hear of citizens of Maryland jeering Minnesota recruits as they marched through to the Potomac—one volunteer would report that Rockville, for example, was "a pleasant village, with a rather disloyal population"—that state had, *so far,* not seceded.[7] The rebel stronghold of Richmond, Virginia, was less than a day's ride; and there was diminishing confidence in the Union army. "It is not improbable that there will be difficulty here in the Capitol."[8] As the fuse burned closer to the powder keg, one month before the Confederates opened fire on the federal instillation of Fort Sumter, Wilkinson delivered a speech of defiance before the Senate in defense of the United States Constitution. "If those who are engaged in the destruction of the Government suppose that their treason will add to the power and dominion of slavery on this continent . . . they are warring with an element too powerful and majestic to be materially affected by any effort they can put forth."[9] On March 4, two days after Wilkinson's speech, Lincoln took the oath of office, and a little over a month later, on April 13, Fort Sumter fell. The Civil War had officially begun. Wilkinson accompanied Governor Ramsey, who had just come to town to secure governmental appointments, to meet the governor's old friend from Pennsylvania, Secretary of War Simon Cameron, and offer Minnesota troops.[10]

As more Southern states seceded, Wilkinson hoped that the new administration of Abraham Lincoln was up to meeting the crisis. He knew where Lincoln stood—that the president hated slavery, that he understood the nation was finally at the crossroad when it would either be all free or all slave; and that he stood foursquare for freedom—but Wilkinson was skeptical of the men on the president's team whose actions may have emboldened the Confederates. By July, even though Union troop strength was nearly 200,000 men, double that of the Confederacy, after the first two months of war, the outnumbered and more poorly equipped Confederate army gave as much as it received. That month, Wilkinson openly questioned whether the administration had the resolve to fight: "If the administration had been true, treason might have been crushed out in the start. But I fear now it has gained great headway."[11] But he could not have anticipated just which Republican would compromise first.

In late August 1861, two months after the First Minnesota marched out of Fort Snelling to begin the trek eastward to the nation's capital, guerrilla warfare in Missouri, less than a hard two-day ride on horseback, intensified throughout the state. This emergency was compounded as Confederate forces amassed just across the border with a plan to invade. John C. Fremont, major general in the Department of the West, would have to hold the state for the Union with inadequate troops and matériel. On the thirtieth of the month, hoping to gain a tactical benefit for his position, he issued what would come to be called the Fremont Emancipation, which instituted martial law. But the part of the order that galvanized the abolition community was the declaration that slaves of all Missourians taking up arms against the United States would be freed. The *Boston Daily Evening Transcript* reported that Northerners took to the streets cheering.[12] Harriet Beecher Stowe exclaimed, "The hour has come, and the man."[13]

Just as breathtaking was President Lincoln's order to modify the declaration; when Fremont refused, Lincoln, using the rationale of Fremont's incompetence in running the department, removed him from command. He did so to avoid alienating the border states (such as Maryland) and to punish Fremont's insubordination; and, in doing so, the president alienated the Radicals in his party, including in Minnesota, where Lincoln's action was viewed as a "cowardly retreat."[14] Even the moderate *St. Paul Press*, the leading Republican journal in Minnesota and organ for the Ramsey machine, felt a temporary loss of confidence in the wisdom and ability of the national administration, but upon reflection apprehended "no serious result from this step backward."[15]

Minnesotans around the state disagreed and they held public meetings to air the issue. On September 27, one such meeting occurred in Plainview, Wabasha County, where a committee was appointed to ask each of the state's

U.S. senators and congressmen his "position on the doctrine enunciated by Gen. Fremont." Rice's response was unsatisfying because it was frustratingly ambiguous. In contrast, Senator Wilkinson's response was both clear and expansive: he endorsed Fremont's proclamation and strongly criticized Lincoln's action. The fact that the president saw fit to remove Fremont from command for incompetence—especially in light of the failed leadership of many of the generals in the eastern theater—meant nothing to Wilkinson. "Whether Fremont is successful, as a military commander or not, has nothing to do with this question. I approve of the course he took in his proclamation."[16] To Wilkinson the president's action was a compromise with slave interests. No such quarter would be given to anyone who he felt was disloyal to the Union. Indeed, in Wilkinson's view compromisers and outright rebel sympathizers could be found anywhere provided one was vigilant, even within the U.S. Senate, even among federal lawmakers.

Between December and February, assuming the role of the senate's chief prosecutor, Wilkinson submitted the first of three separate resolutions that proposed to expel senators for conspiring with a rebel sympathizer.[17] On February 5, the senators voted 32 to 14 to expel Jesse Bright, which prompted applause from the galleries.[18] Fourteen days later, Wilkinson submitted a passionately worded resolution calling for the expulsion of Kentucky senator Lazarus Powell on grounds of disloyalty to the Union.[19] Then, on February 26, a resolution to expel was filed against Benjamin Stark of Oregon.[20] But by now the Senate was running out of resolve. On March 14, 1862, after a long list of duties—receiving, debating, and passing bills—senators, weary over what had become continuous, unconvincing, and increasingly inflammatory debate over the meaning of loyalty and treason, and "free speech" during a time of civil war, turned their attention to the greater concern: the war was not going well.[21]

Earlier that year, on January 27, President Lincoln issued a war order authorizing the Union to launch aggressive action against the Confederacy. General George McClellan, commander of the Union army, simply ignored the order. In March 8, out of impatience with the general's inactivity, Lincoln issued an order reorganizing the Army of Virginia and relieving McClellan of supreme command. Given command of the Army of the Potomac, he was ordered to attack Richmond. This marked the beginning of the Peninsular Campaign, which would result in a humiliating defeat of the general in July under the aggressive leadership of Robert E. Lee. Illinois senator Lyman Trumbull, chair of the Judiciary Committee, which first vetted the expulsion resolutions, expressed growing concern over the distractions of the debates and wanted to debate the confiscation bill. Taking the property of rebels might prove more effective in prosecuting the war, he argued, than expelling the pro-Confederate Benjamin Stark from the Senate.[22] He was overruled. For the time being, senators balked at confiscating rebel property and emancipating slaves within the nation's capital even if doing so would disrupt the rebel economy. But Wilkinson, who had brought the charges and participated in the debates, often putting forth detailed, time-consuming, lawyerly, and, when the spirit moved (which was often), ad hominem rebuttals, knew he was ready for that fight.

On March 26, 1862, Wilkinson rose in the Senate chamber to speak on the emancipation of slaves within Washington, D.C. The otherwise unsentimental senator from Minnesota was about to contribute to a family legacy that had advanced the cause of freedom. Until 1827, when slavery was finally abolished, and years later, his father had spirited fugitives through central New York State to Syracuse, from which his uncle, a leading businessman in the region, took them to Canada; his extended family included noted abolitionist Reverend Samuel May and novelist and poet Louisa May Alcott.[23] But until now, the senator had not distinguished himself beyond the small political world of Minnesota, where Democrats had largely been in control, where compromise was unavoidable, where principles were expendable: the voice he was now about to unleash had before been tactically muted. In calling for freeing slaves, he was freeing himself. This was his moment, a rare moment in which principle and practical military benefit were conjoined; but he knew it needed to be the "practical" argument that would win the day.

"Mr. President [the presiding officer of the Senate], I am prepared upon this, as upon all other questions, to conform my action to the plain dictates of justice and of right." Slavery, he argued, was not only morally repugnant, but the very act of slaveholding was so immoral that it even corroded the soul of the master. "Believing, as I do, that human slavery is the great sin of this country, that it is in violation of every principle of justice and of truth, that its influence upon this country, and upon this world, has a tendency alike to encourage everything that is evil, and to repress everything that is good in the State; that its evil influences are visited alike upon the master and slave; that it affects us for evil in our political as well as in our social relations, and that it is the primary cause of this wicked rebellion which has risen up against the constitutional authority of the Government, I feel bound, by every vote which I am called upon to give, and by every word which I may utter upon this question, to do everything in my power towards its final extinction; and, so far as my influence goes, to blot out the last remains of slavery on this continent."[24]

He reminded the opposition, especially the senators of slaveholding states, that the bill only sought to abolish slavery in the District of Columbia. "It goes no further; it does nothing more; it does not propose to interfere with the institution in any of the States, nor does it in anywise affect the relation of master and slave in any portion of the communities beyond the limits of this District." But, he said, "If there is a place upon the face of the earth where human slavery should be prohibited, and where every man should be protected in the rights which God and nature have given him, that place is the capitol of this great Republic. . . . It is an insult to the enlightened public sentiment of the age, and those who meet here from the free States of the Union, and the representatives of the free Governments of the earth—lovers of Liberty— should be compelled in the capitol of this free Republic daily to witness the disgusting and shocking barbarities which a state of human slavery continually presents to their view."[25]

The travesty of it all, he argued, was that those who had perpetrated the insults and threats on the representatives of the nation had actually benefited from the bounty of the nation. "Yes, more, when the hour of peril came upon the country, when acts of treason followed each other in quick and rapid succession, when the slaveholders were stabbing at the very heart of the nation, when the heavens were all black with the impending storm, and no one knew wither to return to escape the coming danger, we were here surrounded by slaveholding traitors who were daily plotting for the destruction of the Government which had fed them."[26]

He reminded the senators how dangerous it had been for antislavery senators in the city. "A little more than a year ago these galleries were daily filled with a mob ready to cheer every eulogy pronounced for slavery and to applaud every utterance of treason. Senators well remember the terrible sense through which we passed when vile traitors as Toombs, Davis, Wigfall, and Breckinridge were lionized by the slaveholders of this; and when, upon this floor, these men defiantly proclaimed their treason, there was no power to check them, for the whole authorities of the city were on their side. The city police was in sympathy with the traitors, and there was no security until the freemen of the North rushed to the defense of the Capitol." And why, he asked, "Had this Government been unkind to the people of this District? No; the Government had built them up. It had given them all the prosperity they had. Why, then, were they opposed to its existence?" The answer was simple: "This District is under the influence of slaveholders. That is the reason why so many people here were on the side of treason."[27]

He reminded the senators of the night during the earliest days of war, when he and other Union men realized the extent of the danger they faced within the city, and the determination they felt to defend the national edifice against what they were certain would be an imminent rebel attack. "We all remember the fearful night when members of Congress and other citizens of the free States then in this city met in the large hall of one of the hotels here, and, organizing themselves into a company under the lead of the noble and brave Cassius M. Clay, and sending to the War Department for arms, they resolved that they would peril their lives in the defense of the Capitol. This little company was nearly all the defense against treason that this city at that time had. But, sir, they were not long held in suspense. The telegraph conveyed to them the cheering intelligence that the freemen of the North were rushing to their support."[28]

But it was not an easy march, for the earliest troops had to traverse the hostile soil of Maryland, "now claiming to be loyal; now interposing her objection to the passage of the [confiscation] bill; now asserting her right to prevent the abolition of slavery in this District, and the progress of free sentiments here, then lay as a wall of fire between the seat of Government and those who were determined to uphold it, determined to repel and drive back the loyal people of the North."[29] He then told of the violent assault of a massive Baltimore mob on federal troops marching to Washington. "I believe that the first blood shed in this wicked rebellion was poured out in Baltimore by the brave troops of Massachusetts while a little band of them, not more than one hundred in number, were forcing their way through the maddened and infuriated mob of from eight to ten thousand, which resisted their passage through the city on the 19th of April, 'the first slaughter that took place in this war.'"[30]

When information was received at the depot of this attack, the Pennsylvania regiment, which had just arrived in the city and which was unarmed, was sent back. Some were also wounded in the melee. Wilkinson reported that the governor and the mayor, "entirely at the mercy of the secessionists," ordered that no more troops pass through town, and requested the owner of the railway to transport the troops to the border of the state. Such was the level of chaos in the city that the bodies of the dead soldiers, wrote the mayor in his letter of sincere regret to Massachusetts governor John Andrew, could not be sent home for burial. Wilkinson said, "The people, debauched by slavery, corrupted by its degrading influence, and maddened by the evil passions which it engenders, broke lose from all the restraints of law, and wildly trampled civil authority under their feet. . . . There is nothing in it to cheer the heart of the true patriot; there is no bright spot here upon which the eye of the lover of the Union rest."[31] Only coercion, Wilkinson insisted, worked with traitors.[32]

Wilkinson reported on the massacre of Union troops in Guyandotte, Virginia, on the Ohio River, in the extreme western part of the state, loyal soil that soon would become West Virginia. The tragedy occurred on Sunday night, November 10. Two hundred and fifty federal troops composed of loyal Virginians were bivouacked in town. Rebel civilians established friendly relations with the soldiers, eventually inviting them to their homes on various pretexts. The invitations were accepted by all of the men who were off duty; and while they were being entertained, at about half past eight that night, the rebel cavalry dashed into town. "Signals were displayed from every house where the loyal Virginians were unsuspiciously enjoying themselves, and into these the rebels rushed, *murdering the unarmed solders in cold blood.* The rebel citizens, men and women, rushed to arms, and aided the cavalry in the slaughter." Wilkinson's point was simple: "Nothing but the barbarity of human slavery could ever so turn men and women into brutes! . . . There is no way to defeat their designs but to meet and rush them in the storm of battle; and that, sir, is what we northern men propose to do."[33]

His blood was up when he then took on Unionist Virginia senator John Carlile, pro-slave Unionist Garrett Davis from Kentucky, and Republican conservative John Cowen of Pennsylvania.[34] Days later, when Davis heatedly responded to Wilkinson's attack, the senator from Minnesota felt no need to respond, confident in the fact that the votes to pass the measure had been secured. "Mr. President, I regard this measure to abolish slavery in the District of Columbia as eminently just, humane, and Christian, and as tending to obliterate all treasonable sentiments in this District, and to rear up here the standard of the Constitution and the Union. For this reason, I support the measure."[35] When all had been said, it was time to vote for the bill.

On April 16, President Lincoln signed what would be known as the First Confiscation Act and issued the following message: "The act entitled 'An act for the release of certain persons held to service or labor in the District of Columbia,' has this day been approved and signed." As Lincoln noted in signing the bill, Congress had used its lawful authority to emancipate slaves, a provision that opponents of the bill had asserted in debate, and that he was "gratified that the two principles of compensation and colonization are both recognized and partially applied in the act."[36] Wilkinson had supported neither principle. But in the name of emancipation, and the opportunity to drive a stake into the heart of the slavers he hated, compensation and colonization were two concessions he reluctantly made. "I am," he said, "for stripping these rebels of everything they possess."[37]

On April 23, one week after Lincoln signed the First Confiscation Act,

Democratic senators, in their own rear-guard action, began attacking the new law on the grounds of its being unconstitutional. Wilkinson, expecting this reaction, declined to engage the principal proponent of the issue—his "dear and respected friend" Senator Garrett Davis from Kentucky. However, when Republican senator Orville Browning joined Davis, Wilkinson went on the attack. The chief villain in Wilkinson's eyes was Browning, moderate Republican from the state of Illinois.[38]

With the loss to Lee's much smaller Army of Northern Virginia at Chancellorsville after a weeklong campaign between April 30 and May 8, and now the Peninsula Campaign just then being waged and not looking good for the Union army, Wilkinson's blood boiled over. More than 18,000 federal troops, to 11,400 Confederates, died at Chancellorsville; 15,000 (to 19,000) would die on the peninsula. The day before, June 27, he swiped at the incompetence of the administration's prosecution of the war effort, when, after expressing support for a bill to proscribe favoritism, he quipped, "I wish they were guilty of a little more such malfeasance in office, if . . . this war would go on a little better than it is going on now, and I think that in this case we should have a set of men at the head of the war who believed in it, and that we should have the contractors who were anxious to furnish the Army in the field to the end that this rebellion should be put down."[39]

Now, Wilkinson was saying that Senator Browning, as reflected in his criticism of the confiscation bill, was not one of a set of men at the head of the war who believed in it. "Gentlemen are found here in the Senate, who seemingly close their eyes to the monstrous wrong of this rebellion, and the terrible sacrifices of our people in their efforts to suppress it, and they seem anxious to avail themselves of all excuses and subterfuges in order to evade or defeat such a revolt."[40] Congress, Wilkinson argued in support of the president's position, had the constitutional authority to free slaves. In this, he had shifted his position from a year earlier when he criticized Lincoln for reversing Fremont's emancipation order in the military district of Missouri. Lincoln, Wilkinson reasoned, was no longer the man who had sought to appease the slaveholders in the border states by reversing Fremont's order, but rather was now viewed to have acted in the defense of the constitutionality of congressional authority. "He places himself, in regard to the legitimate prerogative of Congress, on the platform where every man who was acquainted with him knew he would stand." Conjuring the spirits of Daniel Webster and Henry Clay, Wilkinson declared, "The liberties of this country, if they were defended at all, must be defended by the immediate representatives of the people. The sovereignty of this nation lies buried with the people of this country. It is not in the President, nor is it in the judicial department of the Government. It rests with the people."[41]

By June, the "people" as represented in the United States Senate spoke again by enacting the Second Confiscation Act "to suppress insurrection, to punish treason and rebellion, to seize and confiscate the property of rebels, and for other purposes."[42] As the law moved forward to approval, Wilkinson, now seeing the exigent need to compromise, argued that $500,000 be allocated to facilitate Lincoln's plan for colonization. He detested this portion of the First Confiscation Act, but here he was apparently reversing himself, just as he seemed to do in the debate to expel Lazarus Powell from the senate. Rather, it speaks to a special trait in Wilkinson's unique character as an advocate: even in the heat of battle, he listened to the opposing argument, sometimes imperiling the alliances he had struck. If colonization was to be the law, the allocation could make relocation more humane.

Born in the tradition of his father, who spirited fugitive slaves through Skaneateles, New York, to Syracuse and from there to Canada, was the notion that the African American—especially one recently out of slavery—might never find acceptance and opportunity within a society that so long had condoned his enslavement and the stigma of his race in Southern and Northern states alike. If freed slaves elected to go elsewhere, the nation owed them resources to get them set up in their new homes. With this, Wilkinson moved to amend the confiscation bill with a provision that allocated sums "not to exceed $500,000" for colonization "to lands or countries in Mexico, Central America, or South America, or in the islands of the Gulf of Mexico."[43] His intent was to draft an amendment that was "broad enough to enable the President to accomplish what is desired; but it seems to me there should be some money appropriated."[44] However, Wilkinson received no support from his allies, who made up the voting majority.

On Monday, June 30, the Senate approved the Second Confiscation Bill by a vote of 28 to 13. Senator Edgar Cowan, acting under pressure from Pennsylvania officials, voted with the majority that included Senators Charles Sumner, Trumbull, David Wilmot, and Wilkinson. Browning voted with the minority that included Senators Davis, Carlile, Powell, and Stark, the last two of whom had escaped Wilkinson's efforts to have them expelled from the Senate.[45] In the end, when the bill became law in July 1862, the impact was more symbolic than real. Slaves were taking fate into their own hands by leaving the fields to pour into Union camps for sanctuary, and the president, increasingly criticized by Republicans for not prosecuting the war more aggressively, would in time be poised to elevate the struggle to a higher plane of human freedom with the Emancipation Proclamation.[46] But Wilkinson was not wait-ing for that day, for two days after the Second Confiscation Act was signed into law, he argued for black enlistment into the army.[47] If slaves should be able to fight, their families should go free.[48] Wilkinson took it further when he, a lawyer by profession, argued that a man defending the Union should have the right to give testimony in court.[49] With these positions, he fully embodied the concept of a champion of the black man. But it was only this one class of man of color to whom he could show benevolence; with the Indian, it was much more complicated.

# 3

# THE INDIAN'S GUARDIAN

*" 'Tis hard to live in a world*
*where all look upon you as below them."*

JAMES FENIMORE COOPER, *THE DEERSLAYER*

When Wilkinson was growing up on a farm near the tall woods of central New York State, his father—affectionately called the "Socrates of Skaneateles" for his love of learning—filled their house with books that young Morton devoured in his free time. They provided his restless mind with adventurous tales and romantic images of the early frontier as depicted by James Fenimore Cooper, and of the full range of noble and villainous characters as exhibited by the Indians who encountered the writer's white hero, images that nevertheless reinforced within the young reader the sense that they were an exotic and wholly separate species of mankind. The novels had been Wilkinson's only exposure to these people, for since his birth, throughout his youth and adolescence, he had lived in places where Indians had just given way to white settlement, leaving only their names on lakes and rivers that whites had graciously chosen not to replace, or the lone personage of the odd uncommunicative fellow who lived on the edge of town.[1] It would only be when Wilkinson came to Minnesota that he first felt the palpable presence of a people who outnumbered his kind. In those early days, it wasn't so much that they were threatening, for they seemed harmless enough to white men. If they fought at all, it would be against rival tribes. Even so, their ubiquitous presence was disquieting.

Now, entering into what would be the second year of civil war that had drawn away more able-bodied men into the army, Wilkinson felt even more uncomfortable for the security of his family and their neighbors in Mankato (the town in Blue Earth County was on the edge of Dakota land where the Indians freely ventured about). At times, they seemed to him to be everywhere, like dark clouds that had silently gathered without thunder or rain, yet portended that bad weather was near, clinging to their blankets and exhibiting in their dress and manner no signs of civilized habits, no sense that they wanted to be civilized despite their proximity to white culture, no sense that they respected their own people who had adopted white ways. He believed that some of the same Indians he frequently saw roaming the streets harassed the Dakota farmers at nearby Hazelwood, killing some of the livestock, uprooting crops, and damaging farm tools.[2]

In town, they proved to be a nuisance as they milled about the streets, loitering in front of stores and sometimes asking for hand-outs, sometimes staring too long at shoppers and passersby or touching ladies' garments. They had learned nothing from their proximity to white culture. As a Methodist by faith and a reformer by inclination, part zealot and part naïf, Wilkinson saw it as his duty to bring the ways of civilized people to all of the tribes. He, like reformers of the day, like even the leaders of Minnesota's old fur trade, men to various degrees he had always distrusted since the earliest days of the territory—Henry Sibley, Joseph Brown, and Henry Rice—believed quite fervently that coexistence between whites and Indians was feasible, provided the native communities were given opportunity, education, and time to acquire the "capacity . . . for all the duties and requirements of civilization." Even once formidable chiefs, such as Wabasha, Wakute, and Mankato, were coming to realize that survival might require their people to adopt the white man's ways.[3] But much time had passed and valuable resources squandered by unscrupulous Indian agents had created among the Indians a new sense of desperation. As the war progressed, Wilkinson viewed these people who inhabited the Union's rear flank with increasing concern: the vast majority of them who most clung to their primitive ways posed a threat, not just to the spread of a republican civilization, but to life and limb.

In Washington, throughout the legislative season Wilkinson had focused on the security of the Union, whether the military had the resources it needed to fight the rebels, or whether this hallowed chamber was secured from traitorous senators. But as a senator from a state with a large Indian population, he was sucked into the quagmire of Indian affairs where corruption thrived and where even the best-intentioned man lost his moorings. As a senator with close ties to President Lincoln, whom he viewed as honest but naive about his ability to identify ethical men to be appointed to sensitive jobs, Wilkinson waded into the muck of the notorious Indian system with the same degree of self-righteousness that led him to prosecute disloyal senators and call for emancipation. Thus, he kept close watch over Indian affairs and the many tribes affected by a vast federal agency that was unmonitored even more now owing to the exigencies of the war effort. In such a convulsive time, when good intentions were like lighted candles easily extinguished with a sudden gust of wind, Morton Wilkinson was out of his depth.

Watchful of fraud involving federal dollars, he reviewed reports of the secretary of the interior for contracts made to transport goods to tribes, checking to see if they were given to the lowest bidder "or by special contract"; banning the sale of liquor; and sponsoring resolutions for funding to relieve tribes of the adversities of war, providing for "the immediate necessities of the loyal portion of these several nations [of Creek, Seminole, and Chickasaw Indians] who had been driven from their homes [to Kansas] in consequence of their loyalty."[4] On February 19, the day he called to expel Lazarus Powell from the Senate, Wilkinson submitted a resolution instructing the secretary of the interior to inquire into the expediency of purchasing land within the bounds of Minnesota in an effort to defray costs for holding a council to negotiate a treaty, in the likelihood of expediting the state's plan to build a railroad connecting St. Paul to the head of Lake Superior. He soon submitted to the Senate a memorial from the Minnesota legislature's request for land and money to support the project.[5]

As a member of the Senate Committee on Indian Affairs, Wilkinson introduced a bill to protect the property of Indians who had adopted the habits of civilized life.[6] During the debate Senator William Pitt Fessenden of Maine asked Wilkinson to define what constituted a "civilized life," a phrase that had appeared in many of his resolutions. Wilkinson, seemingly perturbed by a question for which the answer was for him all too obvious, responded, "I mean simply this: to induce the Indians to labor. Labor is a great civilizer-up in our country; and as the white men are pretty well civilized, because they all labor, so we think if we can induce the Indians to labor and earn their own living by cultivating farms, that will be one of the highest evidences of civilization."[7] If given the opportunity, Wilkinson was saying, Indians, in short, could live and be as productive as white men. The very act of industrious labor as the proprietor of one's own land not only would have a civilizing influence but would forever remove from the Indian's makeup the infirming qualities of his aboriginal character. In this Wilkinson felt that his intentions were good. Willard Hughes Rollings's comment about the expectation of well-meaning white men who supported Indian suffrage equally applies to their expectation of Indian acculturation and survivability: "Throughout the nineteenth and twentieth centuries, well-intentioned white people sought to protect the Indians; however, they believed that Indian people could only survive if they abandoned their culture and embraced the white European way of life. These so-called friends of the Indians rallied for the assimilation and inclusion of Indian people into the American fabric, but not as Indians, rather, as assimilated 'white Indians.'"[8] For Wilkinson, this was a point of departure that had made for him an uneasy relationship with his Republican brethren who were divided enough on whether their ideology should or could include foreigners and blacks.[9] But for now, the Indian should be given more tools to be civilized. There was no alternative.

This for Wilkinson was the crux of the matter, and it was emblazoned on the state seal of Minnesota—a farmer working the soil in the foreground and an Indian fleeing westward away from fields that he did not cultivate. Characteristic of the times, the inheritor of the earth was one who worked it. It was a classic Jeffersonian notion of the inherent virtue of farming, and it was, felt Wilkinson, in the Indians' best interest to adopt the lifestyle that could provide an opportunity for further advancement. It had been the lesson of his family legacy. His father, Alfred, lived on the same farm where he was born and was buried in the year of his son's election to the United States Senate. From the same homestead would come his uncle John, Alfred's younger brother, who became a lawyer, founding resident of Syracuse, New York, prominent businessman, and abolitionist. It all had been the result of hard work, for which there was no substitute. The Negro understood this as he labored on his master's land. Through freedom, he would acquire industry. The Indian could achieve the same if offered, and he accepted, the opportunity Wilkinson was determined to provide. Race and culture, insisted Minnesota's Yankee Protestant from central New York State, need not be a problem for advancement. It was only one's commitment to hard work that mattered.

He also knew the many challenges to achieving this goal. Unlike the slave whose desire for freedom was denied by a vengeful master, the Indian clung to his "savage" traditions like the blanket he clutched around him. The more money that was spent to change Indians' hearts and minds, the more opportunities there were for Indian officials to enrich themselves. In other words, Wilkinson had come to believe that Indians' resistance, which seemed encouraged by certain religious leaders, enabled Indian ways, thwarted Indian development, the expansion of civilization, and the security of the Union. He doubled his effort. On March 6, to induce "civil life" for Indians,

Wilkinson introduced a bill to pay them, as well as whites, for any damage to property done by "wild Indians."[10] But the bill did little to induce more Indians to become "civil." An exasperated Wilkinson shifted the burden to the Indians, believing they were "idle barbarians" incapable of being civilized. He and Cyrus Aldrich, Minnesota representative in the House, would soon openly express their doubt that the Indians would profit much from any attention.[11]

He was convinced that his work was being thwarted primarily by the Reverend Henry Whipple, the new Episcopal bishop of Minnesota, who had become incensed at the corruption he found in the federal government's Bureau of Indian Affairs and, by extension, congressmen who had a hand in its operations. Wilkinson was annoyed with the bishop, who could have been a strong ally but chose instead, in Wilkinson's view, to interfere in his senatorial efforts, placing the burden of transforming Indians on the government instead of on the Indians. Earlier, on March 6, 1862, Whipple addressed an open letter to President Lincoln in which he summarized the inequities of the Indian system and insisted on the supreme importance of placing the Indians under a government of law, administered by honest and capable men selected for their merit and fitness and not as a reward for political services.[12]

He had by then become a seasoned and, in Wilkinson's view, most irritating lobbyist to reform the Indian system. On April 16, Whipple explained to Lincoln that Indians had no protection against theft and murder—no legal framework for protection or self-government. Whipple's contention was that the entire system was rife with thievery and corruption. On another occasion, Whipple repeated this insight to Alexander Ramsey: "It is based on a falsehood that these heathens are an [independent] nation and not our wards. We leave them really without any government—then after nurturing every mad passion, standing unconcerned to witness Indian wars with each other looking on their deeds of blood, and permitting every evil influence to degrade them we turn them over to be robbed and plundered and at last wonder if we have reaped what we sewed [sic]."[13]

Throughout that spring the bishop managed to engage the president and the secretary of the interior in discussions on reform. He reinforced this small beachhead by obtaining endorsements from Washington friends, including general and former secretary of the treasury John Dix. Dix praised Whipple to the president: "I know him as a most able, indefatigable man, and am satisfied that any confidence the administration may repose in him will be faithfully responded to."[14]

Whipple next asked for help from his old friend, Senator Rice. Rice told the bishop, "I will do all in my power to carry out your views." The senator complained that he had little power. He was a Democrat, and the Republicans had taken the places on the Indian Committee, with Morton Wilkinson assuming his seat. Minnesota's Cyrus Aldrich, another Republican, served on the Committee on Indian Affairs in the House. Rice's view of Lincoln's Washington was cynical: "All, everything country, Constitution, right—sacrificed upon the altar of party." The Republican congressmen controlled the Indian patronage in Minnesota and "the secretary of the interior and the commissioner of Indian affairs give much attention to their suggestions." Rice believed that making Whipple's plan into law would mean nothing "so long as Agents and Superintendent, even commissioners are appointed as regards for political services." Rice told Whipple he would try, "but I fear the demagogue, the politician and those pecuniarally [*sic*] interested [shall win out]."[15] Whipple refused to be discouraged. He asked Rice to see Lincoln and urge "the appointment of a commission—simply to devise a plan." Whipple believed Lincoln to be "an honest man." "I believe he is not afraid to do his duty. If he could hear the cries which ring in my ears, if he could see what I have seen, if [he] had prayed as I have 'how long, how long O lord!'—he would act."[16] At the time Lincoln was following the reports from the Peninsula Campaign and soon Shiloh.

On April 13, Whipple lobbied both Wilkinson and Aldrich. Aldrich had already experienced Whipple's reach of influence that came from another direction. His House Indian affairs committee had been asked by the secretary of the interior to "give very special attention" to Whipple's proposals. Aldrich, however, intended to sidetrack the reform plan. The congressman, not interested in contributing to the destruction of a portion of his own power base, denied the need for change. He accused the bishop of making "general allegations and indefinite charges." Aldrich said he knew the Indian agents were honest because he helped select them. In fact, he insisted, the real problem was not the system but the Indians. Reform would mean nothing because of "the capacity of the Indian race."[17]

Wilkinson's response to Whipple was so similar to Aldrich's that they must have discussed it. He too accused the bishop of making "general [and insubstantial] charges." As he had said in a debate on May 13, he contended that Lincoln's appointments had eliminated the problem of corrupt agents, thus ignoring the bishop's fundamental point concerning the political premises of the appointment system.[18] Later that year, following the outbreak of the Dakota War in Minnesota, in the company of his friend and cousin General Henry Halleck, Whipple visited Lincoln and found the president sympathetic to his point of view. Lincoln is said to have told a friend that Bishop Whipple "came here the other day and talked with me about the rascality of this Indian business until I felt it down to my boots." He later pledged, "If we get through this war and I live, this Indian system shall be reformed."[19] Whipple got the commitment he sought.

In the meantime, old practices continued. On May 13 Senator James Doolittle of Wisconsin and chairman of the Senate Committee on Indian Affairs sponsored an appropriations bill that included $20,000 for treaty making between the government and tribes in the Red River valley, in the upper western corner of Minnesota. During debate, it surprised lawmakers, who were accustomed to officials inflating allocations directed to their states, when the senator from Minnesota proposed that the amount be reduced to $15,000; the bill as amended, insisted Wilkinson, would be of "significant diplomatic and economic benefit to the country and the State."[20] The two thousand or so Indians who lived along the Red River made navigation difficult, extracting tribute from boats and "annoying [the boat owners] in various ways." Wilkinson proposed to buy them off with a small sum "so that the channel of communication shall be unobstructed."[21] No extra sums would be available for plunder.

Wilkinson had in mind what had happened eleven years earlier in Minnesota when the government negotiated the Treaty of Traverse des Sioux with Dakota tribes that resulted in thousands of dollars ending up, not with the Indians, but in the pockets of fur traders, not to mention into those of Minnesota's first and (he believed) second governors.[22] Before the Senate, however, Wilkinson refrained from naming names. But did the "small sum" guarantee against corruption? asked Ohio senator John Sherman, thinking of the similar appropriation the year before by the "incompetent man" Goddard Bailey, who later squandered "the whole of it" and the money disappeared. The unscrupulous Bailey, who had passed himself off as a "dealer in government bonds," was in fact a Department of the Interior clerk who had embezzled funds, in another scheme, from the department's Indian trust fund. On December 22, 1860, he sent a letter of confession directly to President Buchanan, who had appointed him. Subsequently he was arrested for taking $870,000 in bonds out of the safe at the Interior Department.[23]

To Sherman's question Wilkinson responded that he had faith in the president and the "worthy officers at the head of this Government" and that he trusted that the secretary of the interior "will not allow this money to go to the hands of dishonest agents as the late Administration did. . . . If we cannot trust our officers, if because under the late Administration there were thefts here, we must stop all appropriations, we might as well abandon the Government at once." Then tellingly he said, "I believe there is integrity somewhere, although occasionally corrupt men get into high places."[24]

As to Senator Fessenden's question of why Indians should be paid off at all to enter into a treaty, Wilkinson pointed out that no treaty with Indians could be made "without some presents." He added, "You must give them blankets; you must give them medals; you must subsist them while the negotiations are going on, and the Indians will not make a treaty in a day, nor in two days, nor a week. You must have beef there to feed them, and blankets and trinkets to pay them: It is utterly impossible to make a treaty with them unless you make them presents."[25] He attested to the honesty of the new regime of Indian officers in Minnesota who would negotiate the treaty: "I know if they have anything to do with it they will render an honest and correct account of every dollar of money that goes into their hands. . . . I feel confident that every dollar will be accounted for. I would not vote for it if I did not think so."[26]

One of Minnesota's new Indian officials to whom Wilkinson referred was Clark Thompson, a campaigner and presidential elector as well as a banker, railroad speculator, and state senator in 1861. Clark had been placed into heading the Northern superintendency, whose territory included Wisconsin, Michigan, Indiana, and Ohio. This position was considered a great patronage prize, not just for the man who filled it but especially for Wilkinson, who, in winning this presidential appointment for "his man" over candidates sponsored by powerful men in Washington, displayed the considerable influence he had acquired within a relatively short period of time in office, owing in large part to his connection within the executive branch. William Henry Seward, Lincoln's secretary of state, had come to Minnesota the year before to canvass for Lincoln.[27] Wilkinson, who invited Seward, had known him for some time, in particular through ties with the Underground Railroad that ran across central New York State into Skaneateles (where Wilkinson's father worked) and Syracuse (where Wilkinson's uncle worked). But now as secretary of state, Seward had become the second most powerful man in the Union. But in recent months, as Union defeats mounted, he was accused by Wilkinson's Radical cohorts of having "an improper and evil influence" on the administration and the military.[28] Nevertheless, the two men maintained their useful ties.[29]

Thompson did not end his business practices when he began his superintendent duties. He continued to speculate in railroads and retained his interest in his St. Paul banking firm, Thompson Brothers. In July 1862, his brother

Edward was assigned to the Sioux Agency, where he complained about the sluggish delivery of annuities, supervised by his brother, the superintendent. "I have been here sometime waiting for the payments seeing the sights." He lobbied on behalf of his friend for patronage jobs under his jurisdiction, reminded frequently of his duties to the party faithful. Congressman Cyrus Aldrich: "Clark, keep your ears open and your eyes peeled. . . . Write us occasionally, & give us the 'points.'" His first annual report suggested he cared less about the welfare of the Indians under his supervision, and more about business transactions and the disbursements of Indian funds that benefited Thompson and his associates.[30] Nonetheless, the senate took Wilkinson at his word when his appropriation amendment was called and approved.[31]

Even though Wilkinson had let the serpent into the tent, he continued to insist that all money that belonged to the Indians should be paid to them. Indeed, the government, he said, was "duty bound to pay what belongs to the Indian whether the agents steal it or keep it, or not." There was a circumstance in which the federal government should not be responsible, however, and that was when the welfare of the Union was at stake.[32]

In acquiring Indian land, the government agreed to place payments in the form of interest-paying bonds through federal government bonds. But in 1850, it was instead decided to place the payments in state bonds. About $3 million due to Indians was invested in stocks of different states—most of it in Southern states, and in some instances, Southern cities. In 1855, George Manypenny, the commissioner of Indian Affairs, directed $390,970 to Northern securities, reserving about $150,000 of Ohio stocks for himself. "I believe," noted Wilkinson, "he was an Ohio man." In 1860 securities held in Northern states totaled $316,000, in contrast with Southern states, where the sum was $2,828,911.82.[33]

Wilkinson found that the securities directed to Southern states were going to Southern tribes who organized regiments to fight federal troops. "The sum [owed in interest through the present appropriation bill] it strikes me, ought not to be paid any more than you would pay interest to Jefferson Davis and Robert Toombs. . . . This portion of the appropriation, it is very clear to me, ought not to be paid. These Indians, as I stated before . . . had a full regiment . . . organized at home to resist the Government forces if [federal troops] should come through [their region]. It strikes me that we might as well set the precedent here and now of refusing to pay these Indians . . . until the question of their allegiance and fidelity to the Government is fully settled." To Wilkinson the arrangement abetted treason. "By referring to the fact of the case it appears very evident now and no Senator can look at the record without becoming convinced, that from 1855 to the present time, there has been a fixed plan to run all the money that has arisen from treaties with the Indians, and from the sale of Indian lands, over into the southern States."[34]

The year 1855 was a harbinger of the fate of Southern interest, for, one year earlier, the North formally mobilized against the spread of slavery, starting with the founding of the Republican Party. From that moment on, Southerners anticipated the day of armed conflict. Wilkinson reported, "Enormous amounts of money have undoubtedly been made by the officers who have negotiated these transactions, in the purchase of these stocks. . . . While all these purchases were being made during the time to which I have referred, in stocks of southern states, there was not, after Mr. Manypenny was in the Indian office [as commissioner], a single dollar bought of the stocks of any northern state. . . . In no event do I think we are bound by any principle of law or morals to pay his money to the Indians who have taken up arms against the Government; and, at all events, I would not do it now."[35]

Three weeks earlier, on April 21, 1862, Senator George Collamore of Kansas wrote a letter to Commissioner Dole providing an account of his "recent visit to the Loyal Indians who were obliged to flee from their pursuers (the rebel Indians and Texans) in the dead of Winter . . . [now] encamped on the Neosho River" in southern Kansas. Collamore stated that these Indians— numbering about eight thousand men, women, and children—had suffered and many have died from guerrilla warfare, exposure and lack of food.[36] Appropriations to "rebel" Indians would only be used to persecute other "loyal" Indians. Wilkinson's amendment to exclude appropriations to tribes fighting on the side of the rebels was approved.

In all, he insisted on accountability. "If there was a commission appointed, Congress should provide that that commission should make a report, and that report should be submitted to Congress for its action hereafter. I would not consent to leave a roving Commission to settle claims in this way." Yet, even as he took pains to secure a degree of oversight, the integrity of the commissioner prompted him to interject an amendment to add to the official's contingency fund to cover unexpected expenses that he might incur during the course of his duties. "In the management of Indian affairs a great deal must necessarily depend upon the discretion of the Department," Wilkinson said. "There are many things that frequently arise requiring an expenditure of money."[37] Wilkinson's gauge of rectitude was now in full effect when he again endorsed the integrity of the commissioner though there had been problems in the past that had remained in the present. "I believe that the Commissioner . . . is a strictly honest and intelligent officer. That he may have made some mistakes when first entering upon the duties of his office . . . but that he has discharged his duties as faithfully and as economically as any officer in this Government, I have not the least doubt."[38]

In light of how thoroughly corrupt the Indian Bureau was, it is hard to conclude that Wilkinson actually believed what he said, or the alternative, that he could be so naive. In the best light, he may have been blinded by his growing regard for Lincoln, who, like Bishop Whipple, he believed to be an honest man. The president's Indian policy, with which Wilkinson fully agreed, never seemed to question the proposition that Native Americans should give way to white settlement, though Lincoln did, on a few occasions, act mercifully toward individual Natives who had been on the losing side against the government, as would seem to be the case at the end of the year. Upon his inauguration he joined a federal government that had long provided Native Americans with shoddy, and often malicious, care. Senator James Nesmith of Oregon argued, "If there is any one department of our Government worse managed than another it is that which relates to our Indian affairs. Mismanagement, bad faith, fraud, speculation, and downright robbery had been its great distinguishing features."[39]

Lincoln appointed a man from Illinois named William P. Dole as commissioner of Indian Affairs. Dole and the president proved unable to undo the bureau's system of what one observer called "institutional corruption," for the annuities that were dispersed became an irresistible magnet for corrupt officials and opportunists intent upon separating Native Americans from their treaty monies. Fraudulent claims by white men drained tribal annuities. Congressmen used their influence to direct construction to political friends and licenses to sell food to the Indians at exorbitant prices. Dishonest bookkeeping was geared to keep Indians in perpetual debt, and the Indians had no machinery for processing their claims against whites. Corruption was rewarded and whistle-blowers were attacked.[40] As one agent told Lincoln, so many people wanted these jobs because shrewd agents could "in four years lay up a fortune more than your Excellency's salary." Another observer told Lincoln how these positions were used "to plunder both the Indians and the government," and the Lincoln administration seemed impotent to clean up the mess.[41] Such widespread practices to pillage Indian funds could only exist within a climate created by corruption among the higher officials in the Lincoln administration, who included Commissioner Dole, John P. Usher, secretary of the interior, Hugh McCulloch, comptroller of the currency, and John G. Nicolay, Lincoln's personal secretary.[42]

The Indian system seemed to bring out the corrupted streak in everyone who came near it, and Wilkinson understood the powerful allure of pilfering, especially when funds passed without accountability through many sets of hands. Thus, he argued against the government insuring goods through private companies, which he felt would only enrich middlemen.[43] "I think," reported Senator Pomeroy, an ally on this matter, speaking from his experience trading on the upper Missouri River, "the Government had never yet collected a dollar of insurance in that country, and I do not believe they will for years to come; and yet every agent will insure, for the reason that there are so many applicants for the insurance." Wilkinson's amendment to drop the insurance provision was agreed to.[44]

And yet he seemed to feel that with the right men in key positions, at least that part of the system was likelier to shape Indians into "adopting the habits of civilization," and that Dole was the right man to lead the effort. Wilkinson was determined to help Dole in that work. When news reached Wilkinson of the deprivations suffered by the Indians in southern Kansas, "who were entirely destitute in the middle of winter, frozen, and starving to death," he reminded the Senate that it was "obliged" to appropriate contingency funds to the commissioner, "this faithful officer," who had been "prompted by the highest considerations of Christianity and humanity" to now tend to their needs.[45] That amendment was also agreed to.[46]

But he viewed efforts that directed resources to those determined to hold on to their savage ways to be foolish, for it wasted funds as well as fostered corruption. The sincerity of Indians to be civilized, Wilkinson felt, filtered out the prospect for corruption. "The efforts to improve and civilize the Indians are misdirected," he wrote to Bishop Whipple. "So long as an Indian feels that his mode of savage life is preferable to the civilization of his neighbor, just so long as your efforts to educate him will prove abortive because education in no wise aids him in the gratification of savage ambition."[47] Rather, the funds would be better directed to those men whose proven effectiveness was reflected in the quality of the lives they led. He could see promising impressions of the progress of the Indians in his own neck of the woods, the county he and his family called home—Blue Earth County in southern Minnesota—and of the dynamic young leader in Indian Affairs working as the Sioux agent:

> [In Blue Earth County] some of the best fields of corn we have
> seen were on the Sioux reserve cultivated by the Indians. We were
> surprised to see the amount of land they were cultivating, compared
> with the amount of previous years and also the manner in which it
> is cultivated. That may be attributed the superior management of

Major [Thomas] Galbraith. The Major has made a great improvement in the condition of affairs during the past year. Many of the Indians who, until the present year, have done nothing, now have the best-cultivated farms on the reserve. Many new farms have been opened up, and for miles along the river there is every indication of civilization and (if you can see the people) no one would suppose he was seeing a nation of savages.[48]

Thus, in one of the final actions of the session, Wilkinson offered a joint resolution that authorized a portion of the Winnebago funds held in the treasury, at the request of the tribe, to be used for improvement on their land, located within the same county as his hometown, Mankato. With approval from his Senate Committee on Indian Affairs, he said, "It appropriates nothing out of the Treasury, the money belongs to the Indians; it is their fund." The joint resolution was ordered to a third reading, read the third time, and passed.[49] The funds would benefit all involved. In a letter to his protégé Clark Thompson, "[The appropriations] will give [fellow protégé St. Andre Durand] Balcombe a chance to employ our friends this fall."[50] If men were to benefit, Wilkinson would not be one of them, for despite his associations, naïveté, and poor judgment, at no time during or afterward did he reap financial benefit. He did, however, overestimate the extent of Indian docility.

The next day, July 17, the president pro tempore proclaimed the work of the Senate of the Thirty-Seventh Congress to be concluded: "And now, Senators, wishing you all a safe and welcome return to your constituencies, and to your homes, I have only to perform the last act of a long and laborious session, in declaring the Senate of the United States adjourned without delay."[51]

Four weeks later, Senator Morton Wilkinson led a delegation including Commissioner Dole, Superintendent Thompson, and Nicolay on a mission to negotiate a treaty with the Red Lake Chippewa Indians, when they were told that it was too dangerous to proceed: "The Sioux were in open warfare and had commenced murdering, burning, and destroying, and that the party to make the treaty must not go out without a strong guard of troops!"[52]

**4**

# A WILD PANIC PREVAILS

*"Is it justice to make evil, then punish for it?"*

JAMES FENIMORE COOPER, *LAST OF THE MOHICANS*

On August 19, 1862, at 11 in the evening, William H. Shelley rode full gallop into St. Paul from St. Peter, ninety miles away, carrying a dispatch from Thomas T. Galbraith, U.S. Sioux Indian agent: "There had been an outbreak among the Sioux at Red Wood, firing into the stores, buildings and killing and laying waste everything within their reach. Messengers have also arrived from Mankato, bringing information from New Ulm that the Indians were on the move, marching on from Red Wood, down to that place, murdering people, destroying grain, and creating the greatest consternation through the valley."[1]

Jane Grey Swisshelm, reporting on a massacre at Acton, wrote, "It seems that seven or eight Indians came to the house of Mr. Jones, the postmaster, on Sunday last, evincing an unfriendly disposition. Mr. Jones . . . with his wife went to the house of Mr. Howard Baker, a neighbor, where they were followed by the Indians. The Indians [tricked them into going outside] and, after getting out of the house, all of a sudden they turned and fired upon the party, mortally wounding Mr. and Mrs. Jones, Mr. Baker, and a Mr. Wheeler. The Indians then returned to the Jones' house, which they broke into, and killed an adopted daughter of Mrs. Jones, who had been left there. The wounded all subsequently died."[2]

For the white settlers who lived in Minnesota, the U.S.–Dakota War seemed to begin without warning. Most whites were relatively new to the region, the Dakota people, and the treaties under which they had lived for

43

eleven years. For the Dakota, the war was the inevitable result of festering animosity surrounding the negotiation and implementation of treaties with the United States. In a series of treaties executed between 1837 and 1851, the Dakota lost nearly all of their land in the state of Minnesota.[3] These treaties were negotiated using intimidation, trickery, and outright fraud by the United States.[4] Most prominently, in 1851, Congress investigated Alexander Ramsey for his role in the negotiations of the Treaty of Traverse des Sioux that led to the mishandling of $450,000 in Dakota money, and the amount of money that passed directly to traders.[5]

By mid-decade, all that remained of the Dakota homeland was a long and narrow reservation 10 miles wide and 140 miles along the Minnesota River in southwestern Minnesota, on the prairie, far from the woodlands they favored.[6] On this small strip of land the Dakota were unable to sustain themselves through their traditional means of hunting and gathering. A few turned to farming, which was part of the assimilation program advanced by the United States; but many resisted this and other assimilation policies, thereby relegating their lives to depend more on the annuities of cash and goods promised to them in the treaties. These annuities were always late in arriving, and when they did, traders took the bulk of the money, claiming that it was owed to them for goods purchased on credit. Robert Hakewaste, a member of Little Crow's band, later testified before a commission that "we were in a starving condition and in a desperate state of mind."[7] The Dakota were indeed in "an extremely destitute condition."[8] Federal agents did little to reduce these frauds, as they were often complicit in them.[9] Instead, agents exacerbated the rifts growing within the Dakota community by making resources available only to those, as Wilkinson proposed, who were willing to participate in the United States assimilation programs. Starvation, trader fraud, and corruption in Indian affairs; the late delivery of annuity payments; and rumors that, because of the American government's preoccupation with the Civil War, payments might be made in paper money rather than the stipulated gold, or might not be made at all, or that what payment was eventually made, might be the last, were all factors that contributed to the uprising.[10]

Meanwhile, as white settlers continued flooding the area, encroaching on what little Dakota land remained and crowding ever closer to the reservation boundaries, they began clamoring for a further reduction of the Indian territory. Thus, in the spring of 1858 several Dakota chiefs, tempted by the thought of increased annuity payments, accompanied their agent, Joseph R. Brown, to Washington, D.C., to sign still another pair of treaties. They agreed to give up the strip of land along the north side of the Minnesota River—nearly a million acres—for a price to be fixed by the United States Senate, but it was two years before Congress appropriated thirty cents an acre in payment. After the usual traders' claims had been satisfied, the Lower Sioux received little cash, and the Upper Sioux had coming only about half the original amount voted by the Senate. Such traders' claims soon became a source of bitter complaint among the Indians of both bands.[11] Bishop Henry Whipple strongly agreed. On March 6, 1862, he addressed an open letter to President Lincoln, in which he summarized the inequities of the Indian system and insisted on the supreme importance of placing the Indian's payments under government law, administered by honest and capable men selected for their merit and fitness and not as a reward for political services.[12]

In 1861 Brown, who had successfully persuaded over two hundred Sioux to become farmers, was replaced as agent by highly inexperienced Thomas J. Galbraith, a political appointee and newcomer to the frontier. That fall the Dakota encountered major crop failure, which resulted in near-starvation conditions during the winter. Adding to these dire straits, the annuity goods and cash, traditionally received around the end of June, did not arrive. This delay was probably the most important and immediate cause of the Dakota War. There were two reasons why the money did not reach the Indians as scheduled: the tardy action of Congress in appropriating the funds, and a monthlong discussion in the Treasury Department concerning whether to pay the Indians in paper currency instead of scarce gold. On July 14 Galbraith was surprised to find some five thousand Indians assembled at the Upper Sioux Agency. All were hungry and demanded to know why they should not be fed from the warehouse full of provisions that belonged to them. On August 4 approximately five hundred Dakota—mounted and on foot—surrounded the infantry camp of one hundred soldiers from the Fifth Minnesota Volunteer Infantry Regiment, while other Dakota broke into the warehouse and carried off sacks of flour. Lieutenant Timothy Sheehan ordered his men to aim a loaded howitzer at the door, but avoided violence as Galbraith, who held the Indians in disdain, allowed for the distribution of a tiny quantity of food.[13] On August 15, at the Lower Agency in Redwood, a Dakota representative met with Galbraith and representatives of the traders who resisted pleas to distribute provisions in agency warehouses to starving Dakota until the annuity payments finally arrived. Trader Andrew Myrick summarized his position bluntly: "So far as I am concerned, if they are hungry, let them eat grass or their own dung." Those present at the meeting did not know that the gold had finally been sent. On August 16, $71,000 in the customary gold coins arrived in St. Paul but a few hours too late to prevent the outbreak of violence.

On Sunday, August 17, near Acton, Minnesota, four young Dakota warriors were on a hunting trip when they came across some eggs in a hen's nest along the fence line of a settler's homestead. When one of the four took the eggs, another in the group warned him that the eggs belonged to a white man. The first young man became angry, dashed the eggs to the ground, and accused the others of being afraid of white men, even though half-starved. To disprove the accusation of cowardice, another said that to show he was not afraid of white men he would go to the house and shoot the owner. He challenged the others to join him. Soon three white men, a white woman, and a fifteen-year-old white girl lay dead.

The attack, apparently unprovoked by any immediate act, was fueled by the increasing tensions between the Dakota and white settlers. If serious grievances against the Americans had not built up over the previous several years, the Dakota might have delivered the four men to the Americans for punishment, as the Sisseton had done in surrendering a tribal member who had stabbed an American soldier,[14] or delivered punishment themselves, as a Dakota observer reported of the fates of two of the Dakota who killed at Acton and were consequently shot in punishment by their own people.[15] The Dakota did not take killing whites lightly. Even so, the line had been crossed. Many of the young Dakota men urged their leaders to initiate war against the American settlers to try to drive them from the Minnesota River valley. A war council was held that night. Many expressed reluctance or even opposition to the war. Some felt sympathy with or had ties to the American community; others realized that a war against the superior numbers and firepower of the Americans could not be won, even though many of the Minnesota men had been sent east to fight in the Civil War. Many others felt that the Americans would stop payment of the annuities and take vengeance upon the whole tribe in retaliation for the Acton killings, particularly since women were among the victims. They argued that the Dakota should strike first rather than wait for the inevitable. The council decided on war.[16]

Many who called themselves the friend of the red man were shocked by the "sudden" violence of people whom many viewed to be exotic but primarily harmless adornments of frontier life. "Before going to Minnesota," Swisshelm wrote, "I had the common [James Fenimore] Cooper idea of the dignity and glory of the noble red man of the forest; and was especially impressed by his unexampled faithfulness to those pale-faces who had ever been so fortunate as to eat salt with him. In planning my hermitage, I had pictured the most amiable relations with those unsophisticated children of nature, who should never want for salt while there was a spoonful in my barrel. I should win them to friendships as I had done railroad laborers, by caring for their sick children, and aiding their wives. Indeed, I think the Indians formed a large part of the attractions of my cabin by the lakes."[17]

Swisshelm insisted that they had been incited to commit the deadly work of misguided Indians or foolish and unscrupulous whites. "No one pretends that western settlers have injured Indians, but Eastern philanthropists, through the government they control, have, according to their own showing, been guilty of no end of frauds; and as they do not, and cannot, stop the stealing, they pay their debts to the noble red man by licensing him to outrage women, torture infants and burn homes. When gold is scarce in the East, they substitute scalps and furnish Indians scalping-knives by the thousand, and they may collect their dues at their own convenience. This may seem to-day a bitter partisan accusation, but it must be the calm verdict of history when this comes to be written by impartial pens."[18]

Many closer to the fighting blamed Indian attacks on Southern sympathizers. On August 28, the day after Wilkinson's alarmed telegraph to Lincoln, 62,000 federal troops engaged 50,000 rebels in the Battle of the Second Bull Run. Two days later, the Union army suffered yet another defeat with an incomprehensible toll of 14,000 federals dead and wounded to the rebels' 8,000. In the wake of Confederate general Robert E. Lee's latest victory in the South over the superior number of Union forces, and half their state being consumed by Indian hostilities, a pall fell over white Minnesotans as they struggled to comprehend it all. Rumors circulated that Confederate sympathizers within the state missed no opportunity to tell stories that "would poison the minds of the Indians and inflame them against the present agent and government. To make matters worse, Union defeats on the battlefield tended to lend credence to their tales that the Great Father 'was whipped' and that Indians would receive no further annuities."[19] Swisshelm was more succinct. "The outbreak was mysterious. It was of course in the interests of the South, and meant to prevent the troops leaving the State."[20]

Indeed, as Republicans claimed, "The traders had generally belonged to the Old Moccasin Democracy of the territory and state and had no expectation of better times under the 'Black Republican' rule. Altogether there was a considerable 'Copperhead' element on the reserve."[21] Not so subtly, the message was simple: Indian annuities and black freedom were incompatible. Galbraith reported that literate mixed-bloods kept the Dakota informed of the progress of the Civil War as well as the defeat of General George McClellan at Gaines' Mill and the poor outcome of the Peninsular Campaign in Virginia. Folwell writes: "The Great Father, they were told, was whipped—'cleaned out'—and 'niggers' would get the money due the Indians."[22] In other words, as the Dakota starved, blacks would be enriched.

Such sympathizers, it was said, were adept in working "upon the fears and hopes of the dissatisfied and restive Sioux." As one victim of the outbreak who later had been held captive wrote, "I was assured by many of the wisest among the Indians that it was what the traders told them more than anything else that caused the uprising."[23] Even the missionary preacher Stephen Riggs, who should have known better, minimized the privations of the Dakota when he emphasized the influence of the war: "If there had been no Southern war, there would have been no Dakota uprising and no Minnesota massacres!"[24] He noted that some Dakota actually anticipated possible aid from the British. Believing that the Civil War had disrupted Anglo-American relations, some of the older Dakota thought that in gratitude for the help they had given Great Britain in the War of 1812, the British would now return the favor, or at least provide sanctuary. Little Crow, after the defeat of the Dakota, escaped to Canada; later, accepting that his end was near, he returned to Minnesota and to the Big Woods of which he had so many pleasant memories. On the evening of July 3, 1863, while picking berries with his son, Little Crow was shot to death.[25]

Swisshelm, speaking for many, even chided certain clergymen for their misguided ways: "When the Sioux, after the Bull Run disaster, arose as the allies of the South, and butchered one thousand men, women and children in Minnesota, the Quakers and other good people flew to arms in their defense, and carried public sentiment in their favor. The agents of the Eastern people had delayed the payment of annuity three weeks, and then insulted Mr. Lo by tendering him one-half his money in government bonds, and for this great wrong the peaceable Quaker, the humanitarian Unitarian, the orthodox Congregationalist and Presbyterian, the enthusiastic Methodist and staid Baptist, felt it but right Mr. Lo should have his revenge."[26] She insisted that hypocrisy shrouded their "unique brand of Christianity," which at once condemned polygamy among the Mormons while tolerating the same practice among the Indians. The "do-gooders," she wrote acidly, did nothing to cause the Indians to become civilized, even while wringing their hands in sympathy for them. "All the property of every tribe must be held in common, so that there can possibly be no incentive to industry and economy; but if the Indian refuse to be civilized on that plan, he must go on taking scalps and being excused, until extermination solve the problem."[27]

It was exactly the type of circumstance that had alarmed Wilkinson about the conditions faced by other tribes, that under the worst circumstances—as clearly the fall of 1862 seemed to be for the future of the Union—fools and traitors on the nation's vulnerable rear flank could easily incite the Indians to rise up. And now these circumstances had come to pass, right under his nose, on his watch, in his state, within miles of his own house, desperately near his wife and children. All the work he had done for their welfare, to reduce opportunities of fraud and to make funds available at their request, as he had done for the Winnebago on the last day of session, was all for naught. Simply put: he reacted not just as a representative of the victims of the region would, but as one who felt betrayed. It is unknown whether he knew the supplies and annuities had been locked in the warehouse and held while the Dakota, to whom the supplies were directed, starved. But he was remarkably shortsighted—indeed, willfully blind—in these affairs despite what he claimed in the Senate debate. Corruption within Minnesota's Indian system was rampant, committed by faithful party men, many of whom he placed in positions to exploit Indian funds or enable it to happen; and his hands were bloody from culpability.

Thomas Galbraith, the Santee Sioux agent, presented Thompson with a $52,000 claim for reimbursement in January 1862, suggesting the Indian Office cooperate in helping them perpetuate a "little fraud" while processing the claim.[28] "The biggest swindle," he wrote, "pleases them best if they but have a share in it." Galbraith advised Thompson to "riddle" his report as he saw fit, and mentioned that the assistant commissioner of Indian Affairs and fellow Minnesotan, Charles Mix, "would aid you & I think old Mix would easily go in."[29] With regard to issuing contracts that advanced the business of Indian affairs, Wilkinson instructed Thompson, in late 1861, that he wanted to punish newspapers that were "politically disloyal" by giving printing contracts to friendly newspapers—to the *St. Paul Pioneer and Democrat*, a Rice organ and rival to the Ramsey press, if at all possible. If this proved impossible, Thompson should manipulate the bid process so that the chosen papers received the contract.[30]

Special arrangements for contracts were numerous in the Northern superintendency. Assistant Commissioner Mix wrote to Clark Thompson about a friend who "has a little business transaction with you." In November 1861 Aldrich advocated that a contract to sell pork to the Dakota and Winnebago be given to O. D. Webb, "an active and devoted Republican" and "deserving of and entitled to a share of the spoils, and if you can consistently give him the contract he desires, you will greatly oblige him and all his friends." Wilkinson also had friends who wanted contracts. For example, he wrote to Thompson on behalf of E. C. Wells, who sought a contract for plows for Indians.

Mindful, however, of the unseemly impression of making the Indian system work for him politically, he preferred to preserve the appearance of propriety, cautioning Thompson, "I shall like to see [Wells] get the contract in the proper way, if possible."[31] Notwithstanding the head fake to propriety, Wilkinson had indeed played a role in depleting funds allocated to the welfare— indeed, the very survival—of the Indians.

Saint Andre Durand Balcombe at the Winnebago Agency was accused of misusing annuity funds and an investigation was launched. In testimony, Balcombe allegedly told a man "that he intended to make money out of his Agency and that the only reason why he accepted so small an appointment as Winnebago agent was for the purpose of making money."[32] A month after the investigation ended, Balcombe was still on the job and Thompson had approved a $100,000 appropriation request from the agent and passed it on to Commissioner William P. Dole. Thompson called the charges against Balcombe "mainly general in character" and claimed the accusers were mostly traders who had been refused licenses by the agent. "Thompson was correct about the identity of the accusers," observes historian David Nichols. "In Minnesota it was sometimes difficult to tell the old crooks from the new ones."[33]

When Wilkinson, at the end of the term in July 1862, introduced a bill to appropriate $50,000 of Winnebago funds for "improvements" on the reservation, the committee, as it routinely did out of courtesy to fellow committee members whose states were affected, approved the measure. The vote did not come easily. On the floor, under questioning from Senator John Sherman of Ohio, Wilkinson managed to refute objections with generalities. In a letter to Thompson shortly afterward, Wilkinson revealed the real reason for the appropriations: "It will give Balcombe a chance to employ our friends this fall."[34] In this, the senator from Minnesota appeared to become a full-fledged member of the corrupt Indian system.

But none of this seemed to matter, upon first hearing of the killings. The hostilities had erupted not just within his state but in proximity to where his family lived; and this made it quite personal. "After all I had done," he wrote to his law partner Cameron Burt, "and this is what the heathens show!"[35] On August 27, one week after the hostilities erupted that had aborted Wilkinson's delegation's negotiation of a treaty with the Red Lake Indians, the senator dashed off a joint telegram to the president that read in short, "We are in the midst of a most terrible and inciting Indian war. Thus far the massacre of innocent white settlers has been fearful. A wild panic prevails in nearly one-half of the state. All are rushing to the frontier to defend settlers."[36]

One of those who rushed to the defense of the settled frontier was Thomas Montgomery, a twenty-year-old corporal in the newly formed Seventh Minnesota Volunteer Infantry Regiment, Company K. Having enlisted just ten days earlier, on August 12, the Protestant Irish immigrant whose family had settled in Cleveland Township, in Le Sueur County, not far from the fighting, was motivated as much by the desire for heroic adventure as by a desire to serve and protect. To his family, Montgomery wrote, "A great many families came here to claim our protection. There have been hundreds of soldiers sent from here to the frontier posts to defend them and prevent the savages [from taking over]. The wildest excitement and rumors prevailed here for days."[37]

Despite the mobilization of a military presence of troops marching into the region, Swisshelm chided President Lincoln for not doing more for the people in western Minnesota, writing in mocking exasperation of a recent meeting he had held with a delegation of black leaders over the issue that had been nettlesome to most Radicals: colonization. Why not, she queried, send the "colonized" blacks to Minnesota, where they could provide defense against the Indians? "The President, that precious old imbecile, has had a meeting with a committee of enlightened colored men to see how much they will take and remove a few hundred thousand loyal men out of this country in which their presence is very offensive to his Kentucky brethren of the 'secesh' stripe. As our poor imbecile and bewildered President is over-burdened with loyal men, will he be kind enough to colonize 500,000 of them in Northern Minnesota?"[38]

When a miffed Swisshelm wrote it was seldom without mocking and multidimensional irony, and this letter to the *St. Cloud Democrat* was no different. Minnesota Radicals were already impatient with Lincoln's failed military and conservative racial policies, which included, for them, his contemptuous advocacy for colonization, not to mention their sense that Minnesota was being treated as a backwater of little political and military significance: even now, some fumed, despite the exigencies of war he had never set foot in the state. Since the beginning of his term in office, Lincoln often expressed that he did not feel free blacks and whites could ever coexist without conflict. With freed blacks out of the country blacks and whites could separately flourish. But free blacks rejected the plan even with the provision that freedmen and -women would not be forcibly removed.

In August 14, Lincoln invited a delegation of men from Washington's black churches to meet with him at the White House "for the first time in the history of the country." What he said to the delegation, another cause for Swisshelm's mocking tone, would become one of the most controversial moments of his presidency. "You and we are different races. . . . Even when you cease to be slaves, you are yet far removed from being placed on an equality with the white race. . . . It is better for us both, therefore, to be separated. . . . Blacks could never be placed on an equality with the white race. . . . Whether this is right nor wrong I need not discuss."[39] If Lincoln, "our poor miserable, bewildered President," was so intent on sending blacks abroad, Swisshelm reasoned, then why not as soldiers to remote northern Minnesota where their presence would be valued by white Americans?[40]

It was not altogether a flight of fancy. With the joint crises of the Dakota War and the routing of Union troops at the Second Bull Run, weeks later, after prompting from several senators, including Morton Wilkinson, Lincoln made the momentous decision to enlist black troops into the Union army. As late as August 6, Lincoln had rejected the policy outright for it would disrupt the delicate alliance among the North and border slaveholding states, but slowing enlistment of white troops and defeats in the South forced a change of mind.[41] Singularly, in terms of black enlistment, Wilkinson had been on the right side of history. In terms of the Dakota, the same was decidedly not so. The national emergencies in the South and Minnesota were transforming the president, but in the senator's view, not in the right direction.

By the end of September, the Dakota War was over. It was now time for retribution and Colonel Henry Hastings Sibley intended to mete it out, issuing an order on September 28 to impanel a five-member military commission.[42] Its charge was to try and find guilt "for murders and other outrages upon the Whites, during the present state of hostilities of the Indians."[43] On the same day, Sibley wrote to General Pope to report that he had seized sixteen men suspected of being participants in the "late outrages" and planned to try them. The guilty, he said, would be executed immediately despite his expressed doubt whether such action was within his authority. "An example," he wrote, "is imperatively necessary, and I trust you will approve the act."[44] Apparently General Pope would have, for on the same day of Sibley's letter, the former commander of Union forces who had been humiliated in the recent defeat at the Second Bull Run, wrote with all vengeance to Sibley, "It is my purpose utterly to exterminate the Sioux if I have the power to do so and even if it requires a campaign lasting the whole of next year. . . . They are to be treated as maniacs or wild beasts, and by no means as people with whom treaties or compromises can be made."[45] Not waiting for the general's approval, with the military commission impaneled—all of the officers appointed had fought in the war against the Dakota—and hardly impartial, the trials began on September 28, the very day Sibley had issued the order.[46]

The haste to dispense justice precluded time needed for credible search for the truth. The commission had set a brisk pace, trying sixteen men on the first day, convicting ten and sentencing them to hang; acquitting six and apparently setting them free. Sibley apprised General Pope of the progress of the trials and his plans for the convicted. On October 2 Pope responded to Sibley that he "altogether approve[d] of executing the Indians who have been concerned in these outrages." And he reiterated his distrust of Indians, whether or not they professed to be friendly, saying that he would not sanction any treaty with them and that he had enough troops to "exterminate them all, if they furnish the least occasion for it." Sibley held off executing the guilty so as to induce the Dakota still on the frontier to surrender, thinking they would receive mercy if they did so. When several hundred more Dakota arrived at his encampment, Sibley informed Pope that he expected to imprison all the men except the very old and that the Dakota would "receive but small mercy" at his hands. Indeed, although he had not yet reviewed the proceedings of the commission, which had by October 7 condemned twenty Dakota to death, Sibley told Pope that he probably would approve the results and "hang the villains" even though the proceeding might not be "exactly in form."[47]

Between October 7 and 10, Pope wrote several times to General Halleck to inform him that trials were in progress and that many of the Dakota who participated in the "late horrible outrages" would be executed. On October 13 Pope expressed his first doubt that he and Sibley were proceeding correctly, and he asked Halleck if they needed any further authority to execute those condemned by the commission. Meanwhile, Sibley planned to send the convicted Dakota and the other disarmed men to Fort Snelling and to continue the trials there. On October 15, Sibley received new orders from Pope, instructing him to proceed with the trials, to execute those found guilty, and to send only the remainder to Fort Snelling.[48]

In Washington, Lincoln read Pope's report on the status of the trials to the cabinet, who as a group rejected the proposed executions. Secretary of the Navy Gideon Welles noted in his diary, "I was disgusted with the whole thing; the tone and opinions of the dispatch are discreditable." Taking specific note of Pope's intent to "punish" the Winnebago, a separate tribe that lived on a reservation south of Mankato and who did not join the Dakota in the war, Welles pointed to one factor that must not have escaped Lincoln's attention: "The Winnebagoes have good land which white men want and mean to have."[49]

But pressure to execute the Indians was mounting in Minnesota. Governor Ramsey quickly sent to Lincoln the argument that would become standard for the pro-execution forces—executions would abate the taste for mob violence. "I hope that the execution of every Sioux warrior condemned by the military court will be at once ordered. It would be wrong upon principle and policy to refuse this. Private revenge would on all this border take the place of official judgment on these Indians."[50] Apparently disturbed by what he read and of the planned executions, Lincoln moved to prevent any precipitous action. On October 17 Pope wrote to Sibley that "the President directs that no executions be made without his sanction." By the time Sibley received the dispatch on October 21, he had reported to Pope that the commission had tried more than 120 cases, with nearly 300 remaining.

By November 3, the last day of the trials, the commission had tried 392 Dakota, with as many as 42 tried in a single day. Most were charged with joining or participating "in various murders and outrages committed by the Sioux Indians on the Minnesota Frontier." Most trials were but mere formalities; some lasted less than five minutes. No one explained the proceedings to the accused. None was represented by a defense. Of the 392 men tried, the commission convicted 323. Of those convicted, the commission sentenced 303 to be hanged; only 20 were sentenced to terms of imprisonment; and the remaining 69 were acquitted.[51] Sibley quickly approved the sentences. Mankato resident Morton S. Wilkinson, as he would soon make all too clear, did not think Sibley went far enough.

# 5

# LINCOLN'S DECISION

*[This is] a cause lost, and the country ruined.*

MORTON S. WILKINSON, 1862

Believing that the summary trials were necessary to avoid vigilante justice by angry mobs of Minnesotans, Sibley ordered the removal of the entire Dakota people from the Lower Agency at Redwood. "I have learned," wrote missionary John Williamson on November 5, "that orders have been issued to convey all the Indians who have not been convicted to the neighborhood of Fort Snelling. They will probably take up their march tomorrow. The men who have been convicted are to be taken to Mankato for what disposal is not made known. It is a sad sight to see so many women & children marching off—not knowing whether they will ever see their husbands & fathers again."[1]

Before departing from the Lower Agency for Fort Snelling, Lieutenant Colonel Marshall, trying to mitigate some of the fury that both convoys would surely encounter, wrote to assure Minnesotans that "some 300" of the "guilty Indians . . . are to be executed." But he admonished would-be troublemakers to restrain themselves. "I would risk my life for the protection of these helpless beings, and would feel everlastingly disgraced if any evil befell them while in charge. . . . I want the settlers in the valley . . . to know that they are not the guilty Indians . . . but friendly Indians, women, and children."[2]

But as the train of wagons and riders passed through Henderson, they were attacked by an "angered mob . . . cursing, shouting, and crying." Men, women, and children, armed with guns, knives, clubs and stones, rushed upon the Indians as the train was passing by, and, before the soldiers could interfere and stop them, succeeded in pulling many of the old men and women, and even children, from the wagons by the hair of the head and beating them, and otherwise inflicting injury upon the helpless and miserable creatures. A sympathetic observer, Samuel Brown, called the settlers' mob "as bad as savages," and wrote that he witnessed "an enraged white woman . . . snatch a nursing babe from its mother's breast and dash it violently to the ground." The baby was returned to its mother, but it later died and its body was "quietly laid away in the crotch of a tree," according to Dakota custom. Brown also recalled another incident at Henderson: "As the train was passing through the town one of the citizens with blood in his eyes and half-crazed with drink rushed up with a gun leveled at Charles Crawford [Samuel Brown's uncle], one of the friendlies, and was about to fire, when 'the bold charger of the Indians,' Lieutant Colonel Marshall, who happened along on horseback, rushed between them and struck down the gun with his sabre. He got Crawford out of the way, thus saving a life at the risk of his own."[3]

Meanwhile, farther south, Sibley led his convoy of convicted prisoners to the camp in Mankato. On November 9 the prisoners, shackled together in horse-drawn wagons, were attacked on the outskirts of New Ulm by a mob that pelted them with bricks and other missiles, seriously injuring some prisoners and guards. The crowd was driven back by a bayonet charge, and some fifteen men were arrested, marched with the wagon train to camp, reprimanded, and released. Two of the prisoners later died from their injuries.[4] By the time the convoy arrived in Mankato, Sibley's nerves were frayed. Corporal Montgomery, one of his men, heard him say, "If the guilty were released by God he would resign; [and he would] notify the citizens to come . . . [and] do as they pleased with them."[5] The young and wide-eyed corporal did not seem as affected by the pressure mounting around him until he took in the sobering spectacle of the condemned Dakota prisoners:

We have here all the Indians who were captured and found guilty numbering about 400. They are all chained together by two's and confined in a long narrow shed in the form of a square and in the center of the encampment. They are shoved together so close as they can sit and have little fire here and here among them. They are fed on crackers and in addition they have the care of a dozen squaws who administer to their wants by giving them water and soup made from the offal of bones of cattle killed. These squaws and Indians present the most haggard species of humanity that I ever saw—dirty, filthy, and lazy. . . . They are contracting diseases in their close confinement and cannot stand it here in winter.[6]

On November 10 Lincoln wired Pope for "the full and complete record of their convictions," requesting distinctions be made as to the seriousness of alleged crimes. Pope complied with a characteristic commentary: "I desire to represent to you that the only distinction between the culprits is as to which of them murdered most people and violated most young girls." He then echoed the governor's dire warning characterizing what had happened in Henderson, just days earlier. "The people of this State . . . are exasperated to the last degree, and if the guilty are not all executed, I think it nearly impossible to prevent the indiscriminate massacre of all the Indians—old men, women, and children."[7]

Pope stepped up the pressure by sending Lincoln daily descriptions of the funerals for white settlers killed in the uprising, and he wanted the president to know that his troops fully sympathized with the citizenry. He offered Lincoln a relatively painless way out of the situation: "I would suggest that even if the gov't be unwilling at so great distance to order the execution of the condemned Indians the criminals be turned to the State Gov't to be dealt with."[8] For more than a month, Lincoln and his aides labored over the trial transcripts. They discovered an appalling lack of evidence against most of the accused, who had merely been warriors in battle. Lincoln's fears had been justified. The Minnesotans were seeking blood vengeance, not justice.[9]

Meanwhile, on the evening of November 13, one week after they set out from the Lower Agency at Redwood, and four days after the attack in Henderson, Marshall's convoy of "friendly" Dakota arrived at Fort Snelling. On the first night the group camped on the bluff above the river, but the next day Marshall moved them down to below the fort. Soldiers guarding them were ordered to allow no one to enter without a pass from the fort commander. In a few days a stockade was built to keep the Dakota from wandering and to protect them from curious and vengeful whites, who included some of the soldiers. And there for months they would languish.

On November 15 Sibley appointed Colonel Stephen Miller to take command of "Camp Lincoln." A resident of St. Cloud and cousin of editor Jane Grey Swisshelm, the Pennsylvania native came to his commission as lieutenant colonel without military experience; but his sixteen months of service were filled with much distinction. In two years he would be the fourth governor of Minnesota. He had demonstrated courage at Bull Run and at other battles when he was summoned back to help put down the Indian uprising. Miller arrived to take charge of the Seventh Regiment, but only after the Dakota's surrender at Camp Release. When Sibley turned over the command at South Bend to Miller, his primary orders were to protect the Indian prisoners while President Lincoln weighed the fate of the 303 Dakota who had been sentenced to hang.[10]

Shortly after Sibley left Mankato, Miller received a visit from Colonel Milton Montgomery (not related to the corporal), who commanded Wisconsin troops barracked in Mankato. Montgomery reported his "serious apprehension" regarding the safety of the Dakota. Miller reported to Sibley that he learned of "extensive secret organizations including men of character in all this upper country, and many soldiers" who will only relent provided they are assured that the Dakota will hang. "Should such a calamity occur, [we] will of course sell our lives as dearly as possible, in obedience to the laws, and our superior officers. . . . If an attempt is made at all it will no doubt be of the most formidable character. I was informed on yesterday that the Sheriff was very busy exciting the citizens upon this subject." An attack was imminent and the camp was undermanned, a perceptive missionary Thomas Williamson shared. As of November 21, he wrote, he had only 102 men on duty, hardly a sufficient number to resist the pending threat.[11]

The next day Williamson wrote, "I have constant advice of secret meetings here and throughout the country, and a firm and almost universal determination on the part of the citizens to execute the Indians by violence, should the government much longer postpone it." Any attempt, he wrote, to remove the convicted Indians from the region would surely spark attacks by white mobs who would view removal as an official act of leniency. "There is a deep determination, and extensive as it is deep, to never let the Indians be removed alive, and should any official intimation of Presidential leniency or postponement reach this place—to execute prisoners by a mob. And it is daily hinted to me that too many of the soldiers participate in this feeling and determination." Nonetheless, he recommitted himself to what he knew he had to do. "I know my duty in the premises and shall fearlessly perform it; but the consequences with the small force at my disposal, must be dreaded. I shall certainly use all peaceable means to prevent any such riots, and—that failing—will resort to the only measures left to me."[12]

The next day Miller met with a group of civic leaders who feared the Indians would be "sent below"—to Fort Snelling—but knowing nothing of what the president had been considering, the colonel could only listen and appeal to their civic pride and willingness to uphold the law. Before they left, he warned them that he would not hesitate to execute his orders to defend the Indians "to the letter." The meeting ended cordially, but Miller knew the potential of violence remained. "I suppose that the next wagon train will be a new source of threats and excitement."[13]

Considering the vulnerable ground on which they were encamped, Miller called for the prisoners to be moved into the heart of Mankato, both for the added security of the Indians and for the comfort of his troops. Given the shoddy blankets supplied by swindling public contractors, inadequate tents, and tick-infested beds the men had to sleep on, Minnesota cold and snow loomed as an adversary almost as serious as the lynch mob. He complained that his men were without stoves in their tents and had "only one thin blanket each," and that the condition of both the Indians and his troops was rapidly worsening. Miller wrote, "A few more like the last one will kill many of [the prisoners], and sicken most of my command."[14] On the night of November 29, five to six inches of snow fell. "The prisoners and soldiers are suffering intensely."[15]

Miller indeed had reason to worry whether his soldiers—especially those men, like Thomas Montgomery, who came from the area—would do their duty at the moment of truth. As soon as Company I joined his ranks, Miller sought to have the Wisconsin troops reassigned from Mankato, not only to gain space to house his troops, but more importantly, because he did not fully trust them to defend the prisoners since they had lived in close proximity with the irate townsfolk. "Indeed," he reported, "if attacked I should hesitate about calling upon them at all."[16]

The time had arrived on December 4. At 7:00 p.m. Colonel Miller received two messages: one came from St. Peter attesting that an attack by whites on the Dakota was under way; the second was from New Ulm reporting that "a body of men" planned to "attack and murder the Indian prisoners" at eleven that night. Even before the letters arrived, Miller's "scouts and spies" had already reported that "large numbers" of men from St. Peter and Traverse des Sioux were arriving in Mankato, "[drunk] with beer to gain courage." Lieutenant Theodore Carter later recalled that the lynch mob expected little opposition from the troops, "as it was generally supposed that the soldiers would not fire upon them." And "there was some ground for this belief," for many soldiers had friends who had been massacred. "But," Carter added, "they didn't know old Col. Miller."[17]

Miller called for reinforcements from St. Peter and the Winnebago Agency who arrived within two hours, increasing his command from 196 men to 500; but he did not assume that the camp was secure. Indeed, one soldier wrote to his wife that "nine-tenths" would "never fire on the citizens." Greeted with derision when he instructed his troops to prepare to defend the prisoners, Miller declared "he would shoot the first man that refused to shoot [any] citizen that dared to attack us." To prevent sabotaging the weapons to render them unusable, he ordered his officers to watch as each man properly loaded his gun.[18] Not all soldiers felt in sympathy with the mob. For some, like Corporal Montgomery, it was simply the work at hand: "We received word at camp that a multitude of civilians were coming to camp that night for the purpose of killing the Indians or taking them from us which we took as an insult."[19]

At the designated time, Miller ordered his men to conceal themselves near the Blue Earth River Bridge. On horseback at the head of his men, the colonel was the first to confront the mob, who "were largely unarmed except with clubs, axes, knives, hatchets, and forks." Miller called out, "Who comes here?" Someone from the mob replied, "We have come to take the Indians and kill them." Miller responded, "Well you will do nothing of the kind." At that point his cavalry appeared out of the dark to the rear of the mob, and this was enough to unnerve the vigilantes.[20] "The colonel went up to them and talked a while and told them to go home as it was rather cold to be out."[21] It was below zero. Before they dispersed he arrested a group of ringleaders, placing them under the management of Lieutenant Carter, but releasing them upon receiving promises of good behavior.[22]

In the end, the soldiers had acted rapidly and in good order to put down the attack, and with good results. In acknowledging this, Miller issued a proclamation commending them for helping to defeat the attackers. Further, he recognized the soldiers' own desire for "the prompt and universal execution of the guilty savages," but cautioned agitators that the soldiers would do their duty "so long as the avenues of government point to the final and certain vindication of right and justice."[23]

Although Miller kept the guard up, there were no more attacks from civilians. Governor Ramsey issued a proclamation urging the people of Minnesota to act with restraint and to obey the law. The proclamation was a double-edged sword, however—it suggested that Lincoln ultimately would agree to execute the prisoners, and warned that the state courts and legislature would take action if the federal government did not.[24] It was a statement that reflected frustration that the president was taking so long to decide on such an obvious matter. Ramsey did not know that the president had made his decision—nor, as of yet, did the senator who had first brought the uprising to the president's attention.

✦ ✦ ✦ ✦ ✦

The day before, on December 5, 1862, Wilkinson, in an effort to force the president's hand, introduced a resolution demanding that the president account to the Senate concerning the Minnesota war and projected executions. He began by criticizing the charity and advocacy that easterners showed toward the Indians:

> Committees have visited the president of the United States, requested him to extend to these convicted Indians his executive clemency, and I fear that they have so wrought upon the President as to shake his purposes and to render him doubtful as to what he ought to do. Those who sympathize with these Indians seem to place their sympathy upon the ground that they occupy the relation of prisoners of war, and that being savages they should be treated with greater mercy even than white prisoners. This is an entire mistake.[25]

The Indians rose up to murder whites for no reason. "Suddenly, without any pretext, without any cause, without any apparent motive, they rose up almost simultaneously along our whole frontier line, for one hundred and fifty miles in extent." Then he listed in graphic detail the atrocities done to white settlers and criticized those who counseled the president against the executions. "In one case . . . they killed the father and the two sons at the wheat stack; they went into the house, murdered two little children, and took the mother who was very feeble with the consumption, and a little daughter into captivity . . . and the next morning took the little girl, out of the lodge where her mother lay, took her clothes from her person, pinioned her arms, laid her upon the ground, and ten or twelve of them violated her person, until she died within ten feet of her sick mother! I understand the Quakers of Pennsylvania wish to have these men pardoned!"[26]

He talked about the military trial that was held under the direction of former governor Henry Sibley, "who is known to many senators as a very moderate, conservative man." Yet, Wilkinson was not satisfied with his work. "I think Governor Sibley did not go far enough. He ought to have killed every one of the Indians as he came to them, but he did not; he established a court, and they were tried." Then he threatened the president, as Governor Ramsey and General Pope had done earlier, that unless something was done, there would be mob violence.[27] "The result will be that either the Indians must be punished according to the law, or they will be murdered without the law. The people of Minnesota will never consent that they shall be turned loose in their midst." The resolution was adopted.[28] The senator's remarks, reproduced in newspapers around the state, "fueled a growing execution fever."

✦ ✦ ✦ ✦ ✦

On December 6 Lincoln finally issued his decision. In his message to the Senate, he explained that he had been "anxious to not act with so much leniency as to encourage another outbreak, on the other hand, not with so much severity as to be real cruelty." He had, accordingly, called for a review of the transcripts with the intention of ordering the execution of only those who had been "proved guilty of violating females." Lincoln indicated that, contrary to his expectations, only two men had been convicted of rape, so he determined to draw the line by executing those who had participated in "massacres," as distinguished from those who had participated in "battles." The distinction between massacres and battles was suggested to Lincoln earlier in communications from the Reverend Riggs and Bishop Henry Whipple, who wrote, "There is a broad distinction between the guilt of men who went through the country committing fiendish violence, massacre-ing women and babes with the spirit of demons, and the guilt of timid men who received a share of the plunder or who under threat of death engaged in some one battle where hundreds were engaged."[29] Of the forty men fitting this description, Lincoln wrote, one had been recommended by the commission for leniency, leaving thirty-nine to be executed on December 19. The man to whom he referred was Joseph Godfrey, the only slave to be born in Minnesota, who had escaped his master, Oliver Faribault, and found sanctuary among the Dakota.[30] As for the remaining prisoners, Sibley ordered that they be held "subject to further orders, taking care that they neither escape, nor are subject to any unlawful violence."[31]

An exasperated Wilkinson sponsored a resolution demanding that the president "furnish the senate" with any documents "touching the late Indian barbarities." Lincoln responded on December 11 by forwarding the transcripts, his staff's recommendations, and other trial-related materials to the Senate. In his cover letter Lincoln referred to the list of forty Dakota men and offered a simple explanation (the only one he ever gave) for Godfrey's reprieve: "One of the number was strongly recommended by the commission which tried them, for commutation to ten years of imprisonment." Lincoln mentioned neither the name nor the race of "one of the number." "But Lincoln," Walt Bachman observes, "could not resist aiming a subtle zinger at Wilkinson." Returning the letter that he had received from the Minnesota delegation that luridly described the Indian assaults, the president wryly noted that it "contains some statements of fact not found in the records of the trials." The extravagance of their reporting had undercut their credibility, especially Wilkinson, the chief author of the missive.[32]

In Minnesota events were now moving quickly. Three hundred Dakota warriors were chained together in an encampment that could at any time be overrun by mobs. The longer they remained, the more precarious their fate. Anticipating this, Whipple wrote a letter to Senator Rice that he hoped would be delivered to the president. "We cannot hang men by the hundreds. Upon our own premises we have no right to do so," he wrote. "We claim that they are an independent nation and as such they are prisoners of war. The leaders must be punished but we cannot afford by any wanton cruelty to purchase the anger of God."[33]

Soon Whipple was not alone. Quakers, clergy, and even the commissioner of Indian affairs, William Dole, cried out against execution. Stephen Riggs, who generally supported the convictions, also felt private misgivings throughout the trials that had condemned the three hundred men. To his son he wrote, "I told the members of this commission several times that I should be sorry to have to have my life placed in their hands."[34] He later felt compelled to be public with his doubts when he wrote to the *St. Paul Pioneer*, "I have a very high regard for all the gentlemen who composed the military commission. I count them individually among my personal friends. But they were trying Indians; and my sense of right would lead me to give Indians as fair and full trial as a white man. This was the difference between us."[35]

Still the outcry for blood only intensified as the citizens of St. Paul sent a resolution to the president demanding that all of the Dakota prisoners be executed and that every "Dakota Sioux Indian" be banished from the state. This was not good enough for some Minnesotans. "Exterminate the wild beasts," Swisshelm wrote, "and make peace with the devil and all his hosts sooner than these red-jawed tigers whose fangs are dripping with the blood of the innocents."[36] As Senator Rice reported from his conversation with Lincoln, the Minnesota congressmen were causing trouble. In fact, they were only part of a coordinated effort to pressure the president into approving the executions or at least handing the responsibility over to the state. Ramsey again had warned Lincoln that mob violence would be unavoidable if the executions were not immediately carried out, echoing Pope's wire four days earlier: "If you prefer it turn them over to me and I will order their execution." Lincoln sought legal counsel on just this question and learned that only he had that authority. On the same day of Ramsey's offer, Wilkinson and Aldrich met with Lincoln to make similar arguments, securing assurance that Lincoln would issue "a final determination upon it after completing his [annual] message."[37] The president was holding them at bay.

To Whipple, the concept of lumping every Indian into a single category was offensive: a just people needed to be a discriminating people, especially in matters of life and death. In a letter to the editor of the *St. Paul Pioneer,* Whipple crafted words that would influence the president enough for the sentiment to reappear in the president's final order on the matter: "There is a broad distinction between the guilt of men who went through the country committing fiendish violence, massacring women and babes with the spirit of demons, and the guilt of timid men who received a share of the plunder or who under threat of death engaged in some one battle where hundreds were engaged."[38]

In December Bishop Whipple published in the St. Paul newspapers a calm, clear statement of the train of events that led to this terrible explosion. So far as is known, he was the only public man in Minnesota who had the courage to face the whirlwind of public denunciation of all Indians, and of all Dakota in particular. To punish the guilty would avail little if the traditional Indian policy was to be left unreformed. "In some quarters," wrote historian William Folwell, from whom there was little sympathy, "the Bishop came in for denunciation almost as spiteful and unsparing as that directed against the Sioux themselves, but he never retracted a syllable nor budged an inch."[39]

In public, Sibley maintained a stoic silence, swallowing his humiliation when Lincoln overruled 270 of his sentences. His attempt at legal process had, in fact, pleased no one. While Whipple maintained that the civilized world could not justify putting surrendered enemies on trial, Morton Wilkinson had declared to the United States Senate that Sibley "ought to have killed every one of the Indians as he came to them." The general was left with little choice but to stonewall the whole question. Nevertheless, Sibley, who had made his fortune working with and developing close ties with the Dakota, was clearly disturbed over the moral issues that were raised by his contemporaries and by the ambiguities of his own position.

The role Sibley had readily assumed in commanding an army intent on quelling the Dakota and bringing them to justice—indeed, the role he readily assumed to command the forces—had appealed to a darker side that he had managed to restrain. He had spent a lifetime cultivating an ongoing private correspondence with Whipple and strained to justify his actions. When the bishop objected to hanging men who had come in under a flag of truce, Sibley insisted that he had made it perfectly clear that the guilty would be punished. He argued that those who resisted his police action had made themselves willing accessories to mass murder. "A great public crime had been committed," he told Whipple, "not by wild Indians who did not know better, but by men who have had advantages of some religious teaching." He himself had been forced, he said, to turn his back on long associations and even "personal attachment" to some of the condemned. Duty demanded it, for the hard fact that every one of them deserved capital punishment was a thing of which "I have no more doubt than I have of my own existence."[40] Most white Minnesotans would have agreed fervently, but unlike Sibley, they drew little distinction between the guilty and the innocent. All were Indians. It is not likely that this impression would fade when the president came to act upon the findings of the military commission. A disgusted Gideon Welles, likely reflecting Lincoln's views, recorded in his diary:

> When the intelligent Representatives of a State can deliberately besiege the Government to take the lives of these ignorant barbarians by wholesale, after they surrendered themselves prisoners, it would seem the sentiments of the Representatives were but slightly removed from the barbarians they would execute. The Minnesotans are greatly exasperated and threaten the Administration if it shows clemency.[41]

On December 5 that threat became real in Congress when, during the new session that had hardly begun, Morton Wilkinson rose in the Senate to introduce a resolution that the president account to the body concerning the Minnesota war. In this speech, Nichols writes, "Lincoln faced the irony of defiance and vigilantism in a key northern state, aided and abetted by congressional representatives and elements in his own party."[42] But for Wilkinson, this was no longer just a matter of seeking vengeance against the Indians; this was a moment for opportunity.

On December 16 Wilkinson again took to the floor to introduce a bill to compensate Minnesotans for losses in the Indian war. He also presented bills to remove from the state the Dakota and the Winnebago.[43] He realized that an opportunity had presented itself, as he indicated in a letter to Ramsey: "If the people will be patient we will be able, I think, to dispose of those condemned, and will also succeed in removing the Sioux and Winnebago Indians from the State."[44] The thirst for vengeance yielded to an appetite for Indian land, just as Secretary of the Navy Welles had said would happen.[45]

Indeed, for years, farmers had campaigned for the removal of the Winnebago.[46] At last, the time was right. To most Minnesotans, exterminating all of the Indians was the desired solution: removal appeared far more humane.[47] Lincoln, on the other hand, who watched the morale of his nation flag even more as thousands of his soldiers died at Fredericksburg and in the pyrrhic victory of Antietam, was open to placating the Minnesotans, and the Winnebago act would become law on February 21, 1863, and the Dakota act on March 3. Neither encountered debate. In general, the acts specified that the Indians were to be relocated on unoccupied land "well-adapted for agricultural purposes" but beyond the limits of any state and that money derived from the sale of their old reservation lands should be invested for the tribe's benefit.[48]

Jane Grey Swisshelm, who would hold firm on executing more Dakota, felt that the bills were misguided in their leniency to "undeserving savages," and that the author was treading on dangerous ground: "Unless the [bills are] different than what was implied . . . Senator Wilkinson is getting himself into the position that will soon be 'too hot to hold him!' "[49] Wilkinson obviously disagreed, feeling the speedy enactment presaged a new day for Indian affairs: "I believe there has been a great revolution in the conduct of our Indian Affairs since this Administration came into power."[50] But, as Nichols notes, "abundant evidence existed that very little of importance had changed."[51]

Nichols was not questioning the senator's judgment, as Swisshelm had done: his critique, understandably within the context of the immediate issue, was of Wilkinson's veracity. Evidence that the dreadful state of Indian policy did not change during the remaining years of Lincoln's term in office was indeed overwhelming. And the defender of the system, a role Wilkinson seemed to embrace, had become a formidable foe to reform, as he equally wielded a singular bias against Indians and willful distortion of their welfare, for when his blood was up, he tended to speak in broad and sometimes overheated terms, sometimes undercutting the message he sought to convey. One senator reportedly scolded him during a debate for "not knowing what he says when he gets excited."[52] After hearing that soldiers from Minnesota had been detained by their commander in Missouri, admittedly "after they may have committed some little act of insubordination in not obeying the command of General Brown," an incensed Wilkinson took to the senate floor on January 13, 1864, to condemn the general and demand a full report from the secretary of war. "One thing is very certain," Wilkinson asserted. "If we want these men to fight they must be treated a little differently."[53]

By the end of 1864, reports circulated around Washington of the horrific treatment of Union soldiers at the Confederate prisoner-of-war camp at Andersonville, Georgia. Especially angered at Lincoln's disinclination to seek vengeance, Congress wanted reprisal, and Wilkinson led the initiative. On December 20, reports historian Mark Neely, "[Wilkinson], a sharp tongued and unforgiving Radical Republican," offered the following resolution that would limit "rations, clothing and supplies" that the Union prison camp gives to rebel captives to the same meager amount that rebel authorities give Union prisoners.[54] "The resolution," Neely observes, "was in fact a directive to starve and freeze Confederate prisoners of war to death as a deliberate government policy."[55] Senators Benjamin Wade and James Lane joined Wilkinson in arguing that it would force the Confederacy into providing Union prisoners with better food and shelter and appropriate clothing.[56] S.R.85, or the Retaliation Act, as this resolution came to be called, was referred to the Committee on Military Affairs.

Lincoln was not persuaded after being advised earlier by one of his own generals, Dan Sickles, that the act was pointless: "The enemy are reported to be without the means to supply clothing, medicine, and other medical supplies even to their own troops." Senators Thomas Hendricks of Indiana and Charles Sumner of Massachusetts challenged the implicit cruelty of the act, which they said was based on "vague rumors" and "uncertain reports" and violated the laws of nations governing prisoners. Nonetheless, whether the reports and rumors were accurate, Union prisoners were dying at Andersonville. The resolution passed Congress on January 1, 1865, by a vote of 24 to 16.[57]

Meanwhile, ten days after Wilkinson presented his bills, on December 26, in the largest mass executions in American history, thirty-eight Dakota were hanged in Mankato as if in macabre tribute to the city's most prominent resident, Senator Wilkinson. Corporal Thomas Montgomery's unit was assigned to stand guard over the condemned and to secure the gallows:

Dear Parents and Brothers,

I wanted to come home about Christmas but I see no chance now of getting home till after New Year. This is owing to unforeseen events that have transpired since, and which require the presence of all soldiers here. By an order received by the Colonel—night before last—39 of the convicted Indian prisoners in our possession will be executed by hanging on next Friday, the 26th, and for that reason he will allow no furlough to be granted till the tragedy went transpired.

Several of the Indians are recognized by some in our company as the murderers of their parents or brothers or sisters, and it is hard for them to stand in the prison as guard over them with guns in their hands and not revenge their death.

The trains that brought Mr. Manning's family up here are about to start. . . . I would like to see some of you up here next Friday. It will be a great day. There will be thousands in attendance from the whole country, soldiers as well as citizens. They will be hung in the public street, 20 at a time. It is a sure thing.

I remain your son, T. Montgomery. My love to all.[58]

As the time of their deaths approached, the Dakota asked the missionary Riggs to record some thoughts to be sent to their friends, "and also," as he reported, "to the white people." He acceded to their request and spent a whole day with them, writing down such things as they wished to say. Most of them claimed they were innocent of the charges laid against them of killing individuals, "but they admitted, and said of their own accord, that so many white people had been killed by the Dakotas, that public and general justice required the death of some in return. This admission was in the line of their education. Perhaps it is not too much to call it an instinct of humanity."

The executions took place. Arrangements were made by which *thirty-eight* Dakota men were suspended in mid-air by the cutting of one rope. The other prisoners, through crevices in the walls of their log prison-house, saw them hung. And they were deeply affected by it; albeit they did not show their feelings as white men would have done, under like circumstances.[59]

♦ ♦ ♦ ♦ ♦

Though Lincoln, by the end of the year, had said nothing about his plan for the 260 Dakota who had not been hanged, it was Sibley, even more than the president, who now became the lightning rod both for critics who favored more executions and for those who opposed more hangings. The most vocal crusaders in the former camp attacked Sibley for having started down the path of military justice, choosing it over the more expeditious lynch law. As the *Faribault Central Republican* opined, "Gen. Sibley didn't half execute his duty. He ought to have shot every Indian who approached his command, for in point of fact the guilt of the recent massacres is about equally shared by the entire Sioux nation."[60] This was the same message that Jane Grey Swisshelm held when she took it upon herself to go to Washington to lobby the president, whom she had once called an "imbecile," to finish the work he had constrained Sibley from doing.[61]

In Washington, the Minnesota delegation secured the use of Dr. Sutherland's church, where Swisshelm could address large crowds regarding the urgent need for more executions. In one lecture she intoned, "If justice is not done . . . our people will hunt them, shoot them, set traps for them, put out poison bait for them—kill them by every means we would use to exterminate panthers. We cannot breathe the same air with those demon violators of women, crucifiers of infants. Every Minnesota man, who has a soul and could get a rifle, will got to shooting Indians; and he who hesitates will be black-balled by every Minnesota woman and posted as a coward in every Minnesota home."[62] She would later write that her lecture was "enthusiastically applauded." Swisshelm biographer Sylvia Hoffert gives a more accurate assessment: "Despite her provocative and inflammatory rhetoric, she found that her audiences were more curious than concerned about either the Dakotas or their victims. Distracted by the Civil War, they did not seem interested in the West and appeared to be bored by the subject of Native American depredations."[63] Proper Washington, aside from genteel curiosity, had taken its lead from the White House. "The Secretary of the Interior assured me it was not worth while to see the President, for 'Mr. Lincoln will hang nobody!' and our Minnesota delegation agreed with him."[64]

Together Senator Wilkinson and Mrs. Swisshelm, leveraging her weight as the "mother of the Republican Party"—an appellation that had adorned her effigy as it was set afire by a mob of Democrats in St. Cloud years earlier and one she wore now with great pride—went to see the president in a last-ditch effort to change his mind, but it was for naught.[65] It is likely that Lincoln declined the meeting, knowing what the Minnesotans would say; and he had heard enough. The matter was settled. The Dakota War was over.

Besides, the Civil War had entered into a new phase, and with it the very character of the nation. In January he signed into law the Confiscation Act and the Militia Act that approved black enlistment in the army, and on the first day of the year, he had issued the Emancipation Proclamation. With these laws the federal government had taken its first steps to elevating the black man to the level of every white man, a goal for which Wilkinson and Swisshelm had energetically advocated but now had seemed to lose sight of in their thirst for vengeance.

A deflated Swisshelm saw no point to meeting anyone else, but reluctantly agreed to attend a presidential reception despite her bitter feelings for him. "He had proved to be an obstructionist instead of an abolitionist, and I felt no respect for him; while his wife was every where spoken of as a Southern woman with Southern sympathies—a conspirator against the Union. I wanted nothing to do with the occupants of the White House, but was told

I could go and see the spectacle without being presented." But she was transformed when she saw him from afar. "I watched the President and Mrs. Lincoln receive [their guests]. His sad, earnest, honest face was irresistible in its plea for confidence, and Mrs. Lincoln's manner was so simple and motherly, so unlike that of all Southern women I had seen, that I doubted the tales I had heard. Her head was not that of a conspirator. She would be incapable of a successful deceit, and whatever her purposes were, they must be known to all who knew her. . . . I could not resist going to [Mr. Lincoln] with the rest of the crowd, and when he took my hand I said: 'May the Lord have mercy on you, poor man, for the people have none.' He laughed heartily, and the men around him, joined in his merriment."[66]

# 6

# PIKE ISLAND

*Humanity requires it.*

MORTON S. WILKINSON, 1863

On January 1, 1863, Lincoln issued the Emancipation Proclamation, which applied only to slaves in rebellious states, excluding those who lived in parts of Virginia and Louisiana as well as other slaveholding states then under federal control. Missouri, the site of unrelenting guerrilla activity by proslavery forces, was one of the slaveholding states that nonetheless stood officially under the Union banner. In other words, emancipation did not extend to slaves there. But to certain Missouri slaves the legalism was nothing more than a distinction without a difference. For them the president had freed the slaves. They were now free to go wherever and do whatever they wished, including joining the army to fight their masters, including following the North Star to freedom. Their desire, as free men and women, now superseded the president's wartime design. Missouri-born Robert Hickman was one such slave.[1]

He was a man of many gifts. A natural leader and talented speaker and one who had found salvation in spreading the Word of God: with the permission of his master he preached to other slaves on neighboring plantations. But when news of emancipation came, he made plans to collect his flock and leave. Because the whole region swarmed with rebel guerrillas, traveling at night on water seemed to be the better way to escape, especially considering that the Northern steamboats frequently connected St. Louis to ports upriver. Finally, on a moonless night, on or about May 3, they crowded with simple provisions onto the raft to depart. However, Hickman having failed to equip the raft with oars, sails, or any device that could propel it, the raft simply drifted on the black waters of the Mississippi.[2]

On the following day a steamboat carrying mules and wagons for the government churned northward from St. Louis to St. Paul. Somewhere in the vicinity of Jefferson, Missouri, the *Northerner*, owned by the St. Paul and Galena Packet Company and commanded by Alford J. Woods, came upon the strange raft and its occupants, drifting helplessly in the center of the wide river. Hickman explained to the captain that he and his followers wanted to go North where they could live and work as free men and women. The captain, perhaps partly motivated by altruistic impulse, was also following the orders of his employer, Henry Sibley, who wanted him to bring "contraband" to Minnesota to address the severe labor shortage. Captain Woods ordered that the raft be towed in the wake of his steamer to his homeport. Neither Woods nor Hickman anticipated the reception they would receive in St. Paul.[3]

On May 5, the *Northerner*, with the raft of fugitive slaves in tow, approached the levee in Lowertown. A crowd gathered and grew restless, then boisterous, as it became apparent who the new arrivals were. Men in the crowd—mostly Irish laborers—became so threatening that Captain Woods ordered the steamer to bypass St. Paul altogether and head upstream to Fort Snelling instead. The *Press* reported, "The police were very much alarmed at the appearance of such a thunder cloud, and thinking they were to land here, proposed to prevent it on the ground that they [Hickman and his followers] were paupers. The Irish on the levee were considerably excited, and admitted by their actions, that the negro was their rival, and that they fear he will outstrip them. On finding [the negroes] were bound for the fort, [the Irish laborers] resumed their whiskey and punches with great equanimity."[4] "It was impossible," wrote an observer, "for the impartial spectator, who witnessed the scenes on the levee . . . not to assign the negro to a higher type of civilization than the white barbarians who howled around them as if, like beasts of prey, they thirsted for their blood."[5]

By the spring of 1863, the labor shortage in Minnesota had become acute. The war effort had drawn many of Minnesota's men to military service in the Civil and the Dakota Wars. Thus farmers were forced to reduce the acreage under cultivation because of the difficulty of planting, harvesting, and transporting their produce without help. The *St. Paul Daily Press* reported, "Since the absorption of so many of the laboring class in the army, many of our farmers have found it necessary to reduce the quantity of land under tillage from sheer want of putting their usual crops, and even then, much of it has gone to waste from the deficiency of help at harvest time."[6]

The federal troops at Fort Snelling were also under severe pressure. In an effort to free soldiers from various forms of menial work General Sibley contracted for contraband labor to be brought from St. Louis for work under federal supervision. Contraband workers could also alleviate the labor shortage in the private sector. Although Hickman did not know about Sibley's desire for contraband labor, he probably would have welcomed it: work meant opportunity.[7] Regardless of the obvious shortage, state legislators and opinion makers from St. Paul condemned efforts to bring blacks to Minnesota, for, they argued, the Mississippi would become a conduit for such people to stream northward, bringing unfair competition for jobs normally filled by poor white laborers. This was their stance as early as 1854.[8]

The concern was heard again in 1859, when St. Paul legislators introduced a bill to prevent the migration of free blacks and mulattoes into the state and require the registration of those already in residence. Like their predecessors, these legislators insisted that blacks would compete for jobs customarily held by poor whites, thus denying that class of citizens a livelihood. Just the year before, the St. Paul and Galena Packet Company, along with the La Crosse Company, dispatched agents to St. Louis "to engage Negroes as deckhands on the steamboats" after their white deckhands struck for higher wages. Sibley, in addition to his other accomplishments, was a founder and director of the Galena company, which enjoyed government contracts and employed black strikebreakers. This was, after all, a time of war against the Confederacy in the South and the Dakota within the state, and these hostilities compounded the need for steamboats carrying supplies for troops to operate unimpeded by aggrieved laborers. Indeed, the financial viability of Minnesota now depended on uninterrupted steamboat service.

But it was argued that whites unwilling to work with blacks would resort to violence. At worst, blacks would become paupers and wards of the state.[9] As late as February 1863 many St. Paul residents opposed to the use of contraband labor were circulating petitions on the city streets requesting that the legislature again consider the issue. Even persons sympathetic to the black migrants wondered aloud about the efficacy of Sibley's plan. Referring to Hickman's group, the liberal editor of the *Press* conceded, "This is rather more than was bargained for, and the question arises, what will be done with them?"[10] Despite the vast acreage in the state to be tilled, black labor—especially those who had experienced plantation work—seemed of uncertain value rather than an answer to an economic and agricultural need.

The reaction to white settlers arriving four days later was different, for, as the *Press* reported, "We record with much satisfaction an unmistakable increase of immigration to this state. . . . They are nearly all agricultural and are all of a solid, intelligent and well-to do class, who will make good settlers. Nearly every family has its horses, cows, etc., and have evidently 'come to stay.' The proportion of children is unusually great. . . . On a recent trip the McLellan left La Crosse with 98 bright-eyed little boys and girls, to become the future legislators, farmers, and merchants of Minnesota."[11] Three days later the *Press* pronounced "the arrival of a large contingent of 'Hollanders' as laudable as that of the earlier group of immigrants, for too are a hearty and industrious looking people," likewise in possession of farming implements, household gear, "and plenty of money—regular 'shiners' too, and nothing else."[12] These were the kinds of settlers Minnesota leaders viewed as the right people to repopulate the southwestern region of the state after the Dakota and Winnebago had all been removed. Where the colored people would fit in was another matter altogether, something that would remain to be seen. Once they reached the landing below Fort Snelling, their first hesitant footsteps on the soggy free soil of Minnesota, especially after the hostile reception at Lowertown, they had to be struck by one more unsettling visage of humanity that had been gathered together on higher ground.

◆ ◆ ◆ ◆ ◆

Pike Island, in the shadow of Fort Snelling, was the site where in 1806, a twenty-one-year-old lieutenant named Zebulon Pike first negotiated with the once powerful Dakota chief, Little Crow, to purchase the cliff on which a future Fort Snelling would perch. Fifty-seven years later the people of the mighty chief were huddled in defeat, illness, and despair, and his grandson— their leader by the same name—continued to elude Pope's and Sibley's armies. Since November 13, 1862, when the contingent of Dakota women, children, and old men, and soldiers arrived in the evening at Fort Snelling after a grueling six-day march from the Lower Sioux Agency at Redwood, life had grown even more desperate. The first night the group camped on the bluff above the river, but on the next day Colonel Marshall moved them down to the point below the fort, near the spot where supply boats landed. There they were guarded by soldiers. No one was allowed to enter without a pass from the fort commander. In a few days the Dakota anxiously watched as soldiers constructed an enclosure of wooden planks to keep them from wandering and to protect them from curious or vengeful whites.[13]

Disease was a significant problem among the Indians. In the weeks while they were still on the frontier a measles outbreak had started and spread among both soldiers and interned Dakota. From October to November, disease spread quickly throughout the densely confined Indians, many of whom died during their November march to Fort Snelling. Measles affected the Dakota on the frontier, where up to twenty died from the disease or its side effects, which included pneumonia and dysentery. Other diseases affecting the Dakota in Fort Snelling were typhoid fever, smallpox, and scarlet fever. Soldiers were also widely affected by disease at Forts Snelling and Ridgely, as were people in St. Peter, Shakopee, and Le Sueur. Morticians reported a sharp increase in deaths.

"Amid all this sickness and these great tribulations," remembered Gabriel Renville, a mixed-blood who was held in the stockade along with his family, "it seemed doubtful at night whether a person would be alive in the morning." At the fort, burying the dead became a challenge. Graves outside the fort were sometimes dug up and the bodies were desecrated. Riggs reported, "They are now keeping their dead or burying them in their tepees." Twenty or thirty people died in one day. Good Star Woman remembered that both the children and elderly were buried together in a long trench; the older people at the bottom of the trench with the children placed on top of them. She recalled that a Roman Catholic priest brought a box for each body to be properly buried in the spring.[14] Somewhere between 160 and 300 people died that winter in those squalid conditions.

The Indians sold personal possessions in order to purchase food to supplement the military rations they were given. Some of the mixed-blood families owned land vouchers that had been granted them in treaties with the U.S. government. These vouchers granted the head of each household up to 640 acres of any unsurveyed, nonfederal land in exchange for giving up claim to land in Minnesota. Many sold these vouchers to local businessmen at deflated prices in order to have cash in hand to provide for their families while in the stockade. Businessmen like Sibley ally Franklin Steele profited by purchasing these vouchers and later selling them to land developers for large profits.

As months passed while officials deliberated what to do with the interned Dakota, the Dakota prisoners at Mankato and internees at Fort Snelling developed an interest in learning to read and write so that they could communicate with each other, especially for the families that had been separated. By February, as Riggs reported, writing paper and spelling books were in demand, and missionaries would carry written messages back and forth.[15] During this same period religious conversions began to increase at both Mankato and Fort Snelling. "Many were convicted; confessions and professions were made; idols treasured for many generations with the highest reverence were thrown away by the score. They had faith no longer in their idols. They laid hold on Christ as their only hope. On this ground they were baptized, over a hundred adults, with their children."[16]

While there was some suspicion that the conversions may have been calculated or a convenient way to gain favor with the officials, it is just as likely that the missionaries exploited the dire situation and despair for the uncertainty of their circumstance to win more souls. In any event, the number of baptisms markedly increased.

On May 4 the first group of Dakota interned at Fort Snelling, numbering 771, was put on the steamer *Davenport*. About half an hour on its way, the steamboat stopped at the St. Paul levee to take on freight, and there a crowd gathered. Some of the crowd, urged on by a soldier wounded at Birch Coulee, the site of some of the bloodiest fighting of the Dakota War, hooted and threw stones at the Indians, easily hitting their tightly packed targets on the boiler deck. The *Daily Press* reported, "Some of the squaws were hit upon the head and quite severely injured." To restore order, Captain D. C. Sanders of Company G, Tenth Regiment, commanding the guard consisting of forty men, ordered the crowd to desist or "he would order his men to charge bayonets among them."[17]

The next day, the steamer *Northerner,* which had come to Fort Snelling to transport the remaining Dakota, encountered a mob at the St. Paul levee, this time inflamed by the appearance of more blacks who had been brought up from Missouri. The *Weekly Pioneer and Democrat* snidely commented, "The Northerner brought up a cargo of 125 niggers and 150 mules on Government account. It takes back some eight or nine hundred Indians. We doubt very much whether we benefit by the exchange. If we had our choice we would send both niggers and Indians to Massachusetts, and keep the mules here."[18]

Later that day, May 5, upstream, the *Northerner* arrived near the flooded landing to transport the remaining 547 Dakota waiting to be herded onboard. It was one of those rare moments in history that best summed up how the United States in the nineteenth century looked upon its two principal peoples of color. The strange sight of bedraggled black men and women crowded on the raft being towed forward must have given the wary Indians a sense of curious diversion. And Hickman and his followers, for their part, had to be similarly struck by the sight of these strange and defeated people huddled together on dry ground just above their flooded, fenced-in encampment— the strange and horrible smell moved farther as they witnessed the Indians file mournfully past the very site of their sorrow to board the same steamer that had brought Hickman and his group from Missouri to this wretched spot and now would take the Dakota dependents to whatever fate awaited them.[19] "One of them leads in prayer, after which another hymn is sung," observed J. P. Williamson, who accompanied them, "and so they continue till all are composed; and drawing their blankets over them, each falls asleep."[20] Theirs now would be a time bygone. Williamson reported:

> Many died at Fort Snelling. The steamboat trip of over one month, under some circumstances, might have been a benefit to their health, but when 1300 Indians were crowded like slaves on the boiler and hurricane decks of a single boat, and fed on musty hard tack and briny pork, which they had not half a chance to cook, diseases were bred which made fearful havoc during the hot months, and the 1,300 souls that landed at Crow Creek June 1, 1863, decreased to one thousand.[21]

• • • • •

As Hickman and his followers climbed the steep path to the fort, their unintended destination, they must have felt great trepidation with each labored step that brought them closer to the huge walls looming over them.[22] Little about this "Promised Land" made much sense. With President Lincoln's armed soldiers escorting them up the path to northern soil, some may have wondered whether this was what freedom looked like. What were they to make of those strange unfortunates who were huddled below on the boat now making its way to St. Paul? Would those Indians get the same reception when they arrived? What was behind those wary Indian eyes? What had created all that human wretchedness? Were the soldiers here their saviors or their tormenters? Was this a place for them? Down south the blue uniform meant protection. But everything they had experienced in the short time they had been in the North Star State may have caused some to feel ambivalent. Now on the grounds in front of the gates to the fort they took in all the riders galloping by and wagons racing about. This was the first time they had stood amid this kind of busyness, so many soldiers, guns, and cannons. And then there was the fort itself, with its high thick walls that commanded the entire valley and all the waterways. It was one thing to see the fort from the raft on the river; another, altogether, when standing under its immense shadow.

Construction of the fort was completed in 1825 on the bluff above the confluence of the Minnesota and Mississippi Rivers. For almost thirty years, Fort Snelling was the hub of the Upper Mississippi and meeting place of diverse cultures. Dakota and Ojibwe gathered at the agency and fort to trade, debate government policy, and perform their dances and sports. Traders stopped at the fort while their goods were inspected. The American and Columbia Fur Companies built headquarters nearby and the mixed-blood families and employees settled at nearby Mendota. The fort was racially and ethnically kaleidoscopic, and for much of the antebellum period, a very busy place; twenty-three years earlier, it had been the home of Dred and Harriet Scott.

As later treaties opened much of the new territory of Minnesota to settlement and pushed the frontier farther west, Forts Ridgely, Ripley, and Abercrombie took over the frontier duties; Fort Snelling became a mere supply depot, and eventually the private property of Minnesota entrepreneur Franklin Steele. The outbreak of the Civil War brought renewed activities to the fort, however. Between 1861 and 1865 Minnesota expanded the fort as a training center for thousands of volunteers who joined the Union army.[23]

What Hickman would have seen as he approached what Thoreau called the "tawny and butterish" walls of the fort, was a stone wall about nine feet high that enclosed the fort, and rested, on the east side, nearly on the edge of the bluff.[24] If viewed from the air, the fort would appear to have an irregular diamond shape that fit the terrain of the bluff while the towers overlooked the two rivers and the plains behind.[25] The quarters of the officers and men are built of stone. The hospital was a stone row house. The stable, workshop, icehouse, and other necessary buildings were outside the wall on the bank of the Mississippi. Hickman would have also seen a number of wooden barracks, storehouses, and stables erected a short distance above the post.[26]

If they were led into the fort, Hickman and his flock would have seen immediately along the right the gate wall, shops, and the hexagonal tower in the far corner; to their immediate left were the guardhouse, the blacksmith shop, and, in the far corner, the distinctive round tower with its conical roof installed the year before. Proceeding forward they would have passed between a long row house on their right that served as the hospital, and on the left, a smaller structure that served as the school with the well in front and powder magazine (with its six-foot-thick walls) just beyond; moving forward, they would come out onto an expanse that served as the parade ground.[27] Along the far walls were two more row houses that served as barracks, and in the far right corner stood the house of Colonel Robert M. McLaren, fort commandant, "a stern, soldierly man." A great, round, wooden bastion, a famous lookout, projected from the back of his house over the precipitous cliff and the narrow stream where the Minnesota and the Mississippi Rivers joined. From this guns were mounted that had been trained on the "representatives of the Sioux . . . tribes encamped upon Pike island, or, as we called it, Grape Island, below, compelling by this measure a treaty of peace."[28]

Were they encamped within the walls they would have daily witnessed dress parade, as blue columns marched and countermarched to the strains of the wartime music. In the evening, the lowering of the flag at the sunset gun gave, to one civilian witness, an especial thrill. But they also would likely see the odd juxtaposition of frolicking children one moment, pausing only to watch a punished soldier being forced, as Mary Newson witnessed, to "[march] under guard up and down . . . in a barrel bearing in huge letters the words, 'I Was Drunk Last Night.'"

Newson, who lived at the fort during this period, described other trials of fort life during this period: "Some mornings we watched the soldiers open barrels of flour—a most exciting pastime—for frequently I saw ferocious rats as large as half-grown kittens jump into the faces of the soldiers, who muttered unpleasant things about the government even as they released their rat terriers upon their prey." Newson recalled that "heartache everywhere [was] present in the fort." Between 1861 and 1863, one out of every four families was down with typhoid, and there were few families who did not lose at least one or more members to the dread disease. They never forgot that this was wartime. "Everywhere, we partly understood the anxiety on the faces of those who daily surrounded the bulletins of the latest disasters, and we wondered curiously why some, women especially, broke down and ran sobbing to their quarters."[29] With the new Conscription Act about to go into effect, the gravity of war set in as once-vital young men increasingly listed as "disappeared," "wounded," or "dead" would be replaced by men with no choice but to serve as draftees in a war to free the slave, the very type who now appeared at the fort, the very type at whom the curious young Minnesota recruits could not help but stare.

And what did Hickman and his followers see? Some of the soldiers were immigrant laborers from St. Paul, where antiblack activities had occurred frequently since 1854.[30] As early as February, petitions circulated to oppose the use of contraband labor.[31] In March, with the enactment of the Civil War Military Draft Act, Congress essentially forced the immigrant laborers, who most feared black labor set free by the Emancipation Proclamation, into the blue uniform, igniting riots in New York City and other cities with a large white underclass. In St. Paul, a provost guard would soon be posted in response to the threat of mob violence.[32] When the time came for them to march off to the South to fight and die to free the slaves, more Negroes like Hickman would come here to take their jobs. Though the uniforms said that they were President Lincoln's men, their stares conveyed something else altogether. After what they had gone through, some of the newcomers from Missouri had to wonder whether Minnesota was for them.

At least one set of eyes watched them both with curiosity and with benevolence, especially when they gathered to give thanks for their deliverance. Some of the missionaries, who had come to work among the Dakota captives while they were held in the compound, had not yet left. Now that the Indians had been sent away, their mission had ended. Some would go back home; the Reverend Stephen Riggs returned to his family living in St. Anthony. Thomas Williamson would leave with the last of the Indians, one week later. The Reverend William Norris, who was still at the fort when Hickman and his followers arrived and settled in, was attracted to these people, who so desperately embraced the grace of God. It would be Norris who provided a pivotal connection to their future in Minnesota.[33]

To accommodate the large numbers of new recruits, several large wooden barracks were constructed outside the fort's stone walls. On the grounds, recruits learned the basics of soldiering and spent the majority of their time marching, drilling with their weapons, and standing guard duty. Once a military unit's term of service was done, Fort Snelling also served as the mustering-out point before the men returned to civilian life. Between 1861 and 1865 nearly twenty-five thousand soldiers passed through Fort Snelling on their way to Southern battlefields. Throughout the summer and fall months, Hickman and his people would have witnessed all the activity. It must have strained the patience of junior officers scurrying about trying to find a place on the crowded Fort Snelling reservation for the unexpected blacks to stay.

They were not the first blacks to be at the fort. Since the beginning, commandants, many of whom were Southerners accustomed to holding slaves as part of their retinue, brought their bondsmen with them when posted at Fort Snelling. Even the second commandant, Josiah Snelling, who completed the construction of the fort and after whom the fort was named, had slaves. The fact that he was Massachusetts-born illustrated how deeply entrenched this practice was in the officers corps. The practice ended, however, at the outbreak of the Civil War.[34]

The people from Missouri and some of the men who came with the second arrival of contraband found paid work at the fort. Under the catchall listing "Citizens employed at the Fort," Colonel McLaren's monthly records seemed to reflect that those who had been categorized as "contraband" were listed as "laborers" by September, and paid the same as other laborers who presum-

ably were white.[35] Some evidently went on to the frontier to serve as army
teamsters. Corporal Montgomery referred to them in a letter to his parents,
"There are now between 200 and 300 wagons in camp and we expect 100 more
shortly. Also [there is] a heavy squad of niggers for teamsters. Mules here are
numerous now."[36]

♦ ♦ ♦ ♦ ♦

A few days after the Dakota left Pike Island on May 4, Saint Andre Durand
Balcombe, the Winnebago agent, was ordered by Commissioner Dole to assemble the tribe, inform them that they would soon be removed from their
land, and above all disarm them. Balcombe, a fellow New Yorker and supporter of Wilkinson, had served in the territorial legislature and as presiding
officer in the Republican caucus of the state constitutional convention; but
in this capacity as Indian agent, he benefited greatly from the patronage he
enjoyed from his leader, Senator Morton Wilkinson. Now with the order to
begin the removal process, he stood to profit even more.[37] But it was to be a
delicate matter, for he understood, as Commissioner Dole clearly did, that
violence between the whites and the Winnebago could erupt at any time. The
settlers were eager to begin spring planting on the patches of ground cleared
for cultivation by the Winnebago; yet, even as they wanted the land, the settlers and long-term white residents in the area were anxious to have the Indians strictly confined to the reservation until they were permanently removed.
Balcombe waited two weeks before he held a council with the Winnebago
to officially inform them that the government intended to remove them to a
reservation on the Missouri.[38] Their reaction, which Balcombe anticipated,
was not good. The chiefs, who had already seen much relocation of the tribe
to this point, objected to the order. But it was only after Balcombe had closed
the traders' houses, and had packed and freighted supplies into Mankato, that
Chief Baptiste and Chief Little Priest relented. The presence of troops at
both the reservation and in town no doubt influenced their decision.[39]

In February 1855, the Ho-Chunk people (the Winnebago) ceded 697,000
acres of land near Long Prairie, Wisconsin, in exchange for 200,000 acres
along the Blue Earth River. The new area was better suited to their needs as
farmers than the dense forests of the Long Prairie region, and was considered
the finest cropland in the territory: a prize for white farmers and speculators.
White settlers already living on the land had been forced to leave in order to
accommodate the incoming Ho-Chunk. By June the tribe began to settle on
the new land, irritating groups of white residents who gathered in Mankato to
protest their arrival. The Ho-Chunk attempted to live in peaceful coexistence

with the whites. Many adopted the customs of white men, cutting their hair, building houses and schools, and wearing "white" clothing. In 1859 Charles Mix reported to his superiors that the Ho-Chunk had acclimated to their new life and had a bright future in front of them. According to Mix, farming activity, educational progress, and the general health of the Indians were at their highest point since their arrival at Blue Earth.[40]

In 1859, however, their old annuities expired, and they needed money to pay their debts, improve their farms, and purchase equipment and stock. Knowing that the value of their land had been enhanced because of increased settlement in the area, they signed a new treaty with the government relinquishing the western portion of the reservation. The people of Mankato and surrounding areas were jubilant over the treaty and welcomed the opportunity to settle on the ceded land, no doubt seeing their new United States senator as the patron of this bounty. Yet, two years passed and still the new treaty had not yet been ratified. Whites began demanding the government completely remove the Ho-Chunk from Minnesota, and began occupying the land. Many business leaders in Mankato believed the growth of the city depended on the opening of the reservation to white settlement. Capitalizing on economic and emotional pressures, therefore, some prominent men in Mankato organized the semisecret "Knights of the Forest," a group whose single aim was to get rid of the Winnebago.[41] In the same year, the Civil War began, and sixteen months later, the Dakota attacked the Lower Sioux Agency. When the Winnebago bill passed the House on February 21, the *Mankato Independent* announced, "GLORIOUS NEWS, THE WINNEBAGOS WILL BE RE-MOVED."[42] Wilkinson proclaimed, "Humanity requires it. The welfare of the Indians as well as the peace of the whites demand [Indian removal]."[43] The Dakota and the Winnebago would be transported to barren ground at the mouth of the Crow River, in the south-central Dakota Territory.[44]

On the day Hickman and his group and the Dakota internees at Fort Snelling crossed paths near the flooded land of Pike Island, the Winnebago began arriving at Mankato at a place that had been called Camp Porter, after John J. Porter, a Mankato tanner and politician who had actively fomented local demands for the Winnebago deportation. Justus C. Ramsey, the governor's brother, supervised their arrival as special agent. A few days before, warriors of Little Priest's band had killed two Dakota—one believed to be married to a Winnebago woman—who were seeking refuge on the Winnebago Reservation; evidently the two men were slain because some of the Winnebago blamed their expulsion from Minnesota on the Dakota War and thought they could win favor with President Lincoln by killing his enemies.

When they arrived in Mankato, the Winnebago paraded the scalped and dis-membered bodies before the whites, whose anxiety deepened as the number of Winnebago coming to town increased.[45] Soon they could not all be held at Camp Porter. Spilling out into the town they milled up and down Front Street, visited stores, and examined the scaffold on which the thirty-eight con-demned Dakota had been hanged. Some of the warriors, in paint and mud, held scalp dances accompanied by drums and chants.[46]

Finally, on May 9 and 10, three Minnesota River packets awaited to take the Indians downriver to Fort Snelling. The all-night scalp dance that began on the eve of debarkation continued during the actual departure. As one of the boats, the *Pomeroy*, left the dock, "the war party of about twenty young bucks, half-naked, their bodies daubed with mud and paint, and with wreaths of green weeds and grass on their heads . . . next to them [squatting] a number of other warriors, all chanted in time with two or three tom-toms a monoto-nous 'He-ah, he-ah' as they journeyed down the river, a scene quite in con-trast with that presented by their Sioux brethren on their departure two weeks before."[47] Though the Winnebago and Dakota could hardly be called "breth-ren," as reflected in the trophy Dakota scalps that Little Priest's warriors band proudly displayed, the manner in which the Winnebago were removed from the state, in brutal contrast to the Dakota's trail of tears during a week of November, touched on the burlesque.

Although the land on Pike Island had flooded annually for the previous several years, the water level of the Minnesota was quite low that year, expos-ing more than an ordinary number of snags and sandbars.[48] Over the next three days, the *Eolian* struck a snag between Henderson and Belle Plaine, rip-ping a thirty-foot hole in the hull and sinking the boat in three feet of water. It was bailed out and the hole was repaired, but continuous use of pumps was necessary during the remainder of the trip. The *Favorite*, loaded with 350 Indians as well as wheat, ran aground just out of Mankato and broke a shaft, rendering one of the wheels inoperative. After it was repaired in St. Peter, the boat hit an exposed reef at Little Rapids just above Chaska. In order to pass through the rapids, it was necessary to unload the Winnebago and three hundred sacks of wheat.[49]

Upon arriving at the landing at Fort Snelling the Winnebago disembark-ing the *Pomeroy* enraged the beleaguered Dakota internees by waving the two bloody scalps and shouting insults at them. Since none of the Indians were armed, troops were able to avert a clash between the two tribes by keeping them apart. Nonetheless, during their brief stay at the fort the Winnebago held two scalp dances and sold trinkets to sightseers.[50] Late in the afternoon of

May 12, the *Davenport* arrived at the Fort Snelling landing to unload supplies; but what must have caught the attention of the Winnebago and soldiers, and everyone else working at the fort, including Robert Hickman and his people, who had arrived the previous week, was the latest and larger contingent of black contraband brought up from Missouri, who encountered, just as the earlier group had faced, a hostile reception at St. Paul's Lowertown. The same battered boat that had transported the Dakota passed the same rock-throwing mob hours later. Now, one week later, the *Davenport* was being prepared to transport the Winnebago southward.[51]

Like the Dakota, the Winnebago would be transported to barren ground at the mouth of the Crow River, in Dakota Territory.[52] Even General Alfred Sully—not a friend of the Indians—complained to the secretary of the interior that the vanquished Indians—Winnebago and Dakota alike—were forced to give up good land for inferior soil. "The land is poor, a low sandy soil. I don't think you can depend on a crop of corn even one in five years, as it seldom rains here in the summer. There is no hunting in the immediate vicinity, and the bands of Sioux near here are hostile to them."[53] The general would later add, in protest to his superiors, "I feel it to be my duty as a Christian and a human being to make known the sufferings of these poor human beings, though they are only Indians." Sully was outraged at the secretary of the interior, who instructed him to furnish troops to protect the Winnebago when they hunted buffalo. The trouble was the Winnebago had no horses. "Afoot it is impossible to hunt buffalo," the general stormed.[54] Removing them from Minnesota was far more important than ensuring their survival.

Nonetheless, on May 15, 1863, the Winnebago climbed aboard the *Davenport* and were accompanied by forty soldiers of the Tenth Regiment under the command of Lieutenant Michael R. Merrill. Observers in St. Paul were treated to an unexpected spectacle. Unlike before, when boats carrying the blacks and Dakota attempted to dock at Lowertown, this time no mob assembled to attack the passengers. Instead, during the three hours the boat was at the dock, large numbers of citizens came to look at the Native Americans and buy their trinkets.[55] These Indians, along with the last contingent scheduled for exile, were called "Red Christians."[56] The message of this portrait was clear: this enterprising band of Indians would do well wherever they went.

For most white Minnesotans the removal of the Dakota and Winnebago had represented the end of an unfortunate era in state history. At last, they had hoped, this mark in time would always mean the end of all contact with the troublesome Indians. It therefore came as a surprise when they learned in October that a wagon train was being organized to provide relief to the relo-

cated tribes. Few knew or cared about the desperate conditions under which
the Indians lived, and virtually no white man or woman felt that Minnesota—
against which the Indians had risen up in a murderous frenzy—owed them
anything. Many felt the Indians should have been grateful, having been allowed to leave the state with their lives and in relative peace. They had sealed
their fate by being born red.[57]

Few knew what a handful of white men knew. In addition to General
Sully's comments to the secretary of the interior, S. D. Hinman, a missionary with the Dakota, told Bishop Whipple that the land was "parched with
drought" and that the Indians "had neither guns nor horses" to hunt game:
"Bishop, if I were an Indian, I would never lay down the war-club while I
lived. They are right, to be savages is the only hope of the Indian."[58] Missionary John Williamson saw the same thing at Crow Creek, the new home of
the Winnebago, and adjacent to the Dakota: "I think the land is too barren."[59]

It had been disastrous planning all around. Superintendent Clark Thompson had selected the site of relocation and had stocked meager supplies and
provisions to sustain the Indians. By the time they arrived, it was too late in
the season for them to plant a crop. On June 9, Williamson reported that the
daily rations were slightly less than one-quarter pound each of flour, pork,
and corn. There was no extra food or medicine for those who had been ill during their winter confinement at Fort Snelling. By July 22 seventy of the thirteen hundred Dakota had died from want of proper food and medical care. It
was not until September 15 that Thompson reported that no provisions had
been made "for the subsistence of the Winnebago and Sioux . . . after the first
day of October next." Commissioner William P. Dole later complained that
he knew nothing of the conditions at the reservation except for newspaper accounts and private letters protesting the condition of the Indians. The expedition, starting from Mankato, would alleviate their suffering.[60]

But many felt that the humanitarian motive behind the relief effort was but
a ruse to further exploit the Indian issue for personal enrichment. Thompson
had either shown exceptional incompetence in administering the relocation or
created a circumstance that could only be resolved by those in the best position to act. The men of Mankato were such people. James B. Hubbell and Al-
pheus F. Hawley, both licensed traders with the Winnebago who resided and
operated from Mankato, and Hubbell and Thompson had known each other
well for several years. Before 1860 they had been active in the Minnesota Republican Party and had worked particularly in support of Morton Wilkinson's
candidacy for the United States Senate. Wilkinson's influence with President
Lincoln got Thompson and Hubbell their posts; and in October, the senator

cleared the way for Thompson to procure flour and corn. The *Weekly Union* reported, "Through the efforts of Senator Wilkinson, the Secretary of Interior has empowered Col. Thompson, the Superintendent of Indian Affairs, to establish a depot for the purchase of Indian goods, provisions, cattle, etc., at Mankato." In a glowing editorial the newspaper envisioned the expedition as the forerunner of a new "Minnesota System" of supplying the upper Missouri, and painted a glowing picture of a great trail from Mankato to the Missouri dotted with stages, express riders, and gold seekers and protected by an extensive line of military posts. The writer estimated that the new "system" might be worth as much as $100,000 or $150,000 annually to the people of Mankato and its vicinity.[61]

As Lass noted, "Provisioning a Dakota Indian agency from Minnesota was unusual enough, since traditionally supplies had been carried up the river from St. Louis, but even more strange was the timing. The editor of the *St. Paul Press* wondered publicly if undertaking such an expedition across the northern plains in the late fall were not as foolhardy as Napoleon's ill-fated invasion of Russia. A 'Moscow Campaign' was under way, the *Press* announced on October 18, 1863, and soon other newspapers as well as many of the people involved in the enterprise were calling it the 'Moscow Expedition.' "[62] It would become a term of ridicule.[63]

One week later, Hubbell received a contract to supply the tribes with beef. Thompson's brother Edward helped Hubbell acquire cattle throughout southern Minnesota. The quality of the animals prompted Hubbell to remark that the "Indians will not get out of beef very soon, if toughness has anything to do with it."[64] In other words, the beef contractor had deliberately bought old cattle; and with the help of Wilkinson, who was in Mankato at the time, Hubbell procured wagons for the expedition. To John C. Wise, fiery editor of the Democratic *Mankato Record,* the entire affair seemed a final desperate attempt by Senator Wilkinson and his associates to exploit the Indians and was "a complete farce."[65]

◆ ◆ ◆ ◆ ◆

Months earlier, in late August, Montgomery's unit, the Seventh Volunteer Infantry Regiment, had begun its long march back to Fort Snelling after the expeditionary campaign into Dakota Territory.[66] The seventh regiment, commanded by Colonel William R. Marshall with Captain Theodore C. Carter, had covered during the fall of 1862 about 675 miles; and during the next summer, in 1863, they marched from Mankato to the Missouri River, then back to Fort Snelling, covering 1,250 miles, marching a total of 1,925 miles throughout Minnesota and Dakota Territory. On this march, reported James T. Ramer, referring again to the teamsters, "we had our tents and knapsacks hauled for us."[67]

In late September, Hickman watched as the regiment filed onto the fort grounds, scanning the parade of exhausted soldiers and creaking, heavily burdened wagons for his fellow pilgrims who had worked on the detail. Two weeks later, he watched the same soldiers file out, turning to descend the incline he and his people had climbed a few short months earlier, down to the heavily trampled muck at the landing on Pike Island and to the boats that would transport them south.

# PART II
## *An Officer and a Gentleman*
### Thomas Montgomery
### 1863–1867

# 7

# THE FIRST LIEUTENANT
# TAKES COMMAND

*We'll see many hardships greater than we can now imagine
but we hope to have courage to overcome all cheerfully and
be able to come back safe in the folly. Still we can't forget
the logic of the song "Brave Boys Hurrah! We've gone at
our country's call. And yet, and yet, we can never forget,
that some of us must fall."*

THOMAS MONTGOMERY TO HIS MOTHER
JUNE 1863, JUST BEFORE THE DAKOTA EXPEDITION

In October 1863, after spending more than a year chasing and fighting the Dakota, the Seventh Regiment Minnesota Volunteers under the command of Lieutenant Colonel William R. Marshall sailed downriver from Fort Snelling to rendezvous with other Union forces in St. Louis, Missouri. Twenty-one-year-old Thomas Montgomery, corporal of Company K, could already say that he had seen adventure and had been tested through the crucible of fire, far beyond the trees that surrounded the small farm that was his home in Cleveland Township, Le Sueur County; but what he was about to see and experience on assignment in the South further influenced his wide-eyed perception of the world, his place therein, and his sense of justice, duty, character, and self-awareness.[1]

In a letter to his parents he wrote, "Times are rather exciting although not anything in comparison with what we will yet see."[2] A month later, he wrote, "From when I left home, until recently I have been constantly exposed to new and varied scenes, exciting the imagination and giving substance for conversation not yet exhausted."[3] The horror of the abysmal conditions that led to widespread disease among the white troops of the Seventh Minnesota included three men who had mustered in with Montgomery.[4] "Thank God my own health continues very good although sickness is quite prevalent in the Regiment. From 100 to 150 report sick daily from our regiment. The weather being much more worse than in Minnesota, the men are more liable to catch colds and then again the boys have to stand night and day in the rain, when it does rain, and going from the heated guardhouse into the cold and moist air makes a person take a cold quite readily."[5]

But it was when he saw a black man for the first time that he was exposed to the personification of the struggle. "There for the first time I saw negro soldiers. They do good duty here in the city."[6] In fact, black men had been in uniform for some time, the result of a plan that had been in the offing since the month before Montgomery and other young men from Le Sueur County had mustered into service.

In the spring of 1862 the war effort for the Union was not going well. As demoralization began to spread throughout the North, enlistment for volunteers showed signs of decline. The Lincoln administration had wrestled for months with the issue of recruiting black troops, concerned that such a move would prompt the border states to secede. When General John C. Fremont, commander of the Department of Missouri, and General David Hunter, commander of the Department of South Carolina, issued proclamations that emancipated slaves in their respective military regions and permitted them to enlist, President Lincoln nullified their orders. By midsummer, however, in the midst of declining white enlistment, escalating numbers of former slaves reached Union lines, and increasingly pressing personnel needs of the Union army forced the government to reconsider the ban.[7]

As a result, on July 17, 1862, Congress passed the second Confiscation and Militia Act, freeing slaves who had masters in the Confederate army. Two days later slavery was abolished in the territories of the United States, and on September 22, Lincoln presented the preliminary draft of the Emancipation Proclamation to his Cabinet. After it was subsequently announced, black recruitment was pursued in earnest, with volunteers beginning to fill the first black regiments. Minnesota Democrats were told "the negro soldier experiment was not only failure, but that under the emancipation proclamation the negroes are fleeing from instead of coming to our lines." As for Negro brigades, the *St. Paul Pioneer and Democrat* declared, "The negroes are deserting, casting aside the scarlet trousers, gaudy buttons, and glittering muskets. Massa Lincum has [set] them free, and their interpretation of freedom is no work of any kind; hence they do not desire to exert their energies in the common labor performed by white men."[8]

The St. Paul newspaper was hardly authoritative. In late January 1863, Governor John Andrew of Massachusetts received permission to raise a regiment of African American soldiers. This was the first regiment to be organized in the North. The pace of organizing additional regiments, however, was very slow. That March, in an effort to change this, Secretary of War Edwin Stanton sent General Lorenzo Thomas to the lower Mississippi valley to recruit African Americans. Thomas was given broad authority. He was to explain the administration's policy regarding these new recruits, and he was to find volunteers to raise and command them. Stanton wanted all officers of such units to be white, but the policy was softened to allow for African American surgeons and chaplains. By the end of the war there were at least eighty-seven African American officers in the Union army. Thomas's effort was very successful, and on May 22, 1863, the Bureau of Colored Troops was established to coordinate and organize regiments from all parts of the country. Created under United States War Department–issued general order number 143, the bureau was responsible for handling all matters concerning the colored troops. All African American regiments were now to be designated United States Colored Troops (USCT). At this time, there were some regiments with state names and a few regiments in the Department of the Gulf designated as Corps d'Afrique. All these were ultimately assimilated into the USCT, even though a small number retained their state designation.

As the war progressed, black regiments included infantry, cavalry, engineers, light artillery, and heavy artillery units. Approximately 175 regiments, composed of more than 173,000 free blacks and freedmen, served the last two years of the war.[9] Their service bolstered the Union war effort at a critical time. By war's end, the men of the USCT composed nearly one-tenth of all Union troops. The USCT suffered 2,751 combat casualties during the war, and 68,176 losses from all causes. Disease caused the most fatalities for all troops, black and white. By the time Montgomery first saw black soldiers, several black regiments, made up largely of the former slaves of Missouri— many of whom had fought gallantly at Port Hudson and Milliken's Bend— were standing garrison duty at strategic points of St. Louis. By war's end, sixteen black soldiers would be awarded the Medal of Honor for valor.[10]

On December 16, 1863, Montgomery wrote to his parents, "Colored regiments rapidly are forming in this state. One whole regiment was formed last week. The First Iowa Volunteer Colored Infantry passed through here on Monday for the South. They looked fine. They had colors and music. One company was from Minnesota. They looked well under arms and I guess will fight, as well as an equal to any white [unit]."[11] During the war, 104 African American men from Minnesota volunteered for service in the army's African American units, including the First Iowa African Infantry, as well as the Eighteenth and Sixty-Eighth Regiments of the United States Colored Troops. It was this service that offered Montgomery his best opportunity for advancement.

◆ ◆ ◆ ◆ ◆

Thomas Montgomery was born on June 4, 1841, of Protestant heritage in Mount Charles, County Donegal, Ulster Province, Ireland. When he was four years old his father, Alexander, and mother, Margaret, brought him to Lower Ontario, Canada, and in July 1856 to Minnesota to settle on a farm in Le Sueur County. Showing early on in 1862 an interest in real estate, he located a claim of 160 acres in Meeker County, which he planned to homestead until, in August, he heard the call to arms: the Dakota were on the warpath. Later that year, on December 16, Corporal Montgomery was ordered to Camp Lincoln, where he guarded Dakota prisoners. There he stood in formation and witnessed the mass execution of thirty-eight Dakota men. Later, at Camp Pope, he was elected second lieutenant and participated in the Dakota campaign on the Missouri River. At twenty-one he had found what very few men of his age could, and that was his road to being an officer and a gentleman, a true man of honor and distinction. "I presume you have heard this, that I have left the old 7th Minnesota and am now associates with the colored population, those of dusky hue and who all their lives have been slaves, but are now (thanks to the war and Old Abe) free men." He was a young man who was as proud of his promotion as he was of himself. To his parents and brothers, he wrote, "Great changes will sometimes occur in a man's life and undoubtedly it has in this instance in mine."[12]

The black soldier and every member of his race were for whom this war was being fought. The president, Montgomery felt, had said as much on January 1, when he issued the Emancipation Proclamation. Montgomery and white men like him wrapped themselves in the nobility of leading the struggle to make all men free. He with his combat experience from fighting the Dakota in Minnesota (mainly chasing them; there were few encounters) would be privileged to lead these black men in this mighty effort, a privilege indeed that colored his sense of duty, race, and good intentions. Because of the otherwise controversial nature of black military service the Negro, many whites assumed, could not be expected to fight without proper leadership. The Lincoln administration thus determined that whites should serve as officers in the new black regiments. African Americans were barred from the officers' ranks.[13]

By offering commissions to whites, the War Department hoped to appease critics in and out of the army. Whites who supported black military service and assisted in its execution could gain commissions and promotions to higher ranks. Critics were assured that no black man would hold commissioned rank over enlisted white men.[14] Montgomery's company was "composed entirely of slaves," and he expressed compassion for their desperate state. "They come here almost entirely destitute of clothing and look pretty hard. But Uncle Sam is a transformer just now and they are not here long till they get clothes. My company here already got their blankets and I intend to clothe them on Monday." The regiment had thirteen officers and nearly all were Minnesotans.[15] Montgomery's temperament made him a perfect choice.

The federal government decided to screen prospective officers carefully. Some were men whom prominent politicians knew to be sympathetic to black people, and they received direct commissions. But the rapid expansion of black regiments in the latter half of 1863 and throughout 1864, and the ensuing demand for white officers, forced the government to devise more efficient means for selecting officers. The problem was that there was no sure-fire method to determine an individual's sincerity, capacity for leadership, and attitudes toward African Americans. The best the government could do was to seek out the moral white men with military knowledge who also had a liberal arts background, which reflected a more well-rounded individual. This is reflected in the battery of examinations that Montgomery took to qualify for rank. By mid-1863, the adjutant general's office established boards to formalize the process. While many officers in the USCT were political appointees, a majority passed an examination that assumed a higher degree of selectivity and competence among officers of black units that did not exist in white regiments. Most officers of white troops obtained their commissions through political contacts or election by their comrades. Montgomery attained his first promotion by election while serving in his Minnesota regiment. He, like other officers who had served in rank, learned on the job. Nearly all of the officers in the USCT assumed command with knowledge of their duties, which unquestionably facilitated the development of most units.[16]

Some viewed service in the USCT as an extension of their prewar antislavery activities. One example was Ozora Stearns, future Olmsted County attorney, mayor of Rochester, Minnesota, U.S. senator, and judge. Others joined because they wanted to uplift the black race. Some coveted commissions in the USCT exclusively for the increase in pay and rank, and such men tended to have no interest in leading black soldiers in battle. Many of its officers, after fighting a couple of years in white units, entered the USCT because they felt this was the best way to contribute to the Union war effort. Whatever the motive for joining, nine of every ten white officers had at least some combat experience. Montgomery had fought in the Dakota War. They had "seen the elephant" and knew how to prepare recruits for the hazards and chaos of the battlefield.[17] Occasionally an officer, outwardly fitting the bill of a proper officer, exploited the opportunity to encourage their charges to work on their homesteads. In Goodhue County, for example, five enlistees joined the United States Colored Regiments, two of whom were brothers, Benjamin and Daniel Densmore, who sent contraband to Red Wing farms.[18]

In several ways, Montgomery embodied many of the traits that characterized white officers in the USCT, and he knew it. But his excitement for the new promotion and assignment was soon tempered by the sober reality that faced African American regiments, especially those assigned to posts in the lower Mississippi River valley—disease. In a letter to his brother Alexander he commented on widespread illness among the ranks. "Sickness is very prevalent here. A great many of our old regiment have been confined by sickness to quarters, and several have died: some 8 or 10, mostly by small pox or varioloid [sic]."[19] "I have now about 18 men in the hospital."[20]

Montgomery set to the administration of his new detachment, tending to the basic necessities of men who had escaped slavery to come with nothing to the company's swelling ranks. "Since I last wrote of 33 men . . . my own company [grew to] 111 recruits. These men I had to provide for with food, quarters, and blankets and make-out their muster in rolls, have those mustered and assigned to different companies to fill them up. After their physicals 31 were rejected, mostly old men and boys. I then took 35 of [those who passed the examination] to fill up my company and give the balance to other companies. I then had to make out the discharges of those rejected men and get them signed and delivered . . . to the contraband camp, free men. I then had my new recruits to arm and clothe. I now have the company clothed and well-armed and not behind any other company in drills."[21]

Now he set to addressing his needs, selecting from among the rejected men a waiter named Washington Barton, who had run away from his mistress. Thanks to Barton the young lieutenant could afford to dress in a manner befitting an officer and a gentlemen. "From [Barton] I borrowed $39 which helped me to get my [new] uniform [purchased due to the recent promotion to First

Lieutenant], which pleased me very much." And Montgomery thought very well of his new waiter who helped him afford his new military dress. "[Barton] is a fine boy, well-clothed, and had been a waiter in a hotel." Indeed, he wanted his mother to know how much his men trusted him, as they began entrusting him with their wages. "Today another of my men entrusted me with $120 for safe keeping for his family. This I will deposit in interest, keeping enough to buy me pants, shoes, hat, and shirts." He was proud of the men he was forging into a military unit. "Yesterday being Sunday, we had regimental inspection. I have the pleasure of saying that I was complimented several times by the Colonel and all decided I had the cleanest and most orderly quarter in the Regiment," and he was impressed at how willing the men were to be molded, even though it taxed him: "I could fill an interesting letter with scenes and tales of these darkies. . . . I endeavor to read the Bible and do my duty as a Christian more than ever."[22]

Never far from the mundane activities of regimental responsibilities was a constant presence of sickness and death. When the company was deployed to Port Hudson, Louisiana, Montgomery had hoped that the conditions that led to illness would likewise be left behind. But he soon learned better, as illness spread even more throughout the ranks. "I like this place pretty well but I won't be sorry at leaving for sickness and death have been very prevalent. I have lost by death already 13 men. There were 70 in the regiment who died in the Post Hospital in February and other regiments in proportion." As his men feared for the worst, to ensure their wages would be secure they gave their earnings to Montgomery to hold. "I had over $300 which I drew for men in the hospital. I pull out about $100 [for my efforts] and have still over $350 in trust for the boys. One man gave me $100 and has since died, but I intend on sending it to his family if I ever can find them."[23]

◆ ◆ ◆ ◆ ◆

In late March 1864, ten months after Union forces attacked Port Hudson, Louisiana, and gave the federals absolute control of the Mississippi River—Vicksburg had been taken in the summer of 1863—Montgomery's unit was deployed to the site where he spoke reverentially about the heroic actions of the African American unit that fought there, giving the highest accolade he could offer: "The colored soldiers who have been here and are well-drilled beat any white soldier I *ever* saw, in guard duty."[24]

The First Louisiana to which Montgomery referred was a part of the famous Corps d'Afrique that was formed in New Orleans after the city was taken and occupied by Union forces. It was formed from the Louisiana Native

Guards, which initially were militia units formed by the city's property-owning free people of color, or as they were called *gens de couleur libres*. Free mixed-race people, often referred to as "Creoles," had formed a third class in New Orleans since colonial years. Although many members of this class also were property owners and had wanted to prove their loyalty and bravery to the Confederacy like other Southern property holders, the Confederates rejected them and confiscated their arms. When Union forces occupied southern Louisiana in 1862, the Creoles stepped forward to serve.

As the Corps d'Afrique formed, the Union recruited freedmen from the refugee camps. Liberated from neighboring plantations, they and their families had no means to earn a living and no place to go. It had been the same story along the river since the fall of Vicksburg. Local commanders, desperately needing replacements because of an increasing mortality rate among black troops owing to disease, started equipping volunteer units with cast-off uniforms and captured weapons. The men were treated and paid as auxiliaries performing guard and picket duties to free up white soldiers for maneuver units. In exchange their families were fed, clothed, and housed for free in the army camps; often schools were set up for them and their children. Montgomery would later comment on this kind of school. Through this period the army had no confidence in their capacity to be a fighting force. In May 1863 the corps proved skeptics wrong when the unit served with distinction at the Battle of Port Hudson.

In the spring and early summer of 1862, Union forces began the conquest of the Mississippi River by taking New Orleans and Memphis. The river between those two cities, however, remained under Confederate control; this section included the river between Vicksburg and Port Hudson, just north of Baton Rouge, which fell to Union forces in June 1862. Well-fortified Port Hudson, unlike Baton Rouge, was one of the strongest points on the river, with batteries placed upon the bluffs that commanded the entire riverfront. When President Lincoln stated that "the opening of the Mississippi River was the first and most important of all our military and naval operations," Port Hudson became central to the war effort and was a chief target.[25] In May 1863, General Grant commenced operations against the Confederate fortified position at Vicksburg, the northern part of the last section to be conquered; General Nathaniel Banks moved against Port Hudson at the southern end.

The assault on Fort Hudson proved quite costly because of both friendly and enemy fire. Union soldiers got bogged down in deep ravines; dense vegetation and rebel crossfire from ridge-top trenches accounted for high Union casualties and resulted in halting their advancement. Seeing that the advance had been stopped, General William Dwight ordered the First and Third Louisiana Native Guards forward into the attack. These troops were not intended to take part in the attack because of the general prejudice against Negro troops on the part of the Union high command. Dwight was determined to break through the Confederate fortifications, however, and committed the Native Guards to the attack at 10:00 a.m. on May 27. Since they had been deployed as diggers and workers on the pontoon bridge near the junction of Big Sandy Creek and the Mississippi, these soldiers were in the worst position possible for the attack than all of the white units of the assault group.

The Guards had first to advance over the pontoon bridge, along Telegraph Road with a fortified ridge to their left manned by rebel sharpshooters supported by a light artillery battery and heavy guns. The Louisiana Native Guards advanced with determination and courage, led by Captain Andre Cailloux, a free black Creole from New Orleans. Filing orders in French and English, Cailloux led the Guards regiments forward until he was killed by artillery fire. Taking heavy losses, the Guards were forced to retreat to avoid annihilation. Yet, even in defeat their reputation grew.

White officers who witnessed the assault took note. In a letter home, Captain Robert F. Wilkinson wrote, "One thing I am glad to say, is that the black troops at P. Hudson fought and acted superbly. The theory of negro inefficiency is, I am very thankful at last thoroughly, exploded by facts. We shall shortly have a splendid army of thousands of them." General Banks also noted their performance in his official report: "The severe test to which they were subjected, and the determined manner in which they encountered the enemy, leaves upon my mind no doubt of their ultimate success." The repulsed attack, due to its hasty implementation against a magnitude of opposing conditions, was eventually fully reported in Northern newspapers, thereby doing much to dispel the belief that black troops were unreliable under fire. On June 13, 1863, an editorial in the August *New York Times* stated, "They were comparatively raw troops, and were yet subjected to the most awful ordeal. . . . The men, white or black, who will not flinch from that, will flinch from nothing. It is no longer possible to doubt the bravery and steadiness of the colored race, when rightly led."[26]

♦ ♦ ♦ ♦ ♦

Good leadership required establishing discipline and orderly quarters. "We are all making camp as comfortably as possible," Montgomery wrote. "We are provided as long as we stay here with wedge tents for the men and wall tents for the officers as we have the privilege taking a steamboat and going down the river foraging, we will get good lumber and fix up comfortably." Officers' quarters required special accommodations in the way of an adequate number of servants. "We have two boys and a woman to wait on us, wash and sew, so we have no trouble but attend to our duties."[27] But he was exceedingly proud of how well he transformed his unit. "I found this company in a rather dirty, slovenly and undisciplined condition. Now they are clean, their camp and tents are kept clean, they are prompt and do their guard duty 3 times as well. I had to enforce discipline to maintain any credit in my position as provost guard." For this, he won the attention of his superiors. "I am also proud to announce that Company B had been complimented more than any other company in the regiment for their cleanliness and good order."[28]

But smart appearances did not mean his men were battle-ready. Though Montgomery had confidence in their potential, he knew they needed more training. "The Missouri [colored] troops need much drilling yet before they can be efficient in the field. General Banks has held the colored troops in reserve, [Confederate general John B.] MacGruder [sic] having said [the Confederates] would take no prisoners of any kind, if the blacks were found fighting. It was well enough to be cautious at first till he knew how he stood, but he ought to disregard any thought, as the blacks will make their mark if they have a chance."[29]

By May he and his unit got their chance. "I have been selected twice to go on a special mission by the General." On May 14 he and fifty of his men were ordered to take command of the steamboat *Louisiana Belle*, and sail down the river about six to ten miles to Prophets Island, where he was to arrest a Confederate named "Fullems." Montgomery landed on the island and marched with some of his men down along the shore, leaving the remaining unit on the boat to come afterward. Learning where his man was from "some colored folks (the only reliable authority for information)," he rushed onward to capture and arrest the "Reb." Soon they were on their way back to camp.[30] On another maneuver, he was likewise sent into an area controlled by Confederates to arrest another rebel and bring him back in custody. He did so, bringing as well food and supplies that his men had foraged while in route.[31]

But they were deep in rebel territory and it soon became necessary to redeploy to a new position. The heat and humidity alone, which got worse by the day, taxed the men to near breaking point:

Monday witnessed a hard march for the poor men. Before we stopped
for the night, nearly ½ of the men had given out. Several were
sunstroke, one lieutenant among the number. That night we slept

under our shelter tents near Morganza. The next morning, Tuesday, we marched to our present camp in rear of this place. I had to watch with an eagle eye on my own [men] and company properly. If I had not been very watchful I would have lost nearly all.

The object in going to Morganza was to relieve "another colored brigade who were to take our place at Port Hudson." Once they arrived, the men were ordered to build a fort. Montgomery estimated that 20,000 troops were in the encampment. "There are Rebels all around us now. We captured some a short time since."[32]

The lieutenant showed his mettle when he imposed discipline, "even over a popular non-commissioned officer": "I reduced my Sergeant to the ranks this AM for misconduct. He was until lately a good sergeant and had the name among the officers of being the best in the regiment, but lately I did not like his actions. He was reported to me for the pernicious act of stealing, but last night I caught him. He entered my cook's tent and filled his haversack nearly full of flour which I had just purchased, and took it to his tent."

For the first time, Montgomery mentions Elizabeth ("Lizzie") Estell by name and what she meant to him. Lizzie told him that she had suspected the sergeant pilfering flour. Yet, when she accused him of it, the sergeant denied it. But she had watched him closely and saw him take the flour under his arm and hide it in a hollow tree, where it was found and brought to Montgomery. Though the sergeant continued to deny his thievery, Montgomery had him reduced in rank. "I had lost confidence in him [and] so had the Captain and all the boys." Though he maintained confidence in his men—"I must say, they are very honest and trustworthy"—his cook was special: "Lizzie, I can trust."[33]

# 8

# LIZZIE AND THE TROUBLES

*You accept my offer of sending Elizabeth there.*

THOMAS MONTGOMERY, 1864[1]

Lieutenant Montgomery's mother had not been feeling well lately. In June 1864 he offered a solution. In the household that he left, which included his father and two younger brothers, Charles and James, the lone woman in the house, his mother, needed help with the chores. The lieutenant felt that his girl would be a considerable help. She was a good cook, laundress, and washerwoman "all together in one person" and the wife of one of his corporals, "a fine yellow gal," an always preferable color of Negress, almost white and well formed; and she had always been "kind and good to me, and always very great and industrious," and she made splendid pies, biscuits, and dumplings, and could make a plain dress in half a day. "She can also make a pants coat." Montgomery's mother was growing weak, and he knew she had more work to do than she could manage, so he proposed sending Lizzie to the family homestead in Le Sueur to live with his mother and work for her until he returned. "I know you want a girl badly and I have spoken to her on the subject and she is willing to go and live with you." Her name was Elizabeth Estell.[2]

"She ran away from her mistress in Missouri and has been with me ever since. She is not saucy or haughty, but is willing to be taught. I don't like to spare her but it would be to your and her advantage, as she can do all of your work and you can teach her to read and make a woman of her. Her husband (so-called) is in my company, a corporal, one of my best men. They have no children to trouble her."[3]

In fact, she did have children who were somewhere in Missouri. Whether Montgomery knew this when he wrote this letter to his mother is unclear. It is plausible that as a regimental commander in the occupied but still un-stable region of southern Louisiana, he had little time and interest in learning much about the personal life of his contraband servant girl, even though her husband was his corporal. On the other hand, as his subsequent letters sug-gested, Montgomery seemed disposed to convey a rosier view of the truth. Therefore, in persuading his mother, likely a bit concerned that Lizzie would be distracted from her labors on the farm if she had children whose welfare she could not know, Montgomery was quite intent to proving that Lizzie, free of all encumbrances, would best suit her needs. History does not record whether Lizzie knew of this exchange. In any event, it was Montgomery, and later his mother, who spoke for her, for she could neither read nor write. Her story says more about those who wrote about her.

Black people in Montgomery's hierarchical world, in which he represented absolute protection and hope for a life of freedom, were a source of curiosity to be observed from afar. In an August 11, 1864, letter to his brother James, after watching the "unusually" emotive style of worship by his men, Mont-gomery wrote, "Preaching prayer meetings are frequented more among the Darkies, seeing they have a place to hold faith in." He did not note how the threat of death heightened their sense of religious fervor, even while looking at the events that surrounded them. Sickness continued to ravage the troops. Even Montgomery got sick but recovered thanks to the medicine he received, which was not available to the troops. "Two of my men died this morning which leaves us now 62 men." Soon officers would be dispatched to St. Louis to enlist new recruits.[4]

* * * * *

To mother, August 16, 1864:
    You accept my offer of sending Elizabeth there. This pleases me
as it will be much better for her as it will be an immense help for you.
Being a great help to me I am loth to let her go but I guess I will get
along without her help better than you can. I will send her up as soon as
a favorable opportunity presents itself. I would like to go up myself this
fall and take her along but that is doubtful. If she could read and write
I would not fear sending her alone, but somehow I fear that she may get
lost or get into difficulty being alone. I can send her safely to St. Louis
and from there she would have to make her own way but she thinks she
can go and is very willing. I will find out about this in a few days.[5]

Montgomery made arrangements for Colonel Alonzo Edgerton's son, "a fine Christian man," who promised to take her with him to Mantorville, where he lived. From there, he would place her on a stagecoach to Mankato and from there to St. Peter, where she would be met by Abner Tibbetts, who would "take care of her valise" while she waited for the connecting stagecoach to Le Sueur. Tibbetts was a family friend who also served as the federal agent of the St. Peter Land Office; he had given Montgomery and his father counsel on real estate investments. With the removal of the Dakota and Winnebago from their land in the southwestern counties of Minnesota in 1863, Tibbetts would also be responsible for handling bids for parcels once the land was opened to settlement the following year. It was in Tibbetts's care that Montgomery entrusted the security of the valise.

Montgomery itemized the contents as follows: clothes, some writing paper and pens for the boys, a pair of gloves and a knife, a package of old letters, a box of seashells picked up on the coast of Texas and lost by some officer on the Red River, Louisiana, campaign. He gave her fifty dollars to pay her expenses; she could keep anything left over. "I trust," writing to his mother, "[Lizzie] will find the way home without any difficulty and be a satisfaction to you. I hope you will all treat her well for she has been good to me in sickness and health. She will probably want clothes for cold weather. You will find her very willing to work at any housework. She relieves you of so much hard work, sewing and washing. I hope you will teach her to read."[6] When he hadn't heard whether Lizzie arrived in Le Sueur, he wrote to his brother, "I suppose Lizzie is with you now. At least, I hope she is. I hope she pleases you although she is colored. Tell her everything is the same as when she left."[7] When she had not arrived by the end of September his worry changed to irritation with her, assuring his equally frustrated mother that he "would have some other person to do the rough work. Never fear the expenses. I expect to send some three or four dollars in a few days which will pay all expenses."[8]

Meanwhile, the mortality rate within his unit grew because of illness. "The men continue to die off. I have lost 18 during the last two months."[9] By mid-September, Montgomery expressed frustration with his troops for falling ill, an apparent reflection, he thought, of poor character, and one that threatened to undermine his command:

> The frightful ravages of death in this brigade are appalling. In
> our regimental hospital, only three or four rods from my tent,
> five men died yesterday, the day before, five, and the day before 3,
> only thirteen in three days. These men die at a considerable rate.

They will be walking along and fall down dead in the morning
in or at their tents or at the sinks. They have no tenacity of life
whatsoever.[10]

He reported that the mortality in the New Orleans Hospital was dreadful and
that two companies were constantly at work digging graves. There was no
talk of recruiting more men. Montgomery worried that the unit would soon
have no men left. There was talk of sending them farther South into the Louisiana swampland for the good health of the men.[11]

As weeks passed with constant drilling and guard duty, Montgomery's
attention to detail earned him more attention from his superiors. By October
1864, ten months after mustering into the USCT as an officer, Montgomery
was promoted to captain. In a letter to his father he expressed satisfaction in
his achievement and with himself, relieved that the regimental enlistments
remained high enough to warrant the promotion. "Well since I left home I
have endeavored to do the best I could. So as to advance my temporal and
spiritual interests and have no reasons to complain of the result of my efforts to God's Blessing, however, I owe all. From an enlisted man in the
ranks I have advanced to the highest position in a company. This under God
I owe to my own individual efforts." It is evident that he was concerned the
decline of able-bodied men in his regiment might impair his chance at promotion. "I was fortunate also in being mustered in as captain when I was. I
would not have succeeded a month later. I am afraid that there is not enough
to warrant such promotion. We are under 500 men in all present. My company is reduced to 50. The scurvy is very prevalent in my Brigade. More
than half of the men have it. If not soon recruited I presume we will be
consolidate."[12]

Finally, the strain of facing the mounting death rate among his men got
to him. The men he was selected to lead, the men he had elected to lead, had,
in his view, let him down, as well as the Union's crusade for freedom. "One
thing is clear. Missouri negroes cannot stand the climate. Much of the mortality no doubt arises from the change of food and manner of living, and the
lack of vitality characteristic of whites." But it wasn't just an issue of the frail
constitution of the men; it seemed, in Montgomery's view, to be a general lack
of character that made them subject to illness. "It would appear that they can
die when they please." He continued:

They make no effort to live when taken sick. They give in at once.
Not a day passes but one or more funeral escorts leave this regiment.

I have come to the conclusion that the present race of black men will
not be of any account to the next generation.

He felt that some of his men were so indifferent they could as easily have returned to Missouri and to the rule of their old masters, "with no higher object
apparently than to see their wives and children." Apparently, missing one's
family was exclusively a trait of the black recruit.[13] Montgomery was generous
toward white officers who wanted at that time to leave the service. "Our chaplain's resignation was accepted and he is going home. He is well-pleased to get
away. I would like to go home too but I can't afford to go on one-half pay."[14]

Many soldiers in the Sixty-Fifth died not only in battle but from the horrific conditions at the Benton Barracks. In October 1864, less than a year after the first recruits entered Benton Barracks, a medical board convened. Its
findings showed that more than a third of those enlisted had died of various
undiagnosed diseases. Others expired due to poor sanitary conditions, as well
as lack of proper food and the means to prepare it. One hundred soldiers,
thinly clad, with no shoes and hats, died during their first two months of duty
at Benton Barracks, beginning December 1863. Two hundred soldiers were
recommended for immediate medical discharge. Black regiments were most
often bivouacked near swampy or poorly drained areas of the camp. The condition and treatment of these troops were a direct result of the racism and
discrimination that was prevalent throughout the army.[15]

◆ ◆ ◆ ◆ ◆

Elizabeth Estell, after setting out for Le Sueur in late August, finally arrived
sometime in early October. Had it been Montgomery traveling home, it would
have taken him a week. So why did it take Lizzie so long to make the same
trip? Montgomery chose not to raise the question. It was more important that
she had finally arrived. His patience may have been propped up by what other
similar-intended officers had experienced. While working with freed slaves
the brothers Ben and Daniel Densmore realized that they could send some
to their hometown of Red Wing, where they would work as servants. Ben
specifically received word from neighbors that they could use contraband to
help them on their farms. The trouble of "delivery," as Ben would later record, was the distance the contraband would have to travel to the Minnesota
farm: "they are not the most reliable people in the world—they are apt to be
trifling."[16]

In any event, Montgomery was pleased to hear that Lizzie had finally arrived at his Le Sueur home: "The best news to me was that Lizzie has arrived

safely with you—and she seemed to be in good spirits." She had apparently gone through the money he gave her. His mother wanted to withhold the cost for the trip from her wages, which had yet to be determined; but Montgomery decided against this, not wanting to do anything that would upset Lizzie. "I have made no bargain as to her wages. The expense of sending her up was considerable and would go a long way in paying her wages [but] don't calculate in that way. The intention is that she will remain with you."[17] This seemed to have pleased Lizzie, who sang his praises. "I am afraid Lizzie blows too much about me and I was well pleased with her day's work that you mentioned."[18]

The exotic appearance of this "yellow gal" from faraway Missouri soon became the source of curiosity and the uncomfortable ever-present stares from the Montgomerys' Le Sueur neighbors, most of whom had probably never seen an African American before, the very embodiment for which the Great War was now being waged, the reason why their fathers, sons, and brothers were fighting and dying; but he suggested to his mother what she could do to help Lizzie through the disorienting process of transition into her new life in Minnesota. "I suppose you receive many visits to see Lizzie and I hope she will not be lonely. Give her a chance to ride horseback and send her the enclosed letter from William, her husband." Now, all seemed at peace with him: "We drill a little every day. I have plenty of time to read and write. . . . I am taking an interest in learning my boys to read. I now have just for a company of 42 men. The other company has much less.[19]

Within the week, he learned that Lizzie wanted to return to Missouri. He insisted that all that could be done should be done to persuade her to stay. But then it began to outrage him that she could be so ungrateful. He did not consider that homesickness or discomfort was a sufficient reason for wanting to leave Minnesota. If she had a better reason for wanting to leave, he would let her do so, though he would insist on keeping her valise and other articles that she had taken to Minnesota. "Tell her she will make me feel bad if she leaves you now after all my expense and trouble for her present and future good. Tell her I say she is a hundred times better off than here or elsewhere. Try to divert her mind. Let her ride on horseback or anything till this wears off." In leaving, she would be casting herself among strangers. But she was not his slave, nor was he her master. "She promised me to stay with you till I returned at least. I want her to be contented and to fulfill her promises to me but if she is bound to leave, I would let her go. Perhaps she is best judge of her own feelings." He finally resigned himself to the peculiar trait of her race: "Privately I would say if Lizzie is determined to leave, or she has left you, it may be better now than later. One thing I observe, a large portion of the race of negroes don't appreciate efforts for their future elevation and good." He nonetheless wished her well but closed by reiterating the point: "I would be sorry if she leaves you now. It would not be treating me fair."[20]

In the midst of war and mounting deaths in the regiment owing to disease, Montgomery instead remained agitated over the prospect of Lizzie's leaving the farm. In the letter he wrote to his mother the next day, he passionately recounted the reasons why Lizzie was better off in Minnesota; she obviously did not know what was good for her. It was, he wrote, for her own good that he insisted on her going to Minnesota, even though she had wanted to return in Missouri. Besides, he explained, there was no reason for her to return to the unit. All the women servants had left.

At the heart of his frustration was that she was upsetting his "plan." "It is my profound belief that she would suit you if she would be contented not to be so homesick as it were. She must remember that she is no longer a slave, but if she attempts to leave Minnesota, ten chances to one she will be kidnapped and returned to slavery or be arrested by the rebel government and put on some plantation. It is irresponsible for her to go back to St. Louis, or even to leave [Minnesota]." As if to seal the deal that she was to stay put, he added that no money was forthcoming: "We are not yet paid and consequently William can't send her money, yet."[21]

Twelve days later, on November 8, Abraham Lincoln was overwhelmingly reelected to the presidency. To his brother, Montgomery rhapsodized poetic: "The news of the election is such as we had reason to expect. Lincoln is reelected! God bless him. This is glorious news to Union-loving people and very bad news for Copperheads and rebels. May the country be saved entirely, Slavery entirely abolished, and peace and union perpetuated in the Land. For this we endure hardship, toil, and privation so the country is saved and the Union preserved even at the cost of my poor life." Elsewhere in the letter, he mentioned the surplus clothing he was able to send them. "They will be worth a great deal to you."[22]

It was now December and Minnesota was frozen in winter, a time of the year that probably gave Lizzie pause in wanting to leave the farm. Montgomery was pleased to hear that she was making the best of the situation, and he made certain to include positive reports about Lizzie's husband, Will. "Tell her that I will give Will the lock of hair and he was glad to hear from her and send her his love. Tell her that he is now the best boy in Company B. He is always glad to hear from her and hopes she will take good care of herself."[23]

Throughout the month Montgomery underscored his pleasure with Lizzie in staying at the farm by reminding her that Will was also pleased with her decision: "Will was delighted to hear from her and of her doing well."[24] Montgomery imagined how tranquil his home was, as the family sat around near the blazing fire. "There is mother on the right of the table with her knitting and a book open before her. . . . There is Lizzie looking wondrously wise and sewing with all her might, now and then stopping to ask a question about her lesson. She is on the left of the table. Father is absent on business of a public character. Alexander in the background is now making some fancy sketches on his slate, and then again biting his lip or scratching his head. . . . Yourself [James] has just come in from town," "Oh," he often concluded, "how I miss being there with you all."[25]

In January, he must have surprised his mother when he stated that after the war, he did not want to return to a life of farming; rather he wanted a life of learning, one of breeding. "I used to like farming very much but my mind has another bent now. Much as I have been educated, I feel the lack of education very much and I believe if I returned safely from the army, I would go to college or high school and store my mind with useful knowledge. When I look at the poor darkies, I think I know something; but when so much lies before me to be learned, I confess I feel ignorant."[26]

"Breeding" had become important to the captain even before he enlisted in the army. It had prompted him to invest in land. During the previous August, he indulged in stereotype as he wrote about Dr. Charles Eliot, whom he had met in Missouri. The good doctor, though a graduate of the Iowa Medical University, "would make you laugh to hear of his uncouth manner and gestures and peculiarities. He dresses very rough, wears old shoes, sticks his fingers up his large nose and hitches up his britches. When I saw him I thought he was a common old Irishman, as he looks and accents his words much like one."[27] Despite his education, Eliot displayed the absence of refinement normally associated with a man of his professional status, an Irishman from whom the Irish-born Montgomery dearly wished to distance himself. His captaincy made him an officer. Education would make him a gentleman. He closed by wishing Lizzie well. "She is ten times better than she would be here. William her husband is well and is always glad to hear of her welfare."[28]

Montgomery's mother had never been exposed to African Americans, so Lizzie must have been quite a curiosity for her. Stories Lizzie shared about her life and marriage may have been so foreign to Mrs. Montgomery that the facts probably invited more questions that "proper" people may have felt too inhibited to raise, questions like the nature of her marriage to William. What Lizzie conveyed about the sacred institution within the prism of slavery may have prompted Mrs. Montgomery to wonder whether the holy union between her servant and her servant's husband was in fact legitimate.

Montgomery seemed to handle the delicate matter in a roundabout manner, by first reminding his mother how fortunate she was to have Lizzie. "You have much need of help. I think Elizabeth is learning fast. She will yet learn to write a letter perhaps." Then he reported that his men had just been paid. "The Darkies are having a regular jollification since pay-day. Poor boys, they are much in need of money. Some throw their money away while others save it all." Then he got to the hedged point. "You talked of getting certificates concerning Lizzie's marriage. I may attend to it but I don't think it is necessary. [William] is willing [to legally marry her]. . . . They are man and wife in the eyes of the law and are married as nearly all their race is: common consent of both parties as long as they agree. There is genuine affection between some, and others if too long separated will marry again, anyway."[29] What he meant was that enslaved people could not legally marry in any slaveholding state. Laws considered them property and commodities, not legal persons who could enter into contracts, and marriage was very much a legal contract. This meant that until 1865, when slavery ended in the country, slaves—indeed, the vast number of African Americans—could not legally marry. Nonetheless, many enslaved people entered into relationships that they treated like marriage; they considered themselves husbands and wives even though they knew their unions were not protected by state law.[30] Perhaps assuming it necessary to vouch for William's character, Montgomery later wrote, "He is now a corporal with a hope of soon being sergeant, all this for good behavior and attention to duty. He is well. So are Lizzie's friends. All send love and tell her that Mary left here last week for St. Louis."[31] It seemed that Lizzie's friends had not left the camp as Montgomery had previously claimed in a desperate effort to discourage her from wanting to return to the unit. But since she seemed happy in her new Minnesota home, all, for now, was well with her.[32]

◆ ◆ ◆ ◆ ◆

*I am anxious to do all I can for them but I will not involve myself in any trouble.*
THOMAS MONTGOMERY

With the removal of the Dakota and the Winnebago from Minnesota in 1863, the federal government claimed their now-vacated land and prepared to open it for purchase. By June 1865, the government was poised to begin the process for receiving bids. The St. Peter Land Office would administer the work that officially was to begin that summer. The land agent—more officially known as the register of public lands for the General Land Office at St. Peter, and a presidential appointee—was Abner Tibbetts. One month earlier, he had inquired whether Montgomery's troops would be interested in staking their claims in rich Minnesota farmland. It was an extraordinary gesture, considering that there were loud voices in the region of Minnesota that were hostile to black migration. Talk of changing the state constitution to include black suffrage had set the spark to the fuse, and Tibbetts would have known about this. Still, he made the offer.

Tibbetts had known the Montgomery family for some time through, initially, previous land dealings, but their relationship had deepened over the years. Curious about the war effort and what he had learned from Montgomery about the sights he had seen, as well as the blacks he commanded, Tibbetts visited his friend in St. Louis in early 1864. That firsthand exposure left in him a lasting impression of the nobility of Montgomery's men, ex-slaves, the type whom many questioned could be counted on in battle, who had nevertheless rushed forward to take up arms against their former masters and defend the nation, if need be, at the cost of their own lives. Not even Tibbetts was making this sacrifice. Perhaps he at least could contribute to the cause in some small measure. The idea may have come to him later in August when, as a favor to Montgomery, he sat with Lizzie Estell in St. Peter as they waited for her stage on the final leg to Cleveland Township.[33]

Though there is no record of what transpired between them, one may surmise that they conversed with proper restraint, a curious Minnesotan in his first conversation with a black woman, a so-called contraband with light-colored skin, who now huddled within her borrowed coat against all the unfamiliarity around her and the chill of Minnesota's autumnal air: she embodied what the war was truly about. Reading about Confederate atrocities in the South, it was hard to imagine a South where black people like Elizabeth and her husband, William, could ever securely live in freedom. She struck him as a person of high character and industry, married to a man of equal carriage, deserving of a homestead where she could live at once as a wife and mother in a unified family under the same roof on the free and richly fertile farm soil of Minnesota. Clearly, Tibbetts concluded, their best opportunity for a bright future resided up north and in Minnesota, the state that was the first to respond to Lincoln's call to arms when the war broke out. He could offer Montgomery's men the opportunity to acquire the soon-to-be available and soon-to-be purchased land parcels on the Dakota and Winnebago reservations. This would be his contribution to the cause for freedom, giving Montgomery's troops the opportunity that white men of privilege, many of whom had not fought in the war, always had: the advantage of bidding early.

Montgomery responded that his men were interested. "I spoke to the men about it and they seemed to be gratified that any person had taken such an interest in their future welfare."[34] He had "no doubt that he could form a good colony but the men," as well as himself, wanted to know "on what conditions we are to base our actions." For their benefit, Montgomery wanted more information. Will the land be timber or prairie? High or rolling or wet or marshy? Good soil or sandy or poor soil? Will it be convenient to market or to the Minnesota River? To timber if prairie, and can wood and good water be found easily? About how far and in what direction from St. Peter? Will the land be safely held for the men till after the war, free from taxes, in case they should die or be killed while in the army. They, "of course," wanted to know about the climate. "The object of asking these questions is to make my own action secure and furnish the men a guarantee that there is no deception":

> All my men are without houses and are desirous of procuring them
> and they could each bring their friends along. Some are tradesmen.
> All of them I have no doubt would make good industrious citizens.
> I don't want to have them misled or disappointed. If your answers
> will be satisfactory and you will guarantee a good selection as I have
> no doubt you will, I will hasten to send you the names and money.
> I think they will be quite willing to go to Minnesota. One of them
> said, "We will go anywhere to get away from the secesh." The plan
> is a good one and I like it well and it will induce them no doubt to be
> saving of their money.[35]

But despite his support he expressed one condition. If there was resistance to the plan, he would let the idea drop. "I am anxious to do all I can for [the men] but I will not involve myself in any trouble." It seemed that there was "trouble" with the plan for a black colony, though Montgomery never confirmed this in subsequent letters. In fact, he mentioned nothing more about the scheme. It was as if the overture had never existed.

He changed the topic. The unit had received new recruits the day before. They were from Wisconsin, and most could read and write. One was "perfectly white"; another was from Winona, Minnesota, and a number of them had friends in his unit. One apparently knew Montgomery's corporal, William, and told him that Lizzie's two children "were well and well taken care of and at the same place as where she left them." In persuading his mother to receive Lizzie as a helper, he had earlier assured her that Lizzie had "no children to trouble her."[36] This was now the first time he mentioned that she indeed did, a fact quite plausibly he may have known from two persons he trusted—his cook, whom he had sent to work for his mother, and his cook's husband, William, Montgomery's corporal. He seemed unaware of yet one more reason why Lizzie might have wanted to return south.

On April 9, 1865, General Robert E. Lee of the Army of Northern Virginia surrendered to Union general Ulysses S. Grant at Appomattox Court House, Virginia. Montgomery rejoiced at the news. "We have had the official announcement of the surrender of Lee with his entire army into the hands of Grant on terms proposed by the other. It is glorious."[37] Five days later, on April 14, President Abraham Lincoln was shot. "With feelings of utter sadness I refer to another subject—that all but absorbing topic of the day, the horrible assassination of President Abraham Lincoln and the Sec't. of State William Seward and others." In fact, in a botched attempt by one of Booth's coconspirators, Seward was severely wounded at his home but was not killed.

> My heart grieves at every mention of the atrocious deed. I never endured such sad and mournful feelings as I did during the 24 hours succeeding the mournful intelligence. The noble honest pure patriotic and magnanimous Lincoln is no more. He has fallen in his manhood at the height of his excellence and devotion for the country's best interest. Our great and good President has been cut down in his glory and that by the devilish assassin's bullet without any cause or provocation. Freedom has lost a champion: the oppressed, their truest friend.[38]

Presidential appointee Abner Tibbetts tendered his resignation the day Lincoln died, April 15, and returned to his home in Lake City.[39]

◆ ◆ ◆ ◆ ◆

> *When young folks grow up, and leave the home of their*
> *childhood they are so engrossed with so many strange*
> *objects and see so much that is new that they nine cases*
> *out of ten forget all about home.*

THOMAS MONTGOMERY

May brought a new sort of trouble for Captain Montgomery when he learned that his teenage brother Alexander had run away from home. Though he could understand why any young man might feel restless, "gone to seek abroad those advantages [and] privileges that he was denied at home," the captain nonetheless was perturbed to learn that his brother could be so "reprehensible." Alex, insisted his oldest brother, had responsibilities to the family to stay and help work the farm. Yet, he said, he was "not prepared to judge." As for himself, Montgomery, who was "used to the city or public life," was "fully aware that farming in the woods of Minnesota furnishes few inducements to a mind bent on the acquisition of knowledge," declaring that he himself did not want to return to the farm. "My choice today would be to go to college to further my education as yet only commenced. I feel my disadvantages very much at times. It is a sad thing to grow up in ignorance while so much remains to be known. Such a person should live in the backwoods all their days."[40]

With the realization that two of her three sons might not be coming back to her, Mrs. Montgomery grew quiet, or she was at least nonresponsive to the added blow of the captain's plan, which for him was the logical progression of a young gentleman in training. Left behind was her husband, who seemed always away from home, investing in land deals, and James, the son who seemed to be the only man left to share the hard labors of farming with their increasingly "restless" servant, Lizzie. What exactly could Mrs. Montgomery say to her oldest son who was serving their nation that now needed him more in the aftermath of the killing of their president? Finally, on May 31, the captain prompted her to respond to his plan with other news: "When you write next, our regiment will probably be consolidated. William Estell is with us and is doing well." He then asked what he really wanted to say: "What do you say to me leaving the service and going to college?"[41]

♦ ♦ ♦ ♦ ♦

Dear Brother James, June 4:

This being the twenty-fourth anniversary of my birthday I seat myself to write you a few lines. My health today is good and I hope it will continue. . . . I have been unwell for the past month, my bowels have been deranged, but I feel now as if I was entirely well. I was not very sick [nor] was I confined to my bed but was quite weak. I am now improving fast. God be all praised.

The captain later ruminated on his near future in the army if his unit was to be consolidated with another regiment. Compensation was a key factor to his desire to remain in uniform. "The War Department will decide who [of the officers] go and who stay, at least as it is said. Most of our officers wish to go home. I choose to stay some time longer, unless I am refused a leave of absence when I will ask to be mustered out. My pay is good. An officer who is mustered out honorably with his command receives 3-months additional pay proper being for me $1800. We also receive one-day pay for 20-miles travel from his place of muster in. These are inducements." He also wanted Lizzie to know that he was being well taken care of. "[Servant] Henry Hershey does all our cooking, washing, and cleaning up and does it scientifically to[o]. He is an active boy full of fun all the time amusing us with his drollery. He has only one eye but he is death on Rebels."[42]

One night William Estell came to the captain's tent to tell him "something to write to Lizzie." He had been "in feeble health for some time" though he thought he was getting better. But the main point of the letter he wanted the captain to write was that he wanted her to be "a good girl and remain there [until] he comes out of service after her. He would rather she would stay there than to leave."[43] The time was remarkably convenient, especially as it related to Lizzie's recent murmurings about leaving the farm. Her restlessness seemed to have abated for the time being. The Minnesota winter had a way of dampening wanderlust. Brother Alex's sudden departure was a sign of the times. And now that Lizzie was sounding off, it meant that his mother would have no one to help around the farm, which would create a burden on the oldest son. His sense of duty would have compelled him to return to the farm. Montgomery's letters would increasingly reflect one who understood the loneliness his mother feared and now anticipated. It became critical to him that Lizzie should stay on the family farm, not, as he would write, that it was what he wanted, but what her husband William wanted, especially in his weakened state. It was a message he was prepared to make to his corporal's wife in person. "You say that Lizzie is getting restless and is anxious to leave[.] If she has not kept her promise to me I will shortly be up there perhaps and see her for it. . . . She should be well-paid for staying with you, but if she is headstrong and disobedient, I would not keep her if I could better myself." He had to concede, however, that laborers like Lizzie could make more money elsewhere: "She has lived with you longer than I expected [especially] for one who has been around with the army. Women have made as high as $25 per month, cooking the mess, washing and sewing."[44]

But he also wanted his mother to buck up, conveying, for the first time in any letter he had before written, edgy displeasure and impatience with her. "There is something mysterious in consequence of getting that letter which I cannot fully comprehend. You are doubtless greatly perplexed in these times. So many things as here are written on your mind." Then, softening his tone he wrote, "I can faintly imagine how you feel now being so secluded and lonely since Bro. Alex left, but you must strive to bear up under the dispensation of Providence and to put your trust in the One Almighty to save all, who noticed even the fall of a sparrow. May God uphold you in His Grace to the end. I know you must feel grieved but perhaps it is all for the best. I will try to visit you as soon as possible and then we can talk more freely on the subject."[45] He added, "I suppose I could leave the army if I would try but as it pays very well I don't care to go on the farm. It is not my intention however, to remain in too long." His own health had been bad: "I am troubled this summer, much as I was last, with diseases of the bowels which has reduced me in flesh coincidentally. I do not suffer any, however, but would like cool weather to come again."[46]

Two weeks later both mother and oldest son were in better spirits. "I was glad to hear that inspite [sic] of our case of anxiety for Bro. Alex your health was so good that you could ride out and that your spirits were not as despondent. I suppose that you are well pleased to hear from your dear sisters in Ireland." One of his aunt's sons, his cousin Thomas Morrow, had like Alex suddenly left home. "It is a little strange that [they] don't hear from Cousin Thomas Morrow. But it is much the way of the world. When young folks grow up, and leave the home of their childhood they are so engrossed with so many strange objects and see so much that is new that they nine cases out of ten forget all about home. If they have been well brought up, they will sometimes think seriously of their loved ones far away. It is my experience that were it not for writing so frequently, I would seldom think of home being so much engaged with my everyday affairs." Turning his focus on his wayward brother: "I feel sorry for Bro. Alex very often. I think it strange that he don't write to either of us. He will surely be brought to a sense of pain it inflicts over you and ought to relieve your anxiety by writing. May God take care of him."[47]

◆ ◆ ◆ ◆ ◆

Later in June 1865, Montgomery got a leave of absence to return to Le Sueur. No record exists of what transpired while he was at home. By mid-September he had taken a circuitous route in return to his regiment, by way of Faribault, Red Wing (where he visited Hamline University and met with Reverend J. Brooks, president, who gave him a catalog), Madison, Wisconsin, where he searched for brother "Sandy" (Alex), Milwaukee, Chicago, St. Louis, and

Cairo, Illinois. By the time he reached his regiment, now in Baton Rouge, Louisiana, he found major changes.[48]

In the fall of 1865, Montgomery's Sixty-Seventh Regiment was consolidated into the Sixty-Fifth Regiment because of the considerable number of deaths due to disease. In the Sixty-Fifth, in particular, 749 enlisted men and 6 officers died to cholera and smallpox. Black regiments posted along the lower Mississippi River valley encountered similar problems. Whether stationed in Louisiana, Arkansas, or St. Louis (Benton Barracks), the mortality rate was alarmingly high. One company in the Sixtieth lost more than a quarter of its men to sickness. Another unit, within six days after arriving at its post in Arkansas, lost 65 percent of its men. Black troops were not only far more likely to contract smallpox while in service, but they also were more likely to die from it. The Union army required vaccinations of its troops but the vaccine used—sometimes taken from men who were sick from other diseases—often led to severe complications. "However I am thankful for things as they are and am willing to conform to circumstances as ordered for me and accept changes as they occur."[49]

He wanted Lizzie to know that William was now in the Sixtieth Regiment, Company A, though he remained sick for a good while and was in Post Hospital. "For wont [sic] of time I have not yet seen him but will soon and write again."[50] However, William Estell's name does not appear on the roster of Company A, Sixtieth Regiment, also known as the First Regiment Iowa Volunteer Infantry—African Descent. On October 15, 1865, the regiment mustered out at Devalls Bluff, Arkansas, and was discharged on November 2.[51] In fact, subsequent letters from Montgomery indicate that Estell never left the hospital, suggesting that he was too ill to travel.

The prevention and treatment of disease were as important as combat operations in the campaigns along the Mississippi River during the Civil War. Throughout the Vicksburg campaign, many more soldiers were disabled by disease than by combat injuries. While this held true for both sides, a greater proportion of the Union army was healthier than the opposing Confederate troops. In the last two years of the war, however, the North tried to occupy the Confederate states along the Mississippi valley. The failure to accomplish this goal was largely due to the deteriorating health of the Union army.[52]

Doctors did not understand that mosquitoes spread disease and, in particular, yellow fever. Once an infected mosquito bit a person, the onset of the disease began within a few days. The patient suffered head and body aches, along with high fever and nausea; damage to the liver resulted in the yellowing of the skin and eyes. More than half of victims of yellow fever died within a few days; those who survived gained immunity against the disease. There were many severe epidemics throughout the Civil War. The disease was common in the swamps within the Mississippi valley, where Montgomery's unit was now encamped. Even senior officers were infected. "The Colonel has been sick for a few days but is getting well."[53]

Seven days later Montgomery reported that as long as the weather was dry, "the officers were in good health but when wet weather set in, nearly every one was taken down sick. I have had no chills or fever since last Sunday. My stomach now is only a nervous weakness." But he also acknowledged that the officers had not fully recovered. "For the last two dress parades the Company officers were the 9th and 10th Captains and only one line officer was present beside the Adjutant. This shows how we are reduced by sickness. The Major and Adjutant are both sick now." William had been "feeble" "nearly all summer" and "he looked quite thin." But, in a hopeful note to Lizzie, Montgomery wrote, "He is not confined to bed. He is out every day and sent his love to her." Montgomery reported that William regretted not writing more frequently: "He says it is difficult to get anyone to write for him." William also wanted to know whether the forty dollars he had sent to Lizzie by Captain Whitford ever arrived.[54]

It was not unusual that enlisted men would hand over their wages and savings to trusted officers of their units, for it seemed that the officers would survive them all. It had seemed that the health of officers tended to fare better and because of the privilege of rank, the officers had relative freedom of movement. There was always a chance they might venture near a distant loved one and convey personal regard just as a lifeline would do. And as their officers—indeed, white men who chose to lead them into battle to win their own freedom—they were imbued with a special, in some units, reverential status. But under the cloak of an officer and the veneer of "gentleman," the man within was ultimately a man with flaws. In the midst of the greatest crusade there was always the opportunity of personal benefit.

By mid-October William Estell was still in the Post Hospital, but he was "improving rapidly." As to Lizzie's restlessness, Montgomery wanted her to know that "William is uneasy to hear from Elizabeth and sends his love to her. Give my regards to her to be a good faithful girl and learn to read."[55]

In Minnesota, voters were being asked to elect a new governor, and Montgomery was a Marshall man though he was ambiguous on the companion question that would be posed: whether the state constitution should extend the right to vote to black men. "I am anxious to hear the decision of the election this fall. I hope [William] Marshall is elected but I think it will be a close run on account of the point at issue—negro suffrage."[56]

Montgomery had a special interest in William R. Marshall, his old commander in the Seventh Volunteers. The lieutenant colonel had done well since they fought the Dakota together in 1862, and in November 1863, Marshall was promoted to colonel. He fought valiantly in the Battle of Nashville, where he took command of Colonel Sylvester Hill's brigade after Hill was killed on the first day of the battle. He continued in brigade command when transferred to Mobile, Alabama, to take part in the Battle of Fort Blakely. Colonel Marshall was brevetted brigadier general of volunteers on March 13, 1865.

In 1865 the Missouri-born war hero was elected governor of Minnesota and would serve for two terms. In 1865, however, despite his support for black suffrage, the question failed statewide by a vote of 14,651 to 12,138; Marshall defeated Democrat Henry Rice, 17,318 to 13,842. Montgomery's skepticism of the success of black suffrage was well founded, for he understood his community's views on race and knew Marshall's support might undercut his candidacy. In 1865 black suffrage and Marshall both fell short in Le Sueur County: Marshall lost, 422 to 729, and the black suffrage amendment lost, 224 to 839.[57] Montgomery did not state his position on the issue of whether black men should have the right to vote.

♦ ♦ ♦ ♦ ♦

Montgomery could never forget that he and the unit were in danger. "There is now and then some shooting between us and the Rebel citizens. They don't like us any too well. Doctor Moore, of our Regiment on duty at Clinton with the Seventh Kentucky, was shot through the head by a Rebel." During these months, the Union army was able, though barely, to enforce the law. "The murderer and his accomplices are safely in a cell of the Penitentiary here in irons, awaiting trial."[58]

# 9

# FREEDOM
# AND EDUCATION

*There are hundreds of colored children being*
*educated in this city and will soon outstrip the white*
*children in general knowledge.*

THOMAS MONTGOMERY TO HIS MOTHER
DECEMBER 15, 1865

After the requisite number of twenty-seven states of the then thirty-eight
states ratified the Thirteenth Amendment, Congress, on December 6, 1865,
adopted the new law that abolished slavery in America. On December 16,
Secretary of State William H. Seward officially proclaimed the ratified
amendment to be a new law. But already the effort to free all those who had
been enslaved was systematically being curtailed. Shortly after its adoption,
in many counties throughout the South blacks walking around without papers could be detained for vagrancy and forced into involuntary servitude as
"punishment" in accordance with newly enacted statutes drawn up expressly
for that purpose. Within the week after Seward's announcement, all former
slave states adopted such laws and other similarly draconian statutes called
Black Codes that restricted the freedmen. While the Southern states pursued readmission into the Union, they enacted laws that limited freedmen to
second-class status with no voting rights. Southern plantation owners feared
they would lose their land and power in the absence of a coerced labor force.
Thus, Black Codes became necessary to preserving the old order. The North

was outraged at the proliferation of these new laws for it seemed the South was creating a form of quasi-slavery to negate the result and purpose of the war. Spurred on by mounting resentment to Union military governors and Freedman's Bureau officials, the Southern states defiantly continued more detailed restrictions of the black man.

Since autumn, most of the old Confederate states had held all-white constitutional conventions, all under the approving eye of Andrew Johnson, who succeeded President Lincoln after his assassination. By the end of the year, most of the Southern states had held elections under the new state laws. Not surprisingly, ex-Confederate leaders won elections for state government positions and for the U.S. Congress. The newly formed legislatures quickly addressed needed public projects, including the creation, for the first time in the South, of a public education system, although the new schools excluded black children. Other laws were passed to limit the freedom of the former slaves that denied voting rights, the freedom to travel, and work in the occupations of their choice. In some states, even their marriages were outside the law.

During the last months of 1865 a rumor spread among freedmen that the federal government was going to grant forty acres and a mule to every ex-slave family on Christmas Day. Although the federal government had confiscated Confederate land and had in certain counties given parcels to freed slaves, it never planned to do this on a massive scale. Nonetheless, blacks expecting their own plots of land heightened the concern of white landowners, who now worried that the freedmen and -women would refuse to return to work on the plantations of their former masters. Meanwhile, the white owners circulated their own rumors that the black population would rise up in rebellion should they not receive the land on Christmas Day. These fears led to the first Black Code, enacted by Mississippi, which proved to be harsh and vindictive. South Carolina followed with its own code. On December 21, four days before Montgomery recognized his fourth Christmas in the army and away from home, the Louisiana assembly enacted its Black Code, which included a restriction of movement and a concerted effort to return former slaves to a servile status.[1]

St. Landry Parish, which neighbored Baton Rouge, where Montgomery's units were encamped, had its own Black Code that included a prohibition on a black man passing within the limits of the parish without special permit from his employer. African Americans were not permitted to rent or keep a house. Every African American was required to be in the regular service of a white person. No public meeting of African Americans was allowed within the parish after sunset. No African American could preach, exhort, or otherwise declaim to congregations of colored people without special permission from the president of the police jury. No African American who was not in the military could have firearms, nor could he sell, barter, or exchange any articles of merchandise within the parish without permission. Negroes who intermarried with whites were guilty of a felony, punishable by a long prison term.[2] The Louisiana Black Code, enacted in the same city where Montgomery was encamped, was enforced with white violence against black men and attempted to turn the clock backward to the antebellum period. It was within this context—one in which the tide of white supremacy was rising up in clear view—that Captain Montgomery described his uneventful day:

To Mother, Headquarters Co. I, 65th Regiment,
USCI, Baton Rouge, December 25
    Another Christmas Day is past and it being the fourth I've spent in the army and away from home. Were it had been a day of pleasure but not unmixed with pain. There being no religious exercises in any but the Catholic Church, I spent the forenoon with my company in practicing with the ball cartridge, the different modes of firing by file, rank, platoon, and company, to get used to firing as skirmishers. Unfortunately, one of the men shot a cow which came up out of a ravine in a wrong moment. . . . I found the owner of the cow and offered to settle by buying the cow or paying the damages for wounding the animal. My men were in favor of buying the cow which I done, paying $45. Some of the officers I am sorry to say disgraced the day (Christmas) and themselves by becoming beastly intoxicated.

He described in the same letter a tour of the Intermediate Colored School he had taken with other officers and that left a profound impression on him. "I went and such a sight I never saw before." The house was crowded with black children—an estimated "200 scholars were in attendance." They demonstrated their proficiencies in reading, spelling, arithmetic, geography, and history, "and they completely surprised me at their rapid advancement." Some of the scholars were under twelve years of age and yet they could name all the countries on the different maps, tell their capitals and the rivers that flowed nearby; also the islands, capes, and lakes. "One little girl almost white spelled a word of 21 syllables, repeating each syllable over and over from first to last. Afterwards, the students demonstrated their skills in declamation, recitation, singing and speeches. The whole thing was a splendid affair and effected good credit on the manager." The teachers were white ladies from the Northern states. The schoolroom was very tastefully decorated with evergreens, mottoes, and behind the teachers' desk and on the opposite wall over the American flag was arrayed the word "Excelsior." On another wall was printed "Freedom and Education," and on the last, "Lincoln and Books." Still lower down were three mottoes, "Sobriety," "Industry," and "Tomorrow." "The examination of the Primary Colored School of this city will be by Mr. Tinkner, Supt., and the next day, the refugee white school. I propose attending."[3]

Montgomery's experience contrasted with other Negro schools set up by Northerners in southern Louisiana that were routinely burned and razed. White teachers from the North were ostracized and occasionally run out of the community.[4] Yet, he saw a more hopeful scene. "There are hundreds of colored children being educated in this city and will soon outstrip the white children in general knowledge. Our officer who visited the examination was satisfied that the Blacks could be taught and that they were eager to learn." He closed his Christmas letter in what was becoming the usual manner: "My health is splendid and the weather is warm. Tell Lizzie I have seen William and he is pretty well and sends his love to her. I also send mine to all. Your son, Thomas Montgomery, Capt."[5]

Federal troops in Louisiana were being pulled out. Montgomery expected that his regiment would soon follow, as he indicated in his letter dated January 2, 1866: "Several regiments have left here having been mustered out. All the rest except ours will follow within ten days. I think our turn will soon come."[6]

Demobilization, the military operation to return just over one million volunteer soldiers back to civilian life in the wake of the Civil War, was generally well organized and rapidly executed. As of May 1, 1865, just three weeks after the surrender of Robert E. Lee's command at Appomattox Court House, 1,034,064 volunteer soldiers, both white and black, were slated to be mustered out and discharged. By November 1, 1866, a year and a half later, that number was reduced to 11,043 men, or approximately 1 percent. By November 1865, six months after demobilization began, approximately 801,000 men had been processed. Yet significantly, as impressive as this achievement was, it occurred before the close of hostilities. Edmund Kirby Smith, the last full general of the Confederate army, surrendered arms on June 2, 1865; still, guerrilla bands and irregulars continued skirmishing with remaining federal troops. In those areas of engagement, the war was not yet won. A significant amount of redeployment of federal troops was necessary to accomplish the required garrisoning of conquered areas of the South.[7] Montgomery's unit was one of these.

Though the morale of Union soldiers yet to demobilize tended to be high, or they had developed the sense that the process was working quite well even while some of them remained for the time at their posts, troops bivouacked within the range of ex-rebel snipers had to feel a unique kind of anxiety: the war is over and I am packed and ready to go home, and still I can be shot.[8] In fact, as the commanding officer of the Eighty-Fourth USCT noted, it was dangerous for a federal official [from the Freedmen's Bureau] to travel more than eight or ten miles outside the state capital of Louisiana.[9] An officer in Montgomery's regiment, assigned to provide security for the officials, was himself threatened with assault. "Lieutenant Roberts of my company . . . is in the Freedman's Bureau looking at the schools. He says his life is often in danger."[10]

The Bureau of Refugees, Freedmen, and Abandoned Lands, known simply as the Freedmen's Bureau, was created by Congress in March 1865 to assist for one year in the transition from slavery to freedom in the South. Run by the War Department, the bureau's first and most important responsibility included a system of free labor, overseeing some three thousand schools for freepersons, settling disputes and enforcing contracts between white landowners and their black labor force, and securing justice for blacks in state courts. Congress extended the bureau over the veto of President Johnson, who thought it unconstitutional. Southerners were basically opposed to blacks having any rights at all, and the bureau lacked military force to back up its authority as the army had been quickly disbanded and most of the remaining soldiers assigned to the western frontier. Though the bureau would accomplish some of its goals, especially in the field of education, Southern whites commenced a steady effort to frustrate the work, including intimidation and assaults of bureau agents and the sabotage of bureau projects. Agents soon became targets of ex-rebel terrorism.[11]

Despite some of its successes, the bureau was headed to even more troubled water. White supremacists had taken aim against it. But the very nature of the bureau—namely, federal "intrusion" into state affairs—proved controversial. Jealous of African Americans' prerogatives of self-government, white Southerners maintained toward the bureau an attitude ranging from indifference to hostility, ignoring or taking lightly bureau suggestions that lawmakers not enact discriminatory laws against African Americans. When agents of the bureau interfered with the policies of state governments, they were not always safe from the wrath even of the federal government. Historian John Hope Franklin gives as an example the assistant commissioner for Louisiana, Thomas W. Conway, who had found himself in "deep water" with state officials by September 1865, and was summarily removed by Washington because of the lobbying of Governor J. Madison Wells. President Johnson did what he could to frustrate the bureau's work.[12]

And he felt supported, not just by Southerners, but by slivers of the Northern population as well, winning support from conservative business interests. Eric Foner notes that the mass meeting at New York's Cooper Institute to endorse Johnson's veto to extend the tenure of the bureau attracted some of the city's most prominent bankers and merchants, who criticized the bureau for interfering with plantation discipline essential for the revival of cotton production. But even more insidious, throughout the region, though much less obstreperous, was a spreading sense of Northern apathy to bureau difficulties. While most had taken to the cause to free all men as inspired by their martyred president, and at least retained a passing if not complaisant interest in the welfare of freedmen and -women in the face of mounting white supremacy, for many, awareness of the events in the Old Confederacy masked the persistent notion white Northerners had of Negro inferiority. Foner notes that not only was racism deeply embedded in Northern as well as Southern public life, but, as Frederick Douglass observed, "no political idea" was "more deeply rooted in the minds of men of all sections of the country [than] the right of each state to control its own local affairs."[13] Even among Lincoln Republicans, it was the basis on which they later viewed the Civil Rights Act of 1875, which banned discrimination in public places, with skepticism, defeated the provision that banned school segregation, and turned an eye away from the proliferation of Jim Crow laws and lynchings in the Deep South: all fundamentally were "local affairs." Senator Morton Wilkinson of Minnesota would be one such example when during the 1870s he attacked President Grant for keeping federal troops in Louisiana despite the outrages of the white supremacists.

But in the winter of 1866, the die was cast. Within such an enabling climate, so soon after the war ended, vengeance and desperation honed the resolve of ex-Confederate soldiers to continue the fight. They had, of course, lost the war; but they had also lost everything at home, "trusting to the hospitality of the people for food."[14] All they had was the color of their skin to find any sense of purpose and honor. In contrast, Union soldiers who were not deployed to hot spots had come to have relative confidence in how they would be demobilized, for those coordinating the process had taken pains to provide good transportation and food on their return home. This circumstance may well explain why Montgomery's letter seemed airy and more casual. "I suppose you have had very cold weather. The weather here has been delightfully warm in fact." Then showing the eye of a future land salesman, he wrote,

"Many of the officers are looking after the land to buy or rent. Hundreds of plantations can be purchased or rented cheap. I have no particular desire to stay down here among Rebels and contraband chattel although I believe I can make five times more money that I would at the North. I would rather spend a few years at a good school or enter business."[15]

In fact, a number of Union officers stayed in the South after purchasing plantations, and they experienced considerable hostility. A lieutenant colonel of the Eightieth USCI reported that there was "very little change" around Alexandria, in central Louisiana. "Union men whether of northern or southern birth are living in extreme jeopardy of their lives," and he mentioned "extremely bitter feeling against Henry Frisbie," former colonel of the Ninety-Second USCI, who ran a plantation some twenty miles from Alexandria. "The only ground . . . for this hostility," wrote the lieutenant colonel, "is the fact that Col. F. treats his [black] laborers decently, and accords to them the common rights of humanity." Largely due to frequent threats, Frisbie armed his plantation hands that spring. Hundreds of former Union officers shared his experiences. Some thirty-five miles northeast of Vicksburg, Morris Yeomans's plantation was home to fifty veterans of his former regiment, the Seventieth USCI. Surrounded by "those who have not ceased to be our constant and unrelenting foes," Yeomans's men were necessarily "thoroughly armed," as he reported the murders of seven freedmen in his neighborhood since the beginning of the year.[16]

Yet, within this charged climate, in viewing another black school, Montgomery saw only progress. "The pupils [in another Freedmen Bureau's school] are the enlisted men of this regiment who are learning as fast as any white children I ever saw. The colored people are becoming a power in this land, and are more respected in their rights as citizens by the sensible people here then they are by their would-be friends at the North."[17]

Montgomery finished his letter home as usual, "I hope Elizabeth is well and that you agree better together. William is about the same. Nothing very bad is the matter with him, I think."[18]

# 10

# MASONIC TIES

*My religious training and impression of right before
entering the army were of incalculable benefit to me. Was
it not for that I would have yielded to temptation long ago.
I thank God that it is not worse for me.*

THOMAS MONTGOMERY TO HIS MOTHER
JANUARY 16, 1866

Writing on February 9, Montgomery told his brother James that it was a virtue to seek knowledge, which was why he applauded James for wanting to
become a teacher. As for himself, he, too, had plans that did not include returning to laboring on the farm. "I had a very good start but my six years on
the farm did not forward me much intellectually. I will never regret acquiring
useful knowledge wherever obtained, and if I get out safe, neither will I regret
having entered the service of my country." But now that the war was over, he
saw his opportunity in a military career, provided he could retain his present
rank. He was by now living in the encampment with Lieutenant Hutchens, his
"genial friend . . . and brother Mason." During this period of normalcy, the
captain frequented the local Masonic lodge. "I attend the Masonic Lodge here
regular and found so good hearty friends even among what we would call 'Secesh.' They have a fine lodge here. I will never be sorry for being a Mason."[1]

Montgomery was a Freemason. As he indicated in his letter, during the
Civil War, Freemasons fought on both sides. Soldiers in the lowest ranks to
the highest, including Union generals George B. McClellan, Winfield Scott
Hancock, and Winfield Scott, and Confederate generals Lewis Addison

Armistead, P. G. T. Beauregard, and George E. Pickett served both as combatants and proud members of the fraternal order. Masons formed military lodges within their regiments. Some 94 Union and 150 Confederate military lodges are known to have existed. Near the end of the war it was estimated that 11 percent of the soldiers in both armies were Freemasons. Military lodges allowed the men to share a lodge at home to continue their traditions, and also to induct unknown numbers of comrades in arms.

Just as the brotherhood appeared to transcend politics after the cessation of hostilities, as reflected in Montgomery's letter, it occasionally appeared in the least expected moments on the battlefield. Masons on each side obtained special treatment while injured or dying in combat (being given water, emergency care, or respectable burial), while imprisoned (being given provisions or even allowed to escape), while in danger of being captured or killed, or while being robbed by enemy soldiers. Masonic burials were attended by soldiers on both sides hours after active fighting. Masons attempted to save the homes of fellow Masons from ransacking, and in one instance Union soldiers moved a rebel Mason's body off the field at Gettysburg while under Rebel fire in order to provide a decent burial.[2]

Nothing in Montgomery's letters conveying his Masonic ties—"even," as he wrote, "among what we would call 'Secesh'"—amounted to fraternizing with the enemy. Technically, by February 1866, they were no longer enemies. But while there were no longer clashes between the great armies of the blue and gray, aggressions of Southern whites against Southern blacks escalated beyond the conventional rules of engagement as ex-secessionists eroded the meaning of the Thirteenth Amendment through terror. Unlike with those Union officers who protected freedmen or officials of the Freedman's Bureau and thus remained the enemy to ex-rebels, Montgomery's war, for all intents and purposes, had ended. If he could not transfer in rank to the regular army, he was ready to get on with his life, to go home. For opposite reasons, the ex-rebels wanted the same thing.

In the time and place where they were, Montgomery's troops could see what was happening around them. Some may have known when he attended lodge meetings with former Confederates. The troops had reason to be wary of their future, for once out of service, their lives would be subjected, not to the protection of martial law, but to the oppressiveness of the Black Codes, which had been enacted in every former slave state. Abraham Lincoln was gone and soon all of the Union troops would be too. "As President Johnson is not in love with colored troops," Montgomery wrote, "I think that we will get out of this soon."[3] No doubt, many looked forward to mustering out of the service. But others surely realized that once out of uniform, it would be open season.

As a War Democrat from Tennessee who believed in slavery and states' rights, but stayed with the Union because he opposed secession, Johnson had seen early in the war the military benefit of black troops.[4] Yet he was not a friend of black men, in or out of uniform. Johnson had played an important role in the enactment of the Black Codes, encouraging the Southern states to pass such laws that he felt, remarkably, would deal with the civil protections of blacks. He understood that without some kind of safeguard, as he felt Black Codes could provide, Southern blacks would be vulnerable to the restoration of slave codes. He had made this clear in his communications to his provisional governors and also in his December 1865 Annual Message. But the codes that were adopted by state conventions and legislatures exceeded what Johnson had sought or imagined. Frequently Black Codes authorized police officials to force black men to work on plantations.[5]

Nonetheless Johnson did not intervene to insist that the laws be revoked or altered to eliminate their reprehensible provisions. Whereas most of the Codes throughout the South provided for basic rights—the right to acquire and sell property, sue and be sued, and marry, on the whole more liberal than in St. Landry Parish—most also severely restricted the rights of black laborers and excessively limited movement by blacks about the towns and countryside. "The postwar legislation of the Johnson government was unequivocally discriminatory and designed to keep blacks in subordinate economic and social relationship with whites."[6]

Montgomery showed his lack of understanding of Andrew Johnson, presuming that because he had been Lincoln's vice president, Johnson supported Lincoln's ideas and policies concerning the black man. "We [Unionists] think down here that Pres. Johnson turned his back on his friends and those who . . . [put] him in office." His policies only consoled the South, "who has in him a friend who is aiding them all he can, contrary of the expressed views of the majority of the whole people." Montgomery wrote, "Despite what is said, the entire South has still a concealed hatred of the North and are only kept in their proper place by the presence of Government troops." Proof of this assessment: "A plot was discovered here a few days [ago] to blow up the arsenal's magazines [in Baton Rouge]. Such a plot could only be [conceived] by the Devil himself for it would be the destruction of the whole town."[7]

The state of race relations in 1866 foretold of bad things to come in Old Dixie. But it was for Montgomery to remain an officer and a gentleman in the United States Colored Infantry, and not a politician. He wrote to his mother,

"Last Saturday I attended a concert or exhibition of the Lincoln School (colored). Three young ladies teach there, have a piano, and discoursed some splendid music. The darky children spoke, sang and declaimed in a credible manner. The band of our regiment attended and gave them some music. The colored people here are attempting to organize a church. They intend to raise $2500 to put up a church under the management of the [Methodist Episcopal] Church (white)." About this same time, at the other end of the Mississippi, in St. Paul, Minnesota, a small band of black men and women approached a prominent white church to help them start their own house of worship.[8]

In June, a racial incident involved some of Montgomery's troops and white men in a Baton Rouge saloon. His first sergeant and five black soldiers went into the saloon and asked for beer but were refused it. A white man present who was drinking saw fit to insult and strike Montgomery's orderly and demanded "in an insulting manner" that they leave. Some of the party left but three remained and were attacked by the more numerous whites. Fleeing, because they "had no means of defense," they "used brickbats from the street." A mob of white men formed and "fired twenty or thirty shots wounding my orderly in the leg only slightly while one of their number was also shot in the leg by one of his friends." One of Montgomery's corporals attempted to "prevent someone from firing at the Sergeant and was struck several times over the head with a revolver." When order returned, the colonel "destroyed the liquor of one of the saloons but done nothing further":

> The affair is not over yet and unless the authorities use some means
> of punishing the perpetrators of such outrages, the men will execute
> the law themselves, and I won't blame them one bit. I would like to
> see a few of those lawless villains meet their just deserts. If they see
> fit to reenact the Memphis riot we are prepared to give them a warm
> reception and could give them the worse, I rather think.[9]

Montgomery was referring to a violent racial incident that occurred in Memphis one month earlier. On May 1, 1866, a black man and a white man, each driving horse-drawn carriages, collided on a street in Memphis. When the police arrested the black driver, a group of recently discharged black veterans intervened and a white crowd began to assemble. In short order, three days of racial violence ensued, with white mobs, mostly composed of Irish policemen and firemen, attacking blacks on streets and invading a black shantytown in South Memphis that housed the families of black soldiers stationed in nearby Fort Pickering. Before the rioting subsided at least forty-eight people (all but two were black) lay dead, five black women had been raped, and hundreds of black dwellings, churches, and schools were pillaged or destroyed by fire.[10]

The first year of reconstruction was a time of lawlessness, and black troops occasionally found themselves in a new role—that of seeking reprisal against white plantation owners who savagely beat black people for resisting their demands to return to work on their estates. Although Freedman's Bureau agents tried to investigate as many reports of wrongdoing as they could, black soldiers sometimes took matters into their own hands. Near Columbia, Louisiana, "where the cruel punishment of all colored people [was] indulged in to the 'heart's content' of white residents," men of the Fifty-First USCT threatened the life of a former slaveholder who had "shot and killed one of his negroes." The man's former slaves reportedly told the soldiers about the incident and urged them to act. White residents used the incident as a pretext to argue for the closing of the Union garrison in their midst, especially one made up of black soldiers.[11]

As early as 1864 Union troops could not always identify enemy combatants. It was difficult for them to distinguish properly enrolled but poorly dressed Confederate soldiers from guerrillas, or guerrillas from common bandits. Neither was it entirely certain whether armed Southerners were pro-Confederate or anti-Yankee. "Whatever the root of its animus," William Dobak notes, "home-grown opposition, not the main Confederate armies, was the day-to-day worry of Union soldiers in occupied Louisiana during the last year of the war."[12] By late 1865, however, Union occupation authorities were more inclined to blame disbanded Confederate soldiers—whom Montgomery called "rebels"—for the unrest that roiled the South. The commanding officer of the Seventy-Fifth USCT, for one, noted "large numbers of armed men of the late rebel army roaming about" near Washington, Louisiana. Fifty miles to the east, a captain of the Sixty-Fifth USCT serving as provost marshal at Port Hudson drew charges up for the military trial of a Confederate veteran who had been robbing and killing freedmen nearby. In August a lieutenant of the Fourth United States Colored Cavalry told the commanding officer at Morganza, Louisiana, about a secret society of Confederate veterans in a nearby parish "organized . . . to drive out or kill all persons whom they termed Yankees."[13] Montgomery gave an account for another incident. "The citizens took a colored teacher from the town [of Jackson] who was teaching at a school there and ducked him in a creek, pounded him almost to death, and ordered him to never return. They would do the same here if he dared [to return]."

As commanding officers in the South looked around them in the summer of 1866, what they saw was not encouraging. A lieutenant colonel of the Eightieth USCT reported "very little change" around Alexandria, in central Louisiana. "Union men whether of northern or southern birth are living in extreme jeopardy of their lives."[14] Ten of the mob who abused the colored teacher at Jackson were arrested one night and sent to New Orleans for trial. While coming in, their guard or escort was fired upon by "bushwackers." "The Rebel spirit is becoming more rampant." Complaints of abuse to Negroes were a daily occurrence. Many were murdered, others beaten, and some sent away without their wages. Montgomery wrote, "I fear when the coming crop of cotton is secured, many of the poor people will suffer from a breach of contract and they look in vain to the civil authorities for succor. Troops ought to be scattered all over. Stationed in every county and parish of the South until they learn to do justice to the blacks."[15]

The issue of contracts between black laborers and plantation owners in Louisiana arose from a policy initiated in 1862 by General Benjamin Butler, who wanted a process that transitioned slaves into paid laborers. To do this, the policy authorized the army to keep slaves from running away from plantations and required them to continue working on the plantations of loyal landowners. The blacks were to receive wages on a fixed schedule as well as food, medical care, and provisions for the aged and infirmed. Corporal punishment was prohibited, but under the system blacks could be disciplined for refusing to work.

Beginning in 1863, under the administration of General Nathaniel Banks, the system, likely drafted to appease plantation owners, imposed stricter consequences on blacks caught leaving their plantations without permission of their employers. In all, the provost marshal, charged with enforcing the policy, balanced his role between opposing ends—being an agent for emancipation and a slave catcher. Nonetheless, at the root of the system was an effort to establish a better quality of life for the African American on Louisiana plantations; and the success of the policy rested fundamentally with the army's ability to enforce the arrangement. But by late 1866, a year after demobilization had begun, a markedly reduced military presence in Louisiana weakened the army's ability to force employers to comply with the terms of the contact.[16] White violence against black people characterized Louisiana during the late summer of 1866, and it would only get worse.

Montgomery's concern for African Americans revealed a relative lack of acuity about the moment for he knew that his regiment, soon to be mustered out, was one of the last units to be in Louisiana. To James he wrote, "I have good reason to believe that we will be mustered out of service before 2 months. Some applications for furlough have returned disapproved from Department Headquarters saying as reason that this Regiment will probably soon be mustered out."[17] Though replacement troops were expected to arrive, that force would likely have minimal impact on curbing racial violence. One week after his last letter he reported that he received his army pay on time. "I have now over $1000 here with me, nearly all bonds." William Estell was not so fortunate. "I went over to the hospital last evening and saw William Estell. He had chills and fever and a sore back and is confined to the hospital. He did not get his pay but said he thought he could be down to camp in a few days and get his money and send some to Lizzie. He hopes she won't think bad of him as he had been sick a long time. He sends best love."[18]

On July 28, Minnesota governor William R. Marshall, commander of Montgomery's former unit during the Dakota War, sent a letter to the secretary of war recommending Montgomery for a commission in the regular army. "He is an officer of good capacity, well-instructed in military knowledge, and of excellent moral character."[19]

Two days later, in the Crescent City of New Orleans, at the opposite end of the Mississippi River, African Americans, after attending an assembly of Republicans, were gunned down in the streets by a white mob that included police officers. Fifty African Americans and a number of white supporters were killed and nearly two hundred people were wounded. "The rebels were the aggressors of course and commenced the outrages. Policemen and city officials shot down negroes indiscriminately. . . . The negroes were marching to the Institute in procession with music and flags. Shooting commenced without provocation and the convention was broken up but the worst feature was that President Johnson seems to sustain the City authorities in their proceedings." The military was called out to place the city under martial law. The soldiers were camped out on the squares in tents. Batteries were parked. Sentinels patrolled the streets. "The citizens don't like it."[20]

The tragedy was months in the making. Over the veto of Republican governor James Madison Wells, early in 1866, the state legislature—the same body that had enacted the state's Black Codes—mandated new municipal elections, which, in New Orleans, returned to power the ex-Confederate mayor of New Orleans. In response, Wells endorsed a radical plan to revoke the constitutional convention of 1864 that had limited suffrage rights to white men. A new convention would be convened in late July 1866 at which black suffrage would be established. The governor's revocation would also result in denying rebels their vote and establishing a new state government, inflaming conservatives with the belief that Louisiana was to be "Africanized" to the detriment of white men.

For weeks, Wells's opponents feared the prospect of a "revolutionized" Louisiana, and, as Foner writes, "it appears that certain of the city police, made up largely of Confederate veterans, conspired to disperse the gathering by force." On the appointed day, July 30, only twenty-five delegates in fact assembled, soon joined by about two hundred black supporters, mostly former soldiers. Fighting broke out and the police descended on the area, and the scene degenerated into what General Philip Sheridan later called "an absolute massacre," with blacks assaulted indiscriminately and delegates who attempted to escape being shot down despite hoisting white flags of surrender.[21] The son of former vice president Hannibal Hamlin, a veteran of the Civil War, wrote that "the wholesale slaughter [in New Orleans] and the little regard paid to human life I witnessed here" surpassed anything he had seen on the battlefield.[22]

The handful of black regiments that remained on duty in rural Louisiana tried to maintain order. "Much abuse of the freedmen are being perpetrated," reported a colonel of the Eightieth USCT to department headquarters in Shreveport that September, "and the parties go free from punishment . . . as we are powerless to reach them with infantry troops. . . . Civil authorities will not protect the negro when calling for justice against a white man. The people are as strongly united here against . . . the U.S. Government as . . . [at] any time during the rebellion." Despite the ineffective performance of infantry, the colonel added, "Take away the troops and northern men must leave or foreswear every principle of true loyalty and manhood to the prejudices of the masses."[23]

Similarly, officers of the Sixty-Fifth USCT, Montgomery's unit, reported failures throughout the summer to arrest mounted lawbreakers around Lake Providence, on the Mississippi River. Officers of the regular infantry, which had necessarily taken on an increasing share of occupation duty as black regiments mustered out throughout the year, complained of similar unsatisfactory results. Simply put: they had won the war, but, as it would be said of future wars, they were losing the peace.[24]

While federal troops struggled to control what seemed to be a rising tide of disorder during 1866, Congress and President Johnson became increasingly estranged. Many Northerners blamed him for the lack of preparation and protection for the constitutional convention in Louisiana. The local army commander had cabled Washington during the days leading up to the event about the danger of violence, but nothing came of it. Secretary of War Stanton failed to forward the warning to the president, and Johnson informed the lieutenant governor the convention could be dispersed. The fact that nearly all the casualties were black and convention delegates, and the police, far from maintaining order, had participated in the assault, led many Northerners to agree with General Joseph Holt that Johnson's leniency had unleashed "the barbarism in the rebellion in its renaissance."[25]

In August and September 1866, Johnson undermined his own political support on a speaking tour of Northern states. Meant to establish a coalition of voters who would support Johnson in the upcoming midterm congressional election, the tour instead destroyed his reputation when reports of his undisciplined, vitriolic speeches and ill-advised confrontations with hecklers swept the nation. Through the rancor he called for reconciliation between the North and South, affirmed the loyalty of Southern whites, and argued that suffrage rights should be restricted to whites only. He never mentioned the Fourteenth Amendment. Instead of increasing support, the midterm elections led to a veto-proof Republican majority in Congress. The Radicals were not only able to pass civil rights legislation but also wrested control of reconstruction from the president and took the reins themselves by carving up the old Confederacy into five military districts.[26] This only inflamed those set against the rights of African Americans. For them, a new and ominous chapter of reconstruction was about to begin.

# 11

# GOING HOME

*You have plenty to do and yet you have enjoyments that I*
*cannot possibly have. It will not do you to complain.*

THOMAS MONTGOMERY, 1866

The letter he wrote on August 4 to his brother James was the last time Captain Montgomery mentioned racial tensions in Louisiana. He knew that his tour was coming to an end and the uncertainty of his future loomed ahead. Though his plan for the future was unsettled, he knew that he did not want to return to his family farm. He shared his thoughts with James:

> You say I must come to relieve you on the farm at home. I fear that
> you will not see me back for some time at that work. A good salary in
> the army is very much easier. But I never enjoyed myself better than
> when I had plenty of hard work to do. And I could return to it again
> if obliged to. Much will depend with me on whether I stay in the
> army or leave it. If I get out of service safely I do not think I would
> go home to farm unless I meant to settle down for life. In fact, having
> spent four years without performing manual labor to any extent, I
> did not feel able or willing to go back to it if I can help it. It would go
> hard for me at first. But you are situated differently. You have been
> altogether used to farm life since you were able to and are not trained
> for any other pursuit or profession. You have plenty to do and yet
> you have enjoyments that I cannot possibly have. It will not do you
> to complain. You are infinitely better off than thousands of poor

people and remember that you could not engage in anything else that would pay you half as well. Farming in Minnesota will pay better in the future than it has done in the past so I would strongly advise you to stick to the farm. If your work is too laborious, get help. I would not hurt myself working if I could help it. Accept my best wishes and believe me your affectionate brother. Thomas.[1]

Meanwhile, cholera continued to ravage his men. "I lost one man with it last week. He was well at dark and was dead next morning. Three others have died with it but it is confined to a few cases as yet." But he wasn't worried, "being all the time constipated." Besides, the weather was cooling.[2] By the end of two weeks, he had lost several men and William Estell's condition had not improved. "It is a good thing that Elizabeth is staying with you this winter. I am really glad of it."[3]

He soon learned that all, once again, was not good with Elizabeth. Her children, whom she could not have seen for three years, remained somewhere in Missouri, and her husband William appeared to be desperately ill. She clearly had reasons to want to return to the South, especially since the war had ended. Little of what he wrote conveyed the full dimension of racial violence in Louisiana, and the encroaching Minnesota winter meant that she would be sequestered on the farm, unable to see her family. But she had not yet been taught to record her thoughts. In any event, Montgomery, upon getting news of her renewed "restlessness," was quite exasperated with Elizabeth's temperament. On September 23 he wrote, "If Elizabeth gives any trouble you should settle with her and send her away. I should be sorry to hear of any trouble. I never want to return home to witness any more troubles. I don't like them."[4] Elizabeth stayed on the farm. "I'm glad to hear that Lizzie is well. I hope she is still of great help to you."[5]

His unit finally received orders to return home. By the tenth of January, the regiment would move to St. Louis for discharge and final payment. In Baton Rouge, they would turn over all property except their arms and colors. He did not look forward to returning north. "The prospect of going North now is in no-ways encouraging. It will go hard with us to leave this delightful climate for a country of ice and snow. I shudder at the thought but I suppose we will soon get used to it. What I fear most is the danger of getting chills again. If I do, I will certainly return here."[6]

The country to which he was willing to return to escape the cold was changing for the worse. White terrorists continued to harass, beat, and murder African Americans and white Republicans throughout Louisiana with virtual impunity. Judge Thomas Crawford, who was later assassinated by white conservative vigilantes, acknowledged that no jury in his parish would convict a white man accused of assaulting a black man, and that legal authorities had taken no action in response to the many instances of the murder of freedmen in the parish. Similar dynamics occurred in Bienville Parish in August 1866, including, as attested by Captain N. B. Blanton, severe floggings administered by vigilantes known as "nighthaulkers." In St. Landry Parish in 1867 and 1868, outlaws Benjamin and Cyriaque Guillory orchestrated several murders of freedmen with ties to planters whom they viewed as their social enemies.[7]

On May 22, 1867, the Knights of the White Camellia, Louisiana's Ku Klux Klan, which formed in 1865, organized to step up the campaign to turn the clock back. What they could not do against the Union army, they would strive to do against the freedmen and -women of the state. Their activities set the context for an even greater atrocity that occurred on September 28 and 29, 1868, in Opelousas, St. Landry Parish, when over two hundred African Americans were murdered on the threshold of the presidential election. On the day of balloting, no Republicans—white and black alike—went to the polls.[8]

Farther North in Missouri, where so many of the troops in the Sixty-Fifth Regiment were from, bands of "bushwacker" militias terrorized Republicans and blacks, committing "all sorts of horrible outrages" that included "shooting negroes for carrying the *Missouri Republican.*" The *New York Times* reported, "President Johnson declined to interfere in Missouri affairs on the ground that each State should be left free to preserve peace."[9] If Montgomery worried about his troopers who were about to reenter that world as civilians, he did not mention it in his letters.

But the "cold, frozen North" to which Montgomery was about to return had also undergone unsettling changes during his years in the South. The Dakota War of 1862 had resulted in the defeat of the Indians, their removal, and the occupation of their land by white settlers. White Minnesotans in the southwest region of the state remained traumatized. In the town of New Ulm the mocking of the German residents resulted tragically in vigilante justice and revenge. On Christmas Day, just days before Montgomery's last letter dated December 30, two men were lynched, "causing great excitement in all that region [of the state], especially in Mankato, where the lynched men resided and were well-known." Two white men, Alexander Campbell and George Liscomb, had come in around two in the afternoon from a trapping expedition and gone into Zeter and Howenstein's, a New Ulm saloon, where they proceeded to get intoxicated. A witness noted, "The term 'Indian' [was] not a very favorable one with the citizens of this place." As the two men drank they behaved provocatively "acting the part of Indians, dancing their scalp-dance, and cutting right and left with their knives." Their actions incited the onlooking residents. John Spenner "saw a storm brewing" and "tried to persuade the men not to go any further in their dangerous proceedings," but the men stabbed him, killing "the only man who had tried to shield them from harm."[10]

The sheriff arrested Campbell and Liscomb, and while on their way to jail handcuffed, they were attacked by a mob and beaten with stones and sticks of cordwood. "Campbell was stabbed three or four times by a drunken soldier on furlough from Company A, Tenth Regular Infantry, stationed at Fort Ridgley." Then they were taken from the sheriff and hanged. The mob cut and hacked the men's bodies "in a shocking manner." Their bodies, left hanging until the next day, were frozen stiff.

Influential citizens in New Ulm had refused to allow the bodies to be returned for burial, inciting the "well-armed" friends of the lynched men to retrieve the bodies "at all hazards . . . or [they will] make a few more funerals in New Ulm. . . . Another collision is feared, as great exasperation exists on both sides." It was later discovered that the bodies had been dropped through a hole in the ice and into the river. In Mankato and St. Paul "they were well-known and respected by all who knew them." Both were members of Company H, Second Regiment Minnesota Infantry.[11]

Four long years of war had scarred the humanity of the nation, not just in terms of relationships between the North and South, or between black men and white, but even among Minnesotans during the relative peace of the early postwar era, even among those who had fought on the right side of history. The tragedy at New Ulm reflected unresolved tensions exacerbated by the festering trauma of 1862. But it was also the rapid immigration of foreign-born homesteaders competing with native-born settlers for farmland—land that could and would destroy dreams, that imposed extreme hardship and demanded endurance. The horror at New Ulm occurred on the threshold of the galvanic shifts of a new and unforgiving economy setting farmers against business monopolies. It was only during the long, cold Minnesota winter that the tensions lay temporarily hidden just beneath the otherwise placid veneer of snow and ice, unless someone foolishly stomped through the surface in a rousing mockery of ghosts.

Although the tragedy at New Ulm was made newsworthy to a broad readership by the national newspaper of record, the *New York Times,* Montgomery never referred to the event in his final letters. After spending ten months at war with the Dakota and three years in war-torn Louisiana, he had found his path in life and "a proper lady born in London" to be his wife, and he would seek to live a life of honor, free of troubles.[12] History credits him for asking about a black colony, but says nothing about how he chose not to pursue the project at the first apparent sign of "problems." And regarding Elizabeth's recent "bout with restlessness," he never wanted to return home to witness any more troubles. "I don't like them."[13] The troubles between the men of Mankato and New Ulm would seem to be no more an issue for him than the troubles engulfing African Americans in Louisiana, nor did he utter a word of concern about the men who served under his command.

In January 1867, Montgomery set sail northward on the steamer *Julia* on his last trip home. In his last letter as an army officer, he wrote:

> After two weeks of preparation we were mustered out of the service of the U.S. as a regiment. Last Sabbath we had our last Dress Parade. This morning the camp we have been occupying for 14 months was demolished and before noon not a vestige remained of this old campground. Lumber, brick, and everything else was carried away by the citizens. The steamer *Julia* arrived about 1 pm and the regiment formed for the last time on our old parade ground and passing through the principal streets of the city, we embarked for St. Louis. Hundreds of the soldiers' friends thronged the levee and remained until we left at 2 pm. The colors at the arsenal were run up and down, waving us a salute as we left.[14]

He concluded his letter:

> Another epoch in my life has become reached and I am now about to bid farewell to the South, the theatre of most of my military life, and start finally, perhaps, for the cold, frozen North. But although the latitude may give me a chilly reception, I shall hope to have a warm and hearty reception from those I love.[15]

♦ ♦ ♦ ♦ ♦

On May 1, 1867, with Brigadier General William Marshall's endorsement, Montgomery was brevetted major for faithful and meritorious service during the war and his rank was dated as such for March 13, 1865. Throughout the summer, other than a visit or two to the family farm, civilian Montgomery made plans for a new business venture. By September, nine months after he mustered out of the army, Montgomery left the farm for good and settled in nearby St. Peter, where he married English-born Sarah A. Purnell. Soon afterward he formed a partnership with Captain T. K. Carter, whom he had known since the Dakota uprising, and engaged in law, real estate, and insurance, as well as a collection business.[16] In the years to come, he would develop the Masonic lodge in Nicollet County.

Nothing more was recorded about Elizabeth Estell, her children, and her husband William, who never appeared on the muster rolls of the Sixty-Fifth Regiment after it was consolidated with the Sixty-Seventh in the fall of 1865; and nothing more was mentioned of the plan for a black colony.[17] Much of the land Montgomery bought and sold was the land Tibbetts mentioned in 1865. In the winter of 1869, Thomas and Sarah delivered their first child, whom they named Edmund.[18] They seemed to have had little interest in the events that had just transpired with the black folks in St. Paul, yet occasionally he would long afterward think fondly on his service in their behalf.

PART III

# The Man on the Seal

## Morton S. Wilkinson
### 1865–1869

# 12

# BY CHICANERY
# AND DECEPTION OF
# A FEW POLITICIANS

*I believe the United States will come out
of this war redeemed and purified.*

MORTON S. WILKINSON, 1865

On January 10, 1865, Morton S. Wilkinson, "the best Senator of the West," as the *Mankato Union* called him, had lost his bid for reelection and the defeat was painful. He loved the Senate. He loved grappling with the momentous issues of the day, indeed, of the century. By January 1865, the war was drawing to an end. Lee's armies were crumbling before the merciless onslaught of Grant's forces. And, most important of all, Abraham Lincoln had been reelected as president. As a United States senator, Wilkinson could join in the greatest work facing any American, participating in the grand design of founding a new nation this time free from the taint of slavery, united under God, indivisible, with justice and liberty truly for all. But he had lost the election and the way he lost was especially painful.[1] Democrat David Norton had won and the opinion makers of both parties crowed at the result. As the Democratic *St. Paul Pioneer* wrote, "[Norton's victory was] an event which indicates that we are approaching the end of the dynasty of such venal demagogues as Wilkinson and Ramsey."[2]

Yet, this was hardly the case. The truth of Wilkinson's defeat was far worse, one that he did not contemplate could happen. Going into the contest he had had solid backing starting, no less, with the Great Emancipator himself, to whom Wilkinson had been zealously loyal. Contemporary H. P. Hall described him thus: "His admiration and support of Lincoln was unstinted, and he was one of the few senators with whom Lincoln was wont to consult before adopting some radically aggressive policy." Indeed, the president was quite vocal in endorsing Wilkinson for reelection through an open letter to the voters, so there was every reason to conclude that he was the leading candidate.[3] Thus, as he entered into the contest Wilkinson had every reason to believe that the preelection posturing of so-called rivals would end once the tally showed Wilkinson's "inevitable" victory. The supporters of Republican William Windom would of course, as most of them did, join his ranks, and, as allies, would soundly defeat the true rival.

But this did not happen. "A portion of the opposition to Mr. Wilkinson for reasons sufficient to themselves," reported the *Winona Republican,* "saw proper to unite in an agreement to defeat his nomination at all hazards."[4] The nomination had, in effect, been stolen from him, and not by Democrats, but as Wilkinson later said, "by chicanery and trickery of a few politicians who, unable to secure the nomination of their candidate, made a combination with their bitter enemy."[5] It was nothing less than betrayal by his own kind, fellow Minnesota Republicans, Congressman William Windom, in particular, who had two years earlier pledged that he would never run against Wilkinson only to change his mind by declaring that he should be elected. Worse, he encouraged his men to assail Wilkinson's character and resort to the basest of maneuvers to frustrate the senator's bid, "to indulge," as the *Mankato Union* reported, "in a style of abuse and calumny against Senator Wilkinson which was entirely uncalled for, and did not prove of any material benefit to himself. His adherents made gross personal attacks on Mr. Wilkinson's private character, because they could find no tainted spot on his public record."[6]

The *Mankato Union* further asserted that the Windom men "brought everything to bear upon [Wilkinson's] supporters to induce them to desert the Senator, and endeavored to get one of his friends drunk to prevent his attending the caucus. Was there ever treachery so base, friendship so rewarded, or gratitude so blinded by selfishness as has been shown by this 'dead cock in this pit.'" Even a party stalwart and Windom supporter who joined Wilkinson's column reportedly expressed "his deep regret at the action of Windom after the contest," remarking, "Windom is the worse beaten man of the whole crowd. He will never rise again."[7]

Until 1913 and the ratification of the Seventeenth Amendment to the U.S. Constitution, legislators, rather than the general electorate, elected men to represent their respective states to serve in the United States Senate. Procedural rules allowed for the contest to go as long as was needed to present a clear-cut winner, regardless of the number of ballots taken. In 1869, only one ballot would be cast in a close contest between Wilkinson and Alexander Ramsey. But in 1865, it took thirty-two. In a crowd of five candidates, between the second and thirtieth ballot Wilkinson led in votes, but in the end, he failed to win the nomination by only two votes. Reviewing the tally, it appeared that Republican Henry Swift and Democrat Edmund Rice were every bit as culpable in denying Wilkinson the requisite number for victory; but William Windom, because of his tactics, was deemed to be the villain of the contest and not David Norton, who ultimately won, considered by many, including even the incumbent himself, to be "the best man of the opponents of Senator Wilkinson."[8] Norton's qualities were not a main reason for Wilkinson's defeat, however. Rather, it was Ramsey.

The history between Ramsey and Wilkinson had been tense since 1849, when the Pennsylvanian first arrived in the territory of Minnesota as its first governor. Already a seasoned Whig politician from Pennsylvania, Ramsey understood that the effectiveness of the party to hold power rested fully on its organization, which, in turn, depended on individual loyalty. And key to this was patronage, the ability of party leaders to secure the allegiance of men by offering jobs and other favors. Ramsey knew this brand of politics very well. He had caught the eye of party leaders as an effective builder of a Whig organization in a crucial district in Pennsylvania during the election of 1848; and in selecting Ramsey to be territorial governor, Zachary Taylor, the nation's first Whig president, hoped that the young Pennsylvanian would do the same within Minnesota, which was then dominated by Democrats. In setting up his new government, surely Ramsey would include the only Whig who was an elected official, a delegate at the Stillwater convention of 1848 at which Minnesota reputedly was established, and a legislator in the first territorial legislature. Instead, Ramsey chose to snub Wilkinson. In those days, it was more expedient to court the most prominent and collaborative Democrat and territorial delegate to Congress—Henry Hastings Sibley—rather than a fellow Whig who brought virtually no political capital.

Throughout the 1850s, their relationship was pragmatic though uneasy. But in 1859, the tension between the two men once again appeared when, as Wilkinson was about to clinch the votes for the U.S. Senate, Ramsey tried to spoil the bid by persuading liberal John North to run for the office. Nonetheless, the senator-elect and the governor-elect worked together, though their cordiality merely glossed over the tension that by then was literally as old as Minnesota itself.

With the election of Lincoln, suddenly the new party had a real bonus for political success: the power to appoint; and for a while, the Republicans enjoyed a period of party harmony. But it was short lived, with the defeat of a real political foe. Fissures began to form, or in some instances, reemerge, especially when President Lincoln adopted a policy for determining the distribution of patronage by consulting with the congressional delegation rather than the governors. Suddenly, Wilkinson and Congressman Cyrus Aldrich no longer felt compelled "to consult and satisfy" Ramsey with regards to appointments; they could have their own men appointed against Ramsey's wishes. For Wilkinson, the new arrangement afforded him the leverage to return a snub with a snub.[9]

In the summer of 1861, claiming that Ramsey's organ, the *St. Paul Press*, was hostile to the congressional delegation, Wilkinson and Aldrich transferred the federal public printing contract to the *Pioneer and Democrat*, a Democratic paper that for the privilege had agreed to endorse the Republican Party and its principles. "This it did with relation to national policy—a course which was neither unusual nor particularly inconsistent for a paper that, like the *Pioneer and Democrat*, had traditionally supported the free-soil wing of the Democratic Party."[10]

This same newspaper, Wilkinson's choice, initiated the darkest political deed of the period when it insinuated in an article titled "Who Is Responsible?" that Ramsey was responsible for the Dakota War. While the Dakota War raged in the Minnesota River valley the paper argued that the cause was the governor's failure to protect the settlers on the frontier. And in making its case the paper exposed an even more tender spot by reviving the long-standing blight on the governor's record: the Dakota payment investigation of 1853 by the U.S. Senate, which examined allegations that Ramsey cheated the Indians; the investigation itself proved to be nothing more than a whitewash. "And now, when his acts have been culminated in a Sioux War; now when the chickens from eggs of his own hatching have come home to roost, he meanly attempts to cast the blame upon others."[11] The *Press* responded by reminding readers that the Senate had absolved Ramsey of the allegations and that Aldrich, "an ex-Land Officer in the State of Illinois" and rival for the Senate in 1863, had been convicted of defrauding the government. For weeks, the two papers exchanged epithets against each other's patron.[12] Elections had a way of gouging the wounds of the past, and none were more open than those coming from the recently ended war with the Dakota people. In January 1863, after a very difficult campaign to garner votes from legislators, Ramsey barely won the Senate seat, defeating Aldrich, one of his chief rivals. Two years later, he pulled the necessary strings to defeat his other rival—Wilkinson. Further, because of the new office, Ramsey could now enhance his own political power and neutralize Wilkinson's influence at the same time.[13]

Wilkinson's style in conducting business also contributed to his vulnerability. A contemporary observed that no one questioned his party loyalty or zeal. But in the end, he had violated a cardinal political rule—developing and maintaining relationships, especially during a period when patronage was a political given. Being fiscally conservative and therefore critical of a bloated governmental administration, the thin-framed senator from Minnesota recoiled from creating unnecessary positions in the transparent guise of solving a bureaucratic problem. Thus, though he filled existing positions within Indian Affairs with his allies, he shied from making new jobs for men seeking his patronage. Thus, as Thomas Hughes wrote in 1909, "Senator Wilkinson in his distribution of government patronage had made many enemies in his own party. Not one in ten of the various applicants for office could receive appointments and the nine unsuccessful ones felt ugly towards him."[14] Publisher and contemporary H. P. Hall made a similar observation:

> In those days the senate was not as liberal in furnishing clerks and private secretaries for the senators as at present, and Mr. Wilkinson lacked the element of a successful politician as a correspondent with his constituency. Letter writing to him was drudgery, and, while he would attend to important letters, hundreds of trivial ones, such as every senator and congressman receive, went unanswered. Thus, between failure to devote his entire time to writing letters, to the neglect of his real senatorial duties, and his disappointing fifty men for every appointment he made, Wilkinson went down in defeat, notwithstanding he had the direct request from Abraham Lincoln for his re-election.[15]

But, as Hughes further noted, one more trait sealed his fate. "In spite of his great ability and integrity, [Wilkinson] had one very vulnerable point. He was addicted to intemperate habits, which drove from him the support of many of the best people of his party. The result was that he failed of re-election, and a man of very mediocre ability succeeded him."[16]

By 1865 Wilkinson's side had lost. With Ramsey's ascendency to power, winning statewide office did not seem likely. He missed the Senate. During the nation's greatest crisis, he had participated in the most important issues of the day, and wanted to resume that work. In time, he began to nurture thoughts of a future campaign to return to Washington. Yet despite the widespread support he enjoyed, the growth of Ramsey's power now made it less likely that Wilkinson could win over the majority of the people's representatives in the legislature.

For now, he needed to heal from his defeat. Fresh from the loss, Wilkinson had to speak at a charity function created to provide support to Minnesota soldiers. Organizers of the Sanitary Fair, held in St. Paul, highlighted such notables as Governor Stephen Miller and General Cadwallader Washburn as well as the senator, just the kind of affair where politicians tested their powers of oratory. After the Reverend J. D. Pope, pastor of one of the city's most prominent churches, the First Baptist Church, gave a blessing to the occasion, the normally fiery Wilkinson spoke, his tone this time, as one reporter noted, was markedly subdued, mourning it seemed, the death of forever lost opportunity.[17] The pain of defeat mingled with uncertainty and worry, for he was not a wealthy man. In his years in the Senate he had handled hundreds of thousands of dollars and had seen, even helped, men grow rich. He must now have regretted not taking full opportunity to make his family more comfortable and provide for his infirm son. He had not measurably improved his financial status since his election, when he received the generosity of a friend who bought him a suit of clothes to wear in Washington.[18]

But that could have changed if acquiring wealth had been his central focus. In keeping with the courtesy of assigning such tasks to the legislator representing the area, as well as placating the temperamental senator from Minnesota, the government appointed Morton Wilkinson to make the arrangements for distributing Winnebago land. Wilkinson nominated the appraisers, and Secretary of the Interior John Usher "continued his happy relationship with the senator by summarily approving those nominations." Among the firms authorized to finance the land sales was Thompson Brothers of St. Paul, Clark Thompson's old firm. Wilkinson supervised everything, including advertising, and Lincoln placed his official approval on the whole transaction. On August 23, 1864, Lincoln signed the order for sale of fifty-four thousand acres of Winnebago land.[19]

Wilkinson was now in a position to attract favors from would-be entrepreneurs and newfound friends of opportunity. The large stone Italianate house in the prestigious Lincoln Park district of Mankato that he would call his residence was a gift.[20] But everything Wilkinson had done since he arrived

in Minnesota in 1847, and afterward, conveyed that he was not primarily motivated by personal enrichment. Rather, he preferred public service, or what
he called "public service" as reflected in his appropriation bills in Indian affairs and his vituperative campaign against the Dakota. He seemed to prefer
bestowing favors on associates than appropriating such favors for himself.
But now, in unexpectedly losing his Senate seat, Morton Wilkinson had been
cast into the wilderness.

During the first of the remaining weeks in the Senate he seemed disengaged, and he remained silent until the end of February, seeming to vote ar-
bitrarily and on matters that were inconsistent with his senatorial legacy, like
the issue of black relocation during the debate over the Freedman's Bureau
bill.[21] But he became more engaged by the close of February, when, within a
week of the end of his senatorial career, he introduced a bill to grant public
land for the "use and benefit of the Southern Minnesota Railway Company"
and spoke in favor of a Ramsey-sponsored bill to secure additional lands for
railroad construction, a bill that appealed to businessmen and farmers alike.[22]
"Our Senator," reported an approving Washington correspondent for the
*Mankato Union*, "has made of himself a record of which many men might
be proud. His bold and unflinching advocacy of radical measures and firm
cordial support of the administration, have made him a popular favorite, not
only with the people of Minnesota, but those of other States."[23] On the day
before the Senate adjourned, Wilkinson introduced an amendment that would
authorize the payment of damages to white settlers who had lost land in Blue
Earth County when the former Winnebago reservation was first established,
damages that now could be used for venture capital. One such recipient was
John Willard, who purchased parcels on Winnebago land that he in turn
would begin to sell for a profit.[24]

Only after attending Lincoln's second inauguration on March 4, the day
after the adjournment of the Senate, did the senator finally shift his focus to
the next chapter of his life. He felt a new opportunity awaited him when he
heard of the effort to force William P. Dole to step down from his post as
commissioner of Indian affairs. Wilkinson believed he had served ably on the
Senate Committee of Indian Affairs, acted honorably during the crisis of the
Dakota War, and led his neighbors to accept the far more "humane" policy
of removal over extermination; and now he was responsible for the sale of
Indian lands. Who, better than Wilkinson, had more experience to work in
Indian affairs, and he told Lincoln so.[25] Filling the post answered so many
needs—status and employment, and a position in which he could expand his
political base, not to mention his financial opportunity. The so-called Indian

system that for so many had been a veritable cash cow now seemed to offer him his best avenue for opportunity. In fact, few offices would prove better than the one currently held by Commissioner Dole. To keep up the pressure, Wilkinson marshaled his friends in the congressional delegation to lobby the president for the appointment.[26] But Lincoln, who thought well of Dole and was reluctant to replace him, seemed disinclined to act in the favor of his Minnesota friend.[27]

One month later, he and the rest of a nation were faced with sudden tragedy. On April 14, his president, Abraham Lincoln, was assassinated. In a letter to his fourteen-year-old son, who remained ill in Mankato, Wilkinson wrote,

> Yesterday I went to the funeral of President Lincoln. The service
> was held in the large reception room of the White House. . . . I wish
> you had been there with me, and then after the services in the house
> were over the coffin was put upon a hearse made for the purpose and
> drawn by six white horses to the capitol and the body was placed
> in the rotunda and there left as that people might see it. Everybody
> seems to be in deep sorrow and the poor people in particular, the
> colored, seem to mourn the most bitterly.[28]

He had been a gadfly, a frequent visitor to the White House, who, despite his early complaints of the lame manner in which the war was being prosecuted, as well as the reversals of the orders to emancipate slaves by Lincoln's generals, he remained nonetheless a loyal friend, boisterously rejecting overtures from Republican leaders who conspired to deny Lincoln the party endorsement for a second term in office.[29] Stung by electoral defeat, grieving the loss of his president, and worried about his son's health, Wilkinson entered the unfamiliar civilian life in Mankato and a new circle of "friends" who saw a way to benefit through an affiliation with a man of his stature.

By May land parcels on what had been the Dakota reservation were surveyed, plotted, and ready for bids. Together with the available Winnebago tracts, the prime land of southwestern Minnesota was fully available to that lucky number able to take advantage of the moment. In the same month, J. J. Thornton and Company of Mankato opened as an investment firm whose board of directors included businessman and attorney John Willard and Kate Hubbell, wife of James Hubbell, who with Willard would start a railroad line. Connecting Mankato eastward to Winona, the Southern Minnesota Railway Company was the same company for which Wilkinson, in one of his final acts as senator, had sponsored a bill to grant public land. Now out of office, Morton Wilkinson joined them as board director.[30] "The senator," observes Mary Wingerd, "was to benefit quite handsomely from the sale of Winnebago land. Given the oversight of reservation land sales he embarked on a 'happy relationship' with firms that handled the subsequent appraisals and financing."[31]

By 1868—in a matter of three years—J. J. Thornton and Company would become the First National Bank of Mankato with John Willard serving as its president. James Hubbell, another cofounder of the bank who in 1861 was a licensed trader to the Winnebago and large-scale farmer, built the Mankato Linseed Oil Works; and with Willard, became principal promoter and builder of the Wells Railway. In 1871 Hubbell was elected to the legislature and, after a desperate fight, pushed through both houses the Internal Improvements Land Act (in the common parlance of the day, the "Land Grab Act"), which, had it not been vetoed by Governor Horace Austin, would have ensured the building of the Wells road to St. Cloud, giving Mankato an inestimable advantage as a commercial center.[32]

By then, however, in a move that probably forever cost him financial security, Wilkinson charted a different course by leaving the board and the prospect of wealth that would be available to him were he to stay. He left no record explaining this move. But considering the political stance that he would soon take—advocating farmer equity and checking the growing power of the business and political elites—it is likely that his departure was one of conscience. He knew the plans of the investment company to speculate in the Indian land that he would soon open up for acquisition, as well as provide seed capital for other ventures.[33] That intention was why the firm was established and why Wilkinson had been invited to join the board; and he certainly could use the money. But Wilkinson had already concluded that as an able lawyer and one still widely regarded, he could make his way in a manner that aligned with his principles.

Years later, at the dedication of a granite monument to Wilkinson at Mankato's Glenwood Cemetery, Daniel Buck, a Democrat and former justice on the Minnesota Supreme Court, eulogized about the former senator, "Generous to a fault, he lacked thrift and died penniless in 1894. During his whole legislative career, there was no dark stain of corruption that rested upon his character. In this age of municipal and governmental corruption, no grander and nobler legacy can be left to the people than an official character and reputation unstained and unsullied by corruption. . . . Fault he may have had [appointing without personal benefit corrupt men into positions of responsibilities] but as an incorruptible office holder he was an honor to his home, his State, and his Country."[34]

By the fall of 1865, just as bids were being submitted, Wilkinson had relinquished his seat on the board of directors. Politics, something for which he had a passion, would be his venue. It was within that venue that full equality and opportunity could be attained and secured. Though no longer, for now at least, an actor on the federal level, Wilkinson would renew his commitment to completing the unfinished business of fully enfranchising the black man, even if just on the state level; and to his primary concern—the well-being of the farmer whose likeness was emblazoned on the state seal, the true Minnesotan.

# 13

# WILLEY'S AMENDMENT

*Sit not quietly in your homes and shed crocodile tears over the barbarism of slavery and the inhumanity of slaveholders when you have the opportunity to go and take this oppressed race not only to live in your midst, but to take them to your heart and to cherish them as philanthropic men should cherish the object of their pity.*

WILLARD SAULSBURY, 1864

For people who watched Wilkinson closely, his departure from the board of directors of the J. J. Thornton investment firm would not have been a surprise. If anything he did was surprising, it was his decision to occupy the board seat in the first place. The firm represented everything he had long despised: men and women of privilege exploiting their access to capital and contacts in order to get an advantage over the common man. But such was the former senator's disorienting extent of disappointment, stress, and sorrow, and now perhaps he had one more to add—shame. Stepping down from the board to refocus his energies on politics and law offered him an avenue to redemption that would come only when the image of the state seal was fully realized. He had begun with his legislation to remove the Dakota and Winnebago from the state as the part of the work that was represented in the image of the Indian riding westward and forever away. What remained was to attract humble settlers to the state to homestead their claims on Minnesota's fertile land. But in the spring of 1865, the question for the champion of black freedom was, with the war over and slavery abolished, would there be room on the seal for the African?

· · · · ·

Two years earlier, on the same day Lincoln issued the Emancipation Proclamation, the Homestead Act of 1862 went into effect.[1] Both were intended to free men, both legally and economically, and though both received the enthusiastic support of Senator Wilkinson, it was the Homestead Act that offered his state the more immediate, widespread benefit. He embraced the Jacksonian ideal of a society that empowered the common man against the privileged few and the Jeffersonian ideal of the superiority of agriculture as a necessary means to that end. Thus, as he had argued during the debate in April 1860, "it would be 'scarcely' necessary to remind the Senate that the monopoly of land by the few, as against the many, and the parceling out of public domain in immense tracts among venal courtiers, have been, all over the world, the most powerful auxiliaries of absolute and despotic power." The result had been that "the monarchies and the aristocracies of all ages have been enabled to hold the masses subject to their will. . . . Millions of the human family," he continued, "have been reduced to penury and degradation, because they were deprived of the right to earn the subsistence from the common earth, which was intended alike for the rich and for the poor."[2]

In the United States, "even now, with all of our vast expanse of territory, labor is outweighed by capital, and the rights of the settler are but slightly regarded when brought into comparison with the money of the speculator." Wilkinson argued that the homestead measure would be directed to "the laboring masses of the country, to those who are most often crushed down by the cruel and unequal conflict between capital and labor; to the poor man who earns his bread from day to day by the sweat of his brow; to him who feeds upon the uncertain crumbs which fall from the rich man's table."[3]

He shifted his argument to the conditions of poverty in the urban North and challenged his fellow senators "to pass through our great cities" where they would "see the boys of all ages who swarm around the streets, many of them willing and anxious to labor, but finding nothing for their hands to do." They were "exposed to temptations of every kind, day after day looking upon the equipages of wealth with the hungry and cannibal eyes of poverty." The Homestead Act was "the measure of the working, suffering class of our people; those who were struggling on from day to day, from week to week, and from year to year, vindicating the dignity of labor against the oppressions and aggressions of capital."[4]

A poor man intending to be a homesteader needed to be the head of a family, twenty-one years or older, a citizen of the United States or one who formally intended to be as required by the naturalization laws of the United States; one had never borne arms against the government or given aid and comfort to its enemies; and one who registered the appropriate paperwork and paid a nominal fee. The applicant, above all else, needed to pledge that "such application was made for his or her exclusive use and benefit, and that said entry is made for the purpose of actual settlement and cultivation."[5] In other words, as Wilkinson argued in 1860, these public lands were reserved for farmers, not speculators, corporations, or investment firms, and the provision sought to guarantee that the common man stood a chance at acquiring the land.[6] "The measure of granting free homes to the actual settlers upon the public lands," he said, "is one which I have long felt a deep interest."[7]

Wilkinson felt the government had been a central culprit in making monopolies against the public interest, for time and again it sought to replenish its Treasury from the proceeds of a traffic in the public lands as a source of revenue. The spirit of the Homestead Act was simple. It was about equal opportunity. "Laws, in order to be just, must be equal in application."[8] The design of the act authorized the distribution of public lands up to 160 acres to citizens or intended citizens who paid a minimum filing and registration fee. After five years' residency and the completion of prescribed improvements to the land, the homesteader would receive title.

Hundreds of thousands of settlers streamed onto the public land seeking to take advantage of this new opportunity. Yet, even though they secured their claims, many were confronted by a very basic matter. The desperate reality for the type of settlers for whom the act was intended—namely, the farmer whose only currency was his willingness to work hard—placed him in a position of being in debt, for he needed to borrow for seed, feed, and basic necessities until his harvest would allow him to pay the creditor back. Lenders, banks, and merchants, all of which were roles to be played by the investment firm of J. J. Thornton, soon prospered while homesteaders lived a Sisyphus-like existence.

Another obstacle confronted settlers when subsequent congressional enactments designed to promote railroad interests (like the Union Pacific bill that Wilkinson rejected) and facilitate the development of colleges and universities (which Wilkinson also rejected), exempted vast amounts of public land from homesteading. Passed the same year as the Homestead Act, the Land-Grant Act (also known as the Morrill Act for its supporter Justin Morrill, a congressman from Vermont) offered states parcels of public land to use as funding sources for new institutions for higher education. A number of western congressmen opposed the measure, either because of an apparent lack of interest in establishing schools or through a vociferous hostility to the act's potential loopholes. In the latter category Kansas senator James H. Lane insisted that the passage of the act would "ruin" his state.

It was soon apparent that the intent of the Homestead Act to protect the interests of settlers, could not, as Wilkinson feared, filter out speculators, who grabbed great swaths of the best parcels of the public domain through inventive, if unscrupulous and illegal, tactics in the West and elsewhere. Corporations quickly found out that they could use proxy filings by individuals as a way to accumulate vast acreages of western land; tried-and-true methods of graft and corruption often proved just as successful.[9] As a senator, Wilkinson railed against speculators as "a remorseless class of vampires," who he was certain would benefit most from the new legislation.[10] This was the key reason why Wilkinson wanted to oversee the arrangements for the sale of the Indian lands.

The Dakota Removal Act of March 3, 1863, provided that the Dakota reservation be surveyed, appraised, and then offered for sale at its assessed value, with proceeds to go to the displaced Indians. The third section of the act directed, as in the Homestead Act and the Winnebago Removal Act, that "before any person shall be entitled to enter any portion of the said land, . . . he shall become a bona fide settler." Speculators were persona non grata, and entry was restricted to those persons who would settle and cultivate the land. In June 1865, with the completion of the survey and appraisal, the area was opened to entry at the St. Peter Land Office, which would also be assigned the task of selling Winnebago land.[11] This was just one month after the small Mankato investment firm named J. J. Thornton and Company was established.[12]

During the first thirty days after the St. Peter Land Office opened for business, only four persons, well situated by their contacts in government, filed claims on the Dakota reserve. Three of the four men were public officials and friends of the senator. John B. Downer and Henry Swift were officials of the St. Peter Land Agency. Downer served as receiver of public moneys, and Swift, a former territorial governor, was register of land sale. Another public official was Judge Charles Vandenburgh, who had presided in 1860 over the Eliza Winston case, the only slave emancipation trial to occur in Minnesota. The remaining months of 1865 saw no significant increase in sales.[13] Thousands of acres of land remained unclaimed and open for auction. Land was available to anyone who understood how business was conducted. By November 1, 16,859 acres of Winnebago land had been sold for $49,076.26.

As reported by the secretary of the interior, $4,249.88 in receipts was in the bank.[14] Many more thousands of acres remained to be sold.

Absent from the bidding process were the black soldiers who served under the command of Captain Thomas Montgomery, Sixty-Seventh Regiment, U.S.C.I. Earlier, in late March of that year, three months before the St. Peter Land Office opened, Abner Tibbetts invited his friend from Le Sueur County to have his men bid, which Montgomery was excited to facilitate. His men jumped at the chance to establish homes away from the rebels. But the captain also knew that such a venture would be controversial, something with which he did not have the stomach to contend: he well knew the sentiment of his neighbors. "I am anxious to do all I can for [his black troops] but I will not involve myself in any trouble."[15]

In the end, there evidently was "trouble," for Montgomery wrote nothing more about the venture, and the Land Office received no bids from the black veterans. Moreover, even though President Lincoln had assigned full authority to Wilkinson to oversee the sale of Indian land, there is no indication that the ex-senator intervened in any way. It is, however, implausible that he knew nothing of it or that any of his men were not involved. Bids— even prospective bids—from black men would have been quite noteworthy, especially since for the remainder of 1865, few others stepped forward to bid on the land. Nonetheless, plans to establish a black colony on tracts from the Dakota and Winnebago reservations dissipated into thin air.

It would seem that the senator would have favored black settlement in Minnesota. During the previous spring of 1864, Senator Wilkinson introduced a bill to withdraw all funds for Lincoln's colonization plan that intended to send fifty thousand free blacks to an island near Haiti. Congress passed Wilkinson's measure on July 2, and the president signed it.[16] Wilkinson's bill reflected the emergent view that African Americans were indeed Americans. But it would seem that in Wilkinson's view they were Americans whose movement and settlement should remain limited. The savage backdrop of war set the context for his unexpected position.

It was impossible to imagine a war-torn South where freedmen and -women would be left alone to live and prosper. On June 28, 1864, during the debate to extend the Freedmen's Bureau, Republican senator Waitman T. Willey of West Virginia proposed a solution for the safety of the freedmen and -women who still resided in a hostile South that had recently seen a series of Confederate victories: relocate them, he proposed, to places in the North and West. Specifically, his amendment would authorize the commissioner of the Freedmen's Bureau to initiate correspondence "with the Governors of States, the municipal authorities of the States, with the various manufacturing establishments, and farmers and mechanics," precisely the sort of livelihood that white native- and foreign-born laborers coveted. Willey continued, "Homes might be provided for them, and they might not only find good homes but humane persons and employment at fair compensation, and it might supply to these districts that lack of labor which has been occasioned by the withdrawal of laboring men in the ranks of our armies. It seems to me," he concluded, "that here is a proposition which will accomplish more good for the freedmen."[17]

The amendment divided the Republicans and produced an unusual alignment across party lines. The arch conservative Willard Saulsbury of Delaware joined with antislavery men such as B. Gratz Brown of Missouri in supporting the Negro relocation plan, although Saulsbury took a circuitous route to his conclusion: "I could not vote for the amendment of the Senator of West Virginia as an independent proposition; but as an amendment to an obnoxious bill, with a view of perfecting that bill, I shall vote for the amendment." On the other hand, conservative Democrat Charles Buckalew of Pennsylvania, denounced it as "monstrous" and said that "our states to the North may well object to any such exertion of power . . . of this Government." He was certain that Northern states would "prohibit the introduction of this element of the population within their borders." Charles Sumner, the "best friend of freedmen" in the Senate, whom Willey no doubt was seeking to persuade, set the tone for opposition from the Radicals when he said that "with great reluctance" he felt the amendment "went too far": "It seems to me the whole idea is entirely untenable: it is out of place on this bill."[18]

However "untenable" the amendment was, by summer, 1864, Union armies, even with superior numbers, had not shown that they could defeat Lee in the field, let alone protect the multitude of freedmen still living on Southern soil, whether occupied or not. At any rate, the amendment was being misconstrued as compulsory relocation. Willey insisted that "[i]t is not my design to organize a system of compulsory emigration . . . The whole design and spirit of the section is that it shall be a matter of mutual consideration between the three parties—the commissioner, the freedman himself, and the person who desires to employ him."[19]

This was Willey's strongest argument and one that had to appeal to Republicans who worried about the growing number of voters back home who were tired of war, angered at mounting casualties, lacked confidence in Lincoln and the Republican Party, and now, with the prospect of black relocation, threatened by the influx of black laborers competing for work, not to mention the prospect of continued racial violence, the sort of which they witnessed in the last year in New York and Detroit. Mob violence erupted even in St. Paul in the spring of 1863 when steamers delivering contraband slaves from Missouri attempted to dock, and again when the same steamers, on return voyages, attempted to dock. This time the passengers were the Dakota and Winnebago who were being removed from the State. Weeks later, a provost guard was ordered when it was learned that more riots would ensue, this time against the draft. But the measure required that "reasonable white men at home," with an investment in a stable community and vital local economy, would make the deal, not ham-handed bureaucrats in Washington. Indeed, under these best of circumstances, the proposition offered an additional benefit: it could transform the brutish former slave into a productive member of society. Willey expressed (perhaps disingenuously) his amazement at the controversy:

> And I did think that such was an obvious advantage to the freedman himself in securing a home where he would obtain the protection of the law, the kindly sympathies of the people around him, and good labor at fair compensation, that there could hardly be an objection from any quarter to it.[20]

But Wilkinson knew—as he realized Willey knew as well—that the notion of "kindly sympathies of the people around [the new black arrival]," could hardly be so in his section of the northern states. As early as 1861, the *Chicago Tribune*, as Edward Pluth notes, had observed that northerners feared that freed slaves would "overrun the North." Likewise, as Leslie Schwalm has observed, "Many northern whites shared the fear that removing the bonds of slavery would bring unwelcome change to the 'place' of African Americans—and, by implication, the place of whites—in a postemancipation nation. . . . Revealing a deep-seated belief in the benefits and necessity of a racially stratified society, many [midwestern] whites assumed that any black gains in the region would diminish their own status and citizenship."[21]

And as the violence in St. Paul in 1863 attested, Wilkinson knew that many in his home state felt no differently, as such fears of a pending black deluge fell unhindered upon the fertile minds of people inclined to think the worst. "In the last census I see that at least of every 100 negroes born," wrote C. A. S., "17 are mulattoes—nearly one-fifth. And now we have in the free states 155,994 blacks and 69,855 mulattoes. Thus, you see, over one-third are mixed now, in the free states, and the ratio is gaining every year if the political and social ties are given, as the census shows mixing goes on more rapidly in freedom than in slavery, not because of intermarriage, as that has so far been prohibited to a great extent, but because of the licentiousness of negro worshippers in the free states. Let those former restrictions be taken away all over our land, and it will not require a prophet to foresee the result. Mexico and South America present a limited view of our condition in the future."[22]

But it was more than a justification of the exclusion of people singularly on the basis of skin to many white people calling Minnesota home. It went to the very heart of what "civilization" was. Nineteenth-century European Americans used it to describe a culturally specific set of beliefs about proper land use and, more generally, what constituted civilization.[23] Thus, settlement was not merely the presence of people but the introduction of various features that symbolized Euro-American society and provided the basis for an ordered way of life. Essential to the concept was agriculture, defined as planting crops on a large scale or raising domestic animals. The settlers of the 1850s were, in their own terms, engaged in imposing agriculture and the agricultural way of life, which they believed to be wasted on its original inhabitants, on a region that lacked order.

It was believed that race, and its demarcation, brought order to the "savage" land. As historian Bruce White notes, "More and more Americans in the midnineteenth century believed that human beings could be categorized according to racial groups, not all of which had the same intelligence and capabilities. Those considered superior were described as Anglo-Saxon, Germanic, Caucasian—or, simply, white. Indian people and blacks, as well as, on occasion, Irish, Italians, and others, were thought to be inferior and without a part to play in the making of American society. In keeping with these new attitudes, settlement and civilization came to be described as the accomplishments of white people, even if other groups might live an orderly, cultured existence. From this point of view, the history of settlement in the Minnesota region, as described by post-territorial historians, was essentially the story of how Minnesota came to be white," that is, passed from a time when most Minnesotans were Indian and mixed.[24] Conversely, the white race as a whole, they believed, would "dissolve" into "any number of tan-colored grandchildren."[25] The future of the state, they felt, rested firmly in the hands of the idealized Minnesotan indelibly embossed as the man in the state seal, a white farmer at the plow, laboring on his land.

But it was the cranky Senator Saulsbury who summed up the matter. In the wake of Congress approving the resolution to send to the states the Thirteenth Amendment, Saulsbury argued that those who supported the abolition of slavery were hypocrites if they rejected the Willey amendment:

> Sir, tell me not, tell not the honest people of this country that the professions of the abolitionists are sincere; and they are honest in their efforts to set free this race unless they are willing to take them home, and give a practical illustration to the world of their sincerity by admitting them to an equality of rights to themselves.[26]

For Wilkinson, in particular, Saulsbury hit a nerve, for Minnesota had yet to approve suffrage rights for the black residents it already had. The friends of the freedman, it seemed, could support emancipation so long as the emancipated did not live among them. Racial equality was good as long as freedmen lived among white Southerners. The Delaware Democrat continued to scold the Radicals. "I am surprised that any man or any party professing to have at heart so much the interests of the negro race should refuse to avail of the privileges offered by the amendment of the Senator of West Virginia." Ridiculing the Republicans, he said, "If this amendment be rejected by such votes as I have indicated, I apprehend that it will be impossible hereafter to make even the most stupid believe that modern abolitionism is anything else than absolute hypocrisy."[27]

Wilkinson knew that what made the provision untenable, beyond mere logistics, was the widespread antiblack sentiment in the North. Since the start of serious emancipation efforts in 1862, black migration to the northward had been a controversial issue, and though many freedmen had made their way north there was strong unpopular opposition to government actions to assist their relocation. In the fall of 1862, the War Department, facing great resistance from Illinois officials, abandoned efforts to arrange for the employment and support of black refugees in that state. Nor was eastern opinion any more favorable to blacks on this issue than in the west, as Governor John A. Andrew of Massachusetts showed in declining the offer of Union commanders to send two thousand blacks to the New England states.[28]

Indeed, Northern prejudice made congressmen acutely sensitive to the issue of black migration from the start of Freedmen's Bureau planning. In the first meeting of the House Select Committee on Emancipation in December 1863, Representative Godlove Orth of Indiana proposed that no action should be taken to encourage emigration by freedmen. Sharing this viewpoint,

Democrat Anthony Knapp of Illinois moved an amendment to the bureau bill, stating that nothing in it should authorize the introduction of any persons of color into any state whose laws prohibited them. Massachusetts congressman Thomas D. Eliot's committee rejected this motion by a vote of six Republicans (including Orth) to one Democrat, but the result signified a desire to steer clear of the issue rather than support the migration of blacks.[29]

By June 1864, the issue of black relocation had become political theater. Republican opponents of the Willey amendment acknowledged political reasons for avoiding any reference to black migration in national legislation. To open public correspondence on the subject, Samuel C. Pomeroy of Kansas declared, would enable "a political party to make A FUSS about it, and it will become an unpopular thing." Henry Wilson of Massachusetts held that the provision for official correspondence with state governors was liable to misrepresentation and would excite opposition. Wilson said he supported black relocation only if it were carried out by private voluntary means, for any governmental intervention could result in more contention in Northern communities. Considering that antiblack sentiment was particularly strong in the west, many felt that some of the western Republicans actually supported black migration to embarrass easterners who voted against a bill for black advancement. After all, the amendment was primarily not so much about homesteading as about labor, and urban labor at that, where white laborers had already demonstrated a penchant for mob violence. Nonetheless, other westerners knew that for many settlers, the town could be a springboard to homesteading, a lifestyle ordained to the white man, and that the freedman was a creature of the South. In any event, many senators anticipated that the House would not approve the provision.[30] The Willey amendment vote would thus quietly recede into the shadows.

This needed not be a party-line vote; senators could vote any way they wanted on the matter. The Radicals had established their bona fides in the struggle for freedom when they approved the resolution to send the Thirteenth Amendment to the states for ratification in April with a 38–6 vote; and it was a defining vote, one that each senator knew would stand the test of time.[31] The Willey amendment was of a different stripe, permitting each senator to march to his own drummer. On June 28, the Senate approved Willey's amendment, 19–15. It was one of the few issues concerning the freedmen that confronted the wartime Senate when men within the same caucus opposed each other. Such was the case with the senators from Minnesota. Ramsey voted to approve the amendment while Wilkinson voted to reject it.[32] Two men of similar minds on the advancement of the freedman stood on opposing sides of the political divide, a precursor of the politics to come in terms of racial opportunity during the fratricidal age of reconstruction. It would therefore seem that in Wilkinson's mind, the farmer etched onto the state seal was to be literally construed as white, only. And Montgomery, who within a few years would himself become a successful businessman in real estate, would have concurred.

14

# A LESSON IN LEADERSHIP

*Negro suffrage is but a stepping stone to universal equality
in everything, even to the detestable and God-forbidden
principle of miscegenation.*

CHATFIELD DEMOCRAT, 1865

One year after the 1864 debate over the Willey amendment, Willard Saulsbury's words still stung. Though he was not talking specifically about Minnesota, he might as well have been. Minnesotans had indeed not extended voting
rights to the black men of the state. What moral integrity they had over the
Delaware senator and his slaveholding constituents was lost in Minnesota's
duplicity with the antiblack impulse within its own borders; and by extension,
for such a proud man as Wilkinson, his own. In 1864 Wilkinson supported
black suffrage in the Senate during the debate over the organization of Montana Territory. While the House of Representatives had limited suffrage to
white male inhabitants, Senator Wilkinson moved to enfranchise "every free
male citizen and those who have declared their intention to become such," and
got his bill passed by a vote of 29 to 8 on the Senate floor. Even in the House
of Representatives fifty-four Republicans supported the Wilkinson bill, and
only twenty voted against it.[1]

But Wilkinson had not been successful in his home state. As a member
of the first territorial legislature in 1849, he had supported an amendment
to remove the word "white" from the voting eligibility provision, a change
that would have extended the franchise to Minnesota's black men, but soon
relented to political pressures to exclude that class.[2] Seven years later, in 1857,

during the constitutional convention, as a nondelegate, he could only look on as fellow Republicans shot down all efforts to enfranchise the black man.[3] In 1849 there was no Republican Party and the Democrats controlled the territory; but in 1857 there was a Republican Party, and it would soon have control of the state government. Still, the will for that sort of change was not there.[4]

Politicians—including those whom Wilkinson considered sincere and high-minded—continued to defer to the prejudices of the voters. Even after the current Republican-dominated legislature had approved a referendum on black suffrage to be held in the November election, party leaders nonetheless seemed ambivalent and opinion makers were divided. The die for an anemic and disorganized campaign was already cast by the time Wilkinson came home from Washington. Too many men were choosing the wrong side. Righting the ship would be complicated, because for far too many Minnesotans, black suffrage and black homesteading were one and the same. Promoting the first without the other, which only exacerbated the politics of black suffrage, would be like threading a needle. The circumstances around the unfortunate timing of the prospective black colony in March would have to be handled delicately. It was fortunate that Captain Montgomery of Le Sueur County was an ambitious young man with an eye to his own future. On the larger matter of black suffrage, Wilkinson, as a recently unseated but still widely respected senator, though now of diminished political stature and no patronage, had to figure out how to lead from the rear.

Already some of his most influential and reliable friends had staked out strong opposition against the amendment, a harbinger of the fading prospect for success of the measure. No less than the Wilkinson-leaning *Mankato Union* now called on voters to "effectively kill it."[5] Cheering on the paper and all other Republicans who agreed was the city's Democratic newspaper, the *Weekly Record,* which reported, "We are gratified that at least two Republican papers of this State . . . have come out manfully in opposition to the proposed amendment of the Constitution . . . [for] they are sustained by the more intelligent and responsible members of their party."[6] Despite this apparent meeting of minds, their reasoning, as the *Weekly Record* conveniently ignored, was quite different. The Democratic editor argued that with ratification of the measure, Minnesota would be the only state in the North to enfranchise African Americans, which would induce "wholesale immigration of that class of person. While there are doubtless some respectable and worthy exceptions, they are, as a people, ignorant, indolent, and addicted to petty thieving."[7] The editor was wrong on both counts. Wisconsin had enacted a black suffrage amendment in 1849, which would be affirmed by the state supreme court in 1866, to no measurable increase of the black portion of the general population.[8]

Nonetheless, the *Weekly Record* editor had touched a nerve, not only among Democrats but also many Republicans who had supported Lincoln, the war, and emancipation, but who feared undue competition from those whom they had fought to free. With Negro suffrage came the impression that Minnesota was receptive to Negro empowerment, which would promote Negro immigration, Negro employment, and in turn Negro residency, resulting, within the farm state of Minnesota, in the dire inevitability of Negro homesteading. Here for them, the interests of suffrage and homesteading threateningly converged. The editorial was nothing less than a rallying call to protect what rightfully belonged to the white man.

On the other hand, the *Union* argued that the measure was too broad. In its opposition, under the unfortunate and misleading title, "Nigger on the Brain," the editor argued that the well-intended, but unwise, legislature missed the opportunity to require citizens to be intelligent. Unlike the editor of the *Weekly Record,* who intimated that "intelligence" was on full display when Republicans supported Democratic principles (in this instance, a former slave could never be "intelligent"), the *Union*'s notion was more nuanced. Intelligence was not exclusive to race. Black men, just because they were black, were not incapable of being thoughtful, enlightened, or at least what lawyers referred to as "reasonable," and were not relegated by their race to impulsive, uncouth, and irresponsible behavior; not, in short, like the Irish, a large number of whom supported the Democratic Party. The problem was that legislators, through the measure, wasted the opportunity to elevate the level of civilization by requiring a higher standard of character from its citizens. "We are in favor of allowing every intelligent man of lawful age, whether black or white, to vote; but we are not in favor of allowing a man who is not intelligent, to exercise this vote privilege. . . . No doubt an ignorant negro is just as well qualified to become a citizen of Minnesota as an ignorant Irishman, but no more nor no less. Because an error has been committed in our present State constitution allowing a man to vote simply because he was white, no matter how ignorant, is no reason why we should commit another error by allowing ignorant negroes to stand on an equality with our ignorant whites."[9]

Fault rested with the legislature for failing to grapple with the criterion against which the lofty qualities of "intelligence" should be measured. The editor seemed to be espousing the kind of intelligence that came from a liberal arts education, which exposed the student to a wider range of subjects and encouraged the development of critical thinking skills, which fostered within the learned man the capacity for independent thought. In the end, it was left to the editor to offer what he had to know to be a more practical, albeit inadequate, criterion: "We should be glad to see our Legislature turning its attention towards making an amendment to our constitution allowing none to exercise the right of the Legislative franchise who are not sufficiently intelligent to read our State constitution."[10] This, he argued, would filter out ignorance. In the near future, starting in South Carolina and Louisiana, Southern states would soon use the same kind of law to filter out not ignorance but the entire black electorate.[11] This was not what the *Union* editor had in mind.

By the time Wilkinson returned to Mankato the readers of the *Union* were embroiled in heated debate over the newspaper's position as well as whether the measure should be approved. To the credit of the newspaper, it, more than any other paper in the region, had opened its pages to opposing views on the matter. One reader argued that black men should be allowed to vote or else relieved from all taxation. Another argued that ignorant Irishmen should be disenfranchised. But it was a reader who signed his piece "C.A.S." who feared that the measure would usher in miscegenation and competition for jobs and land. The antidote for him was colonization, a position he insisted black men would accept. "As I do not intend to come into competition with the negroes, I have no personal fears on that question." The black man, the reader insisted, never asked for the privilege.[12]

A reader named John Kellett took issue with the paper's perceived racism against the Irish: "I may be called an ignorant Irishman. My education was obtained fifty years ago in a school house built of rolling stones and road mortar thatched with straw, no table, no chair, only those used by the teacher; yet few countries have given more facilities for education during the last forty years than Ireland has, and the ignorance of those you allude to is not a want of knowledge of reading and writing." But he took equal offense at the appearance of the word "nigger" in the editorials and published letters: "We can afford to call [him] 'black man' or 'colored man' or any such name without descending to a nickname or anything bordering on it." Then Kellett turned his sarcastic attention to C.A.S. "He says, 'the negroes do not want the privilege.' That is a blunder. They want all the rights of man[;] nothing more or less will satisfy either themselves or their advocates throughout the Union."[13]

C.A.S. responded, holding that black men at arms had not shown themselves worthy of suffrage: the war would continue for another month before Grant and Lee would meet at Appomattox: "In the present struggle in the United States, what part have they taken? Has there ever been a regiment of negroes raised in the free states, out of a population of 225,84[?] . . . The negro North and South has remained the idle spectator in the present struggle so far as he could. The negro enlisting South in our armies have no choice. They are marched in like so many cattle, having no means of support, and getting none unless they enlist. Ask our returned soldiers about this and see if I am right. . . . While the struggle goes on, [negroes] still look on, unless forced to enlist, notwithstanding they are the most interested or should be, in the result. If freedom from slavery is not worth fighting for in the name of heaven, what is?"[14]

There was no ringing endorsement of what C.A.S. wrote. In fact, in the weeks that followed, several letters appeared taking issue with aspects or the totality of his argument. John Kellett, "the ignorant Irishman," wrote with blunt eloquence on the moral and historical duty to support black equality. "We are not asking any favors or privileges for the colored race. We are not. We demand justice. Rights are rights. . . . The measure of the rights of God and men are thus defined by the best authority: 'Thou shalt love the Lord thy God with all thy heart and thy neighbor as thyself.' "[15] But even though more letters printed in the *Union* generally favored the abolition of slavery, and an inherent equality between the races, few spoke in favor of the present measure. Few readers expressed outward support for the views of C.A.S., but it would seem, given the election returns in November, that many subscribers to this Republican newspaper came to embrace some aspect of his view: black suffrage was a bridge too far.

Throughout the month of March, a wounded and preoccupied Wilkinson had not stated his position on the subject, and few seemed for now willing to seek it out. Simply put: he was a man out of office, not because he had chosen to retire, but because his bid to return had failed. In the political world, this was worse. The party had rejected him and he was no longer at the head of a ticket. His views, simply put, meant less than when he was a United States senator. But he was still a loyal Republican, capable of delivering a spellbinding speech; of tapping into the hearts of those who had seen him as their leader; and whose opinion, despite his diminished stature in Minnesota's political world, still mattered. In this regard, he remained a political asset, a person with whom major candidates wanted to share the stage. And if he was considering a run for office in the near future, a consideration people who knew him best recognized as realistic, and a triumphant return to, perhaps, his beloved seat within the old Senate chamber in Washington, campaigning for as popular a candidate as Colonel William Marshall could be of considerable mutual benefit.

In these appearances, as on October 26 before a Mankato crowd, Wilkinson's role was simple: appear on stage, offer a few words of endorsement before introducing "the next Governor of the State," and then step aside.[16] He was only to support the candidate and his views, and Marshall was for black suffrage.[17] Marshall was another member of that rare breed of mid-nineteenth-century Minnesotans who championed black equality at a time when the concept was unthinkable even among some of the most upstanding citizens. He had cofounded the Republican Party and early showed the capacity to breach the line separating pro-abolitionists and antiblack sympathizers, and men in between those two camps. As a Missourian by birth, raised among yeomen stock within slaveholding country, he possessed a commoner's touch that made him that much more accessible to the working man; and as a dashing commander, he enjoyed the admiration of his troops, even those who otherwise disagreed with his racial views. And yet he was at ease facing racism, for he understood as a result of growing up in the South, that, as he had told a Mankato audience in 1865, racism was something learned, not inherent to nature.[18] He was the ideal candidate to run for high office, to be the standard-bearer of his party.

As for Wilkinson, weeks before the election, he appeared nightly in different towns in southern Minnesota, keeping a full expression of his views on black suffrage to himself. He was a Marshall man. In that role Wilkinson spoke in the smaller towns throughout the southern counties of Minnesota. The region had become Wilkinson's political base and it was there that he stumped during the final days of the campaign, appearing nightly in a different town, sometimes with a candidate for lesser office, sometimes by himself. Whether he wanted once and for all to divulge his position on black suffrage or was bowing to public demand, Wilkinson finally scheduled a time to speak on the matter.

He would speak on three occasions in three separate towns. None would be in Mankato or anywhere in Blue Earth County, but only in neighboring Faribault County.[19] It was as if he was testing the political waters to assess not just his ability to bring an audience to a particular issue, but to draw an audience to him. At this late hour, it was improbable that he would say anything to controvert the Marshall and Republican position on black suffrage even if he was so inclined, given his now-recognizable aspiration to return to Congress, even if in fact it meant repudiating the *Union*'s position. But there would not be a public quarrel between Blue Earth's favorite son and his organ. It was as if they had agreed to disagree in silence. The *Union* announced the scheduled speeches, saying simply, "We are not certain as to what Mr. Wilkinson's views

are, or what he will counsel the Republican voters in reference to negro suffrage, but we trust the people will give him a full hearing as his acknowledged
abilities as a statesman, and his experience as a counselor of the actions entitle
his opinions to be respectfully considered."[20] As improbable as it was that the
*Union* knew little of Wilkinson's views, at least officially the paper and its
readers would remain in the dark.

The only known account of Wilkinson's remarks appeared in a sarcastic
letter in the Democratic *Weekly Record,* yet it depicted some sense of what
happened that night. "Last Saturday evening the citizens of Blue Earth City
were somewhat surprised by the appearance of the former United States
Senator Wilkinson. . . . This being his first appearance in this section since
1861, there were just 28 individuals who felt sufficient interest in the drama to
obtain a room and listen to Wilk's oration." Wilkinson, according to the correspondent, was not in his best voice. "I have heard Wilk talk before, when
I thought he spoke well, but he seemed to be oppressed with some great and
terrible thoughts, and this oppression was naturally communicated to his audience, most of whom went away feeling rejoiced that the terrible scene was
over. [Nonetheless,] he spoke long and quite loud," wrote the correspondent,
snidely referencing Wilkinson's evident purpose in being there really to prepare for another run for Congress. Then the correspondent got to the point—
namely, Wilkinson's stance on black suffrage and his avowed endorsement of
black-white political equality. "*He thought that Jeff Davis' nigger was as good
as himself.* Here he was in good rapport with his listeners. This seemed [to
spark] cheering."[21]

It would seem that the reported "cheering" was meant to be sarcastic:
what intelligent white man could ever support black suffrage? A week later,
when the votes were cast, Marshall defeated Rice for governor, and the entire
Republican slate won their seats. However, the measure failed not only statewide but, in particular, Blue Earth County. In Faribault County, however,
where Blue Earth City was, the measure was approved nearly two to one.[22]
Most Republican officeholders supported the measure. However, as noted by
U.S. Supreme Court Chief justice Salmon P. Chase, two men were notably
absent from the column. Senator Alexander Ramsey and Congressman William Windom had distanced themselves from the issue, for which both were
roundly criticized by the party brethren.[23]

It is hard to know whether Wilkinson could have swung Blue Earth
County to support black suffrage in 1865. What is evident is that he did not
appear to try. The year 1865 was peculiar. At the beginning of the year his
own party had wounded him politically. If he wanted to return to the Senate

he needed the support of Republicans in Blue Earth County, who were divided over black suffrage, as well as from the state party, which officially was not. Wilkinson may have felt that he was caught between a rock and a hard place. Moreover, at the time, as a board director of an investment firm he had a fiduciary duty to avoid attracting controversy to J. J. Thornton and Company and obstructing the business it did. Its business would principally be acquiring and selling land. How could its most prominent director, especially without the backing of the *Union,* be the champion for black suffrage and not, in effect, endorse its logical progression—black homesteading? Marshall could do it but his political star was on the rise. This was not the case for Wilkinson, who in 1865 could not predict that the same would be his fate, and without that certainty, it would be harder to rebuild his machine. Conceivably he could have aggressively campaigned for black suffrage without losing standing within his home base, but for Wilkinson this was a year of caution. He had not been a part of the caucus that launched the campaign.

Besides, too many people saw and feared the connection between suffrage and homesteading, seeing, as "C.A.S." saw, the inevitability of unseemly competition, a curious perception since freedmen and -women remained mostly unskilled, unpropertied, and, in a word, impoverished. Yet, as historian Leslie Schwalm has written, "Steady inflation had already brought home the cost of war, and some midwesterners felt that Federal aid to fugitive slaves was depriving more worthy citizens of support. . . . In the Midwest, it was particularly because of the juxtaposition of the Federal government's conduct regarding the Dakota Sioux, white citizens, and former slaves that some came to believe Washington was failing to act in the best interests of white citizens, even demonstrating preferential treatment of nonwhites . . . In a region where the very presence of white settlers was sanctioned by the state-supported effort to dominate and expel Native Americans, the Federal government's failure to divert manpower and resources to a more immediate and brutal military response was viewed by whites as a deep betrayal. That sense of betrayal was sharpened by the belief among white settlers that even while their needs were ignored, large sums of public funds were being spent to support fugitive slaves in the South."[24] In other words, many whites, like many Indians at the outset of the Dakota War, held one belief in common: black people were unduly getting resources that should have gone to them.

How, some wondered, could a laboring white man compete against that, especially after Congress had discontinued the colonization effort, which could have diverted the pending flood of freedmen away from the North and Midwest? The antifederal government seed had been planted, and with it the deeper bias against the black man and woman. "Negro suffrage . . . means much more than the simple fact of conferring the right of voting upon the released slaves of the South, and their little less enlightened brethren of the North," argued the *Chatfield Democrat*. "It don't mean that the privileges of Sambo are to cease when he shall march to the polls and affect your vote with his, but you must take him to your home, have your wife wait on him, let him kiss your sister, set up with your daughter, marry her as he wants her, and raise any number of tan-colored grandchildren," concluding breathlessly, "[Negro suffrage] is loaded with the fetid breath of mongolism and carries with it the putridity that will blot from earth the white race of this continent."[25] Other papers published similar views—stories that insisted interracial rape was the logical product of black suffrage.[26]

To further legitimize the antisuffrage sentiment, the Democratic press claimed that the heroic Civil War veterans were also against the measure.[27] It was not hard to find Union soldiers who felt that slaves, contraband, and freedmen enjoyed privileges that the white soldiers did not receive. The testimonials had special cachet for readers in the southwestern counties when they came from "our boys" who served in the Seventh Regiment of Minnesota Volunteers, a unit made up largely of young farmers from the same area of the state who joined initially to fight the Dakota in 1862. One soldier from Blue Earth County reportedly said in 1862, "I am as much in favor of abolishing slavery as anybody . . . but since I have been in the Army and seen them better treated than white men . . . I lost all my love for the colored Gentlemen."[28]

Later that year, the *St. Paul Pioneer* exaggerated reports of contraband receiving better rations of fresh bread than white soldiers, who were issued "hard, mouldy wormy crackers."[29] And in July 1864, even Senator Wilkinson added to this resentment when he advised the Senate that he wanted to see more "black soldiers enter into the contest than to have all our white men annihilated before the war shall be over."[30] The words came back to haunt him when they were used to echo the sense that many white men felt: white men had carried the inordinate burden of fighting for black freedom.[31]

These were testimonials from enlisted men who, due to their deployments, had no encounters with, for example, the consolidated Sixty-Fifth and Sixty-Seventh regiments of the U.S. Colored Infantry, bivouacked in the disease-laden swamps of southern Louisiana, sent there under orders from their white commanders. Nevertheless, it was common to report in 1865 that white soldiers would vote monolithically and that black suffrage would surely be defeated. In the midst of intense patriotism and when freedom was no longer the issue, it was a powerful argument but hardly authoritative.[32] What mattered more was that white men proudly saw no conflict embracing freedom while rejecting equality. It was a position validated by what civilians presumed the soldiers would take. Because the soldiers had marched through fire, they, more than any politician, had moral authority on the matter. If, in fact, there was a soldiers' voting bloc, it would be a powerful bloc indeed.[33] Few proponents were willing to challenge the presumption by showing leadership.

Within this vacuum, the sentiment against black suffrage grew. During the suffrage campaign, the *Weekly Record* reported that Minnesota's soldiers were almost unanimous in support of ex-military men Marshall and Christopher Columbus Andrews, the latter running on the same ticket for lieutenant governor, but against black suffrage. "Ninety-nine, one hundredth percent of the returned soldiers are opposed to negro suffrage, and while they might admire Marshall and Andrews personally, none can be mislead [sic] by them to favor this fanatical proposition."[34] The admiration was indeed felt deeply, forged in battle, solidified in grace. The man running for governor—William Rainey Marshall—showed mythic courage during the Battle of Nashville.[35] On another occasion, after an exhaustive march, the men were allowed to slaughter sheep for supper. "When the men had their supper ready, seeing that Col. Marshall and some of the officers had nothing to eat, they were invited to eat with us."[36] Perhaps the most poignant moment, summing up a series of such "moments" that endeared the colonel, by now a brevet brigadier general, to his men, occurred at Fort Snelling on August 10, 1865, after being mustered out of service. One soldier characterized Marshall's men's profound regard for him: "After receiving our discharge and pay we bade our comrades good-by. . . . We expected some of our officers would be there to see us off. Only one came, Colonel Marshall; he bade us good-by, shaking each one by the hand, the tears rolling down his cheeks. The boat started off, and he stood looking after us as though he had parted with his best friends."[37]

Despite Marshall's courage, inspiring leadership, and the extent to which his men admired him, he did not leverage his popularity to lead his men to support black suffrage. As a result, while many rejected the measure, many more seemed to reflect the ambivalence of a Lincoln Republican serving as an officer in the colored regiment. To his brother James who lived on the family farm in Le Sueur, Captain Thomas Montgomery wrote, "I am anxious to hear the decision of the election this fall. I hope [William] Marshall is elected but I think it will be a close run on account of the point at issue—negro suffrage."[38] Marshall did not go to the front, and as rebel bullets whizzed by, draw his saber and exhort his men, "Follow me, boys, Follow me for the Union and our martyred President!" That November, black suffrage failed at the polls. The Democrats succeeded in carrying ten counties, "their greatest achievement since soldier balloting had been inaugurated."[39] In Blue Earth and Nicollet, counties that could have been sites for the black colony Tibbetts foresaw, Marshall won the election while the Negro suffrage measure failed.[40]

For Wilkinson, the lesson was clear. It was not an issue of timing: when could there have been a better time to ask Republicans to approve a black suffrage measure than in the immediate victorious aftermath of the Civil War and the echo of the assassin's gunshot. Rather, the lesson was that in order to ask men to do what they were disinclined to do, one had to lead from the front. Wilkinson, focused and determined, would have to be able to say that he would be the first to take the bullet for his men.

# 15

# "GOOD NIGHT"

*It was the duty of Minnesota Republicans to work
for [the amendment] and talk for it, and urge your
neighbors to vote for it.*

MORTON S. WILKINSON, 1868

In January 1866 the state party renewed its commitment to black suffrage. Republican legislator Stephen Hewson proposed a strategy to coordinate the amendment campaign statewide with local campaigns led by party leaders. The party's enthusiasm was, however, tempered. In his inaugural address, Governor-elect William Marshall declared that while he supported black suffrage, and public support had increased, he would let the legislature determine whether the time was right for a new campaign. Outgoing governor Stephen Miller, who had been Marshall's commander during the Dakota War, was less supportive, urging the legislature to instead submit a proposal for a qualified suffrage amendment enfranchising all males able to read and write, who held property valued at last at $300, or who had received an honorable discharge from the U.S. Army.[1] However, the House Republicans overwhelmingly rejected the proposal, 24 to 8. According to one reporter, the 1865 defeat had dampened Republican resolve, and support for any form of universal suffrage might mean political suicide: "Some few of the men voted against the bill on the professed ground that the question of Negro suffrage, having been so recently decided against, it was not expedient to bring it up in any shape as present."[2]

Others, whose support had always been reluctant, got colder feet as they watched the events in Washington unfold. President Johnson, having troubles with the Radical Republicans, was forming the Conservative Party, a coalition of Northern Democrats and conservative Republicans who strongly opposed black suffrage; the new party attracted such notable Minnesota politicians as Daniel Norton and William Colvill. Some Republicans had even accepted the endorsement of the Democratic Party in 1866. The Republicans seemed on the verge of breaking apart, and their support for black suffrage seemed at its lowest. The national elections buoyed them, for despite the president's strong campaign against the Radicals, voters nationwide overwhelmingly returned Republican majorities to Congress in a clear repudiation of Johnson's policies. Minnesota Republicans themselves experienced an important victory when they decisively won two congressional districts against candidates supporting President Johnson. These victories prompted many moderate Republicans in Congress to return to the fold, supporting efforts to revive the momentum for black suffrage. In January 1867 Congress enfranchised blacks residing in the District of Columbia as well as all federal territories and insisted that black suffrage be a requirement of statehood for Nebraska. In March Congress required black suffrage as a condition for readmission of former Confederate states.[3]

With renewed vigor, Governor Marshall called for the legislature to submit a suffrage bill to the people. Representative B. F. Perry sponsored and guided the bill through the House and Senate, where it met virtually no resistance. It was not until October that the Democrats began their attack.[4] As in the 1865 campaign, they appealed to the same racial prejudices of foreign-born Minnesotans and laborers, claiming they would lose their jobs and opportunities if blacks got the vote, and shocked supporters with stories of rape and miscegenation, arguing that America belonged to the white man. In terms of stating whose nation this was, before the Civil War, Republicans had delivered the same message.[5] But four years of war and an assassinated president had shifted the racial and political landscape for most Republicans.

Throughout the remainder of the campaign season, Republicans used a creative ploy to obscure the true intent of the provision that appeared on the ballot, identifying the question as not expressly about black suffrage but referring to the referendum cryptically as "Amendment to section one (1), article seven (7) of the Constitution," evidently to avoid repelling unknowing, anti-suffrage Republicans. The *St. Paul Daily Pioneer* described the provision's language as a "Republican sugar coat of a bill so that voters may not know its character" and an "elegant euphemism."[6] In the November election, the referendum once again failed, though the margin was smaller than in 1865.[7] Nonetheless, opinion makers felt that its defeat was in large part due to this bit of obfuscation as well as poor organization. Instead of the question being placed on the ballot, county committees (mainly because they received no directions from the central committee to do otherwise) placed the question on a separate ballot where it was overlooked, ignored, or misunderstood by voters who otherwise voted the Republican ticket. As a result, as the *St. Paul Daily Press* reported, "Thousands voted for the general and local tickets without thinking anything about the amendment, and so cast no vote on that question, or were confused by the multitude of amendments and cast no votes on them."[8] It was a painful lesson to have lost by votes they could have won.

On January 10, 1868, Governor Marshall called for a third campaign for black suffrage in his annual message to the House and Senate. Appealing to the highest principles of the Republican Party that he had cofounded in 1855, he said that Minnesota was ready to move forward on this issue. Referring to the election returns of 1865 and 1867, he insisted that public opposition had declined. The black man had served his country well and, Marshall maintained, tapping into a theme that had inspired the American Revolution, was being taxed without representation; moreover, Republicans, he said, had a duty to protect the rights of oppressed people. His comments were warmly received.[9] Three weeks later state senator Hanford L. Gordon sponsored the bill to place it on the November ballot, recommending that it should not be identified in arcane parliamentary language as it was in 1867, and that it be placed on the general Republican ticket rather than on a separate ballot. With a large Republican turnout expected for the presidential election, in which the greatly admired General Grant would be their candidate, Gordon and his colleagues believed the provision would draw enough new votes to guarantee the amendment's success.[10]

And this time, taking to the field and exhorting all Republicans who would appear on the ballot to inextricably link their bids for office to black suffrage, Morton Wilkinson, now running for a seat in Congress and showing needed leadership from the front line, insisted that the duty of Minnesota Republicans was "to work for [black suffrage] and talk for it, and urge your neighbors to vote for it." In other words, he told candidates to say, *a vote for me is a vote for black suffrage.* Other prominent Republican candidates began to do the same. Christopher C. Andrews, running for another congressional seat, said, "I would rather be defeated a dozen times over than have the suffrage amendment lost." Their strategy succeeded. The amendment passed with a wide margin. In November more than 90 percent of the votes cast for the Republicans supported the suffrage amendment, and Morton Wilkinson, who got credit for the victory, was returning to Congress.[11]

• • • • •

In the eleven years since Wilkinson settled in Mankato, he had witnessed its change from a distant outpost of white civilization on the edge of Indian country, through the ordeal of the Civil War, the trauma of a threatened attack by the Dakota, and the macabre resolution of mass execution and removal of two Indian tribes; thousands of acres of fertile farmland had opened up for homesteading, a plague of speculation and opportunism occurred, and finally the region saw a major influx of settlers.[12] The people who flooded into the region were humble stock, from all parts of the North and Northern and Western Europe, who transformed the complexion of the region from red to white.

These were his people, and in terms of his future, it was they who would be his constituents, not the men who dominated the legislature, most of whom by now were subject to Ramsey's influence. Though law dictated that senators be elected by that body, a congressman was elected by popular vote from Wilkinson's district, and for this reason the former senator shifted his congressional sights. The change that had occurred in and around Blue Earth County was not just in terms of demographics, which outstripped Democratic influence in the region: it was for him a matter of political opportunity. With virtually no threat of black homesteading, both new and older voters could afford to be high-minded.

Boosters for settlement in Minnesota were already looking for native- and European-born settlers streaming into the state to farm. In the Congress of 1864, Ignatius Donnelly rose to speak, in effect, to the world: "With nearly a billion acres of unsettled lands on one side of the Atlantic and with many millions of poor and oppressed people on the other, let us organize the exodus which must come and build if necessary a bridge of gold across the chasm that divides them that the chosen races of mankind may occupy the chosen lands of the world."[13] As such, the state had invested resources into creating an agency whose focus was on native- and foreign-born immigration.

To draw attention to the state, the Board of Immigration sent out pamphlets in Norwegian, Swedish, German, and Welsh, as well as English, to be dispatched by agents who fanned out throughout states in the east and northeast as well as Europe. The board cooperated with railroads to get cheap fares for immigrants and their families and built immigrant-receiving settlement houses for their temporary accommodation. Swedish-born immigrant Hans Mattson, appointed as the board's secretary, went to Sweden in 1868 to recruit immigrants, describing his adopted home as a land of milk and honey.

While in Sweden he organized two shiploads of emigrants to accompany him
to Minnesota. In 1871 Mattson, now an emigrant agent for the Northern Pacific Railroad, returned to his native country to search for prospective settlers
and returned to his new homeland in 1873 with another contingent. Agents
representing the state were also sent to Milwaukee and Chicago to give aid to
immigrants, and one was delegated to give them protection and advice when
they reached St. Paul.[14]

The state also consigned Paul Hjelm-Hansen, a Norwegian journalist, to
write a series of articles that appeared in Norway and Norwegian American
communities touting the beauty of Minnesota. Elsewhere other writers told
of exaggerated accounts of Minnesota's fresh air and healthy climate. Edu-
ard Pelz and Albert Wolf, German immigrants who worked as agents of the
St. Paul and Pacific and later the Northern Pacific Railroad, wrote pamphlets
and articles about the "humanistic and public-minded effort to concentrate
German emigration to Minnesota." These and other ethnic Minnesotans all
whetted the appetites of their countrymen who in turn established ethnic
communities that dotted the state. As Theodore Blegen wrote, "The Yankee,
German, Norwegian, Swedish, Irish, Czech, Welsh, and other settlements
and 'colonies' that took root in the 1850s expanded in numbers and deepened
in their special character in the decades after the Civil War. . . . More revealing of the complexion of the people [of Minnesota] is the fact that by 1880
seventy-one per cent of the total 'represented European blood of the first and
second generations.' "[15]

No similar outreach effort to African Americans was made. Their opportunity for landownership lay instead within another homestead policy geared
to inducing freedmen to remain in the South, a policy conventionally termed
"forty acres and a mule," but in practice one born of the reluctance of Republicans to move, as Eric Foner writes, "very far toward the goal of land
for the freedmen," a policy that essentially and intentionally denied blacks
the full opportunity to land otherwise made available to white homesteaders.[16] In Minnesota, by 1870 759 African Americans were counted as residents.
Anoka, Blue Earth, Dakota, Goodhue, Le Sueur, Rice, Pine, and Winona
Counties each had at least fifteen blacks, though most were laborers.[17] John
Alfred Boone and John Green, who were veterans of Company K of the
Sixty-Seventh Regiment and served under Montgomery, may have been part
of the group on whose behalf the captain wrote; the two men did move to Le
Sueur County in 1865, but both worked as laborers.[18] This was the role their
patrons could only seem to imagine for black people, as reflected in an 1863
article heralding the arrival of contraband from the South: "The people of

the State are prepared to welcome a large accession of Negroes to our laboring population."[19]

Forty years later 8.7 percent of the African American population in Minnesota lived in rural areas, but only twenty-nine farms out of 156,137 were
operated by black families. "Of these," recorded David Taylor, "sixteen
[farms] were owned by the operator, twelve were farmed by tenants and one
was managed."[20] As "colonies" of foreign settlers took root on Minnesota's
farmland, not even the intimation of similar settlements of black homesteaders occurred since the Tibbetts-Montgomery correspondence in 1865. In 1870,
when the legislature established the Board of Immigration, a man named Dr.
H. W. Ward proposed founding another black colony in the Lake Osakis area,
whose residents had supported Lincoln and black suffrage, but after encoun-
tering "a number of difficulties," Ward noted, he abandoned the scheme.[21]

A few black men in rural Minnesota could and did escape the limitations
of farm labor if they possessed the skills to barber and charm to attract white
customers. Prince Honeycutt had served during the Civil War as camp boy
for Captain James Compton. After the war, Compton brought Honeycutt
home with him. In time the former slave became a barber and married a white
woman, living out his life in Fergus Falls and speaking against the rise of antiblack activity that had appeared in the area,. Mark Cane was once sold as a
slave for a thousand dollars to become an orderly in the Union army and later
moved to New Ulm, Minnesota, where he became a barber and his wife was a
hairdresser.[22] The chance of a reasonably comfortable life existed not on the
farmland but in towns; and few towns needed more than one barber. Thus,
the "bridge of gold" for black Minnesotans, most of whom had come from a
hopeless life in Southern agriculture, led, not to Minnesota's farmland, but to
the cities. For some who made that journey to reside in St. Paul's Lowertown
and serve the needs of white employers and clients, Wilkinson's admonition
to the newly minted black citizens, whether hypocritical or myopic, nevertheless must have sounded hollow: "Do not be content to be barbers and porters
in hotels, but be men, hard-handed, laborious men."[23] Though the purpose
of the grand event in January, where he would speak these words, was to
joyously mark the ratification of black suffrage, it was also a moment when
Republicans could celebrate themselves, their own good deeds and expectations of a truly grateful audience.

The year Mankato became an incorporated city, the J. J. Thornton investment firm that began in 1865 became the First National Bank of Mankato with
John Willard as its president, and Wilkinson's Blue Earth County experienced
unprecedented growth and economic vitality.[24] Though homesteaders could

be found in virtually every corner of the old Winnebago Reservation, according to census data of 1870, none was African American. Even so, it is worth
noting that more Blue Earth voters—all males—supported the black suffrage
amendment than there were black men, women, and children residing in the
entire state; and the margin of victory within the county was greater than it
was the year before. The same was true in Nicollet County, where Brevet
Major Thomas Montgomery, whose real estate business thrived, was pleased
to be of use to a patron destined for Congress, reminding each new buyer that
the lofty principle of voting for black suffrage and Republicanism was every
bit as important as enlistment in the army of their adopted and welcoming
country. But in contrast to the returns in Nicollet County, the amendment
once again failed in neighboring Le Sueur County, by a nearly two-to-one
margin, just as it had one year earlier.[25] It was time to show thanks to the black
man's true friend.

In St. Paul, on the evening of November 13, a delegation of black men
visited the International Hotel where congressman-elect for the first district
Morton S. Wilkinson was staying. Thomas Jackson, one of the organizers of
the evening, as well as the convention that would be held in January, stepped
forward and delivered a statement of appreciation of Wilkinson's labors:

> We, the colored citizens of St. Paul, have called on you this evening
> to return you our hearty thanks for the part you have always taken
> in our behalf. You, as one of the great Republican leaders, have ever
> stood up manfully and battled for the great principle of giving to the
> black man his rights as citizen of this State, the franchise of the ballot
> box. Though quite unpopular, the issue was manfully sustained. You
> took the ground at the risk of defeat, and maintained it until at last
> your efforts have been crowned with success; and to you we return
> our hearty thanks. We have long watched the efforts of our friends.
> We know them, and shall ever remember them. And to you, as one of
> the leaders of this great principle, we pledge to the party our hearty
> and undivided support. The battle has been fought. The victory is
> won, and to the victors belong the spoils. We again thank you for
> your efforts in our behalf. [26]

When he finished, the congressman-elect responded. "It was not for you
alone that I labored during long and weary years to produce this grand result. . . . The success has elevated the people of our State to a higher plane,
and a loftier platform, than they ever occupied before." Perhaps still thinking

about Willard Saulsbury, he said, "I shall be proud to represent in Congress the people of a State which forms the vanguard of the army of liberty and re-publican progress—a State whose people have proven that they can conquer their prejudices and perform an act of justice; notwithstanding the teachings which for a hundred years have been warping the judgment of the American people in favor of tyranny, oppression and slavery." In closing, and laying out fully his and the party's expectation of their new brethren, he said,

I am sure that you will exercise the right which is now conferred upon you with that intelligence which will verify the wisdom of those who have labored so long and so faithfully to confer the right of suffrage upon the black man. Again, thanking you for this honor conferred on me, I bid you good night.[27]

PART IV

# The Man in the Shadows

### Daniel D. Merrill

### 1864–1871

# 16

# "OLE SHADY"

*Oh, ya ya! Darkies, laff wid me*
*For de white folks say ole Shady's free . . .*
*Good bye hard work, and never any pay,*
*I'm goin' up Norf where the white folks stay.*

BENJAMIN RUSSEL HANBY, 1861

During the week that followed the breaking news that the white men of Minnesota had extended citizenship to them, Robert Hickman and the black barbers of St. Paul reflected in communion on what it all truly meant. Indeed, they could now vote as political equals to any white employer and Irish laborer, friend and foe, gentleman and ruffian; and as real men they could now hold policy makers accountable for protecting their interests. They could stand tall anywhere and command the respect they were due as men. One could say that it was inevitable. On January 16, 1867, Minnesota's House and Senate, through joint resolution, approved the Fourteenth Amendment—finally, on July 8, 1868, it was ratified. They were citizens of the United States, despite anything Roger Taney had to say eleven years earlier.[1] But this last statewide vote, just a couple of weeks earlier, was special: the state in which they had made their home and staked their future had just made it personal for the very same white men of Minnesota—who had not always been as forward-thinking as their elected officials—and who now seemed to be saying, *you are a part of us.*

Still, some of the black men who assembled that evening had to wonder what it meant when white communities with virtually no black residents supported black suffrage while the city with the most—St. Paul—did not.

It would seem those friendly counties had more to offer if all that mattered was a chance to farm or work in some small town among neighbors who took seriously their support of the Republican Party and legacy of the Great Emancipator. It seemed those counties offered more opportunity, more exposures to the tiny graces of everyday life, the "hellos" and "thank-yous" of white shopkeepers to black customers; the nurturing teacher and welcoming classmates of their children. It seemed that those communities embodied the true Promised Land where the color of their skin was not the emblem of inferiority. Possibly, in time, black people might relocate out there, especially those seeking sanctuary from the increasingly vengeful, unrepentant South, especially those who felt trapped in the poverty and racism that increasingly characterized life in Minnesota's capital city.

And yet, it could also mean that those whites were friendly precisely because there were few blacks in their world. Wherever large numbers of blacks moved, fear and prejudice stood to meet them. This, paradoxically, had been the black experience on free soil. For those who had escaped the agrarian drudgery of slavery, farming had little appeal, as did laboring on a white man's farm, even if he was a Minnesotan. Down South, living in the countryside had meant for some, vulnerability, and St. Paul at least provided the potential of safety in numbers among people of your own kind. There were a few—a very few, indeed—like Maurice Jernigan and R. J. Stockton, who had done quite well in the city. Living in the countryside would mean living away from the contacts they had established, contacts that had made them financially comfortable, contacts with party leaders who had ultimately brought the franchise to the black man. And then there was Robert Hickman, who found in the capital city the best opportunity to establish a church. Ultimately, it was in the city, even in the face of Democratic prejudice and ridicule, that a black man could proudly join other black men to openly celebrate being black, free, and equal, all at the same time.

On Friday evening, November 13, 1868, Robert Hickman, the spiritual leader of the Pilgrim Baptist Society, hosted a gathering of residents of St. Paul's black community. Meeting in the room he and his followers used for worship at Wabasha and Third, they came to celebrate the recent passage of the state referendum that made them politically equal. After the meeting they joined Seibert's Band, which they had previously secured for the occasion, climbed into wagons and carriages, and set off to serenade some of the Republican leaders who had championed their cause. They first went to the residence of Governor William Marshall, where the band played the governor's favorite tunes. After brief speeches, the governor, one of Lincoln's generals who had fought the Indians and then the rebels, invited the group inside, where he served them refreshments, then requested "one of the newly made voters" to sing "Old Shady," a favorite freedom song of Mississippi contraband that he may have first heard in 1864 during the Tupelo, Oxford, and Arkansas campaigns:[2]

> *Oh Massa got scared and so did his Lady,*
> *Dis chile breaks for old Uncle Abby,*
> *"Open the gates out here's old Shady a comin', a comin'."*
> *Hail mighty day.*
>
> *Den away, away, for I can't wait any longer;*
> *Hurra! Hurra! I'm goin' home.*
> *Den away, away, for I can't wait any longer;*
> *Hurra! Hurra! I'm goin' home;*
>
> *I've got a wife, and she's got a baby,*
> *Way up Norf in Lower Canady,*
> *Won't dey shout when dey see ole Shady*
> *Comin', comin'! Hail mighty day.*
>
> *Den away, away, for I can't wait any longer;*
> *Hurra! Hurra! I'm goin' home.*
> *Den away, away, for I can't wait any longer;*
> *Hurra! Hurra! I'm goin' home.*

Considering that some of the leaders had neither been slaves nor were from the Deep South—Jernigan had lived in Minnesota since the beginning of the decade and Grey, from Pennsylvania, had lived in the state since 1857—the colloquial lyrics of the song may have seemed quite foreign to their lips. Nonetheless, those who knew the lyrics, likely including Robert Hickman, a Missouri slave before 1863, gladly obliged the governor's request.

Then they took their leave to next visit the International Hotel, where former senator and now congressman-elect Morton S. Wilkinson stayed. He was the man who perhaps more than any other political leader took the most principled stance, tying his electoral fortunes to the suffrage question, insisting that black suffrage was more important than political gain. From there they went to the homes of St. Paul mayor Jacob Stewart and *St. Paul Press* publisher and editor Frederick Driscoll, before retiring for the evening. Five days later they reconvened at Pilgrim to plan the convention that would be held in January.[3]

The worship hall for the Pilgrim Baptist Society was the appropriate place to meet, for it was not simply a site that had been consecrated through baptism, but one born of the quest for deliverance from slavery. It was their place, and as such, not a space for whose use they needed permission or favor from powerful white men. By 1868, within a span of a few short years, they had acquired the favor of the white men in high places, the same men whom Democrats described seven and a half years earlier as "nearly all the business men of the city";[4] men who in time would arrange a hall for them to use in mass celebration of black suffrage on the first day of the coming year, men who could supply railroads and stage lines to transport at a reduced rate black outstate Minnesotans who wished to join the celebration, men who could join in the glittering array of political luminaries to showcase what undying loyalty to the Party of Lincoln could do for "the late accessories to the Republican ranks."[5]

These were men who had probably helped to commission Seibert's Band for the occasion. Indeed, these white men of power and influence were their friends, men who believed in the promising future of black Minnesota, men who saw in emancipation and black political equality the very essence of a republican civilization truly worthy of enlightenment and the never-ending progress of mankind. And herein lies the paradox of their situation—the pilgrims seemed to know, for all these accumulated reasons, to remain grateful to the gentlemen bountiful; they understood that with their limited numbers, wealth, and education, not to mention the persistent stigma of two centuries of slavery, the dimensions of equality for them, for now, largely existed in compromising degrees, which was why the choice to meet in Pilgrim Baptist's place of worship was so important. November 13, 1868, would be a very special occasion marked not just for the momentous reason for the meeting but also for the fact that they did not need to ask for someone else's room in which to quietly note that they stood equal to all. This was what meeting at Pilgrim meant, officiated by Pilgrim's chosen leader, what Pilgrim itself meant, what manhood and freedom fundamentally meant—having a place of your very own to do with what you wished, to serve God in His Image. Except the Friday meeting would be the last meeting of a political nature that would be held at Pilgrim Baptist for the next eight years. Paradoxically, it seemed that these freedmen, on the safe free soil of Minnesota, and on the threshold of their citizenship, could no longer celebrate the essence of their own freedom.

◆ ◆ ◆ ◆ ◆

*We ought to obey God rather than men.*

ACTS 5:29[6]

Until coming to Minnesota, Hickman only knew a life in slavery. Since before his birth in 1831 his station in life, like that of every other slave living in the state, was a condition of national politics and compromise. In 1820, Missouri, when becoming a state, provided the opportunity for national leaders to strike a plan that many hoped would avert a growing sectional crisis over the spread of slavery into the West. By drawing a line along the southern border of the state, from the Mississippi River to the western border of the Louisiana Territory, the nation then had a demarcating line that would settle the matter between pro- and antislavery forces. Territories north of the line would be free; territories south, slave. But Missouri, no longer a territory, but situated nonetheless north of its southern border, would remain slave, surrounded on three sides by free soil, and it was to become the epicenter of national strife.

Thus, logistically understandable and legalistically clear, Missouri, the basis for a political solution and the gateway to western expansion, would inevitably become a house of cards especially when war was finally declared. No amount of legalism alone could change the heart and mind of a resolute people. Established as a means for sectional peace and nurtured as a Union state, it would in time become the site of some of the most vicious fighting ever witnessed during the Civil War as pro-Union "red legs" and Jayhawkers and Confederate "bushwackers" waged an unrelenting campaign of reprisals against each other and the civilian population caught in between. It was a time when men of God cited economic determinism and "a legalistic interpretation of the Scriptures" to justify or condemn the practice of slavery.[7] One observer noted, "Both sides used the Bible to bolster their argument."[8] Churchgoers were choosing sides. Even the Baptists were divided over the issue of union and slavery, a division that continued years later.

The division between Baptists in the southern states over the issue of slavery had roiled since the first quarter of the century. Many of the first opponents of slavery came from the lower economic brackets of society—the yeoman farmers found among the non-slaveholding majority of the population of the South. In the Upper South, where plantation life was not on a scale so extensive, this was especially so. In Virginia and Kentucky, from which many of the earliest Missourians would come, Baptist associations passed resolutions against slavery. In 1828 the Cherokee Creek Baptist Church sent a statement to the Holston Valley Baptist Association, in eastern Tennessee, against the trafficking of slaves.[9] In Kentucky, Baptist churches and associations, known as the "Friends of Humanity," passed resolutions of nonfellowship with slaveholders. Many of these Baptists left Kentucky for Missouri, to escape a system that was as debilitating economically as it was injurious to their sensibilities, in either instance strengthening the antislavery sentiment in that state. David Marshall, later father of the fifth governor of Minnesota, was one of those men. Another head of a Baptist family, Thomas Lincoln, father of Abraham Lincoln, left Kentucky for Indiana and Illinois. Church historian William W. Barnes wrote, "Of all the divisive issues in American life in the second quarter of the nineteenth century, slavery cut the deepest because it was at once a political, economic, social, moral, and religious issue." But it was not until 1833 that the first tremor from a leadership body was felt.[10]

In December of that year, the Board of the General Convention for Foreign Missions, located in Boston, a city by now identified with abolition thought, received a communication from the Baptist ministers in and near London on the question of slavery. During the previous year, under the leadership of English Baptist missionaries in Jamaica, the slaves on that island had been emancipated. In celebration of that victory, the London ministers urged the American Baptists to end slavery in the United States. Nine months later, however, on September 1, the Boston board politely declined: "Resolved, That while, as they trust, their love of freedom and their desire for the happiness of all men are not less strong and sincere than those of their British brethren they cannot as a board interfere with a subject that is not among the objects for which the Convention and the board were formed."[11] In his most hopeful of terms that Baptists in the South would come to realize the error of their slaveholding ways, the Reverend Dr. Lucius Bolles, editor of the *Cross and Journal*, issued what seemed to be an apology for his brethren:

> There is now a pleasing degree of union among the multiplying
> thousands of Baptists throughout the land. . . . Our Southern
> brethren are liberal and zealous on the promotion of every holy
> enterprise for the extension of the gospel. They are generally, both
> ministers and people, slave-holders, not because they think slavery

right, but because it was firmly rooted long before they were born and because they believe that slavery cannot be instantly abolished. We are confident that a great portion of our brethren at the south would rejoice to see any practicable scheme devised for relieving the country from slavery.

The issue was so delicate that more would be forever lost—the union of the Baptist community—than gained—the emancipation of slaves:

> We have the best evidence that our slave-holding brethren are Christians, sincere followers of the Lord Jesus. . . . We cannot, therefore, feel that it is right to use language or adopt measures which might tend to break the ties that unite them to us in our General Convention and in numerous other benevolent societies.

Simply put, "It is not the duty of the Baptist General Convention, or of the Board of Missions, to interfere with the subject of slavery."[12] In this, the editor of the *Cross and Journal* likely expressed the attitude in the 1830s of the vast majority of Baptists, North and South, "working together in the General Convention . . . evinc[ing] a wise precaution and respect to subjects irrelevant to the single and grand purpose of the Baptist General Convention, which is the publication of the gospel to the heathen world."[13]

But working together proved increasingly difficult. "If the members of the Board in Boston had continued this attitude," Barnes wrote, "there might have been no break. But abolitionists were active and persistent. Churches and associations were won over, first to condemnation of slavery and then to nonfellowship with those who had any sort of connection with slavery."[14] A Northwest Convention, which covered northern Illinois, northern Indiana, and parts of Michigan and Wisconsin, was formed in 1841 by Baptists who migrated from the East. Thomas Ward Merrill, a young New Englander who settled in Michigan, and father of the man who would be the patron of Robert Hickman, was part of this migration. To Dr. J. M. Peck, an influential missionary, they constituted "a dangerous element of abolitionism and sectional strife."[15] Barnes noted that "many Baptists in New England preferred to remain with the Boston Board in the hope and expectation of influencing the Board to do some act that would cause a rupture with the South."[16] Slave ownership, insisted the Southerners, was a constitutional right that "insurrectionists" (the abolitionists) were determined to deny free and loyal

Americans. "Abolitionism was unscriptural . . . against the national constitution," declared the alarmed Southerners; "was against the peace and prosperity of the churches, and dangerous to the permanency of the union."[17] They insisted that their contributions to the Board of Foreign Missions and to the American and Foreign Bible Society should be withheld until they were assured that these agencies "had no connection with antislavery." They concluded, "If satisfactory information be not obtained upon this subject, we recommend the formation of a Southern Board, through which our funds may be directly transmitted."[18] Barnes noted, "Baptists in the South were almost unanimous for separation."[19] The die was cast. By 1845, Northerners had accepted that disassociation was inevitable, as reflected by the statement drafted by New York Baptists:

> For ourselves we deplore the necessity of division, but when things
> reach such a crisis as they appear to have done, deplore it as we may,
> there is no prospect of peace or comfort in the continuance, and
> weakness rather than wisdom would yield to efforts to affect it. . . .
> Why is it not best that our Southern brethren take their position on
> one side of the line and we take ours on the other, and engage in
> the various deportments of benevolent effort with renewed zeal and
> increased liberality?[20]

In 1845 the split was finalized, and in 1846, the Missouri Baptist General Association joined the Southern Baptists. Yet, not all Missouri Baptists shared the view of the new Southern Baptist Convention. In the 1850s, the First Baptist Church in Springfield hired Rev. George White to preach to the growing congregation. While still living in Kentucky, White had come to the conviction that slavery was wrong and freed his slaves before heading west. "The willingness of the church to call a man of strong anti-slavery convictions to slavery was still alive in Missouri in the 1850s," Rev. Wayne Bartee wrote. "Although most people in Springfield were Southern in their background and political viewpoints, they elected an 'unconditional union' man to oppose Missouri's secession when the moment of decision came." In the Springfield area, church buildings were taken over by armies, and church services were nearly nonexistent, save for the well-armed parson. As Bartee wrote, "The outbreak of the Civil War in 1861 shattered all plans and hopes for the church's growth, cancelled all services for over five years and nearly destroyed the congregation."[21]

No more violent a place was Boone County, situated in the heart of the state, known as "Little Dixie," where residents commonly embraced but one opinion: "Little Dixie is of the very essence of the Old South, more Dixie than Dixie . . . and to this day it remains unreconstructed."[22]

> *It's the heart of Missouri, blooded of three,*
> *Virginia, Kentucky, and Tennessee,*
> *It's a tall spare man on a blue-grass hoss*
> *It's sugar cured ham with raisin sauce,*
> *It's coon dog, coon, persimmon tree,*
> *It's son, or brother named Robert E. Lee.*
> *It's tiger stalking a jay hawk bird*
> *It's the best hog-callin' that ever you heard*
> *It's fiddler fiddling you out of your seat,*
> *Fiddler fiddling you off your feet*
> *It's blue bird singing in a hawthorn thicket*
> *It's vote to a man the Democratic ticket.*[23]

Organized in the same year as statehood by a small group from Kentucky led by David McClanahan Hickman, others from upper Southern states, notably Kentucky, Tennessee, and Virginia, brought slaves and the slaveholding traditions with them to cultivate crops they had always known—hemp and tobacco. Over the years, they enacted laws that prohibited speaking and writing against slavery, teaching a slave to read and write, and allowing freed slaves into the state; slave marriages were not recognized. But Hickman was a curious breed in that his interests did not just reside with tending to the business of his plantation but also included a profound commitment to education, to which he devoted much of his efforts as a politician and businessman. He bred the same passion into his son, who charted the family ventures even further than his namesake.[24]

Within the community of slaveholders, David Henry Hickman could be considered, in the context of the times, an enlightened man following in his father's footsteps and contributing, as he did, to early education in Boone County, education for women, and securing the work of his father, who sponsored the bill in the state assembly to create the University of Missouri. Hickman's business ventures spread beyond the plantation, into railroads (he built and owned two), insurance, livestock breeding, banking, brokering real estate, hauling freight, and serving in elective office. He was able to do all this because he understood how to read the signs and make the adjustments necessary to advance his interests.

*Crisp brown cracklin's and hot corn pone*
*It's cat tail clean fried to the bone,*
*It's hominy grits and none of your scrapple,*
*It's mellow pawpaws and the Jonathan apple,*
*It's sorghum sweetenin' and belly-warming corn*
*It's old Jeff Davis a-blowin' on his horn,*
*Unreconstructed, it rares and bites,*
*At touch of a rein that will curb its rights.*

In the 1850s, while serving in the state assembly, young Hickman was a Whig who cowrote legislation that required 25 percent of the state's revenue to be apportioned for common schools in Missouri, which the general assembly approved. But when the Whigs disbanded, he joined his Boone County constituents in forming the Democratic Party, supporting the ever-amplifying voices that espoused states' rights and slavery. Yet, even as a plantation owner Hickman's wealth was increasingly focused on developing Boone County into one whose economy did not heavily rely on the plantation system or slave labor. To do this, he needed and increasingly relied on infusions of federal dollars, whether in his hauling business for Fort Leavenworth or building railroads. In either case, they gave him an investment in having Missouri remain in the Union.

Such work was dangerous, however. Survival was paramount, and Hickman showed his ability to maneuver away from the crosshairs. In July 1864, "Bloody Bill" Anderson and his guerrilla band raided Huntsville and robbed five merchants of $30,000, and the Randolph County treasury was rifled for $18,000. On September 27, Anderson's men perpetrated the massacre of Centralia. Merchants and bankers in Columbia worried that they were next. Three days later, the First National Bank of Columbia issued a notice that it was closing. Three months later, Hickman, the bank president, opened the Boone County Savings Association, a state bank that was intended to draw sympathy from supporters of states' rights.

Through all the turbulence his fortunes appeared to remain secure and he was an ever-devoted member of the Baptist church. Having united with the church at fifteen years of age, he served for years as moderator of Little Bonne Femme Association, and at the time of his death, as moderator of the General Association. He was by many accounts "a most amiable Christian, and one among the most liberal of the denomination, contributing generously to an endowment at William Jewell College of which he served for several years as trustee and for one year as President of the Board. He was foremost in establishing the Baptist College (later named Stephens College) at Columbia. The rule of his life was to give 'as the Lord had prospered him.' "[25] And, as time passed, his prosperity would rely less on the slaves on his plantation. Nonetheless, it would only be the military victory of the Union army and ratification of the Thirteenth Amendment that would ultimately force Hickman the master to relinquish his slaves. Hickman the slave did not wait for that glorious day, leaving as he did two years earlier.

Despite the laws, Robert had learned to read and write, likely with the tacit support of his master, and he was allowed to preach off the plantation, which was possible because as a rail-splitter working on one of his master's railroad ventures he could travel and preach to whomever he met. Indeed, he had been called by the Lord and his master seemed to respect that. Yet, while his soul was free, as a slave his body was not. Thus, he felt incomplete as a creation of God; only through freedom could he be made whole.

The Baptists had split over the issue of slavery, and in 1846, the Missouri Baptist General Association joined the Southern Baptist Convention, an explicitly proslavery denomination.[26] Theirs was a belief that a stout wall existed between spiritual and temporal equality, and they upheld the doctrine expressed in the following passage: "The Scripture, far from making any Alteration in Civil Rights, expressly directs, that every Man abide in the Condition wherein he is called, with great Indifference of Mind concerning outward circumstances."[27] Simply put: Robert Hickman, the slave, could not serve God here. Not even his master could protect him during these terrible times. Only God could. Religious freedom necessitated personal freedom, the kind of freedom that allowed him to give voice to his conscience—his Lord's will. Northern Baptists understood this. In accordance with the tenets of the Baptist faith, he would lead his flock to the Promised Land.[28]

> Den away, away, for I can't wait any longer;
> Hurra! Hurra! I'm goin' home.
> Den away, away, for I can't wait any longer;
> Hurra! Hurra! I'm goin' home.

# 17

# CALLED TO SERVE

*Fear not them that kill the body but are
not able to kill the soul.*

MATTHEW 10:28

Setting foot on the free soil of St. Paul in the spring of 1863 was as threatening for Hickman and his followers as had been fleeing through the Confederate-guerrilla-infested Missouri countryside and ending up drifting on a barge on the calm waters of the Mississippi. A mob in St. Paul, already agitated by the rumor that this boatload of contraband had been brought to the city to take jobs from white laborers, stoned the boat until the captain ordered that they continue upstream to Fort Snelling, where they could safely disembark. But their Promised Land was not there under the protection of Union arms nor in the surrounding countryside, nor on the farmland they passed as they sailed northward, land that required the kind of labor they hoped to leave back in Missouri. Most of them came to realize that, despite the hostile reception at Lowertown, it was within the city of St. Paul that they faced the greater prospect of finding a new kind of freedom.[1]

They found temporary housing in an old building located on the bluff near the corner of Hill and Third Streets and remained there until housing and employment were secured, holding prayer meetings wherever they could, including in the home of a black woman named Mrs. Caroline Nelson, on Fifth Street between Washington and Franklin Avenues. In November 1863, the group succeeded in renting the lodge rooms of the Good Templars in Concert Hall on Third Street between Market and St. Peter, meeting "once or twice a week." In time, being too strapped to pay the rent, they were forced to worship in several other locations around the commercial district.[2]

By the end of the year, realizing they needed help in order for their church to secure a stable footing, they decided to approach the one church that was best situated to help. Thus, in January 1864, Hickman and group member Thomas Scott wrote to the largest in the city, the all-white 162-member First Baptist Church. On behalf of the fifteen "Colored Baptist members of Saint Paul," they said, "we have organized ourselves but we do not feel satisfied without been [*sic*] united to the church and then bee [*sic*] a branch from your church buy [*sic*] a request from the members."[3] J. H. Randall, church clerk for First Baptist, later reported:

> In the month of January, we read a communication from a company
> of col'd people then meeting in the Ancient Hall requesting to be a
> branch of our church. They being Baptists, their request was granted
> and since then we have had them under our watch care and supervi-
> sion as members with us of the Church of the Living God. Of the
> [numbers] rec'd by baptism 9 were from the Col'd branch and 13
> col'd people have been rec'd upon the Christian experience. We have
> been compelled to exclude 4 of the col'd members for grievous sins.[4]

The "grievous sins" that compelled First Baptist to exclude nearly a third of the people who had escaped from slavery in Missouri were left discreetly undefined. Thus, the mission for the colored Baptists of St. Paul was created, worshipping under the tutelage of First Baptist. The word "pilgrim" had not yet become their formal name.

Within mission status, members of the colored branch wished to receive the sacrament of baptism from an ordained minister; and since Hickman was not ordained, they had to go to First Baptist. Thus, throughout the winter members of the mission attended church services at First Baptist "to relate their Christian experience at the Colored Branch and ask for the sacrament of baptism."[5] Still, Hickman recognized that as supportive as First Baptist had been, it was time to move closer to his dream of an independent church. In October 1866 he and a delegation of his members took the first step. "A letter from the Col'd Branch [was] signed by nine of the members requesting letters of dismission so as to enable them to form a separate organization. On mo-tion the following committee was appointed to meet and confer with them—Deacon Cavender, Bros. Prescott, Sherie, Randall, and Merrill."[6]

In light of the quick succession of major decisions, three key issues were addressed: the sincerity of their calling to be an independent church, their commitment to remaining with the small but growing Minnesota Baptist Association, and the acquisition of a permanent place for worship. It was during these meetings that Hickman probably laid out the long-term vision in which he foresaw Pilgrim Baptist Church as the center of all manner of religious, social, and educational uplift for the small but growing black community of St. Paul. Hickman's ambitious and enterprising spirit impressed the men from First Baptist, all people of considerable standing within the business community of St. Paul.[7] It had to be gratifying to hear the aspirations of those who, so recently out of slavery, were highly motivated and best poised to advance their race and larger community all in the service of their Lord and Savior.

These men, no doubt seeing Hickman's potential, could help him avoid being ensnared by unscrupulous speculators by introducing him to the right people, prominent realtors and bankers—men like Charles Oakes, the senior partner of St. Paul's largest and oldest banking house, Borup and Oakes, and brother of George H. Oakes, a member of First Baptist Church.[8] And knowing the impecunious status of the group of the new arrivals, the men of First Baptist understood how to sort through the intricacies of capital and property while acting fully within the service of their faith, their church, and their colored Baptist brethren.

It would prove to be the thirty-two-year-old Daniel David Merrill who became central to the work. Born in Comstock, Kalamazoo County, Michigan, on February 16, 1834, and educated at Kalamazoo College from 1851 to 1854, Merrill brought a remarkable degree of business acumen and experience to service. He came to St. Paul in 1855, when the city was in its infancy, to immediately become engaged in real estate before taking office as deputy city treasurer. In 1856 he joined First Baptist Church, by letter, and helped to organize the YMCA in the city, serving as its secretary and treasurer. Meanwhile, his considerable business skills helped him to soon become eminently successful.

During the Civil War, Merrill was secretary and treasurer of the United States Christian Commission, and would become treasurer of the Minnesota Baptist State Convention from 1865 to 1890, when he would be elected its president for the next four years. In 1857 he stumped the territory with Carl Schurz, Galusha A. Grow, Schuyler Colfax, and other nationally prominent Republicans of the day. Within a very short time he had impressed powerful men in the financial and political quarters of the city and soon-to-be state. As such, he was in the optimum position to negotiate a property deal on behalf of the Baptists.[9]

His service was very much in keeping with his family legacy of religious and educational entrepreneurialism that started in Maine at the turn of the century. "There has, without any doubt," noted D. T. Magill, a chronicler of the family, "been no family which has had so large and so long-continued an influence in Baptist affairs as the Merrills of Maine, Michigan, Nebraska, Minnesota, New York, and Maryland, from 1805 to 1907."

His grandfather, the Reverend Daniel Merrill, was born at Georgetown, Massachusetts, and at seventeen enlisted in the militia, serving until the end of the Revolutionary War. After military service he attended Dartmouth College and studied for the ministry; once ordained he settled in Nottingham West, New Hampshire, and afterward at Sedgwick, Maine. He was for years a member of the Governor's Council, and was one of the founders and promoters of what is now Colby College, at Waterville, New Hampshire. His impressive skills in organizing and weaving political favor were quite evident in his work to build a society of Baptists. In 1805 Daniel Merrill, pastor of the Congregational church in Sedgwick, Maine, was converted by his own studies to the Baptist faith and was baptized by immersion along with 120 members of his church. The town voted to call their society a Baptist church, and elected Daniel Merrill as its pastor. When the Sedgwick church was a Congregational church it was the largest and most influential church in Maine. Merrill was evangelistic and had a number of young men studying for the ministry. He had formed an educational society, of which he was the president and the chief contributor, to help these young men. This society received some funding from other churches. When he became a Baptist the society and its work went with him, and it was for several years the first and only Baptist educational society in America.[10]

From the start Merrill called for the establishment of a college and seminary in the Maine district. In 1811 he secured a charter for the Maine Literary and Theological Institution, which later developed into Colby College. He was a member of the first board of trustees and remained one of its most important and influential members until his death. He was also chairman of a committee whose action resulted in the organization of the Northern Baptist Educational Society and of the Newton Theological Institution.[11]

Three years before Merrill converted to the Baptist faith, his third son, Thomas Ward Merrill, was born. "The most natural fruit of the thought-provoking circumstances in which he was reared was to create in the boy an energetic loyalty to Baptist principles and prospects and a love for knowledge." In 1820 Thomas entered the Latin school at Waterville (later to be known as Waterville College) and was under the instruction of George Dana

Boardman, who would later join the Baptist board for foreign missionary work in India. Thomas Merrill was one of the young men who came to him with the intent of becoming a missionary. After four years of study, he graduated from college and entered Newton Theological Institution, graduating in 1828, to teach in the New Hampton (New Hampshire) Literary and Theological Institution. Within the year he set out westward for the frontier in Michigan.[12]

He spent the summer and early fall of 1829 traveling by foot to the western part of the territory. In October he was at Ann Arbor village, preaching there and in the vicinity. On November 23, he opened a school in Ann Arbor but was denied a charter from the territorial legislature. Instead, the legislature granted a charter to an academy whose trustees were residents of the village. By the fall of 1831, Merrill's school had closed, leaving an open field for the rival. The chartered academy eventually became the University of Michigan. That September Merrill went to Pontiac to present and receive endorsement for a new academy to the Michigan Baptist Association. Traveling to New York in October, he gained an endorsement from the Baptist Convention "by the leading brethren present," and later, on April 27, 1832, from the American Baptist Home Mission Society in New York. Later that year, the society would grant him its first commission. Eventually, on April 22, 1833, with the help of important political allies, he received at last a charter for the establishment of the Michigan and Huron Institute, "location not designated."[13]

With the school now chartered but not yet located, Merrill made "long journeys over primitive roads to meetings" at Clinton, Troy, Comstock, and any number of other towns, both large and small. Finally, after several frustrating letdowns, Merrill secured a site at Bronson (now Kalamazoo), where the school was set in operation and developed into what eventually became Kalamazoo College. Thomas Merrill served for many years as one of its trustees and later as endowed chair of practical theology. In 1847 he moved to Lansing, where he lived for thirty years, during which time he amassed a considerable fortune and attended all meetings of the association conventions as the agent of benevolent societies.[14] At his death he left a considerable estate to the institution he had founded.

Thomas Merrill's younger brother, Moses, followed in the family tradition, when, at the age of thirteen, he was converted by a sermon his father preached. Licensed to preach in April 1829, he left Sedgwick to join his brother Thomas in Ann Arbor to help him establish the school. But in the summer of 1832, Moses and his wife accepted an appointment to work among the Indians at Sault Ste. Marie; by the spring of 1833, the board ordered them to "a more promising field in the great Indian Territory of the West." In late fall they arrived at Bellevue, now Nebraska, where the Otoe Indians were located, two hundred miles from the nearest white settlement. There they built a school for children, preached through an interpreter until they had learned the language, and provided medical assistance. It would be here that Moses succumbed "to tubercular troubles" on February 6, 1840, and was buried on the eastern bank of the Missouri River.

The tradition of religious leadership continued with the Reverend S. P. Merrill, the son of Moses and a graduate of Rochester Theological Seminary, who held pastorates in New York and Maine, and who served as secretary of his alma mater for over fourteen years. G. E. Merrill, son of St. Paul's D. D. Merrill, would become a successful businessman like his father, who strengthened "all manner of Baptist interests" in Annapolis, Maryland.[15] It was into this tradition—the religious, educational, financial, and missionary zeal in the name of the Baptist faith—that Daniel David Merrill, "the Minnesota Merrill," and son of Thomas Ward Merrill, was born.

Acquiring and holding the title to the property in trust for Hickman and his followers for a mutually agreed time was considered more Christian-like than engaging the church in "the unholy practice of usury." Protocol required, however, that such an arrangement be requested by Hickman. On November 13, Hickman formally requested the trustees of First Baptist to purchase in trust for them the lot on the southwest corner of Thirteenth and Cedar Streets. Adhering every bit as much to formality, the trustees approved the deal.[16]

One day later, on November 14, the committee reported back to the church membership recommending that they approve the request of Hickman's congregation to form a separate church.[17] "After the prayer meeting the committee appointed to meet with the Colored Brothers and Sisters reported . . . the following recommendation—that all of the colored members who desired to form a new organization be granted letters [of dismission]." Trustee Merrill made the motion: "That the following named Colored Brothers and Sisters be granted the letters of dismission from this church for the purpose of organizing an independent Baptist Church." The motion was seconded and approved. Fielding Combs, Adeline Combs, R. Hickman, Matonia Hickman, Henry Moffitt, Charlotte Moffitt, George Chambers, Eliza Chambers, Melvinia Asak, and Giles Crenshaw, all in attendance, joined in singing with the congregation; then they left as a group, as the total membership of the newly formed Pilgrim Baptist Church. Motivated by their own early history the First Baptist leadership—all New Englanders and religious descendants of America's first Pilgrims—agreed "to assist the Colored Brethren and Sisters in forming a new church."[18] In this, they were carrying on the tradition that was incumbent to the soul of their church legacy. As future pastor the Reverend John Brown would later say in a sermon he delivered during the seventy-fifth anniversary of First Baptist, "In New England we find entire congregations setting up their light and their churches in the wilderness, having been driven from across the ocean for conscience sake."[19]

◆ ◆ ◆ ◆ ◆

*A Teacher should bring books with her sufficient to begin a school, as there is no bookstore within three hundred miles.*

THOMAS WILLIAMSON, MISSIONARY AT KAPOSIA,
TO WILLIAM SLADE, MARCH 1847

In 1846 the Board of National Popular Education was organized in New England. Its object was to supply the new settlements of the West with competent female Christian teachers—all evangelical denominations uniting in the movement with William Slade, former governor of Vermont and now its general manager and corresponding secretary. In May 1847 the first class of thirty-three teachers was convened at Albany, New York, for general instruction and individual assignment. In anticipation of this, three months earlier, Presbyterian missionary and physician Thomas S. Williamson, while at Dakota chief Little Crow's village, Kaposia (now South St. Paul), asked his friend Slade to recommend a teacher for a school he hoped would be established "near the [principal] village of white men," named St. Paul.[20] He specified that the desired qualities for the new instructor must include not only competence but also racial tolerance: "A teacher for this place should love the Savior and for His sake be willing to forego not only many of the religious privileges and elegancies of a New England home, but some of the neatness also. She should be entirely free from racially intolerant on account of color, for among her scholars she might find not only English, French, and Swiss, but Sioux and Chippewa, with some claiming kindred with the African stock."[21]

Harriet Bishop answered the call and arrived in Minnesota in 1847, after having trained with Catharine Beecher, a reformer and sister of Harriet Beecher Stowe, who believed that women needed to be well educated in order to devote themselves to the moral development and education of their children and their homes.[22]

Bishop established a school in an old blacksmith shop—a mud-walled log hovel covered with bark and chinked with mud, "where on July 19, 1847 ten pioneers, Indian and mixed-blood children came to learn." Six days later she invited them back to attend Sunday school. "The children should not only be taught to read and write," she wrote, "but also to be taught the Word of God."[23] On July 25 she wrote that the first Sunday school was held. Seven students attended, and the mixture of races and ethnicities was such that an interpreter who could speak English, French, and Dakota was required. She invited everyone in town to attend Sunday worship. By the third week, Sunday school enrollment had increased to twenty-five children.

No Baptist church and Sunday school existed north of Iowa, and Bishop was the only person present to provide the community with ministry. This changed in 1848 with the overland arrival in wintry December of Abram Cavender, a blacksmith from New Hampshire. Bishop later noted that when he arrived in St. Paul in 1848, the religious element in the village was greatly reinforced. Together they carried on the work of leading Sunday worship.[24]

Constant petitions to Heaven and to the Baptist Home Mission Society resulted in the appointment of the Reverend John Parsons as missionary to St. Paul on February 8, 1849, one month prior to Minnesota's official recognition as a United States territory. Within six months, a church was formed of twelve members who were settling in the city, including some whose names would later be prominently associated with Minnesota history—Lyman Dayton and Charles Stearns.[25] The island south of St. Paul and one of the largest lakes in what would be Minneapolis were both named after Miss Bishop. But in 1849, she initially only had herself to persevere in creating a religious gathering within "an utterly godless community" that "was not prepared for the rigorous gospel for which the little congregation stood. . . . It was in this village on the edge of an almost [unlimited] wilderness whose only exits were down the river and to the Red River Valley by ox carts that the First Baptist Church began to let its light shine."[26]

The leadership of the First Baptist Church may have felt that they could indeed relate to what Hickman's followers must have been experiencing as these people just out of bondage had followed their "star of destiny" into an unfamiliar and isolating, if not totally hostile, wilderness to wholly devote their lives to God.[27]

The church's reception of the people from Missouri was based, in part, on a liberal sense of ever-evolving purpose and relevance to society. "There is an inescapable social law that if an institution does not make positive and constant contributions—changing them with the needs of the time—it becomes a cumberer of the ground and is doomed either to extinction or to absorption to some larger institution." And proof of its relevance was found in the rapid growth of its membership even during its first year of existence—from twelve members to over forty souls.[28]

A crucial factor to this growth was in the care the church took in rejecting severe and exclusionary prescriptions of faith. In the early days, steeped in the tradition of evangelistic purpose—taking the word to the wilderness— the church was quite wary of beliefs in anything that seemed like "final creedal form," ways that could obstruct the forging of relationships, reaching souls. In fact, at the time of the organization no articles of faith were adopted at all. Instead, that group of twelve bound themselves by a covenant of conduct and life in which the great principles of the gospel were involved but were not stated in definite language. Not until four years later, in 1853, did the church adopt what might be called a set of principles for conduct and life, rejecting the New Hampshire Confession of Faith, only recently adopted as an amendment of the same confession of 1833, which had been a concise statement in harmony with the older doctrines, but expressed in milder form. It was widely accepted by Baptists in the northern and western states; but the St. Paul Baptists chose instead to "maintain the tenets and ordinances now obtained and observed by the American Baptist Home Society and the American Baptist Missionary Union." These two organizations, while never holding a formal creed and while always recognizing the freedom of faith among Baptists, have done much to stabilize the opinion and procedure within the denomination without exercising any direct authority over the churches whatever:

> The minutes of the church are remarkably free from references of any doctrinal controversy. There are indications that at different times over-zealous persons tried to get the church to make certain statements of doctrines or an emphasis of certain doctrines which the majority of the church would not accept. Every such attempt was voted down. To this day the church has kept the reputation of the freedom of the faith without wavering. All types of mind and doctrine are represented in its membership.[29]

Theirs, in short, was intended to be a legacy of inclusion.

In 1817 John Mason Peck, a pastor from New York and commissioner for the "domestic mission" in the Missouri Territory, established the first Sunday schools, women's societies, and missionary societies in the region. He organized the first Baptist churches west of the Mississippi, ordained the first African American clergy in St. Louis, and helped found Alton Seminary in Alton, Illinois, which later became Shurtleff College. Peck also served two terms in the Illinois legislature and was a strong advocate for the abolition of slavery. Though he faced harsh criticism from the antimission, "old school" Baptists who did not believe in Sunday schools, colleges, seminaries, or missions, and the Triennial Convention, which had instructed him to work among the Indians, Peck continued to work in St. Louis, receiving financial support from supporters in Massachusetts and the American Baptist Home Mission Society. It was there that he met John Berry Meachum.[30]

Reverend Meachum, a former slave and skilled carpenter who bought freedom for himself and his family, assisted American Home Mission pioneer Peck with the church and Sunday school Peck founded in St. Louis in 1817. Black and white, free and bond worshipped together in First Baptist until 1822, when black congregants formed a separate branch. Peck ordained Meachum in 1825 when he founded the first African Baptist Church, the first Protestant church established for African Americans west of the Mississippi River. Shortly after a brick church was erected, Meachum and Peck opened a day school, the "Candle Tallow School," so called because classes had to be conducted in a secret room with no windows to avoid being discovered by the sheriff. Missouri law forbade teaching free or enslaved blacks to read and write. In 1847 even more restrictive laws were enacted by the general assembly of Missouri. Undeterred, Meachum, with the help of black and white friends, raised the necessary funds to purchase a steamboat that he would sail on the Mississippi; the river was federal territory where slavery was not recognized. Within months, he stocked the boat with a library and classrooms, and christened it "Freedom School."[31]

It was a testament to the importance of strong leadership and it was coincidental, for it was in this same year—1847—that Harriet Bishop first arrived in the village of St. Paul. "To two persons, Miss Harriet Bishop and A. H. Cavender, are due the qualities of mind and leadership that kept the First Baptist Church alive in the first two years."[32] It was this same legacy that framed the discussion when the delegation from First Baptist met with Hickman's followers on the subject of naming a pastor.

# 18

# A CHURCH IS BORN AND
# A PASTOR IS FOUND

*A church may be a peculiar institution in a community but
it was not free from those laws of social change through
which all institutions have to pass.*

REVEREND JOHN R. BROWN, OCTOBER 5, 1924

In the antebellum South, slaves were allowed to preach only with permission
from their owners and normally were restricted to the area of the local parish.
The duties of black preachers included conducting funerals and sanctifying
marriages among slaves, and acting as crucial mediators between Christian
belief and the experiential world of the slave. "In effect, they were helping to
shape the development of bicultural synthesis, an Afro-American culture, by
nurturing the faith of Christian communities among blacks, slave and free."[1]
At the root, however, was the unavoidable fact that while gatherings were
at times clandestine, such gatherings, funerals, and weddings that preachers performed always rested on the permission of masters and were subject
to their whims. Yet it was the ceremony that was the life's blood of a slave
community.

Funerals were the last in a cycle of ceremonies during the life of a slave.
Sunday worship, prayer meetings, revivals, Christmas "baptizings," weddings, funerals, all came and went, alternating like the seasons of the year,
from day to day, from week to week, from month to month, in the life of
the plantation. To the slaves, these services and celebrations were special
times, counteracting the monotony of life. Slaves asserted repeatedly in these

seasons of celebration that their lives were special, their lives had dignity, and their lives had meaning beyond the definitions set by slavery. In their meetings, slaves enjoyed fellowship, exchanged mutual consolation, and gave voice to individual concerns. And here too, some slaves found a place to exercise their talents for leadership.[2]

Presiding over these ceremonies was the slave preacher, leader of the slaves' religious life and, in turn, a dominant figure in the slave community. Usually illiterate, the slave preacher often had native wit and unusual eloquence, and was inspiring enough to preach and minister in a very difficult situation. Carefully watched and viewed with suspicion, the preacher had to straddle the conflict between the demands of conscience and the orders of the masters. In many instances, masters thought preachers were ruining their slaves. "The slave preacher who verged too close on a gospel of equality within earshot of whites was in trouble." But if he was deemed trustworthy, he was permitted to travel to neighboring places to conduct prayer meetings, allowing him, at safe moments, to share information about events and relatives who lived in distant places. Essentially it was eloquent preaching that drew and inspired his congregation. Vivid imagery and dramatic delivery were characteristic of the slave preacher's sermon. One white observer said, "[Slave preachers] acquire a remarkable memory of words, phrases, and forms; a curious sort of poetic talent is developed, and a habit is obtained of rhapsodizing and exciting furious emotions." The preacher, even within the strictures of bondage, occupied a position of esteem and authority.[3]

This was the tradition that Hickman and his followers knew when he was a "jackleg" preacher in Missouri. He was the logical selection since he had brought them together and led them to the Promised Land up north. In Minnesota, a Baptist minister (as he was envisioned within the First Baptist tradition) had to be both ordained and formally educated with administrative experience to lead an organization; inspiration was not enough. First Baptist pastors all held advanced degrees. Nothing less was permitted for one of their missions that had requested dismission, and Hickman seemed to recognize this fact. Though he had been called, had the gift of an inspirational speaking manner, and was able to minister to the spiritual needs of the congregation, he lacked experience in administering a Northern Baptist organization that possessed property and had to raise funds and pay bills.

Nonetheless, it was desirable that the pastor-select would not be just any pastor but one who understood and was respected by the members of this congregation of pilgrims who shared in the same adversity to get to Minnesota. That experience crystallized a sense of themselves as devout Christians and sharpened their identity as proud black people. They had not just survived slavery; they had prevailed over it when they broke free of the chains that had bound them, for subjugation was complete when the subjugated capitulated to it. Their flight from Egypt into the Land of Canaan proved them to be children of God doing his will. The legitimate pastor was one who understood and respected this birth of a legacy.

It was the spring of 1863 when the Hickman group arrived at Fort Snelling, the same moment when the Dakota and Winnebago were about to be removed from their Minnesota homes. Hickman and his followers caught the eye of William Norris, a missionary who was there to minister to the spiritual needs of Indians who had converted to Christianity, and at some point they talked, Baptist (as they had come to realize) to Baptist. The issue became, where could the people from Missouri go? Their hostile reception at Lowertown in St. Paul had convinced many of them that the Saintly City was not a safe haven. The missionary would have known about First Baptist Church of St. Paul, for it was the largest and most established church in Minnesota where the Christian spirit was generous and true. Indeed, Norris himself, the first white man they had befriended since arriving at the fort, seemed likewise to be generous and true. On his word, they returned to St. Paul.[4]

Three years later, in 1866, as the delegation from First Baptist worked with Hickman's group in starting their independent church, Hickman may have suggested that the Reverend Norris, who seemed not to be known at First Baptist (his name does not appear in church records), be their pastor: therefore, the expanded delegation, in the name of Baptist faith, may have interviewed him in that they were still relatively new to the Minnesota Baptist community. According to the Baptist tenets of selecting a pastor, however, it probably was formally left to the members to appoint Norris without need of denominational approval. Accordingly, he was selected to lead the church. Two days later, Hickman and his group formally organized Pilgrim Baptist Church and on November 18, "the ordinance of baptism by immersion was administered from the Pilgrim Baptist Church (Colored) today between 12 and 1 o'clock, by Reverend William Norris, at the Lower Levee."[5] The *Daily Press* proudly repeated the announcement a week later:

A Baptist Church was organized in this city on the 18th last, composed of colored people. Their preacher, W. Norris, baptized eight persons in the Mississippi, near their place of worship. This shows much enterprise among the two hundred people of African descent now living in St. Paul.[6]

It is ironic that the site of their immersion baptism was near the place where they were stoned as they approached the dock, two and a half years before.

Meanwhile, the negotiations with seller Charles Oakes over the property transfer continued for the next several months until an agreement was finally reached. On April 30, 1867, Wakefield recorded,

> The matter of holding in trust, a building lot, in behalf of the
> Colored Baptist Church in St. Paul was presented and voted. We as
> Trustees of the First Baptist Church received the lot in question in
> trust as above and made the proper management with Charles H.
> Oakes the balance due. On motion [the Trustees] voted that
> D. D. Merrill be approached to attend to the matter.[7]

On this lot on Sibley near Morris Street in downtown St. Paul, the members of Pilgrim Baptist, who numbered nine at the time, intended to build a stone-and-wood structure that had an ambitiously large seating capacity of three hundred. Pilgrim was intended to be the center of activity for black St. Paul—the community's church. Notably the members of First Baptist did not appear to see the aspirations of Hickman as extravagant, for it was within the ethos of their own congregation to appreciate such a vision for place of worship. In 1862, in a sermon dedicating their new chapel, Pastor John Pope said,

> Worship in the sanctuary involves other and different conditions. It is
> the united offering of our hearts. It lays under tribute a due proposi-
> tion of pecuniary means. It requires the offering of the heart and
> with it also money. It has in it much that is designed to cultivate and
> gratify a judicious and sanctified taste. It was instituted as a power-
> ful means to affect the interests of the people. As a general thing in
> Christian lands, church edifices reflect the social and religious study
> of the community. Well-located, tasteful, comfortable and liberally
> furnished sanctuaries are never built by a groveling, narrow-minded,
> covetous people. A congregation in an ordinary intelligent and enter-
> prising locality cannot long maintain a respectable position while it is
> contented to serve God in a mean and shabby house.[8]

In 1874 First Baptist Church burned down, but within the year a new building was constructed. When it opened on May 31, it was the largest and most costly church in St. Paul, described in the *Pioneer Press* as "the finest piece of architecture west of Chicago."[9] The Pilgrims needed someone to help them construct an edifice befitting their work in the Lord's name.

♦ ♦ ♦ ♦ ♦

*We empower him to obtain any funds which the friends*
*East may be willing to place at his control for religious and*
*educational purposes.*

D. D. MERRILL, 1853

Born near Aberdeen, Scotland, in 1815, Andrew M. Torbet received an early
education in Edinburgh. While he was still a young man at a mercantile house
his father sent him to America; the rest of the family followed in June 1836.
Settling in Paterson, New Jersey, Torbet became a member of the First Baptist Church of that city. It was here that he received his calling for a life in the
gospel ministry and where he was licensed to preach. Accepting the calling
to a church in Piermont, New York, he was ordained on August 22, 1839.
On that same day, after his ordination, he baptized his mother and father off
the shoreline of the Hudson River. In 1845 he became pastor of the Baptist church in Zion Hill, near Suffield, Connecticut, where he married Caroline Hosmer-King, with whom he had six children. He soon left Zion Hill
for a pastorate in Medina, Ohio, and later served a church in Canton; and in
November 1852 he accepted the call to the pastorate of First Baptist Church
of St. Paul. On December 2 he was formally installed.[10] When he arrived
in the pulpit, the church could already see qualities in him that were critical
to its survival.

Within a year of Torbet's appointment as pastor of First Baptist Church,
in 1853 the trustees felt that rather than have him stay in St. Paul during the
critical early years when its survival was most tenuous, he would better serve
the immediate needs of the church by traveling throughout the territory and
out east to raise money:

To Whom It May Concern: I hereby certify that at a meeting of
the Church held this day, it was resolved that we send our pastor
(Rev. A. M. Torbet) to represent us as a church, and the religious
interests of the territory, at the anniversary of the various societies in
New York, and that we empower him to obtain any funds which the
friends East may be willing to place at his control for religious and
educational purposes and for our own Church edifice founded.
Done by order on our behalf of the First Baptist Church. Daniel D.
Merrill, Church Clerk.[11]

As the financial status of the church stabilized and membership grew, Torbet's stature as a church leader was enhanced. He was then asked to join a fledgling institution of higher learning:

> Feeling, after what I trust has been a full and prayerful consideration of the whole subject, that it is my duty to accept the Financial Agency of the Minnesota Central University pressed upon me by the Board of Trustees. I therefore tender my resignation of the Pastorate of this Church. I shall ever cherish with grateful remembrance the many tokens of kindness which I have received at your hands, and the pleasant years of toil it has been my lot to perform among you. With my poor prayers to God for the continued prosperity of the Church, I remain yours in Christ. A. M. Torbet.[12]

Indeed, the university was a brainchild of the church. The territorial legislature chartered Minnesota Central University in 1854 through the efforts of the Reverend Timothy Cressey, pastor of First Baptist and Torbet's predecessor. The cornerstone was laid in Hastings in 1857 when Torbet joined the university, with territorial governors Alexander Ramsey and Henry H. Sibley, and Cressey present. But the timing for the enterprise and for Torbet's career was unfortunate, because in 1859, when the school doors opened, the university was already in decline owing to dwindling financial support following the Panic of 1857. The building consisted of only one room.[13] Torbet began looking for a new pastorate.

For the next three years, he worked in churches in Taylors Falls and St. Croix Falls, though not as a pastor. By 1862, realizing there were no pastorate opportunities available—his successor, Reverend John Pope, stayed at First Baptist until 1866—Torbet moved to the far Northwest, finding work eventually with the government mail service. In 1868 the board of the Minnesota Baptist Association reported a year of "healthy growth" of 130 Baptist churches embracing a membership of 4,208, ninety-four of whom are ordained ministers. "The people have twenty-five meeting houses in Minnesota and thirty others in the process of erection."[14] The increased possibility of returning to a Minnesota pulpit may have attracted Torbet back to St. Paul. On July 26, the fifty-three-year old former pastor preached a sermon at First Baptist titled "Truth."[15] It was not until September that his son-in-law and church trustee, D. D. Merrill, may have contacted him to expect a call from Robert Hickman requesting on behalf of his congregation that he become Pilgrim's new pastor.

The church had been without an ordained pastor since February, the culmination of tensions that became apparent at a fund-raiser in December. At first all had gone well. "The members of the Colored Baptist Society, called 'Pilgrim Church,' gave quite a festival at Mozart Hall last night, the object being to raise money to build a church." About three hundred persons were in attendance, approximately one-third of whom were white. A string band was in attendance and provided some very fine music during the evening.

"The colored people were all in their holiday dresses," and seemed to enjoy themselves hugely. All were orderly, quiet, and happy. "Every shade and tint of color was visible, from the blackest Aunt Dinah to the brilliantly handsome brunette, with not a drop of negro blood apparently." A supper had been prepared that did great credit to the Pilgrims and it was enjoyed by all. Previous to partaking of the supper, Rev. Mr. Paterson [pastor of First Baptist Church] made a statement in regard to the object of the festival. He said the Pilgrim Baptist Church had recently purchased at great sacrifice among themselves a lot worth $500, and were now anxious to raise means to build a small church on the lot. This was the purpose of the gathering, which went on until late in the evening.[16]

Then what followed best reflected the vulnerability that Norris, Hickman, and the Pilgrims faced in holding a function open to all members of the community, including those whose character was other than that to which the members of Pilgrim Baptist Church aspired and sought to be identified. Two days later, the *Pioneer* could not resist printing the follow-up of the event. Apparently, a group of young blacks, intent on having a more raucous time, wanted to dance later into the evening. The Reverend Norris attempted to oppose this and when they refused to leave, he went into the adjoining room and turned the gas off at the meter, leaving the hall in utter darkness. Two or three young men "mounted his reverence," and were about to rough him up when a policeman came in "and nipped the melee in the bud." Instead, Norris's intervention created more of a commotion. The officer decided that the minister had no right to turn off the gas, but he advised him to prevent the band from playing as it had been hired by the church and was under their orders. When Norris tried to tell the band to leave, the musicians refused to leave because they had made a new contract with the "worldlings" who wished to dance. "The shepherd of the flock," evidently too ineffective in managing his parishioners, "left in disgust, and the dance went on until a late hour."[17]

The reference to Norris as "shepherd of the flock" seemed intended to implicate the so-called worldlings as members of Pilgrim Baptist Church. That idea is implausible, however, since such an association would undermine the respectability of the congregation and their wish for the support of the white community. Still, it seems evident that the bond between the pastor and congregation had ruptured—on one hand, Norris felt abandoned by the congregation and publicly humiliated; on the other, Hickman did not have confidence in Norris's leadership. The festival had commenced without opening words from the symbolic host, the pastor of Pilgrim Baptist. Only Paterson spoke, a man whose church had proved itself to be a genuine patron, a man who within the six months of his arrival, knew enough to show support for Hickman.[18] Within this circumstance William Norris concluded it was time for him to leave, egged on by the mischievous editor of the *Pioneer* who wrote a noxious account of the event titled "Row at de Church":

> Last evening, a poor-looking, shriveled up old darky, blacker than the ten of clubs, or ten black cats in a dark night, handed in the following advertisement for insertion: "The Pilgrim Baptist is a regular nuisance. They are drunkards, liars and adulterers. No confidence can be put in them. I believe that they are a disgrace to the community and much more to the cause of Christ.—Rev. W. Norris, once pastor."
>
> In answer to the question "What's the row?" he straightened himself up to nearly five feet, and with an air of dignity that repelled undue familiarity or further inquiries, exclaimed, "It's all writ down on dat there paper." Now we have no idea that the allegations on "dat paper" are true, and regret that our colored friends, in imitation to white christians, have got into a church brawl. It don't look well, even to "worldlings." We fear "Rev. W. Norris, once pastor," has allowed his passion to get the better of his judgment, to say nothing of his christian character.[19]

With no one speaking in his defense, leaving his reputation to sway alone in the wind, Norris was gone and with him went the official, if not the authentic, leader of Pilgrim Baptist. That role, as far as the congregation was concerned, was still filled by Robert Hickman.

In 1867, within a few months after Merrill secured the property, Pilgrim was able to acquire the lot from First Baptist on which to build a new church, but they had no funds for construction, and the last venture in fund-raising did not go well; the *St. Paul Pioneer* did not help matters.

Within the black community, Hickman was being recognized as a race leader. If the community had its own wealth, his standing alone could generate the funds he needed; but it didn't and he couldn't. The black community, at the end of the 1860s, was predominantly composed of semi- and unskilled laborers. Pilgrims needed the help of white St. Paul, and the *Pioneer* had done its best to taint the Pilgrims as a truly devout congregation. Hickman knew his church needed someone whom the white community already knew. Moreover, he needed to further redeem himself from being associated with an unfortunate incident involving the inebriated behavior of some black picnickers. The *Daily Press*, which was usually supportive of the Pilgrims, reported:

> The colored populations of St. Anthony, Minneapolis and St. Paul united in a massive picnic at Hansen's Gardens in the outskirts of this city. It was designed as a kind of celebration of the anniversary of the emancipation of the slaves of the West Indies, though not exactly in the anniversary day.
>
> The assembly was much divided on opinion as to the best mode of celebrating. Some of those wanted speeches and music, singing, etc., while others desired a grand dance and a celebration of that kind. Brief addresses were made by Rev. Mr. Hickman, pastor of the Colored Baptist Church, and by Rev. D. Cobb of the Jackson Street M. E. Church, he being sent for especially. Shortly after the addresses were over the gayer parts of the congregation began to form with a dance.[20]

The titles "reverend" and "pastor" were misleading since Hickman had not yet been licensed and ordained; but their use may reflect the honorific light in which his members had always seen him—as the only recognized leader of Pilgrim Baptist Church. The article continued:

> The selection of the place for celebration was hardly judicious as some of the men and brothren [*sic*] showed themselves rather weak on the beer question. When our informant left the youths and maidens were whirling in the giddy manner of the dance.[21]

Though the *Press* did not implicate Hickman in acting in a low-class manner, any affiliation with such people might sully the reputation he sought to create, one that was "blameless, the husband of one wife, vigilant, sober, and of good behavior." Indeed, the tenets of the church dictated that a minister should be free from all vices, and "have a good report of them who are without."[22] It would have displeased church officials and it mattered what people thought of him—righteous Christians as well as likely donors.

Weeks later he learned from Trustee Merrill, by now a confidant, that he might be able to secure the services of a highly respected clergyman and fund-raiser—indeed, a former pastor of First Baptist itself as well as a former member of St. Paul's Board of Education, someone who had appreciation for the value of a friendly press. The overture itself would make Hickman and his pilgrims appear to be the epitome of responsible stewardship, the kind of upstanding people whom St. Paul would do well to welcome to its bosom. The proximity of the proposed site to the home of William Marshall, the Missouri-born governor of Minnesota and popular Civil War commander, in itself underscored the rectitude of the venture. On September 13, the *Daily Press* reported:

> The Pilgrim Baptist Colored Church, we understand, have, if the funds necessary for the purpose can be obtained, resolved to build a church edifice upon their lot, situated about half a block west from the residence of Governor Marshall. They have requested Rev. A. M. Torbet to supervise the work for them, and as he is well-known in this city, being formerly the pastor of the Baptist Church here, the community may rely upon the faithful application of any funds. They may subscribe and pay towards the erection of said building. [Members of t]he church are to circulate a subscription paper for this object, and as it is a want deeply felt, we hope our citizens will be ready and willing to assist those who have moved in this matter to supply it, and thus furnish the colored people in our midst with the phase of worship. This work is to be pushed as fast and as far as the funds will permit immediately.[23]

On the same day, "several" black men and women were baptized in the river "at the foot of St. Peter Street. Quite a crowd was in attendance."[24] The message was simple: these colored people, cleansed by God's grace, wishing to be Pilgrims, were not like those other colored people who danced and drank too much and otherwise gave their race and what should have been their most prized possession—the church—a bad name. Yet, Torbet's role, as tactfully described—the same statement appeared in the *Pioneer* and *Dispatch*—was "to supervise the work" rather than pastor the church.[25] It was the *Pioneer*, in its last unfortunate reports on the experiences of Norris, that had made the pastorate too public and undesirable as the newspaper enthusiastically mocked the *inevitable* misadventures of being " 'shepherd' of a colored flock." This characterization largely reflected a city whose history with its black residents was far from stellar, one that had evolved in the twenty years since officially becoming an American settlement.

19

# UNDER HIS STEADY HAND

*Cold! Oh how cold! The bleak, north wind nearly pierced
the vitals on my long walk to Sunday School. No fire had
been made and this prefaced the duties to follow; but was
very happy in telling children and adults the story of the
cross, and pressing their need of a risen Savior.*

HARRIET BISHOP, JANUARY 9, 1849

In 1841 Father Lucien Galtier secured a site for a chapel, a garden, and a
graveyard on the river bluff near the landing that would become the territorial and later the state capital. Here he built a humble log church "so poor," he
said, "that it would well remind one of the stable in Bethlehem." On November 1 he blessed "the new *basilica*, and dedicated it to St. Paul, the apostle of
nations," the namesake so chosen to reflect the variety of races and cultures
that could be seen in the area's earliest population, a population that included
white Americans, Europeans, French Canadians, Dakota, Cree, Ojibwe, and,
to a much smaller degree, African Americans, a place where a black man's
character could often preempt the stigma of color, before the time when the
prejudices of Jacksonian America were enacted into the local social contract.[1]

By 1848 the signs of change were imminent: power was inexorably moving into the hands of men who were white, American, and Protestant, and
codified by laws they promulgated in 1849 that strengthened their position in
matters concerning governance and property. At St. Paul's Central House,
where the territorial legislature met, Gideon Pond, Morton Wilkinson,
and a handful of legislators had argued in vain for a law that would extend

citizenship to all men over twenty-one years of age, instead of white men only. From then on, it would primarily be St. Paul that would witness a history with its black residents that would be far from stellar.[2]

As a city that offered opportunity no other place in the state provided, St. Paul attracted the largest concentration of black residents in the state. And yet, the very concept of a growing black presence had always been the source of consternation among city policy makers and their constituents. Situated at the head of the navigable waters of the Mississippi throughout the 1850s and much of the 1860s, St. Paul was the last stop for blacks running away from slavery, the abject racism of the lower Midwest, or the drudgery of farm labor that was in some ways a slight improvement over what they had left in the South.[3] But in the view of much of white St. Paul the attraction of the city was its own threat. In 1854 legislators representing the city proposed a law that would create a black code for Minnesota. The measure failed, but in the face of the defeat, a legislator from St. Paul reportedly threatened to propose a bill in the next session that would require blacks to live in Hennepin County. Though nothing came of that measure, the message to black arrivals was clear: go anywhere else but here.[4]

By 1863 Minnesota suffered a major labor shortage due to the high numbers of young men who had gone off to war, a need, as the *Daily Press* reported, that not even "five thousand Negroes" could satisfy.[5] Alarmed at the possibility of contraband flooding northward, several state legislators and a segment of the white community began characterizing the Mississippi as a "conduit for blacks and mulattoes fleeing southern states bordering the river." Legislators feared that blacks would compete for jobs customarily held by poor whites, thus denying that class of citizens a livelihood. Furthermore, it was felt that whites unwilling to work or compete against black labor might resort to violence. They had seen it happen in other Northern cities. At worst, the detractors claimed that black migrants would become paupers and wards of the state.[6]

The concern expressed by the legislators was not entirely unfounded, for in the opening years of the Civil War blacks and fugitive slaves came to Minnesota. Between 1860 and 1870 the black population nearly tripled in size, growing from 259 to 737. In January 1860 a bill was introduced into the state House of Representatives that would have prevented the further migration of blacks into the state and required registration of those already in residence. The 1860 bill would have discouraged the further migration of blacks. Though it failed, as late as February 1863, petitions were being circulated on the streets of St. Paul requesting that the legislature reconsider the issue.[7]

An aspect of this message appeared in 1857 when the Board of Education proposed to "separate children of African descent if thirty requested formal education." When fewer than that number stepped forward, the board, overseeing the education of more than six thousand enrolled schoolchildren, lowered the limit to fifteen, relegating black children to abysmal classroom conditions. Despite the order, because of the high cost of the Civil War and the Dakota War, by 1864 the city was unable to maintain even the most decrepit facilities and allowed black children to attend white schools. The *Press* reported, "Many white parents were taking away their children on that account."[8] In October 1864 the school board reaffirmed its commitment to segregate black children with whatever resources it saw fit to invest.[9]

On August 10, 1865, a group of black veterans who had served in units of the U.S. Colored Infantry published in the *Daily Press* a petition criticizing the school board and its chair, Colonel Daniel Robertson, for the appalling conditions of "black" classrooms and the exclusion of "their black children from public schools"; the men threatened to withhold their payments of school taxes.[10] In response, the board issued an official notice that a "School for Colored Children" would be open in a building on Ninth and Jackson Streets. Soon after classes began, however, the board discovered "problems of maintaining and operating" the school. Not until two years later did the superintendent of schools announce that "the colored school will not be opened until further notice." Yet, despite Superintendent Mattocks's report on May 6, 1867, that the average monthly enrollment of colored students was 25 with the average attendance being 18, no teacher had been hired. In contrast, total enrollment of all of the city's children was 1,983; average attendance, 932. Fifty-two teachers were paid that month.[11]

On November 30, 1867, the *Daily Press* reported, "The colored students of this city are excluded from the free schools which are located in convenient and comfortable buildings, well-supplied with maps, charts, blackboards, and usual equipment for such institutions." Rather, the school reserved for black children remained "in an very dilapidated condition." Some of the windows had been broken out, the plastering was falling off, "and the keen air of winter will find entrance through many a crack and cranny." To keep out a part of the cold that would otherwise seep inside, the windows had been partly boarded up, so that while the room might be warmer, there would be very little light.[12]

As board secretary and chair of two standing committees—accounts and census—D. D. Merrill, very much mindful of how unpopular it would be to criticize the quality of resources set aside for black students, said nothing during the one term he served on the board, or of how he perceived such

inequity. Several of his fellow board members were both prominent Democrats and business associates, and the educational welfare of black children
was the least of their concerns. The streak of pragmatism led Merrill to keep
his misgivings to himself.[13] The policy of school segregation remained until
March 1869, when the state legislature, three months after the celebration of
black suffrage, passed a bill that denied state funds to schools that segregated
on basis of race. The St. Paul school system, the only district in the state that
officially segregated black and white children, was the only district affected.
It was now essentially mandated that the capital city's black and white children were to learn in the same classrooms.[14] The board recorded wryly, "The
colored school which has been in operation for the past three years has been
abandoned by virtue of an act of the last Legislature of the state, making it a
penal offense to maintain such a school."[15]

Before the week had passed, voices complained that there was no room
in white classrooms and black pupils were being turned away. "Some feeling
has been already manifested upon this subject, and it is very far from certain
that the law will prove beneficial to the colored pupils, in whose interest it was
framed and passed."[16] By April, thirteen students were admitted into white
schools "after due examination" just instituted that month.[17] According to the
*Pioneer*, they displaced white students who would otherwise be enrolled in
school. "Three of four pupils have been taken out of the public schools on
account of the admission of colored students."[18] By May 15, 1869, the total
number of students enrolled was 1,302. The average number of students who
attended district schools that month was 1,148.[19] In that the legislature allocated school funds according to the number of children living in the city, the
St. Paul School District received enough to serve nearly twice the number
currently enrolled. The reason for the surplus was the large number of children who attended Catholic schools.[20]

November 1865 was notably reflective of another form of antiblack sentiment in St. Paul, standing in high contrast to the tumultuous events earlier
that year. After the deaths of 620,000 men the Civil War had finally ended at
Appomattox. One week later, President Lincoln was assassinated. As Radical Republicans in Congress enacted a series of civil rights laws, they jousted
with Lincoln's successor, Andrew Johnson of Tennessee, a Democrat and
former slaveholder whose prickly temperament prompted fighting between
the executive and legislative branches of the federal government. In Minnesota the party of Lincoln was just as determined to extend its martyred president's legacy by granting the vote to black men residing in the state. That
year, however, the question failed, 12,138 to 14,651. In St. Paul, the "nay"

vote prevailed by more than a three-to-one count. In response, in 1867 the Republican-controlled legislature adopted a series of resolutions expressing the belief that "Southern traitors, vanquished in arms, were still hostile." No truer strike for equality could be taken than to try again; but again, the referendum failed statewide by over one thousand votes, with St. Paulites voting against the measure by over a two-to-one margin.[21] By 1868 voters were being prepared to address the issue for a third time. The city with the largest black population would likely continue to be the most resistant to black suffrage.

On January 10, 1868, Governor Marshall fired an opening salvo in the new campaign for black suffrage in his annual message to the state House and Senate. Appealing heavily in that speech to the principle of Republican values, he argued that Minnesota was ready to support black suffrage. Throughout the state the remarks were largely well received. Throughout the year, Republican voters statewide were strongly lobbied by party leaders, spearheaded by Morton Wilkinson, to support the amendment. By September they were prepared to vote yes.

The problem was, despite the city's being the site of Republican-dominated state government, the residence of the Republican governor, the seat of a Republican mayor, and the home of the state's most influential Republican newspaper, the majority of the men of St. Paul were decidedly Democratic. The *Daily Pioneer,* the voice of Democratic grievances, reported, "The amendment was [supported] by nearly all the businessman of the city."[22] Under the title "Minnesota for a White Man Government," the paper editorialized a sentiment that was as pertinent in 1867, when it was written, as it was in 1868: "Whether Flandrau or Marshall is elected, the white people of Minnesota can lay this emotion to their souls, that the negroes who live in this state are not their political equals."[23] In another section under the heading "Attempted Outrage," the *Pioneer* compounded a story on "negro suffrage" with another—"A Nigger attempts to violate a white woman on the steamer *Milwaukee,*"[24] fusing three of the most inflammatory topics of the nineteenth century: race, sex, and politics. A year later, weeks before the 1868 vote, the editor urged his readers, "This is the greatest importance that everyone opposed to the negro voting should vote against the proposed amendment."[25] Elsewhere the *Pioneer* editor was more expansive:

> For the third time, we are called on to decide whether the elective franchise shall be extended to negroes or whether the purity of the ballot box shall be maintained and WHITE MEN alone be permitted to exercise this sacred trust. Twice has this proposition been voted

down by large majorities. This time, in order to make the odious
thing sure, the law says it shall be voted upon the regular ticket.
The Republicans sugar-coat the pill so that voters may not know its
character, by describing it simply as "amendment to section seven
of article one," while it is explained on the Democratic ballots.
The Democrats to a man oppose the proposition and thousands of
Republicans will vote against it if they understand the method if
submission. Remember to scratch out the "Yes" and write "No."[26]

Simply put: the thorny politics of the day made quite uncertain the prospect
of raising money for a black church that was intended to grow into a dominant
platform for black Minnesota. Many whites would support what Hickman was
trying to do. But many more, some being Baptists, could be influenced against
the venture if there was a sense the church could attract an uncomfortably
large number of irreligious, unskilled, and unassimilable Southern black arrivals to the city, or any other hint of controversy. Hickman's group needed
someone to help guide them through these treacherous waters, someone who
understood the white people who would respond to their call, who could convince potential donors that building Pilgrim Baptist Church would "civilize"
the unruly black masses in their midst, while remaining politically nonpartisan, or at least not a platform for the Republican agenda. It was an act of
faith to reach out to a man whose history they could not have known, who
understood the white people who would respond to their call, who had been
of that community, having served on the Board of Education in 1857, someone whom Merrill most clearly favored: the Reverend A. M. Torbet. The announcement of his "superintending" role appeared in both the Republican
and Democratic press.[27] Yet, even as the Democratic *Pioneer* printed notices
of Pilgrim's ("colored") services amid the listing of white churches every
Sunday, it also periodically reminded its readers of disturbances caused by
black residents.[28] In doing so, the paper demonstrated that a truce had been
struck, but it was a very fragile truce.

◆ ◆ ◆ ◆ ◆

*What has been the positive service which this church has
rendered in the community apart from its contribution of
Christian life through its individual members? It has given
to the community that subtle something called the Christian
sentiment which always challenges any community. . . . The
membership of this church has always had a high reputation in*

*the city's life. To call the roll of earlier days is to name the men
and women who were creative forces for the building up of a real
commonwealth. Members of the First Baptist Church have been
found in all the relations of the city's life and that contribution
has not been lessened in the least in the years just behind us.*

JOHN R. BROWN

Robert Hickman had no other choice but to rely on the advice of one who
seemed to understand it all: D. D. Merrill, senior trustee and devout Baptist
(he would become a deacon in 1870), successful businessman, a leader of the
Chamber of Commerce, former inspector of the St. Paul Board of Education: he was the man in the middle, sometimes the man in the shadows, who
whispered the right words to the right people, who in turn had the influence
to change the course of events.[29] He knew when to push and when not to
push, and he understood the tactical complexities of advancing the interests
of Hickman and his followers within the racial and political maelstrom of a
city that had never supported the interests of African Americans. He did so
within the sectarian tenets of the Baptist faith; he appreciated the delicate and
sometimes duplicitous balance of wielding influence without provocation,
showing virtue through compromise, embodying conscience without expression or voice. And presumably he knew that an uncomfortable number of
fellow Baptists, many who considered themselves to be genuine friends of the
black man and sincere Lincoln Republicans, may view black suffrage as over-
reaching on the part of black aspirants and ill advised on the part of radicals.

The *Pioneer,* strident as ever against black suffrage, wrote often against
the proposition, publishing articles about "outrages committed by Southern
blacks and white renegades" against white women, all in an effort to provoke
the view that granting the ballot to black men was the epitome of civic irre-
sponsibility. Even the friends of the colored man had severe misgivings about
the wisdom of black suffrage. "The *Chicago Standard* of October 2," reported
the *Pioneer,* "which is the organ of the Baptists of the Northwestern States
and is of course, sufficiently radical in its politics, says, 'We doubt seriously
whether it has been for the interests of the colored race themselves to excite
among them such expectations as they seem now to cherish, or to encourage
them in putting forward so prominently, and at so early an hour, their chance
to political equality.' "[30]

This missive was directed not only to the party faithful—the Democratic
voter, the white man on the street—but also to the Baptists of St. Paul, who
might confuse a vote for black suffrage with an endorsement of the society

of Pilgrims to become an institution of black political empowerment. In fact, as the *Pioneer* reminded readers, white majorities in other Northern states, as those within the North Star State had done twice before, drew a clear distinction between black freedom and equality. Although willing to fight for emancipation, good white Union men should continue to reject black suffrage, which explained why their legislature betrayed the public trust by now resorting to undemocratic organizing tactics and deception:

> In Minnesota, the radical legislature which again proposed this vote, attempted to twist it up inextricably with the national and general political issue. They provide that the vote should be taken on the general ballot, that the rules of party discipline might be applied to the subject. The order was gone out to radical communities and candidates to print on their ballots with "Amendment to Section One, Article Seven of the Constitution—Yes."
>
> This is the delicate way in which the question is put. The ballots are not to read "For" or "Against" "Negro Suffrage." But an elaborate euphemism was adopted—the pill was sugar-coated for the taste of delicate patients and they are now ordered to take it down.[31]

The editor attacked the referendum process by pointing out that only the majority of those voting singularly on the question would determine the fate of the amendment "whereas the language of the Constitution provides in explicit language that adoption of such provisions 'must be by a majority of all votes cast at the election when the proposition was determined.'" The whole matter was a "fraud," stacked against the will of Minnesota's right-thinking white men. The *Pioneer* continued:

> The vote should have been taken separately, on a separate ballot placed in a separate box, and a majority of all the votes cast at the election should have been required for adoption. As a rebuke to the attempted fraud, a wall as against negro suffrage on its face—see that your ballot reads— "AMENDMENT TO SECTION ONE, ARTICLE SEVEN OF THE CONSTITUTION—NAY!"

To one taking the temperature of the moment in St. Paul, the continued support of white patrons of black opportunity was uncertain especially among the most prominent of supporters. Former U.S. senator Morton S. Wilkinson, who was now running for a congressional seat, was rumored to be plotting a challenge against another (albeit lukewarm) ally of black suffrage, Alexander Ramsey, while Republicans and Democrats alike savaged Congressman Ignatius Donnelly, who was campaigning to return to Washington. August had marked an especially unnerving site of two factions of Radical Republicans—one led by Governor Marshall, Ramsey's chief lieutenant, against Donnelly men—who waged a pitched battle for control over a voting place in the First Ward, blocks from where Pilgrim Baptist was to be constructed:

> Led by Governor Marshall in person, the anti-Donnelly group succeeded in driving out the Donnellyites, but theirs was a hollow victory. The floor of the room collapsed during the struggle, and the beaten Donnellyite forces organized their own poll on the sidewalk in front of the building, hooting and cursing at Governor Marshall as he solicited votes through the window.[32]

Adding to the political complexity was the ethnic loyalty to Republican Donnelly that existed within the large Irish Catholic population of St. Paul that normally voted the Democratic line and typically saw blacks as rivals. In all, these factors gave "the city a long-standing reputation for turbulent politics."[33] In St. Paul, during this political season, anything could happen. Within this climate, it was sage advice to keep one's head down.

On November 3, votes were cast across the state. Wilkinson was elected to the House and Donnelly's bid failed. The *Pioneer* rejoiced in his defeat. "[Donnelly] was generally regarded as a bolter, and this fact, together with the bad reputation he acquired from his blackguard speech in Congress, seems to have lost him the sympathy of the radical party."[34] But it was the suffrage referendum, approved by 39,493 to 30,121 votes, that mattered most to black Minnesotans. In Ramsey County, however, the amendment failed, 1,461 to 1,982. In St. Paul, the question failed in every city ward except the Fifth.[35] After lodging its grievances regarding the manner in which the referendum was held, the *Pioneer* extended what seemed to be a gracious admonition to Minnesota's newest citizens:

> But now that we have got [negro suffrage], we must make the best of it. We advise negroes to read Democratic newspapers, to hear Democratic speakers, to post themselves upon political topics, and to qualify themselves in their minds as they are qualified in law, for the duties of the voter. They should do as a white man should do in Hayti, or Liberia, if the negro governments of those countries

should see fit to let the white man vote. They should not be guided by prejudices, nor be beguiled by demagogues, but should ascertain which party will make the best laws, impose the lowest taxes, wipe out the debt, and make the country what it ought to be: then they should vote for the party.[36]

It seemed that things could settle down.

Hickman was now a full-fledged citizen of the state of Minnesota. As such he could vote, serve on juries, and run for office if he so chose; and as a citizen, standing equal to every white man in the state, he had a right to demand consideration by government leaders. When he came to St. Paul, five and a half years earlier, freedom was all that he desired: freedom to earn a living, freedom to openly worship within a congregation of his kinsmen, freedom to demand respect from any man he met on the street. But it did not necessarily mean that he aspired to political equality. In practice, however, the mere attainment of the vote showed that he already enjoyed the stewardship of the state's most influential political and business leaders. And considering the minuscule size of black men as a voting bloc, there would not be the pandering by politicians often seen directed to the Swedes, Irish, and Germans. And as the returns became evident, it was clear that support for the suffrage came from outside the city. The voting majority within St. Paul voted "nay," and it was from within their midst that Hickman needed support to construct his church. Merrill and his counsel remained quite important.

In the warm reflection of wintry November the event meant something quite profound, however—saving the right to vote was considerable. It was a right that no less characterized the very purpose of the American Revolution, a right that Hickman now possessed by the generosity of white strangers. Indeed, "negro suffrage" was a heady recognition of inclusion into the commonwealth that had *chosen* by its own free will to buck convention, not having it forced on it by Congress or the courts, and in so doing, decided, without coercion, that establishing black citizenship was fundamental to the principle of being Minnesotan. Holding citizenship, in other words, meant holding political and civic worth. And though Negro suffrage by definition was political in nature, it transcended mere politics for a black man who saw his enslavement as a curtailment of God's creation, and in this, it was less political and more spiritual fulfillment, being more fully in the service of God. It was indeed a reason for thanksgiving to be quite appropriately observed when each Sunday he worshipped; but it would begin inauspiciously.

On the wintry evening of Friday, November 13, a group of black men from St. Paul met in the room on Wabasha and Third near the river used for worship by Hickman and the Pilgrims. The night before, St. Paul had been hit by frigid cold and snowfall that drove "workmen from all outdoor work."[37] On Friday, however, the weather tempered enough for the snow to melt in the busy streets, leaving them and everything venturing over them mired in mud. A large procession that had been planned was canceled since "the muddy streets utterly prevented this." Instead, the plan was changed to serenade some of the prominent Republicans who had been "especial advocates of impartial suffrage." By celebrating the work of Republican leaders, the procession would be seen as a partisan affair. "Siebert's band, which had been procured for the evening, mounted in Cook and Webb's bandwagon drawn by four horses," and was "followed by quite a procession of vehicles containing the colored men of the city." It was about ten o'clock before the procession started. The first visit was made to Governor Marshall, who invited them into the home to partake of refreshments and was "handsomely entertained" by the new Negro voters who serenaded him.[38]

The whole affair was like red meat to the editor of the *Pioneer*, who again took every opportunity to report any mishap and indignity to undercut the momentous nature of the event:

> A portion of the members composing the colored celebration party, on Friday night, came to grief on the corner of Third and Meeker streets. The wagon in which they were seated, in trying to turn the corner, capsized the crew into a sea of mud, which they extricated themselves with some difficulty. The party was taken to the *Dispatch* [newspaper] office, where they were provided with a change of clothing, and the editor of that paper accompanied them to [*Press* editor] Mr. Driscoll's house, where a splendid entertainment was provided for all hands—white and colored.[39]

Though the two newspapers represented bitter political rivals—the *Dispatch* was the organ for Donnelly whereas the *Press* was the organ for Marshall and Ramsey—at the end of the day, they were all Republicans helping the "coloreds" within this most Democratic of cities.[40]

In the next several weeks, there was a swirl of activities in preparation for the statewide convention: arrangements needed to be made; accommodations set; speakers secured; resources tapped. Yet the circumstances of the convention made bipartisanship impossible. The powerful friends within the Republican Party and the new leaders of the state's newest citizenry made it so. A cautious man may have worried about the effect of such provocative events. On one hand, there was the demand for discretion on behalf of soliciting funds to build the church. On the other, a cadre of black men who would form the first leadership of a burgeoning social and political elite for Minnesota's black community—barbers Maurice Jernigan, Thomas Stockton, Robert Banks, and Thomas Jackson—saw Hickman as one of the brethren, and it was they who seemed willing to slight the Democrats for their support of policies that kept them in an inferior status. In response to state senator Levi Nutting, who reminded the audience to beware of those who would tell them how to vote and the particular hypocrisy of a certain newspaper, the crowd began shouting *"Pioneer! Pioneer! Pioneer!"*[41] During the morning of the convention, the black leaders met at the home of Maurice Jernigan, who was selected to be convention president. There they spent the morning organizing the Sons of Freedom, Minnesota's first statewide black civil rights organization.[42]

Hickman now stood at the heart of political engagement. But being a politician—or a founding member of a civil rights organization—did not seem to be the reason he was there. In fact, not since his speaking appearance in August at the controversial picnic in Hansen's Gardens, soon before Reverend Torbet had agreed to "superintend" the "work" of Pilgrim Baptist, had Hickman stood up before the larger community to speak. He hosted the November 13 meeting since it occurred in his worship room at Wabasha and Third; but he did not speak during the procession and the visits with dignitaries that followed. And though he participated in planning the statewide convention scheduled for January 1, during the proceedings, after an evening of black and white speakers took the podium, Hickman was called only to lead those assembled in prayer.[43] Though these events gave him exposure, it was not so much as a race leader—one who articulated the dreams and aspirations of his people, inspired them to collectively act in the interest of themselves as a nation within a nation, spoke with the intent of shaping political and economic agenda—as a chaplain of events, one who blessed this momentous point in history. It was an important though not as prominent role.

On stage, Hickman's stature did not equal that of Maurice Jernigan, Thomas Jackson, and Robert Banks, all three of whom were prominently linked with the 1865 and 1866 campaigns and who were successful businessmen within the context of the black experience during the postwar years. In contrast, Hickman was a preacher and semiskilled laborer. As prosperous barbers owning salons in the city's most prestigious hotels, Jernigan, Banks, Jackson, and Stockton had cultivated the style and speech of those accustomed to associating with the state's most powerful men. Hickman worked within a different milieu, serving primarily a very small religious community, ministering to former slaves, but restricted from performing the most sacred pastoral roles—baptizing, marrying, and burying the members of the flock—which were reserved for ordained clergy—white men. Hickman's calling was to preach the Word, movingly, sincerely, without the need for silken eloquence that the new black community expected from its race leaders. Perhaps even in some eyes, standing in contrast to the barbers in style and speech, he embodied the *negro-we-once-were*. Nonetheless, to himself, he was a preacher wanting simply to establish his church and be its pastor.

The reaction of the Democrats in the wake of the convention was noteworthy. Throughout the evening, Republican speakers attacked and ridiculed the Democrats, and in return, Democratic opinion makers counterpunched, though more churlishly, calling the former U.S. senator, congressman, governor, mayor, and legislators "uncommon demagogues," "political shysters," "piddling white radicals," and "white trash." However, the editor of the *Pioneer,* which had been directly criticized, saw fit to portray the black attendees in a better light. It was as if the paper was saying to them, *When the Republicans grow bored with all their so-called benevolence, you will see that we're really not so bad*:

> The colored people filled their part well. They did all things decently and in order. They were temperate, considerate, and high-toned, and gave, throughout their proceedings, many evidences that they were worthy of the possession of their new rights and franchises.[44]

After months, indeed years, of attacking the principle of Negro suffrage, of mocking the social and religious activities of black Minnesotans, of gleefully highlighting the misadventures of otherwise minor events, the Democratic establishment in St. Paul appeared to be having an abrupt change of heart regarding the need to show respect to black voters. Even though the black population had increased over the previous few years, black voting power remained virtually insignificant in singularly influencing the outcomes of policy discussions or elections. The hostility to black suffrage within the body politic of St. Paul, as it had twice before, remained the same in the winter of 1869. Yet, as improbable as it may seem, the *Pioneer*—the organ of the Democratic political establishment—overnight appeared, not just to approve the vote or even show respect to the state's newest voters, but simply to concede to the new political fact of life.

The recent vote on the Negro suffrage amendment gave clear indication that the Minnesota Democratic Party was a minority party. In true fashion of one seeking to regain power or at least influence in the public debate, pragmatism seemed to trump principle. Black voters alone, if they were at all receptive to voting against the Party of Lincoln, would not accomplish this; but if the strategy was to stitch together alliances of disparate interest groups, as the Republicans had done in the 1850s, the party could resurrect itself to relevance, if not dominance.[45] Already the Democrats had established ties to the Order of the Patrons of Husbandry, or Grangers, who included, as history would soon show, leading Republicans, as well. By the early 1870s their efforts would evolve into a reform movement that challenged the Republican Party and its allies—railroad and corporate monopolies, transforming the notion of reform from meaning emancipation and racial political equality to one espousing class equity. Donnelly, who would split from the Republicans to take up the antimonopoly banner, would say one year later:

Let all of those who think alike come together and reason together. The struggle between the North and South having ended, the struggle between the East and West commences. It will not be a conflict of arms but of ideas, a contest of interests—a struggle of intelligence—one side defending itself from the greed of the other.[46]

Notwithstanding black loyalty to the Republicans that for the time being was secure, Democrats took pains to plant seeds of discontent, anticipating a time when blacks might recognize that Republicans had not provided them with genuine opportunities. Coalition building would indeed come to bear in 1884 when Grover Cleveland became the first postwar Democrat elected president of the United States, in part due to the defection of Northern black voters discouraged by Republican lethargy regarding race relations and black civil rights. Mayor Stewart had admonished the black assembly to always distrust their newfound Democratic friends, "who, after [the black man] was liberated, tried to make him a mere menial and serf in the land of freedmen."[47] In response to this kind of statement the Democrats accused the Republicans of hypocrisy. "The radical party, that had conferred upon the colored people the right to vote, and which demands the votes of the colored people for their candidates, did not give them a single office—not even that of a common messenger or fireman."[48] Democratic leaders, determined to place their party in a better light, waited for the right moment.

By March, the St. Paul Democratic Party experienced a steady stream of party bashing, from losing the Negro suffrage amendment and insufferable

Republican crowing that accompanied it, to having to endure the partisan spectacle of the convention in January, to absorbing the legislative blow of a school desegregation law. Leaders knew that a party incapable of getting on the right side of history was doomed to be, at best, a debating society and at, worst, a political fossil.

On March 23, 1869, an opportunity presented itself with the commencement of the trial of a black man named Willis Harris accused of stealing a small sum of money from the room of another black man named Andrew Jackson. All morning, thirty-six men, all white, went through jury selection. Only one survived the cut. By noon, Judge William Sprigg Hall ordered Sheriff Daniel Robertson to summon twenty more men to the opening of the afternoon session. At the assigned time, jury selection resumed. In the end, a jury was impaneled. What made an otherwise mundane trial newsworthy, garnering a statewide audience, was that the new jury included five black men "presenting almost every shade of color, from the deepest black to the most delicate white."[49]

Considering the historical impact of the selection, the appearance of these five black men, the first of their race to serve on a Minnesota jury, would surely create a stir. It is unlikely that the sheriff, elected to his office and a man of significant political and civic stature—publisher of the *Minnesota Democrat*, a former mayor and state representative, and sitting chair of the Board of Education—indeed, the embodiment of the party establishment, would do anything to disrupt the racial conventions without the full concurrence of Judge Hall. In a county with over 3,500 white voters, Sheriff Robertson had brought in within two hours five eligible black men to serve. In other words, the sheriff's deputies had to pass many houses and businesses within the Third Ward—densely occupied with white native-born and foreign-born neighbors who represented every socioeconomic level from unskilled laborer to professional, renter and property owner—to find the black prospective jurors.[50] Nearly three months after the alleged crime, Harris was about to be tried before a jury of his racial peers. Of the jurors the *Weekly Pioneer* reported, "The colored citizens looked dignified and anxious, the 'white folks' curious." One of the five black jurymen was whitewasher and preacher Robert Hickman.[51]

It is evident that party leaders wanted to appoint black men to the jury, but it did not mean that any number of black men would suffice. Clearly, unemployed laborers like Harris and Jackson would not be included. What mattered to the Democrats would be selecting, and in effect, associating itself with black men of acknowledged quality and stature. Assuming that the party was determined to appeal to those blacks who were likely to be future race leaders, those whose names already had cachet, who if brought within the Democratic fold, could bring over others, undercutting, if not the power, certainly the moral authority Republicans now enjoyed. It would indeed be a political coup.

Still, the presence of black men on the jury created a stir, despite the security within the courtroom. The *Minneapolis Tribune* reported that when the court reconvened at 2:00 p.m., the gallery "presented an unusually animated scene":

> Our neighboring city of St. Paul has been greatly agitated over the fact that colored men have been allowed to sit on a jury there for the first time. It created an excitement only equaled by the advent of a tribe of wandering Arabs, and so aroused the refined and delicate sensibilities of the goodly citizens of St. Paul as to fill the courtroom to overflowing, and furnished the principal theme of conversation upon the streets, and in the drawing rooms, and parlors of this aristocratic metropolis.[52]

While the party establishment represented the man on the street, it wasn't made up of men from the streets. Rather, they were of the political and commercial aristocracy of the state who included such names as Rice, Sibley, Robertson, Fisher, Brisbane, and Maxfield. What they felt mattered more; and they wanted black men on the jury despite the outcry from their constituents. Even though the Republicans controlled the state, these Democrats controlled the city, the courts, and Board of Education; and it was in this city that Hickman and his followers resided. Merrill knew these men, having most recently served with them on various civic and business committees and, most recently, with them all on the Board of Education. The former chair of the board, James T. Maxfield, had just been elected mayor, succeeding Republican Jacob Stewart.[53] Thus, Merrill was in the position to aid in Hickman's selection, knowing it might give the black preacher the kind of notoriety that would appeal to potential benefactors and create for him the imprimatur of civic respectability.

It therefore is paradoxical that during these recent unsettling and highly charged months, Hickman, selected in effect by the city's Democratic establishment while enjoying the franchise created by Republican political power, was theoretically in the enviable position of gaining support for his church and, in turn, for himself from Republicans and Democratic leaders alike. The future suddenly seemed bright. Opportunity abounded. His church could get built because both groups recognized that Pilgrim Baptist could be the spiritual, steadying anchor of relevance for this burgeoning black community within this already raucous city, and he at last would be its official pastor, licensed and ordained; all that seemed to stand in the way was the apostolic laying on of hands of the ministers of the Baptist community. However, he had not yet shown himself to be one with their fellowship.

# 20

# TO BE IN GOD'S FAVOR

*From June, 1854, regular Sabbath service was suspended and*
*no covenant meetings until the following November; then the*
*little band rejoiced and again took courage, was strength-*
*ened and rejuvenated with spiritual and material life, by the*
*settlement of Rev. A. M. Torbet, from Ohio. His salary was*
*$1000, of which amount the Church assumed $500 and voted*
*to raise $200 for incidental expenses. Each year the commands*
*of the Church property had been sent when due, and this year*
*it was redeemed from mortgage, for which credit is largely due*
*to women's earnest and persistent efforts.*

LYDIA GATES
"HISTORY OF THE FIRST BAPTIST CHURCH"

In 1860 the population of St. Paul was 10,279—of which 4,659 were foreign-born. By the end of the decade the total population had nearly doubled to 20,030 residents. This increase reflected not only an accelerated birthrate following the return of war veterans but also the renewed influx of foreign immigration. The period between 1867 and 1873 were years of general prosperity and economic growth for Minnesota. The lumber and construction industries revived, agricultural production increased, and eastern capital was again available for financing railroads and other industries. In St. Paul the new wave of prosperity was reflected in the number of growing businesses and temporary housing established seemingly overnight to meet the growing demand. The need for skilled and unskilled labor seemed infinite as building construction and its attendant industries revived from the wartime slump. This was the city into which black migrants entered, enticed by rumors of employment.[1]

In 1860, 259 blacks lived within the state. Of that number 76 lived in St. Paul. By 1865 the black community of St. Paul, including Hickman and his followers, increased the population to 169. Between 1865 and 1875 the population steadily rose to 264 and had almost tripled by 1885. In contrast, between 1865 and 1875 the white population grew from 249,688 to 526,592, and by 1885 to 1,115,984. Though black migration to St. Paul continued throughout the remainder of the century, the black population of the city, after 1870, never exceeded 2 percent of the city's total population.[2] Toward the end of the 1860s the black population was well distributed throughout the city's five wards. The heaviest concentration of housing and businesses were located in Ward Two along lower Jackson Street and Ward Three along West Third, Fourth, and Fifth Streets. This area was then in the heart of the city. Residential housing and business establishments were interspersed in a pattern consistent with a walking city. It was within this area that Pilgrim Baptist rented at least three locations between 1866 and 1870.[3]

During the Civil War, residential accommodations were at a premium in the city, owing in large part to the absence of financial resources, skilled labor, and materials that were more urgently needed for the war effort. The housing shortage was more critical with the arrival of Hickman's group and other contraband making their way to the city in 1863. Many of these migrants lacked skills needed for steady employment or were paid such low wages that they were not able to afford the exorbitant rent demanded for standard housing. Thus, the sites that the Pilgrims used were just as likely to be the result of the pooled resources of the church members as of the generosity of landlords, who likely viewed the religious services as vaguely familiar yet still quite alien.[4] There is no record of their services, but from the research of scholars in the field, one can surmise how the Pilgrims' services might have looked. Nonparishioners might see or hear "true believers" relating their conversion experiences, couching them in certain traditional phrases—*I remember the day and the hour when the Lord spoke peace to my soul.* Worshippers might "get happy" or "shout," flailing their arms about, crying, running up and down the aisles, yelling *Amen* and *Hallelujah!* Shouting might be set off by a prayer or testimony, by singing or a sermon.[5]

The sermon itself, steeped in the "old time religion" vein, painted vivid pictures of a stern father "who gave his only begotten Son to save a sin-sick world," calling on sinners to seek salvation through the "four square gospel"—confession, repentance, regeneration, and sanctification. Other similarly situated ministers preached justification by faith, declaring that a man was not saved because he was good, but could only act good because he was saved. Once saved, a Christian may backslide, but he could be restored to fellowship by repentance and prayer. The immediate rewards of salvation— the "fruits of the Spirit"—were usually described as joy, peace, and a clear conscience. The ultimate rewards, however, are reserved for heaven, the final destination of the "saved." Conversion, baptism, and confirmation were assumed to be the high spots in the Christian's life, and the faithful met periodically at testimonial and prayer meetings to recount the circumstances of their conversion, to detail their "trials and tribulations," and to declare their determination to "press on." Preachers, too, sometimes related the circumstances of their own conversions, referring to that specific moment at home faraway in the South. In doing so, they shared the deepest part of themselves as Christians, thereby strengthening their connections with their flocks and reinforcing their collective sense of identity, which to the ears of white St. Paul landlords, was distinctly "colored" and Southern.[6]

Blacks were not welcome in all sections of the city. As early as May 1866, the *Pioneer* complained of a health hazard existing in the "old rookery" on Wabasha Street. The Second Ward sanitary inspector found the building "inhabited solely by negroes . . . of all ages, sexes, and shades. In one room thirteen persons were sleeping every night." A group of whites attacked the "negro rookery" in an attempt to drive out its occupants and succeeded in destroying the migrants' meager personal belongings. In October white neighbors forced the removal of a large black family living on Seventh Street between Wabasha and Cedar because of an outbreak of smallpox among them.[7]

During the early years of the Reconstruction era the black community in St. Paul was characterized by a majority of families dominated by male heads of households employed in low-paying skilled, or unskilled, and service-related jobs. There was a slight increase in the unmarried male population, which was characteristic of frontier conditions and migratory labor. But male and female heads of households generally owned real estate and personal property. The majority of these families lived in single-family dwellings, behind places of business or in hotels and boardinghouses. Some resided in multiple-family dwellings with white and black neighbors; and while there was no discernible pattern of residential segregation, residents—black and poor white—were concentrated around the city's commercial core.[8]

Black men could be found in a variety of unskilled jobs, but the majority of them filled positions of menial service and common labor. Some managed to establish themselves as independent barbers and others as businessmen, including restaurant and saloon proprietors. Few blacks, however, made it into the ranks of skilled craftsmen. During Reconstruction, blacks were excluded from the burgeoning union movement, which meant they were also denied apprenticeship training. Because of this the percentage of blacks in skilled trades steadily declined during the latter portion of the nineteenth century. Native-born whites and, to an increasingly greater extent, skilled immigrants dominated the craft trades. Locally the trades and crafts were monopolized by small family businesses within which skills passed down generationally. Family businesses tended to hire only relatives or other whites of the same ethnic or religious background. Unless a black possessed a skill before arriving in the city there were virtually no opportunities to acquire one. Until 1886 the St. Paul black community had no professional class. No members had been exposed to higher education. In other words, there were no black doctors, lawyers, or dentists, and not even any municipal or state employees. It was virtually impossible for blacks to compete for jobs above service and menial employment, work that in time became known as "nigger" work.[9]

Discrimination was equally as harsh for black women. Though it is hard to assess how many women were required to work in order to supplement the family income before 1895, or how many were heads of their households, they nonetheless tended to work as laundresses, seamstresses, cooks, and domestics, though in this latter category, they often unsuccessfully competed against white immigrant women. In Red Wing in 1863, the Orrin Densmore family hired a local Swedish woman for domestic duty as they waited for contraband to be sent from the South by their son serving with the U.S. Colored Infantry in St. Louis. The Swede did not like the possibility of having to work alongside a former slave and worried that local people would see her and the African American as equals. She did not want to be "set aside for the ebony article."[10] Black women faced the imposition of compounded limitations in a society that discriminated because of race and gender.

Notably, in 1865 there was near parity in numbers between the sexes. With the increase of migration the city's black population became imbalanced. By 1875 males averaging twenty-six years of age constituted 54 percent of the city's black population, increasing to 62 percent ten years later. Between 1870 and 1885 the black population never exceeded 1.31 percent of the total population.[11] "The surplus of men and the limited resources of the community," historian David Taylor wrote, "directly affected institutional growth and development. One institution, the Black church, suffered more than any other."[12]

These figures reflect the challenge Hickman and the Pilgrims would face over the next twenty years. Their numbers constituted a small minority within a small minority though women's church membership continued to grow. By 1889 women made up 63 percent of the congregation at Pilgrim Baptist in a community in which 60 percent were men. "These figures suggest that the male population was not a church going population."[13] This profile alone was not dissimilar to that of the congregation of St. James African Methodist Episcopal Church, the only early black congregation formed in the city without connections to a white denomination.[14] Indeed, from the late 1870s to 1900 the entire denomination experienced a steady rise in its percentage of female members.[15] Jon Butler has observed that by 1900, when women made up nearly 75 percent of the membership at Pilgrim Baptist, men comprised 60.8 percent of the black population over the age of twenty.[16] Being a small black church within Minnesota's capital city, the vitality of Pilgrim relied heavily on members who characteristically had meager financial resources, were a minority within their own racial demographic, lacked legal standing to vote, and faced the double discrimination of being female and black.

They were the "faithful few," as one black minister said, who attended Sunday services regularly, went to prayer meetings and special services, contributed faithfully to the numerous collections, and organized, coordinated, and facilitated picnics, community celebrations, rallies, and financial drives. "Their lives revolved around religion and the church, and their emotional needs seemed to be met primarily by active participation in the worship ceremonies."[17] Prayer meetings and communion services were the most significant experiences in their common life, and such services were highly charged with emotion. They involved group singing, individual prayers, and "testifying." The early survival of the church was due no doubt to Hickman's inspirational, strategic, and tactical skills incumbent upon able leadership; but the operational viability of Pilgrim Baptist, for decades to come, fell on the shoulders of its women who, unlike their First Baptist counterparts, labored without the benefits of being white, middle class, and married to husbands with political and business ties to the city's power elite. If anything, these black women were likelier to be in their white sisters' employ. Nonetheless, it was they, through no other resource than the hard and usually anonymous labor of their own hands, who served as the backbone of their community's institutional development.

✦ ✦ ✦ ✦ ✦

*Now we were six years old and we numbered sixty-five.
God's favor to Zion had come. After a two-year pastorate of
success in winning souls, quickening believers, and general
up-building, Brother Torbet resigned to become financial
agent of the Minnesota Central University, leaving membership of 87, a net gain of 22 in the two years of arrival work.*

LYDIA GATES
"HISTORY OF THE FIRST BAPTIST CHURCH"

The first planned community function occurred in August 1868, with the celebration of the emancipation of the slaves in the West Indies by Great Britain
on August 1, 1834. The event, widely celebrating in the British Indies, likewise became customary among free blacks and white abolitionists in Northern
cities throughout the antebellum period. The 1868 celebration would mark
the beginning of the tradition in St. Paul. In later years the event, always held
in the summer and open to the general public, would lead with a picnic followed by commemorative ceremonies showcasing some of the leading speakers in the community, and culminate with a grand ball. The tradition would
continue in the Twin Cities until 1915. But on January 1, 1869, the celebration
focused on the passage of Minnesota's Negro suffrage amendment as well as
the sixth annual recognition of President Lincoln's Emancipation Proclamation, and was to be the second such community-wide function.[18]

Both venues were logical places for Hickman to appear if he wanted to
build the membership at Pilgrim. The August 1868 event, being the first,
would indeed place him in front of a large audience. The question was, what
would be his message? There is no record of what he did say yet circumstances
dictated that the stakes were certainly high. This was not a religious gathering and the people present were not all Baptists nor necessarily religious, nor
apparently were they all there for the same reason, as implied by news accounts. As mentioned earlier, typically the portion of black communities in
St. Paul, indeed throughout the North, who attended churches was small in
comparison to the total black population. Married couples and women constituted the bulk of the congregations in black communities where the majority
was young black men. The eminent sociologist E. Franklin Frazier further
noted that the church as a community institution was almost powerless in the
face of sexual promiscuity (especially interracial), vice, and lawlessness. As a

result, two distinct elements coexisted in the community—"sporting" people and Christians.[19] Members of the "sporting" crowd—those, as reported in the *Press*, determined on drinking and raucously dancing into the night—would not be interested in listening to that old-time religion: *Sin is good enough for me.*

Indeed, Pilgrim Baptist's brand of religiosity may not have appealed to many blacks in attendance, even those who were churchgoers. As important as Pilgrim was to the institutional development of black St. Paul, many black churchgoers still preferred to worship in white churches and others still who were "old settlers" or more established in the larger community chose "to worship amongst themselves" for they were "unable to countenance the emotionalism or revivalistic spirit of the Baptist meetings." Some of them had elected to organize the Episcopal congregation of St. Mark's in 1867.[20] Since 1863, the small group of black residents whose numbers grew from new arrivals from the South, some of whom may have ventured to Minnesota with Hickman's Pilgrims and chose to live instead in St. Anthony, organized St. James African Methodist Episcopal Church. In 1869 the congregation would take possession of the church building formerly occupied by a white congregation on Sixth Avenue Southeast and Second Street.[21] Twenty years later, St. Paul blacks drawn to the Catholic faith would finally have a separate congregation named after Peter Claver, a sixteenth-century canonized Spanish missionary to Africans.[22] Given this, Pilgrim Baptist was a small segment of St. Paul's community of black Christians.

It was more likely that Hickman's message would not be about religion but about freedom, a logical topic for a picnic gathered to celebrate the emancipation of slaves in the British West Indies; but even this topic was tricky. It was hotly controversial among the Minnesota clergy, especially in years leading up to the Civil War, to preach politics from the pulpit. Emily Grey, a free black woman who lived in St. Anthony during the years preceding the Civil War, wrote in her memoir that she had selected First Congregational Church in St. Anthony because Pastor Charles C. Seccombe was not reluctant to preach against slavery from the pulpit as most pastors were.[23] During that time, for example, the Reverend John G. Riheldaffer of St. Paul delivered a sermon on "the wickedness of preaching politics." In reaction to this, fellow Presbyterian Henry M. Nicholls of Stillwater cried out, "Chains and Shackles off from the Pulpit! Let there be one place where Truth goes not on crutches."[24] As this related to Hickman, a former Missouri slave, to be black, free, and Baptist was to be political. To separate out any of those facts was to deny the totality of his humanity. But Riheldaffer of St. Paul was more the model of Hickman's patron and it was within this tradition that Hickman worked, removing politics from the religious work of a servant of God.

For the black man and woman, however, freedom, within the historical context, was by definition a matter of military will; equality was very much a matter of political will. Hickman, on that January day in 1869, would have to steer directly into the dilemma. For First Baptist, the line between religion and politics was clear: the tyrant could never be supreme to the will of God; yet where government at last had acted virtuously by fashioning laws that made all men equal, would the same adage hold for men who intended to deny blacks their lawful rights? It was an unprecedented time. No one in the nation, let alone Minnesota, had experienced such a time when a white majority had voted to enfranchise a black minority. For many of the blacks and whites present—an interracial community gathered to celebrate freedom—the issue was inconsequential. It is not clear whether Hickman felt differently. What was plausible is that Hickman was between the white Baptist community whose members were not present, who held a paternal sense of both Hickman and the Pilgrims, a strict ownership of the Baptist faith, and considerable influence in the larger secular community. Different audiences wanted to hear different, more likely conflicting messages from one man, the preacher who had not yet been chosen by his white brethren to be pastor of Pilgrim Baptist Church.

In the end his remarks were not reported, but it seemed sufficiently controversial that his name was mentioned at all in the newspaper. Also mentioned in the friendly *St. Paul Press* was that Hickman spoke at a gathering where the sporting crowd had prolonged an otherwise decorous event with their own more raucous party. Although the *Press* did not insinuate an association between Hickman and the group, the mere mention of their presence proved awkward. Months earlier, a similar crowd had defiled Pilgrim's fundraiser and sent Reverend Norris on his way. By the fall of 1868, Hickman had to be concerned about how his church was being viewed not just by First Baptist, his most dependable patrons, but by the proper members of the black community, who frowned on such lowbrow behavior. Yet, he had attracted the attention of a small group of black men who would call for a meeting to convene in the worship hall of Pilgrim Baptist Society on a night in November. Taking a cue from previous embarrassments, for the festival and dinner to follow the Convention of Colored Citizens, invitations would be distributed to selected whites and blacks.[25] From all accounts the convention went well. Even the irascible *Pioneer,* which attacked the Republican officials who spoke, commended the organizers and blacks in attendance.[26]

Black Minnesotans as well were impressed with what had transpired and the ways in which black men had comported themselves, including the man who blessed the ceremonies, who perhaps embodied the experiences of many in the audience. Within a scant five years after escaping slavery, Hickman had built himself into a man of note, a leader among black men and black women, a leader among leaders, a black man of God, and one who commanded, by virtue of standing onstage, the respect of the state's most powerful leaders. It had been four years since, in the name of fifteen others, Hickman requested to "Bee a Branch" of First Baptist, and two years since Pilgrim was formerly organized. Near the end of 1869, months after the convention had met and Hickman made statewide headlines as a Ramsey County juryman, the membership of Pilgrim Baptist Church had grown to twenty-nine.[27]

It was uncertain where they would meet for worship services, however. They no longer could use the Wabasha and Third site, and newspapers no longer printed Pilgrim notices. A visitor to the city wanting a Pilgrim Baptist experience had to rely on word of mouth to find the service. Hickman and his church had come a long way; yet, for all the new community-wide exposure and acceptance by powerful men in both parties, Pilgrim still had no place of worship. Once again, Hickman's congregation was homeless. Through all the tumult of the last few years, First Baptist, and D. D. Merrill in particular, had been a constant patron who would play a central role in this next phase of Pilgrim's development.

# 21

# OF OTHER
# BAPTIST INTERESTS

*As things are in the Baptist denomination, the minister of*
*any outstanding church must be a denominational servant also.*
*He must do his part on denominational boards and committees.*
*If that service is not rendered, the work of the great whole lags.*

REVEREND JOHN BROWN

A report to the Minnesota Baptist Association told of the straits the members of Pilgrim Baptist were in, and it hinted at something deeper about the relationship between the congregation and its pastor: "The pressure of money matters interrupts our plans of building a house of worship. Have a flourishing Sabbath School, superintended by the Reverend A. M. Torbet, who also for the most part preaches to us once on the Sabbath."[1] Fundamentally, the Pilgrims did not recognize Torbet as their spiritual leader. He did not participate in the religious life cycle of the congregation, which convened throughout the week for prayer sessions, testimonials, socials, and for evening Sabbath services. He had no experience with black people and perhaps found it hard to relate to them. His more formal Scottish demeanor would not have fit easily with their form of revivalism, and it likely caused him to be reluctant to insinuate himself into a community that had its own way of doing things. Not since it was announced that he had agreed to "superintend the work" of the Pilgrims' efforts to raise a construction fund had his name been affiliated with the congregation, and no funds had been raised. What relationships he had once had in 1857 with the men of influence of the day no longer seemed to bear fruit. Until his appointment, he had been away from the city for over ten years, missing the racial events of the decade, and he was now seemingly out of touch with the postwar interrelationship of race, cultural expression, religion, and politics. It remained to be seen whether he would be of any help to his still-unfamiliar flock.

In September, the Minnesota Baptist Association, which now represented twenty-three churches and a total membership of 1,062 Baptists, met at First Baptist Church in Hastings, twenty-five miles southeast of St. Paul. Normally every member congregation in the state would send a delegation composed of the pastor and church clerk to meet and confer about the state of the Baptist community in Minnesota. That year, First Baptist Church of St. Paul, befitting its prominence in the state association, sent the largest delegation, which included Abram Cavender, William Wakefield, George Prescott, and D. D. Merrill.[2] Hickman and church clerk Johnson Discom probably joined them on their trip to the river town as they climbed aboard a train to attend a conference made up largely of white men they did not know. It was in 1863, during his escape from slavery, that he last saw Hastings, and only in passing as they were towed ever northward to St. Paul. Not since then had he been outside St. Paul. He had braved war-torn Missouri, encouraged his followers as they drifted for hours on the wide Mississippi, fully exposed to bushwackers or Confederate sympathizers who might happen along and see them, only to build a home and church in a city that did not want him. Yet, he may now have approached the trip to the convention in Hastings with a different kind of apprehension, knowing that his high-stakes mission was to have his black congregants accepted by these white Baptists. Though they were Northerners— indeed, Minnesotans—recent experiences taught him to be especially careful not to offend; the Promised Land did not guarantee acceptance. He attended the convention but was designated only as a "delegate." Reverend Torbet was absent, the only pastor not in attendance.[3]

It therefore had to be of some comfort to join Merrill and other brethren on the train ride to Hastings. Theirs was a weighty group, since three of the delegates filled prominent roles during the convention. Wakefield was the convention's corresponding secretary, Prescott was the denomination's state Sabbath school superintendent, Randall was president of the Sabbath school convention that followed the association convention, and Merrill was elected state treasurer.[4] They were in the vanguard of the new direction that the Minnesota Baptist Association now committed itself to pursue, as reflected in the keynote address: "Dear Brethren, Let me speak of the church and the children—the today and the tomorrow of Christ's Kingdom. The Sunday School is the tomorrow of the church. . . . The children do not quite so much exist for the Church as the Church exists for the children. . . . We must work at the sapling, and not think to straighten the mature and crooked trunk. We must shape habits while they are plastic and formative. We must popularize the Sunday School by crowding it with the 'ancient and the honorable' among the people, met to study God's words and make it great."[5]

D. D. Merrill, also in charge of collecting the "circular letters" or church reports, assisted Hickman with Pilgrim Baptist's report and was otherwise quite active in the proceedings. In the end, he presented "a resolution of thanks to Milwaukee & St. Paul, St. Paul & Sioux City, and Hastings & Dakota Railroad Companies, and North Western Union Packet Company for their courtesy in passing delegates at half-fare."[6] He would also know the implications of another report issued by the First Baptist Church of St. Anthony, a congregation that had declined to twenty-five members and whose church structure had lapsed into disrepair as bravely referenced in its circular letter: "Our candlestick still abides in its place. . . . Our prayer meetings have been interesting and profitable to the little band. We make grateful mention of our Presbyterian brethren in giving us the use of their house during the winter."[7]

Hickman returned to St. Paul with a broader sense of the issues confronting other churches in the state. He realized that Pilgrim's "flourishing" Sabbath school placed his congregation well within the mainstream of the values the association held, as well as the tenets of the Minnesota Baptists, but also reflected the vision and mission of Harriet Bishop: "She invited them to come together and form [a Sabbath school], and they soon learned to love it very much, and she, too, was very happy in instructing them; and a great deal of good resulted from it."[8] He also learned that they, too, saw in him a soul whom their faith and legacy mandated they embrace, and that his welfare was their welfare: "In this world where gangrene is sin, with its death-producing effects, there is no curative but you."[9] Theirs was a working faith:

> It was a turbulent and worried world to which Jesus came; his great soul stirred within them as he saw the blind leading the blind. He saw their need for light. It is a torn and worried world. Still, all the relations that affect life are disturbed and perplexing, in politics, business, scholarship, society, religion. How shall men understand their right relations to these and the way they ought to go? In that far off time Jesus said, "I am the Light." When He passed into the shadows He said to that first group of followers, and is saying to every succeeding group, "Now you are the

light." Not creeds but you. You must be incarnation of Truth. It must radiate your community from you. There is no light that can illuminate the path from here to the gates of the Eternal City but you. From you is the light that shall lead this old world out of its bewilderment, through its revolutions, out of its political perplexities, resolve its social problems and guide men into the brotherhood of peoples which shall fabricate the commonwealth of God.[10]

Hickman returned determined to learn more about being a Good Shepherd in the mold of the Minnesota Baptists.

On January 3, 1870, the Sons of Freedom, an organization he had participated in establishing the year before, held its first statewide convention at the Pence Opera House in Minneapolis, where between three hundred and four hundred people were in attendance, including "a goodly number of white people who were present as spectators."[11] It was intended to be a celebration of the seventh anniversary of the Emancipation Proclamation, recognition of Minnesota's Negro suffrage amendment (the Fifteenth Amendment had not yet been ratified), and a formal launching of the state's first civil rights organization. Most of the speeches were tributes to the valor of black troops at such notable battles as Fort Wagner in South Carolina and Petersburg, Virginia, but the most significant speech seemed to be that of Robert Banks, who cried out for the importance of education: "Great credit is due Minnesota for liberal provisions for education. It is the principle that will preserve the republic. Let all the children of the state and country be educated mentally, morally, religiously, and physically, and all will be well."[12] Hickman was absent from the proceeding. Instead, he was in St. Paul tending to his churchly duties. Later that month, on January 30, he witnessed the marriage of Alfred Gales, friend, fellow whitewasher, and Pilgrim member; the Reverend A. M. Torbet officiated at the ceremony.[13]

◆ ◆ ◆ ◆ ◆

*But one Monday evening the pastor said to the six deacons, none of them rich at the time, "There is a growing neighborhood out Fort Street where no denomination is trying to meet the need. I have found a good lot and got an option on it. Why should not we seven men buy that lot?" All rose at the impulse. First thing Tuesday morning, D. D. Merrill made a payment for us.*

REV. LEMUEL CALL BARNES
FIRST BAPTIST CHURCH, 1878–1882[14]

In the summer of 1870, three years after he became pastor of First Baptist, the Reverend R. A. Paterson resigned from his duties. He had labored despite persistent illness virtually throughout his entire tenure, at times leaving the pulpit to be filled by visiting ministers.[15] Nonetheless he directed his limited energies to fostering religious education for children and community outreach. "He loved the Word of His Master, and was especially gifted in winning the young to His Service. The Church nursery, the Sunday school, gave large accessions to the visible family of the redeemed ones, during his ministrations."[16] He also made it a point to attend association conferences, though not always participating actively, as well as programs that supported the work of the Pilgrim Baptist Society, being, for example, in attendance at the fund-raiser in December 1867.[17] In June 1870, he officiated at the funeral of James Egbert Thompson, a dear friend and esteemed member of the church who had died suddenly: "While with his family seeking, upon the banks of a little stream, a day's relaxation from the monotonous routine of the bank, of which he was president, he was transported to the other shore of the mysterious river."[18] By July Paterson himself could no longer perform his duties of the pastorate of the state's largest Baptist church, and resigned. "His physical powers were inadequate to the demands of his time and strength, and after three years of service, he resigned for rest and recuperation."[19]

The Reverend E. B. Hulbert was called to succeed Paterson in November 1871, and he would serve for three years, just as Paterson had. Except for Pastor John Pope, who served nine years between the tenures of Torbet and Paterson, on average the pastors of First Baptist Church during the nineteenth century stayed slightly more than three years.[20] A major factor in the relatively short tenures was the amount of work they were expected to do. "As I have read the story of the church," said Reverend Brown at the seventy-fifth anniversary, "I get the distinct impression that while the ministers of this church have been honored, they have been invariably overworked. They have been compelled to carry on an immense amount of routine service which the church might, in many cases, have taken out of their hands."[21] The First Baptist pastor was expected to be of the community, and this required a very special kind of man.

After a number of visiting preachers and candidates, the church would take one and a half years to settle on Hulbert, reflecting the importance of finding the right man for the church. This responsibility gave the deacons influence over policy by virtue of their long-term stature within the congregation and commitment to the larger community, especially when the pastor had answered the call by coming from another church and another state, as

was the case at First Baptist. Essentially, it was they, in the name of the congregation, who set the direction in which the pastor was expected to lead the
church.

First Baptist had created a tradition of "render[ing] service to the community in a unique way in the ministers who [had] not only been pastors of
this church but servants at large to the community itself." Deacons, who for
many years had facilitated the work of this tradition, completely owned it,
and they expected pastors to likewise be "community-minded men" whose
"horizons were always wide enough to take the city's life and development."[22]
Five months after beginning his pastorate, Paterson actively participated in
the Pilgrim fund-raiser in late 1867. It was a time of political uncertainty in a
city where racism could be seen in many quarters. He might have supported
Pilgrim in any event, but the fact that the event itself appeared principally
supported by First Baptist made his presence assured. The deacons embodied the will of the congregation. It was into four months "of this pastorless
season that Brethren D. D. Merrill and J. H. Randall were chosen Deacons,
November 9, 1870."[23]

Merrill's influence within the congregation had already been established
when he received Paterson's endorsement, before he had left, in agreeing
to an idea Merrill proposed in establishing the Walnut Street mission where
George Prescott eventually became pastor.[24]

On November 3, 1870, as the temperature dropped below 30 degrees,
workmen in St. Anthony dismantled the Baptist church that had stood for
twenty years. Considered an old landmark, it was the second church to be
constructed in Minnesota. This humble wood-and-stone dwelling had a seating capacity of three hundred but had recently housed a congregation of
twenty-five members. Now it was being taken down to be moved to St. Paul,
where it would be "rebuilt as a church for the colored Baptist society of that
city."[25] The structure was to be reassembled at Twelfth and Cedar Streets,
near Wabasha, near the Chapel of the Good Shepherd that had been held
in trust by First Baptist Church since 1866. "Our Colored Pilgrim Baptist
Church, I am told," Alice Merrill, wife of Deacon Merrill, later reported, "is
built in a part of the material brought from St. Anthony. [These were] materials that composed really the first Baptist church in Minnesota."[26] The article
that appeared in the *St. Paul Dispatch* ended, "Reverend Robert Hickman is
the Pastor."[27]

In fact, Hickman was not the pastor though his stature among the Pilgrims and within the larger black community, as well as the notoriety he had
acquired in 1869, perhaps led the paper to characterize him this way. Over two

years had passed since Reverend Torbet agreed "to superintend the work"; his name alone, as the imprimatur of honesty, would attract prospective donors. Now, as the work began, his name was absent from notice. The expected cost to move materials from St. Anthony and to construct the church in St. Paul was $2,400. A festival was intended to defray the cost. On November 17, the *Dispatch* reported:

> Mr. Hickman gives notice that there will be a festival given at the Odeon Hall, on Thursday evening, the proceeds to go towards a fund for building a church for colored people. The citizens generally are cordially invited to attend. Mrs. Nichols, a celebrated musician from the East, will preside at the piano.[28]

The festival "was well attended. There was a good supper, good music, and a good time generally."[29] The next morning, "at half past 10," supporters assembled at First Baptist Church, from which they once again marched "in procession to Odeon Hall, where an address [was] delivered by Rev. Mr. Hickman."[30] It was as if even the city's white opinion makers recognized who the legitimate Pilgrim leader was.

By February 1871 the twenty-five Pilgrims of St. Paul, Minnesota, and their visionary leader, Robert Hickman, could finally look on with pride at the new building taking shape that would be, at last, their house of worship, and it would soon be ready for occupancy. To provide seating within the cavernous structure, First Baptist Church had donated black walnut pews.[31] At 3:00 p.m. on March 5, 1871, "the house of worship recently erected at the corner of Twelve [*sic*] and Cedar" at last was dedicated. E. B. Hulbert, pastor of First Baptist Church, delivered the sermon; Amory Gale preached during the evening service.[32]

Deacon Merrill and his brethren at First Baptist had every reason to feel proud of their service to God's handiwork, a new house of worship to praise His Name and a shelter from evil for His children so recently out of slavery. And from here, they would proceed on to other ventures, expanding the membership and influence of First Baptist Church either by direct membership or under its sponsorship "of other Baptist interests throughout the City of St. Paul." Pilgrim Baptist was their first mission to become a church, and more would follow, fueled by the experience they gained and the profound sense of calling.[33] His father, Thomas Ward Merrill, would have been proud. This was a glorious day, a God-sent day to behold.

And for Hickman, this too was truly a glorious day. But unlike for Merrill, it was a day that was not without mixed feelings. It was a paradox that not since his days in slavery had he last preached to his flock as their pastor. On the free soil of Minnesota, however, Hickman could not do so, for he needed a license, bestowed by white pastors, in order to preach; and, of course, as yet, he did not qualify. Of course, on this point he would say nothing, except to express gratitude for the heartfelt support and stewardship of Deacon Merrill and the fellowship of First Baptist Church, never divulging to Merrill that Reverend Torbet, Merrill's father-in-law, as Pilgrim Baptist's legitimate but apathetic pastor, could never serve Pilgrim's people in a manner they deserved. Torbet was not a dutiful church leader who shared their history and travails, a pastor chosen by them who shared their blood. But ingratitude was a bitter fruit. Instead, Hickman, a barely literate former slave who worked assiduously to be accepted by men of high education, social standing, and moral intent, would continue to attend the Minnesota Baptist Convention and to fulfill his labors as an acolyte of Torbet.

Between 1871 and 1876 Hickman would tend to a congregation that grew from thirty to seventy-five members, benefitting from being the only black church to survive the period that saw the demise of all of the other black churches in St. Paul. The church would be the site of the Robert Banks Literary Society and serve as the place where religious, educational, and social activities were held. At last in 1874, Hickman was given a license to preach but he was not present to bless let alone attend the celebration by St. Paul blacks of the Congressional passage of the Civil Rights Act of 1875, which was held at a different site. Later that year, having at last proved himself to be righteously observant of God's will, he was ordained. Still, he would have to wait another three years before he became his congregation's official pastor, fifteen years after he and his followers arrived in St. Paul.[34]

PART V

# *The Buried Citizen*

## Sarah Burger Stearns
### 1866–1875

# 22

# CELEBRATION, 1875

*I believe our success was largely, if not wholly, attributable
to our studied failure to agitate the question.*

SARAH BURGER STEARNS, 1875

In March 1875, when President Ulysses Grant signed into law the Civil Rights
Act, which banned discrimination in public areas, few blacks and opinion makers in Minnesota took note. In a state with a small number of black citizens
and, as it was conventionally viewed by white people, no explosive displays
of racial tension, mob violence and terrorism were perceived primarily to be
Southern phenomena. Even when stories infrequently appeared recounting
flare-ups between blacks and whites on the streets of Minnesota cities and
towns, the incidences tended to be seen merely as isolated, unfortunate, and
rare, and the prevalence of poverty among black Minnesotans was considered
more a matter of character than circumstance. In one of the most enlightened
states in the Union, at least in terms of black-white relations, intelligent white
Minnesotans justifiably felt they had done all they could and should for the
black man—indeed, that they had done their part. But the virtue of some of
that work was dubious, for citizenship was not based on education, or even intelligence, but simply and exclusively on manhood. The Civil Rights Act did
nothing to change that. Unlike with black suffrage where white men worked
to achieve the vote, Minnesota's women would largely have to attain suffrage
by their own efforts. Nine years after Sarah Stearns began her campaign for
women's rights, the fruit of her labors would become evident.

In late 1875, as the day approached for the decision by the voters of

Minnesota to determine whether women should get the right to vote, Sarah Stearns, "wishing to make sure of the votes of the intelligent men of the State," sent a telegram to the editor of the *Pioneer Press,* the leading paper of Minnesota, begging him to urge his readers to do all in their power to secure the adoption of the amendment.[1]

The time, as she later related the plan to be, was right. Since earlier that year the legislature had enacted the bill putting the women's suffrage question to the voters, proponents intended to stay quiet throughout the intervening months so as to lull opponents into indifference. The success or failure of the central issue—women's suffrage—would not be decided directly by the voters of Minnesota, as had been the case with black suffrage in 1865, 1867, and 1868; less controversially, voters were to decide whether the state constitution should be amended to authorize the legislature to extend suffrage rights to women. That their suffrage would be limited to electing school board members and running for a seat on the school board, a right that other states by then had already established, further seemed to minimize the level of rancor. Many men who opposed women voting on "masculine" issues of the day, it was believed, felt less concern if women were seeking leadership roles in nurturing the educational welfare of children, considered yet another aspect of a woman's appropriate place.

Nonetheless, women's suffrage in Minnesota had always been a tricky matter. Nothing should be taken for granted. Men, even so-called enlightened men, simply did not see women as equal to themselves and even, at times, crudely rebuked them for their efforts. In supporting black suffrage, women leaders felt it incredible that Republican leaders, their so-called allies, and in some instances, husbands, had deemed "even the lowest, most ignorant of black men" to be their political equals. To them, Frederick Douglass was one of a kind. But this too was the nature of ignorance that would have to die out in the fullness of time with the passing of each generation. It was this very thing that well-situated intelligent women could change by leading the effort to elevate the quality of public education and, in doing so, improve all of society. This, too, was women's work. To do all of this, they needed to get the votes in the November election.

Just as opponents, it was hoped, would ignore the issue, so too might potential "friends." Timing was of the essence. Inspiring them to vote in the affirmative while not provoking opponents to vote in the negative was like threading a needle. But Stearns's hand was steady when she, at the optimum moment, put pen to paper to get the editor to act. In a private letter, he later thanked her, saying that even he "had quite forgotten such an amendment had been proposed." It was precisely where she had wanted Minnesota to be. Mass *unawareness* was the key, for there had been no debate of the issue that consequently, according to Stearns, created the opening to victory. "I believe our success," she later reported, "was largely, if not wholly, attributable to our studied failure to agitate the question." The opposition, without agitation from proponents of the question, had simply forgotten the whole matter existed, so that it was possible that even "the ignorant classes who could not, or did not read their ballots, voted unthinkingly for the measure." The notice in the *Pioneer Press*, the state's record of note and organ for the Liberal Republican-Democratic Party, a reflection of how much the politics of the day had changed, made it all possible when it triggered the organizations in both parties around the state to print "affirmative wording of all the tickets of both parties."[2] Men following the endorsements of their party bosses— Republican, Democratic, Anti-Monopoly—only knew to circle "Yes" next to the otherwise cryptic phrase, "For the amendment of Article VII, relating to electors." Knowing the implication of doing so was not important.[3]

The simple question of whether the legislature should be empowered to make that decision was a significant shift in tactics, and one that was ultimately successful. When Election Day came on November 2, the relatively innocuous amendment was carried by a vote of 24,340 to 19,480. With the amendment now a part of the constitution, proponents needed only to focus on a handful of legislators, some of whom were spouses or friends. Such was the nature of the political shift of politics in Minnesota by the mid-1870s. The following legislature passed the necessary law, and at the spring election of 1876, the same year when African Americans and liberal-minded whites gathered at Lincoln Park in the nation's capital to dedicate a monument commemorating their martyred president and the Emancipation Proclamation, the women of Minnesota voted for school officials and, in several cases, were elected as directors.[4]

Seeing women at the polling booths, seeing women's names on ballots: it was a start.

# 23

# STANDING ALONE
# IN MINNESOTA

*We can't see why color is not just as good a qualification
for voting as sex, nor why a woman is not just as competent
to choose a member of the Legislature as a negro.*

SARAH BURGER STEARNS, 1866

On February 3, 1866, the *Rochester Post* reported that Representative John
B. H. Mitchell, a farmer from Stillwater, introduced a bill to amend the state
constitution, striking out the word "white" from the qualifications for voters
and requiring that the voter "shall be able to read and write in the English language, *or the language of the country of which he may be a native.*" Essentially,
if approved, the voters of Minnesota would once again vote whether black
men should be given the franchise, a question they had faced and rejected
in 1865, and bar white illiterate men who had previously voted. The writer
surmised that the proposition would pass the legislature and be submitted to
the people. In that the people had voted to reject a black suffrage question the
year before, the writer hoped that the question would be allowed to rest a year
or two. If it were to come to a popular vote again, the writer would support
the proposition:

But as we know of no argument for the extension of suffrage that
will not apply to women, we are sorry that Mister Mitchell did not
strike out the word "male" and make all persons over the age of

twenty-one years . . . voters. We can't see why color is not just as good a qualification for voting as sex, nor why a woman is not just as competent to choose a member of the Legislature as a negro.

Though the writer was especially interested in a proposition that required a certain level of education as a measure for one's qualifications to vote, the writer concluded, "on the whole the amendment will be an improvement on the Constitution."[1]

The *Rochester Post* was owned and edited by Joseph A. Leonard, a Maryland-born Lincoln Republican of the strong reformer stripe. He had come to Minnesota in 1858, the year of statehood, and settled in the small prairie town on the Minnesota border that developed as a stagecoach stop on the road between St. Paul and Dubuque. His entrepreneurial vision for the community was vindicated with the arrival of the railroad in the 1860s, which brought new residents and business opportunities. One such man was Dr. William Mayo, who arrived in 1863 after having served as an examining surgeon for draftees in the Civil War. With a newspaper, Leonard played a central role in promoting the dusty town into a thriving community, and set the moral tone, as leader of the local temperance society and advocate for black suffrage and women's rights, that would later characterize the city as a progressive place.[2]

Those of like minds sought him out, including Ozora Stearns, a young attorney who, with his wife, had just moved to Rochester during the earliest days of 1866, after having served as a colonel in the Thirty-Fifth Colored Infantry. By February the young lawyer was Olmsted County attorney, and by May he had been elected mayor. Every step of his progress was documented in the *Post*. But as impressed as Leonard was with the young mayor, it was the intellect, passion, and talent of Stearns's wife that had impressed Leonard more, so much so that he printed her articles in his paper, articles that were unconventional in the sense that they illuminated the daily adversities that Minnesota women faced.[3]

Sarah Burger Stearns had been an advocate for women's rights since she was fourteen years old, when she began as an editor of her school paper in Ann Arbor, Michigan. Her first article was on the exclusion of women from the state university. Two years later, at age sixteen, she attended a suffrage convention in Ohio, where she was inspired by speeches by such famous leaders as Lucretia Mott and Lucy Stone. By the time Stearns was in her early twenties she had started to turn her ideas into action. In 1858 she and twelve other young women petitioned the University of Michigan to admit women.

Unsuccessful, she entered the State Normal School in Ypsilanti and became a teacher after completing her education. In 1863 she married Ozora Stearns, who had graduated from the very university that refused to admit her. He was in the service and was sent to the front lines in the Civil War shortly after they married. While he was away, Sarah moved back to her family home in Ann Arbor. After the war, in 1866, the couple moved to Rochester, where even as the city's First Lady she partook in the controversial matter of women's rights, "where by lectures, newspaper articles, petitions and appeals to the legislature Mrs. Stearns [did] much to stir the women of the State to thought and action upon the question of women's enfranchisement."[4]

In the same year of their arrival, Republican legislators, who held the majority in both chambers, were still smarting, not just from the recent defeat of black suffrage in 1865 but also from what appeared to be the declining power of the Republican Party at the hands of the reactionary Democrat who then occupied the president's chair in the White House. Skittish about mounting another campaign for black suffrage, for at least the time being, the special joint committee returned Mitchell's bill with a recommendation to "indefinitely postpone" HF No. 18. The motion to postpone passed by a vote of 24 to 2, thus, as they claimed, honoring the wishes of the voters of Minnesota who had rejected the black suffrage question the year before. Still, though black suffrage had been overwhelmingly rejected, Stearns resented that not one legislator was willing even to mention that women should be included in the franchise. She predicted that "the time will come when readers of history will be astonished of the obtuseness of the leaders of the Republican party in not perceiving that every argument they have made in favor of negro suffrage applies with yet greater force to the right of women to the elective franchise."[5]

She asserted that women made up one-half the population of the country—"intelligent, virtuous, native-born American citizens; [who] yet stand outside the pale of political recognition." Her exclusive reference to "native-born American citizens" reflected an ethnocentric streak that was then characteristic of eastern Yankees, suggesting that she had not been in the state long enough to recognize the significance of foreign-born Minnesotans in the political equation. She continued, stating that the Constitution classified women as free people and counted women "whole persons" in the basis of representation, "and yet are we governed without our consent, compelled to pay taxes without appeal, and punished for violations of law without choice of judge or jury. . . . The experience of all ages, the declarations of the fathers, the statute laws of our day, and the fearful revelation through which we have just passed; all prove the uncertain tenure of life, liberty, and property so long as the ballot, the only weapon of self-protection, is not in the hand of every citizen." She therefore called on lawmakers to amend the state constitution, and, "in harmony with advancing civilization, placing new safeguards around the individual rights of four million emancipated slaves, we ask that you extend the right of suffrage to women, the only remaining class of disenfranchised citizens."[6]

Even within this southernmost Minnesota town nestled along the sleepy Zumbro River, yet land-locked by prairie and farmland, it was easy for one with such progressive views to feel isolated; but Stearns knew others felt the same way, or had these feelings that were yet to be born. She was determined to speak to and for her readers, to let them know that they were not alone in their muted awareness and self-imposed silence. She wanted her readers to know that they were part of a larger movement that would amplify their concerns and demands, a movement that was just then gathering momentum in the eastern centers of progressive thought—in Boston and New York and Philadelphia—as well as in the corridors of power. To begin drawing that connection, she reprinted the petition introduced in Congress as senators debated the proposed Fourteenth Amendment, drafted by Susan B. Anthony and Elizabeth Cady Stanton, which called for universal suffrage. And she did so, punctuating the message by reporting that the petition was presented by a Democrat when no Republican could be found to be "bold enough, or manly enough."[7] In this assertion, she was highlighting the dawning of a new political era.

The political landscape had shifted profoundly. The abolitionists, who had labored on the fringes of the political mainstream of the Republican Party, were now firmly planted within the established political order. From there they could influence federal policy; and the policy that now received their more urgent attention was the enfranchisement of the nation's freedmen, most of whom continued to live under the unrepentant specter of Old Dixie. To abolitionists and Radical Republicans, black suffrage best protected freedmen. With abolitionists seated so prominently at the elbows of lawmakers, feminists felt encouraged at the prospect of their friends and allies pressing forward on universal political equality. This was when the rupture between the suffragists and their allies within the party began.

It was the beginning of the postwar era that had been declared "the Negro hour" by Wendell Phillips, leader of the movement for black equality, former abolitionist, and, as many suffragists believed, former ally in the struggle for a woman's right to vote: it was critical for Stearns's readers to see the shifting political landscape through clear eyes, without the tint of sentiment and unrequited loyalty.[8] Phillips had set the tone for the Republican caucus in Congress and by extension, the Republican leadership in Minnesota, when he insisted that women's suffrage, which he had long supported, now for the time being had to be set aside in favor of black male suffrage: "Success," he had stated the month before, "was best obtained by doing one thing at a time." To Stearns's ears, this meant that for the women of Minnesota, where black suffrage had already been soundly rejected and with little hope of future success, Republicans were relieved of any sense of duty to their womenfolk. Worse, they could hide behind the pretext of fatalism. Phillips had spoken in the most respectful way possible, but his words felt like thinly veiled paternalism.[9] Women were being betrayed by so-called friends, and she wanted her readers to know this to be true.

Stearns's message, for some, may have been uncomfortable to read, especially for those who considered themselves devout Lincoln Republicans, investing their hearts and efforts in the cause to preserve the Union and to end slavery once and for all. But within the year following Appomattox and the assassination of their beloved President Lincoln, so much had changed. What should have been a gratifying, high-minded campaign by friends and allies to achieve universal enfranchisement had instead all gone wrong, and what was left was a powerful sense of betrayal followed by a painful recognition that attaining full rights for women would have to be done alone. Stearns's message was discomfiting, for it derided convention that shrouded an ugly truth her readers fundamentally knew about the unique nature of the oppression of women, yet had learned to endure. For many, accepting the message meant that nothing in their lives, including their relationships with husbands and friends, would remain the same. In this, her message was at once cathartic and unnerving. Sacred cows would need to be slain, as she echoed Susan B. Anthony—"The Republicans are cowardly"—with her own experience with Minnesota legislators: "It is a singular fact that while the radical politicians of the country are urging the extension of the elective franchise to all men, *there has not yet been found a man in Congress or even in the Legislature bold enough, or manly enough, to urge the right of women to vote.*"[10]

But for all of the righteous anger Stearns felt about the Republicans, she also recognized one constraining fact: her devoted husband was very much a member of the party's establishment, getting elected county attorney, then mayor, within the first year of their Rochester residency. Throughout the dispiriting year of 1866, as President Johnson railed against the Radicals' control in Congress, Mayor Stearns joined prominent party leaders to offset the resurgence of Democratic power. Ultimately, instead of rewarding the president in the midterm elections of 1866, the voters nationwide repudiated his policies by vindicating the Republicans with a landslide victory that included candidates who had supported black suffrage, revitalized the state-by-state canvass to ratify the Fourteenth Amendment, and revived among Minnesota Republicans a commitment to mount a new referendum in Minnesota for universal male enfranchisement.

On January 15, the Minnesota House voted 40–5 to add the amendment to the Constitution of the United States, which began with the words, "All persons born and naturalized in the United States, and subject to the jurisdiction thereof, are citizens of the United States and of the State wherein they reside." The Senate ratified the amendment the next day. That day, Minnesota legislators ratified the Fourteenth Amendment.[11] It would not be until July 28 of the following year that the campaign to secure support from the requisite number of states—twenty-eight in all—would finally be done. Though in some states the campaign was not easy, in Minnesota the vote was virtually pro forma; the matter was incontrovertible. The Party of Lincoln was indeed securely in control of the body politic, and it was now setting its sights on extending the vote to the black men of the state.

For weeks following Minnesota's ratification, Morton Wilkinson and other congressional nominees reiterated their call for universal manhood suffrage, arguing that the Fourteenth Amendment did not go far enough to protect the rights of black men. Wilkinson was joined by a number of party leaders, including Rochester mayor Ozora Stearns and, later, Samuel Jemison, assistant editor of the *St. Paul Press,* who refrained in his endorsement from speaking for the newspaper. The paper's endorsement would come soon afterward. They all urged their Minnesota constituents to support a constitutional amendment to extend to black men suffrage rights that were not provided by the Fourteenth Amendment. Even moderate Republicans felt emboldened to support black suffrage.

Sarah Stearns did not want them to forget about the women:

> There is no doubt that the next Legislature will provide for the submission of the question of negro suffrage to the people. We hope that we may have among the fifty-six Republicans in that body, one of independence enough to propose universal suffrage. It would be just as easy to strike "male" from the Constitution at the same time as the word "white"; and there can be no stronger argument in favor of the discrimination in sex than of color. But both Legislators and people will doubtless insist on making two bites of a cherry. They will adopt

negro suffrage within twelve months, and after quarreling for years about the right of women, to vote, if they want to, they will amend that, and then wonder why they had not done it long before.[12]

This the legislature did not do. Instead, in their tribute to the tens of thousands of Minnesotans who labored to support the boys in uniform, party leaders linked all that was noble and patriotic to the issue of expanding the franchise. In February Sarah Burger Stearns and Mary Jackman Colburn requested to speak before an expectedly respectful legislature in support of removing the word "male" from the bill, but this presumably easy task would prove byzantine. Stearns's being married to one of their brethren meant little to many of the legislators, as she would soon discover.

On February 7 the House adopted a resolution to invite the two women to address the body at seven o'clock on the evening of the twelfth.[13] The address did not occur as scheduled, however, apparently owing to miscommunications. On the fourteenth, Representative John Sebolski of Hennepin presented a letter from Mrs. Stearns containing the remarks she had intended to make, and it was tabled and ordered to be printed. The petition was formally referred to a special committee of five. Accompanying the letter was a "petition of two hundred citizens, male and female, praying for the extension of the right to suffrage to females." The Speaker announced that the committee would be composed of Sebolski, John Randall of Ramsey, C. A. Wheaton of the Eighth District, C. J. Fetch of the Fifteenth District, and John A. Reed of the Seventeenth District.[14]

The mood was changing, however. Since February 14, when Governor Marshall signed the joint House and Senate resolution ratifying the Fourteenth Amendment of the Constitution of the United States, legislators were not of a mind to have their reform-inspired bona fides tested. On the morning of the twenty-first, the *St. Paul Press* captured the mounting annoyance with the whole matter that could be heard from within the caucus, reporting in mocking terms:

> The meeting announced to take place at the Capitol last night, was a more common failure than the previous one. The lady announced to speak failed to make her appearance and the time was occupied by three of the masculine persuasion, who made the speeches, most of which [were] burlesque and ridiculous.[15]

Nonetheless, Representative Richardson, who had first presented Colburn's request, pressed forward by offering the following resolution: "Resolved,

That Mrs. Mary J. Colburn be granted the use of the hall this evening, to lecture on the subject of female suffrage." The resolution was tabled.[16] It was apparently widely felt among the legislators that uncourtly manners ought to be demonstrated behind the scenes. At this point, Representative Ebenezer Ayres of the Second District introduced a resolution inviting Dr. Colburn to speak in the chamber, this time using far more pointed language aimed at his disrespectful colleague, urging that "gentlemanly courtesy on the part of the sterner sex, in this refined, enlightened and magnanimous age, dictate the tender of the use of the Hall of Representatives for the purpose of said address." The resolution was adopted.[17] The House then adjourned until Saturday evening.[18]

With this, Dr. Colburn was granted a hearing within the state's most august chamber, but despite the gesture, few legislators actually attended. Only the handful who already counted themselves as supporters of the cause appeared. As the *Press* reported the next day, "Owing to [another] lecture in Ingersoll's hall, and the fact that the Governor had a reception last evening, the audience was not so large as it probably would otherwise have been, or as large as the audiences were that assembled at the same place on two previous occasions." Representative Wheaton, a member of the House Committee of Five who now acted as chair for the occasion, "congratulated the audience because this time, the friends of the cause would not be disappointed by having no speaker. On the evening of February 21, she spoke. He was pleased to say that Mrs. Colburn was present, and called on Mr. Sebolski to wait upon the lady to the desk." The *Press* described the guest speaker:

> Mrs. Colburn is a lady of medium height, somewhat thin, about forty-five years of age, and a high prominent forehead and clear eyes. She read from manuscript, and prefaced her lecture with the statement that she had recently been suffering from bronchitis, but hoped to be able to get through her lecture without difficulty. Speaking to the audience does not disturb her in the least. . . . Mrs. Colburn does not have a loud voice, but can be heard with great distinctness in every part of the House.[19]

According to one account from a sympathizer, she made a "carefully prepared argument."[20] The account in the *Press*, however, was more expansive and characteristic of the political establishment. "If the lecture, or address which she delivered last night was her own production, it is very clear she is a lady of no very ordinary powers of mind and who had very positive and clear ideas upon this subject, and the necessary ability to enable her to express them with precision":

> Like all who think with her she goes back to the foundation—to first principles. To her mind the phrase "all men," as used by Jefferson and the fathers, is a generic term and includes women as well as men. From this is induced the right of women to vote.

"Altogether," adjudged the *Press* of her performance, "the address appeared to be an able and forcible presentation of that side of the question."[21] In the end, the women had been placated. Legislators could at last resume the work of the state.

This was not Colburn's first encounter with the legislature. In 1864 the fifty-three-year old medical doctor and Massachusetts native won an essay contest that was sponsored by the legislature. When she went to receive the award, legislators questioned her right to the recognition when they learned that she was in fact a woman: she had signed the essay "M. J. Colburn." Exasperated from the experience, she later wrote in a letter to a friend, "I am but doing little now on the suffrage question, for I will not stoop longer to ask of my congress or legislature for that which I know to be mine." Though her sentiment was sparked then by her reception at the legislature over her duly won award, the words had a deeper meaning now, three years later.[22] The legislative session of 1867 would be the last time she would appear before that body; and for good reason, for increasingly, there was a sense that Minnesota's lawmakers not only held the matter of voting rights for women in disdain, but that any further effort initiated could be trifled with, as would be evident in the sessions of 1868 and 1870.

On the other side of the spectrum, Republican leaders had only to look beyond Dr. Colburn and southwest to Kansas to justify their strategy. They knew the hearts and minds and limitations of the men they represented.

# 24

# THE LESSON OF KANSAS

*At all events, the hypocrisy of Democrats serves us a better
purpose in the present emergency than does the treachery of
the Republicans.*

SUSAN B. ANTHONY, 1866

*If the elective franchise is not extended to the negro, he
dies . . . Woman has a thousand ways by which she can attach
herself to the ruling power of the land that we have not.*

FREDERICK DOUGLASS, 1868

One month after Susan B. Anthony and Elizabeth Cady Stanton founded
the Equal Rights Association, Congress sent the male-exclusive Fourteenth
Amendment to the states for ratification. With the federal government determined to exclude women, Anthony and Stanton resolved to keep the association focused on a strategy that held that black and woman suffrage were
compatible, and to do so on the state level by launching a series of lobbying and petition campaigns to amend state constitutions. In 1866 and 1867,
campaigns began in New York, New Jersey, Kansas, Maine, Massachusetts,
and Ohio.[1] In Minnesota, Sarah Stearns and Mary Colburn began their own
campaign. Despite the best efforts of organizers, however, antiblack riots in
New Orleans and Memphis intensified the belief that freedmen needed further constitutional protections. After passage of the Fourteenth Amendment,
policy makers shifted their focus to black suffrage. Indeed, through black

suffrage, the Union's victory would be secured. As Ellen Dubois has written, "These developments increasingly drew the black man alone to the center of the national political stage."[2] Republicans and Democrats, abolitionists and racists, agreed—the major issue of Reconstruction was the freedmen's political status.

In the face of this consensus, the universal suffrage vision of the Equal Rights Association became more and more problematic. Few believed that white men would support black suffrage if the vote simultaneously made their wives politically equal to them. While Radicals refused to endorse women's suffrage, Democrats supported suffrage petitions and bills, seeing them as a way to embarrass the advocates for black suffrage.[3] Similarly, while the Republican press ridiculed the Equal Rights Association and the *Standard* refused to report its activities, Democratic papers, happy to publicize any split within the abolitionist ranks, gave the association generous coverage and helped spread its message. These were the events to which the *St. Paul Press* would refer in castigating the women's suffrage bill in the 1870 session of the Minnesota legislature. Anthony and Stanton no longer felt they had anything to lose by accepting aid from the Democrats and were under no illusions regarding Democratic motives.[4] The issue was quite clear. "If the Democrats advocate a grand measure of public policy which they do not believe, they occupy much higher ground than Republicans who refuse to press the same measure which they claim to believe. At all events, the hypocrisy of Democrats serves us a better purpose in the present emergency than does the treachery of the Republicans."[5] In time, the tension between abolitionists and feminists deepened until it destroyed the foundation of the Equal Rights Association, leading Anthony and Stanton to an open break with abolitionists. In 1867 the split became unavoidable.

In March, Anthony received a message from Samuel Wood, a Republican state senator from Kansas, appealing to her to come to his state to help campaign on behalf of women and black suffrage. At the time, neither she nor Stanton could leave New York, so Anthony enlisted Lucy Stone to go to Kansas. Stone's husband, Henry Blackwell, accompanied her. The campaign, already poorly financed, was ill fated from the start. Earlier, it had all seemed so promising. Stanton would later write, "As Kansas was the historic ground where Liberty fought her first victorious battles with Slavery, and consecrated that soil forever to the freedom of the black race, so was it the first State where the battle for woman's enfranchisement was waged and lost for a generation. There never was a more hopeful interest concentrated on the legislation of any single state, than when Kansas submitted the two propositions to her people to take the words 'white' and 'male' from her Constitution."[6]

Indeed, Kansas seemed to be a good place to wage a campaign for woman's suffrage, and victory there, as Dubois notes, would counter the charge that public opinion did not support the enfranchisement of women. It would provide the Equal Rights Association with the evidence it needed to convince Republicans that women's suffrage could be safely linked to black suffrage. Many Kansans were veterans of the fighting in the 1850s, and thought to be sympathizers of the abolition movement. The state had a strong record in women's rights. Only in New York was the legislation concerning women more advanced.[7] Blackwell was even more optimistic when he wrote to Stanton, "This is glorious country, Mrs. Stanton, and a glorious people. If we succeed here, it will be the State of the Future."[8]

The glimmer of hope quickly faded. Though Wood had succeeded in getting the Republican-dominated legislature to place the women's suffrage question before the voters, the first signs of trouble appeared when party leaders refused to permit it to be linked too closely to black suffrage, presenting it instead as a separate question. Moreover, the state Republican committee endorsed only the black suffrage referendum. Without that endorsement, women's suffrage was cast adrift. The State Impartial Suffrage Association, which Wood had organized, was being pressured by party leaders to drop women's suffrage and campaign only for black suffrage. Blackwell noted, "There are a great many silent enemies among the Republicans who are paralyzed by our bold strokes and waiting for a lull in our breeze to raise a reaction. This must not be permitted."[9]

To make matters worse, many of the strongest voices of the Equal Rights Association, an organization created to pursue universal suffrage—Frederick Douglass, Theodore Tilton, Wendell Phillips, and Thomas Wentworth Higginson—all refused invitations to come to Kansas to work alongside Blackwell and Stone. In fact, the abolitionist and Radical press, as well as the nation's most prominent paper, Horace Greeley's *New York Tribune*, had all refused even to recognize the work. In May Stone wrote to Anthony, "But the *Tribune* and [Tilton's] *Independent* alone could, if they would urge universal suffrage, as they [do] the negro suffrage, carry this whole nation upon the only just plane of equal human rights. What a power to hold, and not use!"[10] Republican voters were inclined to follow their party's endorsement, and prominent liberal opinion makers heard nothing to support women's suffrage.

What had begun as a campaign for universal suffrage tragically slipped into a fratricidal battle for political survival. This was the moment that both sides—black suffrage supporters and women's suffrage supporters—had long wanted when a people unjustly excluded from the franchise could now be welcomed into the fold. But then it all fell apart. The "black" supporters did not have faith that white male voters would tolerate change that was anything but piecemeal. The "women" supporters, on the other hand, feared that the depth of intransigent sexism was such that this moment of opportunity was fleeting; that the time to act—or at least, *try*—was now, never to return with their generation. The stakes were high. Each saw the ballot as protection against systemic oppression. Neither saw time as a luxury. Both saw the magnanimity of white male voters as a shooting star streaking across the night sky over the Kansas prairie, a sight of wonder, perhaps, and hope, but not one to rely on when charting a navigational direction to permanent safe harbor.

But by April, not quite one month after Wood's request, the allies supporting black and women's suffrage, standing under the flimsy umbrella of "Equal Rights," could feel the momentum change within the Kansas political landscape and their advantage recede as they increasingly slipped into the hubris of mutual distrust. Phillips had already accused Anthony of misappropriation of funds. Anthony accused Douglass, Tilton, and others (including, of course, Phillips), who had all accepted leadership positions with an organization created to promote universal suffrage, of acts of betrayal when those same men refrained from aiding that very campaign. Douglass on several occasions in 1866 insisted that universal suffrage was a birthright of black men and women alike, but now argued that the urgency of present circumstance dictated only one group to get the vote, and that group had to be the black man, whose very life depended on it. Anthony resented the presumptuousness of male colleagues who dictated the strategic goal and then criticized her for being unrealistic and emotional. Blacks questioned Anthony's racial sincerity when she brought Sojourner Truth to New York in a gesture intended to trump Douglass, but not to Kansas, where the presence of the famous former conductor of the Underground Railroad would have turned off potential supporters; and they took exception when Anthony's frustration led her to chide blacks with mockery and stereotype by saying, "It ain't as it used to was."[11]

In this, blacks felt white suffragists, despite their support for universal suffrage, would easily sacrifice black suffrage for their own. Even though audiences seemed receptive to universal suffrage, the power play of the Republican Party and Equal Rights canvassers reduced the suffrage issue to a scrap of meat to be fought over. "The negroes are all against us," wrote Lucy Stone. "These men ought not to be allowed to vote before we do, because they will be just so much more dead weight to lift."[12] A month earlier, a disheartened Blackwell referred to recriminations by blacks directed toward Sam Wood, who had initiated both campaigns in the state. "Wood has helped off more runaway slaves than any man in Kansas. He has always been true both to the negro and the woman. But the negroes dislike and distrust him because he has never allowed the word white to be struck out, unless the word male should be struck out also. . . . So while he advocates both, he fully realizes the wider scope and far greater grandeur of the battle for women."[13]

In fact, Blackwell's reference to "the greater grandeur of the battle" confirmed black suspicions. Earlier that year, in an open letter to legislatures of Southern states, Blackwell advised them of a way to permit Negro suffrage and still maintain white political supremacy. He urged the South to give the vote to women, arguing that the vote of Southern white women would counterbalance the combined vote of black men and black women. If all the whites voted one way and all the blacks voted another, the latter would be outvoted two to one. Thus, through universal suffrage, "the Negro question would be removed from the political scene. . . . [It would be a way to maintain] the political supremacy of your white race."[14] To the Republican Party, this was blasphemy.

The black suffrage referendum in Kansas was a Republican Party measure and represented the success Radicals were having by 1867 in making the freedmen's enfranchisement part of the Republican program. At the same time, it seemed that the universal suffrage message was taking root within the electorate. Dubois notes that the more visible the Equal Rights Association could make its demand for women's suffrage, the more pressure it put on the Republican Party to take a stand on the issue. Although a few Republicans suggested the party take up women's suffrage, antifeminist counsel prevailed and the party moved from implicit opposition to explicit attack. Few of the attacks were philosophical or principled. One Republican canvasser against women's suffrage claimed that Lucy Stone "and that seed-wart she carries around with her—called Blackwood were practicing free-lovers." A black man named Charles Langston claimed to represent the freedmen in their opposition to women's suffrage. Suffragist Olympia Brown described a third man, who asked his audience "if they wanted every old maid to vote" and rebuked the audience with " 'preferring every old thing that had a white face' to the negro." Under such onslaught, the suffragists began to openly seek support from the Democrats.[15]

This could only qualify as a tactical blunder. Grounded in desperation, this new approach at best would appeal to one-quarter of the Kansas electorate. Though the Democratic State Committee had come out against black and women's suffrage, Democratic canvassers accompanied Stanton and former Republican governor Charles Robinson in working in the border town where Democrats were strong; yet, with many of them, the campaign was less about women's suffrage than about mocking the Republican cause. Nonetheless, the Anthony-Stanton faction attempted to cultivate this rather flimsy base of voters. "Although equal rights organizers had quietly sought Democratic votes since the beginning of the canvass," Dubois writes, "they now concentrated on this tactic to the exclusion of others. Their appeals to Democrats became more open and much more partisan."[16] In other words, the suffragists had declared verbal war, not just against abolitionists but also the Republicans as a whole; and in turn, as Republicans saw it, women's suffrage had become a cause that appealed to sympathizers of the Old Confederacy.

In October, the dazzling, wealthy, and racist George Francis Train, a Boston-born Democrat and presidential candidate, stepped onto the stage. As Stanton reported,

> Seeing that the republican vote must be largely against the woman's
> amendment, the question arose what can be done to capture enough
> democratic votes to outweigh the recalcitrant republicans. At this
> auspicious moment George Francis Train appeared in the State as
> an advocate of woman suffrage. He appealed most effectively to
> the chivalry of the intelligent Irishmen, and the prejudices of the
> ignorant; conjuring them not to take the word "white" out of their
> constitution unless they did the word "male" also; and not to lift the
> negroes above the heads of their own mothers, wives, sisters, and
> daughters. The result was a respectable democratic vote in favor of
> woman suffrage.[17]

Years later, Blackwell described the decision to bring Train to Kansas as unwise. "After my wife and I had returned from our campaign work in Kansas, George Francis Train was invited into the State by Miss Anthony, at the insistence of friends in Missouri, to speak in behalf of the woman suffrage movement. While undoubtedly done with the best of intentions, this was most unwise. Mr. Train, as everybody knows, was a semi-lunatic." He added that Train was a "virulent Copperhead" and "the last person who should have been asked to speak for woman suffrage in a strongly Republican State, like radical Kansas."[18] However, Kathleen Barry sees Train's entry in an entirely different light, describing a series of events that characterized yet another challenge the Anthony-Stantonites faced: duplicity from within their own ranks, for it was Henry Blackwell and Sam Wood—and not Miss Anthony, as Blackwell wrote—who had engineered Train's entrance into the campaign:

> [Lucy Stone's] husband told me in the course of a long conversation on the "differences" that Mr. Train went to Kansas on the invitation of one Wood, a republican, to lecture to whomever would hear on Woman Suffrage among other things. . . . Mr. Blackwell & Gov. Robinson & two or three others who were conducting the W.S. campaign thought it might be well for Susan to accompany Train & so get democratic votes—while at the same time she could perhaps keep him straight on the negro question—Train being there against negro suffrage. They accordingly advised & promoted her Kansas trips with Train and she went as General Agent of the Equal Rights Association & with their full approval on that whole Kansas campaign.[19]

In any event, Train arrived on October 21 to begin the disastrous final chapter.

In addition to advocating women's suffrage, he spoke increasingly on currency reform, Fenianism (a movement of Irish nationalism), his own presidential campaign, and the innate inferiority of black men. His speeches, indulgent and often bawdy, entertained audiences with excessive sentimentalism and barroom humor, which at times included prurient insinuations of how he and Anthony, who were traveling together, spent the nights. But "most of all," notes Dubois, "it was Train's racism that violated the historical traditions and political principles of women's rights. Train slandered the freedmen whenever he could and anchored his advocacy of woman suffrage to his racism. Without quite calling for the defeat of black suffrage" (perhaps the high mark of Anthony's effort to "keep him straight"), "he offered women's votes as a weapon to be used against the specter of black supremacy he portrayed."[20] Regardless of Anthony's actual role in bringing Train to the Kansas campaign, it remains that she welcomed him, she worked with him, and she praised his performance. "No other man I ever saw," she wrote to Anna Dickinson, "could *move mountains*."[21] To abolitionist critics who denounced the Equal Rights suffragists for associating with Train, a bitter enemy of black people, Stanton replied,

> So long as opposition to slavery is the only test for a free pass to your platform and membership of your association, and you do not

shut out all persons opposed to woman suffrage, why should we not accept all in favor of woman suffrage to our platform and association, even though they be rabid pro-slavery Democrats? Your test of faithfulness is the negro, ours is the woman; the broadest platform, to which no party has yet risen, is humanity.

Then, recognizing the moral flaw in both camps, she added, "Reformers can be as bigoted and sectarian and as ready to malign each other, as the Church in its darkest periods has been to persecute its dissenters."[22]

In the end, Kansas voters rejected both amendments. Fighting to end slavery was not the same as extending to black men a political say in state affairs. Kansas men had said, *If negro suffrage passes, we will be flooded with ignorant, impoverished blacks from every state of the Union.* On the other hand, the voting majority in the state—Republicans—rejected a cause that so eagerly embraced Democratic votes and the embodiment of all they reviled—George Francis Train, who insisted that the women's vote was "a weapon to be used against the specter of black supremacy."[23] In other words, "Kansas" meant that the voters, as white men, feared black migration and, as Republicans, rejected a vote that supported the Democratic cause.

By collaborating with Train, Stanton and Anthony were reacting to intensifying antagonisms they had not been able to control. Equal Rights organizers had begun the Kansas campaign by trying to forge a joint voting bloc in favor of suffrage for blacks and women, but Republicans had sabotaged their efforts. By turning to Train, they gave substance to the charges of antifeminist Republicans that the women's suffrage movement was a tool the Democratic Party used against the freedmen. Blacks and women did not begin the campaign as enemies of each other's enfranchisement. To the degree they ended that way they were victims of the Republicans' policies of dividing them. Yet, the swiftness and energy with which Stanton and Anthony turned their own abolitionist traditions to Train's racism remain remarkable. At this point, their racism was opportunistic and superficial, an artifact of their Republicanism and alienation from abolitionists. It drew on and strengthened a much deeper strain within their feminism, however, a tendency to envision women's emancipation in exclusively white terms. Encouraged by Train they transformed the racism of white women into a kind of gender pride, which in turn contributed to the awkward fringe of the women's suffrage movement.[24]

In Rochester, Minnesota, despite her frustrations with the state party's singular commitment to passing the black suffrage amendment, Stearns was not ready to sever ties with her own party and the radical wing in particular whose principles she wanted deeply planted in southern Minnesota. Announcing the series of speakers that her group had organized for Rochester during the coming winter months, Stearns wrote, "The lecture committee of the Library Association have, ever since this spring, been in correspondence with other societies and with lecturers and their agents and have after a great deal of effort and much trouble, succeeded in engaging a number of the best lecturers in the United States." It was her intent to bring speakers of different stripes within the liberal camp, including Anna Dickinson, Frederick Douglass, and Wendell Phillips.[25] But as a supporter of Stanton and Anthony, for Stearns the prospect of hearing the last two men promised to try her patience. Indeed, it was already beginning to wane.

In Minnesota, as in Kansas, the 1867 campaign for black suffrage failed. Unlike Kansas, where voters rejected women's suffrage, Minnesotans were never asked the question. Yet it was for black suffrage—and black suffrage alone—that the Republican caucus reaffirmed its commitment. On January 10, 1868, Governor William Marshall stood before the joint houses of the Minnesota legislature and declared in his annual address that it was time to renew the campaign for black suffrage. In that speech, appealing largely to the principles of Republican values, he argued that because of the declining trend of dissenting votes, Minnesota was ready to support the constitutional amendment.[26] Minnesota was poised to be at the vanguard of civil rights at the beginning of the postwar era. There were a few Minnesotans who rejoiced at this prospect and felt it propitious to press the measure just a little further, having confidence that they could avoid the problems in Kansas.

On Tuesday, January 21, Representative John Hechtman of the Fifth District presented the petition of Mary Graves and 349 others, asking for the extension of the right to suffrage to females. It was formally read and referred to the Committee of Elections. Two days later, and barely two weeks after the governor spoke, Representative John Colton of the Twelfth District reported back on behalf of the committee, recommending that the "prayer of said petitioners [to amend the constitution by striking out the word 'male' as a requisite for voting and holding office] be granted." Legislators in the chamber broke out in laughter. Upon a motion from Representative C. D. Davison of Hennepin County, the report was unceremoniously tabled.[27]

＊ ＊ ＊ ＊ ＊

In New York, on May 26, 1868, the American Equal Rights Association met for its second-anniversary convention; but unlike before, when passions were largely held in check as all participants attempted to show at least nominal solidarity, now, because of the deep wounds festering from the Kansas campaign, former friends openly vented their differences. The rupture began to unfold after Stone presented for association endorsement two forms of petitions that would be sent to Congress. One would extend women's suffrage rights within the District of Columbia and the territories; the other petition concerned the submission of a proposition for the Sixteenth Amendment to extend voting rights to women. Olympia Brown supported the proposal, ridiculing the oft-heard assertion that women in politics ran against the laws of nature (*It would take the romance out of life to grant what you desire*). She said, "No one worthy [of] the name man or woman is willing to surrender liberty and become subservient to another. . . . *Now* is the accepted time for the enfranchisement of women. . . . Now is the time for every disfranchised class to make known its wants."[28] Then she took direct aim at the Republican Party: it was no longer worthy of their blind loyalty. "The Republican party is no better than the Democratic." Douglass responded, "There is no deep seated malignity in the hearts of people against her; but name the right of the negro to vote, all hell is turned loose and the Ku-klux and Regulators hunt and slay the unoffending black man." In paternalistic terms that must have felt insulting to the suffragists, he added, "The government of this country loves women. They are the sisters, mothers, wives and daughters of our rulers; but the negro is loathed." Unconvincing to many in the audience, Douglass concluded, "There is a difference between the Republican and Democratic parties."

"What is it?" challenged Brown.

"The Democratic party," responded Douglass, "has, during the whole war, been in sympathy with the rebellion, while the Republican Party has supported the Government."

"How is it now?" she said.

"The Democrat party opposes [President Johnson's] impeachment [presently being litigated in Congress] and desires a white man's government."[29]

"What is the difference in *principle* between the position of the Democratic party opposing the enfranchisement of 2,000,000 negro men, and the Republican party opposing the emancipation of 17,000,000 white women?"

"The Democratic party," Douglass responded, "opposes suffrage to both; but the Republican party is in favor of enfranchising the negro, and is largely in favor of enfranchising [the] woman. Where is the Democrat who favors woman suffrage? (A voice in the audience, "Train!") Yes, he hates the negro, and that is what stimulates him to substitute the cry of emancipation for women. The negro needs suffrage to protect his life and property, and to ensure him respect and education. He needs it for the safety of reconstruction and the salvation of the Union; for his own elevation from the position of a drudge to that of an influential member of society. If you want women to forget and forsake frivolity, and the negro to take pride in becoming a useful and respectful member of society, give them both the ballot."

Then Brown asked, "Why did Republican Kansas vote down negro suffrage?"

"Because of your ally, George Francis Train!

"How about Minnesota without Train? The Republican party is a party and cares for nothing but party! It has repudiated both negro suffrage and woman suffrage."

Douglass responded, "Minnesota lacked only 1,200 votes of carrying suffrage. All the Democrats voted against it, while only a small portion of the Republicans did so. And this was substantially the same in Ohio and Connecticut. The Republican party is about to bring ten states into the Union, and Thaddeus Stevens has reported a bill to admit seven, all on the fundamental basis of constitutions guaranteeing negro suffrage forever."

Brown "again insisted that the party was false, and that now was the time for every true patriot to demand that no new State should be admitted except on the basis of suffrage to women as well as negroes."

Stone took issue with "Mr. Douglass' statement that women were not persecuted for endeavoring to obtain their rights, and depicted in glowing colors the wrongs of women and the inadequacy of the laws to redress them." Stone "also charged the Republican party as false to principle unless it protected women as well as colored men in the exercise of their right to vote."[30] With this exchange, the old alliance within the Equal Rights Association was now at its breaking point.

The Republicans in Congress had begun debates on what would be the Fifteenth Amendment, which would extend voting rights to the freedman but not to women. Nothing—no amount of entreaties, petitions, speeches, rallies, or editorials—changed the hearts of congressional leaders to champion universal suffrage. State parties could not be trusted to support the cause, as they witnessed in Kansas and Minnesota. In Massachusetts, despite the nearly symbiotic relationship between the state's congressional and legislative leadership and the New England Woman Suffrage Association, of which some of the state's most prominent Republicans were members, the legislature— "largely Republican and temperance"—voted 22 to 9 against women's suffrage. This proved, as Anthony stated, that cooperating with Republicans was a "bad bargain." Once the reconstruction laws were enacted, she argued, the question of universal suffrage would be forgotten for another generation.[31]

In July Anthony was made a delegate to the Democratic Presidential Convention; and on the Fourth, she spoke before the convention, saying, in part, "While the dominant party has with one hand lifted up two million black men and crowned them with the honor and dignity of citizenship, with the other it has dethroned fifteen million white women—their own mothers and sisters, their own wives and daughters—and cast them under the heel of the lowest orders of manhood."[32]

When the Equal Rights Association voted to endorse the proposed Fifteenth Amendment, Stanton and Anthony repudiated the men of the organization. "There had been so much trouble with men in the Equal Rights Society," that the two leaders decided to call a meeting at the newly opened Women's Bureau where they invited women only. In October 1868, with representatives from nineteen states, they organized their own independent society and named it the National Woman Suffrage Association, though they eventually allowed men to join. The purpose of the association would be to singularly and independently secure the Sixteenth Amendment to the U.S. Constitution giving women equal suffrage to men.[33]

The opposing faction, composed of such leaders as Stone, Blackwell, and Phillips, believed that this was indeed the "Negro's hour," as Phillips termed it in 1866, a position that may well have been held by the numbers of Minnesota women who turned out to hear Wilkinson speak on behalf of black suffrage during the final weeks of the campaign, a contingent—"the largest audience including great numbers of women"—that did not go unobserved by at least one Republican editor. "We noticed one of the striking differences between [Senator Norton's] audience and the meetings that assembled to hear Senator Wilkinson a week before Norton speak, to a crowd of men—very few ladies were present."[34] Wilkinson's message that black suffrage was timely because the initiative, as he had said a week earlier, "proposed to conform our constitution to the Constitution of the United States," apparently persuaded the women in attendance, and perhaps many more who were not present, who might otherwise have viewed "the Negro Hour" as but mere paternalistic obfuscation.[35] He was being as optimistic about a women's rights amendment to the U.S. Constitution as he was for the Fourteenth and Fifteenth Amendments, neither of which as yet had been ratified.

But it was an optimism that neither Stanton nor Anthony held. For them, too much good faith had been violated. The ideological underpinnings of the party's stature, basic to its political domination during the Reconstruction period, were its claim to be the party of progress. Anthony and Stanton led the first major group of postwar reformers to defect publicly from the Republican camp and to challenge the party's reform pretensions. Brown had insisted that "the Republican Party is a party and cares for nothing but the party!" Historian Ellen Dubois has noted, "In light of the mass defection, four years later, of former abolitionists to the Liberal Republican insurgency, the nature of the threat posed in 1868 by the independent stance of Stanton and Anthony becomes clearer. It was an early indication of what the Republican Party would eventually have to confront, the loss of control over the direction of American reform." The party's involvement in the New England Woman Suffrage Association, and later the American Woman Suffrage Association, "can best be understood as part of their efforts on behalf of black suffrage, an attempt to keep women's rights from interfering with it."[36] Douglass's view was more urgent and alienating: "If the elective franchise is not extended to the negro, he dies. . . . Woman has a thousand ways by which she can attach herself to the ruling power of the land that we have not."[37]

That November, the same month in which the New England Woman Suffrage Association was founded, the white men of Minnesota approved the black suffrage amendment to be added to the state constitution. For Minnesota Republicans, the lesson of the Kansas campaign justified their belief that women's suffrage was something to be set aside for later, always the most prudent approach for such a matter. For Minnesota suffragists, the lesson was to find that delicate balance with assertive restraint, because alliances would always be uncertain.

25

# THE TIBBETTS PETITION

*We have enfranchised niggers, and yet refuse the ballots
to our wives. Are they not as good and as intelligent as niggers? Certainly they are. Schools today are taught mostly
by women—and yet it is said those who would teach our
sons are unfit for the elective franchise. Women are the
guiding spirit of mankind everywhere.*

JOHN MCDONALD, DEMOCRATIC LEGISLATOR, 1869

"The Honorable Abner Tibbetts," reported the *St. Paul Dispatch* on February 5, 1869, "the only man who represented Wabasha County in the Legislature, was at home a day or two last week. He fought a good fight in the interest of Mr. Donnelly thereby carrying out the nearly unanimous wish of his constituents." He had staunchly supported Donnelly's failed attempt to unseat Ramsey for the U.S. Senate, undercut in large part by his ally, congressman-elect Morton S. Wilkinson, who had jumped late into the contest.[1] Tibbetts, the article continued, "is an active working member of the Legislature and commands the respect and confidence of the people of his district."[2] So began a snapshot of the Republican House member, a forty-five-year-old married real estate agent from Lake City who three years before proposed land to a young Captain Montgomery from Le Sueur that could have been the site of a black colony. But on the day before the *Dispatch* profile appeared, Tibbetts had distinguished himself on another count when he introduced a new petition for women's suffrage, "requesting that in any change or amendment of the constitution to extend or regulate suffrage, there shall be no distinction between men and women." However, the motion to send it to the judiciary committee, where it could be reviewed, failed, 22 to 22, amid considerable mischievous jocularity by lawmakers from both parties.[3]

Though the petition lost, it did not die. Only a handful of votes were needed to reverse the action. All that was needed was a little more help. This marked the continuation of a distinctively contentious legislative session. Three days later, the *St. Paul Dispatch,* the progressive rival of the *Press* and organ for reform, welcomed the arrival of Colonel Enos Stutsman, "the champion of female suffrage in Dakota." A colorful lawyer, successful real estate agent, and powerful Democratic legislator from Pembina who had sponsored a bill for women's suffrage in 1868, Stutsman was also well acquainted with discrimination since he was born without legs and an arm. It was hoped by the editor of the *Dispatch* that his presence would result "in the subject being brought before the Minnesota Legislature and it will receive more respectful treatment than the petition a few days since."[4]

As an eyewitness of the rejection of the Tibbetts petition, the *Dispatch* derided the men of the legislature—Democrats and Republicans alike—for toying with such an important matter. "Men may laugh and sneer but female suffrage is the coming political question, which, next to our finances will engross the attention of the pubic for the next few years. It numbers many of the best minds in the country among its advocates and all liberal men are its supporters. Those who look back through the struggle for negro suffrage see a lighter task in this new movement." With a nod to Mrs. Stearns's work taking hold of the state's conscience, the paper added, "We say 'new movement' not in the sense that it has not been talked of and written about for years, but that it is now taking more definite shape and a momentum is gathering with ensured ultimate success."[5]

The *Dispatch,* born of reform-minded irreverence for the established Republican power base, began publishing in January 1868, just as Donnelly focused on a bid to replace Ramsey in the United States Senate. Donnelly, believing that it was impossible to campaign without the support of a metropolitan newspaper, determined that a new paper could satisfy this need. This was the *St. Paul Dispatch,* and it would be his own political organ to combat the Democratic press and the *St. Paul Press,* which supported the Ramsey-Marshall camp and was the chief editorial voice for black suffrage in Minnesota. In January, Donnelly became a silent partner of Harlan P. Hall. The *Dispatch* was initially a cheaply produced tabloid, which faced intense competition from its Democratic and Republican rivals, which sought to ruin it by publishing a special evening edition. "But the *Dispatch* persevered and, for the first time since the *Minnesotan*, Donnelly could count on the support from a friendly newspaper in the Twin Cities."[6] Though its support of the woman franchise was sincere, universal suffrage, which the *Press* adamantly opposed, also served as a proxy for the senatorial campaign. In this, the *Dispatch* found a dual purpose.

Identified by the national suffrage movement as a major St. Paul newspaper sympathetic to universal suffrage, the *Dispatch* received a telegram that parodied the fragile nature of suffragist sensibilities and reprinted "the following unwelcome intelligence" under the eye-catching headline "Failure of the Female Suffrage Movement":

> With much regret, we [the leaders of the Woman's Suffrage Convention of Chicago] are compelled to announce the complete and premature failure of the movement of female suffrage. A copy of the *St. Paul Press* of yesterday having been forwarded to us by telegraph, we read an editorial therein as follows:
>
> "There is good earnest work enough for women in the world without going to Women's Rights Conventions to look for it—the holiest, noblest work that was ever given to mortals. They care for a home with a baby in it, would make politics impossible for a right-minded woman; and with *two or three or half a dozen babies in it,* the sacred duties of maternity almost supplant society. For these are duties which no good mother can delegate."
>
> We have all along been solicitous relative to the course of this journal and knowing that it could not be controlled, made no deposit of bonds for that purpose, but hoped it would be liberal enough to favor us. Feeling that any further efforts to secure suffrage would be useless with the *St. Paul Press* opposed to us, we are reluctantly compelled to abandon the entire movement, and request our friends to do likewise. Though contrary to our previous intentions we now feel compelled to attend to "a home" and perform these duties which cannot be "delegated."[7]

The letter was "weepingly" signed by Stanton, Anthony, Parker Pillsbury, Mrs. M. S. Livermore, Anna Dickinson, and George Francis Train on February 13, 1869.[8]

Supporters of women's suffrage in the House, resolved in the wake of the failure to send the Tibbetts petition to committee, thereby effectively killing it before it received a thorough reading, pressed the matter when, four days later, a formal bill to amend section 1, article 7 was introduced. John Lathrop, a married Republican farmer from Rochester and supporter of the Tibbetts petition, was the bill's sponsor. This was the first bill for women's suffrage to be proposed in the legislature. On February 19, the Committee of the Whole recommended that it be passed on for a second reading. The next day, Representative D. Pile, a married Republican physician from Glencoe, proposed HF Bill No. 91, a resolution for a special hearing for February 25, "and that ladies be invited to seats on the floor, with the privilege of expressing their views on the subject." From here, the legislative road grew bumpy when Representative John C. Rudolph, a married Republican banker from New Ulm, moved the resolution be tabled, and his motion prevailed. The House then adjourned for the evening.[9]

On February 24, supporters moved to hold a special session where Bill No. 91 could be voted up or down. The men of the House debated the measure before a chamber that "was densely crowded, and the lobbies were filled with gentlemen."[10]

The clerk read the proposed amendment to the Constitution, allowing females to vote.

Mr. McDonald (Democrat) moved to go into Committee of the Whole on the bill.

Mr. Chewning (Democrat) moved to indefinitely postpone the bill.

Mr. McDonald asked what reason he had for such a move.

Mr. Chewning asked what reasons he (McDonald) had for supporting the bill.

Mr. Lathrop (Republican) said what we're here for, and hoped the gentlemen in favor of the bill would speak out and perhaps the scales would fall from the eyes of those opposed to the bill.

Mr. Chewning's motion was lost.

Mr. McDonald said that the one reason why he argued against the bill was, the ladies do not desire it. He called on Mr. Pyle to read a petition from his constituents.

Mr. Pyle (Republican) rose and commenced his remarks amid breathless silence. He said the first argument against the bill was based on rebukes and lies. He remembered that when he spoke in favor of the amendment twenty years earlier, he was "rotten egged." Such "gentlemen" who threw the eggs then were still "lurking around" to oppose the measure, "and smut mills in this city are firing off their snubs at me." He said that the reason that prevented the ladies from coming up in one band and asking for this measure was simple cowardice. They had been trained from infancy to shirk from it.

Epithets were thrown at them. Some men were manly enough to come out in favor of it, others opposed it openly, and a third class sneered at and ridiculed it. "We can find no reason in the fitness of things why any distinction should be made in the eye of the law. Females should have the same means of vindication as men have. There are grievous wrongs daily perpetrated on females in this country for which there is no remedy but the ballot. See that mother who once unwittingly bestowed to a being unworthy of her—pleading for her infant child in court—away from the brute who had stolen her food to sell for grog." (This point caused a stir in the gallery.) "These reasons long ago convinced us that the only way to fight those wrongs is to give the ballot to the other sex. They can't be kept under any longer." Dr. Pyle resumed his seat amid loud applause.[11]

Mr. McDonald said this was an important question and he had sustained it so far. The question of suffrage had been "greatly extended" the past few years, and he was "going for the whole figure." (Applause.) It was asserted that it would degrade and unsex the woman. Mr. McDonald strongly disagreed, reading "an eloquent and heartfelt appeal from a lady" whose name he chose to withhold.

Mr. Smith, a Democrat from Dakota County, called for the name.

Mr. McDonald refused to read it.

Mr. Smith objected to reading any more anonymous letters before them. (Laughter.)

Mr. McDonald proceeded: "We have enfranchised niggers, and yet refuse the ballots to our wives. Are they not as good and as intelligent as niggers? Certainly they are. Schools today are taught mostly by women—and yet it is said those who would teach our sons are unfit for the elective franchise. Women are the guiding spirit of mankind everywhere. What, Mr. President, would the world be without women? It would be a universe without a man— the heavens without the polar star of our being." (Terrific applause.) "We ask every man who votes against this bill tonight to remember he votes to declare his mother, daughter, and sister an inferior being."

Mr. McGrew, a Republican from Fillmore County, said that because "no one seemed willing to [argue against the measure]," he would "venture briefly to give some reasons why he felt that he could not support the measure." He rejected the measure because women would be eligible to run for office and that it was "unnatural to place ladies in any such position. . . . Can they go through our heated campaigns, where candidates' characters are always assailed? Who could wish his wife or mother or daughter to pass such an ordeal?" He did not believe that women wanted the law, and viewed it as "a violation of the laws of nature, [nothing that] the Creator evidently designed." There were, however, rights that women should have: the right to own property. "Property rights are far more important to their comfort and happiness than suffrage rights."

As to women in office, Mr. McDonald said that McGrew was wrong about women not having the physical capacity to hold office, and referred to the fact that there were female postmasters. "The State Librarian is a lady, and no objection was made to this."

Mr. Folsom (Republican) said he believed in equality before the law. "How many women carry on business in their own name?" It was a rhetorical question, for Stearns had been writing about female business owners since 1866.[12] "God made women like men—with the same minds and brains, and yet we see them today under the iron heel of the tyrant man."

Mr. L. Smith (Democrat) said he differed with the advocates of the measure. They had not convinced him, and he now desired to hear from the ladies themselves. (Applause.) He understood there was a lady present who was willing to address the house, and moved that she be called upon. The motion was unanimously carried. (Someone inquired about her name; Mr. Smith did not know it.) At this point, Mrs. Dr. Addie J. Ballou, of St. Paul, and an ally of Stearns, arose and said:

> As I have heard my name called, I rise to respond. I came here to listen, not to speak, but will endeavor to give our reasons for asking for suffrage. I am not a citizen of Minnesota, as I am denied the ballot. Yet that starry banner, which is an emblem of this country, is just as clear to me as to anyone (applause) and I have in common with my sisters, I ask to have a voice in the Government. The argument of the gentleman from Fillmore, is very lame. Does he wish to withhold from us the ballot because we may compete with him for office? Then he is not a gentleman, but a coward.
>
> If, as he says, not more than one in twenty will vote if allowed, what harm is done? Why not give us the chance? Even if they so stump the State, they might as well do that as to use their tongues so freely at home. Give women something to do higher than spring fashions, and they will not run after the Grecian bend and such follies.
>
> Women are certainly as capable of following some occupations as men. She teaches school as well, and yet only received one-third or one-half as much as men do, while the expenses are the same.

A woman never embarks in any business to earn a living without
creating scandal. [I am] sorry to say much of it came from women;
but give them suffrage and employment, and they will backbite their
sisters less. Today women are educated, what for? For any useful
stations in life? No, they are taught French, and music, and drawing,
and other almost useless accomplishments, and not taught to earn
their own living. Labor seems disgraceful to most of them. Who ever
saw an American girl employed as a domestic? But every woman
should be independent of a man. We are told we are so much better
off if independent. But a woman feels degraded when dependent. It
gives the man power over her he should not have. But give her suffrage and she can protect herself. I demand the ballot. (Applause.)

I shall offer it at the next election whether you pass this bill or
not. If you refuse me, then I am not a citizen. But I demand a voice in
the laws which govern me. You say men are protectors, but they do
not protect us more than we protect them.

Women will not be less women for having the ballot. They are
called strong-minded—but . . . this is no reproach. She needs to
be strong-minded and strong-muscled too, to earn her own living.
Women have a hard enough time anyway. Give her the ballot to help
her along. It is only a matter of time. It must be given to her sooner
or later. It has been given to the negro—why not her? Is she inferior
to the negro? It will gratify her much to have Minnesota the first state
to adopt it. (Mrs. Ballou resumed her seat amid much applause.)[13]

Mrs. M. R. Smith, state librarian, said she had been requested to speak on
the subject, but would decline such an honor, and leave it in the hands of the
husbands and brothers of the women—hoping that whichever way the question was decided, it would be for the advantage of her sex.

There was a loud call for the question. Mr. Egan (Democrat) moved to
call the roll. Five members were absent (including Chewning), and the sergeant at arms reported that they could not be found. Mr. Aaker (Republican)
moved to suspend further proceedings and Mr. Gilman (Democrat) moved to
adjourn, but he was ruled out of order for not standing by his seat. Mr. Clarke
(Republican) moved the previous question to take up passage of the bill. The
motion failed, 21 to 22, with McDonald voting "nay."

From here on, the suffrage measure began to twist in the wind, as
legislators—predominately Democratic—played with the emotions of suffrage supporters by moving to bring the measure forward, then voting the

motion down, ultimately to be tabled.[14] That evening, the *Dispatch* reported, "the hour for attacking the proposition with ridicule, sneering, or expressions of startled amazement has passed away. Whatever reasons this Legislature may assign for rejecting it, the people will not permanently accept the judgment. It will recur again and again in politics, each time gathering greater strength, until it becomes law of our land."[15]

On February 26, Charles Clarke, a married Republican farmer from Minneapolis, moved to take the bill from the table and offer it for a third reading, normally the last stage of a bill before it was finally decided. The motion prevailed. At last, the questions on the passage of the bill would be presented to the House. Weighing in the balance was whether the women of Minnesota would once and for all get a chance to gain suffrage rights. The next day, February 27, the vote was taken and the measure failed, 21 to 25. Twenty Republicans and one Democrat (Fridley) voted for suffrage. Fifteen Republicans formed the majority to defeat it. "So the bill was lost."[16]

"[Women] have the right of politics and until they exercise that right in their own behalf, the Legislature is not called upon to meddle in that subject," wrote the *Pioneer*. "The members of the Legislature can occupy their time quite well in the endeavors to uplift the burdens of all class of taxpayer, as in futile efforts to redress wrongs which exist only in imaginations."[17] Later in session, the body was regaled by a poetry recitation from Harriet Bishop, titled "Minnesota, Then and Now," just recently published by D. D. Merrill Publishing Company.[18]

◆ ◆ ◆ ◆ ◆

When, in February 1869, Congress passed a version of the Fifteenth Amendment, the schism within the suffragist community widened even more. The New England Woman Suffrage Association supported the amendment and urged its ratification. The National Woman Suffrage Association did not. In fact, they refused to endorse the Fifteenth Amendment unless it was "redeemed" by a Sixteenth Amendment that would be submitted simultaneously for ratification. Republican congressman George Julian of Indiana, a longtime supporter of women's suffrage since 1844, introduced a bill for a sixteenth amendment and Anthony pressed for its passage, insistently denying her endorsement of the Fifteenth Amendment. The New England suffragists charged that the national association was racist.

The assertion was not without good reason. The tactics the Anthony-Stantonites used to advance their cause were often racist. "In particular," Ellen Dubois writes, "they began to use arguments that exploited white women's fear and hatred of black people. To challenge the Fifteenth Amend-ment, Stanton argued the position that it was wrong to elevate an ignorant and politically irresponsible class of men over the heads of women of wealth and culture, whose fitness for citizenship was obvious. 'American women of wealth, education, virtue and refinement,' she wrote in behalf of a sixteenth amendment, 'if you do not wish the lower orders of Chinese, Africans, Ger-mans and Irish, with their low ideas of womanhood to make laws for you and your daughters . . . to dictate not only the civil, but moral codes by which you shall be governed, awake to the danger of your present position and demand that women, too, shall be represented in the government.' Such arguments slandered the freedmen by implying that poor black men were more responsi-ble for women's disenfranchisement than rich white ones."[19] On June 8, 1869, Stanton wrote:

> When a mighty nation, with a scratch of the pen, frames the base
> ideas of the lower orders into constitutions and statute laws, and
> declares every serf, peasant, and slave the rightful sovereigns of all
> womankind, they not only degrade every woman in her own eyes,
> but in that of every man on the footstool. A cultivated lady in Balti-
> more writes us a description of a colored republican reunion, held in
> that city a few evenings since, in which a colored gentleman offered
> the following toast: "Our wives and daughters—May the women of
> our race never unsex themselves by becoming strong-minded."[20]

A month later, Stearns reprinted from the *Pioneer* its account of a black man from St. Paul who had raped a white woman. It was the first time she printed this kind of story, the first time she reprinted anything racially charged from the *Pioneer* or any Democratic paper.[21]

As provocative as their rhetoric had come to be in demonizing the black man, the black woman was nothing more than a convenient symbol. By 1869 Anthony and Stanton made no effort or expressed any interest to bring black women into the rank and file of the movement, cultivate prospective lead-ers, or even share the stage with black women speakers. Not since 1866 when the Equal Rights Association began, did suffragists grapple with the black woman's double disenfranchisement, which, as Dubois writes, "transcended the hostility that Reconstruction politics were generating between the black and white suffrage movements."[22]

However, Frances Gage, who after the war served as chief agent of the Washington, D.C., Freedman's Bureau, specifically advocated for the political rights of the freedwoman. More than any other white leader of the Equal Rights Association, she was immersed within the black community. Soon other leaders took her lead, but only by degree. She still viewed black men with hostility. Using information Gage had collected, Anthony claimed that freedwomen, who had shared equally in the suffering of slavery, were refusing legal marriage and the submission to men that emancipation seemed to require. Anthony added that the black man, trained in the ways "of tyranny and despotism," might be expected to take exceptionally well to the privileges of being a husband. Similarly, Stanton argued that unless the freedwoman received the franchise, she would be doomed to "triple bondage that man never knows." Olympia Brown likewise argued that black women "needed the ballot more than anyone in the world."[23]

But the attention paid to black women was more rhetorical than real. Their overall participation during the three years the Equal Rights Association existed was as minimal as that of black men. Among the more than fifty national officers and speakers at organization conventions, only five black women, the same number as black men, played any role at all. Hattie Purvis and Sarah Redmond were the daughter and sister, respectively, of Robert Purvis and Charles Louis Redmond, two of the half-dozen black men prominent in white abolitionist circles. In addition, Frances Watkins Harper, Sojourner Truth, and Hattie Smith, all ex-slaves and orators, were active, though in no case did they hold positions of leadership. "This sparse record is not surprising," Dubois notes. "Before the war the slave woman had been a central symbol in antislavery propaganda, but blacks of both sexes had been relegated to a peripheral role in the management of the national antislavery movement.... As the possibilities for a joint struggle for black and woman suffrage evaporated, and as the woman suffrage forces became increasingly independent of abolitionism, the image of the black woman—for she had never been much more than an image—receded into the background."[24] No longer relevant to this phase of the movement other than as props to denigrate black men, black women held no value in the rhetoric of universal suffrage as leaders worked to expand the ranks among native-born, middle-, and upper-class white women, and especially when they, as leaders of the National Woman Suffrage Association did, sought to ally themselves with the Democrats.

# 26

# MARRIED WOMEN'S RIGHTS
# AND THE "KING OF MANOMIN"

*Mrs. Knapp, whose husband was murdered and body was bur-
ied in the corn field in the town of Grand Meadows, Mower
County, over two years since, has been on trial in Austin this
week for alleged participation in the murder. He had assaulted
her once too often. The trial has not yet been concluded.*

ROCHESTER POST, SEPTEMBER 9, 1869

The legislature had rejected petitions to place women's suffrage before the
voters, but it served the women of Minnesota in a different, though unexpected, way when this same body of lawmakers voted to amend chapter 69 of
the general statute titled "Married Women."[1] Minnesota's Married Women's
Property Law was a measure intended to secure the economic stability of
married women by allowing them to retain full ownership of the property
they held at the time of marriage.[2] A husband had no automatic marital claim
over his spouse's property. Rather, she held it—and all duties incumbent to
owning property such as selling, renting, leasing, and receiving due mon-
etary profits—"free from the control of her husband, and from any liability
or amount of his debts, as fully as if she was unmarried."[3] In an article printed
months after the law was enacted, Stearns wrote that the new law has, "in
its practical effect, probably more real importance to the sex than would be
attainment of the elective franchise," and that it had passed against "feeble
opposition."[4] It had also passed with no fanfare, even from the suffrage com-

munity, for despite its significance, it nevertheless seemed to some paternalistically intended as a consolation prize, feigned generosity, something to be dismissed.

The final vote was 31 to 13 and the alignment of votes seemed quite peculiar, since fourteen of those who voted against the suffrage bill (among them Rudolph, Smith, McDonald, and Patterson) voted in favor of the property bill. Conversely, five legislators (including Tibbetts) who voted in favor of suffrage voted against the property bill.[5] On the surface it would seem peculiar in light of the defeat of the women's suffrage bill by the same body of legislators. Both bills provided women with a significant degree of independence; and yet, it is clear that the men in St. Paul viewed the two measures as wholly separate policies. Suffrage to them was more threatening to domestic tranquillity than the property law that protected a married woman from being dragged into debt that her husband caused.

The traditional view, as reflected in an 1818 Connecticut court decision, held that a husband acquired absolute rights to the use of the real property of his wife during her life. By allowing women some control over their property, the state, in part, sought to stabilize the family; in case of economic failure, the woman's property could help the family make a new start. But the key to understanding what the property law meant to the legislators was that "economic and legal pressures, not egalitarianism, propelled these changes."[6] Nonetheless, in 1869, friends of suffrage, even those who would passionately advocate for the bill in the next session, saw the property law as having more practical importance to women than would be attained by the elective franchise.

The property law received little attention from its inception. There was virtually no coverage in the press, no editorials, no petitions, no speeches or debates before filled galleries, and, as mentioned, no fanfare when the bill was enacted. Indeed, the supporters of women's rights did not seem to actively campaign for the law though they no doubt welcomed it once enacted. But many felt that rejoicing in its passage would take the pressure off the legislators to address the higher goal of women's suffrage. What they so dearly sought had not yet been achieved, and it could only be achieved through state action. The sting of disdain that came with laughter heard during the session in 1869 signaled the end of courtly formality. It was now clear to Stearns and Mary Colburn that within this political climate, moral suasion would not work on the state party leaders. It was easier for white men to relinquish their racist impulse than their sexist impulse. These men only understood political leverage. It was time to organize. But this would be a challenge, not just because of resistance from political leaders, but also from the sheer isolating quality of distance. As Stearns would later write, "The advocates of suffrage in Minnesota were so few in the early days, and their homes so remote from each other, that there was little chance for coöperation, hence the history of the movement in this State consists more of personal efforts than of conventions, legislative hearings and judicial decisions."[7] Stearns and Colburn were nearly one hundred miles apart. During a Minnesota winter, the distance seemed insurmountable. Nonetheless, they worked assiduously to organize within their respective communities to raise the conscience of women's empowerment. By the end of the year, two suffrage societies would be formed, one in Champlin and the other in Rochester which would hold its first meeting in the Stearns home, numbering up to fifty members, all dedicated to the purpose of extending the franchise to Minnesota's women.[8] "The women," Mrs. A. H. Bright later wrote in 1914, "vowed not to disband until the suffrage law was attained, but unfortunately," she added with considerable understatement, "the effort has been greater than they anticipated."[9]

◆ ◆ ◆ ◆ ◆

*A case of abortion occurred at Owatonna a few nights ago. A hired girl in a private family destroyed an infant at midnight, amid thunder, lightning, and rain. She had retired as usual in the evening, but was discovered in a precarious condition the next morning, which fully indicated that a child had been got rid of. Search was instituted, and no traces could be found, but it was well known that she was absent from the house during the storm. It is supposed she buried the infant in some secluded spot. A bottle of medicine which produced the result, was found in her possession. This crime of abortion is becoming fearfully prevalent among those of both high and low estate.*

ROCHESTER POST, SEPTEMBER 11, 1869

Starting in October, activities in Rochester seemed to speed forward with a series of events orchestrated by Sarah Stearns. First, the Literary Association sponsored a lecture by the controversial racist George Francis Train, "acknowledged," as Stearns reported, "as the most fearless, eloquent and popular speaker in the country." Clearly Republican eyebrows were raised at the news. "Crowded, fashionable and appreciative audiences have attended Mr.

Train's lectures whenever he has appeared. His powers of enchantability are unequaled in the poetic and impassioned eloquence by that of any lecture. We shall expect to see the hall densely packed."[10]

Second, in November as they watched the Fifteenth Amendment gain support from the states and come to Minnesota for approval, Stearns and Colburn were even more convinced if the enlightened men of the legislature wanted, they could persuade the voters to likewise extend suffrage rights to the women of Minnesota. Politicians, many of whom they knew personally, just needed to be inspired, and nothing inspired politicians more than massive appeals from the constituents. At the end of November, Stearns held the first gathering of what would be the Rochester Woman Suffrage Society. "A few ladies of this city met on Saturday last for the purpose of forming an association for the consideration of the question of woman's suffrage." This call to organize appeared in the first article to which Stearns signed her name.[11] As chair of the executive committee, education chair, and corresponding secretary, it was her operation from stem to stern.[12] With this organization, and joining forces with Colburn's Champlin group, Stearns mounted a new campaign to flood the legislature with petitions in time for the session in early 1870.

◆ ◆ ◆ ◆ ◆

*A child is recently born in Wright County, in this State, whose mother was less than twelve years, and whose father, John Slaughter, was thirty-five. The mother of the smart child-mother wrote to the Sauk Centre Herald, under date of January 12th as follows:*

*"We are still alive and doing well. New talk of your smart town and you smart people. Talk of John and Penolla! On the 28th of December, they had added to their household a daughter weighing seven pounds and a half. Where the smartness comes in is the age of the mother. Her age is eleven years, eight months, and twenty days, and her weight before the birth of the child was eighty pounds."*

ROCHESTER POST, JANUARY 29, 1870

◆ ◆ ◆ ◆ ◆

In January 1870, thirteen months after the Minnesota victory for black suffrage, Congress submitted the question of ratification for the Fifteenth Amendment to the states. A minimum of twenty-eight out of thirty-six states, which constituted two-thirds as mandated by the Constitution, were needed, and a handful of legislatures already had voted to support the amendment. The reversal of support by the New York legislature, due to a resurgent Democratic majority that culminated in that body's reversing itself by withdrawing ratification, caused proponents to worry about ultimate success.[13] The concerned *St. Paul Press* rallied its readers: "There is a strong ground for apprehension that the amendment is in great danger of failing. Minnesota can't come too promptly to the rescue."[14] On Thursday, January 13, 1870, Minnesota ratified the Fifteenth Amendment "by strict party vote, every Republican voting for it, every Democrat voting against it."[15] Twenty-one days later the Fifteenth Amendment was ratified.[16] The right to vote did not extend to women, a group that even the *St. Paul Press* would describe as "the only class of citizens wholly underrepresented in the government."[17]

On January 13, by joint resolution of the House and Senate, the legislature approved the new federal constitutional amendment; Governor Horace Austin signed the resolution on January 21.[18] It appeared then that a momentum in favor of universal suffrage had begun among state leaders, so much so that it would overcome the pockets of resistance that had frustrated previous efforts. Especially among their allies, there would be no more reason to reject working for woman's suffrage, since the Negro's hour had come and, with ratification of the Fifteenth Amendment, was about to pass. Suffragists reasoned that it would be hard for Minnesota's Republicans to so blatantly discriminate in favor of black men, a mere abstraction who so few of the party leaders actually knew let alone genuinely saw as their equal, choosing *them* against their own wives, sisters, and daughters. Black suffrage, in a state like Minnesota with a minuscule population of African American men, was more, in any practical sense, an act of loyalty to the Republican banner, nothing more than a symbolic gesture. The time was right for the same brave legislators who supported the joint resolution, many of whom were new to the chamber, some of whom had faced down the enemy fire of Confederate guns, to do the right thing. The time was now. The disappointments faced by Anthony, Stanton, and others in New York, Massachusetts, and elsewhere, would not apply here in the North Star State. After all, it was in Minnesota that, when asked and led by state party leadership, the white men of the state did the right thing, voting before any other state since the end of the war to grant blacks the right to vote. With friends in the legislature, the suffragists of Minnesota began to mount a new campaign.

On February 10, the *St. Paul Press* bitingly reported that in the Senate, "Mr. Fridley came in with his female suffrage bill, proposing an amendment to section one, article seven. This bill is presented by a petition which contained the autographs of 604 females and an equal number of the 'lords of creation.'" It was a bill that would allow women, in this lone instance, to vote alongside men at the polls. Two days later, the editorial voice that had thundered its support of Lincoln, the Union cause, the end of slavery, and the advancement of racial political equality by extending voting rights to the black men of the state, now fumed in a prominently situated space on the front page of its February 12th edition at the dire prospects of female suffrage. The editor mockingly urged readers to look beyond the blush-inducing, puritanical pretense of separating ballots of men from those of women for the sake of modesty and propriety. "Their votes are to be deposited in separate ballot boxes. This precaution against the promiscuous association of the sexes in the ballot box is taken doubtless in the interest of morality, but if the bill passes, as we see no reason why it should not, this provision will seem useful purpose in indicating the precise number of women who deign to go into politics."[19]

With this issue out of the way, the editor sought to discredit women's suffrage as a political boon to "the Democratic element in their midst." He essentially was waving the bloody shirt. "It seems at first sight a little odd that some of the most zealous champions of female suffrage are Democrats, possibly in some instances in the notion that a little affectation of zeal for the extension of political rights in that direction will serve to atone in some measure for their universal and implacable opposition to their extension to colored men." To prove his point of Democratic hypocrisy, he looked to the west. "The Legislature of Wyoming, which recently passed a law giving suffrage to the women in that Territory, is almost wholly Democratic, *of the ultra-rebel variety*; and in their pious haste, says a Democratic paper, to enfranchise the daughters of Eve, they have created a ludicrous blunder of admitting black women to suffrage, while leaving colored men out in the void. We don't see anything ludicrous about this for it is in strict accordance with Democratic precedent—it having been the established custom of Democrats, from time immemorial, to bestow their favors exclusively on colored women."[20] The editor was clearly enjoying himself.

More important, as he continued, Democrats had no compunction in corrupting ladies by forcing them to inhabit polling stations where the worse kind of men and women lounged about intoxicated in the vapors of unrefinement. "In the event of women being allowed to vote, the probabilities are that the great masses of the intelligent, decent, modest women of the country would shrink, with a mutual instinct for modesty, from the rude contact with

Democratic rowdies and loafers to which they would be exposed by going to the polls, which the coarse and brazen Amazons who grace the vicious haunts or enclaves from which a large proportion of Democratic voters come, would swarm in eager crowds, as they swarm to hangings and fires, to await the Democratic votes."[21]

In any case, preached the editor, it was too late to reverse the trying course of events—Fridley's bill. All that was left was to endure the tempest that was sure to come when "the loudest of the loud" lady champions of suffrage will soon descend on Minnesota. "[The bill] would ensure us next fall of Pentecostal visitations of the female stump orators from the Women's Rights Association. Mrs. Stanton, the best politician of them all, would sail in on us benignly, to thaw with her gracious and genial presence the cold of the multitude; Mrs. Livermore, the Juno Titans of the Female Olympus, would unsheathe her lace-edged thunderbolts upon us and make things rattle again; the lovely Anna Dickinson would bedew with her graceful opulence of tears and diamonds, the tender plant of female suffrage of which the great Manomin County Reformer have soon the precious and immortal seed." The editor was now ridiculing the bill's sponsor. "The bashful Fridley smothered with kisses and crinoline, would fly repentant, disheveled and disgusted from the silken suffocation of his own glory to the remote seclusion of some monastery in his own great kingdom of Manomin, after the pattern of Charles the Fifth, to mediate on the vanity of ambition, and resolve never to mention female suffrage again as long as Heaven should spare his virtuous lips."[22]

Abram McCormack Fridley, the sponsor of the bill, seemed in some ways to be a Minnesota version of George Francis Train. He was a Democrat, and the only legislator of his party who, on the final vote, would remain in support of the measure, just as in 1869 he had supported the women's suffrage bill and property bill.[23] And he was a man whose history conveyed one with grandiose sensibilities. "Major" Fridley—the rank came from having served as Indian agent to the Winnebago in Long Prairie, and a delegate to the Constitution Convention in 1857—was a Democrat in politics at a time when Abraham Lincoln was appearing on the national scene and when the Republican Party was rapidly rising to power in Minnesota. The "King of Manomin" as he was sometimes derisively called, kept a firm rein on his "subjects," repressed periodic rebellions in the county, and dominated the ballot box. So effective was his sway that when the presidential elections were held, he saw to it that Lincoln did not receive a single vote in Manomin County; and he continued, even during the war years, to support the Democratic Party. His zeal inflamed much ill feeling, and the antislavery leaders and the antislavery papers went after him rigorously, fomenting preposterous stories that his "secession tendencies" would propel him into leading Manomin County into the Confederacy. The stories were soon found to be baseless and he supported the Union effort for the duration of the war.[24]

His grandiosity notwithstanding, and acknowledging his county to be "a white elephant," by 1868 he had begun lobbying to annex Manomin to Anoka County, which required an amendment to the state constitution and approval from the voters of the state. But before that could happen, the legislature had to approve a bill to submit the question to the voters, just as it had done with black suffrage, as he was attempting to do now with women's suffrage. For three years, the old firebrand Democrat failed to marshal the necessary votes within a Republican-dominated legislature—until 1868. In the midst of the successful campaign for black suffrage, the mood regarding attaching Manomin and Anoka Counties shifted. Writing for the *Post*, Stearns, by now an ally of Fridley and no doubt acting in a quid pro quo, argued for annexation: "Manomin is said to embrace less than a township of land, and contains only some 20 to 30 voters. Such a frivolous county corporation ought, of course, to be abolished."[25] In 1869, the referendum to dissolve Manomin and formally attach it to Anoka County in 1870 was approved by the voters. Nine years later, Abram Fridley, still a member of the Legislature, watched colleagues rename Manomin after himself.[26]

Was Fridley in fact Minnesota's version of George Francis Train? To begin with, Fridley was not a firebrand racist as Train was, nor did he appear to champion women's suffrage to exploit tensions between suffragists and the Republican Party, as Train had attempted to do in the Kansas campaign in 1866. Fridley's support for women's rights seemed true since he had voted in favor of suffrage and the property bill during the previous session. Knowing how little support for suffrage there was within the Republican caucus, the party's supporters of suffrage understood that Fridley's leadership might draw Democrats to the column. But why did he become the bill's sponsor since he had never before sponsored this type of legislation? Though his support of the measure seemed quite sincere, it was clear that he also deemed it to be good politics. The leading opinion maker in Anoka County, the *Anoka Union*, endorsed female suffrage. Likewise, the women's suffrage lobby, whose organization was more formidable in 1870 than ever before, could prove to be a powerful ally. Ultimately, Senator Joseph Leonard of Rochester, co-owner and editor of the *Rochester Post* and an ally of Stearns, committed the support of his caucus for the Manomin deal in return for Fridley's leadership for women's suffrage.[27]

Despite the efforts of opposing members to frustrate Fridley's effort to shepherd along H.F. No. 123, as it was referenced, bringing it at last before its third reading, the last procedural step before a vote could be taken. Representative John Gilman "moved a call of the House" and all but one member—Charles Stewart was ill—arrived for the debate. A. E. Hall rose to explain his vote and in doing so, characterized the thinking of most of his House colleagues. He said he voted against the measure in 1868 and was still opposed to it on principle, but he was now willing to support the measure so that the question could come before the people, though he intended to vote against it at the polls. The twenty-five-year old lawmaker William Jones made light of the moment, noting that he hoped the ladies who looked on (the *Press* noted that a few were present) would remember that he was a bachelor. John McDonald said, "I voted both ways (laughter) but on the final vote, voted against it." But like Hall, he declared that he would vote for the bill, to bring it before the people, and vote against it at the polls. "The question will no doubt be a disturbing element in our politics unless we submit it to the people, although I am against the principle." The yeas and nays were called.[28]

On February 15, H.F. No. 123 passed in the House with a vote of 33 to 13.[29] After the votes were tallied the *Press* commented about the pleased constituents looking on from the gallery: "Several ladies were present when the vote was taken. Mr. Fridley's female constituents, in return for his patriotic effort in their behalf, propose, when the session closes, to welcome him with open arms, and an aesthetic ovation of toast and tea."[30] Despite the hyperbolic disapproval of the *Press*, the manner in which the measure was addressed appeared relatively decorous. Such was not the case in the Senate. As the *Press* reported on February 19, "Fridley's Female Suffrage bill was treated with levity by the Committee of Elections, who were severely rebuked by Senator Leonard who is a convert to the new reform."[31]

Senator Benjamin Sprague of Mower County, a married farmer and chair of the Committee of Elections, reported back to the chamber that the bill should be returned to the Committee of Retrenchment and Reform.[32] Though it had been retrieved from that committee and sent instead to the Committee of Elections, Sprague now sought to return it to the Committee of Retrenchment, the very committee that the body had earlier rejected and where bills were known to languish. In light of this, Sprague's motion appeared to be an effort to maliciously slip women's suffrage into a procedural morass. Senator Leonard rose to take exception to the maneuver, saying, "It could have but one meaning: that to make jest of this subject." He wanted to vote on the bill. Tampering with it through what he viewed to be needless procedural machinations only trivialized the principle of the bill. "It should be treated with the gravity which the importance of the subject demanded." Avoiding the quagmire Sprague was determined to impose, Leonard moved that the bill receive its second reading and go to the Committee of the Whole. The motion was adopted.[33]

During the evening debate, senators offered several obfuscating amendments to the bill, but they were all voted down, keeping the language in its original form. Republican Senator Edson R. Smith, a married merchant from Le Sueur and chair of the Banks and Banking Committee, moved to strike the portion of the bill allowing female suffrage to vote upon the proposition. What followed was a spirited debate among Senators Leonard, Waite, Republican lumberman and chair of Ways and Means Curtis H. Pettit of Minneapolis, lawyer-farmer David Buell from Houston County, Democratic lawyer James N. Castle from Stillwater, and Republican miller Dane E. King from Greenleaf, all of whom, except Castle, were married. After nearly two hours they resolved the debate with "an almost unanimous vote." Republican lumberman and chair of elections Josiah Crooker from Owatonna then offered an amendment to the bill providing the constitution should be so amended if it appeared that the majority of "the females present and voting upon the proposition voted in the favor." The motion was lost. Finally, senators recommended it be read a third and last time. Senator Luther Baxter, a lawyer from Chaska and chair of the Committee of the Whole, then read the bill the third time and was about to put it up for a motion to vote when, as another stalling tactic, a motion to adjourn was made and approved. Two days later, however, the Senate returned to the bill.[34]

In debate, Senator King argued that he was "opposed to female suffrage in the common acceptance of the term, and at the same time voting, as I shall, submit this question to the people, it is but just to myself that I should explain this apparent inconsistency in my course." It was inconceivable to him that the women champions for suffrage could be ladies, and it was this belief that made the bill, for him, unacceptable. "It is to the credit of the sex that no woman of culture or refinement has asked for the right of suffrage. It is left for the strong-minded Amazons of the sex, with a law of our own sex, and whose motives are, perhaps, not really understood, to urge the adoption of this amendment upon the people, and as far as observation has taught us anything of this class of persons, it has shown them to be examples of social unhappiness, either as wives or husbands, as mothers or fathers."[35] He then closed with a heartfelt recitation of a poem that seemed, to him, right for the occasion: the poem began "I believe woman's work to be,"

> *Leading little children,*
> *And blessing manhood's years,*
> *Showing to the sinful,*
> *As God's forgiveness cheers,*
> *Scattering sweet roses,*
> *Along another's path,*
> *Smiling by the wayside,*
> *Content with what she hath.*
> *Letting fall her own tears,*
> *Where only God can see,*
> *Wiping off another's*
> *With tender sympathy.*
> *Learning by experience,*
> *Teaching by example,*
> *Yearning for the gateway,*
> *Golden, pearly ample,*
> *This is woman's work.*

After more debate, the question blessedly was called for a vote and the measure was narrowly approved, 12 to 9.[36] Highlighting the duplicitous role Democrats played in the vote as well as her sister Republicans who she knew worried about the implications of this bill on the party's legacy, Stearns reported optimistically, "The female suffrage bill passed the Senate last week by a bare majority vote. Of the twelve votes for it, six were Democrats and six Republicans, being less than half of the Republicans, and all but two Democrats." It was thought, she wrote, that Democrats voting for the bill would later call for reconsideration, at which time the bill could be defeated, "but no such slaughter had occurred as of this writing, and there is yet every reason to believe that female suffrage will be one of the issues of next fall's campaign. Look for Susan B. and Anna S., *et al. omne genus.*"[37]

A reporter for the *St. Paul Press* saw it differently. Endorsing Senator King's view of the bill as "one of the greatest follies and humbugs of the ages," the reporter saw the majority vote merely "as the same principle that impatient mothers gave sweetments to impudent children, with the view of making them so sick that they will never cry for sweetments again."[38]

Frances Russell, ignoring the *Press*'s condescension, and writing under the name of "Faith Rochester of Silver Lake, Minnesota," was wary after hearing about the Senate deliberations, enough to write sarcastically, "You see what our legislature has done? I like it. Members were begged to vote against the 'Female Suffrage bill,' because there was no strong demand for it from Minnesota women. But why should they? Must women go down on their knees . . . for that which is unjustly withheld from them."[39] Distrustful of the motives of many of the senators who approved the measure that included the provision to allow women to vote on the question, "Rochester" added,

> Our legislators have done their simple duty. Now if the people vote down the amendment which proposes to enfranchise the women of the State the Legislators can tell us, "thou canst not say I did it." Yet it is the intention of many who voted for the bill (and even of its author, I am told) to make it defeat itself, for the bill provided that women may vote on the question, and it was fondly hoped by some of our ennobling lawmakers that the amendment will be voted down by the women themselves, and so forever set at rest the vexed question of Woman Suffrage.

The reference to Representative Fridley was particularly noteworthy, for "Rochester" had simply stated the obvious: duplicity was the very nature of politics when women's suffrage was at issue. In fact, Fridley sponsored the bill in name only. In none of the debates that followed did he argue on its behalf, let alone get caught either in the crosshairs of fellow Democrats or of the *Pioneer*. Indeed, he stood to gain (in the form of annexation of his "kingdom") with minimal political loss, and everyone, it seemed, understood the situation. Fridley was permitted to perch safely on the catbird seat.

He, like so many of his colleagues in both the House and Senate, apparently felt that because the men of the house so clearly rejected women's suffrage, so too would their womenfolk, and this, as "Rochester" had written, would *forever set at rest the vexed question of Woman Suffrage.* "Innocent souls," she called them. She reported sitting quite amused during the debate as she listened to suffrage foe Senator King give his overwrought recitation of "Woman's Work": "If the Senator who repeated that as part of his argument against woman suffrage, saw us laughing at it while he read it, he would probably be puzzled to know where the joke lies, but I hope he will yet see."[40]

"Rochester" then got serious, acknowledging that Fridley's motives were in the larger sense unimportant: "The vote, regardless of the intent of the legislator, now posed the best opportunity Minnesota women ever had for the right to vote, and they were not ready to wage a statewide campaign."[41] This new state of affairs required momentous effort. "I hardly dared hope that the Senate would concur with the House in the passage of this bill, we seem so unprepared for a vote of the people on such an important amendment to the State Constitution. Yet, I tossed up my cup and cried 'Huzzah!' when I learned that the bill had passed the Senate by 12 ayes and 9 nays":

> It almost scares me now to think I did set up a shout, for we are no means "out of the woods" yet—indeed, we have hardly entered the woods. It is no easy task to canvass a state like this—Swedes, Norwegians, Germans, French, Bohemians—whole settlements of foreign-born citizens, and each with a vote as powerful as anybody's. How shall we reach the minds and consciences of all those people?

But she also realized that the foreign-born voters were not the only group who needed mobilizing, admitting unease that the "American" women voters could very well defeat the proposition:

> If the men alone were to vote on this question, next fall, I believe we could carry it, but I am more than half afraid that the women will defeat it. It seems so hard for many simple-minded women to think of voting as anything more than just dropping a ballot into a box at the election. They can't see that there would be any pleasure in that, and they have enough to do at home. What do they care about "the tariff" and such matters? These are they who think "women can't understand politics and guess men could make good enough laws without our help. . . . It would take time to educate most of those people into a proper understanding of the word 'politics.'"

In this, "Rochester" reflected the most fundamental task confronting any kind of reform effort—persuading people—men and women alike—who were complaisant with the familiarity of an unequal status quo to embrace the unfamiliarity of egalitarian change, assuming a role in society that had never before been seen, a role that for some would seem quite unnerving, quite inappropriate, quite unnatural. This would be the work of the suffrage club—men and women, but mainly women—who through their actions would articulate the values and embody the image of the new American woman.

Stearns's work, initially in her hometown of Rochester, and Colburn's work in Champlin, both remote towns at this date, were unlikely to be known to many people in the smaller community of Silver Lake. "I suppose," "Rochester" wrote, "there is yet hardly an organization for Woman Suffrage in the state. Come over and help us—Do!—you of the East who have leisure, and means and hearts and brains for the work. I doubt not there are Minnesota women and men who can do excellent service, but the time is so short!" She concluded with a note of hope. "If victory does not come to Minnesota, friends of equal rights, next fall, it will probably be because we are not prepared for it, but I believe there is a possibility of victory."[42] "Now," reported the *Daily Pioneer* after the Senate vote on the suffrage bill, "[all that was] needed [was] the approval of the Governor."[43] It did not come.

# 27

# VETO!

*"Women's rights"—If a woman has any paramount right it is that of being relieved, if possible, from distressing ailments to which the sex is exclusively liable. Such relief is certain if she resorts to Holloway's Pills as an alternative. Their purifying and resisting operations, and their effort in renewing suspended functional action, recommend them above all other medicines to the confidence of the sex. CAUTION: See that the words "Holloway, New York and London," appear as a watermark on every leaf of the box or pot. No others are genuine.*

*ST. PAUL DAILY PRESS*, MARCH 3, 1870

On March 11 Governor Horace Austin, a former lawyer and judge from St. Peter, vetoed the measure, stating, "I have concluded not to sign this bill for the following reason: Section 1, of article 7 of the State Constitution provides who shall be voters of this State; and section 1 or article 14 provides that no amendment proposed by the Legislature shall be adopted unless a majority of 'voters' present and voting shall have ratified the same. The 'voters,' as used in the section last cited means a 'voter,' as defined in the first section referred. The bill proposes to test the question in a manner not within the Constitution."[1] In other words, women, already barred by the constitution from voting, could not be permitted to vote on changes to the constitution.

The reaction was convulsive. Stearns and her associates had viewed him as an ally. She and her husband, a friend and political ally, had campaigned for him to be elected governor. Never in their wildest considerations did they believe that a veto was possible. They were already preparing to canvass the state. Now the governor pushed everything back. A frustrated Sarah Stearns wrote, "There is no justification for such a veto, and in exercising it Governor Austin displayed the single quality of mulishness. . . . A law of that character, leaving to the people a question as to the qualification of voters which they are perfectly capable of deciding for themselves, is one that a governor has no business to interfere with."[2] Still wounded weeks later she referred to him as "mixed" and "confused."[3]

She was not alone. Another angry writer from Minneapolis, stung by a sense of betrayal, posted in the "friendly" Democratic *Daily Pioneer,* "I do not propose to discuss [Austin's] objections. They are not worthy of it, and unworthy [of] the position of the Governor, if not the man. They are simply the specious plea of a demagogue, whose egotism led him to believe that the *ipso dixit* would be accepted as positive truth. The fact is this bill did not attempt to give women the right to vote upon the *adoption* of the amendment, and the *Governor knew it.*"[4]

More invective rained down on the governor. The pro-suffrage editor of the *St. Paul Weekly Dispatch* had been one of the first to react. "Governor Austin has vetoed the Woman Suffrage bill for the reason that it was to be submitted to women, who are not yet legal voters, and because public sentiment has not called for it. Now, it seems to us that the only method of determining positively whether public sentiment demands this or that reform, is to take a vote on it. . . . This suffrage bill, by virtue of its main provision, is simply a bill making women legal voters for a special occasion and purpose."[5]

For others, for the time, the veto was too much to bear. "Our excellent Governor has hurt the feelings of some of the ladies," reported a reader to the *Daily Press.* "I know one of the most estimable of her sex who actually shed tears of vexation, when she learned that Governor Austin had refused his signature to the bill submitting the question of Woman Suffrage to the people. She could not perceive through her moisture-laden eyelids, the exact point of unconstitutionality, and could only murmur between her sobs, that they would 'remember Governor Austin when they come to power.'"[6]

Later, in a private letter to his irritated friend Mrs. Stearns, the governor rationalized his action. "Had the bill provided for the voting of the women, simply to get an expression of their wishes upon the question, without requiring their votes to be counted as legal in the adoption or rejection of it, the act would not have been vetoed, notwithstanding my second objection that it was premature."[7] In another letter, however, he indicated that his opposition was based on the political calculation that three-fifths of foreign-born Minnesotans were hostile to the measure."[8] In this, he and "Rochester" were similarly concerned with the disposition of this group of citizens. For both, women suffrage was an American issue, a *Saxon* issue, but not one embraced by immigrants, though "Rochester" felt the foreign-born women could be educated as to the benefits.

From Boston, the outraged editor of the recently incepted *Woman's Journal* wrote, "The Woman's Suffrage bill of the Minnesota Legislature was conceived in jest and born in frivolity. Even the author of the bill openly treated it as a joke. The whole thing was coupled disgracefully in levity and fun. [It was an un]worthy way for the people's representatives to spend their time and the people's money. Under the circumstances the Governor's veto was a merited rebuke; as by the Minnesota State Constitution, women are positively prohibited from voting."[9]

"Rochester" was just as troubled, but in the spirit of her unknown sisters in other parts of the state, she was less foreboding: perhaps, even hopeful. "News travels slowly through our snowdrifts. I dare say Eastern people learned before I did of Governor Austin's refusal to sign the female suffrage bill." And they knew of the churlish manner with which legislators acted. "Charity can hardly be stretched to cover the frivolity of our lawmakers in respect to the woman question. . . . Such a great joke it seems to them that women should wish to be free to vote or not, as the conscience of each dictates! *What in the world have we mothers been about, from the days of Eve all the way down, that the men of this generation can mock at women so?*" But it was important that she acknowledge the good men who worked on the issue. "There was some honest men at the Capitol, who voted sincerely for the female suffrage bill, and perhaps before another session of our Legislature, we may convince many more of the reasonableness of our claim, and of a growing desire of Minnesota women to have their freedom."[10]

But Dr. Mary Colburn from Champlin, fueled by a history of insult and rebuke from the legislative body that was longer than even Stearns, her closest colleague in the struggle, had experienced, furiously wrote upon learning of the news, "It seems like the trick of a mean and cowardly foe." Seeing many of these same men casting votes for Negro suffrage reopened a wound and she directed her anger at men of both races. "If it was unconstitutional, that was reason sufficient for the veto, without that talk about little or no evidence or manifestation of any public sentiment [in] favor of the proposed change. What great evidence or manifestation of public sentiment was there when the negro suffrage bill, adroitly managed, forced an issue upon the question of amendment of the constitution? And pray how long and how loud must a woman clamor for political equality with the negro before her cry reaches the gubernatorial ear?" For her—as with Anthony, Stanton, and Stearns—the political equality of black men as a whole was tantamount to being spat in the eye.

The whole affair, it seemed, was an exercise in bad faith. "Many of our would-be politicians affect in ridicule and ignore arguments they cannot refute, and treat with dignified scorn the advocates of this reform. I opine the day is not far distant when men of this class, seized by the epidemic that rages in autumn, will be forced to make their best bow to the laundress and the kitchen maid, for the reason that Bridget's and Kathleen's votes will weigh as much as the votes of Patrick and Hans." Colburn now threw down the gauntlet. "Let the friends of this cause remember that failure is not defeat. We have yet nine months in which to work before the Legislature will again assemble. Let the women see to it that womanhood suffrage be circulated in every county and town throughout the state, and every member of the next Legislature be made the bearer of such petitions as proof positive that the people are willing to meet the need."[11]

This was a call to arms for another legislative campaign, and it seemed supporters might be successful this time. Despite the scurrilous assault over the years on their dignity that suffrage leaders had endured from politicians and opinion makers, the women of the movement, many of whom were married to men who played dominant roles in the Republican Party, had reason to believe they might be successful this time. They had come so close. The campaign of 1871 would demand these men do no more than what they had done for the "illiterate and wretched" black laborer. But this was not to happen. The Fridley bill would be the last of its kind. There was, instead, to be a change in tactics.

## 28

# BACK TO WORK

*[Miss Susan B. Anthony is] a jolly old maid of 50 . . .*
*who had never been beholden one iota to these horrid men.*

SARAH BURGER STEARNS
ON SUSAN B. ANTHONY'S BIRTHDAY

In 1868, after Kansas, Susan B. Anthony struck out to build new alliances for women's suffrage. Democrats had been one group, but they were, as many knew they would be, not just odd political bedfellows but on the whole unreliable. How long could the movement, founded on the principle of universal equality, rely on a political class of men who remained unapologetically racist? Though it was true that Anthony and Stanton had at times allowed their passions to carry them away in rhetoric that played to the prejudices of white people, they never lost sight of what was critical—every citizen of the United States deserved the right to vote. In law, to date, only half of the adult citizen population could do so. Women were still without the franchise. Anthony's focus logically shifted to women who labored outside the home. In September of that year, she and a group of wage-earning women formed the Working Women's Association.

In 1870 approximately 1,300,000 wage-earning women did nonagricultural work, of whom 70 percent were domestic servants and another 24 percent were in textile, clothing, and shoe factories. The women who joined Anthony to create the Working Women's Association came from the smallest, most skilled trade available to women: typesetting. A survey of New York

City revealed female typesetters earned more than any other group, except professionals and the self-employed. "Much like the profession of medicine in the same period, the trade of printing had a strong attraction for women who aspired to a more profitable and honorable field for their labor." As skilled as they were, female typesetters did not earn as much as male counterparts. For them, equal pay and job security were of paramount importance, and men had kept them in an inferior status. Anthony insisted that equality could only be secured with the ballot.

Although the visions of Anthony and those of the association's members overlapped, they differed in some regards. From the beginning, they disagreed over the priority of suffrage in the agenda of the Working Women's Association and the degree to which it would be identified as a suffrage organization. In fact, women's suffrage, one of the most controversial notions of the day, was in the minds of many Americans synonymous with such disparaging labels as "strong-mindedness," "short hair," "promiscuous," and "bloomers."[1] Even the outspoken Minnesota journalist and feminist Jane Grey Swisshelm was frequently at odds with the suffragists, whom she disparagingly called "bloomers."[2] Nonetheless, for the time being, they worked together, agreeing that women needed both the franchise to be politically equal to men and employment out of the home so that women could earn their own money and thus attain economic independence. The prospect of gaining the ballot, and all the benefits it assured them, however, was too abstract for many working-class women. Of more immediate benefit to them was the elevation of women and the value of their labor. To gain this they needed to be unionized, which the men's union of typesetters had always resisted. Suddenly the prospect of a shop cooperatively operated by women attracted both suffragists and typesetters, and the suffragists knew how to organize. The men's National Typographical Union took notice, for it was now faced with a competing union whose members employers were inclined to hire because of their lower rates. If the women worked with the men's union, they would get the same remuneration as the men, promised Alexander Troup, secretary of Local 6. Anthony saw this as success.[3]

The suffragists believed other workingwomen could be organized, and laborers in the needle trade appeared to be ready. But though they wanted higher wages and steady work, nothing in their present situation made the control of all profits of their own industry seem a reasonable goal, or attracted them to the suffragists' vision of opening up more trades and professions to women. Moreover, unlike the female typesetters, who gained support from their male counterparts, no such male trade union had interest in them. The suffragists turned to publicizing the dire circumstances in which those workingwomen labored.

In December, Anthony and Stanton's newspaper, the *Revolution*, established with funds from George Francis Train, published "The Case of Hester Vaughn." Vaughn was a young English immigrant accused of infanticide. She was a domestic servant who had been seduced by her employer, became pregnant, and was dismissed from her position. She gave birth unattended and was found three days later with her dead infant by her side. She was tried, found guilty of infanticide, and sentenced to death. When the presiding judge passed sentence, he said the crime of infanticide had become so prevalent that "some woman must be made an example of."[4]

Hester Vaughn became a symbol of the horrors to which workingwomen were subjected. Stanton wrote, "What a holocaust of women and children we offer annually to the barbarous customs of our present type of civilization, to the unjust laws that make crimes for women that are not crimes for men."[5] The association made this its cause and lobbied the governor of Pennsylvania to pardon Vaughn. She was released and deported six months later to England. This was a different type of gender struggle. Unlike the issues confronting female typesetters, the Vaughn case reflected the kind of obstacles that faced the majority of workingwomen—unskilled in a trade, unprotected by a union, and therefore expendable.

Anthony had envisioned the association as an organization for women to defend themselves. But this was a period of transition, for the women who were credited in doing the most to save Vaughn from the gallows were not the same women whom Vaughn personified. That class of woman—Vaughn's class—instead, became the object of benevolence. Though many of the women who attended meetings to free Vaughn, contributed money, and supported the petition to the governor, were working class, Stanton was most impressed with the "importance [of] women of wealth, education, and leisure study[ing] the laws under which they live, that they may defend the unfortunate of their sex in our courts of justice."[6] Domestic workers—indeed, most working-class women—did not have the time or training to mount sophisticated actions, and the fact that employers could easily replace them made them less willing to take controversial stances. Moreover, the typesetters who had begun the association came from a tiny stratum of skilled workers who were the elite among the working-class, wage-earning women. "Instead of growing beyond the typesetters to include the unskilled workers who dominated the female labor force," Dubois writes, "the association developed outside the working class among a group that might be called middle-class working women."[7]

These were usually women in occupations that involved professional training rather than manual labor and conditions that gave them more control over their work. Frequently they were self-employed or entrepreneurs. Freelance writers, independent businesswomen, and female professionals, they responded to the association's vision. "Because the kind of work they did was socially respectable and relatively well paid, it provided them with a sense of autonomy and individual achievement and some degree of economic independence. They worked out of choice as much as out of necessity."[8] They ultimately, more than the domestic workers, more even than the typesetters, came to be the group who best exemplified the feminist vision of the self-made, self-sufficient woman who embodied their notion of sexual emancipation, and to whom the suffragists best related. Indeed, they moved within the same circles and shared the same values, tastes, and associations, and more fundamentally, a sense of how change must occur. "Suffragists inclined to believe that social changes . . . they wanted to see in woman's sphere and woman's image, came from the top down in society, rather than from the bottom up. . . . Given this framework," Ellen Dubois writes, "suffragists considered middle-class working women strategically important as well as socially desirable, and a critical constituency to attract."[9] It would be this class—the upper middle class—on whom Stearns focused her effort to organize Minnesota women, and in this sense, mirrored Anthony's organization.

Anthony's organization was at a different stage that sought to organize women skilled laborers. By spring 1869, the influx of middle-class women began replacing laboring-class women in the Working Women's Association, so that the regular membership was entirely middle class. In New York, the meetings, which had been held in places where working-class women could attend, were moved to an uptown mansion. Dues were raised from ten cents to twenty-five cents a month, despite the outcry from working-class members that the increase was prohibitive. Anthony, in noting the enthusiasm of the middle-class women who were joining the association, supported both changes.[10] Increasingly, the association took on such activities as providing benevolent programs for "their downtrodden sisters," hosting literary and intellectual activities on self-improvement, or indulging in philosophical debates, and as such, grew out of touch with the bread-and-butter matters that working-class women faced daily. This was especially so when class, gender, and union politics collided.

In January 1869, suffragists and typesetters, the original partners in forming the association, found themselves on opposing sides. Local No. 6 in San Francisco declared a strike against printing companies to raise wages to union scale. The female typesetters supported the men. Previously, employers hired female typesetters to replace striking men; but when the women stood with the men, the union was able to prevail. In return for their help, the National Typographical Union admitted the Women's Typographical Union as its first all-female local. In addition, the national constitution was amended to permit the chartering of other such locals, provided that women did not work below union scale and had the support of local union men. This was a major victory for women, who could now expect equal wages as well as job security. They were now inside the fraternity and Anthony misunderstood what this meant. Seeing the advantages that female typesetters gained by earning union-scale wages, she wanted more women to be trained so that they too could benefit. "Her actions revealed her essential ignorance of trade union principles as well as the dangers inherent in her middle-class approach to working women's problems."[11]

Early in the strike Anthony appealed to the employers' association to establish a training school for women to set type, appealing on behalf of the working-class women who came to the Working Women's Association as a means to gaining better employment. It was convenient for the employers, for Anthony, not they, was proposing a scheme to train strikebreakers.[12] Within a few days, the employers announced that they would indeed train women to set type and place them in shops. The pro-business press applauded "the ladies of the Revolution" in "this practical side of the woman's question."[13] Labor, on the other hand, criticized Anthony for siding with the employers. Though she tried to make amends to the union, claiming that she supported unionism and a woman's right to equal pay, her statements conveyed that she never really understood how her actions weakened the union's position. Indeed, she did not understand the union perspective: it was about protecting the members' jobs from all outsiders. A spokesman for Local No. 6 said, "If a girl is a member of our union, we will give her work . . . but we do not go outside of our organization. You might as well ask why we don't send for the colored men or the Chinese to learn the trade. There are too many in it now."[14]

The National Typographical Union's decision to affiliate with the Women's Typographical Union most decidedly was not the same as a commitment to increase the number of women in the trade. And because strikebreakers threatened their jobs, many of the female members reluctantly agreed. Suddenly the dream of an all-female union that secured union-scale wages for its members could only be realized if it kept additional female workers. The National Labor Congress expelled Anthony as a delegate. In the years to follow, without the vocal advocacy of Susan Anthony, prejudice within the union job placement system led to the bypassing of female members. In time, female membership within the union decreased. In 1878 the National Typographical Union revoked its affiliation with the Women's Typographical Union. By the end of the century the position of women compositors was essentially what it had been in 1867, before women were unionized in the trade. All of the progress made in 1868 was reversed by 1869.

It was at this time that suffragists found a new constituency of middle-class women. "Such women, organized in behalf of their own emancipation and not the uplift of their less fortunate sisters, were the people around whom an independent feminist movement would be built."[15] Even before Anthony's expulsion from the Labor Congress, she and Stanton had expressly begun to organize middle-class women when they formed the National Woman Suffrage Association. Unlike the Equal Rights Association and the Working Women's Association—two groups whose divergent membership inevitably compromised the suffrage movement—the new organization could be completely made in their image, setting its own agenda, its own priorities, and defining its own success. With this new organization, the suffragists returned to their primary purpose.

Throughout 1869 the Fifteenth Amendment circulated through the states for approval. Anthony and Stanton were determined that a country ready to extend voting rights to black men could be receptive to enfranchising some of the most respectable members of American society. The so-called Negro's hour could be transformed into the "universal hour" with a lot of work; but the ratification of the Fifteenth Amendment, which excluded women, was all but a certainty. Their rivals within the American Woman Suffrage Association advocated that any such effort should be directed at legislatures, for competing amendments would threaten approval of the Fifteenth Amendment. The national association's response was to proceed now with a campaign for a sixteenth amendment designed specifically to enfranchise women.

Charging forth from their New York base, Stanton began a nationwide tour to organize state and local suffrage societies. "North, South, East, West, Pacific coast, too!" declared the *Revolution*. "Have you heard the call, and are you heeding it, to organize at once in behalf of the great cause of women's enfranchisement?"[16] In November Stanton toured midwestern states to lecture and organize local suffragists into the national association. State and local affiliates formed in the wake of her visit. Stanton returned to the Midwest later that winter. In late March "Mrs. Cady Stanton delivered a private lecture to ladies at the St. Paul Opera House," and later spoke in St. Cloud on the twenty-eighth of March.[17] At some point, she met with two of the leading figures of the Minnesota suffrage movement—Sarah Stearns and Mary Colburn.[18] It was at this time that Stearns took on the banner of *Revolution*: accordingly, the Minnesotans would shift their campaign from pressuring the legislature to petitioning Congress, in conformance with the agenda of the national association.

By 1870 the relative isolation of the Minnesota movement ended as the work of the suffragists of the *Revolution* began appearing more frequently in the *Post* and other friendly newspapers. In late February, for example, the *Post* announced the semicentenary of Miss Susan B. Anthony, "a jolly old maid of 50 . . . who had never been beholden one iota to these horrid men."[19] In March Stearns reported that Mrs. Myra Bradwell, having applied to the Illinois Supreme Court for a license to practice law, was "denied solely on the grounds the disabilities of her married condition rendered it impossible that she should be bound by her obligation as an attorney."[20] Since its inception, the Rochester Woman Suffrage Society held weekly meetings filled with debates and lectures on the virtues of women's suffrage. The franchise was not only about emancipating the woman but also having the power to do good works. "We believe," Stearns wrote, "that every woman ought to be free to do a part of her work for God and humanity in this way. This is a part of both our religious and political creed."[21] And it was always about high-mindedness and intellectual self-improvement. The programs the association sponsored featured speakers who were for and against suffrage. In one instance the group sponsored one such lecture that "was crowded on Wednesday night, with an audience, chiefly ladies," to listen to Mr. H. H. Young, who spoke against women's suffrage. Stearns's assessment of the lecture was generous: "On the whole, the lecture was more interesting, than profitable or convincing."[22]

In the wake of Stanton's Minnesota lecture tour, Stearns expanded the suffrage organization to prepare for the congressional petition campaign to come, expanding her base of operations from being an association for the ladies of Rochester to a countywide organization, naming it the Olmsted County Woman Suffrage Association. From there, she communicated with editors and other leading citizens around the southern region of the state in hopes that they would print circulars and notices on suffrage activities. Her inquiries were not always well received. "Among others, [she] also sent her circular to Christos of the *Lanesboro Herald,* who publishes it with an answer telling her he is very sorry, but that he is not the man for her business."[23] But it did not slow the work. Just as Stanton and Anthony had discovered the strength of middle-class women—the professional and affluent "working women" of the closing years of the association in New York, women Stearns knew very well—Stearns enlisted them in active service, principally bringing the heart of Minnesota's movement to the state's political and economic center—the metropolitan area.[24]

Stearns convened what would later be called the Organization of the Woman Suffrage Club of Minneapolis, at the home of Martha Angle Dorsett, a New Yorker by birth, who graduated from the University of Iowa College of Law, the first public university in the United States to admit men and women on an equal basis. She would become the state's first woman to be admitted to the Minnesota Bar Association. Her husband, Charles William Dorsett, who joined his wife in lobbying the legislature to change the statute in 1877 that had barred his wife, would unsuccessfully run twice for governor on the Prohibition ticket.[25] Charlotte Ouisconsin Van Cleve wrote a book on her early years growing up at Fort Snelling where her father was an officer, during the period of preterritorial Minnesota; later, in 1875, she would be one of the first women to be elected to the Minneapolis School Board. Her husband, Horatio Van Cleve, was a Civil War general and adjutant general for Minnesota until appointed by Governor Austin to be warden of the state prison at Stillwater, "one of the best acts of Governor Austin's administration."[26] Other women whom Stearns included in her circle were Dr. Addie Ballou, who would be appointed vice president of the National Woman Suffrage Association; Charlotte Winchell, who also served as one of the first school board members in Minneapolis; Mahala Pillsbury, a leader in charitable work in Minneapolis and wife of Governor John Pillsbury; and Harriet Bishop, the first teacher of Minnesota, founder of First Baptist Church of St. Paul, civic leader and namesake of Lake Harriet of Minneapolis and Harriet Island in St. Paul, who would become president of the Minnesota Woman Suffrage Association.[27]

In her own family, Stearns's husband, Ozora, would be elected to the United States Senate to finish the term of David Norton, who had suddenly died. In 1872 the family would move to Duluth, and by 1874 Ozora would be elected to be judge on the eleventh judicial district, where he would serve for the next twenty years. But Stearns would remain the chief influence of the movement as she continued to organize clubs around the state. Though she was quite frustrated with the state party establishment she would not follow the lead of Anthony and Stanton in severing ties.

With this community—women who had the time and resources to meet, discuss, and debate, read and write books, petition the legislature, and attend sessions and rallies without the fear of reprisal, joblessness, or violence, bound together by Saxon race, class, and social status, with the added benefit of political access—the Minnesota women's suffrage movement mobilized to begin the next phase of the struggle for political equality.

\* \* \* \* \*

Since her arrival in Minnesota in 1866, Stearns had chronicled the many challenges women faced on Minnesota's farms and in cities and towns—spousal abuse, rape, abortion, and poverty—but she did not include the experiences uniquely related to women of color. Given the demographics of Rochester during the late 1860s and later Duluth, she likely had no exposure to black women. Although she reprinted a story from a Democratic paper about the rape of a white woman by a black man, she refrained from reprinting a story that appeared in a Republican newspaper about a black mother who had been forced out of her shelter by a white woman; or another story of a landlord who denied shelter to a black woman with children and rent money, solely because of her race; or yet another about a Swedish housekeeper in Goodhue County who forced her employers to release another servant because the woman was black. Sympathy for the African American ended with emancipation. Her story about the black man was a cautionary tale of the inferiority of black men and "proof" of their undeserved status in the political arena; but the racial aspect of the experiences of black women were not of interest to her, other than her abiding faith that the ballot singularly would set them free. However, during the postwar decades to follow, within the increasingly rarefied world of the emergent suffrage leader, clarity of purpose, social connections, and high-mindedness, laced with a cultivated sense of nuance, tended both to shroud and nourish her sense of racial privilege.

It would not be until 1914 that, in St. Paul, a new suffrage group would form. Called the Everywoman Suffrage Club, its motto would be "Every woman for all women and all women for every woman." Though affiliated with the Minnesota Woman Suffrage Association, the chapter that Stearns helped to organize, ESC would be an organization primarily for "colored women." Nellie Griswold Francis, its founder and leader, belonged to the upper class of black society and was consequently able to forge connections with the predominantly white women's social and political clubs that were reluctant to include black women. After a meeting with the ESC, Clara Ueland, leader of the state organization, noted that the members compared favorably with what she termed "ordinary" clubwomen "with one or two exceptionally graceful and charming. But the leader of the club is a *star!* Mrs. Frances [*sic*] is petite and what we call a 'lady,' but her spirit is a flame!"[28]

But in 1870 no such black woman enjoyed that social and financial stature, and this rendered African American women invisible, or at least, inconsequential. They more typically were like Martha Clark Hall, the black servant who worked for Senator Alexander Ramsey. It was evident that Mrs. Ramsey saw her as a valued member of the household. In February of that year, upon hearing of the death of Martha's brother, she wrote to her husband that "Martha seems heartbroken and disconsolate" and that nothing seemed able to "soften her grief" or help her "bear her great loss." The senator quipped, perhaps to lighten the moment over the demise of Martha's brother, a laborer, "If he made no will, Martha will increase her fortune considerably and be infinitely more attractive than ever to Peter."[29] Months later, she married Peter. The *Press* reported the happy affair:

> "Martha," a respected colored woman, who has been attached to the family of Senator Ramsey for over twenty years, was married to a young colored gentleman, a barber of this city, on Tuesday night; but even the bliss of a matrimonial honeymoon could not entice the faithful Martha from her post as Seneschal of the Senator's family, and next morning she departed with them for Washington, leaving her young husband to pine in solitude till her return in spring.[30]

# PART VI

# *The Changed Man*

## Morton S. Wilkinson
### 1869–1876

**29**

# A CURIOUS VOTE
# ON THE BUTLER BILL

*So it must now still further pursue the object of its*
*being, and labor to restrain and keep within due bounds*
*these other great and growing moneyed monopolies and*
*combinations of which threaten to sap the foundation of our*
*free institutions while oppressing the poor about the land.*

MORTON S. WILKINSON, 1870

The same embers left smoldering dangerously and untended in Memphis and in Montgomery's Louisiana sparked to tragic results in other places throughout the South. Soon, it was painfully evident to black folks and their white friends that the time of their advancement was fleeting. Emancipation and political equality were insufficient in securing for black men a place in the new world order. Speaking on the need to continue Reconstruction policies in Georgia, where white terrorism chased black and white Republicans from duly elected posts, Massachusetts congressman Benjamin Butler declared, "I should be glad to have a law passed by which those colored men, who wrongfully, murderously, feloniously, and treacherously driven from their places, should be put back for two years, and the traitorous felons should not get any advantage by virtue of their own wrong. There are some of these loyal legislators who never will take their seats in the Legislature again. By violent deaths they have gone to a brighter and better world. I would give no aid and comfort to this little rebellion, this embryo rebellion in the State of Georgia.

I will not be an accessory neither before nor after the fact of the rebellion by turning out these legislators."[1] The former Democrat and Union general who immortalized the term "contraband" to characterize slaves who fled to the Union ranks for sanctuary, and whose likeness flattered the base of chamber pots that proliferated around New Orleans when his troops occupied that city, was now arguably the most radical and disliked congressman then serving in office. As he spoke, the Honorable Morton S. Wilkinson of Minnesota sat there, wordless, unmoved, yet quietly fuming.

Despite the ratification of the Fifteenth Amendment, and a year after he had welcomed his state's newest citizens into the fold, unchecked violence raged throughout the South coupled with ingenious methods to keep blacks from voting. Tennessee's new constitution included a provision requiring payment of a poll tax to vote, and Maryland imposed a property requirement. Virginia gerrymandered districts to ensure Democratic control, reduced the number of polling places in black neighborhoods, empowered legislatures to appoint local governments, and barred all who failed to pay the poll tax. The future of the New South, they believed, depended on all Democrats being committed to ending the "negro vote," committed to what they called Home Rule, committed to the honor of white supremacy.[2]

Between 1868 and 1871, white Southern terrorism was unprecedented throughout the region. In 1869 Georgia Klansmen forced Abram Colby into the woods and beat him for three hours in front of his mother, wife, and daughter. In 1870 Jack Dupree of Mississippi, president of a Republican club, was murdered by having his throat slashed and being disemboweled all within sight of his wife, who had just delivered twins. That same year, in Chattanooga, Andrew Flowers was whipped after defeating a white candidate in a race for justice of the peace. White Republicans likewise suffered abuse with whippings, beatings, and murders. And in October, a group of armed men broke up a Republican meeting in Eutaw, Alabama, killing four blacks and wounding fifty-four. In the same month, after Republicans carried Laurens County, South Carolina, white gangs scoured the countryside, driving 150 black families from their homes and committing thirteen murders. One of the murdered men was the newly elected white probate judge. In March 1871, in Meridian, Mississippi, during a trial of three black men charged with delivering incendiary speeches, Klansmen began shooting, killing the Republican judge and two defendants. The next day, more rioting followed, resulting in thirty blacks being murdered in cold blood, including "all the leading colored men of the town with one or more exceptions."[3]

In fact, in Washington, a crucial war of principles that threatened nothing less than the underpinnings of reconstruction was being fought, not so much in the U.S. Senate, where Radical Republicans were still in control, as in the House, where ex-Confederates and critics of black equality had grown in influence. This, as fortune would have it, was where Wilkinson's experience, energy, and intellect were most needed. Since 1866 acts of terror against blacks and sympathetic whites occurred rampantly throughout the South. As referenced earlier, in Memphis in 1866, white mobs joined white police officers as they indiscriminately attacked unsuspecting black men, women, and children, leaving over forty people dead and one white man injured. General Stoneham, assigned the task of maintaining order, said at the end of the first day of violence, the Negroes had nothing to do with it except "to be killed and abused." Later, on July 30, in response to a crowd of blacks celebrating black suffrage, a riot erupted in New Orleans in which thirty-four blacks were killed and more than two hundred were injured. Four whites lost their lives and ten policemen were injured.[4] "Violence," writes historian Eric Foner, "an intrinsic part of the process of social change since 1865, now directly entered electoral politics."[5]

The Ku Klux Klan was founded as a social club in Tennessee in 1866, and chapters in nearly every Southern state launched a reign of terror against local black and white Republican leaders and supporters. In 1868 Georgia and Louisiana experienced incredible instances of violence. In the town of Camilla, Georgia, alone, four hundred armed white men led by the local sheriff opened fire on a black election parade and then scoured the countryside for those who had fled, eventually killing and wounding more than a score of blacks. In Louisiana's St. Landry Parish, a mob destroyed a local Republican newspaper, beat and drove the black teacher and editor Emerson Bentley from the area, and then invaded plantations in the area, killing as many as two hundred blacks. Commanding General Lovell Rousseau, a friend and supporter of President Grant, refused to take action, urging blacks to stay away from the polls for self-protection. "The ascendance of the negro in this state," he reportedly said, "is approaching its end."[6]

Terroristic activities in other states had similar effects, discouraging blacks from voting. Eleven Georgia counties with black majorities recorded no votes at all for the Republican ticket. In Tennessee, Alabama, and Georgia, white farmers who had supported the Republicans for economic reasons were returning to the Democratic Party. The Party of Lincoln had taken a beating. Foner writes, "If Grant's election guaranteed that reconstruction would continue, it also confirmed a change in the Republican leadership that would preside over its future." Months earlier, in August 1868, Thaddeus Stevens died, attracting a crowd of mourners in Washington that was second only to Lincoln's. Insisting on being buried in an integrated cemetery, Stevens instructed that his epitaph read, "To illustrate in my death the principles which I advocated through a long life." Now replacing him as party leaders were conservatives James Blaine, House Speaker, and Henry Dawes, who succeeded Stevens as chair of the powerful Appropriations Committee and whose priorities were decidedly elsewhere. "To such men," Foner writes, "Stevens' death seemed 'an emancipation of the Republican Party.' The struggle over the negro, the party's rising leaders believed, must give way to economic concerns." Indeed, reflecting this shift, the first statute enacted after Grant's inauguration was the Public Credit Act, which pledged to pay the national debt in gold. As one federal official stated, "I look to Grant's administration as the beginning of a real and true conservative era."[7]

In 1868 Georgia, embroiled in even more political and economic conflict, was thus kept under military control when Congress realized that the legislature had replaced duly elected blacks with ex-Confederates, who in turn embarked on a comprehensive plan to defeat black enfranchisement by imposing a poll tax and more stringent residency and registration requirements. By 1870 the number of black voters had dropped sharply. In Atlanta, Republicans were eliminated from the city council when it shifted from ward to citywide elections. In Georgia, to demolish the enclave of black political power, the legislature ousted Tunis G. Campbell from his seat as justice of the peace in favor of a white Democrat and appointed a board of commissioners to replace the elected local government. Governor James M. Smith advised blacks to abandon politics and "get down to honest hard work."[8] On March 8 the debate over a bill that would release Georgia from military control and admit its Klan-supported representatives to Congress became one of the most heated debates in the House of Representatives during the Forty-First Congress. Benjamin Butler argued against the bill and in favor of continuing, as a reconstruction measure, military control in that state: "The next we heard from Georgia was that her people by armed bands controlled her elections, that murder was rife everywhere, that many of the members of her legislature, white and black, had been killed, that the Ku Klux was depleting the legislature by the knife and the pistol, that by force and fraud of loyal men of Georgia had been overcome at the polls."[9] He was alone in making the case. In the end, the House approved the measure, 115–71. Wilkinson, who did not participate in the debate, voted with the majority and for the Klansmen who were determined to end Reconstruction, for none of what had been reported now mattered to him.[10] He had indeed become a changed man.

The year was 1870. D. D. Merrill had directed his effort to spread the work of missions throughout St. Paul, leaving Robert Hickman to continue deferring to an apathetic pastor of the flock he had assembled. Thomas Montgomery continued building his fortune in real estate in Minnesota's southwestern counties as the few former troopers who had served under his command made their ways to Minnesota, where they worked as laborers on farms and in towns. And Sarah Stearns and suffragists began a new phase of agitation by shifting their lobbying efforts from the legislature to Congress. Of the four Lincoln Republicans profiled in this volume, Wilkinson was the only one left to deal with the Negro Problem. But after ratification of the Thirteenth, Fourteenth, and Fifteenth Amendments to the U.S. Constitution, a black suffrage amendment to the state constitution, and so-called reconstruction, which to him seemed interminable and counterproductive—it inflamed rather than pacified the Southerners—as far as the black man was concerned, Wilkinson, like the rest, was convinced that he had done his part. The so-called duty to do more was a diversion from the real work at hand. It was said that the honorable man entered public service with an agenda at hand, but was lucky if circumstance allowed him to address it. After one year in Congress, it seemed that Wilkinson would not be so lucky. And he thought the so-called racial problem was due to Republican corruption in Washington, and in St. Paul.

$\star$ $\star$ $\star$ $\star$ $\star$

A little more than a year before, fresh off the victory of the black suffrage campaign and his election to the seat that he now occupied in the House of Representatives, Wilkinson implemented his plan to frustrate the political ambitions of, in his view, a most unworthy man. On January 14, 1869, in St. Paul, two weeks after the Convention of Colored Citizens, the state's Republicans geared up for a caucus fight to determine whether incumbent Senator Alexander Ramsey, who had not attended the celebration, would be replaced. What had been a two-way race between Ramsey and Ignatius Donnelly— the fiery orator, former lieutenant governor under Ramsey, congressman, and now Ramsey foe—took a turn when Morton Smith Wilkinson suddenly entered the fray.[11] In fact, as early as November the two men had discussed how they would proceed to unseat Ramsey.[12] Donnelly, having lost standing among many Republicans for his attacks on party policies, saw that he did not have enough votes to win the caucus ballot. Feeling so strongly about seeing the defeat of Ramsey and the "*Press* ring" of which the senator was the boss,

Donnelly instructed his supporters to back Wilkinson who seemed better po-
sitioned to attract the requisite number of votes to win the endorsement. But
by December, the Ramsey forces knew of the plan. *Press* editor Frederick
Driscoll informed his man Ramsey:

> Wilk has played the dog and I trust he will keep in the field.
> Concentrate the opposition upon him so that we can clean him
> out. Convey to [William] Windom this fact and he will stir up his
> stumps to block him in several important quarters in the Southern
> [counties]. Windom would be of service here during holiday recess,
> not that his friendship with you is excessive, but his hatred for Wilk
> is so intense.[13]

In the end, Wilkinson fell short because of "eleventh hour defections," losing to Ramsey on the first ballot by six votes.[14] The Ramsey faction had already made procedurally certain that there would not be a second ballot, in
marked contrast with the thirty-seven ballots it took in 1859 for Wilkinson
to win his Senate victory. With this, wrote H. P. Hall, "the light went out in
the Wilkinson-Donnelly camp," adding "there is no shadow of doubt that
if there had been a second ballot there would have been no second term for
Ramsey."[15]

This was more than an election for Ramsey. As Wilkinson saw it, it was a
victory for a party that had become Ramsey's plaything, a party that had lost
its bearings to a man who had been slow to join when it was first being formed
in Minnesota in 1855, when it had stood for limiting the spread of slavery,
securing universal opportunity for all workingmen, and assuming the role of
safeguard against corruption, privilege, and exploitation. Although Ramsey
had been slow to support these themes, he could still dominate the party by
exploiting the sentiment of having been Minnesota's first territorial governor.
Under his stewardship, Wilkinson felt, the party had drifted from this mission, and Ramsey's reelection to the senate affirmed this notion.

Clearly, he wanted to deny Ramsey the senatorial seat. But considering
his first year in the House, it is not clear that he now wanted to return to that
chamber, for his view of Congress had already begun to sour, as he saw the
party increasingly promote corporate interests over populist reform. He had
seen enough in both chambers how, in the name of the nation's interest, monopolies were rewarded with appropriations and federal contracts, usually at
the expense of the ordinary man. When the Pacific Railroad bill came to the
Senate that granted public land to railroads, permanently excluding it from

homesteading, Senator Wilkinson voted "nay."[16] Even when his friend and fellow Radical, Benjamin Wade of Ohio, sponsored a bill for federal funding of the construction of railroad bridges over the Ohio River, Wilkinson again voted "nay," arguing that corporate interests were not speaking for the common man, even inferring in the manner in which he tended to view issues in dualistic terms, that Wade's integrity had been compromised. "The mass of the people, the lumbermen who are sawing out the lumber, who are cutting the logs, are not the men who are prowling about Congress for favors . . . but you will find monopolies—railroad men—plotting in advance to control the legislation of Congress, and the only class of men that you will hear of petitioning Congress on such subjects will be the very class of men who want the monopoly of the Ohio River."[17] Although what he said was true, it was also true that the lumbermen would have jobs and, contrary to Wilkinson's argument, small businesses in the area very well could prosper. He came to question whether the interests of the common man could ever be addressed there and whether he, as a Republican, could receive party support.

Wilkinson's experience in the House was no better as its leadership determined likewise to direct the chamber's work to corporate interests. The only thing he and pro-development Speaker Henry Dawes shared in common was frustration with Benjamin Butler and his fixation on the racial problem in the South, in the guise of the so-called Georgia bill. But unlike Dawes, Wilkinson sympathized with the words from Democratic Congressman John Fox from New York: "Congress is a despotic majority, reckless of boundaries and rights, ruling with iron scepter and territorial domain. . . . This Georgia bill is the fruit of our planting. . . . It is fruit rotten ripe, judging by the criminations and recriminations heard to-day. The further we go into this reconstruction the deeper into the muck; the more we struggle to get out the deeper we get in."[18] To Fox, the great injustice was Congress imposing more force on the Southern states in the name of reconstruction and at the expense of state's rights. But for Wilkinson, who agreed that the federal government, now outside the national emergency of civil war—no Confederate armies amassed to renew hostilities against the Union—had overreached, reconstruction only exacerbated Southern repression of its black citizens, serving as a ruse to ignite passions among Republican voters, distraction from the misdeeds of party leaders, and rallying cry to turn out the vote come election time.[19] "The power thus usurped from the states [which the Georgia bill represented]," said New York Democrat Fernando Wood, "will control the whole government of the United States in the hands of a few men composing the majority and ruling power of the two Houses of Congress."[20]

In the closing days of the Forty-First Congress, Wilkinson seemed un-affected by the reports that continued to stream in of beatings, whippings, torture, and murder by the Klan in their violent efforts to discourage black enfranchisement. Two months after the ratification of the Fifteenth Amendment, Congress passed the Enforcement Act to ensure equal access to the polls and to deter those who sought to intimidate black voters. However, the un-restrained violence during the election of 1870 led Radicals to conclude that the act was insufficient in addressing the abuses. It seemed, he felt, that the race problem would be interminable, keeping the nation forever stuck in the past and preventing it from meeting the challenges it would face in the future. Farmers and workingmen and -women, without a federal government that placed their welfare foremost, could only expect a bleak and wretched future run by monopolies and their congressional lackeys. Wilkinson now had no faith that this quality of man would change anything in Washington as long as the people were kept in the dark about the activities of their elected officials. In midsummer of 1870, shortly after the second session of the Forty-First Congress adjourned, he saw an opportunity at home to redress the wrong.

Democrat Daniel Norton, who had replaced him in the Senate in 1865 as a result of an intraparty fight between the Wilkinson and Windom factions, died in Washington on July 13, 1870. Governor Austin appointed Windom to serve until January 1871, when the legislature convened and could elect a man to serve out the remaining six weeks of Norton's term. Despite the con-trol of Ramsey's men of the caucus, it would be a contest, prompted by the irksome Congressman Wilkinson who wanted both to frustrate the Ramsey forces and draw attention to what he viewed as the true agenda of the Re-publican Party. By the fall of 1870, with Ramsey safely reseated in the Senate and Donnelly utterly discredited by his dalliance with the Democratic Party, Republican leadership appeared to anoint William Windom to continue in of-fice.[21] But it proved to be nettlesome. The then-serving congressman began a futile campaign against Windom for the caucus endorsement for United States senator.

At a campaign rally in Winona, sharing the platform with Ramsey, Win-dom, and Governor Horace Austin, Wilkinson staked out his position, argu-ing that the Republican Party was organized to combat and overthrow the unparalleled monopoly of human slavery. "So it must now still further pur-sue the object of its being, and labor to restrain and keep within due bounds these other great and growing moneyed monopolies and combinations which threaten to sap the foundation of our free institutions while oppressing the poor about the land." This, he considered, was the mission of the Republican

Party in the future, and to this object it was his purpose to devote his energies. The *Winona Republican* noted the frequent applause Wilkinson's remarks elicited, showing that the sympathies of his audience were fully in accord with his own.[22]

The contest quickly heated up as the two men and their surrogates in the press exchanged accusations against each other. "The *Minneapolis Tribune*," reported the *Republican*, "having made the assertion that, 'early in this campaign Mr. Wilkinson distinctly stated it to be his intention to coalesce with the Democratic Party to secure the defeat of Mr. Windom and his own success,' the *Mankato Union* gives it a positive and authoritative denial. Mr. Wilkinson never made any such statement. Of course, he did not. The *Tribune*'s declarations concerning that gentleman are simply absurd, as every man who knows him very well understands."[23]

But it was not until the public hearing of the candidates in Minneapolis that the fighting hit a new low. During the question-and-answer period Wilkinson was asked whether he supported the success of the Republican Party. In response, he said, "If nothing unforeseen turned up he expected to vote for the ticket." Then, when asked whether he would stump for Republican legislative candidates, he responded that he would if they "would elect him to the senate." It was the characterization of Wilkinson's equivocation—his "hesitancy"—that inflamed matters, precisely what the Windom/Ramsey faction wanted.[24] In an article titled "The Mask Off At Last," the pro-Windom *Minneapolis Tribune* unleashed its wrath. "Mr. Wilkinson's . . . refusal to say, when interrogated, that he desired the success of the Republican tickets this fall, should warn the Republican committees all over the state, not to send him out to the people as a representative of the party. His unconcealable hostility to that party . . . demands that the Republican committee should, we suspect, put Republicans on their guard against so faithless a representative. . . . Doing what he can to Donnellyize himself, let him have the full benefit of it."[25]

The paper had accused him not only of being disloyal to the party but also of currying the favor of the Democrats just as the "ingrate" Ignatius Donnelly had done. "The Hon. M. S. Wilkinson [is] one of the partners of the political firm of Donnelly, Democracy, and Co."[26] Once again, it must have tickled the Democrats to see the Republicans attack their own, as they had the suffragists. In Wilkinson's case, punishment was excommunication. His "crimes" had really been twofold. First, he stood firmly against the "villainous" high protective tariff that had recently been enacted and joined the Democrats who sought to appeal the measure. Second, but just as inflammatory, Wilkinson had launched an unrelenting attack alleging that Windom had corrupted himself by serving railroad interests. The *Tribune* evidently did not know about Wilkinson's vote with congressional Democrats to admit white supremacists to represent Georgia: the editor, as well, had lost interest in the welfare of Southern blacks. "[Wilkinson] has waged a war on the Northern Pacific Railroad corruption fraud, and all the orators among whom that fraud is being distributed are barking along his track."[27] But extending its hand to the sitting congressman from Mankato, the Democrat-oriented *Weekly Pioneer* stated, "If the radical party can't afford that class of man, the Democracy can afford to make them welcomed."[28]

The *St. Paul Press* and "even the lying little *Dispatch*," which in the view of the *Weekly Pioneer* had become "prosperous and saucy on the share of the Northern Pacific corruption fraud," joined in the call for Wilkinson's excommunication.[29] The *Press* derided Wilkinson for being "so thoroughly disgraceful, so shamelessly recreant" while the *Weekly Dispatch* intoned, "The Republican organization of the 1st District owes it to itself to put none but Republicans on guard in the canvass. We court the opposition of open foes but want no covert enemies."[30] The *Tribune* used a blasphemy in a renewed attack. "When Lucifer changed his base from heaven to hell, it was not understood that his standing in the former place did anything to qualify the infamy of his hell, but only developed the vulgar selfishness which induced him to prefer reining [*sic*] in hell to serving in heaven. This seems to be the political conditions of Mr. Wilkinson just now."[31]

The *Winona Republican* held a different view, expressing appreciation for Wilkinson's value: "The lesson of the day is that both Mr. Wilkinson and those who seek to drive him out of the Republican Party will do well to be a little more considerate of the party's interest, to just go slow."[32] The Democrats would have nothing of that. The Democratic-leaning *Mankato Weekly Record*, reflecting the sentiment of a number of party leaders, held out its arms to Wilkinson, who seemed to be coming over to their side.[33] For weeks the mention of Wilkinson's name in the newspapers affiliated with either party sparked heated emotions. Through it all the Democratic press increasingly advocated his case. "Mr. Wilkinson has taken another view, almost identical with that entertained by the Democracy, upon this subject, and denounces Windom's doctrines with great force."[34]

Deny though he might the accusation that his discontent with the party prompted him to work with the Democrats, the fact was that Wilkinson had done precisely that. Back in Washington, early in December, a congressional delegation of House Republicans from the Northwest referred to as "revenue reformers," met with President Grant to declare that they were as opposed to high tariffs "as they had been in the past to the Democracy," vowing to replace Speaker Blaine and the House leadership with men more sympathetic with them.[35] "In brief the object of their efforts is to destroy the power of the Pennsylvania and the New England manufacturing interests, to utterly annihilate the huge tariff men and to assert the right of the overwhelming majority of the people of the Northwest to seek cheap markets wherever they may be found."[36]

Wilkinson argued that the tariff was so unpopular in Minnesota that Republicans had lost seats to Democrats in the most recent election. He insisted that it was not that the people desired absolute free trade—such a policy would be ruinous—but that a reduction of the tariff was what all the people demanded. He and his fellow reformers said that they hesitated to use the phrase "breaking up the party" but were nevertheless prepared to accept any result that might be forced upon their present position. They were committed to changing the leadership of the House even if they had to unite with Democrats to carry the point, to which the *Republican* replied, "We don't believe the gentlemen will rush headlong to destruction."[37]

The convoluted process for selecting the next U.S. senator began on January 17. The legislature would hold four separate ballots—two in the Senate and two in the House, with each chamber holding one election for the nomination for a full Senate term starting on the fourth of March, and another for the six-week interim term that would end on the fourth of March. In the senate, despite Wilkinson's campaign, "the [Republican] caucus," noted chronicler H. P. Hall, "was less animated than usual."[38] This would naturally be so considering the Republicans held an overwhelming majority, who, in turn, were largely Ramsey men. Of the thirty-nine Republicans present that day, Windom received thirty-four votes; and he won in the house with a commanding thirty votes. The *Weekly Pioneer* wryly reported, "The long agony of the senatorial contest that has been disturbing the Republican happy family of the State for exciting months past is over at last. The Republican caucus has unanimously chosen Mr. Windom as their candidate."[39]

It seemed now that the Ramsey caucus wished to sue for intraparty peace. They could afford to do so. They had won what they sought: their man Windom in the U.S. Senate. But within the context that Wilkinson had helped to create, a party committed to serving the interests of the privileged and doing so at the expense of democracy by wielding its overwhelming might, leaders made the tactical albeit transparent gesture to minimize the perception of a blatant power grab by electing an uncontroversial candidate—Ozora Stearns, "a worthy public man and a prominent Republican" from a southern county within Wilkinson's regional political base. Stearns was a former colonel in the Thirty-Ninth Colored Infantry, former county attorney, mayor of Rochester, and register in bankruptcy for the Southern District of Minnesota, an appointed post.[40] Hall wrote, "The selection of Stearns, for so short of a period, was simply for the purpose of passing the honors about and preventing any formal opposition to Mr. Windom."[41] Indeed, honors would be passed out when, after his term, Stearns moved his family in 1872 to Duluth, where a judgeship would be available. That year he would be elected to the bench where he would securely remain for the next twenty years.[42] It also must have helped the party to do something for the husband of the leader of Minnesota's suffrage movement, which was becoming largely made up of women married to some of the most prominent men in the state, many of whom had continued to support the Republican Party, even one year after Governor Austin's unfortunate veto of the women's suffrage bill.

But the other reason "preventing any formal opposition" was less evident. Wilkinson, perhaps the most vocal opponent in the campaign, was never a threatening contender. In fact, his name did not appear on the ballot nor apparently was he in attendance during the polling of legislators; and when the tally was made, he won a single write-in vote. There was no formal opposition within the legislature, and Wilkinson's intent was neither to win the election nor seek favor from the party. Thus, attempting to placate Wilkinson would have been a wasted effort. After watching the campaign and reading the returns, the *Winona Republican* elliptically interpreted his effort as "an ineffectual attempt . . . made by some outside Republicans to organize a 'bolt.' "[43] But the paper had missed the point. Populist discontent that had taken root in rural Minnesota over high railroad rates during the late 1860s had broken through to the surface by 1870, and Wilkinson was its voice. This was the "formal opposition" the Republicans hoped to prevent. It was the arrogance of power that fooled party leaders into thinking that Stearns's appointment could dampen the resentment of mounting railroad and elevator rates. To Wilkinson, it was all too clear, for he had cast off party unity and consequently had been all but cast out of the party that served as pawns of railroad interests and eastern merchants who benefited from high tariffs.

Party leaders had learned the sleight of hand of distracting the voters— thousands of whom had served valiantly during the war and now labored on their small farms to eke out livings—by casting Republican favorites in the likeness of St. George slaying the dragon of Southern white supremacy, a cynical ploy that doomed the soul of Republicanism that Wilkinson had helped establish fifteen years ago. His newfound friends at the *Pioneer* could see it clearly when it reported, "Ku Kluxism in the South no longer assists Republicans of the North to carry elections. It is effectively 'played-out.' "[44] Other Northern Democrat newspapers reportedly termed Klan violence as mere "sensations gotten up for political effect."[45]

His old ally Ignatius Donnelly, by now another political pariah who had lost his bid for reelection to the U.S. House of Representatives in 1868, the same year Wilkinson was elected, perhaps best reflected Wilkinson's sentiment in an address on the House floor on January 16, 1867, in which he advocated sectional reconciliation despite reports of Klan violence. "All evils will correct themselves. Temporary disorders will subside, the path will be wide open before every man and every step and every hour will take him farther away from error and darkness."[46] Either the change of political and economic circumstances required a change in the party, or the party had to die. No less than Senator Carl Schurz, Lincoln's confidant, one of the founders of the Republican Party and passionate member of the Radical caucus, shared the same sentiment in a speech he titled "The Death of Republicanism, Foretold," which was reported by the *Weekly Pioneer*.[47]

Though Donnelly did not deny violence occurred, he was not going to be distracted from what he viewed as the larger issue: the struggle worth waging was no longer about race but class. Like Wilkinson, he determined that it was now time to end corruption in the federal government. It was time for the poor man to get relief from the high tariffs that reflected the interests of New England, Pennsylvania, and New York monopolies. It was time to end military reconstruction that nurtured a growing bureaucracy, exacerbated tensions in Southern communities, and enriched businesses that supplied the occupying force. It was time to bring the troops home. It was time for reconstruction to bury the bloody shirt forever.

♦ ♦ ♦ ♦ ♦

When Congress convened for the third session, it took steps to deal with the problem of Klan violence. Butler insisted that more forceful legislation was necessary: to pass the "Force Act," as it would be called, which ensured the right to vote in congressional elections by reinforcing the military presence, as well as to investigate the violence in the South. On February 13, 1871, House Bill No. 3011, or "Butler's bill" as it was called, was introduced. Over the objections of the Democrats the bill was promptly referred to Butler's Committee on Reconstruction. One week later, Butler was prepared to formally introduce the bill to the floor.[48]

Butler labored under the urgency to push for action before the end of the session, anticipating that the Forty-Second Congress would be more con-servative. In the days left, Butler would have to act quickly, but House rules dictated that appropriation issues took precedence for the remainder of the session. Appropriations Committee chair Henry Dawes had already rejected Butler's request for a waiver of the rule. Only the House now, by a two-thirds vote, could suspend the rule. On February 28, with only three days left in the lame-duck session, Butler made a final effort to get the bill before the House. During the reading of the bill, Democrats employed a number of delaying tactics, interrupting the requisite reading of the bill with motions to suspend rules to consider unrelated matters like the import duty on coal. The Demo-crats' motions passed.[49]

To avoid further Democratic delays, Butler finally initiated the motion to suspend rules so that he could bring his bill to the floor. To meet the required two-thirds majority of 131 the Republicans had to vote as a bloc. Speaker Blaine and Appropriations chair Dawes voted in support of Butler's motion. Three Republicans joined the Democrats, however—Morton Wilkinson, who said nothing during the debate, was one of them. Butler's motion to suspend the rules failed by three votes. The bill "to protect loyal and peaceable citizens of the United States in the full enjoyment of their rights, persons, liberty, and property . . ." died. In defeat Butler reportedly slammed down his desk lid, threw the bill under his table and stalked out of the chamber, blaming for the loss the Speaker and his ally from Maine, Representative John Peters, who did not vote on the matter.[50] But absent from his ire was Wilkinson. There would be no cross words directed at him, for weeks earlier Butler had learned that the sullen Minnesotan, the man whom the black people of his state would not have now recognized, had just lost his son to scarlet fever. Morton Junior, his only son, was dead at nineteen years of age.[51]

During a term marked by racial violence in the South, Wilkinson's voice was silent and his tenure as it drew to a close remained undistinguished. He had participated in no debates. His votes were largely inconsequential, except for the vote on the Butler bill, which for the moment threatened passage of the Ku Klux Klan Act.[52] The two bills he authored, his only legislative imprints, were far from monumental.[53] His tenure in the House was but a shadow of what he had been as senator; his silence in the face of violent white supremacy diminished the stature of a great man who once stood before the assembly of black citizens of Minnesota and thundered, "Teach your sons this broad do-main is for you, as well as for the white man," or seven years earlier when, as a United States senator from Minnesota, he spoke passionately about the duty of the government to protect its people:

In my judgment it is the bounden duty of this Government to provide for the protection of every citizen of the United States anywhere and everywhere within the constitutional limits of the United
States; and if the people of the State of South Carolina rise up in
rebellion against the constituted authorities of the Government, and
if the people of that state refuse absolutely to protect the rights and
the interests of the people of the several states of the Union whenever they happen to go into and tarry in that state, it is the bounden
and solemn duty of the Federal Government to see that those people
are compelled to do it; and if they refuse it is the duty of this Government to provide that the interests and the rights and the liberties
of every American citizen who happens to tread his foot within the
limits of South Carolina, shall be protected.[54]

For Wilkinson now, it seemed that the rights of white citizens within rebellious states had more value than the rights of black citizens in still unreconstructed states. The more recent words that he spoke at the Convention of
Colored Citizens—"We have done our part!"—were indeed more of a bene-
diction to his commitment to black people. The rest was left to them alone to
achieve. "If you will be respected by good men," he said on January 1, 1869,
"you must hew out your own fortunes. . . . You must carve your way through
the solid rock, as the Caucasian has done, and rise to be dominant among
the nations of the earth. It is work that will do it. . . . It was for such men
that the homestead [act] was passed."[55] Klan violence against black and white
Republicans was no longer more nefarious than monopolies that strangled
the economic opportunities of farmers and laborers. Racism was transitory
and it would correct itself in time. Class struggle was now Wilkinson's great
crusade. Barely over two years after the Convention of Colored Citizens in
St. Paul, he undauntedly tainted his name as one of three Republicans who
voted against his party, his caucus, its leadership, the Southern relatives of the
African Americans who had assembled before him in Ingersoll Hall, and an
issue he once championed. From here on, his people would be the common
man and woman fighting against monopolies that Congress was in the business of propping up. He had given up on Congress and, to a large extent, the
Republican Party, and he was ready to go home.

**30**

# WHERE THE LIBERALS WENT

*The enemy of my enemy is my friend.*

UNKNOWN

Morton Wilkinson's recent halfhearted foray into Minnesota politics, intended more to annoy the Ramsey supporters, was but a slight diversion from a more pressing matter: it was 1872 and the nation was poised to go to the polls to reelect or reject Ulysses S. Grant for president. The issues were clear. The wealth of the nation was accumulating in the pockets of a privileged few; and Reconstruction policies had clearly failed, as indicated by pervasive racial violence that raged in virtually every corner of the Old Confederacy, exacerbated by an infestation of speculators and carpetbaggers and the futile occupation by federal troops, subsidized by lucrative federal contracts, manned by farm boys in uniform deployed into harm's way. People had fought the war to make opportunity a national right, and now, instead, before their very eyes, with monopoly bosses replacing slaveholders, the fruit of that promise withered on the vine. And it was all happening on Grant's watch.

It was time for a change and the discontented Wilkinson was in good company. National leaders, many of whom were closely associated with Radical politics and President Lincoln, men like Carl Schurz, Charles Francis Adams, Lyman Trumbull, and Charles Sumner, came together under the banner of Liberal Republican. The group also attracted moderates and conservatives, as well as many Democrats who saw it as beneficial to join the coalition whose central focus was ousting Grant and ending Reconstruction. Beyond this, the interests were divergent, which in the absence of a strong national organiza-

336

tion, made party cohesiveness far more tentative than for the two most dominant parties. As it was, the broad tent drew together a disparate assembly generally broken down into three groups: reformers, anti-Grant politicians, and
a coalition of four influential newspaper editors known as the Quadrilateral,
who later vied for control of the Republican Convention. With slavery abolished, civil rights amendments ratified, and the Confederacy defeated, the
Liberal Republicans felt that the goals of Reconstruction had been achieved.
Thus, they felt that in the seven years since the war had ended, the tenets of
Republicanism mandated that federal troops be withdrawn from the South,
where they were allegedly propping up corrupt "carpetbagger" regimes,
which had exacerbated Southern frustration and created fertile ground for
violence. The life-and-death struggle of Southern blacks had been reduced
to an unfortunate abstraction. The Liberal Republicans called for general
amnesty by restoring to ex-Confederates the right to vote and hold office,
enacting civil service reform, and holding that the rise of the Ku Klux Klan
was due to Grant's commitment to maintaining a policy of white Southern
disenfranchisement. In all states but Louisiana and Texas, they coalesced with
the Democratic Party in order to run against Grant in 1872.[1]

In May 1872 the Liberals met in Cincinnati to present their program to the
nation and to nominate their own candidate for president. Without a formal
nationwide organization the delegate selection process was haphazard, which
probably distorted their own sense of electoral support among the voters.
Some were self-appointed, but generally the size of each delegation reflected
twice a state's electoral vote, leaving them with an exaggerated sense of the
size of their national constituency. In Minnesota Wilkinson led the delegation that included Dr. W. W. Mayo, Judge Aaron Goodrich, the Hon. James
Hubbell, *Dispatch* publisher Harlan P. Hall, and Samuel Mayall, who as a
Democrat had run against Windom for the Senate.[2] In terms of candidate
selection, the delegation, quite like the convention itself, was far from har-
monious. Goodrich, for example, supported Judge David Davis of Illinois.
Mayall supported Charles Francis Adams. Wilkinson supported his old friend
Senator Lyman Trumbull. The endorsement process went through six ballots,
at which point Wilkinson joined with other politicians to switch their votes
to support Greeley, and the rest followed.[3] Thus, *New York Tribune* editor
Horace Greeley became their candidate for president.[4] Many of the reform-
minded delegates, disgusted with his selection, left the convention.[5]

In Minnesota the Liberal Republicans mounted a swirl of activity to drum
up enthusiasm for a national candidate. Wilkinson was given the honor of
calling a rally to order in Mankato and spoke in several other venues.[6] But the

challenge of mounting support for a candidate who criticized a party that was the most dominant party in the state, personified the voice of the eastern establishment, and embraced high tariffs, was quite daunting. The very fact that Greeley held strong antislavery views but remained a Civil War pacifist made him unpopular with a large number of Republicans and Democrats alike.[7] The campaign needed more oratory power.

Mayo, Hall, and Wilkinson met with the meteoric Ignatius Donnelly, who had been reluctant to get involved. Still smarting from being outmaneuvered during his reelection bid to the House by Ramsey in 1868, and failing to see Ramsey unseated from the Senate in 1869, Donnelly now even more than Wilkinson, the most polarizing politician in Minnesota, had decided to retire from politics, to devote himself to farming and lecturing. Yet he would not be Ignatius Donnelly who considered himself neither a Republican nor Democrat, but a reformer, if a part of him was not open to another fight, another campaign.[8] But he was torn: he disagreed so vehemently with Greeley on the tariff that he could not honestly support him. "I have no love for Grant and less for Greeley," he recorded in his diary, "and I am in a perturbed state."[9] His dilemma was Wilkinson's.

In the end, the voters faced no similar fate. The Liberals' efforts were quixotic, due in part to the lackluster nature of their campaign. "The Minnesota Republicans never worried seriously about the Liberal Republican–Democratic coalition. They ignored the reform issue, concentrated on rebuilding Grant's image of military glory, and talked about slavery."[10] In a state where Scandinavians were one of the largest ethnic groups, the Liberals failed to match the Republican communication machine, which included native-language newspapers and speakers who cemented party loyalty and minimized the reform issues of the rival party. Adding to the Liberals' aggravation was Greeley's passive style of campaigning, which frustrated his supporters who urged him to be more aggressive. To these urgings, the candidate replied, "Let us have patience, God reigns and whatever is best will be."[11] Nationally, Grant was reelected resoundingly.[12] In Minnesota he won with more than 20,000 votes.[13] In Blue Earth County, Wilkinson's home base, Grant won by nearly three hundred votes, 1,906 to 1,617.[14]

Grant had won in the state largely by rekindling the same sense of patriotism that inspired thousands of Minnesotans to be the first Northerners to respond to the call to arms in 1861, a call that Wilkinson and Ramsey were instrumental in initiating.[15] Eleven years later Wilkinson misgauged the resilience of that passion, losing sight of how his fellow Minnesotans were not willing to watch the reemergence of the Confederacy with memories of so many loved ones lost on Southern battlefields still fresh in their minds, and Grant had been Lincoln's man. It annoyed Wilkinson that Minnesotans who labored under such pressing contemporary matters as the economic threat of monopolies, governmental corruption, and protectionism, willingly set these concerns aside when it was time to cast their ballots because they were distracted by Republican candidates waving the bloody shirt, using an ennobling past to effectively place blinders on men that blotted out the realities of the present, prompting them to vote against their own interests.[16] It paradoxically was the party's legacy, perhaps its greatest reform—the crusade for black freedom and political equality, two issues that had defined his political identity seven years before—that now distracted humble Republicans from voting for reform. One of the few men in America who could have reduced the effect of the ploy was Frederick Douglass himself, but he was conspicuously absent. As the reputed leader of black America, to the considerable irritation of leading progressive Liberals like Senator Charles Sumner as well as presidential candidate Greeley, both friends and passionate advocates for the abolition movement, Douglass was not only absent from the convention but also had actively campaigned on behalf of Grant. To a friend he wrote, "My line of argument will be that Grant's position is pure and simple—while that of Greeley's is mixed and ambiguous. . . . Our country wants certainty and wants the confidence and repose which only certainty can give."[17]

To Sumner, Douglass's position seemed incredible, to say the least. They had seen over the past few years how the Republican Party, after leading the effort to ratify the Fifteenth Amendment, had come to disregard the interests of black Americans. Black disenchantment could be felt across the country, and was pricked further when the president, in 1871, publicly slighted Douglass during the "Santo Domingo episode," an ill-fated venture initiated by Grant to annex the Dominican Republic for the purpose of establishing a place to colonize increasingly oppressed Southern blacks. Many knew that subordinates and supporters of annexation saw it mainly as a way to open the door to lucrative real-estate transactions. Senator Sumner, a friend and former colleague from Wilkinson's Senate days, regarded the affair—similar in intent to Lincoln's colonization plan that Senator Wilkinson had killed with his bill to suspend funding—as nothing less than moral bankruptcy, insisting that the United States, instead of exporting its racial problem to a Caribbean island, should be fighting to guarantee the rights of black Americans within the Southern states where they lived. Douglass took a hit for supporting the venture, a position that cast him in the unseemly light of an opportunist. As his biographer William S. McFeely has written, "It would have been entirely consistent for Douglass to feel precisely the same way [as Sumner], but the attraction of a presidential appointment, even to a secondary post as secretary to the commission, was so alluring that he simply looked past Sumner's objections, choosing to see the presidential assignment as an honor."[18]

When the commissioners returned, Grant invited them to the White House, conspicuously omitting Douglass from the guest list. McFeely reports, "A good many black leaders were insulted, and the next year, Horace Greeley, on the campaign trail as the presidential candidate for the Liberal Republican and Democratic parties, chastised Grant, the hero of black Americans, for his hypocrisy." Douglass's friends knew that being excluded was the sort of insult that cut him to the quick (as had the steward who had refused to serve him in the main dining room of the ship returning from Santo Domingo), but he persisted in taking pains in public to say that he took no offense. Such a public gesture would surely be rewarded with an important appointment, provided he campaigned to reelect the president.[19]

"Douglass's stalwart loyalty to the Republican party separated him from many of the reformers . . . with whom he had worked in the antislavery cause," and now many, like Charles Sumner, were Liberal Republicans. Douglass had to work hard to counteract abolitionist Horace Greeley's efforts to bring in black voters. "By winning the war that ended slavery, Grant had become a hero to black Americans second only to Lincoln, but Greeley's antislavery credentials were in good order. Grant's attorney general, Amos Akerman, who had fought the Ku Klux Klan firmly and with some success in 1871, had been driven from the cabinet by the combined pressure of railroad interests and white supremacists, and his departure encouraged talk of bolting Grant's party." There were many reasons for black voters to support the Liberal-Democratic coalition. Douglass's greatest challenge was to remind his kinsmen to look beyond his party's many faults by insisting, "loyalty to the party of Lincoln and Grant was . . . the only course for black Americans."[20]

It would be wrong to disregard Douglass's sincerity, casting him into an image of a mere sycophant, for his suspicions regarding the Democrats, and of the willingness—naive in some instances—of the Liberals to align with them, were well founded. He could not have been clearer than he was in a speech he delivered in November 1870 in Rochester, New York, when he angrily declared, "Talk of dead issues! The Republican Party will have living issues with the Democratic Party until the last rebel is dead and buried—until the last nail in the last coffin of the last rebel is driven."[21] But there were many blacks to be persuaded. A group announced a plan to organize black workers into a national union and, in doing so, exert pressure on the government by threatening to withhold votes from the Republicans. "Douglass challenged this strategy," McFeely wrote, "saying that it would only play into the hands of white-supremacist Democrats at the local level and of Liberal Republicans at the national level—both groups that for the most part were indifferent or even opposed to black interests."[22]

At its root, Douglass most objected to the Liberals' sense that the battle had been won. He railed against their hostility toward Grant's Southern policy and their desire for regional reconciliation. While black Americans and Southern whites who stood for racial equality were being attacked and murdered by supremacists, Douglass viewed Democratic apologists as apostates and enemies, and it was they with whom the Liberals wished to align themselves. "The chief topic" of Liberal Republicanism "is the clasping of hands across the bloody chasm, the great love feast of reconciliation cooked by Mr. Greeley, on which occasion our southern brethren are indirectly promised the first seats at the common table."[23] The welfare of freed people, the cause of black equality, the very meaning of the Civil War and Reconstruction were at risk in Douglass's conception of the Liberal Republican movement and resurgence of the Democrats. He said with a passion that could only come from the heart, "The slave demon still rides the southern gale and breathes out fire and wrath. . . . The smoldering embers of the Lost Cause show themselves in shouts for . . . Horace Greeley!"[24]

As to the Liberals' accusation of corruption, Douglass, in terms that he would soon regret, now simply discounted it as a ploy whose consequent effect was to distract the nation from the unjust actions of white racism. And if they could not address the problems of race relations in the South, there was no way they could confront the more subtle, more nuanced forms of racism experienced daily in the North. Both forms were wearisome, so that in the end neither was worthy of consideration. As Blight observed, "Many Republicans had grown weary of the frustrations inherent in dealing with the woes of the freed people, and as Americans often do when frustrated by a fundamental problem, had turned to the more genteel posture of horror over corruption in high places."[25] But for Wilkinson, persistent racism was not the fault of vengeful former Confederates, but of a government that created that behavior with ill-conceived policies. To Wilkinson, racism was the consequence of frustrated white masses. Remove inequities confronting white men and one removed the racist impulse.

♦ ♦ ♦ ♦ ♦

With Grant and his Republican majority once again installed at the levers of government there was no longer the sense that reform could be advanced at the federal level. To be sure, some of the problems facing farmers were due to global economic factors that fell beyond the control of Congress; yet railroads, through the rates they set, created increasing burdens that exacerbated farmer discontent. Throughout the Midwest they began to organize against railroad interests. With no sense that Congress wanted to regulate rates, there was every reason to expect railroads to charge whatever the market could bear; and if competition along some lines required lower rates, profits could be boosted by setting higher tariffs on other routes. If Congress refused to regulate rates, then the states needed to act. Lawyers such as Wilkinson knew that the law had long held that private carriers had to serve all persons at reasonable rates and without undue favor and that their methods of business, as well as their rates, could be governed by the state's police power and upheld by courts. In other words, if a statute was enacted expressly to advance the welfare of the citizens, the law stood.[26]

In Minnesota, within the vacuum left by the discredited Liberal Republican Party, the only truly potent political force for change that existed was farmers, and as a force they might be persuaded to politicize the Patrons of Husbandry, or Grange. As an organization that originally was intended to meet the social and educational needs of farmers, the Grange was now beginning to promote farmer-owned cooperatives. Soon granges got involved in state politics, which in turn secured the reform legislation they desired, just like the 1873 Illinois law; and it would be good law that even the conservative U.S. Supreme Court would have to affirm.[27] The number of local granges jumped between the close of 1870 and May 1873 from fifty to more than two hundred, a growth that marked a growing membership who were increasingly thinking of public affairs and in particular matters closely related to their home interests. There was so much promise here. These were Wilkinson's people.

"It is everywhere understood," Wilkinson had argued on the floor of the House in 1870, "that the agricultural interests of the Western states are very much depressed; that the great staple production of these states, wheat, is selling at fifty cents per bushel, a price actually below the value of the labor necessary to produce it." He argued that while the western farmer sees every other industry in the land prospering his own is languishing; while those engaged in other pursuits are growing richer at present prices, he is growing poorer. "That system of national legislation, which is intended to uphold the other industries of the people, does not seem to extend to its protection of the farmer. So far as the great interest of agriculture is concerned, it is left by the government to take care of itself."[28]

At the time he spoke Wilkinson viewed Congress as being strong enough to control the monopolies, but he felt that no individual state had the power to withstand the influence of determined monied interests. Now, three years later, after Congress had continued showing reluctance to push for reform, midwestern states appeared ready to collectively stand up to railroads. In Minnesota the legislature would be in the heart of the action as it exerted its authority under the state charter. Wilkinson set his sights on a run for a seat in the state Senate in November.

The fight against economic oppression, as Wilkinson saw it, did not reflect the interests of black Minnesotans, who increasingly appeared in the state's cities to perform the most menial of jobs. Nothing he preached spoke to persuading prejudiced employers to create for blacks the opportunity for apprenticeships and employment as skilled labor, homesteading, public accommodations, let alone speaking out against the many slights and indignities black people daily faced even in Northern cities. To him, the Negro, once freed and enfranchised, effectively lost his right to complain about social and economic inequities.

In March 1873, the staunchly Ramsey-Republican *St. Paul Press*, claiming the high road on the newest issue of black equality by laying the groundwork for equal access to public accommodations, reported that Frederick Douglass was refused entrance "on account of his color" to a hotel in Trenton, New Jersey, an act that apparently "made an impression on the [state] legislature." As a result, reported the newspaper, a bill had been introduced that "by several penalties, prohibited any discrimination between whites and blacks by common carriers, hotel keepers, theatre managers, and in schools . . . whose support is derived by public funds," which if passed would be "an amazing step in advance for New Jersey to take."[29] The urgent tone of the article, suggesting that Republicans were in touch with matters of racial justice, indicated that Minnesota was likewise in need of a similar bill. The newspaper was referring to an incident that had occurred the month before.

In February, the St. Paul Library Association sponsored Frederick Douglass in its third lecture in the city. Titled "Reminiscences of the Anti-slavery Struggles," his speech was "an eloquent recital of personal experience in abolition times, intermingled throughout with strong argumentative points and glowing tributes to the contributors in the abolishing of slavery."

As he spoke at the Opera House before an adoring audience, a crowd formed outside the hall and began jeering and catcalling to disrupt his presentation. Undeterred, he gave his lecture to thunderous applause.[30]

When Douglass ended, Colonel Gilbert Dutcher, proprietor of the Metropolitan Hotel, the most prestigious hotel in St. Paul, invited the speaker to be his guest for the night, "as [Douglass] wished to take an early train to Chicago." But when Douglass later tried to book a room at the hotel, "a stupid clerk" at the Metropolitan, following hotel policy, refused to receive Douglass. The Merchant Hotel likewise refused him service. To his credit, Dutcher, upon learning of the offense which had occurred in his absence from the hotel, extended his apologies "for the unauthorized insult offered [Douglass] by the clerk," and gave a banquet in honor of his distinguished guest.[31] The mere act of reporting the incident—the first time any such story had been published in a Minnesota newspaper, let alone one as prominent as the *Press*—reminded black readers who their friends really were. The full story, however, which mentioned the Republican-dominated legislature that decided against enacting an antidiscrimination law, cast a pall over the rectitude of Minnesota's Republicans.[32]

Even the relationship between black Minnesotans and railroads was categorically different from that of farmers, because since 1869 railroads had been offering reduced rates to black passengers attending social and civic functions in St. Paul and Minneapolis. A negative story appeared in the Democratic press that reported on the two-year-old Harry Robinson case in which the plaintiff alleged discrimination when he was denied seating in the ladies' car, but it did little to alienate blacks against railroads.[33] The opportunity to have blacks share farmers' interests was lost when discrimination locked them out of the ability to own a homestead. In Minnesota by the 1870s, black people were primarily an urban and decidedly Republican people.

Wilkinson's affiliation with the Democrats must have at first confused black Minnesotans and then alienated them. In the South, it was the Democrats who beat and murdered their relatives with impunity. Masked white men who terrorized them there looked alarmingly like the masked white men— also angry at the Republicans—who met secretly throughout Minnesota's farmland. That the Grangers were not white supremacists gave little comfort to black men who escaped the Deep South with their lives to come to the Promised Land of the North Star State. And in St. Paul, the Democrats took every occasion to publicly mock black citizens even over the most fundamental right to assemble and worship, referring derisively to them as "Fifteenth Amendments."[34] To black people, Wilkinson's Democratic ties made his politics seem Faustian. The *Press,* on the other hand, printed advertisements for black businesses and prominently reported the Old Settlers' Association meeting in the Merchant Hotel to which Jim Thompson, "a colored man" and member, was in attendance, an event from which fellow Old Settlers Wilkinson and a number of prominent Democrats such as Henry Sibley and Henry Rice were absent.[35] In time, black leaders would become critical of the party, which enjoyed black loyalty without black inclusion within their power structure. But in the mid-1870s, black Minnesotans focused on securing a community in this brave new world. For now, the fiery debate over tariffs and railroad rates remained largely of white concern. Discrimination, because it seldom appeared in the newspapers, hardly captured the attention of most white Minnesotans, which left most with the opinion that it was either insignificant or nonexistent, Though this was so in the cities, it was especially so in rural Minnesota, and, particularly, in Blue Earth County, where Wilkinson had seen to make the county white when he removed all the Indians in 1863.

Indeed, it is hard to imagine that racism was of much concern to Wilkinson as he prepared to win the voters of Blue Earth County, more than a hundred miles away from the black voters of St. Paul. If, over the past couple of years he had followed the activities of black Minnesotans in Minneapolis and St. Paul, he would have concluded that while they continued to face the boorish behavior of ruffians, on the whole they were advancing quite well as valued citizens, doing what a civilized community did to promote civic-mindedness and uplift.[36] Even Frederick Douglass, in his February speech before the Library Association, said the colored race had made significant progress since slavery. And more examples would follow.[37]

Newspaper editors, with the best of intentions, may have elected to print primarily stories that showed the rapid progress of a people who were just eight years out of slavery, five years after becoming Minnesota citizens, and the embodiment of a political legacy based on the principle of freedom. In turn, blacks saw in these stories opportunities to reeducate the white community about the character of the African American and dispel the demeaning stereotype of the slovenly Rastus character. All high-minded people benefited. And while on his trips to St. Paul, the only blacks he encountered were likeliest to be porters, barbers, and cooks, the only kinds of jobs available to most blacks that offered contact with prominent white men, Wilkinson's impression was probably framed by the newspapers that conveyed a rosy tint to the realities of most black Minnesotans. Discrimination was not newsworthy. Black community building was.

"Locked into a rigid socioeconomic class structure," historian David

Taylor has written, "black people were generally unable to procure employment above low wage levels."[38] In Lowertown, the section of St. Paul where
they lived with other impoverished immigrants, blacks in the coming years
would be left behind as their ethnic neighbors moved out into the city's socioeconomic mainstream.[39] This, in the emerging American city of St. Paul, was
the beginning of a modern ghetto, and most African Americans who attended
the Convention of Colored Citizens lived in Lowertown.[40] What Wilkinson
now faced in Blue Earth County was a campaign for the bread-and-butter
survival of the American farm, not one merely seeking redress for bruised
sensibilities of colored men, and the campaign would be especially challeng-
ing to wage.

Coming from a district that was heavily Republican and had voted for
Grant in the last election, he was faced with a dilemma: should he seek Republican endorsement, which might assure him election but compromise his
political standing and integrity, or seek other endorsements from rival factions, which alone could ward off potential Blue Earth Republican voters who
might not remain loyal to him if he were to wrap himself in the mantel of the
Democracy. It had to appeal to Republicans that Wilkinson endorsed the Republican Party nominee Cushman K. Davis, a man who embraced reform—
regulation of railroads, tariff, and so on. While some criticized Wilkinson for
being too opportunistic, he assured his friends that he had no desire to affiliate
with the Republican Party as long as there was no hope of purging the party
of its corrupt practices. Rather, he insisted that he stood ready, whenever the
element of opposition could be properly marshaled, to work for the reform
the public desired. At this he declared himself to be, as Donnelly had done in
1872, neither a Republican nor a Democrat, but a reformer.[41]

But the simple fact was a reformer seeking to be truly effective in changing policy needed blocs of voters that only an organization could provide.
The Democrats were willing to claim Wilkinson as their candidate. Since the
1870 Republican caucus fight against Windom for the seat in the U.S. Senate, the Democrats openly welcomed him to their ranks, proclaiming, "If the
radical party can't afford that class of man, the Democracy can afford to make
them welcomed."[42] Gaining their support without losing Grange and Republican voters would require delicate but doable maneuvering.

It did not take much effort to gain the support of the Democrats of Blue
Earth. To inspire enthusiasm, the party wanted and needed to proudly announce this most noteworthy of acquisitions. Wilkinson, for his part, needed
to be perceived free of co-optation if he was to be anointed the Democrats'
candidate without *becoming* a Democrat. Instead of simply traditional proce-

dures of nominate-and-ballot, they settled on an unusual tactic: at the party convention, by acclamation the delegates were called to approve a resolution to nominate "the Hon. M.S. Wilkinson . . . to become an independent candidate for the position of State Senator." "It is resolved, that this convention, approving the position taken by Mr. Wilkinson, hereby recommend him to the suffrages of the voters of Blue Earth County as a gentleman in every respect worthy of the position of State Senator, and whose election will insure for our county an able and efficient representative in the legislative halls of our State."[43]

It was a thin line separating "Democratic-endorsed independent candidate" from "Democratic candidate," especially within the rough-and-tumble contest of electoral campaigns in which rivals had a profound interest in exaggerating facts and blurring lines of fine distinctions. The label "independent" was likeliest to stick if Wilkinson won additional endorsements. During the weeks preceding the county Democratic convention Wilkinson's supporters organized the People's Reform Convention, which was meant to attract citizens from all parts of the county, regardless of party affiliation—Liberals, Democrats, reformers, and Grangers who up to now had in accordance with their constitution, refrained from participating as a unified caucus in electoral politics. In October the convention endorsed Wilkinson, "whose large legislative experience and whose public record upon questions of vital interest to the toiling public, [were] in perfect accord with the movement of economy, anti-monopoly and reform."[44]

Later that month, Grangers acting outside their organization affiliation endorsed Wilkinson, breaking from a practice that was born in the intent to be a social and educational organization for farmers; but now they were ready to act on the belief that neither major party was trustworthy, a sentiment encouraged by Donnelly. Though technically the granges refrained from political activity, members were not forbidden to attend, as citizens, certain nonpartisan gatherings that took the name of "county councils." In many instances these councils were composed almost exclusively of Grangers, who thus avoided the constitutional prohibition. In the spring of 1873 Donnelly lectured before many granges, mostly in the first and second congressional districts, on a variety of subjects, such as tariffs, paper money, and patent laws, not forgetting to touch upon railroad abuses. He praised them for the influence they had exerted on bringing railroads under control of the state, but more by suggesting (over the objection of Grange Grand Master George I. Parsons, a staunch Republican) that they were to become the great party of the people that would name the next president.[45]

In September, the Grangers of Olmsted County, at their meeting in Rochester, had earlier rejected endorsing Republican candidate Cushman Davis even though he supported reform measures. But Wilkinson was free of the taint of that party's affiliation as characterized by a *Union* article alleging that politicos acting on orders from the "St. Paul federal ring"—Ramsey and Windom—sought "to defeat Mr. Wilkinson at all hazards. . . . As [the henchmen] are holding federal offices, their heads are in danger unless they take prompt measures to obey success in his defeat is to be the only condition of holding onto public pap." As if to underscore the point, "In Dakota County the office holders have received similar orders in regard to Mr. Donnelly, who is the People's candidate for the Senate in that district."[46] The message was clear: "Wilkinson deserved the support from Anti-Monopolists, Reformers and Grangers," for he would "advocate . . . an unpopular doctrine. He is far in the advance of the people."[47]

The November returns showed that Wilkinson, "with the aid of the Democrats and Patrons of Husbandry," was elected by a majority of nearly nine hundred votes, a veritable landslide within his district of Blue Earth County, and in Mankato he carried every ward except the one where his Republican rival lived.[48] Wilkinson had won as an independent, but his politics would be closely aligned with those of the newly formed Anti-Monopoly Party, "the Independent and People's candidate." The *New Ulm Herald* editorialized, "In Mr. Wilkinson the Grangers and Anti-Monopolists have a champion who can do much to redress their wrongs and effect reform to measure that lead to wring from the farmer his hard earnings. With Donnelly and Wilkinson arrayed on the side of Agricultural interests, we predict an exciting session of the next Senate. That there will be an opening of old sores there can be no doubt."[49]

# 31

# HIS UNCLASSIFIABLE HEAD

*[Wilkinson's] head is nearly bald, and what little hair
there is on it is short. A line drawn from the chin, passing
in front of the ears, would divide the head into two equal
parts.*

ROCHESTER RECORD AND UNION, MARCH 13, 1874

Although historians shed far less light on Wilkinson as a figure in Minnesota history than they do on Donnelly, among opinion makers during the five years of spirited campaigns in the first half of the 1870s, these two men were often mentioned in the same breath as either advocates of reform or traitors of the Republican cause. Since statehood they had played major roles in bringing Minnesota into full partnership within the Union. Both men were noted for their oratory, especially in the crusade to make all men, regardless of race and class, equal, and both were vilified as "bolters" by the very party that earlier had been their political home. Donnelly had followed Wilkinson to the rostrum at the Convention of Colored Citizens in 1869 to likewise extol the promise of black Americans, and it was in their attendance that black Minnesotans could joyfully see the embodiment of a political establishment committed to creating a society whose body politic at last included them.[1] And they did so while mutually shifting their wholehearted energy to the struggle of farmers, as reflected in Donnelly's diary entry: "The struggle between the North and South having ended the struggle between the East and West commences. It will not be a conflict of arms but of ideas a contest of interests—a struggle of intelligence—one side defending itself from the greed of the other."[2] To these two men the country was now embroiled in a class conflict between capitalists and laborers, between men who enjoyed privilege and "hard-handed, laborious" men who were being exploited. The desperate plight of farmers was nothing short of a latter-day form of oppression.

To opinion makers of the day, both friend and foe, they were reflections of each other, "two who hunt," as one editor wrote in 1876, political Siamese twins joined at the hip by black equality and farmer equity. And both felt, as was often the case, that with the end of slavery and the establishment of black political equality, they could shift their undivided attention to the politics of "agricultural interests." And when the two joined with each other to do righteous battle, whether to pass a black suffrage referendum, unseat Senator Ramsey, unseat President Grant, or pass legislation to regulate railroads, as was the case now, onlookers could always expect sparks to fly. Indeed, it had been then as it would be now, a show to behold.[3]

And yet, they were very different men. Visually they made for an odd couple. While at forty-three Donnelly still possessed the countenance of a curly-haired, roguish Gaelic cherub whose "fat sides quiver[ed] and look[ed] as mischievous as an exaggerated Santa Claus," the taller, brooding, and balding Wilkinson, whose face was angular and severe, prompting one writer to refer to him as "the majestic and humorless senator from Blue Earth County," looked every bit of his fifty-seven years.[4] Both could stir men's souls with powerful speeches, yet while the years of battle had seemed to keep Donnelly vibrant, for he would continue to fight in the political arena for years to come, Wilkinson seemed more content to let others carry the standard, relegating himself more to a supporting role as he would when Amos Coggswell introduced the major railroad bill of the session.[5] Donnelly had the sparkle of political celebrity, the one you sought if looking for pizzazz as during the presidential campaign of Horace Greeley in 1872. Wilkinson, on the other hand, seemed barely able to repress his rage.

They did not always arrive at the same point at the same time. Donnelly was late to join the Liberal Republican presidential campaign and Wilkinson came to openly affiliate with the Grange and Democrats after Donnelly had done so. Wilkinson had long been wary of railroads and critical of the privileges Congress bestowed upon them, while Donnelly served as a lobbyist for railroads and for Philadelphia banker Jay Cooke. Donnelly, Philadelphia-born, labeled himself as a "farmer" while Wilkinson, who was born and had labored on a New York farm and was always an advocate for the Jeffersonian sanctity of farming, never looked back at that lifestyle when he left at eighteen. To Donnelly's anticlerical stance (he was born a Catholic), Wilkinson, a

Unitarian, then Baptist, then Methodist, favored the work of the Senate being blessed by a man of the cloth.[6] And through their battles together, it was not at all clear whether they were personal friends. In the end, none of this mattered. What did was that they would be where farmers needed them to be: in the halls of state government where they could initiate the reform Congress was unable—no, unwilling—to undertake.

As Wilkinson gave full attention to the legislative battles to come, the old Dakota and Winnebago lands in the neighboring counties to the southwest of Blue Earth had already undergone a devastating locust infestation of biblical proportions. Counties staggered under the first major invasion of the Rocky Mountain locusts. By the spring of 1874, the insects would spread to the fertile acres of Blue Earth County to become the most recent assault by nature on the Minnesota farmer.[7] Since 1869, when Wilkinson proclaimed to the black citizens of Minnesota in the most ennobling of terms the virtues and promise of farming, the lives of white farmers who had staked their claims had been anything but halcyon. In the best of circumstances, the first year was always at best a gamble; but farmers in the southwestern counties faced an extraordinarily severe number of calamities of nature.

Since 1871, farmers had reported a series of devastating prairie fires that destroyed hay, grain, stables, machinery, livestock, and homes, leaving rural people in desperate need. Hundreds of pleas for relief flooded into the office of Governor Horace Austin. Henry Castle, assigned by Austin to investigate the results of several fires, reported back that several families were in dire straits.[8] One farmer, he reported, had lost all of his hay, his wagon, plow, and harrow. He was very poor "with a family of seven children, a cow, a yoke of oxen, and no money."[9] Hailstorms were also the cause of destitution, doing untold damage to crops. For example, in the Butternut Valley of Wilkinson's own Blue Earth County, in July 1871, quite a number of farmers were reduced to pleading for charity. Similar consequences occurred throughout 1872.

Such natural calamities brought unusual hardship to farmers who had very little capital or ready cash, especially after they had spent most of their money to set up the farm and purchase seed for the first crop. If it was destroyed, as was typical for so many during this period, they were left penniless, needing therefore to turn either to charity or expensive credit. One farmer told Governor Austin that he had mortgaged 160 acres of land for two hundred dollars on which he was paying 20 percent interest.[10] And since the counties most devastated were sparsely populated, the tax base was too meager to provide aid for their residents. Thus, people in the stricken areas needed help from the public coffers and private sources. After Governor Austin appealed to the public for help in 1871, donations began coming in from as far away as the East Coast. Still the suffering continued.

In April 1872, by way of Commissioner Browning Nichols, the governor received an appeal drafted by Abner Tibbetts, a protégé of Senator Wilkinson who had persuaded Lincoln to make him the land agent of St. Peter, and an ally of Donnelly during the senatorial vote of 1869. This time Tibbetts wrote on behalf of an impoverished, widowed mother of two small children. Nichols added, "We have a good many up here in our County that are ve[r]y destitute and really need help and if you have any more funds in your hands for that purpose there is some that I would be glad to see helped. If they could not get more than enough to buy two or three bushels of seed potatoes it would help them a great deal."[11] By the following year, their lot would worsen as the first major grasshopper invasion hit Minnesota.

On June 12, 1873, on a fresh breeze from the west, swarms of Rocky Mountain locusts came across the Dakota border into Minnesota and spread out over thirteen counties. They did not hit the state like a tidal wave that uniformly rolled over flat terrain; rather they flew in like clouds that drifted apart in places to alight on some fields but leaving others unmolested. Even whole towns escaped the blight. But where they landed, their impact was devastating. Succulent vegetation was consumed and the growing crops were greatly damaged, if not completed ruined. In January 1874, Henry Sibley who had been sent to examine the problem, visiting counties he had not seen since he led the Expeditionary Force against the Dakota eleven years earlier, informed governor-elect Cushman Davis that private charitable donations had all but ceased and state intervention was necessary. Davis, in turn, laid the letter before the Senate, which promptly acted on an appropriations bill. In that the locust had stayed within a small portion of the settled area of the state and were believed to have departed with the arrival of winter, the legislature set aside only five thousand dollars to supply food and clothing plus an additional twenty-five thousand dollars for seed grain to be distributed under the supervision of the governor.[12]

With this business completed, the Senate turned its attention to railroad regulation. On January 6, Wilkinson gave notice that he would introduce a bill relating to common carriers, as well as a bill defining the liabilities of corporations engaged in the transportation of goods and other properties, and he submitted the main railroad bill, SF No. 6, to be introduced by his co-sponsor, Amos Coggswell. Coggswell, of Steele County, a conservative Republican who had been a member of the party since statehood, served in the constitutional convention, lost a Senate bid to Wilkinson in 1859, and later as

Speaker, argued against extending suffrage rights to black men. Now he was a committed antimonopolist.[13] The power to determine and set the rates would reside with the legislature, within the hands of the people's direct representatives and, by extension, the people. With the combined force of Donnelly and Wilkinson, as well as a respectable contingent of Grange-endorsed legislators in the Senate and the House, all seemed to understand what was expected of them and what was good politics. The concept would prove to be more elastic than anticipated, as party legislators, feigning the role of being responsive to the people, trimmed the sails of substantive reform.

In fact, the railroad issue grew out of the conflicting needs of a growing society. The land that was open to homesteading, land that made it possible for settlers with no means to make a future for themselves and their families, was located far onto the isolated frontier. Railroads, in some instances in partnership with immigration assistance organizations, helped populate the wilderness and provide farmers with a link to market. For many, it was a lifeline. With such importance and without regulation, railroads inevitably gained leverage over the terms by which business was to be conducted, meaning they set crushing rates. Furthermore, the federal government shared a profound interest in seeing railroads spread throughout the nation, both as a means of integrating the new postwar economy and knitting together a fractured nation. Thus, the nation benefited as railroads grew, and they grew because there was considerable profit to be made. There was no interest on the national level in restraining in any way such an important industry. By the 1870s that responsibility fell to the states.

Founded in 1867 in Washington, D.C., the National Grange of the Patrons of Husbandry began initially as an educational and social organization for farmers, but it was in Minnesota, the home of founder Oliver Kelly, that chapters first appeared. Inevitably, however, Grange meetings became political as members talked about the problems they faced. Soon Grange chapters spread to other midwestern states, and as their ranks grew, so too grew their sense of political potential. Agrarian grievances against Minnesota railroads, particularly the Winona and St. Peter line, stimulated the rapid formation of Grange lodges. The Minnesota State Grange was organized in 1869, and by the end of the year there were nearly fifty active local Granges in the state. The highest Minnesota Grange membership was reached in 1874, just a year after Congress chartered the National Grange.[14]

After the organization of the Minnesota State Grange, reformers concentrated most of their efforts on railroad freight rates regulation. Inspired by Illinois laws, Minnesota Grangers pushed for similar measures. Governor

Horace Austin, formerly a judge from St. Peter, was sympathetic to their demands and signed the first of Minnesota's Granger laws in 1871. It established the office of railroad commissioner and specified rates that could only be adjusted by legislation. Nevertheless, the railroads ignored the new law and set their own rates. In response, supporters of the law filed a lawsuit against the Winona and St. Peter Railroad, and they also began to work for yet stronger legislation.[15]

During their effort to regulate the rates of railroads, Grangers understood that they needed their own political arm.[16] Neither major party was willing or capable of advancing Grange interests. Consequently, farmers and small businessmen united under the Grange banner. If they could not influence senators and congressmen with whom they lost touch once these men went to Washington, where lobbyists seemingly reigned, they could elect and monitor their neighbors who ran for state office. By the mid-1870s, Grangers, many of whom joined to fight the railroad monopoly, were forming viable campaigns for seats in the statehouse.

During the campaign of 1873, the railroad question was the most vital issue in most parts of the state. Dissatisfaction with the men who set the rates found expression through caucuses and conventions, in party platforms, and campaign speeches. In the legislature that met in January 1874, a large majority, regardless of party affiliation, had pledged to support railroad regulation. Of the 106 members of the House 64 were farmers, and there was also a significant number of farmers in the Senate.[17] Most of these were men who considered themselves "express representatives of the Grange movement," filled with the "moral courage to attack iniquity in its very citadel."[18] But their hopes ran head-on into the harsh reality of railroad politics.

In the House, at the opening of the session the more radical members tried to unite all those who were pledged to reform and thus capture the organization of the House. As an indication of how far bipartisanship had come in Minnesota politics, all antimonopolists, without regard to former party ties, were invited to meet in a caucus to nominate candidates for the elective House offices.[19] Their candidate for Speaker, a member of the Grange, lost out by only three votes. Many took the defeat as a harbinger of future battles with a powerful lobby that would not give up control easily.[20]

The Senate committee, on which Donnelly sat, like other major committees, was dominated by the Republican faithful. Indeed, observed the *Mankato Union*, "The organization being in the hands of Republicans, placed reformers either on committees of minor importance or on the tail end of those [in] which the public have the most interest."[21] Earlier in the session,

Wilkinson attempted to change the rules concerning committee appointment to have the body, rather than the Senate president, assign senators, but so as to unofficially slip it away from debate, his resolution was "laid over to future consideration."[22]

Donnelly was left to make his case alone before an unsympathetic committee. Charged with the responsibility of framing the bill, he soon refused to meet with the committee, arguing that it was dominated by Republican establishmentarians determined to draft a law that served railroads rather than the people. Even a few members of the Republican Party took issue with the strong-arm tactics of their party bosses to maintain control of both chambers, but were eventually driven back "by whip and club" to "the party of monopoly."[23] Senator-elect Ignatius Donnelly immediately expressed lack of faith in the legislature and began preparations for a new campaign. He was appointed to serve on the Senate Railroad Committee, but refused to meet with the other members because he did not believe they would support reform.[24] Many of the most radical members viewed anyone willing to dismantle the law of 1871 as suspect, including the governor, who had supported reform.

Governor Horace Austin, who had served as a judge in St. Peter, anticipated, despite his sympathies, the direction of the litigation that would grow out of this kind of legislation: that as long as the law imposed inflexible rates without regard for whether the trains carried freight or passengers, the companies would challenge the law as "too arbitrary and inelastic," unreasonable.[25] Anticipating that the cases would be upheld by the state supreme court—an elected body where Grange sentiment was strong—the companies would then appeal the rulings before the far more conservative U.S. Supreme Court, where the law was destined to be struck down as unconstitutional. Austin advised the attorney general to refrain from prosecution.[26] Instead, he recommended that complaints against railroad companies should be heard and determined by a board consisting of the railroad commissioner and a number of efficient men appointed to serve with him.[27] He approved adopting a plan, fashioned on the French model of strict government inspection and supervision of all roads, the regulation of their charges, and allowing no tariff advances without showing good cause.[28] He also believed as he had before, that cheap transportation could only be secured by developing a viable alternative to shipping by railroad. To this end, he proposed that the waterways be improved and extended.[29] Incoming Governor Cushman Davis, who was equally interested in reform, nonetheless agreed that the law should be modified and that a more reasonable standard be applied in setting rates.[30]

But it was the annual report from Alonzo Edgerton, the railroad commissioner, that appeared to convince many members of the Anti-Monopoly Party that the law needed to be changed. In it Edgerton complained that his powers were too limited to remedy the railroad abuses. He called attention to the fact that he could not commence suits against railroad companies and had no power to prevent extortion, his duties being mainly limited by law to the collection of facts and statistics for the information of the legislature.[31] Edgerton left it to the legislature to determine whether an extension of powers would be advisable. He admonished the railroads against complaining about the wrongs they have suffered, for the revolt against them would grow "greater and greater in magnitude." To buttress his admonition, he reviewed the federal, state, and municipal aid to the railroads of the state, and contended that the people had not shown themselves unfriendly to the railroads as often charged. Rail companies had been liberally dealt with in terms of franchises, land grants, bonuses, and right-of-way donations; and all that the people asked for these "prodigal gifts," Edgerton said, was "security from extortion and freedom from unjust discrimination."[32]

The great question before the legislature of 1874 was the solution of the perplexing railroad problem. Most agreed that something must be done, but there was a great variety of opinion in the legislature, and throughout the state, as to what that was.[33] The old law, whatever its faults, at least drew a clear line between lawful and unlawful practices, a standard legislators had created. Would any revision that allowed for flexibility essentially erase that line? Would it be giving quarter to those who least deserved it? Most believed that the railroads could not be trusted to uphold the spirit of the law; but could the legislators—many of whom were not friends of the farmer, many who were used to the old way of doing things—find middle ground that was just? Could even the reform men come together?

At its annual meeting in December, the State Grange decided against maintaining a "lobbying committee at the capital during the legislative session."[34] However, defying the edict of George Parsons, leader of the State Grange who insisted that the Grange at all costs stay out of politics, legislators, likely at the prompting of Senators Donnelly and Wilkinson, met with members of the executive committee of the State Grange to appoint a committee to confer with officials as to what legislation was desired by the Grange and farmers of the state.[35] Seats were provided for lobbyists in the Senate chamber with the understanding that they were to look after matters of interest to the farmers. But in the end, the committee's only accomplishment was to alienate many of the Granges because it had been appointed against the express wishes of George Parsons.[36] With a division within their own ranks, things did not augur well for the fortunes of reform.

On February 19, the Railroad Committee of the Senate (on which Donnelly served) introduced a comprehensive bill that included all of the provisions Wilkinson had previously introduced, but that had been set aside. On February 24, Donnelly's SF No. 6 was indefinitely postponed in a vote of 26 to 12, with Donnelly and Wilkinson voting with the minority. Then the committee's bill "to create a board of railroad commissioners and to provide for the management of all railroad corporations within the state" was passed, 29 to 7. Once again, Donnelly and Wilkinson voted in dissent.[37] The Donnelly-Wilkinson caucus sought more restrictions for oversight to be determined by legislative action while the senate bill sought more flexibility for men selected by the governor to make those regulatory decisions. Vigorous negotiations ensued between the Senate and House, whose railroad bill was much more stringent, until they agreed on a bill that received wide support in both chambers. The House vote was 83 to 3 and the Senate was 34 to 2. Here, Wilkinson, voting in the majority, parted ways with Donnelly, who cast one of the dissenting votes.[38] Once again, Wilkinson, just as in 1862 when he approved the needed confiscation bill even though it included a provision for colonization, a measure with which he strongly disagreed, voted for regulation, however flawed, because he understood that the law of 1871 would not be maintained. A flawed law, to him, was better than no law at all.

The conflict leading to this vote concerned which body—the legislature or a gubernatorial-appointed commission—should be empowered to set rates. Fundamentally, as Donnelly saw it, the very fact that commission members were appointed made them the beneficiaries of patronage in which loyalty to the party organization or the man making the appointment was foremost. The interest of the people seldom figured into the equation. This was, after all, no longer the Party of Lincoln, but the party of "Bluff Aleck" Ramsey. The law, in short, was tantamount to placing the wolf in charge of the henhouse. It did not matter to him that Ramsey's influence had considerably waned, or that Horace Austin and governor-elect Cushman Davis were of a different stripe, both noted for being sympathetic to reform and, at least in theory, inclined to appoint honorable men. For Donnelly, the law granting governors broad and unprecedented authority, even to men of known character, nonetheless brought with it a corrupting influence, and the three new commissioners proved the point: Alonzo Edgerton, who had served as railroad commissioner since 1871, former governor William Marshall, a Ramsey man who only recently served as president of the St. Paul–Dubuque Railroad, and J. J. Randall of Winona, a former collector of internal revenue from the home and political base of Senator William Windom.[39] Even though the new law required appointees to serve the two-year term with the consent of the senate, and it precluded an appointee from being a "stockholder, trustee, assignee, lessee, agent or employee of any railroad corporation," nothing in the law precluded appointees from having served in those capacities.[40]

Rejecting the entire idea of the rate-making commission, Donnelly placed his faith in legislative regulation. "The people elected a legislature to regulate the railroads," he argued, and any action to the contrary would not work. "After a sixty-day session the Republican majority discard all the bills proposed by the Anti-Monopolists, and coolly tell the people, 'You picked the wrong man; we know nothing about railroads, we are too ignorant and incapable to fix a schedule of charges.' "[41] Ironically, Elias F. Drake, president of the St. Paul & Sioux City Railroad and Republican leader of the Senate, who opposed all regulatory legislation as a matter of principle, was the only senator who joined Donnelly in dissent.[42] Drake was at this moment his only ally, for most members of the Anti-Monopoly caucus favored a bill that authorized a commission like the one that existed in Illinois, a model that later would be upheld in the United States Supreme Court, hardly a body noted for its progressive views.[43] Donnelly's obstinacy alienated many of his cohorts, making it easy for them to vote against him.[44] Wilkinson, however, had resigned himself to the facts of life of this legislative session and supported the bill, not because it gave all the relief desired but because there was no hope of getting anything better.[45]

Most Republican opinion makers around the state seemed to agree with him. The *St. Paul Press,* a paper that had hardly been a friend to him, told of its enactment under the headlines, "The People's Triumph, the New Railroad Law." It claimed that the representation of the railroads in the legislature had been so small that they had nothing to say in its enactment.[46] The *Minneapolis Tribune* did not consider the problem solved, but believed the law to be the best that could have been devised under the circumstances. The legislature had both "killed the iron horse to gratify the insane caprices and spleen of some fanatics and demagogues," but "had at least put a snuffle on him and a curb but to hold his rebellious nose in subjection."[47] The *Rochester Post* gave credit for incorporating the wisest and most judicious thought, deduction, and decision, of the best brains and the clearest heads of that legislature, though the bill was far from perfect.[48] Similarly, the *Rochester Record and Union* believed that while the new law was an obvious advancement from the law of

1871, it would prove "adequate to the consummation desired."[49] On the other hand, the *Dispatch* regarded the law as a triumph of the railroad companies and objected forcibly to the plenary powers, ministerial and judicial, executive and legislative, that had been granted to the commission, and considered its appointment by the governor as a dangerous grant of power.[50] Though some were disappointed that the Grange was not represented on the board, the appointees seemed on the whole to have been quite acceptable to the people.[51]

But it would be Donnelly's prediction of failure that would bear out in history. Because of the financial setbacks in 1873, the debt of railroad companies soared as stock devaluation plummeted and the panic carried over into 1874. In consequence, the commission saw the railroads as a public interest. The avowed aim, the board announced, was not to reduce rates but to remedy abuses. They felt, in protecting the public good, that they had to deal gently with bankrupt companies, and this attitude was frequently interpreted as an indication that they were "in cahoots with the railroads." Accordingly, they decided to raise rates. The commission cost the state ten thousand dollars a year. This was a material increase in state expenses, and it was feared that costly litigation would add to the burden. The Grangers did not work in harmony, and this internal discord had a deafening effect.[52] Donnelly led the wave of criticism. When the legislature assembled in 1875 a new law was demanded.[53] Wilkinson was ready for the fight, though unexpectedly he was about to be given accolades from the political establishment. With this, he had crossed over into a heady realm made transcendent by once-critical opinion makers who, seeing him as both a living "historic" figure and reasonable, now elevated him to the status of statesman.

At the close of the 1874 legislative session, Wilkinson, accompanied by Senators Graves and Talbot, was given the honor of informing the governor of the Senate's intent to adjourn and invite him to customarily give the closing remarks. Governor Davis declined.[54] The next day, March 13, the St. Paul correspondent of the *Rochester Record and Union* published a glowing sketch of Wilkinson as part of a series on the leading state senators currently serving in the legislature:

> Morton S. Wilkinson, for being so long in public life, as U.S. Senator and Member of Congress, is well-known throughout the state, and throughout the United States, and the people everywhere owe him a debt of gratitude for the fearless manner in which he made battle for the cause of freedom during the dark hours of the rebellion. There is no man in the state who cannot respect Mr. Wilkinson

for his unswerving integrity during his public life in Washington. His votes and speeches were all on the side of freedom and in the cause of the great masses. His political opponents knew it was not possible to attack his public life, and so took every opportunity to slander his private character. He possesses many characteristics of strength . . . [and] is a loud talker, and more earnest and much clearer than [most men]. He differs also from the latter in being very companionable, and has many warm friends on both sides of the house.

Mr. Wilkinson is about 54 years of age, tall and slim as a rail. His features are strongly marked, nose thin and long, hanging over the upper lip, deep lines running from his nose to the corners of his mouth. His face is smooth shaven, the mouth large, lips thin and compressed, and prominent chin. Prominent brows hang over keen eyes, which projection gives them the appearance of being deeply set in the head. Wilkinson has got a very peculiarly shaped head, and it is unclassifiable. This prominence of the observing faculties also makes the brow to appear to retreat. The head is nearly bald, and what little hair there is on it is short. A line drawn from the chin, passing in front of the ears, would divide the head into two equal parts.

He is a very energetic speaker, and when warmed up with his subject, becomes eloquent in his earnestness. As against the frauds of the railroad monopolies, he is an uncompromising exponent. In him the Grangers have a tower of strength for the battle of right against oppression in the next session of the legislature.[55]

32

# A REPUBLICAN WITH
# UNCHANGED VIEWS

*That in order to carry out the foregoing resolutions, to bring*
*peace and quiet to all parts of the Union, and to purify the*
*Government, it is necessary that the present [Grant's] National*
*Administration should be overturned, and its place supplied*
*by one heartily in accord with the foregoing principles.*

MORTON S. WILKINSON, 1875

The railroad law of 1874 was a disappointment. It was created to curb the arbitrary power of the railroads and to put them under the control of the people. But because of the financial emergency that began in 1873, it was impossible to give it what its proponents would call a fair trial. Business was at a standstill, and the railroads were unable to meet their obligations that came from times of optimism and prosperity. When the State Grange considered reviving the matter in 1875, the response was tepid. The problem had not been solved. Yet public opinion was fast moving to the opposite position and the newspapers reflected, and in several instances influenced, the shift. "By the winter of 1875 the state press had come to an almost unanimous decision in favor of an about-face in the railroad policy of the state."[1]

The *St. Paul Press* viewed the possible impact of the law as "mischievous in the extreme." Even though it had been administered leniently, the paper nonetheless concluded that as "experience had painfully admitted . . . the experimental legislation of last winter in this state was a monstrous mistake."[2] To the *Minneapolis Tribune,* the farmers' movement was a senseless railroad war. "Ten years will not suffice to repair the injury to the state which the law has inflicted."[3] The *St. Paul Dispatch,* often the more progressive on political and social issues, argued, "The mistake which has been made in this war upon railroads is now very generally conceded, and few have the temerity to longer attempt to ride upon the commune sentiment as a political hobby."[4] "Never before in this country," stated the *St. Cloud Press,* "have the railroad interests felt the result of unjust laws more than now. Never before have the people felt the result of these laws with the same bitterness as now."[5] And in reaction to a speech Commissioner Edgerton delivered in which supposedly he unreasonably limited the rates of a railroad, the *St. Paul Pioneer* editorialized, "[Edgerton] shows that he compelled the Winona and St. Peter railroad to run at a cost of $30,000 a year beyond their receipts, and then he asks: . . . Can we put our hands deeper into the pockets of the owners of this road, until we find whether, after the end of a few months, they have any more money left for us to take?" In other words, the railroad commission was "a cool and deliberate scheme of railroad plunder."[6]

So broad was the opprobrium against the law that the Winona and St. Peter Railroad, which had been the object of complaints sparking the call for regulatory legislation, was now pictured as suffering an injustice at the hands of tyrannical commissioners; and many came to believe that the Grange movement was the cause of the financial depression.[7] In people's minds, the railroad law and the economic panic were cause and effect, and Governor Davis suggested as much. The commercial and industrial interests, and particularly the railroads, were the first to suffer, but the effects of the panic were soon shared by farmers as well. Saby writes, "The grangers had never planned to cripple the railroad industry. They had meant to control the roads for the public interest."[8] But now they felt that more damage had been done than good, with them remarkably looking like the villains. They were no longer militant. In fact, two railroad companies were in the hands of receivers, three had defaulted in interest of debts, and others had maintained their credit only by levying assessments on their stockholders.[9] The *Grange Advance* stated, "It was an illy advised law gotten up in a hurry near the close of the session as an excuse for not doing anything else, providing for three commissioners who should stand between the people and the legislature and bear the odium of the failure."[10] Though they were no longer militant, the Grangers still wanted some form of state regulatory control, but there was no consensus on what the new law should be. They, however, like everyone else, knew that a change to the law was needed. But when the legislature met in January the all-consuming issue was instead the senatorial election.

♦ ♦ ♦ ♦ ♦

In the midst of the political shift, the Grangers' influence had reached and started receding from the high-water point, and the conservatives reasserted their leadership within their respective Republican and Democratic caucuses; this development posed new opportunities for the growing list of men seeking to replace a man who so often in the past had infuriatingly eluded defeat: Alexander Ramsey's time had come and gone. The docket for the legislature of 1875 included deciding who would collect the jewel in the crown of Minnesota politics—a seat in the United States Senate. It was the issue that nearly overshadowed all the others. As Donnelly biographer Martin Ridge has noted, "The Minnesota legislature which convened in January, 1875, faced serious problems, but these were virtually ignored because of a contest for the United States Senate." And once again, Donnelly was in the middle of it.[11]

Shortly after being elected to the state Senate in 1873, Donnelly began his campaign, focusing much of his efforts on gaining Democratic support, soliciting donations from eastern Democrats, and gaining assurances of support from Democrats who allied with "renegade" Republicans. Conservative Minnesota Democrats, however, rejected him. Though they liked his politics, especially when he was a thorn in the side of the Republican hierarchy, they did not trust him as their leader, a view that had only deepened since one of the party's leaders, Louis Fisher, editor of the *St. Paul Pioneer,* rejected his efforts to formally unite all farmers by coalescing under the Anti-Monopoly Party banner. Donnelly had shown himself once too often to be ideologically independent and unwilling to consult with party regulars.[12] With Republican votes splintered into the Davis and Washburn camps, Ramsey barely retained the plurality, holding six more than the second-largest vote getter, Ignatius Donnelly. Davis's men, who normally would have deferred at this stage to Ramsey, remained determined to support anyone but Ramsey—anyone, that is, but Ramsey and Donnelly. Amos Coggswell declared that he would endorse Davis, but "preferred a good old-fashioned Democrat, if you can find him."[13]

Voting for the senatorship began on January 19. Wilkinson, voting with the Democratic-Liberal Republican caucus, supported Donnelly.[14] But by the end of January it was becoming clear to supporters that his standing had not improved and there were calls for him to step out of the contest.[15] By the first week of February the contest had entered into a new phase when Donnelly, realizing that he could not consolidate the opposition votes against Ramsey, dropped out of the race.[16] Already some members of the caucus pushed for Davis to be the standard-bearer, but he was not acceptable to the group. Wilkinson worked with Senators Donnelly, Charles Berry, and House representative Frank Morse on the platform, which, when adopted, was clearly not designed for the policies of Davis. Thus, he, too, dropped out of consideration. The platform was one of protest against the federal military action in Louisiana as illustrated by Wilkinson's sharply worded supplementary resolution to denounce both the policy and to call for the "overturn" of the Grant administration as the necessary effort "to purify the Government."[17] In that Davis was not a Liberal Republican, he dropped out of consideration, making way for a man more to their liking—a man of judicious temperament, an honored veteran of the Civil War, and a Democrat.

On February 1, Wilkinson explained why, "as a Republican—with unchanged views of the sacredness of the Union—in the presence of those who had known and voted for him as a Republican—he was proud to cast his vote for William Lochren." It was the first time since 1870 that he had claimed the party affiliation, but it served him well now in attracting bipartisan support for a Democrat. In response to the characterization by the *St. Paul Press* of the candidate as a "State's Rights Democrat of the extreme school" and his so-called friends who were "greatly surprised and pained" to hear of his endorsement, Wilkinson said, "At a time when the country called its young men to the defense of the Union, and when Minnesota sent out her young men to do battle for the common flag, I had not cared then to what party belonged these young men who followed that flag: I knew they were true to the Union." Employing a tactic that he often criticized Republicans for using to elicit political support from voters, he waved the bloody shirt, and to great effect:

> I remembered soon after the terrible battle at Gettysburg, I was there
> to visit the survivors of our First regiment which participated in the
> perils, losses and glories. I found General Hancock, Col. Colville,
> and Col. Adams and others disabled by their wounds. When I went
> over to see where the Minnesotans were buried, I found a line of
> graves opposite which was a crowd of the rebel dead. There stood
> Lt. Lochren's company [applause] of 34, of whom only seven men
> besides Lt. Lochren came from the field. Through all, till the four
> years of war, Lochren remained in the service, and at last came home

with the tattered flag he had followed so faithfully. [Applause.] . . .
I have only to suggest that in these times there was need for men like
Mr. Lochren, who would regard the constitution and be true to it as
he was to the flag in those days of war.[18]

On the day of the announcement, the votes for Senator were Lochren, 54;
Ramsey, 47; Davis, 22; Pillsbury, 12; and 8 votes scattered among other candidates. On Saturday, the vote remained virtually the same with Lochren at
52 and Ramsey at 47; Davis at 23; and Pillsbury at 13. At one point during
the night caucus it was agreed to cast the Democratic votes for Wilkinson, if
he could rally enough Republican votes to elect him. It is not clear whether
state Senator Wilkinson knew of this plan. In any event, the secret got out
and at an early-morning caucus the Republicans suddenly resolved to concentrate upon Minnesota Supreme Court Chief Justice Samuel McMillan,
though Ramsey's men held out hope that they could secure enough votes.
The deadlock among the Republicans remained so until February 13, when
Ramsey and Davis agreed to withdraw in favor of a compromise candidate,
McMillan.[19] For the Ramsey men, there were regrets, as the *St. Paul Press* of
February 19 indicated, when it declared that the Republican Party in Minnesota was dead and that Chief Justice McMillan would be as good a man as any
"to bury the corpse and administer the estate."[20]

◆ ◆ ◆ ◆ ◆

Meanwhile, the survivors of the locust infestation of 1873 felt, *hoped,* that they
had seen the last of the swarm. They knew that eggs had been laid but had
little understanding of what it meant until the weather warmed and the eggs
hatched. Soon unfledged grasshoppers began their ravages throughout the
eleven counties afflicted in 1873. In some counties, by mid-June news circulated that the wheat crop had been "entirely destroyed." Soon the same report
came from more counties. By mid-July the newly hatched locust sprouted
wings and took to the air. As they flew north and east to neighboring counties,
new swarms from the West replaced them, and the ravage resumed. Calls of
alarm were heard from as far north as Moorhead and as far east as Mankato
as farmers watched helplessly while their crops were completely destroyed.
In July 1874, The *St. Paul Daily Pioneer* reported, "Nearly all the farmers in
that section [from the Blue Earth River westward] are ruined financially."[21]
    They had studied the cycle. After spending the summer consuming the
harvest the adult grasshoppers would deposit their eggs just beneath the surface of the soil in late summer, then the eggs would hatch in late spring, about

the time when the wheat began to sprout. At that time, the fledgling pests would crawl to all vegetation, and satisfy their appetites until they sprouted wings, at which time they alighted on new food sources. Even so, it remained hard to predict where they would land, but once present, the experience would be nightmarish. One farmer claimed that the pests "can be found in our houses on our furniture in our clothing and even on our tables at our meals."[22]

The extent of the devastation in 1873 was too much for charities to address adequately, as Governor Austin had hoped. In 1874 Governor Davis recognized that government had to intercede. His solution was to call on county commissioners to furnish relief for the stricken communities, all of which had meager resources. Generous neighbors divided what resources they had with the less fortunate until whole communities had been reduced to a common destitution. Merchants and men of means had given and lent until they would be ruined unless they too could receive relief, presumably from their respective counties. Not all counties complied, however, questioning whether the governor had the authority to issue such an order. Citizens and donors of all sorts were left to make donations to local funds. An eighty-year-old veteran of the War of 1812 from New York sent one dollar in the name of his sense of "duty and privilege to contribute my mite to help the distressed." The Ojibwe Indians of White Earth Reservation sent fifty-six dollars, together with a peace pipe, to signify that they had always been "the true friend of the white man and that they felt the deepest sorrow for their suffering white brothers." An American in Paris sent one hundred francs.[23]

Twenty-eight Granges contributed $316.80 in addition to $2,000 sent by the National Grange to aid suffering members. Historian Annette Atkins observes, "While the combined contributions of all the Grangers may have been generous, their efforts represented only a minor part of the assistance. Their later claim that 'actual starvation must have resulted but for the nationwide Grange response' can surely be chalked up to organizational pride and exaggeration. In fact, it is surprising that a group dedicated to relieving the social and economic maladies of the farmers did so little."[24]

In January 1875, Henry Sibley, who had been asked to study the impact of the devastation and who himself had raised funds, issued his report to the legislature, as he had the year before. He closed ominously with the admonition that if the state did nothing to help the farmers, "twelve hundred to fifteen hundred farmers . . . 'will, from necessity, seek some other homes.' " He felt that $100,000 was "imperatively demanded to carry the suffering families over to another harvest and half as much more was needed to furnish seed for the next spring's planting," a handful of months away. This amount was unacceptable to legislators, preferring instead to appropriate $20,000 "for the immediate relief of the suffering settlers on the frontier."[25]

At that point, Senator William Murphy from Ramsey County felt this aid was not enough, and tried to raise the sum to $50,000. The debate revealed significant suspicion of the victims, "a suspicion," notes Atkins, "obvious in all of the relevant 1875 legislation." Whereas legislators in 1874 were clearly not in support of extending public aid to victims of the devastation, they did not question their victims' integrity. But during the 1875 session, legislators did. Traditional nineteenth-century rhetoric of "rugged individualism" characterized their pronouncements about the chronically poor. Senator Joseph H. Clark of Dodge County, very much in that vein, opposed Murphy's proposal, arguing that such aid would "tempt the people to sit down and wait for aid." Reports of able-bodied men in frontier counties who had refused work because they were waiting for state relief had apparently convinced him that the needy "should be taught self-reliance" rather than pampered with free aid. Although the senators as a whole may not have shared Clark's attitude, they did soundly defeat Murphy's proposed increase.[26] True to the general sense of distrust that policy makers held for the poor seeking public assistance, the approved bill for $20,000 was filled with severe and exacting stipulations requiring applicants to "[show] the necessity of relief."[27] Better the deserving many suffer than the undeserving few benefit.

On March 1, Wilkinson once again proposed a bill to increase relief funds to $50,000. Future governor John Pillsbury of Hennepin County, reflecting his persona as a penny-pincher, said it would cost too much.[28] Later in March, the legislature appropriated $75,000 for the purchase of seed grain and allowed for immediate relief, if necessary. Instead of granting the governor the authority to distribute the grain, as the 1874 law had, the measure called on him to appoint, with the advice and consent of the Senate, three commissioners to manage and disburse the funds. The legislature did not add specific stipulations for distribution.[29] As for the funds for relief, because of the stipulations, less than the $20,000 in appropriations was given out. "It was not found necessary," reported Governor Davis in his annual message of 1876, "to extend the whole of this sum." However, as one frustrated official in Martin County complained, "[The appropriated amount] seems to be so closely guarded as to be out of reach to nearly all."[30] Thousands of the settlers in the frontier counties would apparently be left to suffer because of a lack of true character, a lack of pluck.

In the spring, the eggs hatched. Many young locusts were killed off by an extended wet-and-cold snap in the northern parts of the state, and a natural parasite did extended damage to the eggs in north-central Becker County. In July when the young developed their wings, they began to migrate out of the state. Unfavorable winds kept most of them from leaving and also shut off new swarms. Damage in 1875 was considerably less than had been feared, with nineteen counties affected.[31] Nonetheless farmers were devastated. Theodore G. Carter—farmer, land agent, and war veteran in Nicollet County near St. Peter—left a record of his trials, just as he had done for the Dakota Trials in 1862. Throughout the period of infestation, he watched his farm, business, and financial security disintegrate. In 1874, he lost most of his nursery stock, including over four thousand grapevines, and in 1875 he recorded that his crops "were either gone or fast going." Before the end of the season he lost fifteen acres of wheat, five hundred cabbages, and all of his cucumbers, beans, onions, carrots, parsnips, and beets.[32] More than half the damage in wheat took place in the counties of Brown, Nicollet, and Wilkinson's Blue Earth.[33]

♦ ♦ ♦ ♦ ♦

On the day of the final vote of the "Grasshopper Bill," the issue of women's suffrage returned to the lawmakers after languishing for six years, when Representative Edwin Berry, a farmer and Baptist clergyman from Martin County, sponsored a bill to extend suffrage to unmarried women. The exasperated editor of the *Mankato Union,* Wilkinson's organ, commented, "What [have] married women done that they are to be cut off from that boon which their spinster sisters would enjoy, and I await with anxiety the appearance of the bill in the Committee of the Whole, where we can hear [Berry's] reasons for excluding our wives and mothers from the right so necessary to their welfare, and conferring it to young and inexperienced maidens."[34] It was time for all women to be given the right to vote, and the paper underscored the notion by reporting on the events of suffragist leaders and the National Woman Suffrage Association, under the reassuring yet curious byline "It's all right now."[35] But most men in the House were not subscribers, and the struggle to gain traction for the bill remained, as before, difficult. For a while, the bill seemed to languish until two weeks later, when "friends of the bill," as *Union* editor Harold Cleveland cleverly called them, revived it.[36]

Another bill, however, one that was acceptable to Cleveland, was introduced into the Senate. "The senate has a sly little bill under discussion now, which will probably pass. This is an act changing the constitution so that women can vote at school district meetings." What made the bill "sly" was that the language only asked voters to approve a constitutional amendment that authorized the legislature to extend suffrage to any class for any purpose it chose. Bill sponsors felt that rather than enfranchising women—even with the limited status of being "unmarried"—to vote on all matters political, the men of the state would vote "no" on the amendment proposal. This was why the Berry bill was untenable. Nowhere in the provision would the phrase "female suffrage" appear. To assure the men that the legislators, once empowered, would act "responsibly," certain newspapers informed their readers that women would only be granted the right to elect school officials. Even so, reasoned the *Union,* the amendment would be a positive, but cautious, first step to full enfranchisement. "This will be a good entering wedge for the subject, and if adopted, the rest of the movement will follow in time. Hadn't the House dropped their bill and adopted that of the Senate? A gradual movement of the kind might succeed, but not a sweeping one as the House measure hardly can."[37] Voters, the vast number of whom would not be following the debate or the campaign to come, would only see on the ballot that November, "Amendment to section four, article six of the constitution—yes." The law would require those opposing the question to laboriously "write or print or partly print or partly write the following words—'Amendment to section four of article six of the constitution—no.'" Intending to stack the deck, Wilkinson and other sponsors marshaled the vote to effectively send the question of woman suffrage for school board elections to the voters in November. On March 8, the bill was adopted.[38]

Two days before Governor Davis signed the "amendment" bill, on March 6, the Senate finally took up the problematic issue with the irksome and erstwhile railroad law. As Saby observed, "Little enthusiasm was shown one way or another." Frank L. Morse, a farmer from Minneapolis and a Democrat, introduced a bill in the House, which substituted a single advisory commissioner for the strong railroad commission under the law of 1874. The bill sailed through without any particular discussion in the Committee of the Whole, but when it came up for the final reading in the House, some members took issue. William Brown, a blacksmith from Rochester, protested that it was being rushed through without much consideration; and though he realized overwhelming sympathy for the railroads and support to get the bill passed, he objected to creating the office of railroad commissioner with merely the clerical powers of gathering statistics. In response, Soren Listoe, a newspaper editor from Breckinridge, summed up his position: "Some farmers howled for railroads, and some against them." Since his people "howled" for them, he would encourage them by voting for the bill.[39] The Morse bill passed the House by a large majority. Such was a vote to repeal the only railroad legislation on the books.

The bill would provide for a single commissioner to be elected for a two-year term. Already the respected J. J. Randall was being considered for that position. He would have the authority to inspect physical conditions of the roads, investigate their finances, and inquire into any alleged violations of law by corporations or their employees. He could issue subpoenas, examine railroad officials and employees under oath, and inspect their books.[40] On the whole, however, the new bill reflected the diminished presence of Grangers in the legislature, for it was clear to reformers that it was a step in the wrong direction. Donnelly argued that the law enacted during the previous session, which he had strongly opposed, was better than this new law. As Folwell observed, "It was the last of the Granger acts, if it may be rightly so considered. . . . If the act had been framed by the attorneys of the companies it could hardly have been more satisfactory to them. The commissioner had power to hold down a swivel chair and transmit the required annual reports of the railroad presidents or managers."[41]

It indeed met with greater opposition in the Senate. The Senate committee on railroads reported against the repeal of the existing law, but later a joint committee on railroads, composed of selected members of the House and Senate, agreed to report favorably on the new bill. Committee members reasoned that the vote was not to be considered a mere repeal of the old law (even though this was exactly how it was being seen and hoped the new bill would become), but rather a positive measure based on good sound principles. A number of the Anti-Monopolists of the previous year rallied to the support of the law of 1874, which was about to be repealed. While they did not favor some of its details, they were in sympathy with its principles of state control. Senator Coggswell, one of the Anti-Monopolists, denied that the law had been injurious to the railroads. Senator Isaac Westfall, a farmer from Rochester, saw problems with the law but considered it merely as a compromise measure. Nonetheless, he committed himself to standing up for the right of the people to regulate freights and tariffs. Donnelly, who had voted against the law in 1874, now defended it, for he "preferred it to be no law at all."[42] But ultimately, the bill passed in the Senate by a vote of 28 to 13, and was approved by the governor. Thus, the Granger law was repealed.[43] As noted historian Solon S. Buck wrote, "While it was perhaps unfortunate that the creation was so thorough and the principle of effective state control so completely given up by Minnesota in 1875, still . . . the act of 1875 was more suited to the conditions prevailing in the state at that time than were the rigidly restrictive railroad laws of 1871 and 1874."[44] Wilkinson had voted with the majority.

This was not the first time he had changed a course that he had previously set. In March 1862, as the Senate's prosecutor against rebel sympathizers in the chamber, he presented charges against Senator Lazarus Powell of Kentucky, seeking to have the Southerner expelled. After presenting his case, Powell was permitted to argue in his own behalf two days later.[45] Addressing the Senate on March 14, Powell insisted that he sought to resolve national difficulties through conciliation and compromise, rather than coercion. "If . . . a senator cannot speak and vote as he thinks proper and right without expulsion," he concluded poignantly, "then the majority are masters and the minority are slaves, and a seat in the American Senate would no longer be desired by an honest man or a patriot." But one of the key points he made was that rebel sympathizers and Union men in his state had called for neutrality. This point would dampen the ardor of at least one of his prosecutors.[46]

Wilkinson, sponsor of the resolution, had a change of heart, and in the end, in a move that frustrated some of his allies, he agreed with Powell. In upholding a state of neutrality that existed in Kentucky, he now reasoned, it was appropriate for Kentucky to resolve to take up arms to repel any invading army whether it was Confederate or Union. This was not a position he took lightly. "I believe that at that very time Minnesota had troops on the soil of Kentucky. I know that the bones of some of them lie there today. How then can I, how can anybody, advocate the retention of a Senator who urged his own people to resist our forces when they were upon the soil of his State defending the Constitution of the country?" His answer was simple. The decision to be neutral was "the position that all of the people of the State of Kentucky took [Union men and rebels, alike]. I must say that it has somewhat changed my feelings in this matter." Releasing his caucus, he stated that he now had "very little feeling about [his own] resolution." That day, on March 14, the Senate voted down the resolution, 11 yeas to 28 nays, and permitted Powell to retain his seat.[47] Wilkinson showed that he was capable, and at very unexpected times, to listen through the trumpet's blare to the opposing side of an issue.

Wilkinson's vote to approve repealing the railroad law won him accolades not from his caucus but from mainstream Republicans and Democrats alike. The *Pioneer* wrote:

The manly and honorable stand of Senator Wilkinson in the railroad question this present session, is the occasion of general remarks. Mr. Wilkinson is one of the few men who scorn to be consistent, when to be consistent means persistence in wrong, and he has shown at many periods of his career that he has dared to be right when to do so cost something of sacrifice and of political peril. The difference between Donnelly and Wilkinson upon the question under review, is the marked distinction between the statesman and the demagogue.[48]

No less than his old enemies at the *St. Paul Press*, echoed in the *Pioneer* and reprinted by the *Union*, sang his praises. "It is so unusual for the St. Paul *Press* to say a word of praise of our Senator that the following comments of that journal upon Mr. Wilkinson's discourse on the Morse railroad bill will excite surprise." The *Press*, reported the *Union*, editorialized the following:

> Senator Wilkinson had risen to a position in noble contrast to those small hucksters of last year's bird-seat. He favored the repeal of the law of last winter, though he then voted for it, because experience has shown it to be a disastrous mistake. It required the courage and the magnanimity of the statesman to then sacrifice the party vanity of consistency to plant himself on the high judicial ground of justice and public policy.[49]

The *Dispatch* likewise praised the senator for the character he displayed in his support of the railroad bill:

> Among the advocates for the Morse bill in the Senate yesterday deserving especial mention, was Senator Wilkinson. In response to a sneering personal allusion by Senator Cogswell, Mr. Wilkinson said that he voted for the law last year to establish the principle of legislative control, and that he still believed in retaining, but the law of last year he believed had proved injurious in its details and he therefore favored the Morse bill. It is so rare for a public man to be willing to retrace his steps, even though he knows that he should do so, that this is noticeable.
>
> No man need have any fear of a revulsion in his political fortunes because he supports the Morse bill. On the contrary, the day is not distant when the people will rise up and call him blessed for so doing.[50]

The world had shifted, and so had a flattered Wilkinson.

# 33

# THE FORCE LAW

*In prohibiting any discrimination . . . the [Civil Rights]*
*bill may possibly be a means of protection to colored*
*people in the Southern States, it can hardly be of any*
*use in any Northern State.*

ST. PAUL PRESS, MAY 3, 1875

In contrast to the provincial necessities that demanded the attention of the upper chamber—senatorial election, grasshopper infestation, women's suffrage
for school governance—a political and racial crisis boiled over in a region at
the opposite end of the Mississippi. Since 1868 Louisiana elections had been
marked by violence and fraud. During the gubernatorial election of 1872, the
Democrats and Republicans escalated tensions that grew worse—even after
the election had been called. When the Illinois carpetbagger William P. Kellogg defeated John McEnery, to appease the Democrats he appointed some to
local offices, but those efforts to secure loyalty from the ex-rebels of Louisiana failed to reach his goal. Still claiming to be governor, McEnery formed a
militia that in 1873 attempted to seize control of New Orleans police stations.
During the following month, anarchy spread throughout much of the rural
areas of the state. The vastly outnumbered federal troops were unable to establish order. In a growing number of parishes, whites refused to pay taxes or
otherwise recognize the state government.[1]

The situation worsened in 1874 with the formation of the White League,
which dedicated itself to the restoration of white supremacy. It targeted local Republican officeholders for assassination, disrupted court proceedings,

and drove black laborers from their homes. The state Democratic platform opened with the words, "We, the white people of Louisiana," and one party newspaper pronounced the inevitability of "a war of races." White League violence and extensive efforts to use economic intimidation against black voters dominated the campaign. Even white veterans of the New Orleans Unification movement, a coalition of free blacks and business leaders working to protect black civil rights and promote educational and economic opportunity, came over to the side of supremacy. "Last summer one hundred of us, representing fairly all grades of public and social status, humbled ourselves into the dust in an effort to secure the cooperation of the colored race in a last attempt to secure good government, and failed. . . . To this complexion, it has come at last. The niggers shall not rule over us."[2]

In Red River Parish, the campaign degenerated into a violent reign of terror, which culminated in August in the cold-blooded murder of six Republican officials. White Leaguers led a full-scale insurrection in New Orleans, hoping to install McEnery as governor. On September 14, some 3,500 Leaguers, mostly ex-Confederates, overwhelmed black militiamen and Metropolitan Police under the command of former Confederate general James Longstreet, and occupied city hall, the statehouse, and the arsenal. They withdrew only when federal troops arrived under orders from President Grant. This incident, which would go down in the annals of Louisiana politics as "The Battle of Liberty Place," would be dredged up in future campaigns to rally Democratic voters and solidify party and racial unity.[3]

The die was cast by the time the Forty-Third Congress returned in December 1874, for the Democrats, through political violence throughout the entire region, had amassed enough representatives to at last become the new majority in Congress. Anticipating the end to the advancement of civil rights lawmaking, Benjamin Butler and others devised a program to safeguard what remained of Reconstruction. Their program included a House counterpart to Sumner's Civil Rights bill, a new Enforcement Act that proposed to expand the jurisdiction of the federal courts. For tactical benefits, however, Butler felt it wise to exclude any reference to the controversial school integration provision, much like what would happen with the Civil Rights bill just then working its way to a final vote. But, in a manner that convinced party critics of true Republican interests, the Republicans included a subsidy for the Texas and Pacific Railroad. As Eric Foner has noted, "Taken together, the package embodied a combination of idealism, partisanship, and crass economic advantage typical of Republican politics."[4]

The events in Louisiana and the president's determination to protect the black vote only weakened the already tentative resolve of the Republican caucus, whose unity was already tenuous. Grant could see the returns, as well. The Republicans had already lost Congress. Butler would have to do what he needed to do. As for Grant, in suppressing armed insurrection in New Orleans, he had committed himself and his administration to not losing the soul of Reconstruction to terror or party disunity. He ordered General Philip Sheridan to sustain Kellogg's administration and put down violence. On January 4, 1875, when Democrats attempted to seize control of the state assembly by forcibly installing party members in five disputed seats, a detachment of federal troops under the command of Colonel Philippe de Trobriand entered the legislative chambers and escorted the five Democratic claimants out.[5]

The following day, Sheridan wired Secretary of War W. W. Belknap, requesting that he establish military tribunals to try White League leaders as "banditti." He reported that since 1866 nearly 3,500 persons—a great majority of whom were colored men—had been killed or wounded in Louisiana. In 1868, the last time an official report was issued, 1,884 were killed and wounded. "There is ample evidence, however, to show more than 1,200 were killed and wounded during this time on account of their political sentiments." The Leaguers had taken "frightful measures" against men on account of their political principles in seven parishes. "In Natchitoches parish the number of isolated cases reported is 33; in the parish of Bienville, the number of men killed is 30; in Red River parish, isolated cases, number of killed, 34; in Winn parish, the number of isolated cases where men were killed is 15; in Jackson parish, 20; in Catahoula, the number of isolated cases is 53; and most of the country parishes throughout the State will show a corresponding state of affairs."

On August 3, 1874, five officials were murdered in Red River Parish along with four black men. "On the 28th of August, 1874, three negro men were shot and killed in Bienville. Just before the arrival of the United States troops in the parish, two White Leaguers rode up to a negro cabin and called for a drink of water. When the old colored man turned to draw it they shot him in the back and killed him. The courts were all broken up in the district and the judge driven off." Detailing more atrocities, Sheridan wrote, "Human life in this State is held so cheaply that when men are killed on account of political opinion, the murderers are regarded rather as heroes than as criminals, in the localities where they reside and by the White League and their supporters." Over the signature of "P. H. Sheridan, Lt. General," he promised a more current and detailed report later.[6]

The fact that Sheridan's telegram—derisively referred to as his "banditti" report—was published in the *St. Paul Dispatch, Pioneer,* and other newspapers throughout the North, suggested that the administration understood the sensitivity of military intervention to its political base. To the extent that this was true, however, it did not change the thinking of a growing number of Northerners—and Republicans, in particular. Though many, in fact, applauded the military action, the number of critics grew, observing Louisiana as an example of the danger of excessive federal interference in local affairs. Foner notes, "The spectacle of soldiers 'marching into the Hall . . . and expelling members at the point of the bayonet' aroused more Northern opposition than any previous federal action in the South."[7] Some voices directed the rage at the commander in chief. "[There is] violent opposition of the country to Presidential usurpation and bayonet rule to the South."[8] In the ten years since Appomattox, Grant the general for union and liberation against Southerners who oppressed blacks, had become Grant the tyrant over Southern oppressors who were now sympathetic victims. The world had shifted underfoot.

In Minnesota, on Wednesday, February 10, outrage was likewise voiced in the Minnesota Senate when Amos Coggswell offered a resolution condemning the military action. Rising to speak in support of the resolution was Morton Wilkinson. Making sure first and foremost to tie the military action to the moral decay of Grantism and to all of those who subscribed to and benefited from it, he began by arguing, remarkably, that such actions existed when people grew fat from excessiveness and complacency. "The greatest danger, which at the present beset[s] our institutions was the indifference of the people to assaults upon constitutional law. . . . The Executive of the nation was also the Commander-in-Chief of the army and navy. When he trounces onto the legislative department, it is an attack upon the liberties of the people. [Neither] he [n]or anyone else [including any State Republican official] had just as much right as Col. De Trobriand to step in and break up the legislature."[9]

Then Wilkinson turned his attention to the general who carried out the order. "Why should we distrust the brave and gallant Phil Sheridan? Because it was men like Sheridan, popular heroes, who menaced the liberties of the people. It was so with Napoleon. It was always so. The tendency of the Executive power in this country was to usurp the functions of the legislative." After paying his tribute to General Sheridan as a soldier, Wilkinson denounced the general's "banditti" dispatch; then reading the dispatches from merchants and others in New Orleans critical of the military action, he bluntly declared that he chose to believe them. Incredibly, he said:

The only truthful and well-behaved people in that State are the
White Leaguers. It is true there is a little very pardonable prejudice against negroes and white Republicans, and by the accidental
discharge of pistols and rifles in the hands of careless White Leaguers, while playfully aimed at their political adversaries, some two or
three thousand negroes have been accidentally shot and killed, and
a goodly number of white Republicans have been disposed of in the
same way. . . . The regrettable thing about it is that the Republicans
of Louisiana, who have lived there, most of them, all their lives,
don't know anything at all about the real state of affairs down there.[10]

Sheridan, he said, had demonized the people of that city by listening too
closely "to the lying statements" of Kellogg and others. In summing up and
closing his "powerful and logical argument," the senator warned the chamber
and the people against the threatened overthrow of constitutional liberty by
the use of military violence.[11] The *Press*, on the other hand, mocked this kind
of fact-finding that took the word of Louisiana white supremacists.[12] The
Coggswell resolution was indefinitely tabled.

◆ ◆ ◆ ◆ ◆

Their blood was already up when word from Congress of the "other" force
law—the Civil Rights Act—settled in. Now with this news Wilkinson and
his cohorts entered into a state of apoplexy. The new federal law was approved by Congress in February and signed into law by President Grant on
March 1, and it guaranteed African Americans equal treatment in public accommodations and public transportation, and prohibited exclusion from jury
service. Litigation brought under the new law would bypass the state judicial
system, where the people elected the judges, who in turn were susceptible
to local prejudice; now, the new law directed cases to go directly to federal
courts, where judges served for life and presided outside of popular accountability.[13] Indeed, state law could not be expected, in terms of racial bias, to be
better than the local white citizenry. By force through the federal courts, as it
was bluntly seen, whites would be compelled to receive blacks into privately
owned businesses, restaurants, opera houses, and the like, where they were
clearly not wanted. The owner would have no say in the matter. While political equality had been granted through the ballot, social equality, as mandated
by the new form of federal intrusion, was a different matter; likewise, the
voters at home, like the owners immediately affected, had no say in the matter. Adding insult to injury, the new law would apply, not just to the South,

which to many Northerners seemed ill conceived because it would only wors-
en black–white relations, as if they were not already horrific, but also to all
sections of the country—North, South, East, and West.

Suddenly, discrimination, as outlined in the new federal law, was not
viewed as a Southern phenomenon. In essence, Northerners, as characterized by the new law, were presented as being no better than Southerners. To
many Northerners, this was an insult from the very government that they had
supported and fought to defend. Even those who generally understood the
spirit of the law were nevertheless ambivalent about its application. The *St.
Paul Press* pointed out, "It is a curious illustration of the tenacity of the social
prejudices generated by slavery that it should be deemed necessary to pass
any such act to secure decent treatment for colored people by the proprietor
of public conveyances, inns, theatres, etc. . . . [But while] the bill may possibly be a means of protection to colored people in the Southern States, it can
hardly be of any use in any Northern State."[14] To place the Northerner on the
same plane with the Southerner was too hard to bear. But whether Northerners liked it or not, despite all the denial, Jim Crow lived among them.

While many blacks in Northern cities fared relatively well during the
boom years of the Reconstruction era, ascending in many cases to the middle
class, as Foner notes, "the bulk of the population remained trapped in urban poverty and confined in inferior housing and menial and unskilled jobs
and even there their foothold, challenged by the continuing influx of European immigrants and discrimination by employers and unions alike, became
increasingly precarious."[15] In St. Paul the story was the same, and the lines
of demarcation among the groups, especially as they related to the African
American community, were quite rigid and were reflected in the residential
patterns of the city. A sign posted on a house in a German neighborhood in
the Fourth Ward stated that "nigger tenants" were not wanted. David Taylor
noted that the physical growth of the emerging black neighborhood was, to
a great extent, limited by the ethnicity of the residential neighborhoods surrounding the commercial district, where most poor blacks lived. On all sides
of the commercial district, ethnic groups zealously guarded neighborhoods
almost as if they were sovereign territories.[16]

Despite these residential cleavages between blacks and immigrant groups
and the desperation of the underclass, it took, as mentioned previously, the
effrontery of a St. Paul street crowd and a hotel clerk carrying out his employer's long-term discrimination policy against America's most famous
"civilizable" black man to finally capture the attention of the state's opinion
makers. That the proprietor of the hotel with such a discriminatory policy

was nevertheless a personal friend of Douglass suggests the policy was as much intended to defer to the prejudices of his high-paying clientele as it reflected the liberal proprietor's bias against black people in general. In any event, the incident underscored the pervasive bias in the state's psyche that no doubt instilled in Minnesota blacks the belief that survival depended on remaining deferential, or at least discreet, in relations with white people, not to mention staying out of trouble and among their own kind. Indeed, the episode is incomplete without reference to the fact that the audience to whom Douglass spoke on the progress of race relations was all white, and the opera house in which he spoke had a policy that banned black admission, a practice that was maintained for the Douglass lecture.[17]

Indeed, there were incidents in which black couples were rudely denied service in restaurants, and in 1873, a black man named Henry Robinson sued a railroad for discriminating against him; he lost the case before an all-white jury. The response from the two leading papers of St. Paul was predictable. The more sanguine *Press*, at least in terms of the paper's position on black equality, argued that St. Paul jurors could not resist the same discriminatory impulses as their white neighbors.[18] The editor even conceded that segregation on certain conveyances in Philadelphia, San Francisco, and Chicago had been found to be unlawful.[19] But the *Daily Pioneer* chose to focus only on Robinson, insisting that a black man who received such gratuities as a ticket to ride a train needed to be grateful. Robinson should have let the matter drop after the first trial. "There is all-together too much disposition on the part of some of our colored citizens to bring this class of action." Then, as if to issue a thinly veiled threat, the editor added, "It is to be hoped that they will take warning by this verdict."[20] That the events of 1873 would be considered "trifling," as the *Daily Pioneer* termed them, was notable enough; the Republicans, who had been their sworn enemies a decade earlier, now stood unmasked as openly sharing, not just the same reactions to the new law, but fundamentally the same prejudices toward black people whom the law was enacted to protect. The *Mankato Union* viewed the Civil Rights bill as yet another fiber of the bloody shirt: "The main purpose of the bill is to carry . . . Grant at the next Presidential election, in the same way that Louisiana has been carried by Republicans the last two years."[21]

To be clear, the liberal-minded Republican men were not questioning the right of black men to political equality. But in their estimation the Republican Congress had gone too far in establishing a right to social equality. Unmindful of the countless slights even to middle-class blacks, for they were the only blacks who could afford to enjoy the conveyances of the white middle class, and therefore sought to avoid such moments where their dignity would likely be impugned, whites concluded that blacks likewise did not desire social equality, let alone a law that mandated it. After all, many concluded disingenuously, there had been no demonstration that blacks, any more than whites, wanted to sit in racially mixed company.

The very essence of the law required that blacks first enter a place where they will be denied services and humiliated. "It was easier," historian C. Vann Woodward has written, "to avoid painful rebuff or insult by refraining from the test of rights. Negroes rarely intruded upon hotels or restaurants where they were unwelcome."[22] In other instances, blacks would not invoke the Civil Rights Act "to make themselves obnoxious," since they "had too much self-respect to go where they were not wanted. . . . Such actions would end only in disturbances" and "colored people wanted peace and as little agitation as possible."[23] "As a rule," observed the *New York Times*, just days after the bill was signed into law, "the Negroes in this part of the country are quiet, inoffensive people who live for and to themselves, and have no desire to intrude where they are not welcome." The paper, which vigorously opposed the law, predicted "there would be little trouble in the North largely because the blacks are in so great a minority."[24] Even black businessmen such as high-end barbers "in particular feared losing white clientele while others viewed the prospect of equal separate facilities as an improvement."[25] In Minnesota, blacks were also divided, though few who learned of Wilkinson's remarks on Louisiana were likely willing to inflame their most prominent and temperamental champion by saying that his handiwork was insufficient to achieving full opportunity, that it perhaps was his fault that black advancement was not greater.

The efficacy of the law was undercut from the beginning. President Grant made no comment about it either at the time he signed it or in subsequent messages to Congress or the public. Members of Congress had little to say about the bill after it passed. Charles Sumner, who sponsored the bill, had died the previous March. At least one member attempted to soften the blow by minimizing its possible effects. Representative Benjamin Butler, who had a significant part in bringing about the bill's passage as well as in deleting the provision that would have desegregated schools, sought to allay the fears of a friend. In a letter to Robert Harlan of Cincinnati, Butler said that the bill did not give Negroes the right to go into a drinking saloon and that he was very glad it did not. "I am willing to concede, as a friend to the colored man, that the white race may have at least this one superior privilege . . . and I never shall do anything to interfere with the exercise of that high and distinctive privilege."[26] "The Republicans of the United States Senate," reported the

*Mankato Union,* "did us right in letting the [school provision of the] Force Bill slip into the wastebasket of unfinished and never-to-be-finished business."[27] It was clearly a state's right to determine education policy.

As controversial as the bill was in mandating the right of black Americans to sit next to whites in opera houses, restaurants, saloons, and other such conveyances, an added provision that was dear to Sumner was even more incendiary, and was therefore dropped—a federal ban against school segregation. In fact, his most vocal opponents were colleagues who came from states where school segregation had been banned. Ever willing to take a shot at Republican hypocrisy, the *Weekly Pioneer* editorialized years earlier, "[Sumner] expressed his doubts as to the probability of such a measure being successful, on account of the opposition that it will encounter from Republicans in Congress who are loud on 'Cuffe' as a man, but down on him as a picaninny. Sumner seems to have learned that the standard Republican politician holds the colored man in about the same estimation that the circus man does his performing dog; he gets his living out of him, and therefore bestows upon him certain necessary proprietary favors, but he takes them not to eat with him, nor to sleep with him, nor do his children enter with the dog in the same gymnasium of instruction."[28]

Sumner's motivation to move forward began at an early age. As a student in Paris at the Sorbonne, he noticed black students performing every bit as successfully as their white counterparts, both academically and socially. In his journal he wrote, "It must be then that the distance between free blacks and whites among us is derived from education, and does not exist in the nature of things."[29] Later as a young attorney, in 1849, he acted on that observation when he sued the city of Boston to permit his client, a black girl named Sarah Roberts, to attend a better-equipped white public school. Citing passages of the Massachusetts constitution that resembled the equal protection clause of the Fourteenth Amendment, Sumner declared that every form of discrimination in civil and political institutions was therefore unlawful. Segregation branded the whole race of black people with the stigma of inferiority and degradation and therefore sentenced the black child to perpetuate a stage of inferiority. Segregation injured white pupils as well: "Their hearts while yet tender with childhood, are necessarily hardened by this conduct, and their subsequent lives, perhaps, bear enduring testimony to this legalized uncharitableness." He lost the suit but the defeat was short lived, for in five years, the state legislature enacted a law that prohibited racial segregation on the basis of race in all public schools in Massachusetts.[30] Through the Civil Rights bill the black children of America would benefit just as those in Massachusetts had.

But the idea of the federal government intruding in the local affairs of public education offended most opinion makers. In 1870 the *Weekly Pioneer* predicted the outcome that would come to pass five years later. "There are certain generic antipathies as irreconcilable in social chemistry that refuse to make a mixture, and any attempt to overcome the natural law that decrees this, results in necessary failure. All legislative effort will fail in making men yield to that which is antagonistic to instincts that are so deeply planted as are any affinities or repulsions that are a part of this mysterious human nature. This being true, Sumner is wasting time in the experiment he is making."[31]

While there may have been some truth in these words of a Democratic writer, accusing Northern Republicans of resisting the schools provision because of hypocrisy, this impression belied the trend to school desegregation already sweeping across the North.[32] In 1869, two months after the Convention of Colored Citizens, the Minnesota legislature, led by then-governor William Marshall, passed a bill that denied state funds to school districts that discriminated on the basis of race, and Wisconsin in 1871, and Iowa as early as 1857, had enacted an outright ban of school segregation.[33] Donnelly had called for an end to school segregation in 1867.[34] So not only was the idea of mixing black and white schoolchildren familiar, the practice also was found to be acceptable to a growing number of Northern voters.

The criticism of Northerners—even former abolitionists—that later resulted in the exclusion of this provision had more to do with easing the tense nature of North–South relations.[35] In terms Wilkinson probably approved, the *Mankato Union* called for the federal government to let the South iron out its local problems. "Beyond repressing violence and insurrection, and protecting the colored brother in the rights of person and property, the Southern States should be left to work out their own destiny."[36] In apparent contrast, almost nine years earlier, a commentator for the *Union* who signed his article with the letter "W" strongly advocated the extension of civil rights to black Minnesotans, arguing that environment and not heredity was the cause of any degradation among black people. In his essay published on March 17, 1865, he added, "Blacks never have had the advantages of an education. They have for centuries been taught their inferiority and stupidity. But the day is dawning when they will show that there is stamped upon their race the image of the same all-wise God."[37] "W" was now silent on the matter. There were not enough black voters in Minnesota, and throughout the North, who could pressure their congressional representation to press the matter.

Indeed, many were relieved when the school provision had been removed. After fighting a war against the rebellion of Southern states and ratifying the

Thirteenth, Fourteenth, and Fifteenth Amendments against the will of ex-Confederate states, mandating school integration would only antagonize the South, and this, too, argued Liberal Democrats, was "the nature of things." Lacking, remarkably, a full and plain understanding of the resilience of racism forged by centuries of social custom and law, or willfully ignoring it in favor of giving full weight to resentment of the intrusive federal government in the name of national harmony and the belief that Southern white supremacists could embrace their black neighbors as equals, the *Union* naively determined that what a state did was a state's business. The paper equated the "force" law with the "daily food of perilous medicine which the Constitution provides for extreme cases of public danger." In other words, in the twisted logic of the time, it was the law, and not Southern white supremacists, that was responsible for the murders. If left alone, the knot of racial tension would loosen to allow the South to be able to solve its problem through the inevitable emergence of due process. The *Union* continued, "[Congress must] try the experiment of leaving the turbulent mobocracy of the South to the restraints of law and [Southern] public opinion."[38] That both "restraints" had actually enabled "mobocracy" was immaterial to the men behind the *Union*.

The otherwise staid *Minneapolis Tribune* took a different tack, arguing that the bill, for all of its drama, was disappointingly halfhearted: "As originally presented by [Sumner], it was intended to fill the measure of national legislation in behalf of equal civil rights to all men, but in its emasculated form, as passed by Congress, it is little more than a mockery." In that the new law had failed to include an educational component, "[it left] the doors of the public schools closed to the colored race in the future as effectually as they have been in the past." As for provision on public accommodations, taking note of the tepid response of black Minnesotans—in St. Paul, only a small group assembled to recognize the bill's enactment—the editor concluded that African Americans as a whole did not even want the law. "It very carefully, however, protects them in those rights which they do not want and which are no value to them. . . . As a rule, they prefer to enjoy themselves socially among people of their own color, tastes, and social standing. They are very much like white people in that respect." On the unfortunate whole, the editor asserted, the Republicans had lost their way. "The great Republican party, which has done so much for the colored race—which gave them their freedom and conferred upon them their political rights belonging to freemen—took fright at this culminating act and proved recreant to its highest duty at the critical moment. . . . [In a cowardly manner] it lost the confidence of the people in a great degree, and paved the way for the triumph of the Democratic opponents. In an attempt to compromise with wrong and injustice, it lost its character, moral force and its strength."[39]

And yet, despite the flaws, critics argued, in that the law supposedly forced whites to be in the company of blacks, it would only foment public disorder. The *Union* took pains to report troubling stories of blacks trying to get service in businesses, characterizing them as perpetrators of misfortune. At Waverly, Missouri, for example, a "desperado" named Hall took a Negro into a saloon kept by a man named Beal, and attempted to place him on a level of equality with white men under the Civil Rights Act. The bartender protested but Hall insisted the Negro be served. The bartender then chased the Negro out of the saloon with a revolver. When another Negro interfered, the bartender shot him dead.[40] In another story, "The civil rights agitation in Nashville increases. The negroes take advantage of the provision, and have forced the closing of several restaurants and other public places."[41]

This was the problem with the law, insisted the Liberal Republican-Democratic editor. It overreached the central function of federal governance—to create policy that advanced interests of the whole nation. The new law fomented disturbances, all in the name of "a dubious sense of justice." To most Americans, it seemed that the new law was clearly unconstitutional. Resigned to its pitiable state, the *Press* editor continued, "The extension of the principle to hotel, theatres, and other places of amusement is of doubtful constitutionality and of still more doubtful utility."[42]

♦ ♦ ♦ ♦ ♦

It was not until the last day of the legislative session that another resolution was brought forward to protest Grant's action in Louisiana. This time, Republican E. F. Drake of Ramsey County and secretary of the Senate, introduced it, asserting that "the constitutional rights of the Legislature and people of the State of Louisiana have been invaded and disregarded by officers and soldiers of the army of the United States."[43]

Viewed by Minnesota Democrats, the resolution—"a distinct and emphatic condemnation" of the military action in Louisiana—passed by "a large majority." The *Pioneer* offered its highest tribute to "one of the ablest and staunchest republicans in the State" and it was with Drake's courage and independence that all could see that "the unconstitutional and destructive acts of the executive can no longer command the entire support of the party, that such support of the party cannot be made a test of republicanism nor even of party fealty."[44]

Across the North, Negro fatigue was setting in, as indicated in part by recent electoral victories by the Democratic Party, as well as the spread of organized protest against military policy in the South. Even in Boston, "the cradle of liberty" and the home of Charles Sumner, Benjamin Butler, and William Lloyd Garrison, one heard the impulse growing in strength as the audience at Faneuil Hall taunted abolitionist Wendell Phillips speaking against the anti-Grant resolution:

> My anxiety is for the hunted, tormented, murdered population, white and black, of the Southern states, whom you are going to consign to the hands of their oppressors. If you pass these resolutions (cries of "We Will! We will!)—if you pass these resolutions (cries of "We will! We will!)—if you pass these resolutions (cries of "We will! We will!)—I say it in the presence of God Almighty (cries of "Sh!" and "Ah!")—the blood of hundreds of blacks and hundreds of whites will be on your skirts before the first day of January next. (Loud laughter.)[45]

The *New York Times* commented that Phillips and Garrison, who also spoke, were "not exactly extinct from American politics, but they represent ideas in regard to the South which the majority of the Republican Party have outgrown."[46]

Wilkinson, on the other hand, was very much a man of the times. Yet, fundamentally, it was not so much that he had become cavalier regarding the fates of black Americans as much as his vision had grown narrow by his rage against monopolies and corruption under Grant, as well as an uncomprehendingly rigid sense of civil liberties when they were obtained through coercion and murder. His contempt for the Republican Party—its corruption, deceit, hypocrisy, and, now, heavy-handedness—tinted his perception of *the nature of things*. He simply did not understand the nature of racism; that in the ten years since Appomattox, white supremacists throughout the South, whose simple interest was to turn back the clock, did not need the provocation of federal bayonets to deny black and white citizens their constitutional rights.

In the end, Wilkinson did not differentiate between civil liberties that included all citizens and uncivil actions that excluded citizens because of race and speech. His lofty and ennobling words defended the actions of those whom he had once condemned in 1862, when he stood in the Senate chamber in Washington to defend a failed bill to emancipate slaves in the District of Columbia: "I feel bound, by every vote which I am called upon to give, and by every word which I may utter upon this question, to do everything in my power towards its final extinction; and so far as my influence goes, to blot out the last remains of slavery on this continent."[47] He did not see that the "last remains of slavery" survived in racial prejudice that was fundamental to what it meant to be a white man and woman in America. Now, instead, Wilkinson found comfort in an interview with a "respectable colored man" of Louisiana who said that it was the Radicals who had cheated in the recent elections:

> He also voted with the white man and used all his influence to get [other blacks] to do so. "The white people own this country and we must live here if we live anywhere. A cold country such as up North don't suit us. This is our home, and we must be at peace with the white people. They will do the fair thing if the colored people do."[48]

Let the people who know each other the best—Southern blacks and Klansmen —discover their own means to achieving racial equality within the comforting embrace of the warm Southern climes. Times had indeed changed.

On March 12, everyone went home, braving the subzero temperatures of this Minnesota winter, one of the coldest on record.[49] Yet, it was considered a successful term. "The 17th session of the Minnesota legislature closed this afternoon. It has been made memorable from the fact that it defeated the head-center of the Minnesota ring, and demoralized the dominant political party, which has so long ruled the State with a rod of iron." The railroad law was considered "the wisest action of the entire session and will lift Minnesota from the ranks of communistic States." Ramsey was gone and cooler heads had prevailed in creating a railroad law that veered away from following Illinois's lead in becoming too radical. Nothing was said in either chamber about the Enforcement bill working its way through Congress, nor about the Civil Rights bill that would soon be enacted within the month. They had enacted a "sly" bit of legislation that, if approved by the voters that November, would allow the next legislature to expand suffrage to all women, if but only to elect and run for school boards.

The Louisiana Resolution standing alone was not an issue that would lead to a major piece of legislation compared to the railroad law, senatorial selection, farmer relief, or women's suffrage. It did, however, represent the degree to which Minnesota senators felt enmeshed within the ever-intensifying national debate over the interconnecting roles of federal and state government, black freedom and equality, the future of Reconstruction. For the time being, the concern of corporate monopolies had abated, for when the issue of regulation came forward earlier in the session, senators chose instead to table it, hoping that the matter would simply blow over. But for some of the senators, the Louisiana Resolution was nothing less than a clarion call against the tyranny of Caesar, when during these times that were filled with burning and complicated issues, the "good" was good enough, and the "bad" was unconstitutional. This was not, as anticipated, a radical legislature. It had appropriated modest funds to help the farmers suffering from grasshopper infestation, returned the railroad law to its former state of impotency, and selected a concession candidate to succeed a man whom opinion makers referred to as "Bluff Aleck." But the resolution was like a tidal wave when the political forces of nature, at a unique moment in time, engulfed all manner of man, drowning out any potential for deliberation and, in the end, reason. The resolution was adopted by a vote of 23 to 7. Wilkinson and Donnelly both voted "aye." Conservative Republican and next governor John D. Pillsbury and Democrat Edmund Rice, brother of former senator Henry, were two who voted "nay."[50]

On the last day of the session, when members wanted to adjourn and leave for home, the matter was returned for a vote. The record does not reflect that there was a debate on the merits, and it would seem to be an awkward vote to combat. Minnesota's pro-Union legacy—something still highly valued—was at stake. It was the first state in the Union to send volunteers into the federal army after South Carolinians had laid siege to Fort Sumter, an arrangement made possible by no less than Governor Ramsey and U.S. Senator Morton S. Wilkinson, whose long-term stance on civil liberties had quite circuitously given him a moral authority that few possessed. Fourteen years had indeed so completely changed night to day. A vote against the resolution had become a vote to prolong a military presence and, in turn, military hostilities in the faraway region of the South, ten years after Appomattox almost to the day. On the other hand, a vote for the resolution really meant that one believed that former slaves and Klansmen, if left alone, could work out their problems and come to see each other as equals; that Grant, Lincoln's man to save the Union, however administratively incompetent, was also truly the enemy of the freedom-loving people of America; that heroic Phil Sheridan had lied. This had to be implausible especially to those men in the Senate who had served under them.

In the end, however, there was no stomach for taking on Wilkinson, who had stood shoulder to shoulder with the greatest men of their party against the greatest crisis of the century, to debate a matter of such national purpose. Certainly no one had the stomach to defend a very unpopular Grant, who was being blamed for the bad economic times and the loss of Congress to

Democrats, who were about to gain congressional power for the first time in eighteen years. No, Grant had to go. Republicans throughout the Northern and western states were already looking for another presidential candidate. Senators, not wanting to stand against the tide on the last day and wanting to go home, and figuring that it ultimately would have little significance (the black men of Minnesota did not have the votes to hold them accountable), took a deep breath and voted "aye." In any event, without the House adoption, the resolution would be nothing more than gesture politics, and on the last day, that was all it became. Representatives in the House acted neither one way nor the other, choosing instead to use what remained of the session in a more time-honored manner. As the *Dispatch* reported, "An effort was made to pass the Senate Louisiana Resolution but they were lost owing to notice of debate. The usual closing fun was indulged in and at 3 pm the House adjourned, sine die."[51] Summing up the session, the editor concluded, "All important legislation was secured and no public interest will suffer in the failure of any measure."[52] Exhausted from legislative battles and creeping age, and ready to return to his new home in Wells, Wilkinson made no additional statement on the issue.

◆ ◆ ◆ ◆ ◆

In a Winona courtroom, on June 8, 1875, Judge R. R. Nelson of the United States District Court, a New York–born, lifelong Democrat, son to a former U.S. Supreme Court justice, and former neighbor of Wilkinson in the earliest days when Minnesota was a territory, handed down a decision resulting from what was "believed to be the first adjudication in this direction by a Federal Judge." He declared the new civil rights law to be constitutional, and in doing so, "produced no little astonishment among politicians as well as lawyers." The opinion was given in response to a request made by the grand jury, before which a case was brought by the district attorney under the Civil Rights Act. After reciting the provisions of the last three amendments to the Constitution, Judge Nelson said, "The power of Congress can be exerted directly to put down all outrage or discrimination on the part of individuals when the motive originates only in race or color. . . . The law, in my opinion, is constitutional."[53]

# 34

# SINE DIE

*The government of the U.S. does not interfere.*

ADELBERT AMES

REPUBLICAN GOVERNOR OF MISSISSIPPI, 1875

A month after the legislative session ended, on April 11, 1875, Wilkinson learned along with thousands of other readers when they picked up their Sunday paper that the Democratic *Pioneer* and the Republican *Press*, had consolidated into one newspaper—the *St. Paul Pioneer Press.* Though it was run by the same men who had managed the two papers, the editorial voice of the new paper would, at least for the time being, take an independent path. Wilkinson, never a friend of the *Press,* was likely pleased with the outcome, understandably concluding that its apparent demise reflected that a nail had been driven into Ramsey's political coffin. The new development, it was believed, would be beneficial to the state for it would give not only a thorough airing of the issues but also a fair hearing of the Liberal Republican-Democratic platform. On the shoulders of the two papers, it would truly become Minnesota's newspaper of note. But though he also likely understood that the emergence of the *Pioneer Press* was not yet indicative of the political sentiment of the majority of Minnesota voters, it was a start. Of course, such machinations assumed that the "independent" label meant third party; but even if the paper thoughtfully assessed the positions of the major parties, the intelligent reader could not help but be well served. This would bear out by the end of the year on the matter of women's suffrage, which Wilkinson, agreeing with Sarah Burger Stearns that the campaign should be low-key, had been working behind the scenes to support. In 1869, while the *Pioneer*'s support was tepid at best, the *Press* was contemptible in its campaign to defeat the amendment. In contrast, the *Pioneer Press* would spark the canvass for suffrage among the men of the Republican, Democratic, and Anti-Monopoly Parties. But even more important: the old Ramsey "ring" was dead. Wilkinson's man, William Lochren, was not sitting in Ramsey's Senate seat, but neither was "Bluff Aleck." The one concern, however, was that Frederick Driscoll and Joseph Wheelock, the business manager and editor of the *Press* and Ramsey's most senior advisers, were still in charge.

Since 1862 Wheelock and Driscoll ran the *Press,* aligning its influence and success with the rise of Ramsey's political fortunes, and sharing in the bounty that followed from their close association with the governor's rise to power. The die of hostility was cast when Senator Wilkinson directed the federal contract away from the *Press* and to the rival *Pioneer and Democrat.* Soon after Wilkinson's defeat for reelection, Wheelock urged Ramsey to persuade senator-elect Norton to return the federal printing contract to the *Press.* In 1867 Driscoll was appointed chairman of the Republican Central Committee and held the position until 1870, skillfully conducting the campaigns that resulted in the second election of Governor Marshall and the first election of Governor Austin, and would be a member of the inner circle who guided the political fortunes of what some called the "Ramsey dynasty." With Wheelock, Marshall, and R. N. McLaren, he managed the appointments of state officers and congressmen, and made several appointments to federal positions. In May 1870 President Grant appointed Wheelock to be postmaster of St. Paul on the recommendation of Senator Ramsey, and in turn, Wheelock made Driscoll assistant postmaster, "thus accomplishing the doubly desirable object of ensuring a competent business supervision of the post office and of securing a welcome recourse, for up-building the Republican party organ, perhaps seven thousand dollars a year from their united salaries."[1] Most recently, they worked furiously behind the scenes to get Ramsey reelected, but failing to do so, "the *St. Paul Press* lost faith in the virtue of the party, if not in the perpetuity of the Republic."[2]

It would seem that the end of the dynasty would mark the end of their influence. One of the earliest official acts of senator-elect McMillan was to demand the removal of Wheelock as postmaster and replace him with the senator's son-in-law, Dr. David Day. Grant agreed; and with Wheelock's departure went Driscoll as well. Shortly thereafter, however, came the "startling announcement" that the *Pioneer* and the *Press* had been consolidated under the management of Wheelock and Driscoll and that the *Pioneer Press* was to be conducted as an independent journal, "a thing then unprecedented in Minnesota politics."[3]

Business concerns, at least for the *Pioneer,* seemed to be the key reason that prompted the merger. Since the Democrats lost political control over Minnesota, the *Pioneer* lost its prominence, being surpassed in business and circulation by the *Press.* Between 1870 and 1875, the paper had as many owners. Recognizing that the paper might not survive, David Blakeley, the last editor, apparently initiated the consolidation. The process went smoothly. "There was no political obstacle to the union of the two papers. The proprietors of the two concerns had for years been personal friends." Blakeley, Wheelock, and Driscoll worked out the business details and the consolidation went off quietly without a hitch. The *Pioneer Press* made its first appearance on Sunday morning, April 11, 1875, "greatly to the surprise of the readers of both papers. Not a whisper of the contemplated change had got abroad, and the actual appearance of the *Pioneer Press* was the first announcement which reached the public." Within days the machinery and all the *Pioneer's* printing supplies were moved into the more spacious *Press* building. The Pioneer Press Company reported capital of two hundred thousand dollars, two-thirds of which represented the valuation of the *Press* in the new concern, while one-third represented the valuation of the *Pioneer.* Wheelock and Blakeley provided the editorial direction of the paper, and Driscoll was still the business manager.[4]

Wilkinson had to wonder whether in fact the wings of the old *Press* leadership had been clipped by the reversal of their political fortune. And what would it mean for these two old partisans to run an "independent" journal? Would the paper truly be independent? Could these men ably don the cloak of opposing principles?

Since statehood, the history of journalism in Minnesota included a few instances in which an editor's politics were not reflected in the editorial voice of the paper. In 1865 Colonel John X. Davidson and H. P. Hall owned the Democratic-leaning, conservative *Pioneer.* Davidson held cultural gatherings at his home for the black community of St. Paul and Hall would soon become editor of the *Dispatch,* Donnelly's organ and the most progressive of Minnesota's major newspapers at the time. Between 1872 and 1874, William S. King of Minneapolis owned the *Pioneer.* He started the *State Atlas* in St. Anthony, which advocated for free soil and the abolition of slavery and was put out of business in 1860 when a proslavery mob destroyed his press; and he served in the U.S. House of Representatives from 1875 to 1877. In 1874 King sold the *Pioneer* to Blakeley, who had been editor of the *Chicago Post* and, from 1867 to 1868, secretary of state of Minnesota. Each was more than a loyal Republican: they were Lincoln men who supported the Union, abolition, and enfranchisement. Yet, each owned the petulant voice of the Democratic Party. It was business.[5]

For dyed-in-the-wool Ramsey men, the reason to print anything other than the established Republican line was the prospect of more subscribers. It was good for business to increase subscriptions, which could happen if Democrats and third-party men found stories that spoke to them. Blakely would see to that. As months passed, the *Pioneer Press* printed stories that appealed to the larger market. In the days leading up to the election, the paper printed the Republican-Democratic ticket on its pages, urging men to vote accordingly, for "The vision of the people demands a new deal."[6] "Vote for the right men. Never mind their politics, their religion, their nationality, their former or latter professions, but only their present standing and efficiency as men."[7] On its front page, the paper reported approvingly of a speech Wilkinson delivered on religious tolerance.[8] The Wheelock-Driscoll bias nonetheless remained where it related to Ignatius Donnelly, a man whom they had gleefully savaged since 1862, when he was the irksome lieutenant governor under Ramsey. Never mind that the senator from Dakota County's politics were quite similar to Wilkinson's—the *Press* had attacked both men with equal zeal during the campaigns of 1868, 1869, and throughout the 1870s—Donnelly had become, since 1873, the pariah. He had jumped from the Republican Party to the Democratic Party, then to the Anti-Monopoly Party. On the hot button issue of railroad regulation, during the last legislative session, Donnelly had stayed true to stringent measures, while Wilkinson, to much fanfare, moderated his stance. Yet it was Donnelly who was demonized for vacillating. "It is not too much to say that if his judgment and reliability were equal to his brilliance, he would be invincible. But unfortunately, they are not."[9] It would appear that the charge of "inconsistency"—which, it could be said, also applied to the editors of the *Pioneer Press*—was nonetheless both convenient and selective; Donnelly's stigma of "unreliability" went deeper, for he had called for a stronger regulatory, what railroads referred to as coercive, role for government over private enterprise. In this, Wilkinson it seemed was willing to go only so far, but not so much as to rattle the underpinnings of those businesses deemed to be financially vulnerable, on which his people—the farmers—relied. In this instance, Wilkinson wanted state government to cast a lighter touch.

◆ ◆ ◆ ◆ ◆

With the enactment of the Civil Rights bill, the Republican-led Congress had steered the federal government into a new and uncomfortable era of national authority, one that seemed to breach the traditional federalist principles for measures that now seemed to be coercive; and it fractured its base. In this regard, Liberal Republicans and Democrats could join forces. A creeping sense that *We have done our part,* as it related to black equality, coupled with a return to free enterprise touched the hearts of established Republicans and attracted the party's disparate members back into the fold. These factors set the stage for a total assault by Southern white supremacists, not just on black rights, but also on black lives, all in the face of misguided Northerners. To them, the villains were not the white mobs attacking blacks, nor even the occupation by federal troops, but Northern carpetbaggers, "that detestable and conscious-less [sic] cabal of moral sappers and miners" who exploited a chaotic South, as well as Southern blacks who were easily duped. In Minnesota, the *Pioneer Press* condemned the "ill-advised, illegitimate, riot-breeding" effort to enlist "loyal whites who will agree to work with the colored republicans to go South to aid blacks. . . . The ignorance and inexperience of the plantation negroes are sufficiently pliant material for those carpet-bagging artisans in mud, without a resort to the skull and crossbones of the midnight convocation."[10]

Likewise, Northerners increasingly felt the same need for Grant to leave, as illustrated in a speech by Wilkinson. In contrast to when he had accused General Grant of not being aggressive enough against the rebels during the Civil War, now, in response to Grant's action in Louisiana, Wilkinson accused him of going to the other extreme; and for this, he had to go.[11] It was an out-and-out repudiation of the president. With Northern Democrats having recently won enough congressional seats to form a new majority in the lower chamber, Southerners could taste absolute vindication, for they were defeating in public opinion a man they could not defeat on the battlefield. President Grant knew that his days were numbered unless he changed the direction of his administration. Tragically this attempt would take the form of his inaction in protecting blacks in Mississippi. His handling of the events in Vicksburg during the elections the year before foretold the fatefulness of his decision.

That summer the white residents organized the White League, which also was known as the White Man's League. At the municipal election, they patrolled the streets in armed bands seeking to intimidate enough black voters to oust the city's Republican officeholders. Meanwhile, planters in the surrounding counties organized White League clubs whose intent was to "rid the region of all bad and leading negroes." In December, inspired by Democratic victories in Northern elections (the party had done quite well reaching out to immigrants flooding into the region), armed league members demanded the resignation of black sheriff Peter Crosby and his board of supervisors.

Crosby fled to Jackson, where he organized a posse of black men. They marched on Vicksburg, only to be dispersed by a white force rallied by city officials. In the days that followed, armed bands of white men roamed the countryside murdering an estimated three hundred black men. Finally spurred into action, in early January on the eve of the military's far more controversial intervention in Louisiana, Grant ordered a company of federal troops to the city and restored Crosby to office.[12]

Still the Northern Democratic electoral victories of 1874 inspired white Mississippians to conclude that the nation had repudiated Reconstruction policy. One man said, "In 1874, the tidal wave as it is called, of the North satisfied us that if we succeeded in winning the control of the government of Mississippi we will be permitted to enjoy it." Though the state Democratic convention adopted a platform recognizing blacks' civil and political rights, the 1875 campaign quickly degenerated into a violent crusade to destroy the Republican organization and prevent blacks from voting. Democratic rifle clubs paraded through the black belt in broad daylight, disrupting Republican meetings and assaulting local party leaders, blatantly thumbing their noses at federal authority, all as Northern Republicans denigrated Southern Republicans as corrupt and stood by watching as they were murdered.[13]

Another "difficulty," as the *Pioneer Press* called it, occurred at Clinton, Mississippi. "As usual the dead list is made up of black men." Several black and white men were wounded and three black men were killed. "No positive information received with regard to the origin of the conflict. About fifty armed whites from [Vicksburg], and fifty from Edwards and Bolton, arrived at Clinton this evening to protect the town."[14]

This is what happened. Four days earlier, on September 1, a mob in Yazoo County chased away the white Republican sheriff and his black schoolteacher wife, then proceeded to murder several prominent blacks, including a state legislator. A few days later a gang attacked a Republican barbeque at Clinton. Men on both sides were killed, but the gang left and scoured the countryside, shooting down blacks "just the same as birds." They claimed about thirty victims, including teachers, clergymen, and local Republican organizers. Even former Governor James Alcorn, after repudiating any association with being a "negro republican," led an attack against the black sheriff in Coahoma County, in which six black men and three white men were killed.[15]

As if to quell the concerns of its readers who might object to the assault on the civil and political liberties of Mississippi blacks, in reporting on a Negro convention in Virginia, the *Pioneer Press* seemed to mock the concept of freedmen even being able to govern. Using the vernacular, the editor wrote,

"'Sho' we've done heard enough of this talk about 'parlamentry' rules. We come here to do 'sumthin or ruther' for the good of the Black race, and here you've been spendin' hours quarrelin' about 'parlamentry' rules and 'parlamentry' laws and 'parlamentry userges.' No this is all stuff. There ain't a man in this here house that knows anythin' about such things and I can't see no use in talkin' about it."[16]

However, the frequency of "difficulties" roiling in Clinton soon eroded the resolve of the paper to present the "independent" spin as troubling accounts increasingly appeared on the front page of the *Pioneer Press* under more lurid banner headings: "The massacre at Grant Park repeated in Clinton / Black men hunted down by white leaguers and shot on sight / 40 to 100 of the hated race and many more wounded / The slaughter still going on, and the officers unable to quell it. Organized bands of whites murdering unarmed blacks at will / Governor [Adelbert] Ames calls on the chairman of the Democratic committee to stop the slaughter."[17] The next day, the banner read: "The Clinton slaughter / Practice Vicksburgers volunteer and do the butchery / Fifty blacks are reported killed by them on Sunday / The bloody work begins at Clinton and extends through the county / It is wholly unsought by the blacks who fought in self-defense."[18] And yet, the editors, in contradictory logic that omitted the lessons of the heroism of black troops during the war, wondered what manner of man—the Southern freedman— could so easily be killed:

> The responsibility of the row in Mississippi between the whites
> and the Negroes [that] occurred the other day at Clinton, appears
> to be about equally distributed, but the mortality, as usual is nearly
> all on the side of the blacks. Either because they are unfamiliar with
> arms, or lacking in intelligence or pluck, they rarely come out of
> the scrimmage with whites except at a sad disadvantage in point
> of sacrifice.[19]

Pleas for help flooded into the office of Massachusetts-born Republican governor Adelbert Ames, who was also the son-in-law of Massachusetts congressman Benjamin Butler. In early September, he asked Grant to send troops to the state. What the president said in response illustrated the North's retreat from Reconstruction. In an unguarded moment, as he vacationed at his estate on the New Jersey shore, Grant said, "The whole public is tired out with these annual autumnal outbreaks in the South . . . and are ready now to condemn any interference on the part of the Government." Another message, however, became the official response: Mississippi must resolve its own problem. Speaking through his attorney general, Edwards Pierrepont, Grant urged Ames to exhaust all of his own resources. "I suggest that you take all lawful means and all needed measures to preserve by the force of your own state and . . . manhood to fight for their state's rights and to destroy the bloody ruffians who murder the innocent and unoffending freedmen."[20]

The *Pioneer Press*, despite what it knew and had told its readers about the events in and around Vicksburg, nevertheless approved Grant's decision as "gratifying proof that the Administration had at last planted itself on solid constitutional grounds, on the question of military arms of the federal government to suppress local disturbances in the South."[21] Morton Wilkinson profoundly agreed. For him, it was the unscrupulous northern opportunist who hurriedly packed his things into his carpet bag and rushed to the South to exploit and inflame a chaotic situation by fooling an ignorant black electorate to put him in office: *let democracy reign!* Down the great river, the men of Vicksburg, who remembered that "General" Grant had taken their city by siege which effectively broke the back of the Old Confederacy, twelve years before, were now experiencing far more than agreement with the decision: they were now getting their revenge.

On election eve, armed white riders drove freedmen from their homes and warned they would be killed if they appeared to cast ballots. "It was the most violent time that ever we have seen," said one black official. In Aberdeen, whites with rifles and a six-pounder cannon "came armed to the polls and drove colored men away." Elsewhere, Democrats destroyed the ballot boxes or replaced ballots with their own. "The reports that came to me almost hourly are truly sickening," Ames reported to his wife, who had elected to stay in their Massachusetts home, adding, "The government of the U.S. does not interfere." "Grant," wrote Eric Foner, "who had sent troops to prop up the unstable and corrupt Republican regime in Louisiana, turned a deaf ear to pleas from the far stronger and more upright government of Mississippi."[22] Essentially, Northern liberals had been released from all responsibility for Southern blacks—politically and otherwise.

After leaving his post as governor in 1876, Ames settled in Northfield, Minnesota, where he joined his father and brother in their flour-milling business. During his residence there, in September 1876, Jesse James and his gang of former Confederate guerrillas raided the town's bank, largely because of the investments deposited there by Ames and his "notorious" father-in-law, Benjamin Butler. An indication of his own notoriety to the former rebels appears in one account of when Ames and the outlaws met on the bridge entering Northfield. They alarmed him when they referred to him as "Governor" and said that he, according to outlaw brothers Cole and Bob Younger, had been their target.[23]

* * * * *

In Minnesota, during the late 1870s, as the African American community turned inward to develop its own religious, educational, cultural, and social institutions, except for the efforts of a few prominent white men and women, and a few moments of public display, it seemed to all that the state's black citizens had disappeared from view. Policy makers had more pressing matters. During the session, the legislature set aside $75,000 for the purchase of seed grain for those who suffered during the infestation, releasing only $25,000 for immediate relief. Farmers qualified for immediate relief if they could pledge that they were wholly without means to purchase food and clothing. The law required the governor to appoint three commissioners to ensure that the funds were spent as they were intended. In March, once the commissioners were named, the legislature released $50,000 of the seed grain fund to be immediately dispersed, along with an additional $10,000 for direct relief. One official sought clarification from the governor, because the standard seemed to demand from applicants that they "cannot have anything at all" in order to qualify. He found out that that was exactly what it meant. If a farmer owned a horse or cow he failed to meet the requirements.[24]

Some farmers refused to take the pledge because of the stigma that came with being labeled a "pauper." Accepting public assistance robbed them of their dignity, forcing them to become precisely what they least wanted to be— dependent on the public dime. An official reported that the Scandinavians in his county would kill their last cow and eat it before they took the oath. Other farmers declined to damage themselves more by getting rid of their last cow or team in order to qualify, for what was sure to be a paltry sum anyway. In Renville County, which was allotted four thousand dollars, farmers who did qualify and desperately needed food and clothing, eventually received one dollar.[25] The standard for eligibility became an empty gesture of governmental magnanimity and a punishment for those who gave in to bad fortune.

Davis reported that it had been unnecessary to allocate all of the $75,000 that was set aside for seed. "It was found," he said, "that the object of the statute could be effectually accomplished with $50,000," and therefore, the seed commissioners only received that amount, "owing to the empty condition of the state treasury." The promised negotiation for additional funds did not happen. The *St. Paul Daily Pioneer* (just weeks before its merger with the *Press*) reported the applications for seed "would exhaust an appropriation of half a million dollars" and that the sum available would not satisfy "more than a meager fraction of the demand." According to Annette Atkins, "Whatever the Governor's arguments to the contrary, most victims agreed that even the whole of the appropriation 'fell far short of being sufficient to seed the ground.'" State relief thoroughly failed to meet the needs of farmers, and the seed that was allocated only provided the barest minimum.[26]

Yet, after two years during which the condition of the farmers had not improved, even as they repeatedly called for public assistance, policy makers, as reflected in the executive office and the legislature of 1875, felt little need to enable "freeloaders." Minnesota's political and social culture adjudged the victims of the infestation, as well as subsequently, Southern blacks, as those who should be blamed for being poor, disenfranchised, and victimized.[27] The newly organized *St. Paul Pioneer Press* would take this editorial stance.

In the summer of 1875, when the grasshoppers did relatively minimal damage, many farmers saved part of their crops. Thus, the need for widespread help abated somewhat and no organized relief effort took place. In the fall, Davis appointed a three-man commission to investigate the habits and characteristics of the grasshoppers. The commissioners personally visited the ravaged counties, sent circulars and pamphlets to local officials, and studied the related entomological reports. Their goal was to give farmers information they could use in protecting themselves against the ravages of the pests. Eventually, the commission published a fifty-page pamphlet summarizing the basic information, including the arrival and departure dates of the grasshoppers, egg laying and hatching patterns, list of vulnerable crops, and known methods of destruction.

In the fall, Davis announced that he would not run for reelection. John S. Pillsbury, a former member of Davis's state relief committee, was elected the eighth governor of Minnesota. A successful businessman from Minneapolis whose life depicted the self-help virtues of Horatio Alger, and one of two state senators who, at the close of the last term, voted against the Louisiana Resolution, his principles set the tone for how his government defined the meaning of relief.

Many Minnesotans felt that Pillsbury was the right man at the right time. The state suffered from the Panic of 1873 and the subsequent depression: the property tax system staggered from high delinquency and the 1874 tax decrease further reduced the state's working capital. Minnesotans were tired of this, and ready for a "modern," more efficient Minnesota, a more bureaucratized and more economically accountable government. A majority of men who voted in 1875 found in Pillsbury the executive they sought: one who shared their frustrations, their hopes, and their interests, and who promised a "businessman's administration of state government."

To restore general prosperity, Pillsbury called for "the practice of a close, methodical, and persistent economy, alike in all public and all private affairs. In my judgment," he said, "the conditions requisite for the promotion of public welfare are precisely those essential to success in private affairs." In the interests of general frugality and efficiency he called for a shorter legislative session, a smaller and less expensive legislature to meet biennially rather than annually—both to cut costs and to avoid "much needless and confused legislation inevitable from the too frequent amendment of untried laws." He called for the consolidation of state offices, a reduction of the cost for public printing that would reduce "the tabulated and minute details which swell the bulk . . . of most the reports." (D. D. Merrill, one of the state's largest printers, would not have been approved.) The governor also called for discharging the financial examiner and a balanced budget.[28]

But two additional items served as the pillars for true advancement— immigration and a full presentation at the upcoming Centennial Exposition in Philadelphia. "It is difficult, in my judgment, to exaggerate the importance to Minnesota of a full presentation at the Centennial Exposition, to commence in May next, of her varied and ample products. . . . Is it not fitting that Minnesota should pay a tribute to the agency to which she owes her existence, and add to the display of a nation of which she is so prosperous a member? She should esteem it a privilege to bear part and lot in such an exposition." Coupled with participating in the exposition was a plan to initiate immigration. "While I deem a credible display of our products at the Centennial Exposition the best possible effort toward that object, I suggest that in connection therewith, a revision of the State Immigration pamphlet, so as to embrace the latest statistics pertaining to population, crops, schools, lands, railroads and company, with adequate means for its wide distribution, would provide an effective aid toward the desired purpose. . . . It should be your aim, *by a counteraction of these adverse influences,* to secure to Minnesota the immigration to which she is justly entitled, both by great advantages and superior prosperity."[29]

By "adverse influences," Pillsbury was talking about the geographic location of the state, which was not situated in "more central and southerly latitudes" in the natural path of westward movement as was Kansas, which showed "an actual gain of population greater than that of our state."[30] "Adverse influences," in Pillsbury's view, were not the grasshoppers that had infested Minnesota cropland every year since 1873. In fact, in his twenty-five-page address, in which he covered a variety of issues confronting the state—Indian troubles, tree culture, and railroad bonds, to name a few—he omitted any reference to the stricken farmers and government relief efforts. This omission might simply have reflected a chief executive and business-man seeking to promote his prescription for a better future, which governors traditionally take the occasion to do, or he sensed (or wanted to believe) that because of the reduced impact of the infestation in 1875, the plague was com-ing to an end. Just as likely, however, it characterized his nineteenth-century notion of a modern and businesslike approach to relief and assistance.

He would develop the theme in a later speech, in which he called the relief program "very questionable policy" and warned farmers against relying on such ill-advised public action in the future. Such relief measures served as "indemnity for past losses," making up for lost revenue rather than providing food, clothing, and other necessities. Moreover, these practices ran the risk of "weakening the habit of self-reliance" among recipients. If people came to depend on relief they would begin to expect it and become a hazard to the welfare of the state and of the individuals themselves. For the good of the state the poor should not expect relief as a right. To protect the poor from their own weak natures, insisted the governor, the state should discourage dependence.[31] Seven years earlier, he had delivered essentially the same mes-sage to the assembly of the newly enfranchised colored citizens of Minnesota.

Both were messages the *St. Paul Pioneer Press* roundly applauded, report-ing that they demonstrated "the characteristic good sense and the sound par-tial judgment of a man exhibited to his first ethical deliverance."[32] It was high praise for John Pillsbury and, by extension, for the voters of the state who made him their eighth governor. He was the paper's man. On a key issue, the paper editorialized that "the better class of people" throughout Minnesota objected to government assistance because it had a very "demoralizing effect" on the state.[33] Theirs was a vote to amend the state constitution that would permit this legislature to extend limited voting rights to women. Wilkinson and Donnelly, however, as "carryovers" from the previous session—no other "grange" senators were reelected—would serve in the upcoming session.[34]

On the whole, it was a legislature the paper deemed praiseworthy—"a more intelligent and good looking assemblage of gentlemen; six or eight of the number . . . who show the fruits of half a hundred winters or hard times, perhaps in a sprinkling of gray in hair or whiskers"—and a legislature that was expected to support the governor's agenda, the will of the people.[35] "Chambers, galleries and lobbies were packed as gavels descended at noon on January 4, 1876, to open the session." Betty Kane reported, " 'The general murmur, which here often attains deafening volume,' as a bemused Swedish visitor put it, was undoubtedly at high decibel."[36] And on the opening day the spectators were presented with the first sign of fireworks over whether there should be a chaplain. "Wilkinson, the majestic and humorless senator from Blue Earth," argued against the "peppery" German farmer from Carver County, A. C. Lienau, that one needed to be appointed: "We would do well," insisted Wilkinson, "to appoint a preacher to do a little praying over the senate." A chaplain was selected.[37]

It was a legislature that could follow Pillsbury's lead in taking Minnesota into the future. But of the forty-one senators and one hundred and six representatives who participated in the eighteenth annual legislative session, of the men who participated in debate and speeches, the paper seemed most impressed, and at times amused, with the senator from Blue Earth, Morton S. Wilkinson; and it was a sentiment that seemed to be shared by most of the men who served alongside him, as illustrated in a display of photographs of the senators and representatives. House members were displayed in a vaguely circular fashion around the likeness of the governor and lieutenant governor. Members of the Senate were arranged differently, however, in the shape of a shield, and at its peak was a likeness of Senator Wilkinson, who was, as the once-critical *Press* described him, "a noble contrast to small hucksters," who had "plant[ed] himself on the high judicial ground of justice and public policy." He was still a Liberal Republican–Democrat, about to become a Democrat, but in 1876, the difference between the two parties was minimal. Clearly his years of public service enhanced his profile, having been Minnesota's first Republican senator and a member of the United States House of Representatives. Four others had served in the House, but until 1895, when Knute Nelson was elected to the U.S. Senate, Wilkinson, in the session of 1876, singularly held that honor.[38]

He was still concerned about the interests of the small farmer and skeptical of privilege, though on most issues he was also one with whom a man could reason. It was a legislature that had fewer voices speaking in behalf of relief because many believed that the plague was coming to an end. Wilkinson served on several committees, but never as chair, nor was he president, nor did he provide any parliamentary leadership.[39] But he had a lot to say on several topics, and he could be quite colorful when he did, which is why he seemed to be—temperament and all—the paper's favorite subject.[40] On one occasion, after a three-hour debate over the state appropriation for a display to be erected at the Philadelphia Centennial, Wilkinson, mindful of the grasshopper sufferers in Blue Earth County, "severely" argued against the proposed bill for $5,000. Losing that battle, he called for an adjournment to avoid further votes from being taken that would enact the appropriation into law. Supporters of the bill protested, yelling, "Oh, no, withdraw your motion, and let's dispose of it now." To them, Wilkinson responded quite stringently (again as the paper reported), "If you do, you'd go home to a late supper, for I propose to make a long speech on this question."[41]

Wilkinson showed flashes of anger on other topics as the session progressed. He hated the reapportionment bill that seemed to give more power to cities, argued to repeal the inebriate asylum in a step to frustrate the temperance lobby, a crusade he once led during the early days of the territory, and he rejected the House's women's suffrage bill that exempted foreign-born, unnaturalized women (the bill would be fixed in time for adjournment); but he viewed the swamp and school land bill "to be the most important matter that had been brought to the legislature this session."[42] Nothing more of significance would be done for farm victims of the plague.

At the end of the session, few were satisfied. Senior senators were reported to have said "that the winding up of the session of the legislature was the most unpleasant, monotonous, and unsatisfactory that they had ever seen," a view the *Pioneer Press* reporter shared. One historian referred to the session as "a case study in lively futility." Little of significance was achieved, though legislators, under the watchful eyes of most of the state's political, business, and civic leaders, including Sarah Stearns and Mahala Pillsbury, a leader in the charity movement and wife of the governor, did approve a statutory amendment "to enable women to vote at elections for school officers and in matters pertaining solely to the management of the schools."[43]

Within two months, the grasshopper eggs would once again hatch, and the adults would wreak more damage than the previous two years; but by that time, Wilkinson, no longer a senator, no longer in a position to do anything to help his neighbors, could only watch. And the "negro" problems in Louisiana and Mississippi would just have to be settled by the people there, once they were able to reclaim control from the corrupt carpetbaggers. It was now a different time in history, and one in which his role, in his fifty-sixth year, would need to be reassessed.

Two weeks later, the *Mankato Union* and the *Pioneer Press* printed a news item about the dedication of a monument to Abraham Lincoln that had just been unveiled in Washington.[44] In both papers, the notice was perfunctory and appeared without commentary: if anything, as Wilkinson might have concluded, the monument was but a thread woven within the bloody shirt, a desperate though transparently cynical grab for votes in a year when the

Republicans might very well lose the White House. In fact, history does not record whether he read the notice or what he felt if he did. But one can imagine, given his view of the world, the vicissitudes of all he had experienced and in some cases caused, that for a battered society that left its most humble, but noble men to suffer alone because their leaders *had done their part,* there was very little to celebrate. In one week, on April 22, the *Pioneer Press,* which had already edged closer to the Republican camp, would merge with the *Minneapolis Tribune,* to virtually hold a monopoly on the journalistic voice of Minnesota.[45] Wilkinson's Minnesota had moved into the era in which the merciless doctrine of self-reliance would have no rival.

# THE CHILDREN OF LINCOLN

*Perpetual reminders of the past humiliation of the blacks are*
*not calculated to hasten the disappearance of race prejudice.*

NEW YORK TIMES, APRIL 15, 1876

Half a continent away, on April 14, 1876, eleven years to the day of Abraham Lincoln's assassination, the great bronze statue of the president stood shrouded under the national flag until the appointed time. The Marine Band played "Hail Columbia" and several dignitaries spoke about the meaning of the day. The crowd, estimated at twenty-five thousand, the "colored population . . . out in full force," assembled on the lawn in Lincoln Park and awaited with great anticipation to finally see the great object.[1] Finally, the moment arrived when President Grant stepped to the front and grasped the rope that was attached to the flag pull, and the Star-Spangled Banner glided down; amid the deafening cheers of the multitude, the playing of music, and the booming of cannons, the beautiful monument stood unveiled. The great bronze casting of colossal size towering twelve feet high, and resting upon a pedestal ten feet high, represented Abraham Lincoln standing erect, with the Proclamation of Emancipation in his left hand, while the right arm was paternalistically outstretched, palm opened heavenly as if bestowing grace over the kneeling figure of a slave from whose limbs the shackles have just fallen. Upon the base of the monument is the word "Emancipation."

The effort to bring this moment to pass began eleven years earlier. In 1865, upon hearing "the lamented, honored and loved Lincoln had been so foully assassinated," as banker James E. Yeatman, founder of the Mercantile

Library and director of the Western Sanitary Commission, both based in St. Louis, Missouri, said on the day of commemoration, Charlotte Scott, a freed-woman of Virginia, who, after emancipation had stayed with the family of her master, went in great distress to her mistress and said, "The colored people have lost their best friend on earth! Mr. Lincoln was our best friend, and I will give five dollars of my wages towards erecting a monument to his memory." "Being her first earnings in freedom," this sum was also the first contribution to a fund "contributed solely by emancipated citizens of the United States, declared free by his proclamation."[2] It would be a memorial that would stand the test of time.

Once news spread about the donation and purpose, colored soldiers under the command of General J. W. Davidson, headquartered at Natchez, Mississippi, amassed the sum of $12,150. The fund eventually grew to $16,242 under the management of the Western Sanitary Commission. The commission, under the leadership of abolitionist and Unitarian minister William Greenleaf Eliot, was a private agency founded in 1861 that operated in the west during the war to deal with sick and wounded soldiers, setting up hospitals and caring for the families and orphans of soldiers, Union refugees, and the freedmen. "In short," as Yeatman said, "all the humanities growing out of the war came under their charge."[3] The commission first came to be entrusted with managing the funds when Scott's employer and former master, William P. Rucker, handed the sum over to General T. C. H. Smith, then in command of the military post of St. Louis, who, in turn, handed it over to Reverend Eliot.[4] It was Eliot who ultimately selected the design.

Thomas Ball, the noted Boston sculptor and painter living in Florence, Italy, had been so moved at the news of Lincoln's death that he felt inspired—"an inward demand"—to sculpt a statue, even though he had not been commissioned to do so. "His aim was to present one single idea, representing the great work for the accomplishment of which Abraham Lincoln lived and died. . . . Mr. Ball also determined not to part with it, except under such circumstances as to insure its just appreciation, not merely as a work of art but as a labor of love—a tribute to American patriotism." For four years, it stood in his studio in Europe, but when he heard that it could serve as a memorial to freedom dedicated by the emancipated slaves themselves, he sought to show it to the commission. "The price to be paid would be altogether a secondary consideration." In 1869 Reverend Eliot visited the Florence studio to see for himself and was so pleased he recommended the statue to the commission when he returned to St. Louis. Upon seeing photographs, "they at once decided to accept the design, and an order was given for its immediate execution in bronze, in accordance with the suggestions made by Mr. Ball."⁵ Yeatman said, "I trust yet that the gratitude of the freed people will prompt them to execute this grand design."⁶

In the original, the kneeling slave was represented as perfectly passive, "receiving the boon of freedom from the hand of the great liberator," Yeatman said. "But the artist justly changed this, to bring the presentation nearer to the historical fact, by making the emancipated slave an agent in his own deliverance." Ball decided that the slave should be represented as exerting his own strength "with strained muscles in breaking the chain which had bound him. A far greater degree of dignity and vigor, as well as of historical accuracy, is thus imparted." Instead of the idealized vision of a slave, he sought "the figure of a living man." Ball based "the face and manly bearing of the negro" off the likeness of "the last slave ever taken up in Missouri under the fugitive slave law . . . who was rescued from his captors. . . . The ideal [design] is thus converted into the literal truth of history without losing anything of its artistic conception or effect." An exact copy of the statue sculpted in pure white Italian marble for the Western Sanitary Commission was later placed, as "Freedom's Memorial," in a public building in St. Louis.⁷ For his bronze statue standing in Lincoln Park, Ball received $17,000. The government appropriated $3,000 for the foundation and pedestal upon which the bronze statue stood, and allowed it to pass freely through the customhouse.

Although most in the assembled crowd were impressed, a number, as they studied the fixed benevolence of the giant figure, were filled with sullen disquiet, for the message to them was unmistakably about how both races, black and white, were to forever regard each other. As the *New York Times* opined, unmindful of the dual meaning of the statue to two parallel worlds sharing the same sphere without ever intersecting, "It is an enduring monument to President Lincoln, and of the gratitude of the colored race."⁸ The monument was created to stand the test of time, initiated and paid for by African Americans, and ultimately designed and approved by white men. To the white patrons, it seemed only appropriate, a dramatic illustration of the advent of freedom and opportunity. But to black people, it was a monument to white paternalism and black subservience forever cast in bronze. The desire of black people had been commemorated in a design chosen by whites in perpetual tribute to themselves. Historian Kirk Savage was more blunt: "Frozen forever in this unfortunate juxtaposition, the monument is not really about emancipation but about its opposite—domination."⁹ The permanent image of the black man, unshackled yet forever bowed, freed yet forever unequal, noted but never really seen, was just as his "children" had presumed it should be; but it was an image their "father" may not have shared.

Eleven years earlier, by midday on a warm April 4, 1865, upon first setting foot on the landing at Richmond, Virginia, the capital of the defeated Old Confederacy, President Lincoln was immediately surrounded by black laborers who exclaimed, "Bress de Lord! . . . Dere is the great Messiah! . . . Glory Hallelujah." Then, first, as Doris Kearns Goodwin reports, a handful of the freedmen followed by several others fell on their knees. But in viewing the spread of the gesture as more blacks assembled around him, the president would have none of it, as he said with emotion welling up in his voice, "Don't kneel to me. That is not right. You must kneel to God only, and thank him for the liberty you will hereafter enjoy."[10] However, to the devotees of the unfurled statue, eleven years later, these facts were not grand enough. Only the more majestic pose of the bronzed form and its outstretched and benevolent left arm that they came to honor would serve as a more fitting tribute as well as serve as a constant reminder of their commitment to protecting his "stepchildren." It was a sentiment that would appear to evaporate within the coming months.

During the presidential election of 1876, sensing a possible defeat to Democrat Samuel Tilden of New York, Republicans worked to inspire their voters to stick with the party, now that Grant was not on the ticket, by reviving the old theme of the bloody shirt. Noted orator and politician Robert G. Ingersoll characterized the campaign when he famously declared, "Every man that shot Union soldiers was a Democrat. The man that assassinated Abraham Lincoln was a Democrat. . . . Soldiers, every scar you have got in your heroic bodies was given you by a Democrat." In response, the Democrats, supported by a considerable number of Liberal Republicans who were determined to see the end of graft and corruption of "carpetbag" and Negro rule, raised the battle cry "Tilden and Reform." To reassure its Republican readers that they would not betray the spirit of the Great Emancipator, the *Mankato Union* printed a front-page speech by a South Carolina black man who explained why he intended to vote for the Democrat. "The Radicals have been ruling this government for ten years, and their motto has been 'Lie, cheat, and steal,' and today there is no money in the country."[11] When votes were tallied in the Electoral College, Republican candidate Rutherford B. Hayes of Ohio, was behind. Twenty disputed votes, mainly from Southern states, could put him over the top; but the stakes were high. In February representatives from both camps met to hash it out in Washington at the Wormley House, the exclusive hotel owned and operated by a black man named James Wormley.[12]

In the end, Hayes edged out Democrat Samuel Tilden by one electoral vote. But his victory came at a price. In return for a Democratic endorsement of the controversial vote, Hayes agreed to withdraw the remaining federal troops from the South. With this order, president-elect Rutherford B. Hayes effectively signaled the end of Reconstruction, as well as the federal government's intent to protect the equal rights and the lives of black people in the South. Even Frederick Douglass, whom Hayes later appointed to the office of marshal of the District of Columbia, largely acquiesced to the president's policies that essentially resulted in the abandonment of the African American.[13] As John Hope Franklin has written, "On the points most important to the white South the North was willing to yield; and on the points most important to the North [in the way of expanded investments] the white South was willing to yield. In a sense, then, both sides were pleased with the outcome of reconstruction. In another sense, however, both sides suffered an ignoble defeat."[14]

None of the four Minnesotans examined in this volume had financial investments in the South; and none had attended the unveiling ceremony, for each of them had more important things to do at home, having long before moved far beyond any further commitment they felt for the welfare of the Negro. For each, that work had been done.

◆ ◆ ◆ ◆ ◆

By 1870 Brevet Major Thomas Montgomery, retired, had established a thriving real estate office in St. Peter, Minnesota, where he lived until 1890 with his wife, Sarah Purnell, and their growing family that would number to seven children, surviving his mother, Margaret, who died in 1887, and his younger brother Alexander, who died in 1892, both residents of Cleveland Township. There is still no record of what happened to Elizabeth Estell. While a resident and real estate agent of St. Peter, Montgomery served for several years as justice of the peace and organized the A. K. Skaro Post, Grand Army of the Republic, a fraternal organization composed of veterans of the Union's armed forces who served during the Civil War, of which he was a charter member and long-term commander.

But it was with his work within the Masonry that he most distinguished himself, beginning in 1873 as one of the founding members of the St. Peter Chapter No. 22, Royal Arch Mason Lodge, and the St. Peter Division No. 2, Sons of Temperance, in 1876. He rose through the ranks within the Masonic community, gaining recognition as an authority on Masonic jurisprudence in the world and being the author of several books on Masonic rituals and jurisprudence that came to be viewed as authoritative.

Eventually he attained high rank in the councils of Masonry, elected in 1889 to the rank of grand secretary of Minnesota Grand Lodge, a position that required him to move his family to St. Paul in 1890. In that position, he also served as the secretary of the Grand Chapter of Royal Arch Masons, grand recorder of the Grand Council, Royal and Selected Masons, and grand recorder of the Grand Commandery, Knights Templar. He was a member of the Order of Ancient and Accepted Scottish Rite bodies of St. Paul, and also the Osman Temple, Order of the Mystic Shrine. He held these ranks until his death in June 1907.[15]

Despite his long service as a leading member of Minnesota Masonry, it remains uncertain whether Montgomery knew of the effort of the Pioneer Lodge of the Masonic Order to be recognized by the Minnesota Grand Lodge. Since 1866, a year before he was decommissioned from military service with the Sixty-Seventh Regiment of the U.S. Colored Infantry and two months before the official incorporation of Pilgrim Baptist Society, five black men in St. Paul founded the Pioneer Lodge under the aegis of the Prince Hall Grand Lodge. On June 3, 1867, fifty black men held a meeting at Pilgrim Baptist Church "to take preliminary steps for the organization of a colored Lodge for Good Templars." As late as 1877, however, the all-white Minnesota Grand Lodge continuously challenged the legality of the existence of the Pioneer Lodge. Denied membership in the Minnesota Grand Lodge, the Pioneer Lodge gained affiliation with the Grand Lodge of Missouri, and after 1882, the African Grand Lodge of Iowa.

◆ ◆ ◆ ◆ ◆

In 1871 Sarah Stearns and the Minnesota suffragists began the new phase of agitation by circulating petitions around the state to be sent to Congress, asking for a declaratory act to protect the women of the nation in the exercise of "the citizen's right to vote" under the new guarantees of the Fourteenth and Fifteenth Amendments. During that year the National Woman Suffrage Association appointed Dr. Addie Ballou its vice president for Minnesota. In 1872 a suffrage club was founded in Kasson. The three organizers, who included Mrs. Almira W. Anthony (married to a cousin of Susan B. Anthony), vowed to each other that while they lived in that city there should always be an active suffrage club "until the ballot for women should be obtained." At a temperance convention in 1874, a women's suffrage resolution was defended by Mrs. Julia Ballard Nelson, Mrs. Harriet A. Hobart, and Mrs. Asa Hutchinson.[16] The next year would showcase one of Stearns's highest achievements—getting women the right to vote in school board elections.[17]

Earlier that year, in *Minor v. Hoppensett,* the United States Supreme Court declared that women had always been citizens but the right to vote constituted an essential privilege of citizenship. The power to award suffrage rights belonged to the states, and the only restraint placed on the power had been that states could not use race to deny the vote. But all sorts of groups lacked the vote. If women were to gain that right, it would have to come from the states. The Constitution, wrote Chief Justice Morrison Waite, stood silent on the issue.[18] The school governance vote, in November 1875, was the last successful effort for the remainder of the century.

In 1872 Sarah and Ozora Stearns moved their family to Duluth after he had served a year in the United States Senate, ending in 1871. In Duluth, he was elected judge of the District Court, Eleventh District, and served from 1874 to 1891. His judicial career, as well as a term as a regent of the University of Minnesota, did not appear to be affected by his wife's work. The couple's finances allowed Sarah to continue her political advocacy, philanthropy, and volunteer work in Duluth while she reared four children.

She was the founding member of the Minnesota Woman Suffrage Association in 1881, its president from 1881 to 1883, and vice president in 1889. Also in 1889, she was president of the Ladies Equal Suffrage League in Duluth when she hosted visiting lecturer Susan B. Anthony on November 9. She wrote the chapter on Minnesota in *History of Woman Suffrage,* volume three, and served as vice president for Minnesota on the National Woman Suffrage Association board, a member of the Duluth School Board, and organizer and first president of the Duluth Home Society, which served destitute women and children. Together Sarah and Ozora Stearns helped found the Duluth Unitarian Church. As early as 1876, she received a U.S. patent for a carpet cleaner.[19]

In 1891 the judge suffered a stroke, forcing him to retire from the bench, and in 1895 they moved to Los Angeles, California. One year later, he died. Sarah survived her husband by eight years, during which time, in 1900, she chaired the Los Angeles Woman Suffrage League. However, her energy and commitment to women's suffrage did not sustain her long enough to see ratification of the Nineteenth Amendment. She died suddenly in her Los Angeles home on January 25, 1904.[20]

◆ ◆ ◆ ◆ ◆

In 1877, at the end of his tenure in the state Senate, Morton S. Wilkinson and his wife, Sally, moved to Wells, in Faribault County, where they would live in the home of their daughter, Ella Brewster, and her husband. The large stone house in Mankato where they lived during his years in the U.S. Senate, "one of the finest houses in the city," was now too large, empty, and quiet to roam within because melancholy threatened to meet him around every shadowy corner. It was here that his son, Morton Junior, had died, and where his wife's ill health began. In Wells, Ella could watch over her. In 1879 Wilkinson was elected Faribault County attorney, but served for one term, possibly choosing not to run for reelection after Sally took a fall that severely fractured her hip. This accident exacerbated her decline and confined her to bed. Finally, in 1888, Sally passed away and was buried at Glenwood Cemetery, in Mankato, next to their son's grave, leaving Wilkinson to face his own mortality, which spread throughout his aching bones, and the darker thoughts ticking away like the clock on the mantel above the living room fire.[21]

The ex-senator was getting to know his daughter, who had grown into womanhood while he was mostly away in Washington or on some campaign. Yet, living in Wells meant he was away from the city that had been his political base for nearly a quarter century, and he still harbored that powerful impulse that had defined his life. The fact that he now needed the care or at least the watchful eye of someone meant that his time and energy were inexorably passing. So, too, was his brand of politics. The cheers of crowds, even the jeers of hostile editors, began lingering in his mind like cobwebs that formed in an abandoned dwelling. He had more to give. Yet even his allies were being passed by the younger generation.

The politics were different while things somehow stayed the same. Though farmers enjoyed a bumper crop after the grasshopper plague at last ended, many remained destitute. Grantism had finally gone away but monopolies, railroads, and eastern banks still had the upper hand. Ramsey, his nemesis, was now Rutherford Hayes's secretary of war. On the occasional trip that the senator took to St. Paul to visit old friends, the few African Americans he noted either swept the floors, toted luggage, or trimmed his thinning hair at his hotel, just like before. In his travels around the state he couldn't recall seeing one black farmer. Their fate was the consequence of having thrown their lot in with the Republican Party.

Within the hearth and home of the loving family of his daughter, at seventy-one years, Wilkinson did not know where he belonged. There was so much yet to do, but doors were now politely closing to the Old Man. He frequently visited Mankato "for business and pleasure and was always welcomed heartily by the old settlers," but they were beginning to die away. In 1890, four years after his tenure as county attorney ended, he was nominated to represent the Second District in Congress by the Democratic Party. Though he ran, he withdrew prior to the election because of his health. In the few years to follow he learned to content himself by attending the local county courtrooms.

It was in 1892 that he first discovered his heart was beginning to fail to perform properly, and he reportedly mentioned to George Brewster, the brother of his son-in-law, John, "This old heart of mine has been pumping away for seventy-four years and is nearly done."

In late January 1894 he took a coach ride to the nearby city of Blue Earth to attend the district court presided over by Judge M. J. Severance. The distance was twenty-five miles and the day was very cold. The court had just taken a recess when Wilkinson made his way down the stairway to rest on a chair in the hallway of the first floor. No one who passed him felt any cause for concern, for they assumed that he was waiting for someone. When Judge Severance came down to speak to Wilkinson but received no answer, he called an attorney named Quinn, who secured medical assistance. Immediately, Wilkinson was taken to his hotel room and sent home to Wells the next day. A short time later he was "prostrated by another attack," which the physicians called neuralgia of the heart. For two days he suffered intense pain, but when this was relieved, he sank into unconsciousness, a state in which he ultimately remained. Morton Smith Wilkinson, seventy-four years old, died in his daughter's home at 2 a.m., on February 4, 1894. Four months later, on June 28, Ella died from surgical complications.[22]

Shortly before he fell ill, in 1892 Wilkinson had received a parcel in the mail. It was a novel written by an "Edmund Boisgilbert, M.D.," sent to him from "an old friend." There is no record of whether he liked or even read it, or who the old friend may have been.[23]

◆ ◆ ◆ ◆ ◆

By the 1890s the very successful stock-in-trade of the devout Daniel David Merrill was in book selling and printing, an enterprise he had built for thirty years. In 1860 Merrill used capital from his investments in real estate to open a little bookstore in a building fourteen feet wide on Third Street in downtown St. Paul, and there his business grew to such a size that eventually a new building was needed. In 1877 he once again was able to leverage his holdings to construct a larger building on Third Street, just below Cedar. In 1879, the business of White, Stone and Company merged with Merrill's company that he partnered with John Randall to form the St. Paul Book and Stationery Company, which later moved to lower Third Street. Every Christmas season advertisements for holiday purchases could be seen not only in the

St. Paul newspapers, but also in the Mankato, Rochester, Winona, and Duluth papers. In some quarters a book or trinket from D. D. Merrill and Company held as much social currency as being seen among people of recognized enlightenment.

Soon the business had to move into even larger quarters on First and St. Peter. The firm name was then changed to D. D. Merrill Company, which now included a publishing house. His holdings by then extended to a printing company in New York City.

And through his mounting success, his commitment to the Baptist faith only deepened, for over forty years he remained a leader of the congregation of First Baptist Church of St. Paul. He was a deacon for many years, served for two years as president of the congregation, and remained prominent in church work in the city and state. He started eighteen churches and missions within the city in the name of the Baptist faith, and served as treasurer of the Minnesota Baptist State convention for over twenty-one years. Indeed, he was one of the most prominent businessmen and church leaders in the city and "was well-known in every reform which was instituted for the benefit of the city." He was a man of considerable influence, and with it, he could do what ordinary men could not do.

The topics of the books Merrill published were wide ranging and included science and art; among the latter was the work of painter Carl Gutherz, who was noted for his grand landscapes of the Northwest and, in particular, a daringly sensual portrait of a semiclad Indian maiden in a suggestive repose. With his status secured, as it had long been since his days as secretary and treasurer of the United States Christian Commission, which raised thousands of dollars for food, clothing, and hospital stores and in which capacity he served for four years without pay, he was indeed a man beyond reproach, which made his last venture rather curious. In 1892, he published a strange little book that began,

> I have made up my mind to tell the whole dreadful story, let the
> consequences be what they may. I know there are those, among my
> friends, who will consider it a species of degradation for me to make
> public the facts that will appear on these pages; while there are others
> who will urge that the world will never believe so improbable a story
> as that which I am about to tell. But it seems to me that I have been
> chosen, by some extra-mundane, superhuman intelligence, out of the
> multitude of mankind, and subjected to a terrible and unparalleled
> experience, in order that a great lesson may be taught to the world;

and that it is a duty, therefore, which I owe to the world, and which
I should not shrink from or avoid, to make known all the facts of that
experience, at whatever cost of shame or agony to myself. Blessed
is the man who can feel that God has singled him out from among
his fellows, and that the divine hand has shaped his destiny; and yet
such men usually bear on their hearts and minds a burden of life-long
woe. Those whom God so honors he agonizes.[24]

Thus began a novel that first appeared in 1891. The main character was a
brilliant young Southern physician infatuated with an intelligent woman who
encouraged him to enter politics to serve mankind but who persuaded him to
keep secret his views on racial equality because they were too radical. As the
story goes, when the good doctor considered entering political life, his soul
and mind were transfigured into the body of the coarsest, most brutal and evil
black man in his community. In turn, the black man took possession of the
doctor's body and status. The story of the steady success of evil in the person
of the doctor's body, and the failures of brilliance, honesty, and courage in
the form of the doctor's soul and mind, were locked in the body of the black
man. Only through religion was the transformed doctor able to find salvation,
but the white community apprehensively saw him as a threat to public safety.
His worse foe was his own body, protected by status although motivated by
evil. The transformation was finally reversed when the black man slew his
own form and the doctor's soul and mind were freed to reclaim possession of
his own body.

*Doctor Huguet,* authored by Edmund Boisgilbert, M.D., was as a fantasy
a startling book that attempted to depict a strong sympathy for the Southern
intellectuals and the impoverished black people who were trying to maintain some semblance of freedom in the face of brutal oppression.[25] Ignatius
Donnelly, who wrote under the pseudonym "Edmund Boisgilbert, M.D.,"
was seeking to strike hard at the opaque discipline of the Southern mind in
dealing with race and its inability to apply standards—good or evil, moral or
immoral, legal or illegal, and the willingness of a group of intelligent Southerners to compromise their principles to gain political power. The book was
doomed. As biographer Martin Ridge observes, "Written forty years too late
to fit into the radical antislavery literature and published at a time when the
Negroes' struggle for legal and personal status was practically at a standstill,
*Doctor Huguet* was not destined for popularity. The book trod too heavily on
the manners and mores of too large a segment of the population."[26]

A few readers appreciated the work. "*Doctor Huguet* is a wonderful tale, so well told that the reader is absorbed to the end, his interest never flags. Then a spirited humanitarian and truly (sic) Christian breathes through it. I could not feel but that the author is involved with the essence of Christianity." The letter was signed "Father Egan, Sea Isle City, New Jersey." From another man: "I feel that I should like to write and thank you for your wise utterances and for the tendency to do good which I am sure is a very marked feature of the book" (Lewis Llewellyn, pastor, First Baptist Church of Hastings).[27]

Donnelly's Chicago publisher, F. J. Schulte and Company, printed a small number of copies and then relinquished the rights to the book because of poor sales.[28] In August 1892, two months after Homer Adolph Plessy was arrested for sitting in a Louisiana railroad car reserved for whites, D. D. Merrill became the only publisher who agreed to reprint Donnelly's book.[29] The provocative nature of the novel, considering Merrill's reputation of staid rectitude, seemed unlike any book with which he would be associated. It most certainly was not likely to realize a profit or satisfy the tastes of the proper, middle-class customers he tended to attract. And yet he decided to risk a financial loss. Doctor Huguet spoke to Merrill, for he had served on the St. Paul Board of Education, presiding over a school district in which black schoolchildren were subjected to abysmal conditions. His association with the Pilgrims exposed him to the desperate straits of black parents who were denied opportunities to learn a trade and treated with no respect in most corners of the community he inhabited, or even the right to dignity that was denied Robert Hickman every Sunday, when Merrill's disengaged father-in-law took his place as pastor of Pilgrim Baptist Church. In other words, Merrill, like Huguet, had witnessed racism and had done very little to confront it. In publishing the thoughts and deeds of Doctor Huguet, Merrill, a righteous man, may have found his own road to redemption:

> This terrible race-prejudice, I said to myself, has continued to exist because there are no great scholars, thinkers and speakers, of the negro race, to challenge and overcome it. White men could not have been suppressed in that fashion. I will lead the way! That may have been the purpose for which this ghastly transformation has been inflicted upon me. And I swelled with pride in anticipation of my triumphs, close at hand.[30]

Apparently in the three years since the novel's publication, what inspiration Merrill may have derived from the fictional Huguet's "anticipation [of his own] triumphs" had waned. As the summer of 1895 approached, two black men, in separate incidences, were chased through the neighborhood streets of St. Paul by mobs intent on lynching them. In that each was accused of raping white women—an allegation that Southern mobs customarily addressed with a rope—the murderous work of the vigilantes received the approval two major newspapers of the city that called the attempted lynching of Houston Osborne, the second man, "thrilling and remarkable" and "a burst of righteous wrath."[31] There is no record that Merrill or any of his brethren protested the prospect of lynch law or those who had cheered the men who carried the rope.

One year later, in late April 1896, Daniel David Merrill contracted a slight cold that rapidly and fatally developed into pleuropneumonia. On Wednesday evening, May 21, days after *Plessy v. Ferguson* was decided, thus establishing the constitutional doctrine of "separate but equal," Merrill died in his St. Paul home, leaving his wife, three sons (two of whom ran the publishing business in New York; the third was an architect), and one daughter, unmarried and at home at the time of his death. "The prominent citizen since was no more."[32]

# NOTES

## INTRODUCTION

1. "Waving the bloody shirt" was a cynical ploy on the part of Republican candidates for elective office who exploited the post–Civil War sentiment of voters to gain their support.

2. Speech by M. S. Wilkinson, *Proceedings of the Convention of Colored Citizens of the State of Minnesota* (St. Paul: Press Printing, 1869), 19–20.

3. See part VI.

4. *St. Paul Dispatch*, February 17, 1877. For commentaries on the shift of focus from black civil rights by the Republicans, see Eric Foner, *Reconstruction: America's Unfinished Revolution, 1863–1877* (New York: Harper and Row, 1988), 343–44; Richard Kluger, *Simple Justice: The History of Brown v. Board of Education and Black America's Struggle for Equality* (New York: Knopf Doubleday, 2011), 55.

5. Thomas A. Woods, *Knights of the Plow: Oliver H. Kelley and the Origins of the Grange in Republican Ideology* (Ames: Iowa State University Press, 1991), 148, citing Theodore Nydahl, "The Diary of Ignatius Donnelly" (Ph.D. diss., University of Minnesota, 1942), 372–73.

6. For example, before emancipation, the New England states had each extended voting rights to black male residents. Wisconsin established black suffrage by a second referendum in 1849. In 1868 Iowa became the first state outside New England to amend its constitution. Minnesota followed a year later. In terms of racial integration of the public schools, for example, Massachusetts did so in 1855; Iowa in 1857, Rhode Island in 1866, Connecticut in 1868, and Wisconsin in 1871. The remaining states in the North and Midwest ended school segregation after Illinois (1874).

7. Taylor, "The Blacks," in *They Chose Minnesota: A Survey of the State's Ethnic Groups,* ed. June Drenning Holmquist (St. Paul: Minnesota Historical Society Press, 1981), 76.

8. Ibid., 74.

9. Until the mid-1860s the black population was distributed throughout St. Paul's five wards. But by the late 1860s, blacks began concentrating in the commercial district of Lowertown, which one newspaper editor called "a negro rookery." Ibid., 76.

10. William D. Green, *Degrees of Freedom: The Origins of Civil Rights in Minnesota, 1865–1912* (Minneapolis: University of Minnesota Press, 2015), 109.

11. Frederick Douglass, *Oration Delivered on the Occasion of the Unveiling of the*

*Freedmen's Monument in Memory of Abraham Lincoln, in Lincoln Park, Washington, D.C., April 14th, 1876* (Washington, D.C.: Gibson Brothers, Printers, 1876).

12. Ibid.

13. Eric Foner, *The Fiery Trial: Abraham Lincoln and American Slavery* (New York: W. W. Norton, 2010), 326.

14. William Carlos Martyn, *Wendell Phillips: The Agitator* (New York: Funk and Wagnalls, 1890), 367.

## 1. THE CANDIDATE

1. Eleanor Gridley, *The Story of Abraham Lincoln; or, The Journey from the Log Cabin to the White House* (n.p.: Juvenile Publishing Company, 1900), 239; David Brainerd Williamson, *Life and Public Services of Abraham Lincoln, Sixteenth President of the United States, and Commander-in-Chief of the Army and Navy of the United States* (Philadelphia: T. B. Peterson and Brothers, 1864), 67; F. Lauriston Bullard, "Abraham Lincoln and George Ashmun," *New England Quarterly,* June 1946, 185; William E. Barton, *The Life of Abraham Lincoln,* 2 vols. (Boston: Books, Inc., 1943), 1:437.

2. Williamson, *Life and Public Services of Abraham Lincoln,* 67; Roy P. Basler, ed., *Collected Works of Abraham Lincoln,* 9 vols. (New Brunswick, N.J.: Rutgers University Press, 1953), 4:50–51, 52; *Illinois State Journal,* May 21, 1860; *New York Tribune,* May 25, 1860.

3. Lincoln to Mark Delahay, May 12, 1860, Basler, *Collected Works of Abraham Lincoln,* 4:49.

4. Lincoln, "Endorsement on the Margin of the Missouri Democrat," May 17, 1860, in Basler, *Collected Works of Abraham Lincoln,* 4:50. In his speech against the Compromise of 1850, Seward developed the "higher law" doctrine that would forever be associated with his name, asserting that not only did the Constitution bind the American people to goals incompatible with slavery, "but there is a higher law than the Constitution, which regulates our authority over the domain, and devotes it to the same noble purposes." Eight years later, he proclaimed that the rising hostility, conflict, and violent incidents that were occurring with greater frequency and consequence represented "an *irrepressible* conflict between opposing and enduring forces, and it means that the United States must and will, sooner or later, become either entirely a slaveholding nation, or entirely a free-labor nation." Doris Kearns Goodwin, *Team of Rivals: The Political Genius of Abraham Lincoln* (New York: Simon and Schuster, 2005), 191; Foner, *The Fiery Trial,* 102; Steven Lubet, *Fugitive Justice: Runaways, Rescuers, and Slavery on Trial* (Cambridge, Mass.: Harvard University Press, 2010), 322.

5. Eugene Virgil Smalley, *A History of the Republican Party from Its Organization to the Present Time to Which Is Added a Political History of Minnesota* (St. Paul: E. V. Smalley, 1896), 166.

6. Foner, *The Fiery Trial,* xv–xvi. Another friend, Pennsylvania Republican leader Alexander K. McClure, wrote, "I regard Lincoln as very widely misunderstood in one of the most important attributes of his character. It has been common, during the last twenty-five years, to see publications relating to Lincoln from men who assumed that they enjoyed his full confidence. In most and perhaps all cases the writers believed what they stated, but those who assumed to speak most confidently on the subject were most mistaken. Mr. Lincoln gave his confidence to no living man without reservation. He trusted many, but he trusted only within the carefully-studied limitations of their

usefulness, and when he trusted he confided, as a rule, only to the extent necessary to make that trust available. He had as much faith in mankind as is common amongst men, and it was not because he was of a distrustful nature or because of any specifically selfish attribute of his character that he thus limited his confidence in all his intercourse with men." Paul M. Angle, ed., *Abraham Lincoln, by Some Men Who Knew Him* (Chicago: Americana House, 1950), 106. For the Davis quote, see Richard M. Current, *The Lincoln Nobody Knows* (New York: Hill and Wang, 1958), 12.

7. For an account of Seward's speech and the observations of Charles Adams, who accompanied him to Minnesota, see "Minnesota as Seen by Travelers: Campaigning with Seward in 1860," *Minnesota History* 8, no. 2 (1927): 151.

8. Lincoln letter responding to an editorial by Horace Greeley in the *New York Tribune*, August 20, 1862; *Washington Daily National Intelligencer*, August 23, 1862; Douglas L. Wilson, *Lincoln's Sword: The Presidency and the Power of Words* (New York: Random House, 2006), 148; Foner, *The Fiery Trial*, 228.

9. Merlin Stonehouse, *John Wesley North and the Reform Frontier* (Minneapolis: University of Minnesota Press, 1965), 123; Frank Crosby, *Life of Abraham Lincoln, Sixteenth President of the United States* (Philadelphia: John E. Potter, 1865), 62; Smalley, *A History of the Republican Party*, 166; Barton, *The Life of Abraham Lincoln*, 1:437–38.

## 2. IN DEFENSE OF THE UNION

1. Wilkinson to Burt, December 4, 1860, Wilkinson Letters, Southern Minnesota Historical Center (SMHC), Mankato State University (hereafter Wilkinson Letters).

2. Wilkinson to Ramsey, January 2, 1861, Wilkinson Letters. Apparently, the letter was mailed on January 3.

3. Senator Clark of New Hampshire, Cong. Globe, 37th Cong., 2d Sess., 475–76 (1861). Senators braced for the worst. On December 27, 1860, the customhouse and post office at Charleston, Fort Moultrie, and Castle Pinckney in Charleston harbor, and the revenue cutter *William Atkra* were seized by the authorities of South Carolina. Three days later, the arsenal at Charleston, with seventy thousand arms, was seized. On January 3, 1861, Forts Pulaski and Jackson, and the arsenal at Savannah, Georgia, were seized by state troops. The next day, the arsenal at Mobile, Alabama, was seized, and Fort Morgan at Mobile Bay, Alabama, seized by state troops. On January 9, 1861, *The Star of the West*, bearing reinforcements and provisions for Major Robert Anderson at Fort Sumter, was fired on in Charleston harbor. On January 11, 1861, the United States marine hospital and the arsenal at Baton Rouge were seized by Louisiana troops. The same day, Forts Johnson and Caswell were seized in North Carolina. On January 12, Fort Barrancas and Fort McRee, the naval yard at Pensacola, and the arsenal at Chattahoochee were seized by Florida authorities. On January 14, 1861, the barracks below New Orleans were seized by the state of Louisiana. And on January 15 the U.S. Coast Survey schooner *Dana* was seized by authorities of the state of Florida.

4. Wilkinson to Ramsey, January 17, 1861, Alexander Ramsey Papers, Minnesota Historical Society, St. Paul (hereafter Ramsey Papers).

5. Cong. Globe, 37th Cong., 2d Sess., 476.

6. Reports continued to stream in. In February alone rebel troops seized Union installations in Arkansas and Louisiana. In Texas they seized Forts Chadbourne and Belknap on February 20, the barracks and other works at Brazos Santiago on the twenty-first, and on the twenty-second, Union general David Twiggs surrendered to Texas

authorities all remaining military posts in the state and attendant property amounting to $1 million.

7. Richard Moe, *The Last Full Measure: The Life and Death of the First Minnesota Volunteers* (St. Paul: Minnesota Historical Society Press, 2001), 73.

8. Wilkinson to Ramsey, January 17, 1861.

9. "Speech of Hon. M. S. Wilkinson, of Minnesota, on the Constitution as It Is; Delivered in the Senate of the United States, March 2,1861." https://catalog .hathitrust.org/Record/009596932.

10. Rhoda R. Gilman, "April, 1861: Minnesota Goes to War," *Minnesota History,* March 1961, 212

11. Wilkinson to Buck, July 7, 1861, Wilkinson Letters.

12. *Boston Daily Evening Transcript,* August 31, 1861.

13. Lyde Cullen Sizer, *The Political Work of Northern Women Writers and the Civil War, 1850–1872* (Chapel Hill: University of North Carolina Press, 2000), 102.

14. Winifred A. Harbison, "Lincoln and the Faribault Fire-Eater," *Minnesota History,* September 1939, 272.

15. *St. Paul Press,* September 19, 1861.

16. Wilkinson wrote, "I have no hesitation in stating that I heartily sympathize with General Fremont in the position assumed by him in regard to the disposition to be made of slave property of rebels in the State of Missouri; and hence I regret that the President has felt constrained to modify the proclamation issued by that officer. In my judgment slavery lies at the foundation of this unholy and wicked war, which is now being waged against the Government and the peace of the country. And I confess, that I can see no good reason why a blow should not be struck at slavery, if such a course would weaken the enemy, and paralyze the arm of him who is laboring to destroy the Government." *St. Paul Press,* October 15, 1861.

17. The three senators accused of treason were Jesse Bright (Indiana), Lazarus Powell (Kentucky), and Benjamin Stark (Oregon). On December 16, the Bright hearing began. Cong. Globe, 37th Cong., 2d Sess., 470.

18. Ibid., 655.

19. Ibid., 891; U.S. Historical Senate Office, *United States Senate Elections and Censure Cases, 1793–1990* (Washington, D.C.: Government Printing Office, 1995), 112–13.

20. Cong. Globe, 37th Cong., 2d Sess., 966.

21. On March 14, the Senate voted down the resolution, 11 yeas to 28 nays, and permitted Powell to retain his seat. Ibid.

22. Trumbull said, "I now move to proceed to consideration of Senate bill No. 151, which is the confiscation bill that we had up yesterday. I am sorry to have to insist on this bill as against the case of the Senator from Oregon; but it has been made a special order, and if it is crowded out by that case, it goes over, and I do not know when we may get it up again. It is a very important public measure, now under consideration, having been discussed yesterday, and I must insist that we proceed with it." Ibid., 963.

23. Heath Hardage Lee, *Winnie Davis: Daughter of the Lost Cause* (Lincoln: University of Nebraska Press, 2014), 92–93.

24. Cong. Globe, 37th Cong., 2d Sess., 1375 (1862).

25. Ibid.

26. Ibid.

27. Ibid., 1375–76. Former U.S. senator Robert Augustus Toombs of Georgia was a

founding father of the Confederacy, its first secretary of state, and a Confederate general. Former U.S. senator Louis Trezevant Wigfall of Texas and Confederate senator was noted for his bombastic oratory. Former U.S. senator Jefferson Davis of Mississippi became the president of the Confederate States of America. Former U.S. senator John Cabell Breckinridge of Kentucky became secretary of state of the Confederacy in 1865.

28. Ibid., 1376.

29. Ibid.

30. Troops from Massachusetts arrived in the city by railway. Because the line to Washington was situated on the other side of Baltimore, the troops had to march through the streets. As they did, a mob formed and began assaulting them with brickbats, paving stones, and clubs, wounding a number of the soldiers and killing two. Ibid.

31. Ibid.

32. Ibid.

33. Ibid., 1376–78. Emphasis in the original.

34. Ibid., 1377. In July 1862, President Lincoln signed the bill that admitted the new state of West Virginia to the Union; Carlile was to be its senator. To Davis, who argued that the emancipation of slaves in the District would threaten slavery in his state, Wilkinson responded mockingly, "[The Senator from Kentucky's] defense of human slavery is more offensive in manner and in argument than any that I have listened to on this floor, if we except the foolish fulminations of the crazy [Louis] Wigfall. The honorable Senator from Kentucky [Davis] contends that the natural right to a slave is the same and rests upon the same authority as our right to a hog, a sheep, or a piece of land." Ibid., 1378.

35. Ibid., 1379.

36. Ibid., 1680. The Second Confiscation Act would be signed in July.

37. Cong. Globe, 37th Cong., 2d Sess., 2992.

38. "Sir," Wilkinson said, "I cannot understand this. Why is it that the Senator from Illinois, on the other side of the Chamber [Mr. Browning], while his own constituents, his neighbors, and his friends who have gone forth to defend and uphold the Government, are wasting away like snow before the influences of the April sun, and while those who were left behind are being taxed to support this war to the extent never before known in this country, stands here and exhibits such unmistakable hostility to a measure which is calculated to make the guilty authors of all this suffering and of all this crime bear some portion of the burdens which he is so ready to place upon the shoulders of the liberty-loving citizens of the loyal States of the Union? Why is it that he is so sensitive when the interests of traitors are attacked, and yet so ready to pour out the property and the blood of Union men like water to save this Union?" Ibid., 2990.

39. Ibid., 2958.

40. Ibid., 2990. He also set his sights on another Republican senator—Edgar A. Cowan of Pennsylvania—and he wondered how both men could "go home to their constituents, where there is a sepulcher in every garden, over which the grass has not yet grown, and in the midst of the gloom and desolation and mourning that surround them. . . . How could they justify to their own people why traitors should not pay for this war?"

41. "[Lincoln] had placed himself upon the record on the question of the right and power of Congress to confiscate the property of rebels. On the 6th of August last [1861] Congress passed, as a war measure, a law confiscating the property and setting free

the slaves of certain rebel masters, and the President at once approved the act. Had he entertained the sentiments of the Senator from Illinois he would have returned that bill to the House in which it originated, with a message declaring that Congress was usurping prerogatives which were, by the Constitution, vested in the President alone, and that it would be dangerous to the liberties of the people were he to permit such an unwarranted exercise of power on the part of Congress. But Lincoln did no such thing; he gave the measure his ready and earnest support." Ibid.

42. *U.S. Statutes at Large, Treaties, and Proclamations of the United States of America,* vol. 12, chap. CXCV (Boston: Little, Brown, 1863), 589–92.

43. Cong. Globe, 37th Cong., 2d Sess., 2996.

44. Ibid., 2997. Senator James Doolittle also made the case for appropriations, but Davis and senators from the border states argued against the amendment, for they maintained that it would destabilize slave ownership of Union men within their respective states.

45. Ibid., 3006. For a reference to Cowan's motive in voting with the Radicals, see B. F. Pershing, "Senator Edgar A. Cowan," *Western Pennsylvania Historical Magazine* 4, no. 4 (1921): 228–29. https://journals.psu.edu/wph/article/viewFile /1265/1113.

46. Cong. Globe, 37th Cong., 3d Sess., 942–44; David W. Hamilton, *The Limits of Sovereignty: Property Confiscation in the Union and the Confederacy during the Civil War* (Chicago: University of Chicago Press, 2007), 23–24; Silvana R. Siddali, *From Property to Person: Slavery and the Confiscation Acts, 1861–1862* (Baton Rouge: Louisiana State University Press, 2005), appendix 2.

47. Kentuckian Garrett Davis insisted that the crisis facing the nation was a white man's war, a fact even Northerners understood. "Sir, I know the soldiery of the Northwest. [He was referring to Minnesotans, Wilkinson's constituents.] They want no negro auxiliaries in this war; they would feel themselves degraded fighting by their side. They feel that the white race are amply strong in numbers, in outrage, in all the elements of a martial people, to bring this contest to a close without the ignominy of enlisting the negro as a fellow." Davis had no objection, however, if they were used exclusively for "all camp and military labor." Wilkinson responded, "The Senator from Kentucky seems to think that negroes are inhuman and barbarous when they once smell blood." Cong. Globe, 37th Cong., 2d Sess., 3204.

48. Ibid., 3249.

49. Ibid., 3355–56.

## 3. THE INDIAN'S GUARDIAN

1. David Roediger notes that in the Northeast, where the white population was most concentrated, direct experience with Indians was less than common. "Anti-Indian racism and frontier myths had considerable staying power." Roediger, *The Wages of Whiteness: Race and the Making of American Working Class,* rev. ed. (London: Verso, 1991), 21.

2. Missionary Stephen Riggs assembled two dozen Christian Dakota and mixedbloods at Hazelwood where they adopted white dress, took up farming, and formed a "republic." Mary L. Wingerd, *North Country: The Making of Minnesota* (Minneapolis: University of Minnesota Press, 2010), 273, 287, 307.

3. Ibid., 267, 273.

4. Cong. Globe, 37th Cong., 2d Sess., 555, 815.

5. Ibid., 891, 916.

6. Ibid., 1228, 1951. His bill would apply to any Indian, not those of specific tribes. Ibid., 2082.

7. Ibid., 2082. Senator Fessenden was referring to the 1851 Indian suffrage provision in the territorial constitution that extended voting rights to civilized Indians.

8. Willard Hughes Rollings, "Citizenship and Suffrage: The Native American Struggle for Civil Rights in the American West, 1830–1965," *Nevada Law Journal* 5 (Fall 2004): 129. See generally Francis Paul Prucha, *American Indian Policy in Crisis: Christian Reformers and the Indians, 1865–1900* (Norman: University of Oklahoma Press, 1976).

9. Eric Foner, *Free Soil, Free Labor, Free Men: The Ideology of the Republican Party before the Civil War* (New York: Oxford University Press, 1995), xx, xxvii.

10. Cong. Globe, 37th Cong., 2d Sess., pt. 3, 2082 (1862).

11. Correspondence between Whipple and Wilkinson and Aldrich, April–June 1862, cited in Prucha, *American Indian Policy in Crisis*, 7n9.

12. Bishop Henry Whipple, *Lights and Shadows of a Long Episcopate* (New York: Macmillan, 1899), 50–52; also see William Watts Folwell, *A History of Minnesota*, 4 vols. (St. Paul: Minnesota Historical Society Press, 1921–30), 2:207–8.

13. Whipple to Ramsey, November 8, 1862, box 40, letter book 4, Henry Benjamin Whipple Papers, Minnesota Historical Society, St. Paul (hereafter Whipple Papers).

14. Dix to Lincoln, April 21, 1862, roll 1, M825, Letters Received, Indian Division, Office of the Secretary of the Interior, Record Group 48, National Archives, Washington, D.C.

15. Rice to Whipple, April 22, 26, 1862, box 3, Whipple Papers.

16. Whipple to Rice, April 30, 1862, letter book 3, Whipple Papers.

17. Aldrich to Whipple, June 12, 1862, box 3, Whipple Papers; David A. Nichols, *Lincoln and the Indians: Civil War Policy and Politics* (St. Paul: Minnesota Historical Society Press, 2012), 134–36.

18. Whipple to Wilkinson, April 30, 1862; Wilkinson to Whipple, May 8, 1862, box 3, Whipple Papers; Nichols, *Lincoln and the Indians*, 139.

19. Whipple, *Lights and Shadows*, 136–37.

20. Cong. Globe, 37th Cong., 2d Sess., pt. 3, 2091 (1862).

21. Ibid.

22. Historian David Nichols reports that Henry Hastings Sibley of Minnesota provides an even clearer example of how the system could be a "pathway to power" for a clever man. While being the territorial delegate to Congress he represented the fur traders at the Dakota treaty negotiations at Traverse des Sioux in 1851, which promised the tribe $475,000 in exchange for land. However, Sibley succeeded in claiming $145,000 of that amount as money due him for overpayments to the Dakota for furs. Over the objection of the tribe, agent Alexander Ramsey, also territorial governor, approved the claim, making the already financially secure Sibley even richer. Charges against Ramsey of collusion that were brought by a rival were later investigated and dropped by a Senate committee. He later succeeded Sibley as governor in 1859. Nichols, *Lincoln and the Indians*, 20; Lucile M. Kane, "The Sioux Treaties and the Traders," *Minnesota History*, June 1951, 79. See generally, Wingerd, *North Country*, chapter 8.

23. Alan Alexrod, *Profiles in Folly: History's Worst Decisions and Why They Went Wrong* (New York: Sterling Publishing, 2008), 173–74.

24. Cong. Globe, 37th Cong., 2d Sess., 2091.

25. Ibid.

26. Ibid.

27. "Minnesota as Seen by Travelers," 151.

28. Walter Stahr, *Seward: Lincoln's Indispensable Man* (New York: Simon and Schuster, 2012), 354.

29. Wilkinson to W. H. Seward, March 15, 1861, box 1, Clark H. Thompson Papers, Minnesota Historical Society, St. Paul (hereafter Thompson Papers); Nichols, *Lincoln and the Indians*, 66.

30. Thompson Bros. to Thompson, April 11, 1862, E. Thompson to C. Thompson, July 26, 1862, I. H. B. Burbank Co. to Thompson, January 28, 1862, box 2, Thompson Papers; Aldrich to Thompson, June 20, 1862, box 1, Thompson Papers.

31. Cong. Globe, 37th Congress, 2d Sess., 2091.

32. Ibid., 2093.

33. Ibid.

34. Ibid., 2093–94.

35. Ibid.

36. Collamore to Dole, April 21, 1862, "Kansas Memory" at State Archives, Topeka Kansas, Kansas Historical Society. Retrieved on May 14, 2015, http://www.civil waronthewesternborder.org/content/george-w-collamore-william-p-dole.

37. Cong. Globe, 37th Cong., 2d Sess., 2162.

38. Ibid.

39. Ibid., 2095.

40. Nichols, *Lincoln and the Indians*, 7, 11–13.

41. Ibid., 15.

42. Ibid., 20–21.

43. Cong. Globe, 37th Cong., 2d Sess., 1692 (1862).

44. Ibid.

45. Ibid., 2163.

46. Ibid.

47. Wilkinson to Whipple, May 8, 1862, box 3, Whipple Papers.

48. "The Progress of the Indians in Minnesota," *St. Cloud Democrat*, August 14, 1862.

49. Cong. Globe, 37th Cong., 2d Sess., 3371 (1862).

50. Wilkinson to Thompson, July 12, 1862, box 2, Thompson Papers.

51. Cong. Globe, 37th Cong., 2d Sess., 3404.

52. *St. Cloud Democrat*, August 16, 1862. The names Chippewa and Ojibwe are interchangeable.

## 4. A WILD PANIC PREVAILS

1. "An Indian Raid," *St. Paul Daily Press*, August 20, 1862.

2. *St. Cloud Democrat*, August 21, 1862.

3. Treaty with the Sioux, September 29, 1837, 7 Stat. 540; Treaty with the Sisseton and Wahpeton Bands of the Sioux, July 23, 1851, 10 Stat. 949; Treaty with the Mdewakanton and Wahpekute Bands of the Sioux, August 5, 1851, 10 Stat. 954.

4. Gwen Westerman and Bruce White, *Mni Sota Makoce: The Land of the Dakota*

(St. Paul: Minnesota Historical Society Press, 2010), 148–54; Folwell, *A History of Minnesota*, 2:216–19.

5. Nichols, *Lincoln and the Indians*, 65–66, 76.

6. Kenneth Carley, *The Dakota War of 1862: Minnesota's Other Civil War* (St. Paul: Minnesota Historical Society Press, 1976), 3.

7. Gary Clayton Anderson and Alan R. Woolworth, eds., *Through Dakota Eyes: Narrative Accounts of the Minnesota Indian War of 1862* (St. Paul: Minnesota Historical Society Press, 1988), 32.

8. Wingerd, *North Country*, 301–2.

9. Folwell, *History of Minnesota*, 2:219–21, 214–15.

10. Carol Chomsky, "The United States–Dakota War Trials: A Study in Military Injustice," *Stanford Law Review* 43, no. 1 (November 1990): 12, 17.

11. Carley, *Dakota War of 1862*, 4.

12. Whipple, *Lights and Shadows*, 50–52; also see Folwell, *History of Minnesota*, 2:207–8.

13. Carley, *Dakota War of 1862*, 5; Nichols, *Lincoln and the Indians*, 77; Michael Keigan, *Heroes of the Uprising* (Bloomington, Ind.: AuthorHouse, 2012), 35.

14. Roy W. Meyer, *History of the Santee Sioux* (Lincoln: University of Nebraska Press, 1967), 115; Gary Clayton Anderson, *Little Crow: Spokesman for the Dakota* (St. Paul: Minnesota Historical Society Press, 1986), 85.

15. "Good Star Woman's Recollections," in Anderson and Woolworth, *Through Dakota Eyes*, 52–53.

16. Chomsky, "The United States–Dakota War Trials," 18.

17. Jane Grey Cannon Swisshelm, *Half a Century* (Chicago: Jansen, McClurg, 1880), 223.

18. Ibid., 225.

19. *New York Tribune*, August 29 and September 5, 1862; *Report to the Commissioner on Indian Affairs, 1863*, 286–88; Isaac V. D. Heard, *History of the Sioux War and Massacres of 1862 and 1863* (New York: Harper and Brothers, 1864), 44 (for the "whipped" quote).

20. Swisshelm, *Half a Century*, 229.

21. The term "Black Republican" was typically a derogatory term used by critics of the Republican Party for its support of abolition. The term was used in the North, as well as the South, whenever such critics felt they could exploit the racial fears of white voters. In 1855 Ohio governor Salmon Chase complained that all Democrats, who had little interest in any issue except race, "simply [talked] about the universal nigger problem, as they call it." Foner, *Free Soil, Free Labor, Free Man*, 264. The term was also widely used in Minnesota in talking about black suffrage and homesteading, as will be discussed in part III of this book.

22. Report to the Commissioner on Indian Affairs, 286: Folwell, *History of Minnesota*, 2:234; William D. Green, *A Peculiar Imbalance: The Fall and Rise of Racial Equality in Minnesota, 1837–1869* (Minneapolis: University of Minnesota Press, 2015), 117.

23. Moses N. Adams, "The Sioux Outbreak in the Year 1862, with Notes of Missionary Work among the Sioux," *Collections of the Minnesota Historical Society* (St. Paul: The Society, 1899), 9:433; Jeanette De Camp Sweet, "Mrs. J. E. De Camp Sweet's Narrative of Her Captivity in the Sioux Outbreak of 1862," *Collections of the Minnesota Historical Society* (St. Paul: Pioneer Press Company, 1894), 6:357; see also Stephen Return Riggs, *Mary and I: Forty Years with the Sioux* (Chicago: W. G. Holmes, 1880), 172–73.

24. Stephen Return Riggs, *Tah-koo Wah-kan; or, The Gospel among the Dakotas* (Boston: Congregational Sabbath-School and Publishing Society, 1889), 331.

25. Alvin C. Gluek Jr., "The Sioux Uprising: A Problem in International Relations," *Minnesota History* 34, no. 8 (Winter 1955): 319; Carley, *Sioux Uprising*, 84; Anderson, *Little Crow*, 177–78.

26. "Mr. Lo" was Swisshelm's derisive term for the Dakota. Swisshelm, *Half a Century*, 226, 227.

27. Ibid., 227.

28. The Santee Sioux, who included the Dakota most involved in the conflict of 1862, were more largely composed of "eastern Dakota," or the Mdewakantons, Wahpe-kutes, Sissetons, and Wahpetons. They resided in the Upper Mississippi River valley, where prairie and forest met to provide a rich array of resources. Wingerd, *North Country*, 4.

29. Galbraith to Thompson, January 31, 1862, box 2, Thompson Papers; Nichols, *Lincoln and the Indians*, 68.

30. William R. Snider to Thompson, January 31, 1862, box 2, Thompson Papers.

31. Mix to Thompson, June 29, 1861; Aldrich to Thompson, November 12, 1861; Wilkinson to Thompson, July 11, 1861, box 1, Thompson Papers.

32. Balcombe was a native of New York appointed by Lincoln in 1861 and reappointed by the president in 1865.

33. Nichols, *Lincoln and the Indians*, 70.

34. Wilkinson to Thompson, July 21, 1862, box 2, Thompson Papers.

35. Wilkinson to Burt, August 23, 1862, Wilkinson Letters.

36. Joint telegram from Wilkinson, Dole, and Nicolay to Lincoln. August 27, 1862, official records, series I, vol. 13, 599–600. Abraham Lincoln Papers at the Library of Congress, transcribed and annotated by the Lincoln Studies Center, Knox College, Galesburg, Ill. https://www.knox.edu/about-knox/lincoln-studies-center/research-and-publication. Also see David A. Nichols, "The Other Civil War: Lincoln and the Indians," *Minnesota History*, Spring 1974, 3, 5–6.

37. Montgomery to parents, August 23, 1862, Thomas Montgomery and Family Papers, roll M235, Minnesota Historical Society, St. Paul (hereafter Montgomery Family Papers).

38. *St. Cloud Democrat*, August 28, 1862.

39. Foner, *The Fiery Trial*, 223–24. Also see Harold Holzer, *Lincoln and the Power of the Press* (New York: Simon and Schuster, 2014), 397.

40. *St. Cloud Democrat*, August 28, 1862.

41. *New York Tribune*, August 5, 1862; Benjamin Quarles, *Lincoln and the Negro* (New York: Da Capo Press, 1991), 153–55.

42. For a thorough review of the work of the commission and trials, see Chomsky, "United States–Dakota War Trials."

43. Order no. 55, issued at Camp Release, September 28, 1862.

44. Sibley to Pope, September 28, 1862, reprinted in U.S. Department of War, *War of the Rebellion: A Compilation of the Official Records of the Union and Confederate Armies*, series I, vol. 13 (Washington, D.C.: Government Printing Office, 1885), 687.

45. Ibid., 685–86.

46. Four of the commission members were Colonel William Crooks, Captain Hiram P. Grant, Captain Hiram S. Bailey, and Lieutenant Rollin C. Olin, who was designated

as judge advocate. Sibley also appointed Adjutant Isaac Heard of McPhail's Minnesota Mounted Rangers as recorder.

47. Chomsky, "United States–Dakota War Trials," 25nn70, 71.
48. Ibid., 26–27.
49. Nichols, "The Other Civil War," 8, citing *Diary of Gideon Welles: Secretary of the Navy under Lincoln and Johnson,* 3 vols. (Boston: Houghton Mifflin, 1911), 1:171.
50. Nichols, *Lincoln and the Indians,* 9, citing Ramsey to Lincoln, November 10, 1862.
51. Chomsky, "United States–Dakota War Trials," 27–28.

## 5. LINCOLN'S DECISION

1. Williamson to S. B. Treat, November 5, 1862. http://usdakotawar.org/history/after math/forced-marches-imprisonment#.
2. *St. Paul Daily Press,* November 8, 1862.
3. Samuel J. Brown, "The Captivity"; "The Experience, Privations and Dangers of Samuel Brown, and Others, While Prisoners of the Hostile Sioux, during the Massacre and War of 1862," *Mankato Weekly Review,* April 27, May 4, 1897.
4. Sibley to Mrs. Henry Sibley, November 12, 1862, roll 11, frame 679, Henry Hastings Sibley Papers, Minnesota Historical Society, St. Paul (hereafter Sibley Papers).
5. Montgomery to brothers, Camp Lincoln, Mankato. November 5, 1862, M235, Montgomery Family Papers.
6. Montgomery to parents, Camp Lincoln, Mankato, November 5, 6, 1862, Montgomery Family Papers.
7. Nichols, "The Other Civil War," 9, citing Lincoln to Pope, November 10, 1862, in Basler, *Collected Works of Abraham Lincoln,* 5:493; Pope to Lincoln, November 11, 1862, U.S. Department of War, *War of the Rebellion: A Compilation of the Official Records,* series I, vol. 13, 788.
8. Pope to Lincoln, November 12, 1862; see Nichols, "The Other Civil War," 9n31. Also see Nichols, *Lincoln and the Indians,* 101.
9. Nichols, "The Other Civil War," 9.
10. Walt Bachman, "Colonel Miller's War," in *Trails of Tears: Minnesota's Dakota Indian Exile Begins,* ed. Mary Hawler Bakeman and Antona M. Richardson (Roseville, Minn.: Prairie Echoes, 2008), 108.
11. Miller to Sibley, November 18, 21, 1862, Letters Received, part 3, entry 346, Record Group 393, National Archives and Records Administration (NARA), College Park, Md.; Bachman, "Colonel Miller's War," 109; Thomas Williamson to Stephen Riggs, November 17, 1862, Riggs Family Papers, Minnesota Historical Society, St. Paul; Bachman, "Colonel Miller's War," 108–9.
12. Miller to Sibley, November 22, 1862, Letters Received, part 3, entry 346, Record Group 393, NARA; Bachman, "Colonel Miller's War," 109.
13. Bachman, "Colonel Miller's War," 109.
14. Miller to Rollin Olin, assistant adjutant general to Sibley, and former commissioner over the Dakota trials, November 26, 1862, Letters Received, part 3, entry 346, Record Group 393, NARA, cited in Bachman, "Colonel Miller's War," 120n16.
15. Miller to Olin, November 30, 1862, ibid.
16. Miller to Olin, November 29, 1862, ibid.
17. "Recollections of Theodore Carter," *St. Peter Herald,* April 13, 1906.
18. Bachman, "Colonel Miller's War," 110nn26, 27.

19. Montgomery to parents, December 17, 1862, M235, Montgomery Family Papers.
20. "Recollections of Theodore Carter."
21. Montgomery to parents, December 17, 1862. Montgomery Family Papers.
22. "Recollections of Theodore Carter."
23. General Order No. 6 (December 6, 1862), enclosed in letter from Miller to Olin, December 6, 1862, Letters Received, part 3, entry 346, Record Group 393, NARA.
24. Proclamation of Govenor Alexander Ramsey, December 6, 1862, roll 39, Ramsey Papers.
25. Cong. Globe, 37th Congress, 3d Sess., 13 (1862).
26. Ibid.
27. Ibid.
28. Ibid.
29. Bishop Whipple to editor of the *Republican Pioneer,* November 1862, Whipple Papers. See also Chomsky, "The United States–Dakota War Trials," 32n118.
30. Walt Bachman, *Northern Slave, Black Dakota: The Life and Times of Joseph Godfrey* (Bloomington, Minn.: Pond Dakota Press, 2013), 42–47.
31. S. Exec. Do. No.7, Cong. Globe, 37th Cong., 3d Sess., 1–2; Lincoln to Sibley, December 6, 1862, reprinted in Basler, *Collected Works of Abraham Lincoln,* 5:542–43.
32. Lincoln to Senate, December 11, 1862, in Basler, *Collected Works of Abraham Lincoln,* 5:550–51; Bachman, *Northern Slave, Black Dakota,* 282.
33. Whipple to Rice, November 12, 1862; Rice to Whipple, November 27, 1862, Whipple Papers.
34. Riggs to his son, November 1862, 144.G.7.1B, Stephen R. Riggs and Family Papers, Minnesota Historical Society, St. Paul. See also "Tried and Sentenced," retrieved May 14, 2015, http://www.mnrivervalley.com/wp-content/uploads/2014/09 /CampReleasepanel3.pdf.
35. Letter to *St. Paul Pioneer,* 1862. Also see http://law2.umkc.edu/faculty/projects /ftrials/Dakota/Dakota_excerpts.html#LETTER%20FROM%20REV.%20 STEPHEN.
36. Jane Grey Swisshelm, "Dakota (Sioux) Indians," *St. Cloud Democrat,* November 13, 1862.
37. Pope to Lincoln, November 24, 1862, in *Minnesota in the Civil and Indian Wars, 1861– 1865,* 2 vols. (St. Paul: Printed for the State by the Pioneer Press Company, 1892), 2:290; Ramsey to Lincoln, November 28, 1862, Lincoln Papers, Minnesota Historical Society, St. Paul. The meeting of Lincoln, Wilkinson, and Aldrich is reported in Basler, *Collected Works of Abraham Lincoln,* 5:493, and *New York Tribune,* November 29, 1862; see also Nichols, "The Other Civil War," 11.
38. H. B. Whipple to editor of the *St. Paul Pioneer,* undated, box 40, letter book 3, Whipple Papers; Nichols, *Lincoln and the Indians,* 103–4. See also Chomsky, "The United States–Dakota War Trials," 32n118.
39. *St. Paul Pioneer,* December 3, 17, 1863; *St. Paul Press,* December 4, 1862; Folwell, *History of Minnesota,* 2:208–9.
40. See, in general, Rhoda R. Gilman, *Henry Sibley and the U.S.–Dakota War of 1862* (St. Paul: Minnesota Historical Society Press, 2012), chapter 3.
41. Welles, *Diary,* 1:186.
42. Nichols, "The Other Civil War," 11.

43. Ibid.

44. Wilkinson to Ramsey, December 9, 1862, Ramsey Papers. See also Board of Commissioners, eds., *Minnesota in the Civil and Indian Wars, 1861–1865: Official Reports and Correspondence*, 2 vols. (St. Paul: Pioneer Press Company, 1890, 1899), 2:291.

45. William E. Lass, "The Removal from Minnesota of the Sioux and Winnebago Indians," *Minnesota History*, December 1963, 354.

46. Thomas Hughes, *History of Blue Earth County* (Chicago: Middle West Publishing, 1978), 60, 97, 99.

47. Carley, *The Dakota War of 1862*, 76.

48. Cong. Globe, 37th Cong., 3d Sess., 100, 104. Also see Carley, *The Dakota War of 1862*, 76, 79; Lass, "The Removal from Minnesota of the Sioux and Winnebago Indians," 354.

49. "What Does Senator Wilkinson Mean?," *St. Cloud Democrat*, December 16, 1862.

50. Cong. Globe, 38th Cong., 3d Sess., 1282 (1863).

51. Nichols, *Lincoln and the Indians*, 204.

52. See generally John Christgau, *Incident at the Otterville Station: A Civil War Story of Slavery and Rescue* (Lincoln: University of Nebraska Press, 2013), 96.

53. Cong. Globe, 39th Cong., 1st Sess., 145 (1864). Wilkinson said, "Sometime in the month of September or October last, five regiments of Minnesota volunteers were sent into the State of Missouri. One of these regiments, the ninth Minnesota volunteers, was sent to and stationed at Jefferson City. A few days after they encamped at that city, a negro came into the camp and told the private soldiers that he was a free man, and that his master was a rebel who had gone into the service of the Confederate government. He also stated to the soldiers that some men, by the permission of the commander of that post, one General Brown, I believe, had the wife and children of the negro on board the cars, taking them South for sale. These soldiers having been recently sent down there from the pure atmosphere of Minnesota, thought that this was an outrage, and about forty of them, as I learn, started for the depot, found the train of cars standing there with the passengers all on board, and took the woman and children out of the hands of the traitors who were conveying them out of the State, and delivered them over to their husband and father. This was probably eight weeks ago. Thereupon forty of these soldiers were arrested and put into prison, where they now remain, as I understand." Ibid.

54. Mark E. Neely, *The Civil War and the Limits of Destruction* (Cambridge, Mass.: Harvard University Press, 2007), 171; Cong. Globe, 39th Cong., 2d Sess., 73.

55. Neely, *The Civil War and the Limits of Destruction*, 171.

56. Ibid.

57. Mauriel Joslyn, "U.S. Policy of Retaliation on Confederate Prisoners of War," in *Journal of Confederate History*, vol. 13, *Andersonville: The Southern Perspective*, ed. J. H. Segars (Gretna, La: Pelican Publishing, 2001), 144–45.

58. Montgomery to parents and brothers, December 19, 1862, Montgomery Family Papers.

59. Riggs, *Mary and I*, 185–86.

60. *Faribault Central Republican*, January 7, 1863; Bachman, *Northern Slave, Black Dakota*, 288.

61. Swisshelm, *Half a Century*, 233–37.
62. Swisshelm to *St. Cloud Democrat*, February 23, 1862, in Jane Grey Swisshelm, *Crusader and Feminist: Letters of Jane Grey Swisshelm, 1858–1865*, ed. Arthur Larsen (St. Paul: Minnesota Historical Society Press, 1934), 184.
63. Sylvia D. Hoffert, *Jane Grey Swisshelm: An Unconventional Life, 1815–1884* (Chapel Hill: University of North Carolina Press, 2004), 153.
64. Swisshelm, *Half a Century*, 234.
65. Regarding Swisshelm's effigy, see ibid., 201.
66. Ibid., 236–37.

## 6. PIKE ISLAND

1. Alfred M. Potekin, "Rev. Robert Thomas Hickman: Preacher (col'd), Rail Splitter and Slave Liberator," box 230, Work Projects Administration—Federal Writers' Project (March 4, 1936), Annals of Minnesota, Negroes in Minnesota, Minnesota Historical Society; "Biographies of Black Pioneers," *Gopher Historian*, Winter 1968–69, 7, 17; David Vassar Taylor, "Pilgrim's Progress: Black St. Paul and the Making of an Urban Ghetto, 1870–1930" (Ph.D. diss., University of Minnesota, 1977), 24–26; Robert Dykstra, *Bright Radical Star: Black Freedom and White Supremacy on the Hawkeye Frontier* (Cambridge, Mass.: Harvard University Press, 1993), 196; Green, *A Peculiar Imbalance*, 129.
2. Ibid.
3. *St. Paul Daily Press*, May 6, 1863.
4. Ibid.
5. "The people of the State are prepared to welcome a large accession of negroes to our laboring population; and unless there should be a great and rapid improvement in the manners and minds of the kind of people who now mainly monopolize the menial branches of industry and claim the monopoly by right of race and natural status—not even the rigorous laws of climate will be sufficient to withstand the more potential law of demand, or prevent such an influx of negro emigrants as may be necessary for the instruction and civilization of the now dominant element of our lowest laboring class." *St. Paul Daily Press*, May 16, 1863.
6. *St. Paul Daily Press*, May 16, 1863.
7. Ibid.; Taylor, "Pilgrim's Progress," 8–9.
8. Minnesota Territory, House Journal, 1854, 258–59, Minnesota Historical Society.
9. Minnesota House Journal, 1860, 242.
10. Folwell, *History of Minnesota*, 2:344.
11. *St. Paul Daily Press*, May 9, 1863; Folwell, *History of Minnesota*, 2:344.
12. *St. Paul Daily Press*, May 12, 1863.
13. Corinne L. Monjeau-Marz, *The Dakota Indian Internment at Fort Snelling, 1862–1864* (St. Paul: Prairie Smoke Press, 2005), 40–41.
14. "Good Star Woman's Recollections," in Anderson and Woolworth, *Through Dakota Eyes*, 264.
15. Riggs, *Mary and I*, 192.
16. Ibid., 219.
17. *St. Paul Press*, May 5, 1863; Green, *A Peculiar Imbalance*, 124.
18. "Contraband-Mules," *St. Paul Weekly Pioneer and Democrat*, May 8, 1863, 8.

19. Green, *A Peculiar Imbalance*, 124. The next time the *Davenport* arrived in St. Paul, ten days later, it towed a barge carrying 218 "contraband" blacks from St. Louis. The reaction of the mob meeting the transport was as threatening as before. The steamboat escort by Chaplain J. D. White and a rather passive contingent of soldiers from Company C of the Thirty-Seventh Iowa Volunteer Infantry Regiment towed the newest black arrivals to Fort Snelling, where they could safely disembark. The next day, however, after returning from Fort Snelling, the *Davenport* landed at St. Paul bearing 417 Winnebago Indians before departing for St. Louis. This time, no mob formed to assault the passengers. Instead, in a bizarre parody of the times, according to the *St. Paul Daily Press*, as the boat docked for three hours, large numbers of citizens came to "view the Native Americans and make purchases of Indian trinkets." One observer found that "the Indians showed their shrewdness by taking advantage of the demand and charging exorbitant prices. Bows, such as they sold at the Fort for twenty-five to fifty cents, brought one dollar and a half and two dollars quite readily. Ten cent arrows at the Fort were twenty-five cents on the levee, and two dollar strings of beads five dollars." *Daily Press*, May 16, 1863.

20. Riggs, *Mary and I*, 224.

21. Ibid., 197.

22. The boat landing for the fort was directly below the end of the bluff. In later years a stairway ran up the steep slope, and a wagon road crept slowly up the bank of the Minnesota River along the stone wall to enter the fort between the two towers. Russell Fridley, "Fort Snelling: From Military Post to Historical Site," *Minnesota History*, December 1956, 180.

23. Marcus Hansen, *Old Fort Snelling, 1819–1858* (Iowa City: State Historical Society of Iowa, 1918), 27; Folwell, *History of Minnesota*, 1:424–28.

24. In 1861 Henry David Thoreau visited Fort Snelling while on a journey to the west for his health. Franklin B. Sanborn, ed., *The First and Last Journeys of Thoreau*, 2 vols. (Boston, 1908), 2:41.

25. Loren Johnson, "Reconstructing Old Fort Snelling," *Minnesota History*, Fall 1970, 88.

26. Ibid.

27. Ibid., 92.

28. Mary J. Newson, "Memories of Fort Snelling in Civil War Days," *Minnesota History* 15, no. 4 (1934): 398.

29. Ibid., 397, 399.

30. See Green, *Degrees of Freedom*.

31. *St. Paul Daily Press*, February 10, 1863.

32. *St. Paul Weekly Pioneer and Democrat*, March 27, 1863; Iver Bernstein, *The New York City Draft Riots: Their Significance for American Society and Politics in the Age of the Civil War* (New York: Oxford University Press, 1991), 43; Tyler G. Anbinder, *Nativism and Slavery: The Northern Know Nothings and the Politics of the 1850s* (New York: Oxford University Press, 1994), 271.

33. Jon Butler, "Communities and Congregations: The Black Church in St. Paul, 1860–1900," *Journal of Negro History* 56, no. 2 (1971): 118–34.

34. Bachman, *Northern Slave, Black Dakota*, 1–22. Also see Lea VanderVelde, *Mrs. Dred Scott: A Life on Slavery's Frontier* (New York: Oxford University Press, 2009).

35. Post Return report, Fort Snelling, June 1863–September 1865, 195//us war dept.

AGO1861–1873 Micro. # 617, Roll 1196. "Citizens Employed at the Fort," in June//1 wagon master ($75 per month), 1 forage master ($75 per month), 5 mechanics ($40), 31 laborers ($25), 3 contraband male ($10); 3 contraband female, 2 contraband children (everyone is paid except questionably for female and children contraband). In September, 41 laborers, no contraband. All laborers were paid the same.

36. Montgomery to parents, June 2, 1863, Montgomery Family Papers. For a full account of the black men who served as teamsters for the Sibley expedition, see Stephen E. Osman, "General Sibley's Contraband Teamsters," *Minnesota's Heritage*, no. 7 (January 2013): 54–74.

37. Office of Indian Affairs (hereafter Indian Office), *Reports*, 1863, 305; Minnesota Legislative Reference Library, "Balcombe, St. Andre Durand," *Legislators Past & Present*, accessed on November 29, 2014, http://www.leg.state.mn.us/legdb /fulldetail.aspx?ID=11120.

38. Indian Office, *Reports*, 1863, 305. See also Balcombe to Dole, May 12, 1863, Letters Received, Winnebago Agency, Office of Indian Affairs, National Archives.

39. William E. Lass, "The Removal from Minnesota of the Sioux and Winnebago Indians," *Minnesota History*, December 1963, 353, 360.

40. MNopedia, Minnesota Historical Society, "Ho-Chunk and Blue Earth, 1855–1863," accessed November 29, 2014, http://www.mnopedia.org/event/ho-chunk-and-blue -earth-1855-1863.

41. Lass, "Removal," 353–54, citing *Standard Historical and Pictorial Atlas and Gazeteer of Blue Earth County, Minnesota* (Minneapolis, 1895), 85–88.

42. *Mankato Independent*, February 20, 1863.

43. Petition for Winnebago Removal (Wilkinson's letter), January 21, 1863, Cong. Globe, 37th Cong., 3d Sess., part 1, 868 (1863); Nichols, *Lincoln and the Indians*, 121.

44. Lass, "Removal," 363.

45. *Mankato Record*, May 16, 1863.

46. Lass, "Removal," 361.

47. *Mankato Independent*, May 15, 1863; Thomas Hughes, "History of Steam Boating on the Minnesota River," *Collections of the Minnesota Historical Society*, 9:132, 151; Lass, "Removal," 361.

48. *Congressional Series*, "Report of the Chief of Engineers, U.S. Army" (Washington, D.C.: Government Printing Office, 1889), 1566.

49. *St. Paul Weekly Press*, May 14, 1863; Lass, "Removal," 361.

50. *St. Paul Weekly Press*, May 14, 21, 1863; Lass, "Removal," 361–62.

51. *St. Paul Daily Press*, May 5, 1863; Green, *A Peculiar Imbalance*, 124.

52. Lass, "Removal," 363.

53. Sully to the secretary of the interior, July 16, 1863, roll 544, M234, Letters Received, Northern Superintendency, Office of Indian Affairs, National Archives. Quoted in Nichols, *Lincoln and the Indians*, 121–22.

54. Sully to J. F. Heine, November 21, 1863, roll 499, M234, Letters Received, Northern Superintendency, Office of Indian Affairs, Record Group 75, National Archives.

55. *Daily Press*, May 16, 1863. See note 19 for further details.

56. *St. Paul Daily Press*, May 16, 1863; Green, *A Peculiar Imbalance*, 124–25.

57. For an overview of the causes and execution of the relief expedition, see William E. Lass, "The 'Moscow Expedition,'" *Minnesota History*, Summer 1965, 227.

58. S. D. Hinman to Whipple, June 8, 1863, box 3, Whipple Papers.

59. Williamson cited in Nichols, *Lincoln and the Indians*, 122.
60. J. Williamson to Thomas Williamson, June 9, 1863, Thomas S. Williamson Papers, Minnesota Historical Society, St. Paul; J. Williamson to Stephen R. Riggs, July 22, 1863, Riggs Family Papers; Lass, " 'Moscow Expedition,' " 228.
61. *Mankato Weekly Union*, October 2, 1863.
62. Lass, " 'Moscow Expedition,' " 227.
63. Ibid.
64. Hubbell to Thompson, October 11, 1863; Wilkinson to Thompson, October 16, 1863; Thompson Papers; Lass, " 'Moscow Expedition,' " 232.
65. *Mankato Record*, October 3, 17, 1863.
66. Thomas Montgomery of Company K, roster of Company K, *Minnesota in the Civil and Indian Wars*, 385.
67. James T. Ramer, sergeant of Company B, Seventh Regiment, Minnesota Infantry Volunteers, ibid., 369; for roster of field and staff officers, see 379 and 382.

## 7. THE FIRST LIEUTENANT TAKES COMMAND

1. Board of Commissioners, *Minnesota in the Civil and Indian Wars, 1861–1865*, 1:349, 355, 385; Earl Spangler, *The Negro in Minnesota* (Minneapolis: T. S. Dennison, 1961), 48.
2. Montgomery to parents and brothers, September 16, 1863. All Montgomery correspondence, Montgomery Family Papers.
3. Montgomery to mother and father, October 31, 1863.
4. Corporals Frank Wilde and Benjamin Damrin, two of the three men who had mustered in with Montgomery and were now listed as sick, were discharged for disability on November 28, 1863. Board of Commissioners, *Minnesota in the Civil and Indian Wars, 1861–1865*, 1:384–85.
5. Montgomery to brother James Charles, October 30, 1863.
6. Montgomery to parents and brothers, October 12, 1863.
7. John Hope Franklin and Evelyn Brooks Higginbotham, *From Slavery to Freedom*, 9th ed. (New York: McGraw-Hill, 2010), 212. See also James McPherson, *The Negro's Civil War* (New York: Vintage, 1965); Edwin S. Redkey, *A Grand Army of Black Men* (Cambridge: Cambridge University Press, 1982).
8. "The Negro as Soldier," *St. Paul Pioneer and Democrat*, January 30, 1863.
9. For purposes here, "free men" means African Americans who were free before the war; "freedmen" refers to those who were emancipated during the war.
10. Budge Weidman, "Black Soldiers in the Civil War: Preserving the Legacy of the United States Colored Troops," National Archives, http://www.archives.gov/education/lessons/blacks-civil-war/article.html. Also see Dudley Taylor Cornish, *The Sable Arm: Negro Troops in the Union Army, 1861–1865* (New York: W. W. Norton, 1965), 288; McPherson, *The Negro's Civil War*, 237.
11. Montgomery to parents, December 16, 1863.
12. About the tests he underwent to be an officer, Montgomery wrote, "You are aware that I was preparing to go before a military examination; this I done on the morning of the 14th and was thoroughly examined in reading, writing, geography, history, mathematics, military terms and phrases, duties of company officers, army regulations and tactics. When examined I went out into the hall and was told to wait a few moments. I was then called in, told I had passed my examination, and was ordered to report for duty to Brig. Gen'l. Pile who has charge to the organization of Colored Troops at

Benton Barracks. . . . I don't remember that I gave you my address in my last. Direct: Lieut. Thomas Montgomery, Co. B, 3rd Reg't., Missouri Volunteers of African Descent, Benton Barracks, Missouri." Montgomery to parents and brothers, January 3, 1864.

13. "The Civil War's Black Soldiers: The Bureau of Colored Troops," National Park Service, U.S. Department of the Interior, updated March 15, 2011, retrieved on February 18, 2013, https://www.nps.gov/parkhistory/ online_books/civil_war _series/2/sec11.htm.

14. Ibid.

15. Montgomery to brother, January 23, 1864.

16. "The Civil War's Black Soldiers: The Bureau of Colored Troops."

17. Ibid.

18. Frederick L. Johnson, *Uncertain Lives: African Americans and Their First 150 Years in the Red Wing, Minnesota Area* (Red Wing: Goodhue County Historical Society, 2005), 19–21.

19. Montgomery to brother Alexander, January 11, 1864. When the old Seventh Regiment mustered out on August 16, 1865, the unit had lost two officers, 31 enlisted men killed and mortally wounded, and 138 enlisted men by disease, for a total of 171. Frederick Dyer, "Regimental Histories," *A Compendium of the War of the Rebellion* (Des Moines, Iowa: Dyer Publishing, 1908), 1299.

20. Montgomery to mother, February 22, 1864.

21. Ibid.

22. Ibid.

23. Montgomery to parents and brothers, March 8, 1864.

24. Montgomery to parents and brothers, March 23, 1864.

25. Ludwell H. Johnson, *Red River Campaign: Politics and Cotton in the Civil War* (Kent, Ohio: Kent State University Press, 1993).

26. Lawrence Lee Hewitt, *Port Hudson: Confederate Bastion on the Mississippi* (Baton Rouge: Louisiana State University Press, 1987), 140–49, 177–78.

27. Montgomery to parents and brothers, March 23, 1864.

28. Ibid.

29. Ibid.

30. Montgomery to parents and brothers, Port Hudson, May 19, 1864. Also see Montgomery to brother Alexander, December 24, 1864.

31. Montgomery to parents and brothers, May 19, 1864.

32. Montgomery to mother, June 25, 1864.

33. Montgomery to mother, May 27, 1864.

## 8. LIZZIE AND THE TROUBLES

1. Montgomery to mother, August 16, 1864. All Montgomery correspondence, Montgomery Family Papers.

2. Montgomery to mother, June 27, 1864.

3. Ibid.

4. Montgomery to mother, August 16, 1864.

5. Ibid.

6. Montgomery to mother, August 31, 1864.

7. Montgomery to brother, September 9, 1864.

8. Montgomery to mother, September 30, 1864.
9. Montgomery to mother, August 31, 1864.
10. Montgomery to father, September 16, 1864.
11. Ibid.
12. Montgomery to father, October 6, 1864.
13. Ibid.
14. Ibid.
15. "62nd and 65th Regiments United States Infantry, Co-founders of Lincoln Institute, Later, Lincoln University," retrieved October 10, 2016, http://www.buffalosoldier.net/62nd65thRegimentsU.S.ColoredInfantry.htm.
16. Ben Densmore to Orrin Densmore Sr., September 22, 1863, Benjamin Densmore Papers, Minnesota Historical Society, St. Paul; Johnson, *Uncertain Lives*, 19.
17. Montgomery to mother, October 12, 1864.
18. Montgomery to mother, October 22, 1864.
19. Ibid.
20. Montgomery to brother James, October 26, 1864.
21. Montgomery to mother, October 27, 1864.
22. Montgomery to brother, November 21, 1864.
23. Montgomery to mother, November 27, 1864.
24. Montgomery to mother, December 12, 1864.
25. Montgomery to brother James, December 17, 1864.
26. Montgomery to mother, January 1, 1865.
27. Montgomery to mother, August 16, 1864, regarding Irish doctor.
28. Montgomery to mother, January 1, 1865.
29. Montgomery to mother, January 14, 1865.
30. Darlene G. Goring, "History of Slave Marriage in the United States," *John Marshall Law Review* 39 (2006): 307–12; Paul Finkelman, ed., *Woman and the Family in a Slave Society* (New York: Garland, 1989); Wilbert E. Moore, *American Negro Slavery and Abolition: A Sociological Study* (New York: Third Press, 1971), 101; Albert J. Raboteau, *Slave Religions: The "Invisible Institution" in the Antebellum South* (New York: Oxford University Press, 2004), 228–31.
31. Montgomery to brother James, February 21, 1865.
32. In his letter of October 28, he strongly argues that she would be alone since her friends had left the camp.
33. Montgomery to mother, June 14 or 27, 1864. Minnesota Census 1865, Cleveland Township, Le Sueur County. roll 2, Minnesota Historical Society, St. Paul.
34. Montgomery to father, March 22, 1865.
35. Ibid.
36. Montgomery to mother, June 27, 1864.
37. Montgomery to brother, April 18, 1865.
38. Montgomery to mother, April 24, 1865.
39. The biography of Abner Tibbetts is found at http://hillsborohistory.blogspot.com/2012/08/so-what-did-abner-tibbetts-do-for.html.
40. Montgomery to mother, May 16, 1865.
41. Montgomery to mother, May 31, 1865.
42. Montgomery to brother James, June 4, 1865.
43. Montgomery to mother, June 4, 1865.

44. Montgomery to mother, June 11, 1865.
45. Ibid.
46. Ibid.
47. Montgomery to mother, June 20, 1865.
48. Montgomery to parents, September 15, 1865.
49. Montgomery to parents, September 22, 1865.
50. Ibid.
51. http://iagenweb.org/civilwar/regiment/infantry/01stA/index.htm.
52. F. R. Freeman, "The Medical Challenge of Military Operations in the Mississippi River Valley during the American Civil War," *Military Medicine* 157, no. 9 (September 1992): 494–97.
53. Montgomery to parents, September 22, 1865.
54. Montgomery to mother, September 29, 1865.
55. Montgomery to brother James, October 18, 1865.
56. Ibid.
57. Board of Commissioners, *Minnesota in the Civil and Indian Wars*, 1:367; Census of the State of Minnesota, 1865, *Annual Report for 1865* (St. Paul: Minnesota Historical Society), 119.
58. Montgomery to unknown, November 27, 1865.

## 9. FREEDOM AND EDUCATION

1. Louisiana Black Code, 1865; Senate Executive Document no. 2, 39th Cong., 1st Sess., 93; Laura A. Belmonte, *Speaking of America*, vol. 2, *Since 1865* (Belmont, Calif.: Wadsworth Cengage Learning, 2007).
2. John Hope Franklin, *Reconstruction after the Civil War* (Chicago: University of Chicago Press, 1961), 48.
3. Montgomery to mother, December 25, 1865. All Montgomery correspondence, Montgomery Family Papers.
4. Franklin, *Reconstruction after the Civil War*, 52.
5. Montgomery to mother, December 25, 1865.
6. Montgomery to parents and brother, January 2, 1866.
7. William B. Holberton, "Demobilization of the Union Army, 1865–1866" (master's thesis, Lehigh University, 1983). Available for download at http://preserve.lehigh.edu/cgi/viewcontent.cgi?article=1167&context=etd&sei-redir=1&referer=http%3A%2F%2Fwww.google.com%2Furl%3Fsa%3Dt%26rct%3Dj%26q%3Dunion%2520army%2520in%2520mouisiana%25201865–1866%26source%3Dweb%26cd%3D1%26ved%3D0CDIQFjAA%26url%3Dhttp%253A%252F%252Fpreserve.lehigh.edu%252Fcgi%252Fviewcontent.cgi%253Farticle%253D1167%2526context%253Detd%26ei%3DME4aUb_oO8iFywH9-oDACg%26usg%3DAFQjCNFaSaIZCtnws7ordDmLBqCbDXosfg%26bvm%3Dbv.42261806%2Cd.aWc#search=%22union%20army%20mouisiana%201865–1866%22.
8. Ibid.
9. William A. Dobak, *Freedom by the Sword: The U.S. Colored Troops, 1862–1867* (Washington, D.C.: Center of Military History, 2011), 488.
10. Montgomery to father, February 28, 1866.
11. Franklin, *Reconstruction after the Civil War*, 35–38.
12. Ibid., 39.

13. Foner, *Reconstruction*, 251.
14. Holberton, "Demobilization of the Union Army," 86, citing Ida M. Tarbell, "Disbanding of the Confederate Army," *McClure's Magazine*, April 1901, 526–38; reprinted in *Civil War Times Illustrated* 6, no. 9 (January 1968): 14.
15. Montgomery to mother, January 16, 1866.
16. Dobak, *Freedom by the Sword*, 494–95.
17. Montgomery to brother Alexander, January 16, 1866.
18. Montgomery to mother, January 16, 1866.

## 10. MASONIC TIES

1. Montgomery to brother James, February 9, 1866. All Montgomery correspondence, Montgomery Family Papers.
2. Michael A. Halleran, *The Better Angels of Our Nature: Freemasonry in the American Civil War* (Tuscaloosa: University of Alabama Press, 2010), 1–7, 78–99.
3. Montgomery to James, March 29, 1866.
4. On March 30, 1863, Lincoln wrote to Johnson, then war governor of Tennessee, "I am told you have at least *thought* of raising a negro military force. In my opinion the country now needs no specific thing so much as some man of your ability and position to go to this work. . . . The colored population is the great *available* and yet *unavailed of* force for restoring the Union. The bare sight of 50,000 armed and drilled black soldiers upon the banks of the Mississippi would end the rebellion at once. And who doubts that we can present that sight if we but take hold in earnest?" McPherson, *The Negro's Civil War*, 171.
5. Paul H. Bergeron, *Andrew Johnson's Civil War and Reconstruction* (Knoxville: University of Tennessee Press, 2011), 83.
6. Ibid., 87–88.
7. Montgomery to father, April 4, 1866.
8. Montgomery to mother, May 29, 1866.
9. Montgomery to brother James, June 4, 1866.
10. Foner, *Reconstruction*, 262.
11. Dobak, *Freedom by the Sword*, 465, citing Colonel A. W. Webber to Captain S. B. Ferguson, 12 September 1865, L-270-D-1865, entry 1737, Letters Received pl. 1, Record Group 393, Department of the Gulf, National Archives; Steven Hahn et al., *Freedom: A Documentary History of Emancipation, 1861–1867*, series 3, vol. 1, *Land and Labor, 1865* (Cambridge: Cambridge University Press, 2010), 165.
12. Dobak, *Freedom by the Sword*, 134.
13. Ibid., 468.
14. Ibid., 494.
15. Montgomery to brother James, July 21, 1866.
16. Foner, *Reconstruction*, 55, citing William F. Messner, *Freedmen and the Ideology of Free Labor: Louisiana, 1862–1865* (Lafayette: Center for Louisiana Studies, University of Southwestern Louisiana, 1978), 21–39.
17. Montgomery to brother James, July 21, 1866.
18. Montgomery to mother, July 28, 1866.
19. Marshall to Secretary of War Stanton, July 28, 1866, Montgomery Family Papers.
20. Montgomery to father, August 4, 1866.
21. Foner, *Reconstruction*, 263.

22. Ibid., citing Cyrus Hamlin to Hannibal Hamlin, August 19, 1866, Hannibal M. Hamlin Papers, University of Maine, Orono. Also see Franklin, *Reconstruction after the Civil War,* 63–64.
23. Dobak, *Freedom by the Sword,* 494.
24. Ibid.
25. Foner, *Reconstruction,* 263n63.
26. Hans L. Trefouse, *Andrew Johnson: A Biography* (New York: W. W. Norton, 1989), chap. 13; Foner, *Reconstruction,* 265. Also see Franklin, *Reconstruction after the Civil War,* 66.

## 11. GOING HOME

1. Montgomery to brother James, August 17, 1866. All Montgomery correspondence, Montgomery Family Papers.
2. Montgomery to mother, August 24, 1866.
3. Montgomery to parents and brothers, September 5, 1866.
4. Montgomery to parents and brother James, September 23, 1866.
5. Montgomery to mother, December 5, 1866.
6. Montgomery to father, December 30,1866.
7. Michael J. Pfeiffer, *The Roots of Rough Justice: Origins of American Lynching* (Urbana: University of Illinois Press, 2011), 84, 85.
8. "Louisiana: The Recent Disturbances in Opelousas—Results of the Investigation Ordered by the Freedman's Bureau," *New York Times,* October 8, 1868; Carolyn E. DeLatte, "The St. Landry Riot: A Forgotten Incident on Reconstruction Violence," *Louisiana Historical Association* 17 (1976): 41–49; Foner, *Reconstruction,* 342.
9. *New York Times,* December 22, 1866.
10. *New York Times,* January 14, 1867.
11. *New York Times,* December 29, 30, 1866; January 1, 6, 7, 14, 1867.
12. For the reference to his fiancée, Sarah Purnell, see Montgomery's letter to brother James, November 3, 1866.
13. Montgomery to parents and brother James, September 23, 1866.
14. Montgomery to parents and brother, January 9, 1867.
15. Ibid.
16. *St. Peter Free Press,* June 15, 1907; *St. Peter Herald,* June 14, 1907; *St. Peter Tribune,* January 20, 1869; Edward D. Neill, *History of the Minnesota Valley Including the Explorers and Pioneers of Minnesota* (Minneapolis: North Star Press, 1882), 665.
17. National Park Service, U.S. Civil War Soldiers, 1861–1865 (database online) (Provo, Utah: Ancestry.Com Operations Inc., 2007). Original data: National Park Service, Civil War Soldiers and Sailors System, http://www.nps.gov/civilwar/soldiers-and-sailors-database.htm.
18. For the family history, see Montgomery Family Papers.

## 12. BY CHICANERY AND DECEPTION OF A FEW POLITICIANS

1. *Mankato Union,* January 13, 1865.
2. *St. Paul Pioneer,* January 12, 1865; *St. Paul Press,* January 12, 1865.
3. *H. P. Hall's Observations: Being More or Less a History of Political Contests in Minnesota from 1849 to 1904* (St. Paul, Minn., 1904), 61–62. See also Folwell, *History of Minnesota,* 2:340–341.

4. Editorial comment in the *Winona Republican* appearing in *St. Paul Press*, January 17, 1865.
5. *Mankato Union*, January 13, 1865.
6. Ibid.
7. Ibid.
8. Ibid. Also see *St. Paul Press*, January 10, 1865.
9. John C. Haugland, "Politics, Patronage, and Ramsey's Rise to Political Power, 1861–1865," *Minnesota History*, December 1961, 324, 326, 328, 330.
10. Ibid., 330.
11. *St. Paul Pioneer and Democrat*, November 2, 1862.
12. *St. Paul Press*, November 4, 16, 1862. For an account of the investigation, see Folwell, *History of Minnesota*, 1:462–70.
13. Haugland, "Politics, Patronage, and Ramsey's Rise," 324, 328, 330. See also Vincent G. Tegeder, "Lincoln and the Territorial Patronage: The Ascendency of the Radicals in the West," *Mississippi Valley Historical Review* 35 (June 1948): 86.
14. Thomas Hughes, *The History of the Bench and Bar of Blue Earth County* (Chicago: Middle West Publishing, 1909), 11.
15. *H. P. Hall's Observations*, 61–62. See also Folwell, *History of Minnesota*, 2:340–41.
16. Hughes, *History of the Bench and Bar of Blue Earth County*, 11.
17. *St. Paul Press*, January 11, 1865.
18. *H. P. Hall's Observations*, 170.
19. Nichols, *Lincoln and the Indians*, 123, citing William P. Dole to Wilkinson, June 13, 1863, roll 71, M21, Letters Sent, Record Group 75, Office of Indian Affairs, National Archives (NA); Wilkinson to Usher, September 25, 1863, roll 936, M234, Letters Received, Record Group 75, Winnebago Agency, Office of Indian Affairs, NA; Dole to Thompson Brothers, July 13, 1864, roll 74, M21, Letters Received, Record Group 75, Office of Indian Affairs, NA; Wilkinson to Dole, July 27, 1864, roll 937, M234, Letters Received, Record Group 75, Winnebago Agency, Office of Indian Affairs, NA; Dole to Wilkinson, August 9, 1864, roll 74, M21, Letters Sent, Record Group 75, Office of Indian Affairs, NA; Order for Sale of Land by the President, August 23, 1864, Basler, *Collected Works of Abraham Lincoln*, 7:515.
20. National Register of Historic Places, United States Department of the Interior, National Park Service, no. 37, section 7, page 15; https://mankatolincolnpark.files.wordpress.com/2015/02/lincolnparknationalregisterofhistoricplacesregistrationdocument.pdf. Also see Living Places: Mankato City (Morrisville, Pa.: Gombach Group, 1997–2017), http://www.livingplaces.com/MN/Blue_Earth_County/Mankato_City.html.
21. See discussion in chapter 17.
22. Cong. Globe, 38th Cong., 2d Sess., 327 (January 19), 1046 (February 24), 1124 (February 27).
23. Letter written on February 28, printed in *Mankato Union*, February 28, 1865.
24. Cong. Globe, 38th Cong., 2d Sess., 327 (January 19), 1046 (February 24), 1124 (February 27), 1302 (March 2). *The Mankato Union* published private land sales of Winnebago tracts, listing, for example, Willard's transaction with Mary Dineen, *Mankato Union*, March 27, 1865.
25. Noah Brooks, a newspaperman and friend of Lincoln, later reported, "A Western senator who had failed of a reëlection, brought his successor, one day, and introduced him to the President. Lincoln, in reply, expressed his gratification at making the

acquaintance of a new senator. 'Yet,' he added, 'I hate to have old friends like Senator W— go away. And—another thing—I usually find that a senator or representative out of business is a sort of lame duck. He has to be provided for.' When the two gentlemen had withdrawn, I took the liberty of saying that Mr. W— did not seem to relish that remark. Weeks after, when I had forgotten the circumstance, the President said, 'You thought I was almost rude to Senator W— the other day. Well, now he wants Commissioner Dole's place!' Mr. Dole was then Commissioner of Indian Affairs." Noah Brooks, *Washington in Lincoln's Time* (New York: Century, 1894), 289.

26. Lincoln's confidant, Dr. Aaron Henry, reported the president saying, "The delegation from Minnesota are pressing very strongly for that place for Ex-Senator Wilkinson." Letter from Henry to his wife, March 13, 1865, quoted in Charles M. Segal, ed., *Conversations with Lincoln* (New York: G. P. Putnam and Sons, 1961), 374.

27. Ibid.

28. Wilkinson to his son Morton Junior on the death of President Lincoln, April 20, 1865. Wilkinson Letters.

29. In a posthumous tribute to Wilkinson, friend and political ally Charles Gilfillan wrote, "[Wilkinson] was honest, earnest and patriotic. One service he did for the country is not well enough known. Near the close of President Lincoln's first term a cabal or organization of Republican senators, some of them prominent, were in the movement, and Senator Wilkinson, then a Republican and prominent in the Senate as a debater and worker was strongly urged to join it. But the great loyal spirit not only refused to favor the reprehensible scheme but denounced it and fought it and was largely instrumental in defeating it, and Lincoln was nominated and re-elected to the great service to the Union and humanity." "Tribute by the Hon. C. D. Gilfillan," in *Mankato: Its First Fifty Years; Containing Addresses, Historic Papers, and Brief Biographies of Early Settlers and Active Up-Builders of the City* (Mankato: Free Press Printing, 1903), 163, https://archive.org/stream/cu31924010437824/cu31924010437824_djvu.txt. For a discussion of the effort of radicals to deny Lincoln renomination in 1864, see T. Harry Williams, *Lincoln and the Radicals* (Madison: University of Wisconsin Press, 1972), 306–333.

30. "Statement by William Dodsworth Willard," *Mankato: Its First Fifty Years*, 115. See also "A Record of Forty Years," *Commercial West*, June 13, 1908, 42–43.

31. Wingerd, *North Country*, 336.

32. *Mankato: Its First Fifty Years*, 115, 240.

33. Thomas Hughes recorded one such example: "Arrangements were also made to lay out another town site on the land of Levi Hauk at Good Thunder's Ford ('crossing'), and a survey of this town was made in April 1871, by Levi Hauk, Clark W. Thompson, James B. Hubbell and John Willard, and a plat filed in which the village was designated 'Good Thunder.' Immediately after the survey in April, John G. Graham, who had been in business at Garden City, began the erection of a store building at Good Thunder. The carpenter work was done by Julius Webber, then a young carpenter at Garden City, but afterwards for many years the honored judge of the Ninth Judicial District, with home at New Ulm." Hughes, *History of the Bench and Bar of Blue Earth County*, 15.

34. "Remarks at Unveiling of Wilkinson Monument by Hon. Daniel Buck," *Mankato: Its First Fifty Years*, 156.

## 13. WILLEY'S AMENDMENT

1. Even though the act was signed into law on May 20, 1862, section 1 stated the act would be enacted on January 1, 1863.
2. "The Homestead Bill: Speech by Hon. M. S. Wilkinson, of Minnesota" (Washington, D.C.: n.p., 1860 [?]), 3–4, 8 (hereafter "Wilkinson's Homestead Speech"). See also John Ashworth, *Slavery, Capitalism, and Politics in the Antebellum Republic*, vol. 2, *The Coming of the Civil War, 1850–1861* (Cambridge: Cambridge University Press, 1995), 270–71.
3. "Wilkinson's Homestead Speech."
4. Ibid.
5. Ibid.
6. William Deverell, "The American West," in *The American Congress: The Building of Democracy*, ed. Julian E. Zelizer (New York: Houghton Mifflin, 2004), 271.
7. Cong. Globe, 37th Cong., 2d Sess., 1508.
8. Cong. Globe, 36th Cong., 1st Sess., 1509–10.
9. Ibid.
10. Ibid.
11. William J. Stewart, "Settler, Politician, and Speculator in the Sale of the Sioux Reserve," *Minnesota History*, Fall 1964, 85.
12. "Statement by William Dodsworth Willard," *Mankato: Its First Fifty Years*, 115.
13. Stewart, "Settler, Politician, and Speculator," 85.
14. "Indian Trust Land—Winnebago Land Account," *Message of the President of the United States and Accompanying Documents to the Two Houses of Congress, at the Commencement of the Second Session of the Thirty-Ninth Congress* (Washington, D.C.: Government Printing Office, 1866), 323.
15. Montgomery to his father. March 22, 1865, emphasis added; Montgomery Family Papers. Also see Spangler, *The Negro in Minnesota*, 48, 54. Muster rolls, Sixty-Seventh Regiment, Company B, USCI; Montgomery to his brother, October 22, 1864, Montgomery Family Papers.
16. Cong. Globe, 38th Cong., 1st Sess., 1108 (1864), and Statutes at Large 13 (1863–65), chapter 210. Michael Vorenberg, "Abraham Lincoln and the Politics of Black Colonization," *Journal of the Abraham Lincoln Association*, Summer 1993, 23, 41.
17. Cong. Globe, 38th Cong., 1st Sess., 3329 (1864).
18. Ibid., 3329–30.
19. Ibid., 3330.
20. Ibid.
21. Edward Pluth, "A 'Negro Colony' for Todd County," *Minnesota History*, Fall 2009, 320; Leslie A. Schwalm, *Emancipation's Diaspora: Race and Reconstruction in the Upper Midwest* (Chapel Hill: University of North Carolina Press, 2009), 82, 83–84.
22. *Mankato Union*, March 10, 1865.
23. Alexander Ramsey, in an 1853 speech to the legislature, made the common assumption that settlers were farmers: "The whole country . . . has the deepest interest in increasing the amount of this cultivation; and the most effectual way of doing this would seem to be by gratuitous grants of land in limited quantities to actual settlers"; Minnesota Territory, Journal of the House, 1853, 70.
24. Bruce M. White, "The Power of Whiteness; or, The Life and Times of Joseph Rolette Jr.," *Minnesota History*, Winter 1998–99, 180–181. On the cultural attributes of the

term "white" and its meaning in nineteenth-century America, White references David R. Roediger, *The Wages of Whiteness: Race and the Making of the American Working Class* (London: Verso, 1991); Reginald Horsman, *Race and Manifest Destiny: The Origins of American Racial Anglo-Saxonism* (Cambridge, Mass.: Harvard University Press, 1981), 154–55, 189.

25. *Chatfield Democrat*, August 19, 1865.

26. Cong. Globe, 38th Cong., 1st Sess., 1490, 3330.

27. Ibid., 3330.

28. Herman Belz, *A New Birth for Freedom: The Republican Party and Freedmen's Rights, 1861–1866* (New York: Fordham University Press, 2000), 90–91.

29. Ibid.

30. Ibid.

31. On April 8, 1864, Wilkinson (and Ramsey) "voted for passage of the joint resolution submitting to the Legislatures of the several States the proposition to amend the Constitution of the United States," joining a majority of 38 yeas to 6 nays. Cong. Globe, 38th Cong., 1st Sess., 1490.

32. Ibid., 3330.

## 14. A LESSON IN LEADERSHIP

1. Chungchan Gao, *African Americans in the Reconstruction Era* (New York: Garland, 2000), 171. Historian Quintard Taylor reports that the first indication of congressional concern about black suffrage occurred when Congress created Montana Territory in 1864. While debating the act that would authorize territorial status, Wilkinson introduced an amendment to strike the word "white" from the voter qualification provision. Senator Charles Sumner echoed support for the amendment and the Senate voted to approve. After negotiations with the House, however, a compromise was struck to limit suffrage to U.S. citizens, leaving blacks temporarily without suffrage rights because the Fourteenth Amendment had not yet been ratified. "Nonetheless, the debate served notice that African American suffrage would no longer be left to the territories." Quintard Taylor, *In Search of the Racial Frontier: African Americans in the American West, 1528–1990* (New York: W. W. Norton, 1998), 121. Also see V. Jacque Voegeli, *Free but Not Equal: The Midwest and the Negro during the Civil War* (Chicago: University of Chicago Press, 1968), 166, 171–72.

2. Minnesota Territory, Journal of the House, 1849, 53, 62; *Collections of the Minnesota Historical Society* (St. Paul: Minnesota Historical Society Press, 1905), 10:420. Green, *A Peculiar Imbalance*, 44–48.

3. *Proceedings and Debate of the Constitutional Convention* (Republican) (St. Paul: George W. Moore, printer 1858), 337, 349–66, 571–22, 575–81; William Anderson, *A History of the Constitution of Minnesota* (Minneapolis: University of Minnesota Press, 1921), 99–101.

4. Republican delegates who supported black suffrage argued against the provision because they feared Republican voters would reject the constitution and thus stall Minnesota's effort to become a state.

5. *Mankato Union*, February 10, 1865.

6. The other Republican paper opposed to black suffrage in 1865 was the *Chaska Herald*. *Mankato Weekly Record*, February 18, 1865.

7. Ibid.

8. The constitutional convention of Wisconsin in 1847–48 resolved the suffrage issue by agreeing that the legislature could allow black suffrage at any time, provided the law was "submitted to the vote of the people at a general election, and approved by a majority of all the votes cast at such election." The compromise appealed to the delegates because a vote for it could be defended as a vote for popular sovereignty rather than black equality or abolitionism. The first state legislature promptly passed a black suffrage law and authorized a referendum, which took place in 1849. The law was approved by a vote of 5,265 to 4,075. However, fewer than half of all voters casting ballots at the election voted on the suffrage issue; therefore, the law had failed. The legislature passed suffrage laws in 1857 and again in 1865; but each time, the voters rejected the measures, although the pro-suffrage vote increased to 41 percent in 1857 and 46 percent in 1865. Ezekiel Gillespie, one of the leaders of Milwaukee's black community, tried to register to vote in 1865, evidently seeking to test the 1840 referendum. In *Gillespie v. Palmer* (1866), the state supreme court accepted the argument and ruled that because suffrage had received a majority in 1849, blacks had been entitled to vote in Wisconsin since that time. John G. Gregory, "Negro Suffrage in Wisconsin," *Transactions of the Wisconsin Academy of Sciences, Art and Letters* 11 (1898): 94–101; Joseph A. Ranney, "Wisconsin's Legal History," *Wisconsin Lawyer* (Madison: Wisconsin Supreme Court, 1998).
9. *Mankato Union*, February 10, 1865.
10. Ibid.
11. Richard Kluger, *Simple Justice*, 67–68; Foner, *Reconstruction*, 447–49.
12. *Mankato Union*, February 27, 1865; March 3, 1865.
13. *Mankato Union*, March 10, 1865.
14. Ibid.
15. *Mankato Union*, March 24, 1865.
16. *Mankato Union*, October 27, 1865.
17. As a delegate to the constitutional convention of Wisconsin in 1847, Marshall had voted for the black suffrage provision.
18. *Mankato Union*, October 27, 1865.
19. "The Honorable Morton S. Wilkinson had made appointments to speak upon the issues connected with the fall election as follows: Winnebago City, October 19, Fairmont, October 20, Blue Earth City (Faribault County), October 21." *Mankato Union*, October 27, 1865.
20. *Mankato Union*, October 14, 1865.
21. *Mankato Weekly Record*, October 28, 1865. Emphasis in the original.
22. Statewide, Marshall defeated Rice, 17,318 to 13,842 votes. However, the black suffrage amendment failed, 12,138 for to 14,651 against. In Blue Earth County, Marshall won, 802 to 597, while black suffrage lost 558 to 707. But in Faribault County Marshall won 501 to 138, and the amendment passed 339 to 196. Census of the state of Minnesota, 1865, extracted from *Minnesota Secretary of State's Annual Report for 1865* (St. Paul: Minnesota Historical Society, 1865), 119. For a discussion on the Minnesota campaign for black suffrage, see Gary Libman, "Minnesota and the Struggle for Black Suffrage, 1849–1870: A Study in Party Motivation" (Ph.D. diss., University of Minnesota, June 1972); see also W. D. Green, "The Long Road to Black Suffrage, 1849–1868," *Minnesota History*, Summer 1998, 68–84.

23. *St. Paul Pioneer*, October 14 and 22, 1865; Libman, "Minnesota and the Struggle for Black Suffrage, 1849–1870," 76–86; Green, *A Peculiar Imbalance*, 145.
24. Schwalm, *Emancipation's Diaspora*, 90, 91.
25. *Chatfield Democrat*, August 19, 1865.
26. *Shakopee Weekly Argus*, September 12, 1865; *St. Paul Pioneer*, November 7, 1865.
27. *Chatfield Democrat*, May 20, 1865; *St. Paul Pioneer*, October 22, 1865.
28. Schwalm, *Emancipation's Diaspora*, 93; *Mankato Semi-Weekly Record*, June 21, 1862.
29. *St. Paul Pioneer*, December 21, 1862.
30. Voegeli, *Free But Not Equal*, 179.
31. Ibid.
32. In reviewing the letters written by soldiers in the First Minnesota Regiment, it appears soldiers were not of a single mind on black equality and suffrage, but rather reflected the range of sentiment held by the general population. Moe, *The Last Full Measure*. However, arguing that soldiers were of one mind suited those most opposed to the measure.
33. Between August 1862 and 1865, Minnesota volunteers were able to vote in state elections, initiated originally by Democrats who noted that solders in Northern states tended to support Democratic candidates. Their admiration for General George McClellan was enough to threaten Lincoln's reelection were an election to be held then. But the Republicans co-opted the issue when citizens who volunteered to fight the Dakota in the western counties during the Dakota War lost their franchise when they enlisted. These citizen soldiers had been good Republicans. It was in the interest of the Republican Party to change the law in extra session, and the argument to do so was overwhelming. What kind of justice was it when citizens who had had voting rights lost those rights they were fighting to protect after they had mustered into service as volunteers? Many questioned a policy that effectively disenfranchised the men who chose to defend their homes and preserve their nation with honor, men prepared to give the last full measure. Thus, legislators mounted a campaign to extend to them the vote to culminate in passage of the bill. By strict party lines, the bill passed.

    Later, on October 7, 1863, Senator Wilkinson, writing for the congressional delegation, sent a similar request to Lincoln asking him to issue an executive order to allow troops the right to vote in federal elections. He wrote, "The greater part of our voters are either in the army or on the frontier fighting the Indians. If our volunteers are not permitted to vote two semi-secessionists [Democrats] will be elected to Congress and will send some of the similar proclivities to the Senate." The soldier vote would send Lieutenant Governor Ignatius Donnelly to Congress and elected legislators who in turn, in January, elected Governor Alexander Ramsey to the U.S. Senate. Theirs was a potent force, and now there were indications that many returning home were skeptical of any mention of black equality. Lynwood G. Downs, "The Soldier Vote and Minnesota Politics, 1862–1865," *Minnesota History*, September 1945, 193; Wilkinson to Lincoln, October 7, 1862, Abraham Lincoln Papers at the Library of Congress, transcribed and annotated by the Lincoln Studies Center, Knox College, Galesburg, Ill.
34. *Mankato Weekly Record*, March 21, 1865.
35. "Colonel Marshall rode his little chestnut horse Don across the field with his men, guiding the colors, and was among the first over the rebel works. He rode on to a rebel gunner that tried to run away, and captured him. One of our men said he wished the

colonel would not so expose himself. A rebel officer, standing with his back against a cannon wheel, said: 'H—l, any man that is brave enough to ride a horse across that field will never be killed.'" Board of Commissioners, *Minnesota in the Civil and Indian Wars*, 360.

Soldiers under Marshall's command relayed numerous stories that illustrated the affection they held for him. In one account, he led his unit on foot out of St. Louis to begin their march to Memphis and Vicksburg. At one point a little girl came running down the way, carrying a small flag in each hand, and saying "Hurrah for the Union." "The Colonel stooped and kissed her, which made the boys in the ranks cheer lustily." Ibid., 355.

36. Ibid., 361.
37. Ibid., 367.
38. Montgomery to brother James, October 18, 1865, Montgomery Family Papers. Montgomery had a special interest in William R. Marshall, for he had been lieutenant colonel and beloved commanding officer of the Seventh Minnesota, rising eventually to the rank of brevet brigadier general. In 1865 he was elected governor of Minnesota and served for two terms. He campaigned for black suffrage, playing an active role in the 1868 referendum, and, as governor, in 1869 signed legislation that denied state funds to school districts that separated children on the basis of race. In 1865, however, despite his support for black suffrage, the question failed statewide by a vote of 14,651 to 12,138; Marshall defeated Democrat Henry Rice, 17,318 to 13,842. Montgomery's skepticism regarding the success of black suffrage was well founded, especially in light of his understanding of his own community. In 1865 black suffrage and Marshall both fell short in Montgomery's Le Sueur County: Marshall lost, 422 to 729; the black suffrage amendment lost, 224 to 839. Board of Commissioners, *Minnesota in the Civil and Indian Wars*, 367; Census of the State of Minnesota, 1865, *Minnesota Secretary of State's Annual Report for 1865*, 119.
39. Downs, "The Soldier Vote and Minnesota Politics, 1862–1865," 209.
40. In Nicollet County, Marshall defeated Rice, 475 to 380, while the amendment narrowly failed, 331 to 374. In Wilkinson's Blue Earth County, Marshall defeated Rice 802 to 597, while the amendment vote failed 558 to 707. Census of the State of Minnesota, 1865, extracted from the *Minnesota Secretary of State's Annual Report for 1865*, 119. For a discussion of the Minnesota campaign for black suffrage, see Libman "Minnesota and the Struggle for Black Suffrage"; see also Green, "The Long Road to Black Suffrage, 1849–1868."

## 15. "GOOD NIGHT"

1. *St. Paul Daily Press*, January 10, 1866 (Hewson proposal); *Annual Message of Governor Miller and Inaugural Address of Governor Marshall to the Legislature of Minnesota* (St. Paul: Press Printing, 1866), 21, 22, 35; Green, *A Peculiar Imbalance*, 145.
2. *Stillwater Messenger*, February 13, 1866.
3. William Gillette, *The Right to Vote: Politics and the Passage of the Fifteenth Amendment* (Baltimore: The Johns Hopkins University Press, 1965), 28–31; Bruce M. White et al., *Minnesota Votes: Election Returns by County for Presidents, Senators, Congressmen, and Governors* (St. Paul: Minnesota Historical Society Press, 1977), 68; *St. Paul Daily Press*, November 18, 20, December 20, 1866; Green, *A Peculiar Imbalance*, 146. Also see Libman, "Minnesota and the Struggle for Black Suffrage," 123–24; John Cox and

LaWanda Cox, *Politics, Principles, and Prejudices, 1866–1867* (New York: Atheneum, 1969), for a discussion of Johnson and the Conservative Party.

4. Minnesota House Journal, 1867, 114–15; Senate Journal, 1867, 154; *St. Paul Daily Press*, February 5, 7, 9, 1867. For opposition to black suffrage, see *St. Paul Pioneer*, October 15, 17, November 5, 13, 1867; *Chatfield Democrat*, October 26, 1867; *Mankato Weekly Record*, October 19, 1867.

5. For example, speaking for many at the constitutional convention of 1867, Republican delegate Charles McClure of Red Wing, said, "We claim to be emphatically the white man's friend [both native and foreign born]. . . . While we sympathize with the blacks, our determination is to protect the whites from the baneful influences of slave labor. Our acts prove that." *Proceedings and Debate of the Constitutional Convention*, 295–96.

6. Records of the State Legislature, 1867, House Bill H.F. no. 1, Archives Division, Minnesota Historical Society, St. Paul; *St. Paul Pioneer Press*, October 17, 1867; *St. Paul Daily Press*, October 20, 1867; for quote, *St. Paul Daily Pioneer*, 3, 14, 1867.

7. Black suffrage lost by 2,513 votes of the 26,789 cast in 1865; it was defeated in 1868 by 1,298 votes out of 56,220.

8. *St. Paul Daily Press*, January 31, 1868. For a discussion of the voting patterns and causes for the defeat, see Libman, "Minnesota and the Struggle for Black Suffrage," 135–46.

9. *St. Paul Daily Press*, January 11, 1868; Green, *A Peculiar Imbalance*, 147.

10. *St. Paul Daily Press*, January 11, 1868; Hanford Gordon Papers, Minnesota Historical Society, St. Paul.

11. *St. Paul Daily Press*, October 23, 1868; *Stillwater Republican*, October 13, 1868; *Minneapolis Tribune*, October 16, 1868. Of the 43,722 who voted for Grant, 39,493 voted for black suffrage. *Legislative Manual, 1868*, 89–93. For a thorough interpretation of the returns, see Libman, "Minnesota and the Struggle for Black Suffrage," 169–84.

12. It would not be until midyear of 1866 that immigration into Blue Earth County began to grow. A year later in neighboring counties, the pace would grow as well. During June and July alone over 6,200 acres of land of the Winnebago reserve were sold at the St. Peter Land Office. In August, J. J. Thornton and Company established a railroad to carry freight and passengers between Mankato and Owatonna. On July 12, 1867, several thousand acres of Winnebago land, ranging from $7.00 to $7.20 per acre, were sold, mostly to speculators. John Willard, a businessman from Mankato, was the sole speculator who bid on land and acquired 4,000 of the 25,000 acres sold. Sales were suspended during winter—speculators could not get to St. Peter—and bidding resumed in May 1868. By summer, 125,000 acres of the 275,000 remaining after December, were sold. Between December 1867 and December 1869, fifty purchasers acquired 159,202 acres. Since 28 percent of the fifty purchasers bought only 750–1,000 acres, Stewart observed, "It is possible that the group included a few actual settlers. But the purchase of three to four times the amount of land a man could farm would seem to indicate entry for speculation." The reserve was a speculators' paradise. The asking price for acreage was unaccountably low for prime agricultural property, and the federal government only served through its hands-off policy to penalize citizens who hoped to improve and populate the broad areas of the West. By selling close to 160,000 acres in the Minnesota River valley to speculators, the federal government in effect was forcing 1,100 to 1,200 future settlers to deal with a middleman. Nonetheless, the prospect of owning land attracted thousands to Minnesota's farmland. William J. Stewart, "Settler, Politician, and Speculator in the Sale of the Sioux Reserve," *Min-*

*nesota History*, Fall 1964, 89. Also see Edward Duffield Neill and Charles S. Bryant, *History of Minnesota River Valley, Including the Explorers and Pioneers of Blue Earth County* (Minneapolis: North Star, 1882), 549. See also Monthly Abstract of Land Sales, St. Peter/Sioux Lands, December 1867–1869; Monthly Abstract of Land Sales, St. Peter/Winnebago Lands, December 1865–1867, National Archives and Records Administration.

13. Theodore C. Blegen, *Minnesota: A History of the State* (Minneapolis: University of Minnesota Press, 1975), 304.

14. Ibid., 304–5.

15. Ibid., 306–7.

16. Illinois senator Lyman Trumbull sponsored a bill that allotted three million acres of public land in the South for homesteading by blacks and authorized the Freedman's Bureau to purchase additional land for resale. When the bill came to the House Thaddeus Stevens sought to include "forfeited estates of the enemy" to the land available to blacks. The proposal was overwhelmingly defeated with a large majority of Republicans, including Radicals, voting in opposition. In the end, the only group of former masters to be compelled by Congress to provide their former slaves with land in those years were slaveholding Indians who had sided with the Confederacy. Republicans were quite unwilling to interfere with the plantation owners' property rights, allowing them to continue monopolizing the best land in the South. Public land, on the other hand, tended to be swampy, timbered in areas too far from transportation, and inferior. The freedmen lacked capital and the land offices were sparsely situated and poorly managed. By 1869 only four thousand black families had even attempted to take advantage of the act, three-quarters of them in sparsely populated Florida, and many of these subsequently lost the land. By far the largest acreage claimed under the act went to whites, often acting as agents for timber companies. Foner, *Reconstruction*, 245–46. Also see Cong. Globe, 39th Cong., 1st Sess., 748; Christie M. Pope, "Southern Homestead for Negroes," *Agricultural History* 44 (April 1970): 201–17; Claude F. Oubre, *Forty Acres and a Mule: The Freedmen's Bureau and Black Land Ownership* (Baton Rouge: Louisiana State University Press, 1978), 90–92, 109–16, 137–42.

17. Taylor, "The Blacks," 87, citing U.S. Census 1860–1880.

18. Spangler, *The Negro in Minnesota*, 46.

19. *St. Paul Daily Press*, May 16, 1863.

20. Taylor, "The Blacks," 87.

21. Spangler, *The Negro in Minnesota*, 55.

22. Ibid., 46. For a discussion of Maurice Jernigan, R. J. Stockton, and R. T. Grey, see Green, *Degrees of Freedom*, chapter 2.

23. *Proceedings of the Convention of Colored Citizens*, 19.

24. "Statement by William Dodsworth Willard," *Mankato: Its First Fifty Years*, 115.

25. In Blue Earth County, 1867, the black suffrage amendment won, 1,246 to 1,168, and in Nicollet County, 551 to 503; but in Le Sueur County, the amendment failed, 516 to 1,010. In 1868 the amendment passed in Blue Earth County, 1,588 to 1,108, and in Nicollet County, 647 to 486, while the amendment failed in Le Sueur County, 791 to 1,159. *Tribune Almanac for 1868* (New York: New York Herald Tribune), 56–57; *Legislative Manual, 1869*, 89; *Legislative Manual, 1871*, 133.

26. *Proceedings of the Convention of Colored Citizens*, 4.

27. Ibid., 5.

## 16. "OLE SHADY"

1. Roger B. Taney, chief justice of the United States Supreme Court, had issued the ruling in the *Dred Scott* decision that held that African Americans could never be citizens. *Dred Scott v. Sandford*, 60 U.S. 393 (1857).

2. *Proceedings of the Convention of Colored Citizens*, 3–5; *Minnesota in the Civil and Indians Wars*, 356–58. An account of where the song came from can be found in an article written in the late 1880s by General Sherman. In the article, Sherman praises the nobility of the composer of the song, "a fine hearty 'darkey,' . . . who was employed by General McPherson as steward and cook at his headquarters" during the siege of Vicksburg in 1863; and by extension, all freedmen who "in the crisis of their fate [as slaves], did *not* resort to the torch and the dagger, as their race had done in San Domingo." In the name of justice, Sherman insisted that all freedmen deserved their full rights to citizenship, and he stated in an ultimatum to Southern repression of the Negro vote that "as there is a God in Heaven, you will have another war, more cruel than the last." William T. Sherman, "Old Shady with a Moral," *North American Review*, October 1888, 362, 367, 366. The lyrics to "Ole Shady" can be found at Mudcat.org: lyr req: Old Shady.

3. *Proceedings of the Convention of Colored Citizens*, 3–5.

4. "Suffrage Amendment," *St. Paul Pioneer*, November 6, 1867.

5. David Jackson in his speech to Frederick Driscoll, November 13, 1868. *Proceedings of the Convention of Colored Citizens*, 5 and 6.

6. Also appears in "Of Civil Government," *Manual of the First Baptist Church* (1877), 13. First Baptist Church Papers, Minnesota Historical Society, St. Paul (hereafter FBC Papers).

7. Earl Sechler, *Our Religious Heritage: Church History of the Ozarks, 1806–1906* (Springfield, Mo.: Westport Press, 1961), 76.

8. Brooks Blevins, professor of Ozarks studies at Missouri State University, retrieved May 12, 2015, http://archive.news-leader.com/article/20110515/NEWS01/105150385/Civil-War-scarred-Springfield-churches.

9. East Tennessee became a center of abolitionism—"a staging ground for the issue that would divide not only the state but also the nation." Wayne C. Moore, *A History of Tennessee: The Land and Native People*, 514, https://sos.tn.gov/sites/default/files/Pgs.%20499-555%20State%20History.pdf.

10. William W. Barnes, *The Southern Baptist Convention, 1845–1953* (Nashville, Tenn.: Broadman Press, 1954), 19.

11. Ibid., 20.

12. Ibid., 21.

13. Ibid., quoting *Cross and Journal*, March 27, 1835, quoted from the *Baptist Magazine* (London).

14. Barnes, *Southern Baptist Convention*, 21.

15. *Baptist Banner and Western Pioneer*, October 14, 1841.

16. Barnes, *Southern Baptist Convention*, 22.

17. Ibid., 23.

18. Ibid., 22–23, citing *Baptist Banner and Western Pioneer*, November 26, 1840.

19. Ibid., 28.

20. Ibid., 25.

21. Wayne C. Bartee, "A History of the First Baptist Church of Springfield, Missouri, 1852–1977" (Unpublished, Missouri Historical Society, Columbia).

22. Albert Edmund Trombley, *Little Dixie* (Columbia: University of Missouri Studies, 1955), ix.

23. Ibid.; Robert M. Crisler, "Missouri's Little Dixie," *Missouri Historical Review* 17 (April 1948): 130–39.

24. R. S. Duncan, *A History of the Baptists in Missouri: Embracing an Account of the Organization and Growth of Baptist Churches and Associations; . . . the Founding of Baptist Institutions, Periodicals, etc.* (St. Louis: Scammell, 1882), 358.

25. James Gregory Clark, *History of William Jewell College: Liberty, Clay County, Missouri* (St. Louis: Central Baptist Print, 1893), 78–80.

26. See generally, Barnes *The Southern Baptist Convention*, which argues that the differences between Baptists in the North and South would have brought separation eventually, even if there had been no slavery-abolition issue. However, when the slave states voted as a bloc in Congress (and particularly in the Senate), threatening to disrupt the political balance, the slave issue became a political football as well as a moral issue. Ibid., 35.

27. Raboteau, *Slave Religion*, 103.

28. "Resolved, That in accordance with the sentiments of our denomination, all preachers of the gospel whom God approves must give evidence that they are born again by the Spirit, called of God to the work, and be set apart by ordination by the authority of the church," Missouri Baptist General Association, August 30, 1834. Duncan, *A History of the Baptists in Missouri*, 339.

## 17. CALLED TO SERVE

1. Green, *A Peculiar Imbalance*, 127–40.

2. Taylor, "Pilgrim's Progress," 26; *Minnesota Baptist State Convention Annual Report* (Minneapolis, 1900), 13; Spangler, *The Negro in Minnesota*, 52–54; WPA Slave Narratives, "Robert Hickman," box 230; *St. Paul Pioneer Press*, December 11, 1887; *St. Paul Daily Press*, November 7, 1863,

3. Thomas and Robert Hickman to (First Baptist Church), January 17, 1864, in Correspondence 1853–1878, 1889, First Baptist Church Papers, Minnesota Historical Society, St. Paul (hereafter FBC Papers). There were about twenty members in the congregation at the time of the petition.

4. *Annual Report of the Chair and Committee, 1859–73*, January 6, 1865, box 2, FBC Papers.

5. For example, Mrs. C. Moffett attended services on December 2, 1864, and Henrietta Murphy came on May 3, 1865. Church Record Book, FBC Papers.

6. Church Record Book, October 3, 1866, FBC Papers.

7. Cavender commenced blacksmithing and wagon building, expanding the business into the large carriage establishment Quinby and Hallowell. He cofounded First Baptist Church with Harriet Bishop. George C. Prescott was superintendent of schools, clerk of court of Ramsey County, and inspector of the St. Paul Board of Education. Sheire also served on the Board of Education from 1868 to 1876. Randall was an attorney and part owner of the Saint Paul and Pacific Railroad. J. Fletcher Williams, *A History of the City of Saint Paul to 1875* (St. Paul: Minnesota Historical Society Press, 1983), 196, 339; St. Paul Board of Education Journal, 1867–69, Minnesota Historical Society, St. Paul.

8. Membership Record Book, 1849–1874, FBC Papers.

9. *St. Paul Pioneer Press*, May 22, 1896; D. T. Magill, "The Merrill Family in Baptist Educational Affairs," *The Standard: A Baptist Newspaper*, August 10, 1907, 13 (1461).

10. Magill, "The Merrill Family," 12 (1460); *Minnesota Society of the Sons of the American Revolution: Year Book, 1889–1895*, compiled by William Henry Grant (St. Paul: McGill Printing, 1895), 369.

11. Magill, "The Merrill Family," 12.

12. Ibid.

13. Ibid., 13 (1461).

14. Ibid.

15. Ibid.

16. Church clerk William Wakefield recorded, "A request having been made by the Colored Baptists of this City, that the Trustees of the First Baptist Church and congregation receive in trust for them, the title of a certain lot on motion. [Voted] That the Trustees of First Baptist Church of St. Paul agree to assume payment of two hundred dollars and receive the title of the lot purchased of Charles Oakes by the Colored people in this City and hold the issue for a Colored Baptist Church, on motion, adjournment." Board of Trustees Minutes Book, 1858–1884, 72, FBC Papers.

17. Church Record Book, November 14, 1866, FBC Papers.

18. Ibid.

19. Reverend John R. Brown, *First Baptist Church: Seventy-Five Years, 1849–1924; Seventy-Fifth Anniversary* (St. Paul: First Baptist Church, 1924), 5 (hereafter *Seventy-Fifth Anniversary*, Brown's sermon), FBC Papers.

20. Williamson to Slade, 1846, Thomas S. Williamson Papers, 1839–1939, Minnesota Historical Society, St. Paul (hereafter Williamson Papers). The letter is also published in part in Lydia J. Rogers Gates, "History of the First Baptist Church of St. Paul, Minnesota," October 7, 1899, FBC Papers.

21. Williamson to Slade, 1846, Williamson Papers. Williamson may have been referring to the children of Jim Thompson, a former slave at Fort Snelling who was freed in 1837 by the Reverend Alfred Brunson, a Methodist missionary. Married to the daughter of Chief Cloudman, an influential Dakota leader in the area, Thompson was the first black man to reside in St. Paul. In 1849 he helped construct the First Methodist Church on Market Street, which probably became their place of worship. Green, *A Peculiar Imbalance*, 17–36.

22. Harriet Bishop, *Minnesota, Then and Now* (St. Paul: D. D. Merrill, Randall, 1869), Minnesota Historical Society PS1099.B78.M5 1869; Zylpha S. Morton, "Harriet Bishop, Frontier Teacher," *Minnesota History* 28, no. 2 (June 1947): 132–41.

23. History of First Baptist Church of St. Paul, https://blog.firstbaptiststpaul.org /history.

24. In Harriet Bishop's account she noted that when Abram Cavender arrived in St. Paul in 1848, the religious element in the village was greatly reinforced. "History of First Baptist Church of St. Paul & Societies, 1874–1880, by Mrs. H. E. Bishop," 68–69, FBC Papers. Also see J. Fletcher Williams, *The History of Saint Paul and of the County of Ramsey, Minnesota* (St. Paul: Minnesota Historical Society Press, 1983), 170.

25. The charter members were Bishop Deacon and Mrs. Cavender, Reverend and Mrs. Parson, Mr. and Mrs. Dayton, Mr. and Mrs. Stearns, Mr. and Mrs. John B. Spencer, Mrs. Samantha Easton, and William H. Townsend. Brown, *Seventy-Fifth Anniversary*, 17.

26. Ibid., Brown's sermon, 9–11.
27. Ibid., 11.
28. Ibid., 13.
29. Brown also surmised that the early church selected the American Baptist Home Society because the organization supplied practically all the money to pay the salary of the first pastor and, for fifteen years after the founding of the church, contributed in part to the salary. Ibid., 13–14.
30. David C. Laubach, *American Baptist Home Mission Roots, 1824–2010* (Valley Forge, Pa.: American Baptist Home Mission Societies, 2010).
31. Ibid.
32. Brown, *Seventy-Fifth Anniversary,* Brown's sermon, 11.

## 18. A CHURCH IS BORN AND A PASTOR IS FOUND

1. Raboteau, *Slave Religions,* 136–37.
2. Ibid., 231.
3. Ibid., 231–35, 237.
4. Jon Butler, "Communities and Congregations," is the only historian who refers to Norris's residing at the fort. Nothing in the census data—state or federal—listed him in St. Paul during this period. And none of the records at Fort Snelling indicate Norris was there. He is likely to have been an itinerant preacher who moved about and who happened to be at the fort when Hickman's group arrived. There is no evidence that Norris and Hickman conversed at Fort Snelling; but it is plausible that if Norris was there for the Indians, the boat intended to remove them from Minnesota had just delivered Hickman and his followers. Hickman's presence at the fort would have drawn Norris's attention, and Hickman's affiliation as a Baptist would have initiated a relationship between the two men.
5. *St. Paul Daily Press,* November 18, 1866.
6. *St. Paul Daily Press,* November 24, 1866.
7. Board of Trustees Minutes Book, 1857–1886, 78, FBC Papers.
8. Address delivered at the dedication of the new chapel of the First Baptist Church by Rev. J. A. Pope, 3–4, FBC Papers.
9. *St. Paul Pioneer Press,* June 1, 1875; Mary Ann Nord, *The National Register of Historic Places in Minnesota: A Guide* (St. Paul: Minnesota Historical Society Press, 2003).
10. Torbet biography, FBC Papers.
11. Church Correspondence and Related Records, May 3, 1853, FBC Papers.
12. Church Correspondence and Related Records, May 28, 1857, FBC Papers.
13. In 1861 the university was placed under the control of the Minnesota Baptist State Convention; it became a preparatory high school, which closed in 1867. By this time, however, Torbet, unable to secure another pastorate, had long been out of steady work. "Minnesota Academy through Pillsbury Military Academy, 1877–1957," by Jerry Ganfield, past president, Steele County Historical Society, Owatonna, Minn. (June 2001).
14. Minutes, Minnesota Baptist Convention, 1868, FBC Papers; *Winona Republican,* October 14, 1868.
15. Church minutes, Sunday, July 26, 1868, 17, FBC Papers.
16. "Festival in Mozart Hall Last Evening in Aid of the Pilgrim Baptist Church," *St. Paul Pioneer,* December 11, 1867.

17. "Fracas at the Pilgrim Festival," *St. Paul Pioneer*, December 12, 1867.

18. Paterson had arrived to be pastor of First Baptist on July 1, 1868. He succeeded John D. Pope, who in turn succeeded Torbet in 1857. Church Membership Record Book, 1849–1888, FBC Papers. It is likely that his reference to the purchase of the lot being set at five hundred dollars is a mistake, either by the pastor or the newspaper. Paterson was not in place at the time of the negotiations.

19. *St. Paul Pioneer*, February 5, 1868.

20. *St. Paul Daily Press*, August 4, 1868.

21. Ibid.

22. William Cathcart, *The Baptist Encyclopedia*, 3 vols. (Paris, Ark.: Baptist Standard Bearer, 2001), 2:98.

23. *St. Paul Daily Press*, September 13, 1868.

24. *St. Paul Dispatch*, September 14, 1868.

25. *St. Paul Daily Pioneer*, September 13, 15, 1868; *St. Paul Dispatch*, September 14, 1868.

## 19. UNDER HIS STEADY HAND

1. Blegen, *Minnesota*, 156.

2. Green, "The Long Road to Black Suffrage, 1849–1868," 69.

3. William Taylor and his wife, Adeline, arrived at Lowertown in 1850 from Galena, Illinois, He started a barbershop while surreptitiously conducting a branch of the Underground Railroad that ended in the Saintly City. Deborah Swanson, ed., "Joseph Farr Remembers the Underground Railroad in St. Paul," *Minnesota History*, Fall 2000, 123–29.

4. *Minnesota Territorial House Journal: Fifth Session of the Legislative Assembly, 1854* (St. Paul: Olmsted Territorial Printers, 1854), 255–56. Green, *A Peculiar Imbalance*, 68–69.

5. *St. Paul Daily Press*, May 16, 1863.

6. *Journal of the House of Representatives: Second Legislature of the State of Minnesota* (St. Paul: Newson, Moore, Foster, 1860), 242.

7. Ibid.; *St. Paul Daily Press*, February 8, 1863.

8. *St. Paul Daily Press*, October 4, 1864.

9. Green, *A Peculiar Imbalance*, 169–72.

10. *St. Paul Daily Press*, August 10, 1865.

11. St. Paul Board of Education Journal, 1867–1869, St. Paul, Ramsey County, School Records, Independent School District No. 625: An Inventory of its Miscellaneous School Materials, Government Records, Minnesota Historical Society, St. Paul.

12. *St. Paul Daily Press*, November 30, 1867.

13. St. Paul Board of Education Journal, 1867–1869.

14. The *Press* reported, "An Act was passed by the last legislature which abolishes schools for colored children in corporate town (which meant simply St. Paul) and hereafter they are to attend the public school." *St. Paul Daily Press*, March 14, 1869.

15. St. Paul Board of Education Journal, 1867–1869, April 1, 1867. FBC trustee Monroe Sheire succeeded Merrill (1867–68), serving from 1868 to 1870. George Prescott was appointed superintendent by Mayor George L. Otis. Ibid.

16. *St. Paul Daily Pioneer*, March 14, 1869.

17. *St. Paul Daily Pioneer*, April 13, 1869. For a reference to the admission examination, see St. Paul Board of Education Journal, 1867–1869, April 1869.

18. *St. Paul Daily Pioneer*, April 15, 1869.

19. St. Paul Board of Education Journal, 1868–1869, May 15, 1869.

20. Ibid.

21. Census of the State of Minnesota, 1865, extracted from the *Minnesota Secretary of State's Annual Report for 1865* (St. Paul: Minnesota Historical Society, 1865), 119; Libman "Minnesota and the Struggle for Black Suffrage: 1849–1870," 213, 215.

22. *St. Paul Pioneer*, November 6, 1867.

23. *St. Paul Pioneer*, November 7, 1867.

24. *St. Paul Pioneer*, November 6, 1867.

25. *St. Paul Pioneer*, October 21, 1868.

26. "Vote Down the Negro Amendment," *St. Paul Pioneer*, October 21, 1868.

27. *St. Paul Press*, September 14, 1868; *St. Paul Dispatch*, September 14, 1868; *St. Paul Pioneer*, September 13, 1868.

28. *St. Paul Pioneer*, September 13, 1868. For example, on October 17, the paper reported a fight between two inebriated black men. "A Colored Scrimmage," *St. Paul Pioneer*, October 17, 1868.

29. "Inspector" was the title for members of the Board of Education. St. Paul Board of Education Journal, 1867–1869.

30. "The Negro and His Northern Friends," *St. Paul Pioneer*, October 15, 1868.

31. "No Negro Suffrage in Minnesota," *St. Paul Pioneer*, October 28, 1868.

32. Rhoda R. Gilman, "Ramsey, Donnelly, and the Congressional Campaign of 1868," *Minnesota History*, December 1959, 300, 304, 305. The rumors of Wilkinson's interest in running against Ramsey were verified in the *St. Paul Pioneer*, November 14, 1868.

33. Gilman, "Ramsey, Donnelly," 304, 308; Green, *A Peculiar Imbalance*, 12, 67–68, 136, 202n28.

34. *St. Paul Pioneer*, November 12, 1868.

35. *Legislative Manual, 1869*, 89; *Legislative Manual, 1870*, 133; *St. Paul Pioneer*, November 11, 1868.

36. *St. Paul Pioneer*, November 14, 1868.

37. *St. Paul Daily Pioneer*, November 11, 1868.

38. *St. Paul Dispatch*, November 20, 1868.

39. *St. Paul Pioneer*, November 15, 1868.

40. Gilman, "Ramsey, Donnelly," 301.

41. *Proceedings of the Convention of Colored Citizens*, 16.

42. Ibid., 7.

43. Ibid., 6.

44. *St. Paul Weekly Pioneer*, January 8, 1869.

45. Rayford Logan, *The Betrayal of the Negro, 1877–1901* (New York: Collier Books, 1965), 57–58. Regarding coalition building by Minnesota Republicans during the 1850s, see Anderson, *History of the Constitution of Minnesota*, 40–41, 88.

46. *Knights of the Plow*, 109–15, 148.

47. *Proceedings of the Convention of Colored Citizens*, 10–11.

48. *St. Paul Pioneer*, January 8, 1869.

49. *St. Paul Weekly Pioneer*, March 26, 1869.

50. St. Paul city directories, 1863–1869; U.S. Census, 1870; Ramsey County Assessor, Ward 3, Minnesota Historical Society, St. Paul.

51. *St. Paul Weekly Press*, March 25, 1869; *Weekly Pioneer*, March 26, 1869.
52. *Minneapolis Tribune*, March 25, 1869; March 26, 1869.
53. St. Paul Board of Education Journal, 1867–1869.

## 20. TO BE IN GOD'S FAVOR

1. U.S. Bureau of the Census, *Census of the State of Minnesota, 1870*; C. C. Andrews, ed., *History of St. Paul, Minnesota* (Syracuse, N.Y.: D. Mason, 1890), 77; Taylor, "Pilgrim's Progress," 39–40.
2. U.S. Bureau of the Census, *Negro Population in the United States, 1790–1968*, 156.
3. U.S. Bureau of the Census, *U.S. Eleventh Census, 1890, Population, Part 1*, 465.
4. Taylor, "Pilgrim's Progress," 42, 43.
5. St. Clair Drake and Horace R. Cayton, *Black Metropolis: A Study of Negro Life in a Northern City*, 2 vols. (New York: Harper and Row, 1962), 2:620–21.
6. Ibid., 615–16.
7. *St. Paul Pioneer*, May 31, 1866; October 7, 1866.
8. Joseph Alexander, "Blacks in Minnesota: 1850–1870," 22–24, unpublished manuscript, 1970, box 375, Minnesota Ethnic History Project Papers, Minnesota Historical Society, St. Paul; U.S. Bureau of the Census, *Census of the State of Minnesota by County, Towns, Cities, and Wards, 1870*; Taylor, "Pilgrim's Progress," 31–32.
9. Taylor, "Pilgrim's Progress," 57–58.
10. Orrin Densmore to Daniel Densmore, April 28, 1864, Densmore Family Letters, Minnesota Historical Society, St. Paul. Also see Frederick L. Johnson, *Uncertain Lives: African Americans and Their First 150 Years in the Red Wing, Minnesota Area* (Red Wing: Goodhue County Historical Society, 2005), 20.
11. Taylor, "Pilgrim's Progress," 52n46, 58–61. In 1870 the white population in St. Paul numbered 20,354. In contrast, the black population numbered 207, of whom 111 were men and 96 were women. In 1875 the white population was 32,914. The black population numbered 264, of whom 148 were men and 116 were women. In 1885 the white population was 110,734. In contrast, blacks numbered 663, of whom 421 were men and 242 were women. *U.S. Tenth Census 1880, Population*, 420: U.S. Bureau of the Census, *Official Census of Minnesota 1890*, 17.
12. Taylor, "Pilgrim's Progress," 66.
13. Ibid.
14. St. James was the only black congregation formed in the city without connections to a white denomination. Its leaders gave little if any consideration to such relations. The nucleus of the congregation was formed in 1870 when the Indiana Conference for the denomination moved Thomas Wise from Chicago to organize a group in St. Paul, but his efforts in time would be unsuccessful, "for the city's Negroes either would not or could not support a second Negro congregation to compete with Pilgrim Baptist." By 1876 the church gained more support and slowly grew to over 100 members by 1900. Edward D. Neill, *History of Ramsey County and the City of St. Paul, Including the Explorers and Pioneers of Minnesota* (Minneapolis: North Star Publishing, 1881), 379; *St. Paul Appeal*, April 19, 1890; Butler, "Communities and Congregations," 122.
15. Butler, "Communities and Congregations," 124–25.
16. Ibid., 125.
17. In the absence of a record outlining the nature of their participation, several traits

characterizing their life experiences were similar to those of their counterparts, as
examined in Drake and Cayton's seminal work on the black experience in Chicago
during the 1930s. They came to the North from rural Southern communities where
their religious zeal was firmly established. They were Protestant, and the experience
I reference was that of Baptists. The women were poor, with little if any education,
unskilled workers, and church focused. Drake and Cayton, *Black Metropolis*, 2:619–20.

18. *St. Paul Press*, August 4, 1868; *Proceedings of the Convention of Colored Citizens*; see
generally, Mitchell Alan Kachun, *Festivals of Freedom: Memory and Meaning in
African American Celebrations, 1808–1915* (Amherst: University of Massachusetts
Press, 2006).

19. See generally, E. Franklin Frazier, *The Negro Church in America* (New York: Schocken
Books, 1963).

20. Organized under the leadership of the Reverend T. H. Gerry in 1867 it was officially
incorporated in 1868. Gerry was also the teacher in the black school that year. When
he died three years later, however, the church disbanded. Taylor, "Pilgrim's Progress," 29; St. Paul Board of Education Journal, 1867–1869; *St. Paul Pioneer*, December
11, 1887.

21. Spangler, *The Negro in Minnesota*, 55–56.

22. Butler, "Communities and Congregations," 121.

23. Emily O. Goodridge Grey, "The Black Community in Territorial St. Anthony: A
Memoir," *Minnesota History* 49 (Summer 1984): 49–50. For an account of the controversy faced by clergymen who preached antislavery sentiments from the pulpit, see
Charles W. Nichols, "Henry M. Nichols and Frontier Minnesota," *Minnesota History*
19 (September 1938): 254–55.

24. Nichols, "Henry M. Nichols," 255.

25. *St. Paul Daily Pioneer*, December 30, 1868.

26. *St. Paul Pioneer*, January 3, 1869; *St. Paul Weekly Pioneer*, January 8, 1869.

27. Minutes of the Thirteenth Anniversary of the Minnesota Baptist Association held
at the Baptist Church at Hastings, September 8–9, 1869, 10, 12, BX6470 M53.A315,
Minnesota Historical Society, St. Paul.

## 21. OF OTHER BAPTIST INTERESTS

1. Minutes of the Thirteenth Anniversary of the Minnesota Baptist Association held at
the Baptist Church at Hastings, September 8–9, 1869, 10, 12, Minnesota Historical
Society, St. Paul.

2. Ibid.

3. Ibid.

4. Ibid., 15.

5. Ibid., 13, 15.

6. Ibid., 4, 6, 7, 11.

7. Ibid., 11.

8. Harriet E. Bishop, *Floral Home; or, First Years of Minnesota* (New York: Sheldon,
Blakeman, 1857), 86.

9. "The Church's Work," sermon by Rev. Herbert F. Sitwell, in Brown, *Seventy-Fifth
Anniversary*, 29.

10. Ibid., 29–30.

11. *Minneapolis Daily Tribune*, January 4, 1870.

12. *St. Anthony Falls Democrat,* January 7, 1870; *St. Paul Daily Pioneer,* January 5, 1870.

13. Douglas E. Larson, "Private Alfred Gales: From Slavery to Freedom," *Minnesota History,* Summer 2001, 274, 281.

14. "The Church's Lord," sermon by Lemuel Call Barnes, in Brown, *Seventy-Fifth Anniversary,* 26.

15. For example, for several Sundays in February 1868, the Reverend John Adams from Chicago preached. *St. Paul Press,* February 5, 1868.

16. Gates, "History of First Baptist Church," 18.

17. "Festival in Mozart Hall Last Evening in Aid of the Pilgrim Baptist Church," *St. Paul Pioneer,* December 11, 1867. For more information about the fund-raiser, see chapter 18.

18. Gates, "History of First Baptist Church," 18.

19. Ibid.

20. Pastors served for various lengths of time: Cressey, 1 year 11 months; Torbet, 2 years 5 months; Pope, 9 years; Paterson, 3 years; Hulbert, 3 years; Cross, 3 years 11 months; Barnes, 3 years 9 months; Riddell, 2 years 9 months; Marie, 2 years 9 months; Butrick, 3 years 4 months. Brown, *Seventy-Fifth Anniversary,* 35–36.

21. Ibid., 19.

22. Ibid., 18–19.

23. Gates, "History of First Baptist Church," 19.

24. Ibid., 18.

25. *Minneapolis Tribune,* November 4, 1870; *St. Paul Dispatch,* November 4, 1870.

26. Entry in "Church History," by Alice K. Merrill (Mrs. D. D. Merrill) (undated), FBC Papers.

27. *St. Paul Dispatch,* November 5, 1870.

28. "Festival," *St. Paul Dispatch,* November 17, 1870.

29. *St. Paul Dispatch,* November 24, 1870. *Dispatch* and *Pioneer* accounts describe the festival as a benefit for colored Methodists and Baptists. This has to be a mistake in that no colored Methodist congregation existed in St. Paul at the time. In 1870 a handful of blacks had tried to establish St. James African Methodist Episcopal Society but they were committed to operating without any connections to white denominations. Though they had a good relationship with Pilgrim, the AME group languished until 1876. In 1870 the black community of St. Paul was too small to support two congregations. Butler, "Communities and Congregations," 122; Taylor, "Pilgrim's Progress," 161–62.

30. *St. Paul Pioneer,* November 24, 1870.

31. Taylor, "Pilgrim's Progress," 162.

32. *St. Paul Pioneer,* March 5, 1871; *St. Paul Press,* March 5, 1871; *St. Paul Dispatch,* March 4, 1871.

33. They would found the First Swedish Church, First German Church, Woodland Park Church, the Norwegian Danish Church, Philadelphian Church, Hebron Church, Immanuel Church, Burr Street Church, and Olivet Church in Minneapolis. In addition, First Baptist would establish the Walnut Street Mission, Fourth Avenue Mission, Ellen Street, Oakdale, Winnipeg Merriam Park, the Second Swedish Mission, Park Avenue, and the Union Stock Yards Mission. Brown, *Seventy-Fifth Anniversary,* 21.

34. Taylor, "Pilgrim's Progress," 163; Butler, "Communities and Congregations," 120.

## 22. CELEBRATION, 1875

1. Elizabeth Cady Stanton, Susan Brownell Anthony, and Matilda Joslyn Gage, eds., *History of Woman Suffrage*, vol. 3, *1876–1885* (New York: Arno Press, 1969), 649.
2. Ibid.; see also *St. Paul Pioneer Press*, October 17, 1875.
3. *St. Paul Pioneer Press*, October 17, 1875.
4. Ibid.

## 23. STANDING ALONE IN MINNESOTA

1. *Rochester Post*, February 3, 1866. Mitchell introduced H.F. No. 18 on January 15, 1866. House Journal 1866, 35.
2. Joseph A. Leonard, *History of Olmsted County, Minnesota* (Chicago: Goodspeed Historical Association, 1910), 49–50, 589–91.
3. In one such article, Stearns wrote about a woman who struggled to survive poverty while she witnessed four of her six children die of disease. Her desperate straits rendered the woman and her remaining children homeless. *Rochester Post*, December 8, 1866. In another article, Stearns reported on a speech she delivered at the Congregational church on the importance of educating women "as to render them independent of matrimony as means of obtaining a home." *Rochester Post*, December 8, 1866.
4. Stanton et al., *History of Woman Suffrage*, 3:649–50; Norma Summerdorf and Sheila Ahlbrund, "Sarah Burger Stearns," in *The Privilege for Which We Struggled: Leaders of the Woman Suffrage Movement in Minnesota*, ed. Heidi Bauer (St. Paul: Upper Midwest Women's History Center, 1999), 29–30.
5. "Universal Suffrage," *Rochester Post*, February 10, 1866.
6. Ibid.
7. Ibid. The petition read in part, "As you are now amending the Constitution, and, in harmony with advancing civilization, placing new safeguards around the individual rights of four million emancipated slaves, we ask that you extend the right of Suffrage to Women . . . and thus fulfill your constitutional obligation to guarantee to every State in the Union a Republican form of government." Also see Stanton et al., *History of Woman Suffrage*, 2:91.
8. "American Anti-Slavery Anniversary," *Standard*, May 3, 1865, 2.
9. "Special Meeting of the American Anti-Slavery Society in Boston, January 24, 1866," *Standard*, February 3, 1866. Stanton to Phillips, May 23, 1865, Stanton Letters, Radcliffe College, Cambridge, Mass. Ellen C. Dubois, *Feminism and Suffrage: Emergence of an Independent Women's Movement* (Ithaca, N.Y.: Cornell University Press, 1999), 105.
10. Anthony to Caroline Dall, January 20, 1866, Caroline Wesley Dall Family Letters, Massachusetts Historical Society, Boston; "Universal Suffrage." Emphasis added.
11. House and Senate Journal 1867, 24–26; *Mankato Union*, January 25, 1867.
12. "Suffrage," *Rochester Post*, December 8, 1866.
13. House Journal 1867, 109.
14. Ibid., 142.
15. "Woman's Rights," *St. Paul Press*, February 21, 1867.
16. House Journal 1867, 191.
17. Ibid., 198–99.
18. House Journal 1867, 199.
19. "Women's Suffrage Meeting," *St. Paul Press*, February 22, 1867.

20. Stanton et al., *History of Woman Suffrage*, 3:651.

21. "Women's Suffrage Meeting."

22. Lyn McCarthy, "Mary Jackman Colburn," in Bauer, *The Privilege for Which We Struggled*, 17. Also see Stanton et al., *History of Woman Suffrage*, 3:650.

## 24. THE LESSON OF KANSAS

1. Stanton et al., *History of Woman Suffrage*, 2:184.

2. Dubois, *Feminism and Suffrage*, 67.

3. See, for example, the comments of Edgar Cowens, Democratic senator from Pennsylvania, in congressional debates on suffrage during the December 1866–January 1867 session: Cong. Globe, 39 Cong., 2d Sess. (1866), 46–47. See also Stanton et al., *History of Woman Suffrage*, 2:103–51.

4. Dubois, *Feminism and Suffrage*, 76.

5. Stanton et al., *History of Woman Suffrage*, 2:322.

6. Ibid., 229.

7. Dubois, *Feminism and Suffrage*, 79–80.

8. Blackwell to Stanton, April 8, 1867, in Stanton et al., *History of Woman Suffrage*, 2:233.

9. Dubois, *Feminism and Suffrage*, 82, quoting Blackwell to Olympia Brown, June 8, 1867, Olympia Brown Willis Papers, call no. A-69; M-133, series III, correspondence 1855–1920, 128, Arthur and Elizabeth Schlesinger Library on the History of Women in America, Radcliffe Institute for Advanced Study, Harvard University, Cambridge, Mass.

10. Stone to Anthony, May 1, 1867, in Stanton et al., *History of Woman Suffrage*, 2:237.

11. Kathleen Barry, *Susan B. Anthony: A Biography* (New York: New York University Press, 1988), 170.

12. Stanton et al., *History of Woman Suffrage*, 2:238.

13. Blackwell to Stanton and Anthony, April 21, 1867, ibid., 2:236.

14. Henry Blackwell, "What the South Can Do," January 15, 1867, ibid., 2:929–81. Also see Benjamin Quarles, "Frederick Douglass and the Woman's Rights Movement," *Journal of Negro History* 25 (January 1940): 35, 40n23.

15. Dubois, *Suffrage and Feminism*, 68–69.

16. Ibid., 92–93, citing Blackwell to Olympia Brown, June 12, 1867.

17. Stanton et al., *History of Woman Suffrage*, 2:243.

18. Henry Blackwell, *The Woman's Journal* (Boston), March 11, 1899.

19. Barry, *Susan B. Anthony*, citing Isabella Beecher Hooker to Susan Howard, January 2, 1870, from notes she took during her meeting with Blackwell in December 1869.

20. Dubois, *Feminism and Suffrage*, 94.

21. Ibid., 95, citing Anthony to Dickinson, November 28, 1867. Emphasis in the original.

22. Stanton et al., *History of Woman Suffrage*, 2:264.

23. Dubois, *Feminism and Suffrage*, 94.

24. Ibid., 95–96.

25. *Rochester Post*, October 26, 1867.

26. *St. Paul Press*, January 11, 1868.

27. House Journal, 1868, 41, 47; *St. Paul Press*, January 24, 1868.

28. Stanton et al., *History of Woman Suffrage*, 2:310.

29. Andrew Johnson, a Tennessee Democrat who supported slavery and despised seces-

sion, became president upon the assassination of President Lincoln. The Radicals, frustrated at the moderate reconstruction policies that Lincoln supported, thought they had in Johnson a man who would support their more hard-line views. When Johnson switched course he offered general amnesty to former Confederates and vetoed legislation that extended civil rights and financial support to former slaves, much of which Congress could not override. This set the stage for the impeachment confrontation between Congress and the president. On February 24, 1868, the House of Representatives approved a resolution to impeach the president for high crimes and misdemeanors, and three weeks later, on March 13, the trial began in the Senate. In May, in the midst of considerable political maneuvering, the Senate acquitted Johnson. David O. Stewart, *Impeached: The Trial of President Andrew Johnson and the Fight for Lincoln's Legacy* (New York: Simon and Schuster, 2009), 207–12. See generally, Eric McKitrick, *Andrew Johnson and Reconstruction* (Chicago: University of Chicago Press, 1960); Hans L. Trefousse, *Andrew Johnson: A Biography* (New York: W. W. Norton, 1989).

30. For the exchange involving Olympia Brown, Frederick Douglass, and Lucy Stone, see Stanton et al., *History of Woman Suffrage*, 2:310–12. See also Philip S. Foner, *Frederick Douglass on Women's Rights* (Westport, Conn.: Da Capo Press, 1976), 83–85.
31. Dubois, *Feminism and Suffrage*, 169, 172.
32. Stanton et al., *History of Woman Suffrage*, 2:341.
33. Barry, *Susan B. Anthony*, 194.
34. *Mankato Union*, October 23, 1868; October 30, 1868.
35. *Mankato Union*, October 16, 1868.
36. Dubois, *Feminism and Suffrage*, 166.
37. "Woman Suffrage," *New York World*, November 19, 1868, 5.

## 25. THE TIBBETTS PETITION

1. A discussion of this campaign will appear in part VI.
2. *St. Paul Dispatch*, February 5, 1869.
3. House Journal 1869, 75. The vote was a loss, pursuant to the rules of the legislature. The issue could be brought back in a later session, however. The question could only return for a vote during the same legislative session if one side won the vote, and a member of the winning side chose to bring the question back to the floor for reconsideration. That was not the case here.
4. *St. Paul Dispatch*, February 12, 1869.
5. Ibid.
6. Martin Ridge, *Ignatius Donnelly: The Portrait of a Politician* (Chicago: University of Chicago Press, 1962), 108.
7. *St. Paul Dispatch*, February 15, 1869. Emphasis in the original.
8. The National Woman Suffrage Association held its first convention one month earlier in Washington, D.C. Immediately after the convention, Stanton and Anthony toured the western states, speaking at various points in Missouri, Illinois, Wisconsin, and Ohio, having been invited to attend several state conventions, of which Chicago (February 12), was one. Stanton et al., *History of Woman Suffrage*, 2:364–69.
9. House Journal 1869, 116, 146, 157, 161–62.
10. *St. Paul Dispatch*, March 5, 1869.
11. Ibid.
12. In 1866 Mrs. Bancroft took over the *Mantorville Express* upon the death of her

husband. Of the then-new editor, Stearns wrote, "One substantial act on the part of a woman is worth more than many speeches of strong-willed lecturesses in bringing about the 'good time coming' when an intelligent woman will be the equal of a man at the ballot." *Rochester Post,* August 9, 1866. See also "Newspapers," Dodge County History, http://www.co.dodge.mn.us/Government_and_Links/DODGE _COUNTY_HISTORY.pdf, retrieved on October 20, 2016.

13. *St. Paul Dispatch,* March 5, 1869.

14. House Journal 1869, 200–201, 214.

15. *St. Paul Dispatch,* February 26, 1869.

16. House Journal 1869, 226, 249; "List of the House of Representatives," *Legislative Manual, 1869.*

17. *St. Paul Pioneer,* February 25, 1869; February 27, 1869.

18. *St. Paul Dispatch,* February 25,1869.

19. Dubois, *Feminism and Suffrage,* 177–78.

20. Stanton et al., *History of Woman Suffrage,* 2:335.

21. "A Swedish woman nineteen years old and married just from her native country, was brutally outraged by a negro in St. Paul last Friday. The negro under pretense of obtaining a situation for her in a family, persuaded her to accompany him a short distance, out on the Stillwater road, and led her off into a ravine where he violated her person. The police have arrested a person named Taylor Combs who was identified by three witnesses as being the person who decoyed the woman away, but Combs claims an alibi even that he was at Lake Como at the time the outrage occurred. About one hundred Swedes collected around the jail on Saturday night with the intention of lynching him, but with the jailor shutting the door against them, and threatening to shoot, they adjourned the hanging indefinitely.

   "The *Pioneer* says that while the crowd was outside banging on the door, a little negro who is in the jail for some minor offense, became terribly frightened. He feared the crowd would get in and get hold of the wrong nigger. He accordingly begged like a good fellow to be locked up in the 'safe.'" *Rochester Post,* June 18, 1869.

22. Dubois, *Feminism and Suffrage,* 68.

23. Ibid., 68–69, citing "Letter from Gage," *Standard,* July 21, 1866, 2; also see "Shall Women Vote?," *New York World,* December 9, 1866.

24. Purvis and Harper served on the finance committee, primarily responsible for solicit-ing donations to cover organizational expenses; Griffith served as a corresponding secretary, a position normally held by whites, which she shared with Anthony, who did most of the work. The black men who served as vice presidents performed primar-ily symbolically. No blacks served on the powerful business committee, which drew up the resolutions, and only George Downing served on the executive committee. Dubois, *Feminism and Suffrage,* 70. Also see August Meier and Elliot Rudwick, "The Role of Blacks in the Abolitionist Movement," in *Blacks in the Abolitionist Movement,* ed. John Bracey, August Meier, and Elliot Rudwick (Belmont, Calif.: Wadsworth, 1971), 108–22.

## 26. MARRIED WOMEN'S RIGHTS AND THE "KING OF MANOMIN"

1. House Journal 1869, 154, 155, 165, 183, 296, 340, 343, 357.

2. The act stated in part, "All property, real, personal and mixed, and choses in action,

owned by any married woman, or owned or held by any woman at the time of her marriage, shall continue to be her separate property notwithstanding her marriage."

3. General Statute of the State of Minnesota, chapter 69, section 1, 1869.

4. "Women Rights," *Rochester Post*, June 5, 1869.

5. House Journal 1869, 249, 358.

6. Melvin Urofsky and Paul Finkelman, *A March of Liberty: A Constitutional History of the United States*, vol. 1, *From the Founding to 1900* (New York: Oxford University Press, 2011), 340.

7. Stanton et al., *History of Woman Suffrage*, 3:651.

8. Ethel Edgerton Hurd, "A Brief History of the Political Equality Cub in Minneapolis," February 23, 1921, Political Equality Club of Minneapolis Records, P1503, box 1, vi, Minnesota Historical Society, St. Paul.

9. Mrs. A. H. Bright, "Experience in Minnesota" (1914), Political Equality Club of Minneapolis Records, Historical Data, 1914–1918, P1503, box 1.

10. *Rochester Post*, October 30, 1869.

11. *Rochester Post*, November 27, 1869; December 4, 5, 25, 1869.

12. "The R.W.S. Association has just received a package of woman's suffrage tracts written by the following persons, and on the following topics: 'Woman's Rights and the Public Welfare' by the Honorable George B. Hoar, 'Ought Women to Learn the Alphabet?' by T. W. Higginson, 'Equal Rights for Women' by George Curtis, 'Women's Influence in Politics' by Henry Ward Beecher, and 'Suffrage for Women' by John Stuart Mill. Those willing for copies for perusal may obtain them of the Secretary at Good Templar Hall, on Saturday, January 8, between 4 and 5 pm, this being the time appointed after the regular meeting of this Association.—S. B. Stearns, Sec'y." *Rochester Post*, December 4, 1869, January 8, 22, 1870; Stanton et al., *History of Woman Suffrage*, 3:65. See also Barbara Stuhler, *Gentle Warriors: Clara Ueland and the Minnesota Struggle for Woman Suffrage* (St. Paul: Minnesota Historical Society Press, 1995), 21; Barbara Stuhler, "Organizing the Vote: Leaders of Minnesota's Woman Suffrage Movement," *Minnesota History*, Fall 1995, 293.

13. *St. Paul Press*, January 8, 1870.

14. Ibid.

15. *St. Paul Press*, January 14, 1870.

16. David H. Donald, ed., *Inside Lincoln's Cabinet: The Civil War Diaries of Salmon P. Chase* (New York: Longmans, Green, 1954), 264–66.

17. *St. Paul Press*, February 16, 1870.

18. Journal of the House and Senate 1870, 29, 40.

19. *St. Paul Press*, February 10, 1870.

20. *St. Paul Daily Press*, February 12, 1870.

21. Ibid.

22. Ibid.

23. House Journal 1869, 249, 358.

24. Merle Potter, "Major Fridley's Kingdom of Manomin," *Minneapolis Journal*, September 4, 1932, magazine section, 3, 5.

25. *Rochester Post*, July 24, 1868.

26. County of Manomin, described in General Statute, was abolished, and the territory attached to Anoka County by Constitutional amendment, adopted 1869. See Const.

Art. 11, Sec. 7. General Statute of State of Minnesota, as amended by subsequent Title I, Sec. 1.

27. *Rochester Post,* November 27, 1869.
28. *St. Paul Daily Press,* February 16, 1870.
29. House Journal, February 15, 1870, 165–66.
30. *St. Paul Daily Press,* February 16, 1870.
31. *St. Paul Daily Press,* February 19, 1879.
32. In fact, Senator Henry Charles Waite of St. Cloud had initially "presented a petition from the citizens of St. Cloud, relating to woman suffrage, which was read and on motion, referred to the committee on entrenchment and reform." Journal of the House and Senate, 1870, 49.
33. *St. Paul Daily Press,* February 19, 1870; *St. Paul Daily Pioneer,* February 19, 1870.
34. *St. Paul Daily Press,* February 22, 1879; Minnesota Legislators Past and Present.
35. *St. Paul Daily Pioneer,* February 25, 1870.
36. *St. Paul Daily Press,* February 22, 1870; *St. Paul Daily Pioneer,* February 25, 1870.
37. *Rochester Post,* March 4, 1870.
38. *St. Paul Press,* February 19, 1870; February 22; February 25.
39. Frances Russell (a.k.a. Faith Rochester from Silver Lake, Minnesota), *Woman's Journal* (Boston and Chicago), April 2, 1870, 99, M-film 4239, Wilson Library, University of Minnesota.
40. Ibid.
41. Ibid.
42. Ibid.
43. *St. Paul Daily Pioneer,* March 11, 1870.

## 27. VETO!

1. Austin added: "There is yet but little or no evidence or manifestation of any public sentiment among the people at large in this State in favor of this proposed change, and it is attempted by this act to force a question upon the people, and inaugurate a campaign upon an issue which they have not made, and in which they have manifested no interest. I deem the bill not in conformity to the Constitution in some of its provisions, and premature." *St. Paul Daily Pioneer,* March 13, 1870.
2. *Rochester Post,* March 12, 1870.
3. *Rochester Post,* April 2, 1870.
4. *St. Paul Daily Pioneer,* March 13, 1870. Emphasis added.
5. "Governor Austin's Error," *St. Paul Weekly Dispatch,* March 15, 1870.
6. "The Female Suffrage Bill," *St. Paul Daily Press,* March 13, 1870.
7. Stanton et al., *History of Woman Suffrage,* 3:651.
8. Stuhler, *Gentle Warriors,* 21–22.
9. "The Minnesota Legislature," *Woman's Journal,* April 2, 1870, 100.
10. "Rochester," *Woman's Journal,* April 2, 1870, 100. Emphasis added.
11. "Letter from Mary Colburn," *St. Paul Weekly Dispatch,* April 1, 1870.

## 28. BACK TO WORK

1. Dubois, *Feminism and Suffrage,* 134–35nn17 and 18.
2. "The anti-negro slavery object of my paper seemed to be lost sight of, both by friends and foes of human progress, in the surprise at the innovation of a woman entering the

political arena, to argue publicly on great questions of national policy, and while men were defending their pantaloons, they created and spread the idea, that masculine supremacy lay in the form of their garments, and that a woman dressed like a man would be as potent as he. Strange as it may now seem, they succeeded in giving such efficacy to the idea, that no less a person than Mrs. Elizabeth Cady Stanton was led astray by it, so that she set her cool, wise head to work and invented a costume, which she believed would emancipate woman from thraldom. Her invention was adopted by her friend, Mrs. Bloomer, editor and proprietor of the *Lily,* a small paper then in infancy in Syracuse, N.Y., and from her, the dress took its name—'the bloomer.' Both women believed in their dress, and staunchly advocated it as the sovereignest remedy for all the ills that woman's flesh is heir to. I made a suit and wore it at home parts of two days, long enough to feel assured that it must be a failure, and so opposed it earnestly, but nothing I could say or do, could make it apparent that pantaloons were not the real objective point, at which all discontented women aimed. I had once been tried on a charge of purloining pantaloons, and had been acquitted for lack of evidence; but now, here was the proof! The women themselves, leaders of the malcontents, promulgated and pressed their claim to bifurcated garments and the whole tide of popular discussion was turned into that ridiculous channel." Swisshelm, *Half A Century,* 140–41.

3. "Women's Typographical Union," *Revolution,* October 15, 1868, 231.
4. "The Case of Hester Vaugh," *Revolution,* December 10, 1868, 357–58.
5. "Hester Vaughn," *Revolution,* November 19, 1868, 312.
6. Stanton, "Hester Vaughn," *Revolution,* December 10, 1868, 360.
7. Dubois, *Feminism and Suffrage,* 147–48.
8. Ibid.
9. Ibid., 151.
10. "Working Women's Association," *New York World,* April 9, 1869.
11. Dubois, *Feminism and Suffrage,* 155.
12. Dubois surmises that employers may have even manipulated Anthony into making such a proposal (155)
13. "The Printers' Strike," *Nation,* February 11, 1869, 108–9.
14. Dubois, *Feminism and Suffrage,* 158.
15. Ibid., 161.
16. "Call to All Hands," *Revolution,* August 26, 1869, 113–14.
17. *Rochester Post,* April 2, 1870; *St. Paul Daily Dispatch,* March 18, 1870.
18. Dubois, *Feminism and Suffrage,* 195.
19. *Rochester Post,* February 26, 1870.
20. *Rochester Post,* March 19, 1870.
21. *Rochester Post,* November 27, 1869.
22. *Rochester Post,* March 12, 1870.
23. *Rochester Post,* April 4, 1870.
24. Stanton et al., *History of Woman Suffrage,* 3:658. By 1883 Stearns had organized in Wayzata, Farmington, Red Wing, Mantorville, Excelsior, Richland, Lake City, Shakopee, and Jordan. Ibid.
25. The House approved the new law with a vote of 63 to 30; she was finally admitted one year later. See Magistrate Judge Susan Richard Nelson, "Law by Women in Minnesota."
26. Stanton et al., *History of Woman Suffrage,* 3:653–54. Charlotte Ouisconsin Van Cleve,

"*Three Score Years and Ten*": *Life-Long Memories of Fort Snelling, Minnesota, and Other Parts of the West* (1888). The characterization of General Van Cleve is quoted from *Rochester Post*, March 12, 1870.

27. Stanton et al., *History of Woman Suffrage*, 3:652, 654.

28. Stuhler, *Gentle Warriors*, 81.

29. Ramsey to Anne Ramsey, January 9, 1870; Anne Ramsey to Ramsey, January 23, February 12, 17, 1870, Ramsey Papers, roll 19, frame nos. 00063–64, 00091, 00121, 00163.

30. *St. Paul Daily Press*, November 14, 1870.

## 29. A CURIOUS VOTE ON THE BUTLER BILL

1. Cong. Globe, 41th Cong., 2d Sess., 1769.

2. Foner, *Reconstruction*, 422–25.

3. Ibid., 426–28.

4. Franklin, *Reconstruction after the Civil War*, 63–64.

5. Foner, *Reconstruction*, 342.

6. Ibid.

7. Ibid., 344.

8. Avery Craven, *Reconstruction: The Ending of the Civil War* (New York: Holt, Rinehart, Winston, 1969), 244; Foner, *Reconstruction*, 423.

9. Cong. Globe, 41st Cong., 2d Sess., 1767–68, 69.

10. Ibid., 1770.

11. Donnelly was finishing his term in Congress after losing to Eugene Wilson, who won with Ramsey's support. By now, Donnelly had begun attacking the party for its support of railroad and monopoly interests.

12. In a letter to his wife dated November 22, 1868, Donnelly wrote, "I will meet Wilkinson on Saturday in St. Paul and arrive home at Sunday. . . . If Wilk and I can agree I shall consider success certain." Donnelly to Kate Donnelly, November 22, 1868, Donnelly Papers, M138, reel 40, Minnesota Historical Society, St. Paul (hereafter Donnelly Papers).

13. Fred Driscoll to Ramsey, December 9, 1868. Ramsey Papers, M203, reel 16, frame 00816.

14. *St. Paul Weekly Dispatch*, January 22, 1869.

15. *H. P. Hall's Observations*, 104. Historians are more critical of Wilkinson, characterizing him as an opportunist who betrayed his friend Donnelly. Ridge, *Ignatius Donnelly*, 123. Also see Folwell, *A History of Minnesota*, 3:16–17. Nothing in Donnelly's papers indicates that he harbored a grudge against Wilkinson, and more likely felt, as his wife had stated, that the greater importance to him was to see Ramsey lose. Ridge, *Ignatius Donnelly*, 123.

16. Cong. Globe, 37th Cong., 2d Sess., 2840.

17. Ibid., 2857.

18. Cong. Globe, 41st Cong., 2d Sess., 1766.

19. Wilkinson would argue this point in the state Senate in 1875.

20. Cong. Globe, 41st Cong., 2d Sess., 1765–66.

21. Folwell, *A History of Minnesota*, 3:73.

22. *Winona Republican*, September 23, 1870.

23. *Winona Republican*, October 3, 1870.

24. *St. Paul Weekly Dispatch*, September 20, 1870.

25. *Minneapolis Tribune*, September 21, 1870.

26. Ibid.

27. *St. Paul Weekly Pioneer*, September 30, 1870.

28. Ibid.

29. Ibid.

30. *St. Paul Press*, September 22, 1870; September 24, 1870; *St. Paul Weekly Dispatch*, September 20, 1870.

31. *Minneapolis Tribune*, September 22, 1870.

32. *Winona Republican*, September 26, 1870.

33. *Mankato Weekly Record*, October 1, 1870.

34. "The Difference," *Weekly Pioneer*, October 28, 1870.

35. Some of the House members were Wilkinson; William Loughridge and William Allison, Iowa; Sidney Clarke, Kansas; Ebon Ingersoll, Illinois; Halbert Paine and Cadwallader Washburn, Wisconsin; William Prosser, Tennessee; and Aaron Sargent, California. *Winona Republican*, December 9, 1870.

36. Ibid.

37. Ibid.

38. *H. P. Hall's Observations*, 73.

39. *Weekly Pioneer*, January 6, 13, 1871.

40. Folwell, *History of Minnesota*, 3:73; Dwight E. Woodbridge and John S. Pardee, eds., "Bench and Bar," in *History of Duluth and St. Louis County, Past and Present*, 2 vols. (Chicago: C. F. Cooper, 1910), 2:567–76.

41. *H. P. Hall's Observations*, 73.

42. Woodbridge and Pardee, "Bench and Bar," 2:572.

43. *Winona Republican*, January 5, 1871.

44. *Weekly Pioneer*, December 2, 1870.

45. *Winona Republican*, March 1, 1871.

46. Cong. Globe, 39th Cong., 2d Sess., 1133–482, 561. See also Martin Ridge, "Ignatius Donnelly: Minnesota Congressman, 1863–1869," *Minnesota History*, March 1959, 173–83.

47. *Weekly Pioneer*, December 12, 1870.

48. Cong. Globe, 41st Cong., 3d Sess., 1762; David Achtenberg, "A 'Milder Measure of Villainy': The Unknown History of 42 U.S.C. Sec. 1983 and the Meaning of 'Under Color of' Law," *Utah Law Review* 1999 (1999): 7–9.

49. Achtenberg, "A 'Milder Measure of Villainy,'" 10.

50. The other two Republicans were Illinois representative John F. Farnsworth and Nevada representative Thomas Fitch, *Biographical Directory of the United States Congress: 1774–2005* (Washington, D.C.: Government Printing Office, 2005); Achtenberg, "A 'Milder Measure of Villainy,'" 10, citing "Washington," *New York World*, March 1, 1871; Cong. Globe, 41st Cong., 3d Sess., 1762.

51. Israel Wilkinson, *Memoirs of the Wilkinson Family in America: Comprising Genealogical and Biographical Sketches of Lawrence Wilkinson of Providence, R.I., Edward Wilkinson of New Milford, Conn., John Wilkinson of Attleborough, Mass., Daniel Wilkinson of Columbia Co., N.Y. . . . and Their Descendants from 1645–1868* (Jacksonville, Ill.: Davis and Penniman, 1869), 288; *Mankato: Its First Fifty Years*, 346.

52. Although the Ku Klux Klan Act was ultimately approved during the Forty-Second Congress, after Grant finally endorsed the measure, Democrats obstructed passage at

every turn. Act of April 20, 1871, chapter 22, sec. 1, 17 Stat. 13. The Ku Klux Klan Act was sometimes called the Civil Rights Act of 1871.

53. House Bill No. 1825 was a bill for the improvement of water communications between the Mississippi River and Lake Michigan via the Wisconsin and Fox Rivers. House Bill No.1484 was a bill to establish a post road between Faribault and Glencoe in the state of Minnesota. Cong. Globe, 41st Cong., 2d Sess. (1870), 1813, respectively.

54. Cong. Globe, 37th Cong., 3d Sess. (1862), 3147.

55. *Proceedings of the Convention of Colored Citizens,* 18.

## 30. WHERE THE LIBERALS WENT

1. See *St. Paul Weekly Dispatch,* April 26, 1872. See also Robert Burg, "Amnesty, Civil Rights, and the Meaning of Liberal Republicanism, 1862–1872," *American Nineteenth Century History* 4, no. 3 (2003): 29–60; James McPherson, "Grant or Greeley? The Abolitionist Dilemma in the Election of 1872," *American Historical Review* 71, no. 1 (1965): 43–61.

2. *Mankato Union,* May 3, 1872; *H. P. Hall's Observations,* 110.

3. *Mankato Union,* May 10, 1872; *H. P. Hall's Observations,* 110.

4. See generally, Burg, "Amnesty, Civil Rights, and the Meaning of Liberal Republicanism"; McPherson, "Grant or Greeley?"

5. Delegates were so dispirited by Greeley's nomination that they openly disparaged the high-minded pretensions of the party, especially as reflected in the manner in which their candidate had been selected. Matthew T. Downey, "Horace Greeley and the Politicians: The Liberal Republican Convention in 1872," *Journal of American History* 53, no. 4 (March 1967): 727.

6. *Mankato Union,* June 7, 1872.

7. Ridge, *Ignatius Donnelly,* 142.

8. Ibid., 144.

9. Donnelly diary, May 29, 1872, Donnelly Papers.

10. Ridge, *Ignatius Donnelly,* 145.

11. Ibid., citing Greeley letter to Donnelly, August 29, 1872, Donnelly Papers.

12. *H. P. Hall's Observations,* 110–12.

13. Ridge, *Ignatius Donnelly,* 148.

14. White et al., *Minnesota Votes.*

15. Gilman, "April 1861," 212.

16. Wilkinson had employed the same tactics in the 1868 congressional campaign. See, for example, *Mankato Union,* October 24, 1868, 2. After James H. Baker, the Democratic candidate, criticized the economic policies of the Republican Party, Wilkinson spent his time reminding the audience that it was the Democrats who started the Civil War.

17. Douglass to Amy Post, July 18, 1872, Frederick Douglass Papers, University of Rochester Frederick Douglass Research Project, letter 117.

18. William S. McFeely, *Frederick Douglass* (New York: W. W. Norton, 1991), 276–77. In June 1870 Sumner, chair of the Foreign Relations Committee, picked up votes to defeat the annexation treaty. In an effort to circumvent the senator, Grant asked the commission to visit Santo Domingo (sometimes referred as the Dominican Republic) and submit the expected favorable report to Congress. Its members were former senator Benjamin Wade of Ohio, Andrew D. White, the president of Cornell University,

and Samuel Gridley Howe of Massachusetts, who was appointed as a ploy to gain leverage over Sumner, his old friend. The appointment of Douglass, another friend of Sumner and compatriot in bygone abolitionist campaigns, was intended to create further pressure on the Senate committee chair; but instead, appointing Douglass as the "assistant secretary" to Allen A. Burton only illustrated Grant's trivial regard for the black leader. Despite the appointments of Douglass and Howe that Grant hoped would soften Sumner's opposition, the treaty fell short of the required votes to pass, with Congress rejecting the recommendation in bipartisan opposition. The Dominicans, likewise, rejected the proposal. McFeely, *Frederick Douglass,* 276; *Dominican Republic: Report of the Commission of Inquiry to Santo Domingo* (Washington, D.C.: Government Printing Office, 1871), 35; Cong. Globe, 41st Cong., 3d Session, 427–28; Foner, *Reconstruction,* 494–95.

19. McFeely, *Frederick Douglass,* 277.
20. Ibid.
21. "Has the Republican Party Accomplished Its Mission?," a speech he delivered on November 10, 1870, in Rochester City Hall, Rochester, N.Y.
22. McFeely, *Frederick Douglass,* 279.
23. David W. Blight, *Frederick Douglass' Civil War: Keeping Faith in Jubilee* (Baton Rouge: Louisiana State University Press, 1989), 213–14.
24. Ibid., 214.
25. Ibid.
26. Melvin Urofsky and Paul Finkelman, *A March of Liberty: A Constitutional History of the United States,* vol. 2, *From 1898 to the Present* (New York: Oxford University Press, 2002), 522.
27. In 1877 the U.S. Supreme Court upheld an Illinois statute that fixed rates for railroads. Munn v. Illinois, 94 U.S 113 (1877).
28. Cong. Globe, 41st Cong., 1st Sess., 871–72. Speech on congressional control of railroads, January 29, 1870.
29. *St. Paul Press,* March 4, 1873.
30. *St. Paul Press,* February 8, 1873.
31. Ibid.
32. For a full account see Green, *Degrees of Freedom,* chapter 4.
33. *St. Paul Daily Pioneer,* May 15, 1873; May 16, 1873.
34. "Five large, healthy colored sisters were baptized in the Mississippi River on Sunday last. Several good jokes were traveling about town at the expense of the ceremony. One heavy lady was so unfortunate as to be batized [*sic*] too much, in consequence of falling from the clergyman's grasp. It is in bad taste to make light of any ceremony, however imperfectly performed, which is sacred to others, still we apprehend that nothing evil was intended by those who make light of this otherwise *dark* affair." *St. Paul Daily Pioneer,* May 14, 1870.
    Under the title "Colored Pic-Nig-Gers": "The Fifteenth Amendments of this City and St. Anthony celebrated the anniversary of Emancipation in the West Indies, yesterday, by an excursion and a pic-nic at Minnehaha. . . . They would have gone to White Bear, but for the existing prejudice against the color of such Bear. About two hundred of the sons and daughters of Ham (not cold yesterday) from this city and St. Anthony participated, and a large

number from St. Paul joined them at the Falls. They enjoyed the day largely, and came home with their teeth clattering." *St. Paul Daily Pioneer*, August 2, 1871.

35. The *St. Paul Press* published advertisements for Maurice Jernigan until 1872. The old Settlers' Association is covered in the *Press*, June 3, 1873, 2, col. 1. For more about Thompson, see Green, *A Peculiar Imbalance*.

36. "1st Colored Juror in Duluth," *Minneapolis Tribune*, December 23, 1871; "Colored Picnic," *Minneapolis Tribune*, June 29, 1872; "Another Church," *Duluth Daily Tribune*, July 15, 1872; "Colored Templar: Colored People Become Interested in Special Temperance Work," *St. Paul Daily Press*, October 19, 1872.

37. *St. Paul Daily Pioneer*, January 22, 1873 (first colored juryman in Anoka County); *St. Paul Daily Pioneer*, March 26, 1873 (colored Tennesseans give concert in Opera House to raise funds for a colored university); *St. Paul Daily Pioneer*, March 29, 1874 (colored citizens celebrate Fifteenth Amendment); *St. Paul Daily Dispatch*, June 25, 1874 (colored concert at First Baptist Church); *Minneapolis Tribune*, September 24, 1875 (colored concert in Minneapolis); *St. Paul Daily Dispatch*, February 25, 1875 (colored literary society established); *Minneapolis Tribune*, April 24, 1875 (colored citizens hold a spelling bee in Minneapolis).

38. Taylor, "Blacks," 76.

39. Ibid., 74.

40. Until the mid-1860s the black population was distributed throughout St. Paul's five wards. But by the late 1860s, blacks began concentrating in the commercial district in Lowertown; one newspaper editor called the area "a negro rookery." Ibid., 76.

41. *Mankato Union*, August 29, 1973. There was also reason to believe that the Republicans had endorsed Davis to thwart the growing power of the Anti-Monopoly Party. Woods, *Knights of the Plow*, 155.

42. Ibid.

43. *Mankato Union*, September 21, 1873.

44. *Mankato Union*, October 10, 1873.

45. Folwell, *Minnesota*, 2:47; Ridge, *Ignatius Donnelly*, 152–54.

46. *Mankato Union*, October 24, 1873.

47. *Mankato Union*, October 31, 1873.

48. *Mankato Union*, November 11, 1873.

49. *New Ulm Herald*, November 18–20, 1873; Folwell, *History of Minnesota*, 3:49.

## 31. HIS UNCLASSIFIABLE HEAD

1. Betty Kane, "A Case Study in Lively Futility: The 1876 Legislature," *Minnesota History*, Summer 1977, 225, 232.

2. Nydahl, "The Diary of Ignatius Donnelly," 372–73.

3. *St. Paul Pioneer Press*, January 5, 1876.

4. Kane, "A Case Study in Lively Futility," 225, 232; *St. Paul Pioneer Press*, January 5, 6, 1876.

5. Senate Journal, 1876, 15.

6. Ridge, *Ignatius Donnelly*, 129–30; Kane, "A Case Study in Lively Futility," 225.

7. Most of Blue Earth County escaped the grasshoppers in 1873. Annette Atkins, *Harvest of Grief: Grasshopper Plagues and Public Assistance in Minnesota, 1873–78* (St. Paul: Minnesota Historical Society Press, 1984), 16.

8. Henry Castle would be in the legislature in 1873, and he would lead a failed effort to

push a bill to prohibit discrimination in public places. *St. Paul Press,* February 8, 1873; Green, *Degrees of Freedom,* 109.

9. Castle to Austen, November 2, 1871, file no. 259, Governor's Collection, Minnesota Historical Society, St. Paul. Also see Gilbert C. Fite, ed., "Some Farmers' Accounts of Hardships on the Frontier," *Minnesota History,* March 1961, 204–11.

10. Affidavit by S. D. Thompson, December 30, 1871, Governor's Collection, file no. 259. Also see Fite, "Some Farmers' Accounts," 205.

11. Nichols to Austin, Governor's Collection, file no. 288; Fite, "Some Farmers' Accounts," 207.

12. Senate Journal, 1874, 81, 154; *General Laws 1874,* 251, 253; Folwell, *History of Minnesota,* 3:97–98.

13. The bill read in part: "[This is a] bill providing for the establishment of a reasonable maximum fee for the transportation of passengers and freight upon the railroads of the state and to prevent extortion and unjust discrimination by railroad corporations or their employees, and to proscribe a mode of procedure, and rules of evidence to relation therein." Senate Journal, 1874, 8, 15, 53 (some sources incorrectly give the name as "Cogswell"). See Secretary of State, *The Legislative Manual of the State of Minnesota, Compiled for the Legislature of 1895* (St. Paul), 94, 95 (which has the name as Cogswell).

14. William E. Lass, *Minnesota: A History,* 2d ed. (New York: W. W. Norton, 1998), 200.

15. During the 1870s, the Grangers also advocated cooperative purchasing ventures as a means to obtain lower prices on farm equipment and supplies. They sought to pool savings as an alternative to dependence on corrupt banks, an early form of credit unions; cooperative grain elevators to hold nonperishable crops until the optimal times to sell; and an abortive effort to manufacture farm equipment, which eventually depleted the organization's funds and was instrumental in its decline. Solon J. Buck, *The Agrarian Crusade* (New Haven, Conn.: Yale University Press, 1920); Dennis S. Nordin, *Rich Harvest: A History of the Grange, 1867–1900* (Jackson: University Press of Mississippi, 1976); Woods, *Knights of the Plow.*

16. Lass, *Minnesota,* 200.

17. *Minnesota Legislative Manual 1874,* 148–15; *Farmers' Union,* July 18, 1874; Rasmus S. Saby, *Railroad Legislation in Minnesota, 1849 to 1875* (St. Paul: Volkszeitung Company, 1912), 135–37, https://archive.org/details/rooailroadlegislatsabyrich.

18. *Farmers' Union,* July 18, 1874; *St. Paul Weekly Pioneer,* February 20, 1974.

19. *St. Paul Daily Dispatch,* January 5, 1874.

20. "Defeated by Treachery," *Daily Dispatch,* January 7, 1874.

21. *Mankato Union,* January 23, 1874.

22. *Mankato Union,* January 30, 1874.

23. "It was to their credit that a few members of the House elected on the Republican ticket came here with an honest purpose to aid reform. It was to their discredit that the ring-master, with whip and club, drove them into the monopoly trap, by which the organization of the Legislature will be handed over in all its parts to those corrupt and venal few who have so long preyed on the vitals of the state. . . . The party of monopoly and corruption is still in the ascendant in Minnesota." *St. Paul Weekly Pioneer,* February 20, 1874.

24. *Farmers' Union,* February 21, 1874.

25. "Governor's Message," *Executive Documents of the State of Minnesota, for the Year*

*1873*, vol. 1 (St. Paul: St. Paul Press Company, 1874), 18; Saby, *Railroad Legislation in Minnesota*, 136–37n573.

26. "Governor's Message," 16.

27. Ibid., 19.

28. Ibid., 20.

29. Ibid.

30. "Inaugural Address," *Executive Documents . . . 1873*, 12–14.

31. A. J. Edgerton, commissioner, *Report of the Railroad Commissioner with Reports of Railroad Companies, 1873* (St. Paul: Press Printing Company, 1873), 38.

32. Ibid., xviii.

33. Saby, *Railroad Legislation in Minnesota*, 139.

34. *Farmers' Union*, January 7, 28, 1874.

35. *Farmers' Union*, February 21, 1874.

36. *Farmers' Union*, March 14, 1874.

37. Senate Journal, 1874, 341–44.

38. Senate Journal, 1874, 481; House Journal, 1874, 563; *St. Paul Press*, February 25, March 4, 1874.

39. *Mankato Union*, March 20, 1874. Marshall was elected president of the railroad in March 1870. *St. Paul Press*, March 5, 1870.

40. *General Laws, 1874*, chapter 26. Also see Saby, *Railroad Legislation in Minnesota*, 143–46.

41. Ignatius Donnelly, *An Address of the Anti-Monopoly Party of Minnesota to Their Constituents* (St. Paul, 1874), 12.

42. Ridge, *Ignatius Donnelly*, 158, citing ibid. Ridge, *Ignatius Donnelly*, 159, citing Donnelly to Drake, December 21, 1874, Donnelly Papers; Drake to Donnelly, December 22, 1874, Donnelly Papers. Regarding Drake, see Senate Journal, 1874, 482.

43. In 1877 the Supreme Court, in *Munn v. Illinois*, would uphold the Illinois Grange law and the legislature's right to enact such laws. Munn v. Illinois, 94 U. S. 113 (1877).

44. Ridge, *Ignatius Donnelly*, 158.

45. *Mankato Union*, March 13, 1874.

46. *St. Paul Daily Press*, March 6, 1874.

47. *Minneapolis Tribune*, March 7, 1874.

48. *Rochester Post*, March 14, 1874.

49. *Rochester Record and Union*, March 13, 1874.

50. *St. Paul Daily Dispatch*, March 6, 1874.

51. Saby, *Railroad Legislation in Minnesota*, 153.

52. Ibid., 153–56.

53. Ridge, *Ignatius Donnelly*, 159.

54. *Mankato Union*, March 13, 1874.

55. *Rochester Record and Union*, March 13, 1874.

## 32. A REPUBLICAN WITH UNCHANGED VIEWS

1. Saby, *Railroad Legislation in Minnesota*, 164.

2. "Repeal of the Railroad Law," *St. Paul Daily Press*, February 26, 1875.

3. "The New Railroad Law," *Minneapolis Tribune*, March 5, 1875.

4. "Paralyzing Business," *St. Paul Dispatch*, January 21, 1875.

5. Reprinted in the *Dispatch*, January 19, 1875.

6. *St. Paul Pioneer*, January 16, 1875.

7. Lass, *Minnesota*, 200.

8. Saby, *Railroad Legislation in Minnesota*, 166–67.

9. *Railroad Commissioner's Report, 1874*, 6.

10. *Grange Advance*, March 2, 1875.

11. Ridge, *Ignatius Donnelly*, 161–62.

12. Woods, *Knights of the Plow*, 157.

13. *St. Paul Dispatch*, January 22, 1875.

14. Ibid.

15. *Mankato Review*, reprinted in *St. Paul Pioneer*, January 29, 1875.

16. Ridge, *Ignatius Donnelly*, 167.

17. *Mankato Union*, February 19, 1875.

18. *St. Paul Press*, January 30, 1875; *St. Paul Dispatch*, February 5, 1875; *Mankato Union*, February 12, 1875; House Journal 1875, 109.

19. *Mankato Union*, February 5, 1875; Ridge, *Ignatius Donnelly*, 162. The *Dispatch* reported the numbers as follows: Lochren, 56; Ramsey, 46; Davis, 27. *St. Paul Dispatch*, February 5, 1875, 8. After two days of backroom wrangling, McMillan received 82 votes to Lochren's 61. *Pioneer*, February 261, 1875. See also Folwell, *History of Minnesota*, 3:87. For another account of the campaign, see *H. P. Hall's Observations*, 135–54.

20. *St. Paul Press*, February 19, 1875.

21. Atkins, *Harvest of Grief*, 22–23.

22. Ibid., 23, 15; *St. Paul Daily Pioneer*, July 8, 9, 1874.

23. Joshua Swann to Davis, July 20, 1874, and Henry Whipple to Davis, August 1, 1874, Cushman K. Davis Papers, Minnesota Historical Society, St. Paul; Senate Journal 1875, 102–4; Atkins, *Harvest of Grief*, 73–74.

24. Atkins, *Harvest of Grief*, 75.

25. Folwell, *History of Minnesota*, 3:100; Atkins, *Harvest of Grief*, 74–75, 78.

26. Senate Journal 1875, 98, 102.

27. *St. Paul Daily Pioneer*, January 27, 1875.

28. *St. Paul Pioneer*, March 12, 1875.

29. Senate Journal 1875, 183.

30. Governor Davis's "Annual Message," January 7, 1876, *Minnesota Executive Documents, 1875*, 34; Atkins, *Harvest of Grief*, 79.

31. Folwell, *History of Minnesota*, 3:101.

32. Atkins, *Harvest of Grief*, 36.

33. Folwell, *History of Minnesota*, 3:101.

34. *Mankato Union*, February 5, 1875.

35. Ibid.

36. *Mankato Union*, February 26, 1875.

37. Ibid.

38. Senate Journal 1875, 294; General Laws 1875, chapter 1, sec. 2 and 3.

39. "The Legislature," *Rochester Record and Union*, March 6, 1875.

40. *Minnesota Executive Documents, 1875*, 91.

41. *St. Paul Pioneer*, March 12, 1875; Ridge, *Ignatius Donnelly*, 164; Folwell, *History of Minnesota*, 3:56.

42. *St. Paul Daily Dispatch*, March 3, 5, 1875; "Westfall on the Railroad Law," *Rochester Post*, March 6, 1875.

43. *General Law, 1875,* 218; *St. Paul Daily Dispatch,* March 4, 1875; Saby, *Railroad Legislation in Minnesota,* 173.

44. Solon J. Buck, *The Granger Movement: A Study of Agricultural Organization and the Political, Economic, and Social Manifestations, 1870–1880* (Cambridge, Mass.: Harvard University Press, 1913), 166.

45. Cong. Globe, 37th Cong., 2d Sess., 1205.

46. Ibid., 1230.

47. Ibid.

48. *St. Paul Pioneer,* March 12, 1875.

49. *Mankato Union,* March 5, 1875.

50. *St. Paul Dispatch,* March 3, 1875.

## 33. THE FORCE LAW

1. Foner, *Reconstruction,* 550.

2. Joe Gray Taylor, *Louisiana Reconstructed, 1863–1877* (Baton Rouge: Louisiana State University Press, 1974), 241–55; 43rd Congress, 2d Session, House Report, 261, part 3:752–53; 46th Congress, 2d Session, Senate Report, 693, part 2:114, 171; Foner, *Reconstruction,* 551; Joseph G. Dawson, *Army Generals and Reconstruction: Louisiana, 1862–1877* (Baton Rouge: Louisiana State University Press, 1982), 197–211.

3. *Nation,* September 24, 1874; Foner, *Reconstruction,* 551; Joy Jackson, "Bosses and Businessmen in Gilded Age New Orleans Politics," *Louisiana History* 5 (February 1964): 387–88.

4. Foner, *Reconstruction,* 553–54.

5. Ibid., 554; Dawson, *Army Generals and Reconstruction,* 197–211.

6. Sheridan to Belknap, January 10, 1875, which appears in total in *St. Paul Dispatch,* January 22, 1875.

7. Foner, *Reconstruction,* 554.

8. *Mankato Union,* February 13, 1875.

9. Ibid.; *St. Paul Press,* February 3, 1875.

10. "Getting All the Truth about Louisiana," *St. Paul Press,* February 28, 1875.

11. *Mankato Union,* February 12, 1875.

12. *St. Paul Press,* February 28, 1875.

13. 18 Stat. 335–37. It passed in the House on February 4, and the Senate on February 27.

14. *St. Paul Press,* March 3, 1875.

15. Foner, *Reconstruction,* 472.

16. Taylor, "Pilgrim's Progress," 43–44.

17. Green, *Degrees of Freedom,* 115.

18. Ibid., 112.

19. *Civil Rights in America: Racial Discrimination in Public Accommodation* (Washington, D.C.: U.S. Department of the Interior, 2004), 13.

20. *St. Paul Daily Pioneer,* May 15, 16, 1873; *St. Paul Dispatch,* May 16, 1873.

21. *Mankato Union,* March 5, 1875.

22. C. Vann Woodward, *The Strange Career of Jim Crow* (New York: Oxford University Press, 1966), 28.

23. Howard Rabinowitz, "From Exclusion to Segregation: Southern Race Relations, 1865–1880," *Journal of American History* 63, no. 2 (September 1976): 346.

24. *New York Times*, March 2, 6, 1875.

25. Rabinowitz, "From Exclusion to Segregation," 347.

26. John Hope Franklin, "The Enforcement of the Civil Rights Act of 1875," *Prologue*, Winter 1974, 226, citing Butler to Harlan in *Harper's Weekly*, April 24, 1875.

27. *Mankato Union*, February 13, 1875.

28. "Sumner's Chemistry of the Schools," *St. Paul Weekly Pioneer*, December 23, 1870. "Cuffe" (sometimes, "cuffee") was an antiblack epithet used in the eighteen and nineteenth centuries. Elizabeth Stordeur Pryor, "The Etymology of Nigger: Resistance, Language, and the Politics of Freedom in the Antebellum North," *Journal of the Early Republic* 36, no. 2 (Summer 2016): 204, 219. In the passage quoted in text, the Democratic critic was mocking the Republicans while deprecating the black man, who was also the subject of his contempt.

29. David McCullough, *The Greater Journey: Americans in Paris* (New York: Simon and Schuster, 2011), 131–32.

30. Richard Kluger, *Simple Justice: History of* Brown v. Board of Education (New York: Knopf, 1976), 75.

31. "Sumner's Chemistry of the Schools," *St. Paul Weekly Pioneer*, December 23, 1870.

32. The following Northern states banned racial segregation in their schools: Michigan (1848), Massachusetts (1855), Rhode Island (1866), Connecticut (1868), and Illinois (1874). Vermont and New Hampshire both had provisions in their constitutions that had no racial distinctions. In 1881 Pennsylvania and New Jersey banned school segregation, and in 1900, New York followed suit. Carter G. Woodson, *Education of the Negro* (Brooklyn: A & B Publishers Group, 1998), 191–206.

33. Ibid., 206; Green, *A Peculiar Imbalance*, 165–72.

34. Green, *A Peculiar Imbalance*, 168.

35. *Mankato Union*, November 13, 1874.

36. Ibid.

37. *Mankato Union*, March 17, 1865.

38. *Mankato Union*, February 13, 1875.

39. *Minneapolis Tribune*, March 3, 1875. Reference to the black gathering to recognize the enactment of the law can be found in Taylor, "Pilgrim's Progress," 163, and Butler, "Communities and Congregations," 120.

40. *Mankato Union*, March 19, 1875.

41. Ibid.

42. *St. Paul Press*, March 3, 1875.

43. Senate Journal 1875, 487–88 (March 5, 1875).

44. *St. Paul Pioneer*, March 12, 1875.

45. *Speech by Wendell Phillips in Faneuil Hall on Louisiana Difficulties, December 31, 1875* (Boston: Wright & Potter), 13.

46. Foner, *Reconstruction*, 554.

47. Wilkinson speaking in behalf of a bill to abolish slavery in the District of Columbia, delivered in the U.S. Senate, March 26, 1862.

48. *St. Paul Pioneer*, March 5, 1875.

49. Between January and March 1875, six days remain, as of this writing, the coldest

on record—January 8 (-30 degrees), February 7 (-29 degrees), February 12 (-30 degrees), February 14 (-25 degrees), February 15 (-25 degrees), and March 19 (-15 degrees). The lowest daily minimum temperature was -30 degrees (Intellicast.com Historic Average, Minneapolis, Minnesota). In January, the first twenty-five days of the month all brought below 25 degrees overnight temperatures to downtown St. Paul. On eleven days temperatures never climbed above zero. Mark Seeley, Minnesota WeatherTalk newsletter for Friday, January 8, 2010, University of Minnesota Extension News.

50. Senate Journal 1875, 488.
51. *St. Paul Dispatch*, March 12, 1875.
52. Ibid.
53. "The Supplementary Civil Rights Bill Declared to Be Constitutional by a Democratic Judge," *New York Times*, June 9, 1875. In 1883 the United States Supreme Court would find the law unconstitutional. *Civil Rights Cases*, 109 U. S. 3. (1883). Two years later, 1885, Minnesota enacted a state public accommodations law. Green, *Degrees of Freedom*, 128–49.

## 34. SINE DIE

1. "Frederick Driscoll," *Minnesota Historical Collections*, 10:695.
2. Ibid., 696.
3. Ibid. Still, it was not unusual for newspapers to adopt the voice of a former rival on select topics. For example, when Republican U.S. senator Wilkinson directed printing contracts to a party rival, the *Pioneer and Democrat*, the editor stipulated that the paper would be friendly to Wilkinson's positions, though it would retain "certain" Democratic interests. John C. Haugland, "Politics, Patronage, and Ramsey's Rise to Political Power, 1861–1865," *Minnesota History*, December 1961, 330.
4. "Frederick Driscoll," 10:695.
5. Neill, *History of Ramsey County and the City of St. Paul*, 357.
6. *St. Paul Pioneer Press*, October 24, 1875.
7. *St. Paul Pioneer Press*, October 28, 1875.
8. *St. Paul Pioneer Press*, October 27, 1875.
9. Ibid.
10. "Black and White Ku Klux," *St. Paul Pioneer Press*, August 31, 1875.
11. *Mankato Union*, February 19, 1875.
12. Cong. Globe, 43rd Cong., 2d Sess., House Report, 265, i–xiii, 108–9, 159, 169–70, 190–93, 400–402, 467–68; George C. Rable, *But There Was No Peace: The Role of Violence in the Politics of Reconstruction* (Athens: University of Georgia Press, 1984), 145–49; Foner, *Reconstruction*, 558.
13. 44th Congress, 2d Session, Senate Miscellaneous Document 45, 206; Vernon L. Wharton, *The Negro of Mississippi, 1865–1890* (Chapel Hill: University of North Carolina Press, 1947), 182–90; Foner, *Reconstruction*, 559.
14. "Another Uprising," *St. Paul Pioneer Press*, September 5, 1875.
15. David H. Donald, "The Scalawag in Mississippi Reconstruction," *Journal of Southern History* 10 (November 1944): 455.
16. "A Delegate from Petersburg," *St. Paul Pioneer Press*, September 5, 1875.
17. *St. Paul Pioneer Press*, September 7, 1875.
18. *St. Paul Pioneer Press*, September 8, 1875.

19. "Blood and Bourbon," *St. Paul Pioneer Press,* September 9, 1875.

20. Foner, *Reconstruction,* 560–61.

21. *St. Paul Pioneer Press,* September 18, 1875.

22. Foner, *Reconstruction,* 561.

23. *New York Times,* May 2, 1876; *Northfield News,* August 2, 1929; *Chicago Times,* September 11, 1876; *Minneapolis Tribune,* September 11, 1876; T. J. Stiles, *Jesse James: Last Rebel of the Civil War* (New York: Knopf, 2002).

24. *General Laws of Minnesota for 1875,* 183; *General Laws of Minnesota for 1876,* 204; Senate Journal, 1875, 511; Walter N. Trenerry, "The Minnesota Legislator and the Grasshopper, 1873–1877," *Minnesota History,* June 1958, 56.

25. Atkins, *Harvest of Grief,* 80.

26. Ibid., 81; Davis, "Annual Message," January 7, 1876, 33; *St. Paul Daily Pioneer,* March 28, 1875.

27. Atkins notes that neither Sibley nor Davis likely shared these views. They believed, like most Americans at the time, that most poverty resulted from personal failing, but such judgment did not apply in these circumstances. Atkins, *Harvest of Grief,* 81–82.

28. *Pillsbury's Inaugural Address, January 7, 1876* (St. Paul: Pioneer Press Printing, 1876), 6–12.

29. Ibid., 12–14. Emphasis added.

30. Ibid., 14.

31. Proclamation of John S. Pillsbury, August 30, 1876, executive record, vol. E, 528–30, Governor's Papers.

32. *St. Paul Daily Pioneer Press,* January 8, 1876.

33. *St. Paul Pioneer Press,* March 7, May 31, 1876.

34. *St. Paul Pioneer Press,* January 2, 1876.

35. "High Expectations of the Session," *St. Paul Pioneer Press,* January 6, 1876.

36. Kane, "A Case Study in Lively Futility," 224.

37. *St. Paul Pioneer Press,* January 5, 1876, 4.

38. *St. Paul Pioneer Press,* October 28, 1875, 2. Also see Kane, "A Case Study in Lively Futility," 223.

39. Kane, "A Case Study in Lively Futility," 223.

40. "Constitutional Dignity," *St. Paul Daily Pioneer Press,* January 7, 1876; January 25, 1876. *St. Paul Daily Pioneer Press,* February 10, 1876 (jokingly referring to Donnelly as a member of the "non-producing class"); February 20, 1876 (attacking the state auditor).

41. *St. Paul Daily Pioneer Press,* February 16, 1876.

42. Criticism of the reapportionment, *St. Paul Pioneer Press,* February 25, 1876; swamp and school land bill, *St. Paul Pioneer Press,* January 29, 1876; and repeal of the inebriate asylum, *St. Paul Pioneer Press,* January 26, 1876.

43. "An Act to Enable Women to Vote at Elections for School Officers, and in Matters Pertaining Solely to the Management of Schools," in *General Laws of Minnesota for 1876,* 29–30; *St. Paul Pioneer Press,* April 3, 1876.

44. *Mankato Union,* April 15, 1876; *St. Paul Pioneer Press,* April 15, 1876.

45. *St. Paul Pioneer Press and Tribune,* April 22, 1876; George S. Hage, *Newspapers on the Minnesota Frontier, 1849–1860* (St. Paul: Minnesota Historical Society Press, 2004), 127.

## EPILOGUE

1. "The Lincoln Monument: Unveiling of the Statue in Lincoln Square," *New York Times*, April 15, 1876.

2. *Inaugural Ceremonies of the Freedmen's Memorial Monument to Abraham Lincoln. Washington City, April 14, 1876* (St. Louis: Levison and Blythe, Printers, 1876), 11.

3. Ibid., 6.

4. Rucker, a Union refugee from Virginia, eventually sought safety for himself and family in Marietta, Ohio, "taking along with him Charlotte Scott, and perhaps others belonging to him." Ibid., 7.

5. Ibid., 8.

6. Ibid.

7. Ibid., 8–9.

8. *New York Times*, April 15, 1876.

9. Kirk Savage, *Standing Soldiers, Kneeling Slaves: Race, War, and Monument in Nineteenth-Century America* (Princeton, N.J.: Princeton University Press, 1997), 90.

10. Goodwin, *Team of Rivals*, 719.

11. The *Mankato Union* report read in part: "These here carpetbaggers and scalawags came around and told me to give them office, and they would tax you so that you would have to sell your land, and then we could buy it, I thought it would be mighty nice to have a big plantation, and I voted for them, and told them to stick on the tax. They stick on the tax, they got land, fine horses, fine clothes, and plenty of money, but I never got anything from them yet." "Colored Men for Tilden," *Mankato Weekly Union*, October 6, 1876.

12. Franklin, *Reconstruction after the Civil War*, 212, 214.

13. Foner, *Reconstruction*, 567; McFeely, *Frederick Douglass*, 289, 291.

14. Franklin, *Reconstruction after the Civil War*, 219.

15. *St. Peter Herald*, June 14, 1907; *St. Peter Free Press*, June 15, 1907; Index of the History of Nicollet and Le Sueur Counties, Minnesota, 1:271, 272, 276; *St. Peter Tribune*, February 15, 1888.

16. Stanton et al., *History of Woman Suffrage*, 3:651–52.

17. Ibid., 652–53. Also see Sarah Berger Stearns, "Women's Interest in Education," *Minneapolis Tribune*, October 21, 1875.

18. Minor v. Hoppensett, 88 U.S. 162 (1875).

19. U.S. patent no. 183,600, October 24, 1876. I am grateful to Patricia Maus for pointing this out to me (email of October 20, 2011).

20. Bauer, *The Privilege for Which We Struggled*, 30–32.

21. "Death of Mrs. M. S. Wilkinson," *Mankato Weekly Review*, June 26, 1888.

22. Wilkinson, *Memoirs of the Wilkinson Family in America*, 288; *Mankato: Its First Fifty Years*, 346.

23. "His Work Done," *Mankato Daily Free Press*, February 5, 1894.

24. Edmund Boisgilbert, M.D. [Ignatius Donnelly], *Doctor Huguet, a Novel* (New York: D. D. Merrill, 1892), 7–8.

25. Ridge, *Ignatius Donnelly*, 289.

26. Ibid., 290.

27. Llewellyn to Donnelly, December 1, 1891, Donnelly Papers.

28. Schultz to Donnelly, February 5, 1892; March 10, 1892; March 19, 1892, Donnelly Papers, roll 102.

29. Merrill to Donnelly, August 31, 1892, Donnelly Papers, roll 104.

30. Boisgilbert, *Doctor Huguet*, 153–54.

31. *St. Paul Globe*, April 15, 1895, June 3, 1895; *St. Paul Pioneer Press*, June 3 and 4, 1895; Paul Nelson, *Frederick L. McGhee: A Life on the Color Line, 1861–1912* (St. Paul: Minnesota Historical Society Press, 2002), 54–55; Green, *Degrees of Freedom*, 253–54.

32. Louis Henry Cornish and Alonzo Howard Clark, *A National Register of the Society Sons of the American Revolution*, 2 vols. (New York: National Publication Committee, 1902), 1:612.

# INDEX

WILLIAM D. GREEN is professor of history at Augsburg University in Minneapolis. His previous books include *A Peculiar Imbalance: The Fall and Rise of Racial Equality in Minnesota, 1837–1869* (Minnesota, 2015) and *Degrees of Freedom: The Origins of Civil Rights in Minnesota, 1865–1912* (Minnesota, 2015), winner of the 2016 Hognander Minnesota History Award.

APR 2 3 2019